INTERVIEWING, COUNSELING, AND NEGOTIATING

INTERVIEWING, COUNSELING, AND NEGOTIATING

Skills for Effective Representation

ROBERT M. BASTRESS
Professor of Law
West Virginia University

JOSEPH D. HARBAUGH
Dean and Professor of Law
University of Richmond

LITTLE, BROWN AND COMPANY
Boston   Toronto   London

Library of Congress Catalog Card No. 90-060588
ISBN 0-316-34571-7

EB

Published simultaneously in Canada
by Little, Brown & Company (Canada) Limited

Printed in the United States of America

To My Parents,
Bob and Hildred Bastress

—R. M. B.

To my teachers for lessons that will last a lifetime:

My mother who encouraged my intellectual curiosity
My father who instructed me on the need to be disciplined
My children who revealed to me the full meaning of love
And most of all to B who taught me how to put these lessons
   together and so much more.

—J. D. H.

Summary of Contents

Table of Contents

Chapter

5

Fundamentals of a Helping Relationship   *109*

Chapter

6

Nonverbal Communication and Techniques   *131*

Chapter

7

Verbal Techniques and Probing Skills   *145*

Chapter
8
≡ *Psychosocial Influences on Communications*   *175*

Chapter
9
≡ *Witness Interviews*   *197*

PART III. COUNSELING

Chapter
10

Planning and Structuring the Counseling Session

Chapter
11

Helping the Client Reach a Decision

Chapter
12
≡
Conflicts in the Attorney-Client Relationship   *283*

Chapter 16

Lawyer Negotiation Models 389

Chapter

19

The Exchange Stage: Preparation   473

Chapter

20

The Exchange Stage: Implementation   487

Chapter
21
≡

An Afterword: Coming Full Circle **523**

Preface

Until recently, interpersonal skills received little attention as a distinct subject for lawyers to study, even though the skills are essential in law practice and to the legal process. In the aggregate, lawyers spend far more time interacting with clients and other lawyers than arguing to judges and juries. Moreover, clients and their lawyers, not courts, decide most legal questions: whether a business should pursue a course of action in light of the applicable regulatory laws, whether litigation is worthwhile, whether a dispute should be settled, how a contract should be structured, and so on. The lawyering skills needed to help clients decide such issues certainly include traditional skills of legal analysis, but lawyers must also have fact-gathering, counseling, and negotiating skills to provide effective representation in these private decisional processes.

To best learn the interpersonal skills, we believe, you must engage in two processes. The first is cognitive: You must know the theory behind the skills and their implementing techniques. Second, you must practice using the theory and techniques.

This text accordingly devotes considerable attention to theory. We have tried to describe the considerable diversity in approaches to interviewing, counseling, and negotiating, and we have drawn heavily from other disciplines. We posit that there is a rich and diverse literature outside of law that can be of great benefit to lawyers. We therefore discuss that literature, deduce from it, and provide references to encourage independent study. Yet we also have our own theories, developed from study of our predecessors and from our own experiences, observations, and thinking. We have unabashedly structured this book to teach those theories.

Our goal is to provide a conceptual framework for using interpersonal skills, much like law schools seek to do in their substantive law courses. Legal education primarily teaches students the skills of case analysis and statutory interpretation. Within each substantive law course, instructors provide a framework students can use in practice to identify issues and solve problems in that subject area. Although law graduates are neither experts in any field nor accomplished attorneys when they finish law school, they nevertheless have the basic analytical skills and knowledge needed to handle legal issues. In similar fashion, we aim to provide the basics for handling the interpersonal aspects of law practice. We do not address special applications of general theories, matters such as multi-client counseling, problem clients, multi-party negotiations, or team negotiations. Those particular challenges can be met by extrapolating from the basic framework. Moreover, while we are occasionally prescriptive, our preferred approach provides alternative strategies, suggests the criteria for making a selection in given circumstances, and leaves it to the individual to determine where a problem fits within the basic framework.

We have striven to put the interpersonal skills in context. We thus liberally use problems to illustrate and enhance substantive concepts. In addition, we recognize the importance of ethical questions in planning strategies for professional relations. We identify those issues, usually discuss them, frequently offer our own resolution, yet admit—as we must—that in the end each lawyer has to reach his or her own conclusions. Finally, we examine each skill in relation to other skills and to the divergent roles lawyers must assume.

We have noted our belief that optimum skills development requires not only cognitive learning, but also substantial practice in applying the theory and techniques. We therefore assume that this text will be used in combination with some sort of experiential learning process, either simulation or representation of actual clients in a law school clinic or law practice. Indeed, our background in clinical education has convinced us that this text will have little utility unless read in conjunction with simulated or live cases. The conceptual learning must be integrated into the practice, and the practice must be subjected to meaningful reflection and analysis.

The book's organization reflects the foregoing premises. Chapter 1 introduces the book's themes, while Chapter 2 delves into other disciplines to canvass helping theories. While Chapters 3 and 4 begin the lawyer-client materials at a logical point by describing goals and initial contacts with clients, the chapters also serve as an overview of the entire interviewing and counseling process. We appreciate the difficulty in trying to understand and apply parts of a process before seeing the process as a whole. We hope the overview will enable you to begin practicing the skills in some meaningful fashion and to better understand the materials that follow. Chapters 5 through 8 then break down and elaborate on the various elements of interviewing clients, and Chapter 9 addresses the specialized issues in witness interviewing. The counseling materials, Chapters 10 to 13, proceed to address the lawyer's role in the decisional stages of the lawyer-client relationship—the planning and advanced skills that will be required and the potential conflicts that can arise.

The negotiation section is similarly arranged. Chapter 14 relates negotiation back to the skills of interviewing and counseling and introduces the bargaining process. Chapter 15 canvasses the theories developed by writers in other disciplines and in the legal literature, and Chapter 16 provides an overview of the models we develop. Chapters 17 to 21 then elaborate on the important components of legal negotiations.

This book has left us in debt to many people. We particularly want to acknowledge the help of James Elkins and Charles DiSalvo, who reviewed and commented on several of the chapters. Colleagues at other schools, among whom are Eugene Basanta, Anthony Bocchino, Barbara Britzke, Robert Dinerstein, Thomas Guernsey, and Elliot Milstein, used portions of the materials in their courses and gave us invaluable feedback. Rick Heuser and Elizabeth Kenny at Little, Brown have contributed greatly to the substance and form of the book and have been an ever-reliable source of encouragement. Our editor, Richard Audet, has earned our gratitude for his thoroughness, sound judgment, and good humor. The persons who contributed their clerical skills to the completion of the manuscripts, and whose good graces we sorely tested, are too numerous to list. Nevertheless, they are dear to us; we remain grateful for, and amazed by, their ability to deal with the two of us. Much-appreciated financial support has been provided by the West Virginia University College of Law, Temple University School of Law, and the Washington College of Law of American University. We must also thank our wives, Barbara Britzke and Barbara Fleischauer, for their assistance on the text, their support, and their enormous patience with us through the various drafts and the years of work.

Robert M. Bastress
Joseph D. Harbaugh

April 1990

Acknowledgments

Excerpts from the following books and articles appear with the kind permission of the copyright holders:

Robert Bastress, Client-Centered Counseling and Moral Accountability for Lawyers, 10 Journal of the Legal Profession 97, 112-113, 117-127 (1985). Copyright © 1985 by The Journal of the Legal Profession. Reprinted by permission.

Carl Bernstein & Bob Woodward, *All the President's Men* 180 (1974). Copyright © 1974 by Carl Bernstein and Bob Woodward. Reprinted by permission of Simon & Schuster, Inc.

William Cormier & L. Sherilyn Cormier, *Interviewing Strategies for Helpers* 14-15 (2d ed. 1985). Copyright © 1985 by Brooks/Cole Publishing Company. Reprinted by permission of Brooks/Cole Publishing Company, Pacific Grove, California, 93950.

James R. Elkins, The Legal Persona: An Essay on the Professional Mask, 64 Virginia Law Review 735, 736-743, 746-747 (1978). Copyright © 1978 by Virginia Law Review Association. Reprinted by permission of the Virginia Law Review Association and Fred B. Rothman & Co.

Mary Clare Eros, Parable from a Patient's Mother (unpublished). Reprinted by permission of the author.

Harrop Freeman & Henry Weihofen, *Clinical Law Training: Interviewing and Counseling* 64-67 (1972). Copyright © 1972 by West Publishing Company. Reprinted with permission of the West Publishing Company.

Charles Fried, The Lawyer as Friend: The Moral Foundations of the Lawyer-Client Relation, 85 Yale Law Journal 1060, 1060-1061, 1065-1067, 1071-1089 (1976). Copyright © 1976 by Charles Fried. Reprinted by permission.

Raymond Gorden, *Interviewing: Strategy, Tactics, and Techniques* 324, 429

Lewis Wolberg, 2 *The Technique of Psychotherapy* 799-800 (4th ed. 1988). Copyright © 1988 by Grune & Stratton, Inc., title assigned to W. B. Saunders Company. Reprinted by permission.

Oran Young, *Bargaining: Formal Theories of Negotiation* 23, 36, 131-132, 134, 138, 303-307 (1975). Copyright © 1975 by the University of Illinois Press. Reprinted by permission.

INTERVIEWING, COUNSELING, AND NEGOTIATING

PART

I

INTRODUCTION

1

Interpersonal Skills and Lawyers

A. THE GOALS OF THIS TEXT

Scene from a Law Office

The secretary's ring signals that my client is here for her 9:00 appointment. My first client! I only hope I don't make a fool of myself. God, my hands are clammy. Do I shake hands or not? What sort of grip? I don't want to come across like a Texas cowboy and rearrange her knuckles, but I don't want her to think she's shaking cold spaghetti either. Moderation. Everything in moderation. There's a knock at the door.

"Mrs. Hoover?" I ask.

"Yes."

"Come in." We shake hands. She recoils as our hands touch. "My name is Jerry Garfield. How are you today?"

She says she is fine and we exchange comments on the weather. The talk is very stiff, as when a 12-year-old gets stuck alone in a room with a rarely seen aunt. Within a moment, however, I try to relieve the awkwardness by turning to business: "What brings you here today?"

"Well," she sighs, "my husband recently died of a heart attack. And then my son committed suicide right after the funeral. So now I need some help to . . . to . . . to sort out all the legal things, you know."

"I see," I say. But I don't see. What the hell do I do now? Boy, does this woman ever need to see a lawyer!

Why, why didn't law school teach me how to deal with clients?

———————————————————

Indeed, the new lawyer raises a good question: "Why didn't law school teach me how to deal with clients?" Legal education has absorbed considerable criticism for its failure to give instruction in the basic skills that lawyers use every day to relate to clients and to other lawyers. Law schools have gradually responded with clinics and with specialized skills courses. Nevertheless, many—if not most—law students graduate without training in the critical skills of interviewing, counseling, and negotiating. This historical and persistent gap in legal education has undoubtedly contributed to the practicing bar's notoriety for its members' unenlightened approach to interpersonal relations. Many experienced attorneys would be as nonplused by Mrs. Hoover's visit as the beginning attorney was in the above vignette.

We take seriously the criticisms and the public's concerns about deficiencies in lawyers' interviewing, counseling, and negotiating skills. We believe those skills are critical to effective representation of clients. We further hold that there are psychological, philosophical, and moral dimensions to the lawyer-client relationship and to the practice of law that legal education and lawyers too often fail to recognize. This text is our response; it provides the information and the structural models you need to understand interpersonal processes, to develop your skills, and to maintain productive relations with clients and other lawyers. Most important, the text constructs a concept for lawyering that envisions lawyer and client as partners working toward a common goal, with the client responsible for the major decisions and the lawyer functioning as helper, adviser, and advocate.

With the information and philosophy from this text, supplemented by experience and by a sense of self-awareness, you can make the most of your natural skills to effectively represent your clients.

B. IMPORTANCE AND INTERRELATIONSHIP OF INTERPERSONAL SKILLS

The need for effective interpersonal skills pervades the practice of law. These skills are essential as you move from identification and development of the client's problem to analysis of alternatives to action step—regardless of whether the ultimate action step is a lawsuit, a settlement, or a document.

The umbrella of essential skills encompasses the interrelated skills of interviewing, counseling, and negotiating (ICN), which in turn include their own overlapping subskills. Interviewing embraces empathy, genuineness, listening, and probing. Proficiency in them enables you to achieve the basic purposes of interviewing—gathering the facts and establishing rapport. In counseling, you seek to identify the client's alternatives and priorities and then help the client select the most constructive option. You manage that by using the skills of interviewing *plus* creativity, foresight, analysis, explanation, cooperation, and advice. With negotiating, you move forward to implement the goals set during counseling. Again, all of the previously engaged skills are used and, again, new ones must be employed. As lawyer-negotiator, you add strategy, persuasion, and conciliation skills to your repertoire. The distribution of the subskills thus resembles a building-block pattern, with the skills of interviewing as the foundation supporting the more advanced skills:

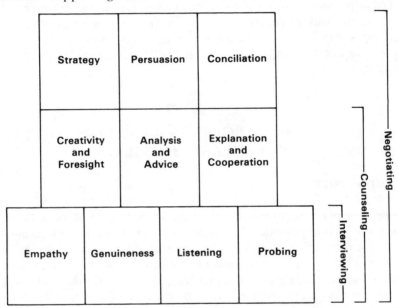

This text structures its skills teaching on the above model.

The ICN processes also interrelate on a second level; that is, the quality of your performance in one stage significantly influences the results in a subsequent stage. You must be effective in fact-gathering and establishing rapport (interviewing) to prepare for effective counseling. Similarly, the success of your action steps in planning, drafting, negotiating, or litigating depends on the quality of the earlier work in interviewing and counseling. For example, your work in counseling calls forth your skills of analysis and creativity to develop solutions to your client's problem. Those solutions then provide the agenda in negotiations as you search for a mutually agreeable outcome with another party. The quality and variety of your proposals in counseling thus directly affect your success as a negotiator.

The skills you use in interviewing, counseling, and negotiating are also basic to other lawyering tasks. For example, deposition and trial examinations, both direct and cross, are simply specialized forms of interviewing. Trial work relies on the same sensitivity to emotions and nonverbal communications that is an essential element in interviewing, counseling, and negotiation. Evaluating a witness's effectiveness, coaching a witness, and assessing jurors are just some of the trial tasks requiring knowledge about interpersonal communications. Finally, negotiation tactics often depend on the lawyer's ability to identify and execute trial tactics.

Thus, mastering the ICN skills will enhance your performance in all aspects of law practice. Moreover (and maybe more important), as you learn about interpersonal skills, you become more sensitive and self-aware, and thus gain qualities that will yield personal benefits well beyond the doors of your law office.

The chart on page 7 breaks down the different phases of the lawyer-client relationship into their component parts. The chart does not necessarily reflect a chronological progression. Counseling, for example, can follow as well as precede negotiation, and interviewing continues throughout the relationship. And, of course, not every client requires a negotiation. The chart does, however, visually illustrate the skills' interrelationships and provides an overview of the concepts that will be developed in the chapters that follow.

C. YOUR ROLES AS A LAWYER: SOME BASIC THEMES

1. Introduction

The practice of law requires you to assume several different roles. Each role makes use of interpersonal skills, and each generates its own issues and problems. In addition, the fact that you are called on to fulfill the different roles can in itself cause personal and professional problems for you. This section reviews those issues and problems. They are fundamental to law-yering; their resolution requires you to articulate your perceptions about relationships with clients, about social and moral responsibilities, and about yourself. The themes identified in this section recur throughout this text and call for constant reexamination. They include:

1. How should you relate to your clients?
2. How does the nature of your relationships with clients affect your ability to interview, counsel, and represent them?
3. What is the appropriate relationship between your professional life and your private life?
4. Should you personally judge the social and moral propriety of your clients' cases? Why or why not?

This section proceeds to cover several subjects. Subsection 2 describes the different roles of lawyers, the relationship between interpersonal skills and those roles, and some of the conflicts the roles create. Your roles as a lawyer, along with your legal training and experience, can threaten to impose on you a "legal persona," which substantially alters your worldview,

	Interviewing (Research and Investigation)	*Counseling (Research and Investigation)*	*Negotiating (Action Step)*	*Other Action Steps (Document Drafting, Trial, Referral, Others)*
PURPOSES	gather facts establish rapport contract for services	gather facts identify alternatives identify client priorities reach decisions	achieve client goals resolve issues without litigation	achieve client goals
SKILLS	empathy genuineness listening probing	Same as Interviewing, *plus:* creativity foresight analysis explanation cooperation advice	Same as Counseling, *plus:* strategy persuasion conciliation	For Referral and Planning, *see* Counseling For Litigation, *see* Negotiation

self-perceptions, and relations with others. That persona is the subject of Subsection 3. Next, Subsection 4 introduces the moral conflicts that can arise in your relations with clients and between your personal life and your professional roles. The final subsection presents material designed to help you reflect on the preceding subsections.

2. The Lawyer's Roles

Much of your work as a lawyer falls within the role of helper. When working as an interviewer or as a counselor, you are an active partner with your clients, helping them to reach a solution that best satisfies their needs. You establish a rapport with the client, gather information, research and analyze the relevant law, and help the client work through decisions and cope with desirable or undesirable consequences. The process of reaching a decision requires a partnership in which you provide understanding, legal expertise, and a structure for decision-making. When in this helping role, you function in an interpersonal, professional, and fiduciary capacity. Predictably, your role as helper is the primary (though not exclusive) focus of this text's materials on interviewing and counseling.

To fulfill the obligations of an effective helper, you must determine what your relationships with clients should be like. What sort of control, if any, should you exert? When, if at all, should you express moral judgment? What "attitudes" should you take toward the client? How do your perceptions of your helping role translate into techniques and actions?

Many theories on the most effective approach to helping have evolved from the various schools of psychotherapy. Selecting a particular theory as the most appropriate calls for scrutiny of your basic philosophical attitudes about life and human relations. Chapter 2 canvasses the most prominent helping theories and describes certain assumptions we have made in setting forth our perception of appropriate roles and techniques for the lawyer as helper.

As a lawyer, you also assume the role of an advocate; you champion and defend clients in a variety of forums. One of those is in negotiating, the subject of Part IV. This text addresses, as well, those aspects of advocacy dealing with the development of a case: gathering facts from clients and witnesses, and scanning, screening, and formulating theories. In addition, law practice requires you to fulfill nonadversarial roles in accomplishing certain action steps for clients. These can generally be described as planning and drafting. For example, you assist clients in formulating strategies, developing plans to meet regulatory laws, preparing contracts, and drafting comprehensive estate packages. As in adversarial cases, you must effectively gather facts, research law, develop theories and alternatives, and counsel clients. Thus, the skills involved in the planning and drafting roles require much the same skills that are used in the developing stages of the adversarial process, even though different skills may be necessary to execute the selected action steps.

These various professional roles can cause drastic changes in your mental and emotional approaches to your work. At one moment, you are an empathic helper, at the next, a fierce negotiator or litigator. Within the same case, or even within the same morning, you could be a caring listener to a family distraught over the loss of a child and also a tough cross-examiner of a 14-year-old who happens to testify for the opposition. In meetings with clients, you are genuine and open, but as a litigator, you may aim only to *appear* genuine and open while consciously attempting to manipulate the fact-finder.[1] As a helper, you are personally involved; you care about your client and genuinely reflect that caring. But as a litigator, you are in one sense an actor or actress—you play a role to create an effect on the audience.

The contrasts within the lawyer's roles extend beyond the comparison of counselor versus litigator. For example, negotiations can require you to play several different parts. In one negotiation, you can be a mediator, a go-between for two (or more) parties, using trust, empathy, and conciliatory skills to be effective. In the next negotiation, you may function solely as an advocate, espousing only the client's cause and using the skills of persuasion.

The critical distinction in these roles lies not in the different skills being used, since, as we have shown above, there is a considerable overlap of skills. Rather, the distinction rests on the fundamentally different attitudes and personality traits appropriate to the varied tasks. The pressures on you can become intense, especially on your sense of self.

No other professional endures that kind of emotional roller coaster. Doctors, dentists, accountants, and social workers are always helpers. Actors and actresses, of course, are always acting. The need to slide in and out of genuineness does not exist elsewhere (except, perhaps, for politicians). The risk of confusing roles is greatest for lawyers. What effect does this juggling of personalities have on your psyche?

3. The Lawyer's Professional Mask

In addition to resolving tensions between your various professional roles, you must also define and manage the interplay between your private self and professional roles. The next two subsections introduce two overlapping problem areas created by that interplay.

Both legal education and the practice of law have traditionally taught particular forms of analysis, attitudes, and bearing that create a professional persona for the lawyer. This can have serious implications for your sense of self and your relationships with other lawyers, your clients, and those close to you. Professor James Elkins has written extensively on these phenomena. In particular, his article, The Legal Persona: An Essay on the

---

1. We recognize there is a substantial argument that litigators, to be effective, must be genuine and must believe in their clients' causes. That is not the generally prevailing view in the Bar, although most lawyers would probably concede some correlation between a litigator's genuineness and his or her effectiveness.

Professional Mask, 64 Va. L. Rev. 735 (1978), discusses several points critical to your development of effective interpersonal skills and relations.

Elkins posits that lawyers possess a "legal persona":

> [L]awyers represent themselves to the world and are perceived by the world through images. That is, in the "presentation of self in everyday life," the self is not shown but only a reflection or image of the self. For the individual lawyer, this image is a mask of the true self—a persona—which defines his professional identity for himself and for society. In addition, owing to his professional training, the lawyer conceives of himself as a "special kind of person both different from and somewhat better than those nonprofessional members of the social order." The lawyer's perception of himself as a lawyer and his perception of his role in society begin to crystallize during his first days in law school. Confronted with the Socratic method of teaching that obliges him to master a new form of reasoning, the law student begins to adjust his view of the world to accord with his changed environment. And through the persuasive efforts of law professors and older law students, the prospective lawyer realizes that he must learn to "talk like a lawyer" and to "think like a lawyer" to *become* a lawyer.[2]

No doubt you can recall the experience of beginning law school and being told your professional education would teach you how to think like a lawyer. The Socratic method in your classes drummed into you the methods for analyzing and synthesizing cases and extracting rules of law. The new vocabulary bewildered you—each case you read required several consultations with a law dictionary. You were then a layperson, much like a client who enters the mystifying world of legal jargon. Over time, you learned to dazzle family and friends with Latin and technical terms such as "res ipsa loquitur," "certiorari," or "substantive due process." You spouted forth the rules from *Hadley v. Baxendale*, *Palsgraf*, and *Shelley's Case*. Soon, you began to think in your new language and then frequently forgot that those about you were not conversant in it. By your modes of thinking and speaking, you acquired an air that set you apart from the general population.

Elkins uses the label "legalism" for this professional worldview that lawyers acquire. Legalism is "the ethical attitude that holds moral conduct to be a matter of rule following, and moral relationships to consist of duties and rights determined by rules."[3] While that unidimensional attitude "creates and molds" lawyers' legal personas, it can be deceptive. "Law professors and lawyers erroneously believe that their legal training and their intellectual tools will enable them 'to strip a problem, any problem, down to its essentials.'"[4] In fact, the "legalism" applied by many lawyers obscures rather than clarifies the real issues. Legalistic thinking too often leads to preoccupation with formal details to the exclusion of what should be (or actually are) the determinative considerations. Thus, for example,

---

2. 64 Va. L. Rev. at 736-737.
3. Id. at 740, quoting J. Shklar, *Legalism* 1 (1964).
4. 64 Va. L. Rev. at 740-741.

lawyers could once argue the separate-but-equal doctrine was constitutional without ever addressing its morality or its impact on minorities.

Elkins also describes the nature of the legal persona in the context of the social roles lawyers play:

> Through membership in a profession, the individual acquires a sense of "identity to the role and solidarity" with other members. Attributes and values of the profession mold and structure the lawyer's role. The collection of individuals, in this case lawyers with similar masks, creates something greater than the sum of the individuals organized: the profession attains an integrity and status as a community within a community. And it is through the professional mask (which signals to clients that the lawyer has the requisite knowledge and skills) that the lawyer is able to play his role. . . .
>
> The lawyer plays other roles of obvious importance outside the legal fraternity—in his private activities and in his relationships with family, friends, and neighbors. Here one must consider "[t]he lawyer's sense of himself as a person [which] is broader and deeper than his sense of himself as a lawyer." Both private roles and identity, and the values associated with the self, constantly shape and define the lawyer's professional life consciously and unconsciously. Unconsciously, the individual may be motivated to select a profession in which certain kinds of relationships are likely and where certain personal needs (e.g., power, self-esteem, control) are met. . . .
>
> Underlying the conflict between the private and professional lives lies a more fundamental tension between professional work and private life. This tension or conflict can be visualized as intersecting circles; the area of intersection represents a merger of the lawyer's professional and private lives. The traditional model of professionalism depicts the lawyer's public and personal lives as largely mutually exclusive. The model is consistent with the attributes of the professional mask: the lawyer must be detached, objective, unemotional, and in control of the client. Here the legal persona is a kind of facade for the public, a mask for the private self of feelings.
>
> The legal persona, however, can touch the private life of the self profoundly. Commonly, the legal persona dominates the individual's personality. Such a lawyer eats, breathes, and sleeps law. He "talks like a lawyer," "thinks like a lawyer," and for good measure dresses like a lawyer. In such a case of psychological identification, the legal persona is internalized and "becomes indistinguishable at a psychological level from other disguises of the self." The effects of overidentification with the lawyer's role lead to rigidity and an inability to change masks as required by society. Ultimately, overidentification with the professional mask may cause psychological problems. Because the lawyer's role is invested with so much status and prestige and because the mask fits so well, the danger of overidentification with the legal persona may not be apparent to the individual.[5]

Does Elkins strike familiar chords here? Do you recognize the legal persona in lawyers or law students? In yourself? How would the legal persona affect you and your relationships with clients? How does it relate to the lawyers' professional roles?

---

5. Id. at 746-749.

As we saw in the preceding subsection, lawyers are called on to fill diverse roles. "The lawyer," Elkins notes, "is counselor, advisor, friend, negotiator, advocate, writer, and problem solver. The paradox for the law-yer lies in the quest for an identity in the midst of constant change."[6] Too often, "legalism as a world view provides the overarching framework" within which lawyers don and discard new roles and "within which the various contradictory tensions in and among the roles converge. The chal-lenge for the lawyer is to resolve not only these tensions but the tensions that arise between his professional roles and his private life. From his 'shape-shifting' posture, the lawyer must take care to retain certain values that mark him as a sensitive, thinking being."[7]

A failure to meet that challenge can seriously affect the lawyer-client relationship: "[T]he elevated status accorded the lawyer as a professional tends to diminish awareness by the parties of their individual role be-haviors. As a result, attorney-client interactions are based on a relation-ship of inequality, with the attorney in the position of dominance. . . . [That] may have profound psychological effects on both the client and the practitioner."[8]

In addition, subsuming self to the legal persona leads to client suspi-cion of the lawyer and to the lawyer's alienation from clients and from "the vital humanity of interaction. This type of relationship especially is charac-teristic of lawyers whose selves are split into professional and private com-partments. Lawyers attempt to protect themselves from the deep feelings which follow psychological identification with client concerns. Maintaining a facade of impersonal coolness precludes a confrontation of the real self of the lawyer with the client: hence, the lawyer relates to the client in terms of functional status, i.e., attorney to client."[9]

Professor Elkins concludes by prescribing self-scrutiny (leading to self-awareness) and greater understanding of the impact—and dangers—of the legal persona as antidotes for the ill effects brought on by overidentification with the persona. The following chapters provide the ingredients for filling that prescription. They elaborate on the symptoms and consequences of the professional mask and, in Chapters 12 and 13, suggest a model for self-scrutiny.

4. The Moral Dimension

In this subsection, we continue to address the interaction of lawyers' pro-fessional and private lives and how that interaction affects the lawyer-client relationship. Professor Elkins considered the issues primarily (though not exclusively) in terms of their personal and psychological effects. This sub-section regards the moral implications of the stated issues.

In a seminal article, Lawyers as Professionals: Some Moral Issues, 5 Hum. Rts. L. Rev. 1 (1975), Richard Wasserstrom examined two moral criti-

---

6. Id. at 750.
7. Id. at 751.
8. Id. at 752.
9. Id. at 754.

cisms of lawyers. The first centers on the lawyer's stance toward the world at large. The second criticism focuses on the lawyer's role in relationships with clients. Both of these criticisms relate to, in Wasserstrom's terminology, the "role-differentiated" behavior of lawyers (i.e., their compartmentalized professional lives).[10]

Regarding his first criticism, Wasserstrom asks "whether there is adequate justification for the kind of moral universe that comes to be inhabited by the lawyer as he or she goes through professional life. For at best the lawyer's world is a simplified moral world; often it is an amoral one; and more than occasionally, perhaps, an overtly immoral one."[11] In the conventional wisdom, the attorney-client relationship and the adversarial system provide the lawyer with a special moral status:

> [I]t is often appropriate and many times even obligatory for the attorney to do things that, all other things being equal, an ordinary person need not, and should not do. What is characteristic of this role of a lawyer is the lawyer's required indifference to a wide variety of ends and consequences that in other contexts would be of undeniable moral significance. Once a lawyer represents a client, the lawyer has a duty to make his or her expertise fully available in the realization of the end sought by the client, irrespective, for the most part, of the moral worth to which the end will be put or the character of the client who seeks to utilize it. Provided that the end sought is not illegal, the lawyer is, in essence, an amoral technician whose peculiar skills and knowledge in respect to the law are available to those with whom the relationship of client is established.[12]

To illustrate, Wasserstrom offers the case of a client who requests help in taking advantage of a tax loophole available only to a few wealthy taxpayers. What if the lawyer believes the loophole gives an unfair advantage to the rich?

> Suppose a client wants to start a corporation that will manufacture, distribute and promote a harmful but not illegal substance, e.g., cigarettes. Should the lawyer refuse to prepare the articles of incorporation for the corporation? In each case, the accepted view within the profession is that these matters are just of no concern to the lawyer qua lawyer. The lawyer need not of course agree to represent the client . . . but there is nothing wrong with representing a client whose aims and purposes are quite immoral. And having agreed to do so, the lawyer is required to provide the best possible assistance, without regard to his or her disapproval of the objective that is sought.
>
> The lesson, on this view, is clear. The job of the lawyer, so the argument typically concludes, is not to approve or disapprove of the character of his or her client, the cause for which the client seeks the lawyer's assistance, or the

---

10. During the past decade, there has been considerable discussion in the academic literature on the issues raised by Wasserstrom. A complete listing of the publications appears in Bastress, Client-Centered Counseling and Moral Accountability for Lawyers, 10 J. Legal Prof. 97, 97-98 nn.2-3, 103 n.15 (1985). More recently, see Kennedy, The Responsibility of Lawyers for the Justice of Their Causes, 18 Tex. Tech. L. Rev. 1157 (1987); Symposium, The Lawyer's Amoral Ethical Role, 1986 A.B.F. Res. J. 613.

11. 5 Hum. Rts. L. Rev. at 2.

12. Id. at 5-6.

avenues provided by the law to achieve that which the client wants to accomplish. The lawyer's task is, instead, to provide that competence which the client lacks and the lawyer, as professional, possesses. In this way, the lawyer as professional comes to inhabit a simplified universe which is strikingly amoral—which regards as morally irrelevant any number of factors which nonprofessional citizens might take to be important, if not decisive, in their everyday lives.[13]

Wasserstrom questions whether this "conventional wisdom" is, in fact, wise. What are the relative gains and costs of allowing lawyers as professionals to operate in a separate, amoral universe? "Is it right that the lawyer should be able so easily to put to one side otherwise difficult problems with the answer: but these are not and cannot be my concern as a lawyer?"[14]

Responding to these questions is made more difficult, Wasserstrom notes, by the alluring simplicity and agreeableness of the role-differentiated lawyer's intellectual world. He elaborates:

> [F]or most lawyers, most of the time, pursuing the interests of one's clients is an attractive and satisfying way to live in part just because the moral world of the lawyer is a simpler, less complicated, and less ambiguous world than the moral world of ordinary life. There is, I think, something quite seductive about being able to turn aside so many ostensibly difficult moral dilemmas and decisions with the reply: but that is not my concern; my job as a lawyer is not to judge the right and wrong of the client or the cause; it is to defend as best I can my client's interests. . . . Role-differentiated behavior is enticing and reassuring precisely because it does constrain and delimit an otherwise often intractable and confusing moral world.[15]

Wasserstrom's second criticism of role-differentiated lawyers charges that their relationships with clients are "morally defective" because they fail to treat clients with appropriate respect and dignity. He concedes an apparent paradox between his two criticisms: How can lawyers be faulted for excessive preoccupation with concern for the client, and yet be simultaneously accused of dominance and indifference vis-à-vis clients? "The paradox is apparent, not real," says Wasserstrom. "Not only are the two accusations compatible; the problem of the interpersonal relationship between the lawyer and the client is itself another feature or manifestation of the underlying issue just examined—the role-differentiated life of the professional. For the lawyer can both be overly concerned with the interest of the client and at the same time fail to view the client as a whole person, entitled to be treated in certain ways."[16]

Wasserstrom sees some "relatively benign" inequalities as inevitable in lawyer-client relationships. Lawyers, and not clients, possess the expert knowledge and the technical language needed to address the clients' prob-

---

13. Id. at 8.
14. Id.
15. Id. at 9.
16. Id. at 16.

lems. In addition, clients are generally unable to effectively evaluate their lawyers' handling of legal issues and procedures. But do those built-in characteristics of the professional relationship justify the dominance typically exerted by lawyers over clients? Wasserstrom responds:

> [T]he professional often, if not systematically, interacts with the client in both a manipulative and a paternalistic fashion. The point is not that the professional is merely dominant within the relationship. Rather, it is that from the professional's point of view the client is seen and responded to more like an object than a human being, and more like a child than an adult. The professional does not, in short, treat the client like a person; the professional does not accord the client the respect that he or she deserves. And these, it is claimed, are without question genuine moral defects in any meaningful human relationship. They are, moreover, defects that are capable of being eradicated once their cause is perceived and corrective action taken.[17]

5. Reflections

How do you respond to the issues Wasserstrom raises? Should you consider the morality of clients' positions in deciding to represent them? Should there be an identity between clients and their lawyers so that the moral stand of clients is attributed to their lawyers? Do you bring your personal views or private morality into your professional life as a lawyer? As a practical matter, what do you do when the moral questions are raised *after* you have accepted the client's case? What if you are working for a firm that takes on a major client whose position you find morally questionable? What if your employer is a corporation that takes a stance you find troubling? Can you be a good person and still represent interests inconsistent with your political, social, or moral views? Can you realistically assert those views without threatening the equality between you and the client?

We leave these questions unanswered and hope you will give them, and other points raised by Wasserstrom, serious thought as you proceed through this text.

The following narrative was written by the mother of a child with a serious kidney ailment. How does her story relate to the questions raised by Professors Elkins and Wasserstrom?

≡ MARY CLARE EROS, PARABLE FROM A PATIENT'S MOTHER

My seven-year-old daughter Janet uses a home kidney machine forty hours each week. Without her machine she would be dead within ten days. We knew nothing of renal medicine when we began to consult with doctors four years ago, but we were educated adults, accustomed to being

---

17. Id. at 19.

in control of our lives. Initially we found that most doctors assumed we did not want to be treated as equals, and we did not want to know the whole truth. They "protected" us. This led to great anxiety since we could only assume something unspeakable was being left unsaid. We could not feel secure in the knowledge that we had faced the truth—however bad it might be. While my husband stayed in the hospital with Janet for over two weeks—sleeping on a cot beside her—he worked a small experiment. Very early every morning he showered and put on a three-piece suit and a tie. Thus he greeted the medical staff. He held a clipboard and pen and recorded his questions and their responses. He asked "why" a lot. The doctors began to spend much longer amounts of time with him. They showed him Janet's chart. They offered to let him look up her drugs in the Physician's Desk Book. He had trained them through his dress and manner to deal with him as a semi-equal. They seemed to be as relieved with the new status quo as we were. Being on the pedestal is lonely.

One doctor, Susan Clark, was different from the start. She listened to what we'd observed. She took notes on what we said to her! She felt that since we'd seen this child every day, we were in the best position to detect small but potentially important changes in her condition. She also realized that if we did not understand orders we might not follow through with the medications, etc. She saw Janet for what she was—the baby of a family that lived on a farm three hours from the city and medical help. She did not see her (as one intern had) as "that incredible kidney slide—the worst biopsy on a kid we've ever seen." She did not ignore the practical realities of this disease and she recommended a hospital social worker who could help us find the way out of the catastrophic financial burden we suddenly faced. Most important, Dr. Clark knew when we needed emotional support. She encouraged us when we were most depressed simply by listening to our litany of horrors and telling us she *knew* we could make it because of what she'd seen us do already. She thought of practical ways to make the home treatment fit our lifestyle. We made it over a lot of rough places because we knew she believed we could.

D. THE APPROACH OF THIS TEXT

We have premised this text on four assumptions about skills development.

First, you must learn how to analyze an ICN session and to clearly articulate your analysis. Even the naturally gifted cannot fully develop their skills until they can break down the interview, consultation, or negotiation into its component parts, describe what has occurred, and identify alternative strategies that were available to the practitioner. To do an effective analysis, you must understand the applicable theories of interpersonal relationships and develop a vocabulary for articulating your insights. By doing that, you increase your sensitivity to the parties' surface and subsurface communications and see more clearly the relationships developing between the parties. With analysis of your efforts, you can gain the means needed to continuously improve on and maximize interpersonal skills within the practicalities of daily work.

Second, you need to build skills incrementally. Begin with the general concepts of the skill in question and then apply these basics to more complex and specialized situations.

Third, you learn skills by doing. They require practice. The theory and cognitive learning will have little meaning until you can apply them in simulated or real settings. You could, for example, read all the books on playing tennis, have exceptional natural ability, and still not be an effective tennis player until you spend long hours on the practice court. Interpersonal skills are no different. You need the theory and the vocabulary, but they alone are not enough. You must also have practice and experience in using the skills before you will achieve real—let alone maximum—proficiency.

Fourth, you must learn how to prepare for meetings with clients or with other lawyers and then put your learning to use. Because interpersonal processes are both demanding and subtly complex, you need to analyze carefully the issues, the format, and any potential problems *before* you interview or counsel clients or negotiate on their behalf. Natural skills and experience (especially the latter) can streamline your preparation, but they cannot provide a substitute.

The chapters that follow build on these assumptions. The text puts forth theories for interviewing, counseling, and negotiating. Comprehension of the readings will facilitate meaningful self-criticism and teach you the essentials of preparation for interpersonal sessions. Experience (either real or in simulated exercises) will then allow you to implement and practice what you have learned. Critiques from peers and instructors can provide valuable responses that, in turn, will sharpen your skills and contribute to an understanding of the kind of self-criticism needed in law practice.

This text will not make you an accomplished practitioner of interpersonal skills. Only extended experience can do that. Rather, we seek to give you a theoretical structure for developing your skills and to raise your intuitions to a conscious level. With careful reading of the text, you should be able to understand and describe the substance of any lawyer-client session or negotiation and to engage in both meaningful preparation and self-criticism. With these goals accomplished, you will be able to optimize natural abilities and improve your interpersonal skills throughout your career.

Chapter

2

Helping Theories

A. INTRODUCTION

Before discussing particular helping skills, we must consider the theoretical bases for the counselor-client relationship. To do that, we refer to the literature on psychotherapy. Why, you ask, are the various schools of psychotherapy necessary—or even helpful—to a lawyer who seeks to be effective in representing clients? That is a reasonable question, and the response requires some elaboration.

First, lawyer-client relations, like all interpersonal relations, require an understanding of people. You need to understand *both* yourself and your client. The psychotherapies discussed here offer respected opinions on what motivates and shapes personality and on what methods are most effective in helping persons with problems. Lawyers are helpers whose profession persistently involves them in their clients' problems. Knowledge of the range of psychotherapies and their premises facilitates greater understanding of self and others. Awareness of psychological forces, personality makeup, and human motivation makes it more likely that you can accurately perceive the nature and extent of a client's problem and can formulate a responsive strategy. That knowledge also allows you to more easily recognize what is going on inside your own mind and how your feelings or needs could affect your handling of a case and your relations with others. That self-insight is essential to effective lawyering.

Second, even if we are not conscious of it, we all hold some opinion about people and about how to relate to them. Knowledge of the prevailing schools helps you to better define what your own theories are and whether you act according to those theories. Several chapters in this book seek to enhance self-scrutiny,[1] and consideration of your views about personality and interpersonal relations is important in that undertaking.

Third, and in keeping with the above, the skills taught throughout this book are premised on certain views about people and interpersonal relations. When those skills are seen as part of a big picture, complete with theoretical bases, then their utility and purpose should be more easily perceived. Grasping theory should permit an easier integration of the various skills into effective relations with others.

Fourth, this chapter—indeed, this book—is intended to entice you to read in other disciplines. The following materials should reveal the usefulness to you of psychology and psychotherapy. Later, Part IV will examine social science fields for theories on negotiation and then apply them to law practice. The legal profession does not exist in a vacuum; we lawyers cannot continue to be so presumptuous as to think our casebooks and treatises contain all the knowledge and training needed to be effective. We, our clients, and the public could all benefit immensely from our careful consideration of the knowledge available in other disciplines.

Two caveats must be made concerning this chapter. The first should be obvious: The following overview of selected psychotherapies is just that—an overview. In no way can this chapter substitute for extended personal study of any one of the theories. We hope only to expose you to the range of theories, which should in turn prompt self-scrutiny and encourage further independent study and reflection.

The second caveat addresses the limits of psychotherapy in the context of the lawyer-client relationship. Psychotherapy essentially strives to identify an individual's problems and to devise solutions. The problems can range from temporary personal crises to major emotional disorders and neuroses, and solutions can vary from reassurance to "cures" that follow intense psychoanalysis spanning several years. Psychotherapeutic efforts typically examine the client's psyche or personality and move toward personal growth or personality changes.

Lawyers also try to identify clients' problems and potential solutions. Working through those stages requires use of many of the skills and knowledge used by psychotherapists. But the overlap stops there. We are not in the business of, and are not equipped for, probing the psyche and helping clients adjust their personalities. That is possible in a lawyer-client relationship, but our goal is necessarily more confined. Thus, the utility of the psychotherapies for you lies in the extent to which they educate you about human behavior and about the skills of problem identification (interviewing) and selection of solutions (counseling). If a solution calls for professional services within your expertise, then you proceed to work with the client toward the selected goal. But if the client needs substantial counsel-

---

1. In addition to this chapter, see especially Chapters 1, 12, and 13.

ing on emotional problems, then you should refer the client to a psycho-therapist. Neither this chapter nor this book should be read as encouraging lay therapy. As the following materials reveal, however, you need knowledge of the various psychotherapies to both fully develop your interpersonal skills and recognize when referral of a client for expert help is indicated.

Each of Sections B through F describes a major school of psychotherapy. The format in each section proceeds through general and background information, a discussion problem, a summary of the school's theory on personality, and its application to counseling techniques and the counselor-client relationship. Each section then concludes by identifying the usefulness and limitations of the particular theory for a practicing attorney. Section G follows with a brief summary of other major theories. Finally, Section H outlines our use of the psychotherapy theories in later chapters.[2]

B. PSYCHOANALYSIS (FREUDIAN)

1. Introduction

No overview of psychotherapy could omit reference to Sigmund Freud and the treatment processes developed from his work. During the first several decades of this century, Freud pioneered studies into the human mind and formulated the basis for modern psychology. He identified a subconscious, as well as a conscious, level to the personality, which he saw as a battleground for continuing conflict between the aggressive and libidinous forces on one side and social and moral pressures on the other. Building on a comprehensive system of psychology, Freud developed psychoanalysis to treat individuals with particular emotional problems. The treatment calls for extended and rigorous exploration of the patient's subconscious and past, especially early childhood. Psychoanalysts have found some success in treating neuroses and interpersonal problems.

Freud's pioneer work not only launched modern psychology but also built a foundation from which all of the psychotherapies (possibly excepting behaviorism) derive a measure of support. Some have simply extended Freud's work, modifying and refining it as experience and experimentation indicate.[3] Others, like Alfred Adler and Carl Jung, have diverged from Freud, relying on different emphases and assumptions. Still others, such as Carl Rogers ("person"-centered therapy) and Fritz Perls (Gestalt

---

2. Each of the sections includes a list of references for further reading. Those sources also provided the basis for the summaries in this chapter. For organizational help, we have relied especially on the essays collected in R. Corsini & D. Wedding, *Current Psychotherapies* (4th ed. 1989).

3. The theories of Adler, Jung, and Perls are briefly described below in Section G. Section C develops the person-centered approach of Carl Rogers.

therapy) have split more radically from Freudian psychology and treat-ment, but would nevertheless concede the insight and accuracy of certain aspects of Freud's theories.

≡ PROBLEM 1 ≡
Samuel Frantz [4]

Samuel Frantz is a schoolteacher who has come to a lawyer upon re-ceiving from his school board a "notice of suspension with the intent to discharge." The action against Frantz followed an incident at school during which, in Frantz's words, he "cuffed" a student. The student and his par-ents were very upset, complained to the superintendent, and have threat-ened to file criminal charges.

Arriving at his initial interview with his lawyer, Beth Jones, Frantz was neatly dressed but covered with a serious skin eruption. Jones's interview elicited that Frantz did, in fact, hit the student after the student had re-fused to follow an order to return to his study hall. Frantz stated he simply had lost his temper and hit the boy harder than was necessary. According to Frantz, he had been feeling a lot of anger for some time but, until this incident occurred, had managed to keep himself under control while at school. Mostly, he said, he went home at night and vented his anger by yelling at his wife, Anita, which naturally had strained his marriage.

Frantz stated his anxiety dates back to four years ago following his mother's suicide. She took an overdose of pills after years of alcohol and drug abuse. She and Frantz had been very close. An only child, Frantz was born illegitimate; his mother never married. At the time of her suicide, she was upset with Frantz because he had married.

Frantz told Ms. Jones that he had served during the Vietnam War in the Navy's Underwater Demolition Team, a very dangerous assignment, and had been awarded the Navy Cross Medal for bravery. He then went on to college, where he played guard on and captained the football team. After college, he began his teaching career. He was set to marry at that time, but broke off the relationship because his mother objected to the woman. He did say, though, that he was not certain he really loved the woman or that she would have been good for him. Besides, he said, had he married then, he would not have developed a relationship with Anita. When she came along, she and Frantz quickly became serious. His mother again expressed disapproval, but he was intent this time. So he proposed, Anita accepted, they were married, and his mother's suicide occurred a few months later. Frantz's anxiety and the skin disorder ensued.

Frantz wants very much to keep his teaching position. He believes the student was being obnoxious and was wrong in not following clear direc-tions, but Frantz also realizes he overreacted. He expressed concern, too, that he might "lose it" again in the future.

---

4. This problem is adapted from K. Lewin, *Brief Psychotherapy: Brief Encounters* 60-68 (1970).

2. *Theory of Personality*

As noted above, Freud saw the personality as an arena for conflict. He compressed the various instincts and inhibitions into a personality triad. The "id" represents the innate, primitive, selfish, aggressive, and sexual instincts in the individual—those that would predominate in a person if he or she were left totally unrestrained by society and feelings for others. Because the id stands for what Freud saw as the individual's "natural" drives, his view of humanity is essentially negative. We are instinctively selfish, aggressive, and irrational. The "superego" comprises the societal, moral, and parental teachings internalized by the person. The "ego" mediates between these competing "internal" forces and the external world. The conflict occurs on both conscious and unconscious levels.

Freud further concluded that our overriding drive is to seek pleasure and to avoid pain or unpleasantness. This is the "pleasure principle." The individual's actions and thoughts reflect a conscious effort toward pleasure. To avoid pain, however, the ego employs a number of defenses to either bar certain unpleasant experiences from consciousness or, at least, to defuse their impact. For example, "repression" occurs when the individual manages to block out entirely a painful experience. "Rationalization," perhaps the most common defense, describes a post-hoc gloss placed by the ego on an unpleasant event to make it appear to have been for the best. Consider Samuel Frantz's case: He recalls that he backed out of a marriage because his mother objected, but he coats that recollection with further explanations that he was not sure of his love for the fiancée and, had he gone ahead with the marriage, his relationship with Anita would not have developed. Perhaps it *was* for the best that he changed his plan on that occasion; but it also seems plausible that Frantz created the gloss as an ego defense to maternal manipulation and to ease the pain that would naturally accompany the dissolution of a serious relationship. In addition, Frantz's ego may be creating a fantasy world for him so he can present himself as (what he perceives to be) a worthy individual. (Did Frantz really serve on the Navy's Underwater Demolition Team? Receive a medal for bravery? Captain his college football team?)

The ego has a whole range of such devices for guarding consciousness against pain and "helping" the individual to cope. In addition to repression and rationalization, they include projection, regression, compensation, intellectualization, and denial. (The ego defenses are discussed more fully in Chapter 8, Section E, below.) When they seriously distort reality, they rise to the level of neuroses.

Another significant principle of Freudian psychology is that of determinism, which provides that personality development and mental processes—on both conscious and unconscious levels—result directly from past experiences. The psychoanalyst assumes that mental and emotional reactions are not accidental, but relate to some earlier event, including (especially) childhood and traumatic events. Thus, when confronting an apparent neurosis, psychoanalysts seek to explore the patient's conscious and unconscious recesses for events that provoked the mental state. The resulting discovery is central to psychoanalytic treatment.

The story elicited from Mr. Frantz illustrates the importance of early childhood experiences and the correlation of present mental states with past events. Obviously, his anxiety appears causally related to his mother's suicide. He may suffer guilt because of a perception that his marriage provoked her demise. The scant facts also hint at other, perhaps deeper, psychological remnants from the mother-son relationship.

In addition, Freud saw the childhood "psychosexual stages" as having a critical impact on personality development. Moving chronologically from the first year through adolescence, the stages include the oral, anal, phallic, latency, and genital stages. Fixation at any one of these stages produces significant personality deviations in later life. For example, the anal stage normally prevails between the ages of eighteen months to three years. During that period, the child derives his main source of physical pleasure from stimulation of the anal erogenous zone and from the activities connected with retention and passage of feces. For a time, the child regards the feces as an extraction of self and thus valuable. When the child encounters disgust from those who care for him, he may lose self-esteem and then grow stubborn, rebellious, and independent. Finally, through a "reaction formation," the child may become compulsively neat, punctual, and possessive.[5]

Psychoanalysts see a distinct connection between mental and physical events. These connections include not only fixations and responses to various sexual stimuli, but also more severe physical reactions to traumatic experiences. Frantz's skin disorder, for example, could well be a psychosomatic reflection of his guilt over his mother's suicide.

3. Theory and Techniques of Psychotherapy

Psychoanalysis is primarily a method for treating neuroses and emotional disorders—that is, psychoanalysis is not a prescription for everyone's mental health. It can be effective when an individual's problem is rooted in unconscious conflicts. By exploring those conflicts, and exposing to patients the unconscious, irrational sources of their suffering, psychoanalysts help them to achieve the knowledge and self-awareness needed to make choices in a sane, rational manner.

Accomplishing these goals requires extended analysis. Treatment often entails several years of frequent sessions. In the treatment, the patient engages in free-flow monologues and the analyst functions mostly as a nonjudgmental, but curious, listener and as an interpreter. Because psychoanalysis seeks to reach information the patient's defenses have barred from consciousness, or at least from everyday awareness, the analyst essentially asks the patient to talk about whatever comes to mind. Absolute honesty is demanded from patients and strict confidentiality is therefore needed and guaranteed by the therapist. Analysts inject themselves only to comment on the significance or symbolism of particular images, thoughts, or events. Special attention is given to patients' dreams because they reveal the unconscious at work. Accordingly, analysts probe dreams

---

5. Arlow, Psychoanalysis, in R. Corsini & D. Wedding (eds.), *Current Psychotherapies* 30-31 (4th ed. 1989).

and ask patients to describe whatever meaning they see in, or thoughts they find provoked by, their dreams. The principle of determinism makes everything that patients do or say relevant. Nonverbal messages are important because many of them are unconsciously communicated.

Psychoanalysis is a process. In its initial phase, the analyst identifies the patient's problem and determines whether psychoanalysis would be helpful. (As indicated above, it cannot resolve all emotional problems.) As the process moves forward, it relies heavily on the concept of "transference." When the treatment reaches a certain point, the analyst takes on in the patient's unconscious the persona of a figure from the repressed past or from fantasies. When that occurs, the patient's perceptions of present events are influenced by his or her past experiences with parental and authority figures. Working with transference helps the patient to understand how the unconscious manipulates present perceptions and relations. Patients work through their misperceptions and rationally address the relation of past events and present behavior. The analysis continues as the transference is developed and the exploration widens and intensifies. Through this process, patients gain awareness of their conflicts and learn to deal with reality.

Ultimately, the analyst attempts to resolve the transference and terminate the treatment. Those tasks can be very difficult, and frequently the patient may reveal an aggravation of the original symptoms. This phenomenon could result from a desire to perpetuate a meaningful relationship, from some sense of dependence left over from childhood, or from a final effort by the subconscious to reassert the fantasy wishes that initially caused the patient's problems. In addition to dealing with those problems, the therapist must prepare the patient for life after analysis. Finally, the analyst must at all times remain sensitive to the potential for "countertransference," in which the analyst reacts to the transference by attributing an identity from his or her past to the patient.

4. Utility for Lawyers and Limitations

As should be obvious from the above description, lawyers are not equipped for, and have no business, conducting a deep psychoanalysis of a client or engaging in extended counseling to explore the client's unconscious. But there is much in psychoanalytic theory of value to the lawyer.

First, you can benefit from an awareness of potential connections between a client's problem and his or her unconscious conflict. Samuel Frantz's case illustrates the point well. A lawyer sensitized to psychoanalytic theory could recognize the possibility that Frantz's overreaction in cuffing the student was a manifestation of a larger emotional problem, a residue from his feelings about his mother and her death. Although unable to treat Frantz's problem, the lawyer can refer him to an expert who has the necessary expertise. The lawyer could also use psychoanalytic theory to advantage in representing Frantz. If the attorney can prove to the school board that the loss of temper was a function of an identifiable problem, for which Frantz is being treated, the board will be more likely to negotiate some compromise short of termination, such as a suspension or a leave of absence. Moreover, there may be financial advantages for Frantz if he agrees to a leave of absence that is medically indicated rather than disciplinary. Referral for expert help may also reveal deeper problems and confirm suspicions that Frantz is fantasizing about his past. At the very least, it seems clear that Frantz will continue to encounter trouble if he is not convinced of the need for expert attention.

Second, you must constantly acquire information from clients, opposing parties, witnesses, and others. Anything that affects recall and information flow, then, is of great importance to the lawyer. The defenses erected by the ego and superego can obstruct information flow.

Third, the phenomena of transference and countertransference occur in attorney-client relationships. When you work closely with a client, the client may unconsciously transpose you with an individual from his or her past just as would occur with a psychoanalyst. Thus, when you find a client behaving irrationally toward you or making extreme demands on you, consider confronting the client or seeking expert advice. Similarly, you may need help when you transpose your client with some symbolically important figure in your experience.

Finally, the psychoanalytical methods bear scrutiny. The use of a nonjudgmental attitude, limited topic control, close attention to nonverbal communication, and maintenance of confidentiality also have utility in law office interviewing and counseling—as we will see in succeeding chapters. Admittedly, you do not want to elicit an unfettered stream of consciousness from a client; your informational goals and practical limitations require a more focused method. Like the analyst, however, you need your client to talk freely and openly to identify what the client sees as important.

REFERENCES

Arlow, J., Psychoanalysis, in R. Corsini & D. Wedding (eds.), *Current Psychotherapies* (4th ed. 1989).
Brenner, C., *An Elementary Textbook of Psychoanalysis* (1973).
Brill, A. A., *Freud's Contribution to Psychiatry* (1944).
Freud, S., *Civilization and Its Discontents* (J. Strachey ed. 1961).
———, *The Complete Psychological Works of Sigmund Freud* (J. Strachey ed. 1976).
———, *General Psychological Theory* (P. Rieff ed. 1972).
———, *The Origin and Development of Psychoanalysis* (1955).
Lewin, K., *Brief Psychotherapy: Brief Encounters* (1970).

C. PERSON-CENTERED

1. Introduction

The person-centered (also called "client-centered" and "Rogerian") psychotherapy has been developed over the past five decades under the leadership of Carl Rogers. The approach is premised on the notion that individuals can best develop and grow toward their full potential—toward self-actualization—when facilitated by a relationship with a helping person who is empathic, genuine, and nonjudgmental. Rogerians believe humans to be fundamentally good. The helper, then, need only nurture that natural goodness. When individuals feel understood, feel good about themselves, and find acceptance, they will respond rationally and positively, in terms of their own growth and their relationships with others.

Person-centered theory thus differs substantially from Freudian concepts, which view humanity as inherently primitive, self-centered, and irrational. The Rogerian perception of human beings and its consequent emphasis on nondirective techniques distinguish person-centered counselors from directive counselors and behaviorists, who view clients as dependent on professional and external influences for personal growth. Rogers has instead aligned himself with the humanistic psychologists, such as Abraham Maslow, and their notions about the individual's dignity, worth, and natural search for growth. If basic needs are met and if not diverted by external forces, people will progress to a stage of maturity, inner peace, productivity, and caring for others—that is, to self-actualization. Person-centered theory also emphasizes the here and now—rather than the past or the future—and how individuals feel about themselves and their relationships—rather than their conformance to the external norms of society, the helper, or others. Rogerians share these latter, "phenomenological," emphases with the Gestalt theorists. (See Section G below.) Finally, person-centered psychotherapy shows a heavy influence from related concepts in Judeo-Christian doctrine, existentialist philosophy (especially the work of Soren Kierkegaard and Martin Buber), and the oriental Taoist teachings.

≡≡≡ PROBLEM 2 ≡≡≡
Reverend Davies

William Davies is a minister in a mid-sized city who has come to see a lawyer, Jill Simmons, about an impending vote of his church council and matters relating to that vote. Davies, 33, has served this church for the past four years and has enjoyed substantial popularity within his congregation. He knows Ms. Simmons from their work together on the city's United Way campaign.

The church council at Davies' church has recently expressed to him its concern about an apparent shortage in church funds. The council is due to meet soon to consider the results of an independent audit. The council has thus far kept the matter confidential.

Davies tells Ms. Simmons that the audit will reveal a $10,000 shortage. He says he borrowed the money over the past year to finance a drug habit he has been furtively feeding for over a decade. According to Davies, he took "speed" in college and then in seminary to sustain his grueling work habits. Since his ordination, he has continued to work a phenomenal schedule. He says that for several years now he has been physically and emotionally dependent on various kinds of drugs. Because of increased government regulation and enforcement of local drug laws, the scarcity and price of black market drugs have increased dramatically over the past five years. Moreover, to purchase drugs in sufficient quantities to satisfy his need, Davies has had to deal increasingly with criminal and other nefarious elements both locally and in nearby cities. Indeed, one of his prime suppliers is a regional pornography kingpin.

Davies has been married for ten years and has two children in grade school. His wife does not know about his habit, although she has been expressing concern for years about his health and his "nerves." Their marriage, though, has remained solid. Davies has always been intensely active in a range of community projects and good works, as well as doing all that can be asked of him as a minister. Indeed, Davies says, that is part of the problem. He feels trapped in a spiral; he has steadily expanded his commitments and his work responsibilities, which, in turn, have thrust him further into his drug habit to meet those commitments and maintain his pace.

About a year ago, his increased usage and the increased costs of acquiring the drugs finally pushed his habit beyond his means. He slowly began to "borrow" church money, thinking that he would pay it back for sure and telling himself that the loans were necessary to support his valuable work for the church and the community. As time advanced, so did the borrowing, and soon he found himself in a situation where he could not repay the money.

Davies is very upset and very worried. He fears public exposure and its effects on his family and his career. He fears losing not only his current ministry but also his ability to continue as a minister anywhere. The possibility of a criminal action also haunts him. He feels embarrassment and shame for his drug dependence, for his embezzlement, for his collection of criminal contacts and his conduct, and for letting down his family and his congregation. Davies feels the need to come clean with the council, but he also wants to be sure he proceeds with a full awareness of all the consequences. He thus seeks advice on how best to deal with the council and the potential legal problems he faces.

2. Theory of Personality

Although Rogerians concentrate on human growth rather than on some comprehensive theory of personality, a theory has nevertheless emerged. From experiential observations and clinical testing, Rogers identified the preconditions and barriers to growth, and from those premises he then articulated a basic concept of personality.

In Rogerian thinking, each individual possesses an innate drive toward self-actualization (that is, toward autonomy, maturity, and self-fulfillment) and away from control by others. As persons grow, they develop through experience a self-concept, which is (in Rogerian terms) "organismic" and personal. They also develop self-regard, which is their perception of how significant *others* see them. Naturally, when a person's actions match up with the expectations of others, his or her self-regard is positive, and when actions fail to meet others' expectations, a negative self-regard results. The ingredients of self-regard—typically derived from family and societal mores or edicts—are called "conditions of worth."

When a conflict develops between organismic needs and self-regard needs, which have incorporated the conditions of worth, the self-regard needs typically take control. Thus, the person in effect subsumes personal needs and drives to social and family strictures. The organismic needs do not, however, disappear. Their persistence and impact on the individual's experience cause anxiety and provoke the person to use defense mechanisms to keep such needs from his or her awareness and thereby maintain self-regard. Self-actualization and self-fulfillment are abated, and neuroses can follow.

3. Theory and Techniques of Psychotherapy

Consistent with the foregoing personality principles, person-centered therapy intervenes to help individuals deal with the incongruence between their self-concept and their experience. When clients find complete acceptance and understanding from a significant other, their self-concept can emerge in an atmosphere that does not threaten their self-regard, and that, in turn, allows the clients to meet their own organismic needs and thus progress toward self-actualization. As they escape the confinement of conflicting conditions of worth, the clients learn to trust their own needs and values. The therapy has a phenomenological basis; it emphasizes the present (not the past, as with psychoanalysis) and lets the clients experience themselves fully through an emotionally meaningful relationship with the therapist.

From his and others' experience in therapy, Rogers identified the three preconditions to helping a client achieve growth: the therapist must be (1) empathically understanding of the client, (2) unconditionally positive in his or her regard for the client, and (3) genuine.

Empathy. To empathically understand the client, the therapist tries to see the world through the client's eyes. The therapist seeks to learn what the client is experiencing—not only events and encounters, but also reactions and feelings. This effort focuses exclusively on the client's present phenomenal experience. The therapist reflects back to the client the essence of the experience and feelings the client has described. At times, the therapist's reflections penetrate beneath the surface of the client's consciousness to feelings or attitudes implied, but not articulated, by the client. Through this process, the therapist pushes clients to recognize their self-concept and organismic needs. The therapist's genuine understanding and acceptance of those needs facilitates clients' growth and progress toward self-actualization.

Positive Regard. The therapist unconditionally accepts clients and their self-concepts and, therefore, exercises no judgment about the clients' values, feelings, needs, or experience. The therapeutic goal is to help each client to identify his or her self-concept but not to reshape it. As clients learn about themselves, articulate what they learn, and are accepted, self-concept and self-regard merge and self-actualization is promoted.

Genuineness. When therapists are genuine, their words match their feelings. They neither create nor hide behind a defensive facade; instead, they meet clients with the feelings they are experiencing. This genuineness permeates their relationships with clients. It infuses the therapists' empathic reflection and positive regard as well as governs their self-descriptions. Genuineness in the therapists' sensing and reporting of their own feelings establishes their "congruence," an essential for effective counselors.

As already implied, empathy, positive regard, and genuineness are interdependent; each needs the other two for successful execution.

Because Rogers' approach to counseling and teaching has been to permit individuals to seek self-fulfillment, his implementing techniques are very nondirective. For example, the therapists rely heavily on questions, exerting the minimum in topic control. Silences can be numerous and long, depending mostly on the clients' willingness to talk and their agenda. The therapists' primary contribution—and the centerpiece of the therapy—is their empathic reflections.

4. Utility for Lawyers

As you will see in the chapters on interviewing and counseling, lawyers have much to learn from person-centered theories. There are many facets and subtleties to those lessons. At this point we canvass only a few of them to provide an introductory appreciation of the theories' utility for lawyers and to adequately address the issues raised by the Davies problem.

First, the underlying value placed by Rogers and other humanistic psychotherapists on the individual and his or her intrinsic worth can provide a theoretical basis for the attorney-client relationship. Each client is entitled to individualized consideration, to be seen and represented as a person with a legal problem and not as a legal problem accompanied by a person.

Second, person-centered techniques offer the most effective means for fact-gathering. By creating an accepting, understanding relationship, you can best encourage most clients to open up and to be more candid about facts and feelings. When your clients know that you will not condemn them and that they will have your acceptance regardless of what unfolds, they will be much more likely to tell you about threatening subjects. Certainly, in Reverend Davies' case, the personally threatening nature of his information would create obstacles to a fully open discussion. If Ms. Simmons empathized with her client's conflicts in a genuine, caring, and accepting fashion, Davies would be more inclined to tell her about all aspects of his predicament. For example, his contacts with criminal elements would be especially threatening to one in his profession and position, and he might be tempted to omit references to them by reasoning such knowledge was not necessary to attend to the immediate problems with finances and the church council. Yet that information would be of considerable value to Ms. Simmons in her representation of Davies' legal interests. She might, for instance, propose to Davies that he make a full disclosure to the police in return for prosecutorial consideration. Davies might also pursue that alternative as a means to atone for his misconduct. At the very least, she should discuss the possible criminal liability that could result from his drug dealings. Such discussions might never occur, however, if Davies cannot expect to find an accepting helper who will understand his problem.

Third, person-centered techniques are extremely valuable in counseling when the client must address and choose from among multiple alternatives. The choice among alternatives often depends more on the client's feelings than on legal analysis. At the very least, feelings are a relevant factor in the client's decision-making. Reaching a decision thus requires a sorting out of feelings as well as an ordering of priorities and risks. Your use of empathic reflection at this stage can help your clients to delineate their feelings and priorities.

A range of issues arises for Reverend Davies and his counselor to resolve. How should he deal with the church council and the fund shortage? How can he save his career? What about the potential criminal charges on the missing funds and drug offenses? What about his drug problem? All of these demand sensitive examination of Davies' own needs and of his concerns for his family and congregation, as well as the legal implications.

Here, Ms. Simmons' empathic reflections can help to sort through the web of issues and considerations. She could reflect on the Reverend's compelling need to serve and to succeed or on the insecurity that caused him to believe he needed drugs to get by. In addition, Davies' misdeeds have left him embarrassed, humiliated, and ashamed, and the embarrassment will intensify with each person who finds out. Measuring these feelings would be important in deciding, for example, whether to force a public hearing or whether to negotiate a quiet retreat out of town. When Davies receives his lawyer's accurate, empathic responses on these and other subjects, he gains a better understanding of himself and his priorities. The lawyer's reflections push him to an even deeper level of self-scrutiny and an analysis of how he feels about the alternatives. That, in turn, produces better decision-making.

Finally, Davies is a good example of a client in need of a nonjudgmental counselor. Davies appears to be sufficiently self-condemnatory so that further reproaches would accomplish nothing. Similarly, he does not need adulation or approval. He has a problem; he must confront that and begin to deal with it. The lawyer cannot take responsibility for the drug rehabilitation, but she can avoid obstructing it. By accepting Davies, and empathically understanding his present turmoil, Ms. Simmons can be a facilitator to help him overcome both his drug dependency and the personal factors that pushed him into that state and kept him there.

5. Limitations

There are, however, limits to transferring Rogerian psychotherapy to the law office. Because your goals do not typically include helping clients to change or to achieve self-fulfillment, you must diverge from the therapist's agenda to meet the task at hand—that is, analysis of the legal ramifications of your client's case. As just noted, the lawyer in the Davies problem would refer the client to a therapist or counselor for help in overcoming his drug and emotional problems while continuing to represent him in his legal matters. The limits of the lawyer's training and expertise dictate such arrangements.

The person-centered school (like all the schools) has its critics. The criticism has largely centered on its preoccupation with problem identification and discussion, and its lack of attention to designing action steps toward resolving the problem. According to traditional Rogerian doctrine, a meaningful relationship with a genuine, accepting, and understanding therapist is, in itself, sufficient to help the patient overcome his or her problem. Sometimes it is. But in other cases, say critics, such a relationship appears to be merely one condition for problem resolution and something more is needed to achieve therapeutic success. (Some psychotherapists, such as the rational-emotive theorists, contend the relationship is not even a condition.) At some point the therapist must do something more than simply listen and reflect.

Thus, Rogers has disciples who have adopted his philosophy and techniques but who also advocate that the therapist should take a more active role after problem identification and the establishment of a meaningful relationship with the client. The active role can include, among other things, making suggestions to the client, assigning tasks, or placing the client in a group discussion. In each instance, the therapist then follows up with additional genuine, empathic, and nonjudgmental listening and reflection.

REFERENCES

Carkhuff, R., *Helping and Human Relations* (1969).
Hart, J., & Tomlinson, T. (eds.), *New Directions in Client-Centered Therapy* (1970).
Raskin, N., & Rogers, C., Person-Centered Therapy, in R. Corsini & D. Wedding (eds.), *Current Psychotherapies* (4th ed. 1989).
Rogers, C., *Counseling and Psychotherapy* (1942).
———, *Client-Centered Therapy* (1951).
———, *Psychotherapy and Personality Change* (1954).
———, *On Becoming a Person* (1961).

D. BEHAVIORISM

1. Introduction

Unlike the psychoanalytical and person-centered therapies, behaviorism focuses on clients' actions and behavioral patterns rather than on their feelings and thoughts. Behaviorists proceed from the premise that all behavior is a function of preceding events. Thus, the means for altering human behavior must be found in external forces and not within individuals themselves. Behavior and behavioral changes are learned; they are not—with the possible exception of cases involving serious psychoses—inherent or organismic.

Behaviorists see behavior as a series of responses to certain stimuli. Thus, when clients want to improve themselves, relieve anxiety or neuroses, or in any way change their behavioral patterns, the therapist begins by identifying the stimuli that produce the undesirable behaviors. The therapist then attempts to alter or extinguish the response and through reinforcement (or occasionally punishment) shape a more desired behavioral pattern.

Behavioral therapists are more directive than their counterparts in other schools. Behaviorists strive to present an image of expertness to the client. Yet they view therapy as a collaborative process; therapist and client together identify schedules and goals and devise a plan for their achievement. Behaviorists claim such plans set them off from the other schools; that is, behaviorists do not just talk about and identify the client's problem—they provide the client with concrete means to resolve it.

≣ PROBLEM 3 ≣
David Bott

Robert and Margaret Bott died in an automobile accident 42 years ago. They left behind two sons, George and David. George was the older by twelve years and was always outgoing and aggressive. Just out of college when his parents died, George took his inheritance and plied it into a modest fortune, eventually becoming the metropolitan area's largest new-car dealer. George never married, but he did take in and rear his younger brother. In contrast to George, David was reserved and rather timid. Preferring contemplative activities, he has worked his entire professional career as a researcher and cataloger for a local museum. Like George, David has remained a bachelor. At George's death, his will left to David a substantial estate of realty, stocks, bonds, savings accounts, the family house, and a summer home. David will also receive an annual payment from the car dealership's profits.

Although he is an intelligent man, David has had no experience in handling money or property. He had relied completely on George to handle all the financial matters and the maintenance on the two homes. Now that he is gone, David has been baffled, distraught, and intimidated by the need to pay bills, field inquiries on his holdings, and manage his money. Mixed with the feelings of loneliness and loss he naturally experienced when his brother died, David has suffered a great deal of anxiety. As a consequence, he has relied heavily and frequently on the family lawyer, Rachel Moore. He has called Ms. Moore about almost everything—from renting the summer home, to purchasing insurance, to managing the bank accounts. Through it all, Ms. Moore has remained patient and helpful and has charged David only for her more substantial services and advice, such as preparation and filing of tax forms.

After six months of this routine, Mr. Bott has begun to feel very badly about his impositions on Ms. Moore's time for trivial and routine matters. Yet he still feels intimidated by the prospect of asserting himself and handling his own affairs. He recently described this dilemma to Ms. Moore during a phone conversation, and she set an appointment for them to discuss the matter in greater detail.

How can Attorney Moore deal with David Bott's anxiety and problems?

2. Theory of Personality

Like the person-centered theorists, behaviorists have not developed an elaborate structure of human personality or explanations of why individuals act as they do. Instead, behaviorists have concentrated on discovering and exploring what, in fact, works in changing personality and behavior. That concentration has led them to see "personality" as a function of learning. An individual learns to adopt conditioned responses to certain stimuli. Behaviorism applies that principle to bring about desired change in personality and habits.

Under the major branch of behaviorism, B. F. Skinner's "operant conditioning," responsiveness is enhanced when the response (operant) is rewarded with a positive stimulus, or "positive reinforcement." "Negative reinforcement" occurs when the response works to curtail or eliminate an unpleasant stimulus. For example, a football coach may negatively reinforce his team's effort in practice on a hot day by ending practice (an unpleasant experience) early. He positively reinforces the team when he throws a watermelon party after a hot, grueling workout. Negative reinforcement should not be confused with punishment, or "aversive conditioning," a stimulus that also occasionally creeps into the behaviorists' repertoire. Our football coach, for example, uses aversive conditioning by requiring extra laps after a lackluster practice.

Beyond these basics, behaviorists have developed a number of corollaries for effecting personality change. By gradually increasing expectations for an adequate response to stimuli, the therapist "shapes" the client's progress to the desired goal. For example, an individual afraid of crowds could be shaped to overcome the fear by progressing from a normal street corner, to a crowded bus, to a crowded department store or sporting event. Behaviorists have also concerned themselves with "extinguishing" maladaptive habits as well as with creating new ones. If responses can be learned, then they can also be unlearned. Similarly, behaviorists realize that some acquired, sought-for responses may dissipate if not continually reinforced in some way.

Behavioral therapy thus rests on the assumption that personality development is a function of learning processes. The learning processes used by the behaviorists are, in many ways, a sophisticated refinement of the basic learning program that parents administer to their children and that has developed personalities throughout history.

3. Theory and Techniques of Psychotherapy

Basically, behaviorist psychotherapy seeks to provide the client with corrective learning. To accomplish that, the therapist moves the client through three chronologically indistinct stages: (1) building a sound therapist-client relationship; (2) developing a functional analysis; and (3) devising and executing a corrective action plan. Each of those requires a brief elaboration.

First, the therapist wants to build a solid relationship with the client.[6] To achieve that relationship, behaviorists use those techniques employed by Rogerians in their client dealings. So the behaviorists strive to be nonjudgmental and accepting, warm, empathic, and genuine. Similarly, the behaviorist wants to impress on the client that he or she is being treated as a unique person and that the two of them will be working together toward client-identified goals. The behaviorists, though, emphasize more than the Rogerians the importance of instilling in the client a perception of therapist expertise. Behaviorists also assume a more directive role with clients than do Rogerians.

Coincident with the efforts to establish a good working relationship with the client, the behaviorist prepares a "functional analysis" to discover the client's problem and the antecedent stimuli responsible for it. This is done by getting from the client a detailed personal history and specific descriptions about the situations in which the client's problems arise. Following this background review and the therapist's analysis, the therapist meets with the client to help identify goals, explain the treatment process, and devise a contract for the treatment.

At this point, the corrective learning begins with intensity through one or more of several different modes. (Frequently, some positive learning occurs during the functional analysis as a result of new insights and the effects of a meaningful therapist-client relationship.) First, the therapist can teach the client by "modeling" the desired skill or by using live or taped demonstrations from other individuals. After observing such models, the client then practices the skill in role-play or, if possible, in "live" (in vivo) settings.

Second, the therapist may find that some cognitive learning by the client is necessary before the desired change can occur. For example, if a client's anxiety about sex is the result of ignorance on the subject, it would be futile to try to change behavior without first dispelling the irrational beliefs. In David Bott's case, he will not be able to overcome his anxiety and dependence regarding financial matters until he learns about money management. In such cases, cognitive learning can be accomplished through verbal instruction, readings, role-playing, and so on.

Third, there are a variety of techniques used for emotional learning. "Flooding" and "implosive therapy," for example, involve intense exposure to the anxiety-producing stimuli. "Systematic desensitization" describes a method by which the anxiety-provoking stimuli are repeatedly paired with relaxation techniques to gradually reduce anxiety levels and,

---

6. Unlike person-centered and psychoanalytic therapies, however, behaviorist therapy is not relationship-dependent. Theoretically, the behaviorist regime can work even in the absence of the "solid relationship" described in the text.

eventually, to overcome the anxiety. "Covert sensitization" is a similar technique in which the anxiety-producing stimuli are paired with stimuli that cause pleasant responses.

Fourth, in "operant conditioning," desired behaviors are immediately reinforced and developed under systematic schedules of progression and reinforcement. The "token economy" is an extension of operant conditioning. Therapists using this technique reinforce client exercises of particular desired behaviors by immediately rewarding the client with tokens, which can then be exchanged for some privilege, specified items, or even money.

This review does not exhaust the behaviorists' entire repertoire, but it should throw some light on how behaviorists implement their theories on corrective learning.

4. Utility for Lawyers

You can put behaviorist teachings to work in your law practice. For example, you can use the behavioral methods to implement a collaborative approach to the professional-client relationship and to achieve a meaningful contract between professional and client. The David Bott case illustrates how a lawyer can use behaviorist techniques to advantage in helping a client. Mr. Bott encountered severe anxiety whenever he tried to tackle finances or personal business. To help him deal with that anxiety and help him stand on his own (and stay out of her hair), Attorney Moore could proceed through the following steps with him.

1. Ms. Moore can begin by discussing with Mr. Bott whether he wants to handle his own affairs or whether he wants to hire a manager.

2. If Mr. Bott says he wants to manage his own affairs, then Ms. Moore can plan with him a schedule for assuming control. She can enhance the probability for successfully helping her client at this point by empathically reflecting on the distress and frustration Mr. Bott feels being alone in an unfamiliar world.

3. After developing a plan, Ms. Moore places it in a contract form so that Mr. Bott knows he is in a cooperative venture. The plan agreed to by Moore and Bott involves several stages.

4. The first stage involves cognitive learning. Ms. Moore needs to instruct Mr. Bott on how to go about handling his personal business. He obviously cannot overcome his anxiety if he does not learn how to manage his affairs. As a lawyer who handles estates and who worked with George Bott on his sizeable holdings, Ms. Moore can certainly convey the knowledge David will need.

5. After cognitive learning, the plan carries Mr. Bott through a series of assigned tasks of increasing difficulty. The first task might be balancing his accounts. Then Mr. Bott could devise a monthly budget. Next, he could undertake to buy and sell stocks and then to negotiate a new lease for one of his properties. The number and extent of the assignments must approximate the variety and substance of the duties required to effectively manage the Bott estate.

6. Upon completion of each task, Attorney Moore should immediately

review and evaluate Mr. Bott's effort and performance. When appropriate, Ms. Moore should positively reinforce adequate performance with some kind of encouragement.

7. When the set of planned tasks is completed, Mr. Bott should be ready to handle daily and routine matters on his own. Ms. Moore should consider occasional follow-ups on his status and encourage him to consult with her about more complex matters. If Mr. Bott's anxiety over managing his affairs has not abated after execution of Ms. Moore's plan, then referral to either an expert counselor or a business manager—or both—would be necessary.

Obviously, you cannot minister to all your clients as Attorney Moore has done with Mr. Bott. Ms. Moore could work with this client as she did because his anxiety-provoking stimuli fell in an area of her expertise, she and Mr. Bott already had a solid professional relationship, Bott could afford to pay Moore for her help, and his problem was not difficult to identify. (Moore, however, may also want to consult an expert about her analysis of his anxiety.) Still, the Bott case does illustrate the potential for use of behavioral methods and theory in the law office.

5. Limitations

Behavioral theory has received criticism on several grounds. Many see behaviorism as treating symptoms (behaviors) only, while leaving unabated the root causes of the client's anxiety (be they unconscious or inappropriate feelings or irrational thinking). Thus, according to these critics, behavioristic successes are short term only; at some point after suspension of treatment, the root cause reemerges in other symptoms.

Another criticism centers on behaviorism's underlying rejection of individual free will. In behavioral theory, behavior is a function of external forces. Thus, an individual's inner forces cannot be responsible for his or her acts. Furthermore, critics charge that behaviorist techniques are highly manipulative; the therapist pulls the strings one way or another to get the client to behave according to a preset script. The high correlation between behaviorist methods and traditional child-rearing methods reinforces the notion that the client is a "child" to be shaped by the professional "parent." Behaviorism is seen as overcoming the person's spirit and free will, as in treatments to "cure" homosexuals or change aggressive behavior in prisoners and the mentally ill. Some people therefore find behaviorist treatment and its underlying premises to be dehumanizing and offensive.

Finally, behaviorism vests substantial power in the therapists. By virtue of their own theories, they manipulate others into a particular course of conduct. The threat is there, then, that those with power will use it to control and standardize their subjects, so the subjects conform to the values (and possibly even the needs) of the trainers. Modern behaviorists have become sensitive to these criticisms. Accordingly, they have emphasized that the therapist-client relationship is a collaborative one and that the client selects the behavior he or she wants to achieve. Still, the threat of trainer control and manipulation remains.

REFERENCES

Bandura, A., *Principles of Behavior Modification* (1969).
Goldstein, A., & Foa, E. (eds.), *Handbook of Behavioral Interventions* (1980).
Leitenberg, H. (ed.), *Handbook of Behavior Modification and Behavior Therapy* (1976).
Skinner, B. F., *The Behavior of Organisms* (1938).
———, *Walden Two* (1948).
———, *Science and Human Behavior* (1953).
Wilson, G. T., Behavior Therapy, in R. Corsini & D. Wedding (eds.), *Current Psychotherapies* (4th ed. 1989).

E. RATIONAL-EMOTIVE THERAPY

1. Introduction

Rational-emotive therapy (RET) was developed by Albert Ellis in the 1950s. It (along with reality therapy) has a cognitive-behavioral basis. RET postulates that faulty thinking leads to anxiety and that people need to restructure their thinking in order to correct their anxiety. Accordingly, Ellis developed the "A-B-C" theory. When an individual experiences an intense emotional consequence (C) following a significant activating event (A), the individual may conclude that A caused C. In fact, however, emotional consequences are largely a function of the individual's belief system (B). Thus, when severe anxiety or another undesirable emotional condition occurs, it can usually be traced to some irrationality in the person's belief system. The therapist's job, then, is to intervene and challenge those beliefs. When the individual sees the belief exposed as irrational, the emotional consequences disappear.

Certain basic assumptions underlie that analysis. Individuals are born with rational and irrational, and with constructive and destructive, potential. RET advocates agree with the humanists and the Rogerians that people have expansive self-actualizing resources. But RET also maintains that people have powerful innate propensities to think irrationally and to engage in self-destructive behavior. These irrational and destructive tendencies are often evoked and intensified by family and culture. Racial prejudices illustrate the point.

Furthermore, say RET therapists, each individual tends to act, think, perceive, and emote simultaneously and interdependently. That is, a person's actions are a function of his or her thoughts, feelings, and perceptions, and those feelings derive from a combination of the person's actions, thoughts, perceptions, and so on. Because of that interdependence, when an individual's thinking is wrongheaded or false, it adversely affects the person's behavior and emotions. Indeed, Ellis concludes that emotional problems nearly always result from poor thinking. In particular, emotional problems derive from irrational self-condemnation, an irrationally excessive need to be liked by others, and irrational demands placed on others.

Perhaps Shakespeare best capsulized RET theory when he wrote, "Nothing's bad but thinking makes it so."

≡≡ **PROBLEM 4** ≡≡
Joe Pignelli

Joe Pignelli is a 50-year-old baker who, for the past 20 years, has operated his own bakery featuring Italian bread, rolls, cannoli, cookies, and other such delights. Throughout the bakery's existence, Joe has worked extremely hard, putting in fourteen-hour days six days a week, from four in the morning until six at night. He has always taken personal responsibility for the baking, leaving his wife and daughter to handle the clerking, cash register, and accounting duties. Joe never made big money on the bakery, but generally managed to get by with a decent middle-class income.

Lately, however, the bakery has fallen on hard times. Joe has had health problems and been forced to cut back on his hours. The cutback in hours has led to a corresponding reduction in his productivity and cash intake. In addition, Joe's neighborhood has changed. It is losing population as major employers in the city have departed and, just as bad, the ethnic mix of those remaining has changed over the years. These developments have caused a lowered demand for Joe's products and forced him to keep his prices low. Inflation has therefore made serious inroads into his profit margin on what he does sell.

As a consequence, Joe is now deeply in debt. He had to take out another mortgage last year to borrow money to buy a new oven, and the bakery has not produced a profit in the last two years. His savings are now depleted.

Joe has come to see his attorney, Samuel Pescatore, because he recently received notice from the bank that it was about to foreclose on the bakery. During his initial interview with Joe, Pescatore learns about the sad state of the bakery's finances and the equally sad state of Joe's physical and emotional health. Joe is depressed, he tells his lawyer; his livelihood is at risk, his friends are moving away or dying, he can hardly recognize his old neighborhood, and he has lost that sense of security and routine that he prized for so many years. When Pescatore suggests that Joe may have to consider bankruptcy as an alternative, Joe resists. For him, bankruptcy would be a mark of disgrace and would rob him of his pride and his purpose.

2. Theory of Personality

We return to Ellis's A-B-C principle to elaborate on the rational-emotive analysis of personality. An individual experiences (A) an unpleasant activating event—let's say he flunks out of college. He then encounters (C) anxiety and depression. RET analysts posit that the academic failure is not, in fact, the cause of the disruptive emotions; rather, the anxiety and depression result directly from (B) the individual's beliefs and values. The individual's thinking at B might develop as follows:

> "I am an awful person because I flunked out. My parents will be mad at me because they will think I didn't work hard enough. People won't like me and won't want to associate with me or hire me because they will think I'm stupid.
> "In fact, I flunked out because my professors didn't like me. They should be damned for not liking me. They have ruined my life and they have no right to ruin my life. Now employers can do the same thing to me. They must treat me fairly."

Here, the individual has, in effect, allowed his beliefs to talk him into a depression. He believes himself to be an awful person because he has breached his family's trust and values. He fears parents and other people will now reject him. Joe Pignelli expressed similar fears in his abrupt dismissal of bankruptcy as an alternative solution to his financial problems. Ellis sees an exaggerated need to be liked as a primary source of self-destruction. To be healthy and productive, a normal individual does require meaningful relationships with others, but a preoccupation with the reactions of others and an excessive need for acceptance cause an irrational fear of rejection. That fear can in turn lead to the attitude, also expressed by this former student, that others and the world must accept him. He demands they cater to his pleasure. Joe Pignelli, too, displayed at least some of those sentiments with his intimations about the new elements in his neighborhood.

RET holds that, once clients see the irrationality of their beliefs and understand that those beliefs have caused anxiety and depression, the clients can then focus on, confront, and overcome their beliefs. When that happens the anxiety and depression will disappear. RET theory, then, has as fundamental precepts that humans are responsible for themselves and their fate; that they have positive and destructive tendencies; that family and social conditioning frequently exacerbate the latter; that irrational beliefs cause adverse emotional consequences; that, however, humans *do* have the ability to understand their own irrationality, once it is exposed to them; and, with that understanding, they can resolve their emotional problems.

3. *Theory and Techniques of Psychotherapy*

Because of these perceptions of the human personality, RET dictates that its therapists assault the irrationality in individuals' belief systems. That is best accomplished, according to Ellis, by therapists who are highly cognitive, directive, and discipline-oriented in their methods. Rational-emotive therapists therefore reject the generally prevailing notion that a warm therapist-client relationship is a precondition to positive personality change. RET does agree with person-centered psychotherapy that the counselor must be accepting of clients as persons, but that does not preclude the counselor from criticizing their behavior. RET aims to provoke clients to examine their values and beliefs and to change those that are irrational or destructive. And RET therapists do not hesitate to communicate their judgment about those beliefs and values.

To accomplish their purge of a client's irrationality and self-destructive forces, rational-emotive therapists engage a variety of methods. These can be grouped into three categories: cognitive, emotive, and behavioristic. Cognitive therapy shows clients the irrationality of their quest for perfectionism, their self-condemnation, and their collection of "shoulds," "oughts," and "musts." As implied by its name, cognitive therapy teaches clients; it teaches them to think, to use scientific methods of deduction. The therapy informs and explains. It is didactic. The therapist's methods include Socratic dialogues with individual clients, group therapy, audiovisual aids, and readings.

Emotive therapy uses assorted devices to demonstrate to the client rational and irrational thinking. The therapist could employ role-playing, modeling,[7] humor, exhortation, and in vivo assignments. In each instance, the goal is to confront the clients with a dramatic illustration of their erroneous thinking and, with the therapist's unconditional acceptance, to convince the clients that others can accept them even with their foibles and perceived defects.

RET therapy employs many behaviorist methods. RET therapists, however, use such methods not only to change the clients' symptomatic behavior but also to correct their cognitive processes. Under this approach, the therapist assigns clients tasks that have a high risk of failure or directs the clients in simulated imagined failures. The therapist then works with the clients to analyze their reactions and ultimately to separate and discard irrational responses.

4. Utility for Lawyers

You can adopt RET theory and methods to help your clients (and witnesses) deal with anxieties related to their legal problems (e.g., divorce, a serious automobile accident, bankruptcy) or to the legal process (e.g., trial or deposition). You could demonstrate to the client the basic RET message—that anxiety is almost always the result of irrational thinking. The message can be communicated through didactic explanation or Socratic dialogue with the client.

In the Pignelli case, Joe presents multiple problems that require multiple solutions. Yet his emotional, financial, and legal difficulties are clearly interrelated. Indeed, Joe's emotional reaction is an obstacle to pursuit of one of the viable alternatives (bankruptcy).

Attorney Pescatore could use RET principles and techniques in a number of ways to help Joe. The lawyer can demonstrate the irrationality of

---

7. "Modeling" is a demonstration by the therapist, or by members of a therapy group, of alternative behaviors available to the client.

wallowing in the past and convince his client that the present requires a new outlook. Joe retains control over his life and has it in his power to look for a new job, learn a new skill, or find a new neighborhood. Which of those would best suit him is a question for counseling (with the lawyer or with someone else), but those are all alternatives that meet Joe's problems and are within his means. Joe still has the potential for growth but his thinking of the past and about his losses currently stands as an obstacle to growth. Therefore, such thinking must be rooted out before Joe can move on. RET techniques, such as Socratic dialogue, modeling, or simple instruction, can enable Joe to adjust.

In addition, RET can inform Pescatore on how to deal with Joe's reaction to the suggestion of bankruptcy. If that course of action is to be rejected, then Joe should do it on its merits and not for what RET would identify as an irrational reason, such as social opprobrium. By thus educating Joe, the lawyer expands Joe's legal options and increases the potential for a full emotional, as well as financial, recovery for the client.

5. *Limitations*

In certain contexts, at least, your use of rational-emotive methods could present some difficulties. For one, boring in on clients' "irrational thinking" while they are in the midst of a tense personal crisis because of a lost family member, marital separation, or whatever could come across as uncaring and insensitive. If you expect to work with clients and need their trust, then any conduct that seems uncaring and insensitive will not be particularly conducive to effective representation. At the very least, then, you should know exactly what you are doing before launching an RET offensive.

Second, rational-emotive theory seems to admit no proper role for values. The theory describes the "shoulds," "oughts," and "musts" in a person's belief system as irrational and destructive. But without them, the individual either vests little importance in values or has no values at all. Thus, RET may encourage amorality.

Third, use of RET risks offending some people because of its pejorative characterization of religion. Because belief in the deity is more a matter of faith than of logical or empirical proof, then, according to RET doctrine, the belief is ipso facto irrational. RET considers religious precepts to be no more than myth or magic. But many clients perceive religion as crucial to their lives and a matter of personal right. If you belittle clients' religion or try to disabuse them of their religious beliefs, you are likely to find yourself summarily discharged.

REFERENCES

Ellis, A., *Reason and Emotion in Psychotherapy* (1962).
———, *Growth Through Reason* (1971).
———, *Rational-Emotive Theories* (1974).

————, Rational-Emotive Therapy, in R. Corsini & D. Wedding (eds.), *Current Psychotherapies* (4th ed. 1989).

Ellis, A., & Grieger, R., *Handbook of Rational-Emotive Therapy* (1977).

Morris, K., & Kanitz, H., *Rational-Emotive Therapy* (1975).

F. TRANSACTIONAL ANALYSIS

1. Introduction

The principles of transactional analysis (TA) were developed by Eric Berne, who popularized his theories with the 1964 publication of *Games People Play*. Berne continued until his death in 1970 to shape and expand the basic principles into a coherent and complete theory of personality. Other psychotherapists have converted to his thinking and contributed refinements and elaborations of TA.

TA combines Freudian, phenomenological, and cognitive perspectives. It emphasizes the here and now, but it also holds that past events have present and serious emotional effects. TA seeks to teach individuals about personality and, thus, about themselves, and through this cognitive acquisition to achieve desired personality changes. TA techniques, however, are much more akin to the phenomenological schools. Moreover, TA proponents insist that each person is responsible for, and can control, his or her life. They also believe in the inherent goodness of each individual. As Berne wrote, "People are born princes and princesses until their parents turn them into frogs."[8]

TA theorizes that each individual functions through three active personality states: the Parent, the Adult, and the Child. These states differ from the Freudian triad because they are dynamic, evolving, observing, conscious, and segregated entities within the personality. The Adult state provides maturity, logic, realism. It relates the individual to the outside world. The Parent state both introjects and identifies with the person's own biological parents. It expresses the individual's values, beliefs, and attitudes. The Parent in a person may be "Critical" or "Nurturing." The Child state comprises the rebellious and nonconforming aspects of the personality, as well as its creative, intuitive, and emotional components. In TA jargon, the individual has both "Free" and "Adapted" child states.[9]

When two persons interact, a "transaction" occurs. When the transactions operate at both overt and covert levels, the individuals are playing "games." These are stereotyped and predictable. Moreover, at some point early in life, the positive and negative "stroking" (human recognition) that children receive from parents and others produces in the children their life "scripts." These determine individuals' views of themselves and of others.

---

8. Quoted in C. Steiner, *Scripts People Live* 2 (1974).

9. The terms used in the text are John Dusay's. See, e.g., Dusay, Ego Games and the Constancy Hypothesis, 2 Transactional Analysis Journal 3 (1972); Dusay & Dusay, Transactional Analysis, in R. Corsini & D. Wedding (eds.), *Current Psychotherapies* 409 (4th ed. 1989).

Emotionally healthy people have a positive view of both themselves and others. This "I'm OK, You're OK" attitude is essential in intimate, close relationships and for emotional and social well-being. Through TA, clients balance their Parent and Child states, develop their Adult state, learn to communicate genuinely and not through games, and acquire positive feelings about themselves and others. They are thereby able to participate in meaningful, intimate relationships and to achieve productive and happy lives. This, according to TA proponents, is possible for everyone.

☰ PROBLEM 5 ☰
Estelle May

Estelle May lives in comfortable style in a small city. She has been working part-time as a salesperson in an art studio since the younger of her two children left for college. Estelle has been married for 22 years to a surgeon, William May. Prior to her present job, she was a housewife. Although she does not have a college degree, she did attend a university for two years until she dropped out after meeting and marrying William. She is an attractive woman who carefully buys only the latest—and most expensive—fashions. She also invests considerable energy in her hair and makeup. Persistent dieting has kept her figure trim.

All of these facts are well known to Lawrence Townsend, the May family attorney for the past 15 years, when Mrs. May consults him following her arrest for shoplifting at an expensive downtown department store. She arrives, as always, carefully and fashionably overdressed. The following dialogue condenses that consultation:

Attorney: Tell me what happened, Estelle.
Estelle: Well, I was downtown for my weekly lunch date with Marie Ballard. We get together and talk, have a few drinks, you know, just share things that are going on in our lives. After lunch, we went shopping, just like we usually do. We'd been looking for about a half-hour when we decided to go into Fox's to see if they had gotten their fall line in yet. Well, they had, and they had really gorgeous things. I just fell in love with this dress they had on display. So I took it back into the changing room to try it on. It looked even better on than it did in the display. But it was very expensive, and I knew my charge cards were all at their limits and I had no more money in my checking account. Lately, Bill's been trying to limit my spending, so he's only been putting so much in my account each month. I thought maybe this part-time job I got would give me some extra spending money, but I go through that almost as fast as I get it. There's not much more to it, really. I was afraid that if I waited till Bill put some more money in my account, the dress would be gone. So I decided to change back into my street clothes and stuff the dress into my bag. I'd been to that store often enough; I didn't think they'd ever suspect me and wouldn't dare do anything to me. God, I was so embarrassed when that detective

stopped me and looked into my bag. I mean I was mortified. My best friend standing right there and all those people around. I don't know what came over me. I felt I just had to have that dress, and, after all the business I gave that damn store, I guess I figured they could afford me this one. Maybe the drinks from lunch affected my judgment, too. I'd had a couple of martinis plus some wine with the meal. I've been depressed a lot lately—since the kids left and I began to realize I was getting older. So these lunches with Marie and the shopping have helped to make me feel better. But now, I'm not even going to have them anymore. I'll be too embarrassed to do them with Marie, or anyone else, after what's happened.

Attorney: I see. . . . I think fighting this charge would get us nowhere. Perhaps our best bet would be to try to negotiate with the prosecutor and the store to work something out.

Estelle: I'm all for anything that would help to get this over with and behind me.

Attorney: You're distressed by all this.

Estelle: Yes. I mean, it was not only embarrassing, it really messed up my life. The only times I was truly happy was when I was out there shopping; I felt comfortable there. I got respect from the clerks. They knew me and I had some status with them. Now, they'll just watch me to make sure I'm not stealing anything. Looking back, I think maybe I got a certain enjoyment out of it—it was sort of like I was getting back at Bill for putting those spending limits on me.

Attorney: You and Bill have been having disagreements about your spending?

Estelle: Oh, it's been an ongoing battle. I want to look my best. That's what makes me feel good. And when I'm not looking as good as I can, things just don't go right for me. It seems that everyone ignores me when I'm not at my best; they don't show me the same respect. And that includes Bill.

Attorney: You know, I have an idea about your experience and the feelings you've described. Do you want to hear it?

Estelle: Sure.

Attorney: It seems to me that you have concluded you are not worth very much except through your physical appearance. So if you don't look good, you can't be worth very much. In order to get the attention you need, you then expend all your energy to look good. To do that you spend a lot of money, and that makes you feel good. You also feel that by spending all that money, you're getting back at Bill for not allowing you sufficient respect and attention. This shoplifting, then, may have been the ultimate effort at getting recognition. You were bound to get either a lovely new dress or lots of recognition plus a chance to fight back at Bill. Is that right?

Estelle: Well, I don't know. It seems so simple. [Silence.] Yet what you've said does make some sense to me.

Attorney: Of course, I'm just throwing some ideas out at you. It's not my job to figure those things out. But I do think you should seek some counseling on the issues and feelings you've discussed with me today. Meanwhile, I will get in touch with the prosecutor and the store to see where they stand. I think that given your reputation, your past conduct, and your past dealings with the store, they should be receptive to talking about alternative ways to handle this matter other than through the misdemeanor process. If, with your permission, I can tell them you are seeking professional help, I believe they might be willing to agree to some compromise. Maybe you could make restitution, or plead to some lesser, totally innocuous charge, like trespass or something. Do I have your authority to proceed in that manner?

Estelle: Yes.

Attorney: Fine. Then I will take the steps needed to carry out that strategy and you must take the steps to begin counseling. I can, if you like, suggest the names of a few experts whom I regard highly. . . .[10]

---

2. Theory of Personality

There are three ego states—Parent, Adult, and Child. A person functions in one of those distinct ego states at any one time. Because TA ego states are observable and real, they differ dramatically from the Freudian concepts of id, ego, and superego. Diagnosis of a particular ego state can be accomplished through direct observation of a person's verbal and nonverbal communications.

The Parent ego state embodies behavior and attitudes inherited from parents and other authority figures. When in this ego state, the person responds, acts, talks, and feels as one (or both) of his parents did when he or she was little. Thus the parent is that part of us that acts as a transmitter of social and moral values and provides a measure of stability in society. As with each of the ego states, though, the Parent is dynamic and complex; it can change as the person encounters new authority figures or new situations calling for varied parental responses. Moreover, individuals can learn to realign the elements in their Parent state.

The Parent ego state has two functional components: the Critical Parent (CP) and the Nurturing Parent (NP). The CP, which has also been labeled the Controlling Parent and the Pig Parent, finds fault, criticizes, directs, limits, asserts, makes rules, and enforces values. Too much CP is dictatorial and overbearing; too little leaves the person lacking in assertiveness and skepticism—the "Wallflower" of years past or the "Wimp" of today. The NP (also called the Natural Parent) protects, promotes growth in, and empathizes with those close to the person. Individuals with too

---

10. The dialogue in this problem does *not* illustrate a model for lawyer interviews. As will be shown in later chapters, the lawyer in this case moves too quickly (even taking into account a long-standing relationship) to assess the root of the client's problem. In addition, the lawyer's method for getting his authority to negotiate with the prosecutor is not consistent with the approach described in Part III of this text. As with Problems 1 and 2, above, we have taken certain liberties to conserve space and to illustrate textual points.

little NP lack sensitivity and feeling for others, while persons with too much NP tend to smother those around them.

The Adult in individuals keeps in touch with the outside world. It is this part of personality that is logical, rational, nonemotional, and nonjudgmental and gets the problem-solving assignments. Persons with a deficient Adult, then, have difficulty in thinking clearly and in acting responsibly, but too much Adult is boring.

The Child ego state, like the Parent, also has subcomponents, although there is some dispute among TA theorists about their designation and classification. The Free Child (FC), also called the Rebellious Child, is creative, spontaneous, vivacious, playful, inquisitive, and intuitive. Artists and performers have a strong FC, but too much FC means the person is too uninhibited and, at times, out of control. On the other hand, too little FC makes Jack a dull boy and Jill a dull girl, unimaginative, and seldom playful or fun.

The Adapted Child (AC) is that part of the person reflecting a child's desire to please his or her parents. Thus, the AC conforms, complies, adapts, and compromises. Society requires a certain measure of AC in its members to maintain some system of order and compliance with law, as well as to permit people to get along. On the other hand, a dominant AC manifests itself as an uncritical robot. Guilt and depression also frequently accompany an excess of AC.

These ego states blend together to form the individual's personality, so each personality reflects the relative strengths of its various ego states. Generally, people experience emotional difficulties when one (or more) of the ego states is particularly low or particularly high. Correspondingly, a balance among the ego states results in a well-balanced, productive individual. In the May problem, for example, Mrs. May's personality includes an impoverished Adult, given her difficulties in reasoning, and a high Adapted Child, as revealed by her efforts to please others (a pattern probably formed in childhood) and by her inability to break a banal, even stultifying, routine.

The individual's personality also corresponds to perceptions of self and others, perceptions that are intertwined with the distribution of the ego states. According to Berne, each individual is born with an attitude of, "I'm OK, You're OK." That too is the attitude of mature, productive individuals. When, however, negative perceptions of self, of others, or of both self and others develop, personal troubles ensue. Predictably, TA adherents see negative perceptions of self or others as functions of an imbalance among the ego states. For example, a high CP usually produces a "You're not OK" attitude, while an "I'm not OK" perception will likely accompany a high AC/low NP makeup.

TA emphasizes how people communicate with each other. As its name indicates, TA looks at "transactions," which are the stimuli and responses between various ego states of two or more people. Transactions can occur at an overt level and be easily recognizable, or they can be psychological and transpire on a covert level through intonations and body language. Transactions may occur between one person's Parent and another's Child, or between two persons' Adults, or between one's Adult and another's

Child, and so on. Moreover, an individual can simultaneously conduct overt and covert transactions in different ego states. For example, the following takes place between a law professor and a student:

Professor: Did you complete the assignment I gave you?
Student: Yes. Here it is.

In the above exchange, there is no (apparent) covert transaction, and each conversant speaks through his or her Adult ego state. So long as the participants remain on the same level (e.g., Adult to Adult or Child to Child), the conversation can continue indefinitely and productively. Now compare the following:

Professor: Did you complete the assignment I gave you?
Student: No, I didn't.
Professor: You knew it was due today, didn't you? How do you expect to be able to function as a lawyer if you don't complete your work on time?

In this exchange, both professor and student begin the transaction in their Adult states, but the professor slips into the CP state when responding to the student. When they speak from two different levels (e.g., Parent to Child), the discussion on that particular subject stops. Now consider a final example:

Professor: Did you complete the assignment I gave you?
Student: Oh sure.
Professor: Well, let's see it.
Student: You can't. My dog ate it.

In this transaction, the overt communication signifies the conversation is occurring between the individuals' Adult states, but the context reveals a covert transaction between their Child states. TA posits that these covert, or "psychological," transactions provide a key to understanding an individual's behavior. The covert communications provide the playing field for psychological games that reveal much about the persons playing them. The games are a rich source of "strokes" for the players in keeping with their personal "scripts."

The need to receive "strokes," or personal recognition, from others provides the most fundamental motivation in human social interaction, say TA enthusiasts. Strokes vary in form and substance. They can be positive or negative, and they can range from physical stroking to praise to mere recognition. Obviously, positive strokes are better than negative strokes, but the latter are better than no strokes at all. A person's emotional (and often physical) health is directly proportional to the frequency and quality of the strokes the person receives. It follows, then, that a hunger for strokes is a driving force in humans, and the ways in which persons give and receive strokes shape their particular personalities. Mrs. May, for example, used a series of contrivances to gain the strokes she needed, and those contrivances (or "games") took over her life.

From early in life, a pattern of stroking develops through interactions between the child and his or her parents (or their substitutes). This pattern induces the child to form an opinion about self and eventually about others. Verbal and nonverbal messages then continuously reinforce those opinions throughout the person's life. Over time, they combine with values received from the Parent ego states of both mother and father and with negative "injunctions" transmitted from the Child ego states of the parents to produce the individual's "script."

A script is the person's "blueprint for a lifecourse."[11] It often incorporates specific elements from myths, fables, fairy tales, popular drama, and the like. Scripts vary, of course. They can prescribe their holders to be heroes or heroines, villains, rescuers, victims, persecutors, bystanders, and so on through the nearly endless variations in characters. Scripts can be tragic, banal, winning, or losing. Whatever the script, it becomes a powerful force in an individual's life; it develops into a strong belief system and sets the tone for the person's life experiences. Unfortunately, because scripts are developed early and prematurely, they often impose destructive scenarios on their holders.

Thus, scripts put individuals through certain recurrent patterns and games. The negative feelings that result from these experiences are the particular person's "racket feelings." During script development, the individual chooses the feelings he or she will rely on in stressful situations. Typically, people select sadness, anger, depression, or fear. They will then use that racket feeling over and over, regardless of its appropriateness.

Although these scripts, with their attendant games and rackets, can radically limit and dictate personal development, TA theorists nevertheless insist that individuals can change their scripts. People remain in control of their lives and with proper instruction and guidance can rewrite the scripts and overcome their destructive elements. Transactional analysis seeks to teach individuals about themselves, to help them read and understand the scripts they have chosen, and to provide them with an environment for change. When that is accomplished, individuals can confront anew their moments of decision and through self-confrontation make informed, mature decisions about life.

Now consider Mrs. May. Her script corresponds to that which Steiner has labeled "Plastic Woman." To obtain strokes, "she encases herself in plastic: bright jewelry, platform heels, foxy clothes, intriguing perfumes, and dramatic make-up."[12] She receives some strokes (particularly from store clerks) for the energy and money she puts into clothes and shopping. She experiences power and satisfaction in her role as a consumer. Her script tells her that she will find respect and recognition if she can present herself as chic and beautiful.

---

11. C. Steiner, *Scripts People Live* 60 (1974).
12. Id. at 213. Steiner classifies "Plastic Woman" among the "banal scripts of women." See generally id. at 210-234. Plastic Woman is depicted at 213-215.

Yet her life outside the department store lacks meaning. She holds little power over what happens to her and devotes her time to putting on makeup, trying on different outfits, and reading movie and fashion magazines. She lives in an emotional void and is subject to her husband's financial restrictions. She repeatedly proves the validity of her script by getting ignored by people when she is not encased in her plastic, superficial "beauty." Over time, frustration, anger, and depression accumulate. She tries to fight back, but her arsenal lacks sophistication. In typical "Plastic Woman" maneuvers, Mrs. May shoplifted and overspent, as if to beat her husband with her plastic charge card. Finally, "when superficial beauty can no longer be bought and pasted on, she ends up depressed: she gets no strokes that she truly values, either from herself or from others. She may try to fill the void with alcohol, tranquilizers, or other chemicals. As an older woman, she often fills her life with trivia and her house with knickknacks."[13]

As in all scripts, Plastic Woman incorporates parental injunctions learned as a child and mythical heroines encountered along the way. She abides by the injunctions of "Don't get old," "Don't be yourself," and "Be cute!" She indulges in the games of "Buy me something," "Schlemiel," and "Alcoholic (Pill-oholic)." Her mythical heroines are the movie starlets extolled in the supermarket magazines.

The trained TA therapist would readily recognize Plastic Woman. Through group and individual therapy, the counselor would help her to reshape her view of herself and her world. If the therapist succeeds, the client will embrace her natural self and take control over her life by accepting responsibility for it. That means she rejects the artificial "power" she felt as a consumer and the escapism she found in drugs or alcohol. She strives to develop herself in meaningful ways rather than concentrate on her appearance.

3. Theory and Techniques of Psychotherapy

To accomplish its goals, TA primarily uses group techniques supplemented by individual counseling. Although TA has demonstrated substantial diversity in its application, TA therapists nevertheless share a number of fundamental views. First, the therapist firmly believes in the ability of each client to both understand the basic precepts of personality and to take control of his or her life. Accordingly, TA insists on a vocabulary accessible to clients and the use, as much as possible, of self-explanatory terms. "Strokes," "Script," and "Pig Parent" are a few examples. With understanding, clients can begin to take responsibility for their lives.

Second, TA places clients in contexts in which they interact with others to gain self-understanding and receive strokes. The contexts include informal greeting rituals; casual, nonmeaningful exercises; goal-directed work; games (which are discouraged); and intimate, straightforward interaction.

---

13. Id. at 214.

Third, the TA therapist uses intervention tactics to guide conversation and to force clients to deal with the meaningful issues. The therapist "interrogates" with direct questions to verify specific points. "Specifications" categorize and synthesize information provided by the client. A particularly important intervention tactic is "confrontation," by which the therapist identifies inconsistencies in the information the client has provided to the therapist or the group. Through confrontation, the therapist hopes to redirect the client's energies and focus. "I see," the client might appropriately respond, "I'm giving away my power again," as he switches from his Child to his Adult. Further, the therapist uses "explanation" to strengthen the client's Adult. For example, the therapist might provide the client with an analysis of the interplay between the client's ego states in the immediate conversation or in a scene described by the client. Fourth, the TA therapist uses "interpositions" to stabilize the client's Adult and prevent him or her from slipping into Parent or Child activities. The therapist does that through anecdotes, humor, encouragement, and respect.[14]

Fifth, TA uses role-playing and simulation to promote client self-understanding. For example, to help a client better identify her ego states, the therapist might ask her to act out a conversation between one of her parents and herself as a child. Members of a group might also be assigned roles in a simulation, which will then form the basis for group discussion and analysis.

Through use of the above and other techniques, the TA therapist assumes an active, dynamic role in the therapeutic process. The therapist confronts, intervenes, interposes, injects humor, assigns tasks, and generally does what is necessary to interrupt the client's habitual patterns of thinking and acting.

4. Utility for Lawyers

As with the other systems of psychotherapy, TA provides a framework for better understanding your clients and yourself. Knowledge of the games people play can enhance any professional's effectiveness. Such insight facilitates your fact-gathering, analysis of the case, and counseling. By observing game-playing, you can better perceive when clients, witnesses, and others are not totally sincere. Awareness of games and scripts can help, too, by directing your questions into relevant topics that might otherwise have gone unexplored. Better understanding of the limitations that scripts place on clients enables you to check your own frustrations. Moreover, your knowledge about your client's decision-making capabilities (or lack thereof) can be invaluable in the counseling process—where decisions are made. You can also use TA to help those of your clients who need it to stand on their own, assert their autonomy, and be more realistic. TA techniques in intervention and interposition can be adapted to meet those goals.

---

14. For further description of interventions and interpositions, see E. Berne, *Principles of Group Treatment* (1966), and Dusay & Dusay, Transactional Analysis, in R. Corsini & D. Wedding (eds.), *Current Psychotherapies* 440-442 (4th ed. 1989).

Estelle May's attorney, Lawrence Townsend, uses his knowledge about the client and her case and proposes a course of action. By recognizing the Plastic Woman script, Townsend perceives the marital relationship as an appropriate topic for probing—a perception that might have escaped him but for his familiarity with TA. He also uses explanation to give Estelle some initial insights into her situation and to prompt her into further self-scrutiny through therapy. Obviously, Townsend cannot engineer a complete resolution of Mrs. May's problems in a limited interview, or even if he counseled her more extensively, but his analysis of her situation may sufficiently impress her that she will seek therapeutic help. He thereby completes important lawyering functions: he scans the facts that the client has provided him, identifies the issues and problems, and formulates (tentative) solutions. Mrs. May presented both legal and nonlegal problems and Townsend met them. TA also could help him in treating the legal problems. An explanation to the prosecutor and the department store that Mrs. May's shoplifting was brought on by emotional difficulties that are now being treated would enhance Townsend's ability to negotiate a result more acceptable to the Mays than a guilty plea to shoplifting.

You can benefit, too, from study of the TA counselor's roles in confronting and challenging the client. Occasions do arise when clients provide inconsistent sets of facts and when clients refuse to accept reality. In such instances, the TA counselor would confront the clients with their inconsistency or their naiveté and challenge them to accept responsibility for their situation. As we will see in Chapter 11, such an approach would be entirely appropriate for the lawyer engaged in a counseling process.

Transactional analysis also has much to inform us about alcoholics and addicts. Persons so afflicted tend toward recurrent, often manipulative, patterns of conduct, and recognition of those patterns (the scripts and games) can help you in representing such clients.[15] Your knowledge of TA would be useful both in your interpersonal relations with the client and in the formulation of evidence. (TA can be valuable, too, in helping lawyers with a substance dependency of their own to recognize their problem.)

5. Limitations

Like the other psychotherapies, TA does not provide a complete package for law office use. Lawyers, of course, have different and more specific goals than do transactional therapists. In addition, the group therapy techniques of TA have little, if any, utility in lawyer-client relations. Thus TA, like the other systems, is most useful for what it tells you about people and the human personality and for its development of certain techniques that are transferable to the law office. Those points were highlighted in the preceding section.

In its rendition of personality, however, TA does have some inherent risks. Because TA sees emotional problems as a function of particular

---

15. See especially C. Steiner, *Games Alcoholics Play* (1970).

scripts, most of which recur throughout the population, reliance on TA can encourage stereotypical thinking about clients and discourage seeing clients as distinct individuals with distinct problems. That, in turn, can lead to a kind of tunnel vision and a tendency to overlook important variations from the identified script. For example, Estelle May's lawyer may have felt very comfortable seeing her as Plastic Woman and setting his agenda accordingly. After all, he had known her for a long time and was thoroughly familiar with her situation. But a lawyer with less knowledge of her circumstances could also reach the same conclusion as Mr. Townsend did; she presented a caricature of the unfulfilled, unchallenged, and unmotivated wife. Yet the complexity and variety of the problems that women face amidst changing perceptions about their roles—in the family, on the job, and in society generally—belie the meaningfulness of neat characterizations smacking of stereotype. Nor are the risks any less when the subject is a male client with a banal script.

REFERENCES

Berne, E., *Transactional Analysis in Psychotherapy* (1961).
———, *Games People Play* (1964).
———, *What Do You Say After You Say Hello?* (1972).
Dusay, J., & Dusay, K. M., Transactional Analysis, in R. Corsini & D. Wedding (eds.), *Current Psychotherapies* (4th ed. 1989).
Harris, T., *I'm OK, You're OK* (1969).
Steiner, C., *Scripts People Live* (1974).

G. OTHER THEORIES

The summaries of the various psychotherapies in the preceding sections do not provide an exhaustive review of the major schools of psychotherapy. Indeed, there are many more, and our exclusion of any one school from specific treatment is not intended to imply a status of lesser importance. Rather, we selected the above theories to provide a reasonable cross-section of different approaches to personality and counseling. To round out this chapter and to meet its stated goals, this section briefly canvasses some remaining theories. During that discussion, the relationships between the various schools should appear.

Freudian psychoanalysis engendered significant offshoots. *Adlerian* (after Alfred Adler) psychotherapy follows the Freudian model in recognizing the purposefulness of symptoms and emphasizing the meaningfulness of the subconscious, dreams, and early childhood experiences. But Adlerians veer off in significant ways. In contrast to Freud's reductionist view of the human personality (i.e., ego, id, and superego), Adler saw the individual as holistic—as being a unity with all parts, including memory, emotions, and behavior, in the service of the whole individual. To Adlerians, man is neither inherently good nor inherently bad; rather, each individual chooses to be good or bad. Thus individuals can exert free will and shape both their internal and external environments. Neurosis results not from psychosexual causes, but from a failure of learning and from distorted perceptions. Adlerians also emphasize the family constellation as being a significant shaper of personality rather than the Freudians' concentration on the Oedipal situation and the stages of sexual development.

Adlerian therapy is a cooperative, educational undertaking between therapist and patient. They work together to identify the patient's perceptions and goals, learn the "basic mistakes" in his or her cognitive map, and reach decisions about whether he or she wants to continue with past patterns or move in other directions. The therapy's primary goal is to develop the patients' "social interest," that is, their other-oriented, altruistic drives, as opposed to their self-interest. In that process, the therapist seeks to decrease the patients' feelings of inferiority, correct their misperceptions about themselves, and foster a feeling of equality in the patients. These goals are accomplished through a solid therapist-patient relationship built on the perceived expertise of therapists and their ability to communicate care about their patients. Generally, the therapists try to present themselves as wise, strong, and assured, use empathic and nonjudgmental listening, and strive to "work through" issues with patients. The therapists will also be alert to identify in patients patterns of behavior that run according to a preset "script." Thus, while remaining a distinctive school, Adlerians can claim common ground on various points with the Freudians, the Rogerians, and the transactional analysts.

Analytical or *Jungian* (after Carl Jung) psychotherapy also evolved, and veered away, from Freud's basic principles. More so than the practitioners in other schools, the analytical therapists emphasize the unconscious and its role in personality development. This emphasis on the unconscious provides the primary bond between Freud and Jung. The latter maintained that the essential goal in life and therapy (they can be synonymous for Jungians) is to become more conscious, to gain awareness. Yet we are all subjects of our unconscious forces, which can be either (or both) destructive and creative in a particular individual. Therapy tries to control the destructive aspects of the unconscious while enhancing the creative forces. The effort derives from the analytical perception of personality as a complement between the two subsystems of the conscious and the unconscious; the more extreme an attitude is in one subsystem, the more pronounced is its opposite in the other subsystem. The interaction between the two subsystems motivates behavior, and all behavior is shaped by both conscious and unconscious forces. The primary route to understanding the unconscious is through analysis of the patient's dreams, which Jungians see as symbolic expressions of the unconscious. Thus, analytical psychotherapy centers around the recall and interpretation of dreams. That process necessarily increases awareness and facilitates the creative forces, especially the human instinct toward "individualization"— the force that directs the individual toward wholeness and that person's particular meaning in life.

Gestalt therapy stands in marked contrast to the analytical and psychoanalytical schools. Founded by Fritz Perls in writings that spanned from the forties through the sixties, Gestalt therapy is strictly noninterpretive, ahistoric, and phenomenological. It concentrates on immediate present awareness of the patient's experience and rejects efforts to explain or interpret its causes. (These characteristics stake out common ground with the person-centered theory.) Gestalt theory emphasizes the whole person; mind and body are interrelated and so are emotional and physical problems. The person is a biological event and every human activity is regarded as a biological process. Gestalt considers the individual as a total organism responding to its environment. Furthermore, all human behavior and experience are organized into succeeding patterns, or gestalts, in which the whole is greater than the sum of its parts. ("Gestalt" is German for "whole.") Everything we are and do is related to everything else we are and do. Gestalt therapists also believe people are born with an innate capacity to deal with life, but learn from significant others that they are inherently bad or selfish. These attitudes then obstruct self-acceptance and reinforce self-distrust. (Gestalt shares these assumptions with a number of other schools. Transactional analysis, for example, certainly begins with those premises.)

Gestalt therapy's primary tool is awareness, or being in touch with one's own existence. An aware person can focus on what exists and is real in the here and now. The therapy achieves that state through the patients' acquisition of the means for changing themselves and their experience of the world. The therapists assume an active and directive role. They force patients to talk and think in the present and refuse them the escapism of daydreams into the past or the future. Therapy pushes patients to teach themselves and their therapists about themselves and to join with their therapists in an open-ended, free-wheeling venture to get to know each other. Clients must learn to take responsibility for their actions and feelings. Gestalt therapy typically pursues these tasks in group settings with extensive use of role-playing, games, and exercises. Successful therapy produces whole persons capable of being self-supported (as opposed to environment-supported), of changing in meaningful ways, of acting in the present on their current thoughts and feelings, and of taking responsibility for their own thoughts and owning them.

The essence of Gestalt theory is perhaps best distilled in a therapy prayer that appeared in one of Perls's principle works:

> I do my thing, and you do your thing.
> I am not in this world to live up to your expectations
> And you are not in this world to live up to mine.
> You are you and I am I,
> And if by chance we find each other, it's beautiful.
> If not, it can't be helped.[16]

Reality therapy is a cross between rational-emotive and person-centered therapies. Like RET, reality therapy is cognitive, rational, and logical and

---

16. F. Perls, *Gestalt Therapy Verbatim* 4 (1969). The prayer certainly reveals why Gestalt became popular in the sixties.

focuses on the advisability of the client's value and behavioral choices. Reality therapists believe two basic instincts shape human personality and behavior: the need to love and be loved and the need for positive self-worth. The therapy tries to help patients meet those needs by teaching them about rational thought and responsible decision-making and by providing a solid and meaningful interpersonal relationship. The therapeutic process requires a warm, open counselor-client relationship. The therapist encourages clients to identify their values and to analyze whether their behavior is consistent with those values. Clients learn to take responsibility for themselves and their actions. To help clients along, the therapist freely offers his or her own analysis and suggestions about the appropriateness and rationality of the clients' thinking and behavior. Over time, the professional relationship should evolve into one of mutual love and respect. The approach used in reality therapy thus closely approximates that employed in Rogerian counseling except that the reality therapists can be very judgmental; they unhesitatingly offer their perceptions to clients on the relationship between the clients' behavior and reality.

There are still more schools of psychotherapy beyond those described above (e.g., Family Therapy, Existential Psychotherapy, Psychodrama). In addition, many therapists advocate the use of a combination of the different approaches outlined above. These latter practitioners settle on the particular method of treatment that is most appropriate for each patient. Some of those therapists can be found in the Human Potential Movement, which encompasses unique aspects of its own but also embraces a sort of eclectic approach to emotional and personal development. Other therapists refuse to confess alignment with any school or overriding theory. But even those helpers must have some basic perceptions about the innate character of men and women, the human personality, and the development of effective relationships with clients. And so must we. The next section sketches some of the basic perceptions we have held to in preparing this text.

REFERENCES

Adler, A., *Social Interest: A Challenge to Mankind* (1929).

Ansbacher, H., & Ansbacher, R. (eds.), *The Individual Psychology of Alfred Adler* (1956).

Fagan, J., & Shepherd, I. (eds.), *Gestalt Therapy Now* (1971).

Glasser, W., *Mental Health or Mental Illness* (1961).

———, *Reality Therapy* (1965).

Glasser, W., & Zunin, L., Reality Therapy, in R. Corsini (ed.), *Current Psychotherapies* (3d ed. 1984).

Jung, C., *Modern Man in Search of a Soul* (1933).

———, *Two Essays on Analytical Psychology* (1956).

———, *Man and His Symbols* (1964).

Kaufman, Y., Analytical Psychotherapy, in R. Corsini & D. Wedding (eds.), *Current Psychotherapies* (4th ed. 1989).

Mosak, H., Adlerian Psychotherapy, in R. Corsini & D. Wedding (eds.), *Current Psychotherapies* (4th ed. 1989).

———— (ed.), *Alfred Adler: His Influence on Psychology Today* (1973).

Perls, F., *Gestalt Therapy Verbatim* (1969).

Whitmont, E., *The Symbolic Quest* (1969).

Yontef, G., & Simkin, J., Gestalt Therapy, in R. Corsini & D. Wedding (eds.), *Current Psychotherapies* (4th ed. 1989).

H. OUR PREMISES

This section could easily become a book in itself. To prevent that, and thereby save the reader from terminal narcolepsy, we can offer only a bare outline of the more fundamental premises that support this book. We leave the development of those premises to the remaining chapters.

As we stated at the outset of this chapter, no theory of psychotherapy transfers perfectly to the law office. Lawyers and therapists have different agenda and different goals. But we can derive from counseling theories some basic understanding about the role of lawyers in their relationship with clients. Through the discussion in this chapter we have tried to demonstrate that each of the schools of psychotherapy can contribute to a lawyer's understanding and effectiveness. Which of those theories are most useful to you will depend on fundamental assumptions you have made about the human personality and about interpersonal relations.

In the chapters that follow, we attempt to build a model for the lawyer in interpersonal relations based on certain assumptions we have made. The lawyer in our model believes in the innate goodness of man and woman and that each person has some instinct, however undernourished, toward self-fulfillment. Furthermore, we believe both individual and interpersonal relations prosper when people deal with each other as equals and with mutual respect. Helpers are most effective when they are warm, empathic, open, genuine, and caring. As a general precept, though certainly not a rigid rule, the role of the lawyer is best filled by a nonjudgmental helper.

To this point, our assumptions share a common ground with a number of the schools outlined above, although the overlap is probably greatest with the person-centered approach. We also believe, however, that the lawyer must move beyond the Rogerians. At some point in the lawyer-client relationship, decisions must be made and action steps must be taken. When that stage is reached, the lawyer must identify potential solutions, advise on their viability, and participate in—perhaps even force—decision-making. In this stage, the lawyer remains empathic, respectful, and genuine, but these attributes assume a more complex meaning, and he or she becomes more active, more involved, and maybe more confrontive. The lawyer may also find it personally necessary in certain circumstances to assert his or her own judgment.

We have reached these premises through experience, observation, and study. With them as our foundation, we turn to consider the interpersonal skills needed for effective lawyering.

PART

II

INTERVIEWING

Chapter
3

The Goals of Interviewing

A. INTRODUCTION

A well-known trial lawyer once described his client-interviewing style in the following manner:

> First of all, it's a total waste of time, and secondly, I want to get to my end by asking questions my own way. I don't want to hear, "We got married in December, 1922, and then we had a fight in 1925." I'll say, "Now keep quiet. Let me ask you questions for 15 minutes and if at the end there's something you think I've left out, then you tell me. What do you want, question number one, do you want a divorce, a separation? Number two, are you looking for money, if so, how much? How much do you need? How much do you need for yourself? How much do you need for the children? Number three, what do you have on your spouse? What do you have that I can use as a compelling argument to get you the amount of money you want? Do they have anything on you?" And, by the time I get through, be it a civil case or criminal case, by asking questions, I have the story and I have not been fed information which I have no need to know. . . . We don't charge an hourly rate because I think that no one will ever persuade me that hourly rates are anything but phony. . . . We like to take a retainer at the beginning of the case that the client can afford and then we like to work out a fee at the end of the case,

based primarily on results . . . [and] mutual consent. . . . If we do a good job, we should be paid for it.[1]

This formula for interviewing, one which is endorsed by a significant number of lawyers, explicitly illustrates one of the primary goals of client interviewing—obtaining legally relevant information. Less explicitly, the approach suggests the importance of a second goal—establishing an appropriate attorney-client relationship. The excerpt also refers to the third goal of the interviewing process—creating the contractual bond between the attorney and the client. These three principal goals of client interviewing deserve detailed examination.

B. OBTAINING RELEVANT INFORMATION

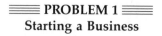 **PROBLEM 1** ≡
Starting a Business

A new client, Eugene Weber, seeks your legal advice about starting a business to counsel executive-level personnel who are interested in changing jobs. During the first three or four minutes of the substantive phase of the initial interview, Weber tells you that two years ago he sold his former business (an employment agency) to a conglomerate for $850,000. The agreement of sale included a noncompetition clause that precludes Weber from "directly or indirectly" engaging in employment placement within a specific area and for a specific time period. To avoid any contractual problems of competition, Weber has decided to establish the new business in his son's name. The son, who soon will receive an MBA degree, has not been informed of these plans because Weber wants to "surprise him with the business as a graduation present." Weber concludes his statement of the problem by noting his "retirement nest egg" has been "somewhat depleted" by the "unexpected" amount of taxes paid on the proceeds of the sale of the former business and as a result of some "bad investments" made at his brother-in-law's insistence. Therefore, Weber notes, he must be on "firm legal ground" in setting up the new business to avoid risking his remaining assets.[2]

QUESTIONS

1. What additional "facts" do you need to obtain from this client? Can these facts be broken down by the type of "problem" involved? Is there a way to characterize problems that will assist you in defining the type of facts that must be obtained?

---

1. The Natl. L.J. 13, 44-45, 47 (Dec. 1, 1980).
2. See Harbaugh & Britzke, *The Basics of Interviewing* (Practising Law Institute 1982), a videotape instructional program, for a complete description of this problem.

2. Are facts limited to past and present events and future intended acts? What other subjects should be included within the definition of facts to be gathered from the client?

1. Scope of Inquiry

Obtaining relevant information means more than mastering "legal" facts that are admissible at trial, are contained in a contract or will, or affect the validity of a particular claim or defense. Certainly, these elements are critical and need to be probed from the outset, but there is much more. For example, facts unrelated to the legal merits yet bearing on negotiation should be explored. Such facts can include whether the client or the opposing party needs money right away, whether the parties fear publicity, or whether they can afford costly litigation or protracted bargaining. Thus, the fact-gathering should explore any information that could be useful to resolving the client's problems by any appropriate means.

In addition, you should independently and thoroughly assess what the client's "problems" are and then develop the facts as to each. There are, for purposes of this discussion, three general categories of client problems that lawyers handle.

(1) Legal Problems Clients Are Aware Of and Articulate. Persons who consult you almost always do so because they have identified one or more problems that they believe are capable of resolution through legal assistance. In the earlier example, Weber determined that there was some legal risk in starting his new business because of the existence of the noncompetition clause. Although he formulated a method to eliminate the risk (putting the new business in his son's name), he needed a lawyer to evaluate his choice or to develop other risk-reducing alternatives. In gathering the relevant facts about this articulated legal problem, you must inquire not only about information concerning operation of the noncompetition clause, but also such topics as the willingness of the client to defer starting the business until after the expiration of the contractual term or to locate the new operation outside of the restricted geographic area; the amount of capital required to establish the new venture versus the client's available resources; and the likely attitude of the conglomerate to the client's entry into this new field.

(2) Problems Clients Are Unaware Of or Do Not Articulate. Quite often, clients do not perceive the existence of a legal problem or, for a variety of reasons, fail to expressly identify the problem. You should not be surprised by this phenomenon since much of legal education is devoted to simply identifying potential legal issues rather than merely unraveling the obvious problem. For example, Weber mentioned in passing the unexpected amount of taxes he paid on the sale of the former business. An examination of his tax return, however, might draw into question the appropriateness

of the tax paid. Perhaps Weber used an unnecessarily low base figure for the business when he calculated his profit on the sale because he had not been taking full advantage of allowable depreciation. The client may be entitled to a refund of taxes or to a recovery from his accountant. Be alert for the unarticulated legal problem and ready to probe for relevant facts about it.

(3) *Nonlegal Problems That Affect a Legal Question.*   It is not uncommon for clients to present nonlegal problems. Many of these nonlegal issues may influence the legal problem confronting you and, therefore, must be pursued through a factual inquiry. The Weber situation illustrates this point. The problem of the client's "bad investments" should be the subject of inquiry because it could reveal the client is financially irresponsible or has poor business judgment. Because the lawyer representing Weber may be forced to rely on the client for financial information and business expertise in finally resolving this matter, the client's credibility in such matters may be crucial. As another example of this principle, Weber's decision to make his son the chief executive officer of the new business may indicate a troublesome propensity to make important decisions for others. Pursuing information about this nonlegal problem should be a priority for a lawyer faced with the prospect of possibly resolving the client's legal problem by depending on the willingness of the son to participate.

Once you identify the problem and topics for discussion, your fact-gathering should be sufficiently thorough to permit an intelligent judgment about the validity, completeness, and appropriateness of the information supplied by the client. Because facts concerning the client's problem form the basis of your future representations to others, you should ensure that the facts are reliable and accurate. To avoid conclusory analysis, seek breadth of information as well as depth. Finally, you must be aware that the facts the client reveals are colored by the client's feelings, intuitions, and perceptions. The potential for distortion means the client's facts must be tested against your common sense and understanding of human nature.

2. *Feelings as "Facts"*

The second important gloss that must be placed on the term "facts" is that feelings are facts. How the client feels about certain issues in the case can dictate how you should proceed. Thus, decisions about whether to file for a divorce or seek marital counseling, whom to name as beneficiaries in a will, or what to do in a child custody dispute can all turn as much on the client's feelings as on the legal merits. In addition, feelings can seriously affect, both positively and negatively, the flow of information in an interview. A woman charging sexual harassment on the job, for example, may experience shame, embarrassment, or guilt in relating her story, thus inhibiting the flow of information. In the "starting the new business" problem, Weber's feelings about risk-taking, about his son's ability to manage the new venture, and about the conglomerate's likely reaction may well be more important in his decision-making than the factual distinctions between the operation of the old and the new business.

3. The "Facts" as Perceived by the Client

Finally, fact-gathering, particularly in the initial session, should focus on the client's perspective. We thus disagree with the approach taken by the lawyer quoted in the introduction to this chapter. He sees fact-gathering from the client's perspective as "a total waste of time." Indeed, for reasons to be explained in later chapters, a nondirective approach ordinarily provides for more—not less—efficient fact-gathering. In addition, allowing clients to develop the facts from their perspective advances rapport between them and you (see Section C, below) and personalizes the process.

The lawyer quoted in the introduction wants to avoid being "fed information which [he has] no need to know." In effect, his expertise has convinced him he can rely on the adage "if you've seen one [(divorce) (personal injury) (noncompetition clause) (fill in the blank)] case, you've seen them all." The approach assumes that all cases of a particular type can be boilerplated and checklisted, reduced to a patented formula for interviewing success. Our experience and the experience of many other lawyers contradict those assumptions.

Obtaining relevant facts from the client's perspective means allowing the client to control the flow of the interview. What is foremost in the client's mind? How does the client see the events unfolding? What would the client like to occur? Encouraging the client to address these and other questions suggested in Chapter 4 fulfills the goal of fact-gathering from the client's perspective.

The client's feelings and views on the facts remain important throughout the attorney-client relationship, but to properly begin representation you must have substantial comprehension of them from the outset. Learning to identify the types of problems clients bring to the interview, developing skill at measuring the necessary depth and breadth of relevant information, and permitting facts to flow from the client's perspective are critical to achieving the fact-gathering goals of client interviewing.

C. ESTABLISHING AN APPROPRIATE ATTORNEY-CLIENT RELATIONSHIP

≡ PROBLEM 2 ≡
The Violent Juvenile Offender

You are an assistant public defender in a large urban office and have been assigned to represent a 17-year-old defendant accused of breaking into the home of a 78-year-old widow and robbing her of $350. Before going to interview your client at the juvenile detention center, you review the available juvenile court and police department information. From that you learn that the accused, a white male from a solid middle-class home environment, had two earlier juvenile violations for possession and sale of narcotics. Following the second offense, the defendant was effectively "disowned" by his family and placed by the court in a residential private school known for its program for dealing with troubled youngsters. When the defendant ran away from the school four days before the present incident, a probation department check with his family members revealed that they have had no contact with the defendant for almost one year.

The police report on the pending offense indicates that the defendant admits breaking into the victim's home, beating and tying her up, and ransacking the house for money with which he purchased drugs. The victim was not found for almost 36 hours, is presently hospitalized in serious condition, and will need extensive treatment for the physical and psychological trauma she experienced during the robbery.

QUESTIONS

1. How would you describe the type of relationship you should have with this juvenile client? Would your description be different if the client were a homeowner consulting you concerning a zoning problem or a business person questioning you about alternatives in a matter involving a corporate merger?

2. What are the goals of an "appropriate attorney-client relationship"? What attitudes should an attorney convey to foster achievement of those goals?

1. Attorney-Client Rapport

From your first contact with a client, a relationship forms that will grow throughout the period of representation. The kind and quality of the relationship ultimately needed to effectively represent a client in a substantial case is likely beyond attaining in the initial interview. But the initial interview is essential to cementing the foundation for the lawyer-client relationship. If the job is poorly done, the foundation will be unable to support the construction of the complex professional relationship needed to conduct a long or emotionally difficult case. Therefore, your initial telephone contact or face-to-face meeting with the client is the moment to begin to establish the appropriate professional rapport.

"Rapport" here has a twofold significance. First, it connotes a certain personal regard between you and the client, though this regard is not necessarily the same as friendship. Rather, the rapport one seeks is one of genuineness and respect; the client knows you care about and respect the client as a person and the client returns those feelings. In the juvenile offender problem, it is unlikely you or any attorney will develop an enduring friendship with a young man who demonstrates his rejection of basic societal norms by beating and robbing a defenseless elderly woman. It is not necessary for you to admire a client to effectively represent that client's interests. It is essential, however, for you to demonstrate to the client that you genuinely care about the client as a human being presently faced with a serious problem. (For further development of lawyer regard for the client, see Chapter 5, Section E, page 130.) Rapport also means that the client respects you as a competent professional who is truly interested in the client's problem. You may have experienced such a relationship with a dentist, physician, or garage mechanic; the sensation is that your professional has taken a special interest in you and that you are more to him or her than just an impacted wisdom tooth, a kidney infection, or a busted radiator.

Second, "rapport" means mutual trust. Clients must trust you in order to open up and be candid. Confidential or sensitive matters are always difficult to communicate. If clients do not trust you, it is unlikely they will confide in you. If, for example, the juvenile offender was experiencing a crisis in sexual identity compounded by a drug dependence and familial rejection, he is not likely to communicate those facts unless he trusts you to deal sensitively and responsibly with this intensely personal information. Correspondingly, you must trust your clients unless you have a reason not to. If you do have reasonable doubts, then your obligation of mutual trust requires you to express your concerns to the client.

It is not only the client charged with a crime and facing deprivation of life or liberty who presents difficult relationship issues. Many clients' legal problems are complicated by personal concerns. The client who seeks counsel on a business problem may be reluctant to deal personally with a difficult partner; the tax client may have family problems that complicate an otherwise appropriate remedy; and a client who is desperate for a quick financial gain may embrace a commercial transaction with doubtful legal protections for important interests. In all of these situations, you must have an appropriate relationship with the client to determine why an apparently acceptable legal alternative does not satisfy the particular client. Unless you identify the underlying reason for the hesitation to accept the legal advice, it will be impossible to structure an acceptable alternative solution to the client's problem.

2. Goals of the Attorney-Client Relationship During the Interview Stage

In the initial phases of representation, you want to establish a relationship with the client that facilitates information flow, encourages assignment of responsibility, and fosters a willingness in the client to seriously consider your advice and engage in frank discussion of alternatives.

Information, whether it be helpful or damaging to the case, is the cornerstone of a lawyer's work and the primary goal of interviewing. The more comfortable a client feels during the interview, the more readily information will flow. With an attitude that encourages, supports, and accepts the client, you make the client more comfortable and facilitate information flow. An attitude that is demanding, challenging, and judgmental is likely to discomfort the client and inhibit the transfer of information. The methods for facilitating information flow vary depending on the individual client. Therefore, you should silently ask in each case, "How can I make this client comfortable?" (Various responses to that question are explored in Chapters 4-7.)

Assignment of responsibility in the client interview is a two-way street. Clients normally assign to you the overall handling of their legal problems. You, in turn, will more likely assign to the client additional information functions, including the production of documents, identification of witnesses, and the like. Thus, both parties to the relationship must be comfortable in exchanging delegated tasks. To facilitate this cross-assignment of duties, clients should have confidence in you as a competent professional and as a caring, considerate human being. With that confidence, clients are more likely to assign to you all facets of the legal problem and to accept your assignment of necessary fact-finding tasks.

Finally, lawyers are givers of advice. This advice, of course, is worthless if the client is unwilling to consider it seriously. While you do not make the decisions for the client, you are in the business of presenting alternative solutions to legal problems and outlining the attendant consequences of those alternatives. A relationship with the client must be established that encourages understanding of your role in advice-giving and the client's role in receiving and acting on that advice. Such a relationship demands your candor and honesty in evaluating alternatives and consequences and your patience and assistance as the client works through the available options.

In applying these principles to the problem of the violent juvenile offender, relationship-building would require you to communicate your concern for a client confronted with serious criminal charges; to create an atmosphere in which you appear as advocate instead of judge; to gather the client's version of the facts; to assign important tasks to the client (perhaps having the client talk to an expert psychiatrist or even help with research); and to display a professional understanding of the basic legal principles involved in the client's case. In this way, you should build the rapport needed to serve the information, delegation, and advice purposes of the attorney-client relationship. These same principles apply to the case of the homeowner confronted with a zoning problem, the businessperson concerned about a corporate merger, or almost any client facing virtually any type of legal difficulty.

D. EXPLORING CONTRACTUAL UNDERSTANDINGS

≣ PROBLEM 3 ≣
Divorce, Custody, and Sexual Preference

Your client, Gina Donato, is a 36-year-old woman married to Dr. Paul Donato, a local surgeon, and the mother of two children, ages 10 and 8. During the initial interview, Mrs. Donato reveals that she and her husband met while in college, they married upon his completion of medical school, and she gave up her career in nursing when he completed his residency. Shortly after their marriage and before the birth of the children, Mrs. Donato "lost interest" in sexual relations with her husband. She continued to have sexual intercourse with her husband "out of a sense of duty." She was "thrilled," however, by both of her pregnancies and has "a deep and undying love" for her children, who have been the center of her life.

About a year and a half ago, Mrs. Donato attended a course given at a local college. The instructor, a woman about your client's age, was a bright, articulate person with whom your client developed a close personal relationship. Within the past year that relationship grew more and more intimate until it involved sexual as well as personal ties. Your client now believes, in light of her fulfilling experience in this new relationship, that all along her interests have been homosexual rather than heterosexual.

Recently, Dr. Donato learned of this homosexual relationship and confronted your client about it. He demanded that your client leave the family home and avoid any contact with the children. Your client acceded to these demands and moved in with her lover. Though she is "barely able to get by" on the small amount her husband gives her each month, your client maintains that she has "never been more satisfied with a relationship with another adult" than in her present setting. On the other hand, she is "desperate about the children" and wants to have custody of them because she needs them and her husband "has never had time to be really involved in their upbringing."

When you mention the existence of a 25-year-old precedent in your jurisdiction that held that homosexual conduct of a parent barred an award of custody, your client admitted she is facing a moral crisis. Everything in her religious upbringing, she relates, "dictates the wrongness" of what she is doing. She adds that divorce is "morally repugnant" to her based on a religious belief in "the sanctity of marriage."

QUESTIONS

1. What criteria will you use in deciding whether to accept this case? Can the criteria selected be applied to other dissimilar cases? Should the criteria be discussed with the client? If so, how should this discussion proceed?

2. Assuming an agreement that you will represent this client, how and when should a discussion about fees take place? What fee arrangements are available in this case? Who should dictate the choice among possible fee arrangements, you or the client?

The lawyer-client relationship is a professional arrangement that entails two related prerequisites. First, both you and the client must decide whether you want to establish a relationship—the client must decide whether to hire you and you must determine whether to take the client's case. Second, you and the client must agree on your mutual obligations under the professional services contract. Neither one of these steps necessarily has to be completed during the first contact between the parties, but there does need to be an exploration of the pertinent issues and, eventually, a final resolution of both questions. How should this exploration and resolution occur? What criteria should you apply in the exploration and resolution process?

In deciding to accept or reject a client's problem, you should examine the issues of professional competence to undertake the case, the willingness of the client to allow you to handle the matter, the availability of alternative assistance, and your personal and professional preferences as an attorney. Each of these criteria deserve further explanation.

Before agreeing to accept a client's case, you must determine whether you are competent to render effective legal service in the particular factual and legal circumstances. Rule 1.1 of the Model Rules of Professional Conduct defines "competent representation" as requiring "the legal knowledge, skill, thoroughness and preparation reasonably necessary for the representation." The comment to Rule 1.1 states that the relevant factors in determining the requisite knowledge and skill include "the relative complexity and specialized nature of the matter, the lawyer's general experience, the lawyer's training and experience in the field in question, the preparation and study the lawyer is able to give the matter and whether it is feasible to refer the matter to, or consult with, a lawyer of established competence in the field in question." In the custody and divorce problem, most lawyers should feel competent by skill and knowledge to accept the case. Though the family law field can be complex, involving knowledge of local procedural rules, statutory authority regulating custody and divorce, and the tax implications of settlement agreements, it is not a field of law that generally requires special expertise as a condition for accepting the usual case.

Competency to handle a case, however, is not limited to an evaluation of your skill and knowledge; you must be able to provide the client thorough, well-prepared services before accepting a case. "The required attention and preparation are determined in part by what is at stake: major litigation and complex transactions ordinarily require more elaborate treatment than matters of lesser consequence."[3] Thus, the time required to provide effective representation versus your available time and ability to efficiently meet deadlines are important competency considerations.

The client's willingness to allow you to handle the problem is an obvious element in establishing and defining an attorney-client relationship. Regarding the scope of representation, the Model Rules note that "[t]he client has ultimate authority to determine the purposes to be served by legal representation, within the limits imposed by law and the lawyer's professional obligations."[4] It is, therefore, the client who determines the objectives of the representation, not the lawyer. For example, in the custody and divorce problem you may determine that pursuing a divorce action will be the most effective method to ensure that the client will obtain custody of the children. If, however, the client is opposed to divorce and unwilling to

---

3. Comment to Rule 1.1, Model Rules of Professional Conduct (1989).
4. Comment to Rule 1.2, Model Rules of Professional Conduct (1989).

consider that alternative, you are precluded from pursuing it. In the earlier problem involving the start of a new business, if the client refuses to open up the tax question for fear of being subjected to a complete IRS audit or for other reasons, you are foreclosed from following that legal issue.[5] This does not mean that you are without responsibility or authority in the objective and means of representation. The premise of client control requires, however, that the client decide and limit the objectives of representation and that you abide by those expressed wishes, at least as long as they remain within legal and moral bounds.

You cannot resolve all the problems that surround and affect a client's case. Indeed, in some instances clients present what they deem to be a legal problem but which, in reality, is a problem that falls within the expertise of another profession. The availability of alternative assistance is an important criterion to be explored before establishing the attorney-client relationship. In the custody and divorce problem, for example, it would be foolhardy for you to attempt to resolve the client's ambivalence toward her sexual preference even though the resolution of that issue may dramatically affect her case. Or, in the starting-the-new-business problem, the client's history of "bad investments" and reduced capital, while relevant to his ability to begin the new enterprise, are issues about which you may be unable to make sound professional recommendations. The comment to Rule 2.1 places the question of the availability of alternative help in the following perspective:

> Matters that go beyond strictly legal questions may also be in the domain of another profession. Family matters can involve problems within the professional competence of psychiatry, clinical psychology or social work; business matters can involve problems within the competence of the accounting profession or of financial specialists. Where consultation with a professional in another field is itself something a competent lawyer would recommend, the lawyer should make such a recommendation.

The exploration of contractual understandings with a client often involves analyzing whether all or a portion of the problem is better left to the competent hands of a professional other than a lawyer.

The final criterion to be applied in deciding whether to contract with a client is your personal and professional preferences. "[A] lawyer is not required to pursue objectives or employ means simply because a client may wish that the lawyer do so."[6] The lawyer is a free agent who may accept or reject a proffered case. Although "[l]egal representation should not be denied to people who are unable to afford legal services, or whose cause is

---

5. The Model Rules attempt to clarify the lawyer's obligation to *advise* rather than *represent* in situations similar to the two examples in the text: In general, a lawyer is not expected to give advice until asked by the client. However, when a lawyer knows that a client proposes a course of action that probably will result in substantial adverse legal consequences to the client, duty to the client under Rule 1.4 may require that the lawyer act if the client's course of action is related to the representation. A lawyer ordinarily has no duty to initiate investigation of a client's affairs or to give advice that the client has indicated is unwanted, but a lawyer may initiate advice to the client when doing so appears to be in the client's interest.

6. Comment to Rule 1.2, Model Rules of Professional Conduct (1989).

controversial or the subject of popular disapproval,"[7] you are otherwise free to decline to represent a particular client on a particular issue. Indeed, there are instances when your personal views may require rejection of a client's case. If, for example, in the custody and divorce problem your personal moral position on homosexuality and divorce could interfere with or adversely affect the exercise of professional judgment on behalf of the client's interests, you should decline the representation.[8]

Application of the four criteria—competence, willingness of the client, availability of alternative assistance, and lawyer preference—should allow you and the client to decide whether to establish a professional relationship.[9] Remaining, however, is the final resolution of the question of joint obligations under the professional services contract. While a number of the joint obligations have been discussed earlier, the issue of professional fees needs attention.

The word "fees" has always been an attention-getter among lawyers and law students. Fees, of course, are a necessary ingredient in a law practice. You need them and clients expect to pay them; few people begrudge lawyers and other professionals their due (although many may quibble about the size of that due). Yet, despite the near universally accepted notion that lawyers do and should charge for their work, lawyers frequently have great difficulty in effectively discussing fees with clients. Many lawyers fail to appreciate the client's perspective and the client's need to have the issue discussed in an open, candid manner.

Inexperienced attorneys, in particular, often feel embarrassed when they talk about fees with their clients; such lawyers fumble their explanations and confuse their clients. On the other hand, experienced attorneys often deal with the subject of fees in a rigid, cursory fashion, as if they are wholesale fruit dealers reciting price lists. Both of these approaches waste an opportunity to enhance and solidify the lawyer-client relationship.

There are three recurrent questions about fees that are tied to the goals of interviewing: when should fees be discussed, how much should be charged, and what payment options are available?

---

7. Id.

8. In discussing the lawyer's obligation of loyalty to the client, the comment to Rule 1.7 of the Model Rules of Professional Conduct notes that "the lawyer's own interests should not be permitted to have an adverse effect on representation of a client." This principle conforms with Ethical Consideration (EC) 5-2 of the earlier Code of Professional Responsibility (1969), which states:

A lawyer should not accept proffered employment if his personal interests or desires will, or there is a reasonable possibility that they will, adversely affect the advice to be given or services to be rendered the prospective client.

This issue, especially as it relates to the lawyer's moral reservations about a case, is further explored in Chapter 13.

9. There are, of course, other ethical issues that may affect the representation decision in some cases. For example, conflict of interest and prior employment questions may arise in a particular setting. See Rules 1.7-1.13, Model Rules of Professional Conduct (1989). A thorough review of the Model Rules and the Code of Professional Responsibility is suggested. As a general rule, "a lawyer should not accept representation in a matter unless it can be performed competently, promptly, without improper conflict of interest and to completion." Comment to Rule 1.16, Model Rules of Professional Conduct (1989).

Rule 1.5(b) of the Model Rules of Professional Conduct is quite explicit about the timing of the fee discussion. "When the lawyer has not regularly represented the client, the basis or rate of the fee shall be communicated to the client, preferably in writing, before or within a reasonable time after commencing the representation." [10] The reference in the Model Rules to an early written statement of the fee arrangement is a significant change in approach. [11] Because disputes over fees are the most prevalent claims by clients against lawyers, the profession is moving toward a prophylactic approach that mandates an early discussion resulting in a clear, preferably written, agreement to reduce the possibility of misunderstanding.

Most lawyers defer the fee discussion until the end of the first interview or to sometime during the second meeting between attorney and client. Except in routine cases, this allows the attorney to evaluate the merits and complexity of the client's case, to estimate the time involved in completing the matter, and to review the other pertinent factors that go into the fee determination formula.

Not surprisingly, the answer to the question "How much should be charged?" is that the fee should be "reasonable." As a professional, you should not exploit the fee arrangement or take advantage of a client. Rule 1.5(a) of the Model Rules of Professional Conduct and the accompanying comment set out the factors to be considered in judging the reasonableness of a fee. The factors include the following:

(1) the time and labor required, the novelty and difficulty of the questions involved, and the skill requisite to perform the legal service properly;

(2) the likelihood, if apparent to the client, that the acceptance of the particular employment will preclude other employment by the lawyer;

(3) the fee customarily charged in the locality for similar legal services;

(4) the amount involved and the results obtained;

(5) the time limitations imposed by the client or by the circumstances;

(6) the nature and length of the professional relationship with the client;

(7) the experience, reputation, and ability of the lawyer or lawyers performing the services; and

(8) whether the fee is fixed or contingent.

Finally, two basic fee arrangements are available to the attorney and client—fixed fees and contingent fees. A fixed fee can be either a set amount for a particular legal service (e.g., $750 for an uncontested divorce action) or an hourly amount (e.g., $75 per hour of work on the client's

---

10. The comment to Rule 1.5 states that "when the lawyer has regularly represented a client, they ordinarily will have evolved an understanding on the basis or rate of the fee." It is unlikely to be disruptive to the relationship with a continuing client to make reference to the earlier understanding about fees as a new project is undertaken by the lawyer. Certainly, if the client's new problem is of such a nature that the billing process shifts from, for example, an hourly rate to a contingency arrangement, the lawyer must initiate a fee discussion.

11. There is no counterpart to Rule 1.5(b) in the Disciplinary Rules of the Code of Professional Responsibility (1969). The closest statement is contained in EC 2-19:

It is usually beneficial to reduce to writing the understanding of the parties regarding the fee, particularly when it is contingent.

case). On the other hand, a fee may be contingent on the outcome of the matter for which the service is rendered. The amount of the fee is typically a percentage of the client's recovery or of a particular fund, although fee-shifting statutes—which provide for "prevailing" plaintiffs to recover attorneys' fees from opponents—have made contingent hourly fees more common. The Code of Professional Responsibility prohibits contingency arrangements in criminal cases and those domestic relations matters in which the contingency is tied to the securing of a divorce or to the amount of the alimony, support, or property settlement.[12] Thus, in the custody and divorce problem, the option of a contingent fee would not be available to the parties. In agreeing on a fixed fee, however, you might spread the payment of the set or hourly amount over a period of time (including a period extending beyond the expected termination of the dispute) to take into account the client's limited ability to pay.

This overview suggests that the exploration of the contractual understanding between the parties to a legal services agreement is at once complex and critical to the nature of the relationship. Fee discussions can affect both the fact-finding and relationship-building aspects of interviewing. The legal relationship between you and the client deserves its prominent position among the goals of interviewing.

E. CONCLUSION

By now it should be obvious that the description of interviewing style provided by the lawyer in this chapter's introduction differs significantly from the interviewing-goals analysis set forth in the subsequent sections. His approach is lawyer-centered; ours is client-centered. Our disagreement with the lawyer-centered model for fact-gathering has been noted. Our view of "facts" is broader, richer, and more comprehensive. Just as important, our emphasis on fact-gathering from the client's perspective substantially affects who controls the flow of information.

Our differences with the lawyer-centered view of the attorney-client relationship are less explicit but just as real. The traditional image of the attorney-client relationship projects a lawyer who dominates the interaction and relegates the client to a subordinate role. Our approach to the relationship, on the other hand, is more like a joint venture in which each partner is responsible for and has expertise in various aspects of the project.

The lawyer's reference in the introductory section of this book to contracting with the client focuses only on the fee arrangement aspects. Though there is some agreement between his and our approach to this question (e.g., fees based on ability to pay and on mutual consent), the

---

12. Model Rule 1.5(d) also specifically precludes contingent fees in such situations. Note that written agreements are mandatory in contingent fee cases. Rule 1.5(c).

differences (e.g., limitation on the types of payment and deferral of establishing the final fee) are significant and can substantially affect the attorney-client relationship.

The disagreements we have with the lawyer-centered model and its commonly used tactics are a function of fundamental philosophical differences. Those differences in philosophy are further reflected in the next chapter, which deals with the stages and tactics of the initial client interview.

Anatomy of the Initial Client Interview

A. INTRODUCTION

The initial interview with the client is an obviously important—and particularly difficult—stage of the lawyer-client relationship. Typically, neither party knows the other well, and that unfamiliarity requires a period of adjustment. A client who has had little or no prior contact with a lawyer usually feels some anxiety about confronting the unknown experience, and that anxiety can inhibit the information exchange. Even the client who has previously consulted an attorney may question whether the new lawyer's conduct matches the expectations created by the client's past experiences. Because little or no information about the client's problem and goals has been exchanged, the lawyer must operate without a detailed agenda and the structure it provides.

Despite the apparent absence of information, you can nevertheless efficiently structure initial client interviews. To be sure, we disavow any intention here of providing a "recipe" for successful first interviews. Yet most of them can, do, and should include a pattern of discernible parts that blend into a harmonious whole to achieve the goals mentioned in the preceding chapter. Those parts include planning for the interview, "ice-breaking," problem identification, problem overview, verification, and closure. This chapter sketches each of these interview parts and succeeding chapters will develop some of them in greater detail.

Before examining the individual interview parts, we insert here the following excerpt from Tolstoy's *Anna Karenina* to stimulate your thinking about analyzing an interview. As you read the excerpt, use the previously mentioned interview parts as a checklist. Try to determine what goals might be achieved during each of the interview parts and whether Karenin's lawyer was successful in using each during his initial client interview.

≡ **PROBLEM 1** ≡
"Karenin Visits a Lawyer"[1]

The famous Petersburg lawyer's waiting-room was full when Karenin entered it. Three women: an old lady, a young lady, and a tradesman's wife; and three gentlemen: one a German banker with a ring on his finger, another a bearded merchant, and the third an irate official in uniform with an order hanging from his neck, had evidently long been waiting. Two clerks at their tables were writing, and the sound of their pens was audible. The writing-table accessories (of which Karenin was a connoisseur) were unusually good, as he could not help noticing. One of the clerks, without rising from his chair, screwed up his eyes and addressed Karenin ill-humoredly.

"What do you want?"

"I want to see the lawyer on business."

"The lawyer is engaged," replied the assistant sternly, and indicated with his pen the persons who were waiting.

"Can he not find time to see me?" said Karenin.

"He has no spare time, he is always busy. Be so kind as to wait."

"Then I will trouble you to give him my card," said Karenin with dignity, seeing the impossibility of preserving his incognito.

The assistant took the card and, though he evidently did not approve of what he read on it, went out of the room.

Karenin approved in theory of public trial, but for certain high official reasons he did not quite sympathize with some aspects of its application in Russia, and he condemned these applications as far as he could condemn anything that had been confirmed by the Emperor. His whole life had been spent in administrative activity, and therefore when he disapproved of anything his disapproval was mitigated by a recognition of the inevitability of mistakes and the possibility of improvement in everything. In the new legal institutions he disapproved of the position occupied by lawyers. But till now he had never had to deal with a lawyer and so had disapproved only in theory; now his disapproval was strengthened by the unpleasant impression he received in the lawyer's waiting-room.

"He will be here in a moment," said the assistant, and in fact, a minute or two later, in the doorway appeared the long figure of an elderly juris-

---

1. L. Tolstoy, *Anna Karenina*, Pt. IV, Ch. V (1878) (L. & A. Maude trans.).

consult who had been conferring with the lawyer, followed by the lawyer himself.

The lawyer was a short, thick-set, bald-headed man, with a black beard tinged with red, long light-colored eyebrows, and a bulging forehead. He was as spruce as a bridegroom, from his white necktie and double watchchain to his patent leather boots. His face was intelligent and peasant-like, but his dress was dandified and in bad taste.

"Come in, please!" said the lawyer to Karenin, and gloomily ushering his client in before him, he closed the door.

"Won't you take a seat?" He pointed to a chair beside a writing-table covered with papers, and himself took the principal seat, rubbing his little hands with their short fingers covered with white hair and bending his head to one side. But hardly had he settled down when a moth flew across the table. The lawyer, with a rapidity one could not have expected of him, separated his hands, caught the moth, and resumed his former position.

"Before I begin speaking of my case," said Karenin, who had followed the lawyer's movements with astonishment, "I must mention that the business about which I have to speak to you must be strictly private."

A scarcely perceptible smile moved the lawyer's drooping reddish moustache.

"I should not be a lawyer if I could not keep the secrets entrusted to me! But if you would like a confirmation . . . "

Karenin glanced at him and saw that his intelligent grey eyes were laughing, as if he knew everything in advance.

"You know my name?" continued Karenin.

"I know you and, like every Russian, I know—" here he again caught a moth—"your useful activity," said the lawyer bowing.

Karenin sighed, collecting his courage, but having once made up his mind he went on in his squeaky voice without timidity or hesitation, emphasizing a word here and there.

"I have the misfortune," began Karenin, "to be a deceived husband, and I wish legally to break off relations with my wife—that is, to be divorced, but in such a way that my son should not remain with his mother."

The lawyer's grey eyes tried not to laugh but they danced with irrepressible glee, and Karenin saw that it was not only the glee of a man getting profitable business; there was triumph and delight, and a gleam resembling the evil-boding gleam he had seen in his wife's eyes.

"You want my assistance to obtain a divorce?"

"Just so! But I must warn you that there is a risk that I may be wasting your time. I have come only for a preliminary consultation. I wish for a divorce, but the form in which it can be obtained is of importance to me. It is quite possible that if the forms do not coincide with my requirements I shall forgo my legitimate desire."

"Oh, that is always so," said the lawyer, "that is always open to you."

The lawyer looked down at Karenin's feet, feeling that the sight of his irrepressible joy might offend his client. He glanced at a moth that flew past his nose and his hand moved, but did not catch it, out of respect for Karenin's situation.

"Although the general outline of our laws relating to this matter is known to me," continued Karenin, "I should like to know the forms in which such cases are conducted in practice."

"You wish me to state," the lawyer said, still not raising his eyes and adopting, with a certain pleasure, his client's manner of speech, "the various methods by which your desire can be carried out?"

And on Karenin's nodding affirmatively the lawyer continued, only occasionally casting a glance at Karenin's face, which had grown red in patches.

"Divorce, under our laws," he said, with a slight shade of disapproval of the laws, "as you are aware, may be granted in the following cases. . . . You must wait!" he exclaimed, addressing his assistant who had looked in at the door; but he rose all the same, spoke a few words to his assistant, and sat down again. "In the following cases: physical defect in husband and wife; five years' absence without news"—and he bent one of his short hairy fingers—"and in cases of adultery," he uttered the word with evident pleasure. "These are subdivided as follows," and he went on bending down his thick fingers, though the cases and the subdivisions evidently could not be classed together, "physical defects in husband or in wife, and adultery of husband or of wife." As all his fingers had been used, he straightened them all out and continued:

"That is the theoretical view; but I suppose you have done me the honor of applying to me in order to learn the practical application of the law. Therefore, guided by the precedents, I have to inform you that cases of divorce all come to the following:—there is, I suppose, no physical defect or absence without news? . . . "

Karenin nodded affirmatively.

"—come to the following: adultery of husband or wife and the detection of the guilty party by mutual consent, or involuntary detection without such consent. I must add that the latter case is seldom met with in practice," and with a momentary glance at Karenin the lawyer became suddenly silent, like a man who when selling pistols has described the advantages of the different kinds, and waits for his customer's decision. But Karenin remained silent, and so he began again: "The most usual, simple, and reasonable way I consider to be adultery by mutual consent. I should not venture so to express myself were I talking to a man of undeveloped mind," said the lawyer, "but I expect it is comprehensible to you."

Karenin was, however, so much upset that he did not at once understand the reasonableness of adultery by mutual consent and his perplexity was expressed in his looks; but the lawyer immediately helped him.

"Two people can no longer live together—there is the fact. And if both agree about that, the details and formalities become unimportant, and at the same time it is the simplest and surest method."

Karenin quite understood now. But he had religious requirements which hindered his acceptance of this method.

"It is out of the question in the present case," said he. "Only one measure is possible: involuntary detection confirmed by letters which I have."

At the mention of letters the lawyer pressed his lips together and gave vent to a high-pitched sound of pity and contempt.

"Please remember that cases of this kind, as you know, are decided by the Ecclesiastical Department, and the reverend Fathers in such cases are keenly interested in the minutest details," he said, with a smile that showed his fellow-feeling with the reverend Fathers' taste. "Letters may certainly serve as a partial confirmation, but direct evidence from witnesses must be produced. In general, if you do me the honor to entrust the case to me, leave me to choose the means which should be used. He who desires a result accepts the means of obtaining it."

"If it is so . . . " Karenin began, growing suddenly pale, but at that moment the other suddenly rose and went to the door to speak to his assistant, who had again come to interrupt him.

"Tell her we have not got a cheap sale on here!" he said and came back again.

As he was returning he furtively caught another moth. "A fine state my furniture will be in when summer comes!" he thought, and frowned.

"Yes, you were saying . . . " he began.

"I will write and let you know what I decide," said Karenin, rising and holding on by the table. After a short pause he said, "I may conclude from your words that a divorce could be obtained. I would also ask you to let me know your terms?"

"It is quite possible, if you allow me full liberty of action," said the lawyer, without taking any notice of the last question. "When may I expect to hear from you?" he added, moving toward the door, his eyes and patent-leather boots shining.

"In a week's time. And you will be so good as to let me know whether you are willing to undertake the case, and on what terms."

"Very well."

The lawyer bowed deferentially, let his client pass out, and being left alone abandoned himself to his happy mood. He felt so cheerful that, contrary to his custom, he allowed a reduction to the bargaining lady and gave up catching moths, having made up his mind to have his furniture recovered next winter with velvet, like Sigonin's.

QUESTIONS

Tolstoy's caricature of the legal interview is as perceptive (and amusing) for us today as it was for Russians more than one hundred years ago. The scene introduces a whole range of issues about client interviewing that will be developed in this and subsequent chapters. Some of those issues are implicit in the following questions.

1. What was this lawyer's view of the lawyer-client relationship? How well did he accomplish the interviewing goals identified in Chapter 3?

2. Did the client's attitude toward lawyers affect the interview? Did the lawyer's conduct reinforce or alter this attitude? Could or should the lawyer have recognized or dealt with the client's attitude? How?

3. What impressions do the lawyer's waiting room, office, and personal appearance create?

4. What important "facts" did the lawyer learn about Karenin's case?

How effective was the lawyer in pursuing those facts? How well did the lawyer explain Karenin's options to him?

5. If you were the attorney, what would you do differently?

B. PREPARING FOR THE INTERVIEW

Ordinarily, you will not face the predicament that confronted Karenin's counsel. In the excerpt, the lawyer had not previously met the client and knew nothing about the facts of his case. Most clients today make an appointment with a lawyer and give a hint about the nature of the problem in the manner of the following example.

≡ PROBLEM 2 ≡
The Angry Minority Shareholder

In your absence, your secretary has received a phone call from a potential client and has left the following message for you:

To: Associate

From: Secretary

Made appointment for Greg Lucchino of the Cougars. Wants to consult you concerning his right as a minority shareholder to block a company's improper action which will hurt the business and injure his reputation.

You know Lucchino is the star player of the area's minor league baseball team. During the past year or so he has appeared on local television advertising a small retail electronics chain, "Video Insights."

QUESTIONS

To get ready for this interview, what steps might you take? How would you prepare for the law, prepare for the facts, prepare for the relationship?

1. Preparing for the Law

Designing a law office system that encourages clients to signal the general area of legal problem in advance of the interview gives you a distinct advantage. You then have the opportunity to prepare for the meeting by reviewing basic legal principles that are likely to apply to the client's situation. Having reviewed potentially applicable legal theories before the interview, you are less likely to miss important, legally relevant questions during the interview. For example, in the minority shareholder problem a review of corporation law should focus your attention on such issues as whether the corporation's actions have been executed or remain executory, whether the action falls within the corporation's express or implied powers, and whether an injunction or a damages action might lie.

By "reviewing" the law, we do not mean you should spend hours of research time in advance of the interview. Extensive research before the facts are developed is undesirable; you could waste time on irrelevancies or, worse, could focus too quickly on certain legal avenues while ignoring other possibilities. Moreover, because you and the client have not yet entered a professional services contract, the client cannot be billed for the research. On the other hand, a brief general review, or a few minutes devoted to rethinking basic legal principles in the appropriate area of law, should sharpen your attention to important facts.

A comment is in order about the various "checklists" that are commercially available to lawyers. While stopping short of outright condemnation, we discourage placing reliance on checklists. Too often the checklist becomes a recipe, with each question asked in a rigid numerical order during the interview. In such a situation, the lawyer turns into a bureaucratic robot completing a form. Not only is this devastating to the attorney-client relationship, but it interferes with creative and client-centered fact-gathering. Rather than depend on a formal checklist, you should conduct a general review of legal principles, jotting down notes of key concepts to stimulate critical thinking during the interview. If a checklist is consulted, you should use it as a general guide or as a reference at the end of the interview to ensure that you covered all the relevant topics.

2. Preparing for the Facts

When meeting a new client, you will often be unable to prepare for the facts that have occasioned the client's legal problem; the client simply has not provided sufficient advance information for you to expand the factual base. In the minority shareholder problem, for example, the client has not revealed enough facts for the lawyer to conduct a pre-interview investigation. The lawyer does not know the name of the company, the nature of the business, the type of action taken or about to be taken by the company, or what the client means by the term "improper." In this situation, the lawyer would be engaging in fruitless speculation by concentrating on the minimal available facts.

There are many times, however, when the client communicates sufficient details before the interview to permit you to judiciously add to the preliminary information base. Consider how the factual situation changes had the client in the minority stockholder problem left the following message:

> Client wants to consult you concerning his right as a minority shareholder in Video Insights, Inc., to block company's plans to produce pornographic video films that will hurt the business and injure his reputation.

By merely adding the name of the company and identifying the nature of the planned conduct, the client has opened the door for productive pre-interview factual preparation by the lawyer. Now the attorney may profit from a telephone call to the jurisdiction's corporate registration bureau to learn more about the legal structure of Video Insights, from conversations with local businesspeople about the economic position of the company in the community and the economic health of the retail video products industry, and from some general investigation of the role X-rated films play in the marketplace.

May now be on-line

Factual preparation for the interview can be a broad factual inquiry about the client's problem (e.g., status of the industry, nature of the services, leading companies, economic trends) or a narrow investigation of the specifics of the client's position (e.g., the specifics of the client's business, how owned, operated, financed). Seldom, however, is it advisable for pre-interview fact investigation to be either time-consuming or extensive. As with advance legal research, the time is uncompensated and too much detail may inappropriately color your view of the particulars of the client's problem.

A proper measure of general or particular inquiry into the known facts before the interview can be advantageous even though the product of such inquiry is not precisely relevant to the client's problem. Combined with reflection about the applicable law, a pre-interview factual analysis stimulates critical thinking and aids in targeting the type and amount of information to be obtained in the initial session with the client. Moreover, advance factual preparation is likely to favorably impress the client with counsel's competence, an important factor in developing an appropriate attorney-client relationship.

3. Preparing for the Relationship

Along with planning for the factual and legal subjects of the first interview with the client, you can prepare both generally and specifically for the relationship aspects of the encounter. General preparation includes consideration of appearances and timing. Specific preparation involves anticipating the client's attitude and adjusting your own demeanor to accommodate the client.

You should consider the setting of the interview and your personal appearance. As will be elaborated on in Chapter 6, the arrangement of a lawyer's office (proxemics) can be an important form of nonverbal communication. For present purposes, it is sufficient to note that you should maintain a neat office (disorder conveys a lack of caring as well as inefficiency) and should, if possible, arrange the furniture to minimize your position of authority (an inhibitor of communication and rapport). Initial impressions based on personal appearance can be powerful and lasting. Although your effectiveness in interpersonal skills will be likely, in time, to override impressions made by dress, the effects on the first interview are of sufficient impact to warrant attention.

You should also plan the timing of the interview to avoid interruptions that detract from the goal of building a relationship. In addition to their obvious inhibitive effects on thought processes and information flow, interruptions can nonverbally communicate to clients that they are not as important as some of your other undertakings. Conversely, when clients learn you have taken steps to ensure an uninterrupted conference, they realize that they will be the focus of your attention for that time and will appreciate the privacy granted their case.

Recalling Karenin's experience with his lawyer underscores the importance of these three concerns about preparing for the relationship. The lawyer's office, particularly the waiting room and the writing desk covered with papers, appeared in the main to have a negative effect on Karenin, reinforcing his dim view of the legal profession. The lawyer's dress, viewed by Karenin as "dandified and in bad taste," suggested self-obsession and thus enlarged the gap between the attorney and his client. The two interruptions by the lawyer's assistant, particularly the second dealing with another client's fee problems, broke the continuity of the interview and destroyed any remaining hope for a constructive attorney-client relationship.

In addition to preparing generally for all client interviews, you should consider measures to develop your relationship with the specific client you are about to meet. When reliable information about a new client is available before an interview, you should sift through it with the goal of making the client comfortable. Such specific preparation can help, for example, to select topics for "ice-breaking" and to decide between a casual or a more formal approach with the client.

The minority shareholder problem illustrates the value of specific preparation in creating a positive relationship with the client during the first interview. Having observed the client at the stadium, on sports shows, and during TV commercials, the lawyer can "picture" the client physically, and thus better plan the seating arrangement and evaluate the personality type. Finding out if the client is currently in a hitting slump or on a batting streak might give the lawyer insight into the client's mood. Finally, brushing up on the client's business and athletic achievements should provide the lawyer with a number of subjects to pursue during "ice-breaking." All of these advance efforts make the development of a productive attorney-client relationship easier and more natural.

Finally, planning the initial interview in the manner we have suggested should give you a head start in understanding the facts, applying the law, and developing a positive attorney-client relationship. That head start helps you in subsequent contacts with clients as you use your knowledge of the facts, the law, and the clients to develop strategies for resolving their problems.

C. INTRODUCTORY ICE-BREAKING

1. Generally

Most clients, from the experienced business client who routinely deals with attorneys to an unsophisticated person seeking a lawyer's advice for the first time, are apprehensive about the initial meeting with their new lawyer. Except for the most gregarious of us, people generally are discomforted by the process of formally meeting another person who, like a lawyer, represents power and authority. That discomfort is exacerbated by the fact that clients seeking legal counsel are usually troubled and concerned about the problem confronting them. Finally, because many clients visit a lawyer to seek help in a matter over which they have little control, they consciously or unconsciously experience a sense of dependency. The combination of these three factors produces people who approach their initial interviews with trepidation.

Even clients who come to the lawyer's office for a follow-up interview or counseling session have some discomfort. Anticipating what the lawyer will say and do about rights and obligations to be enforced for or against them can give rise to a heightened sense of anxiety in clients.

By their very nature, feelings of apprehension, discomfort, and anxiety are inhibitors of open communication. Since these emotional conditions can interfere with the flow of information and the establishment of a trusting relationship between the attorney and the client, it is your responsibility to alleviate the apprehension and diminish the discomfort.

Effective use of your introductory interaction with the new (or old) client and the application of "ice-breaking" techniques should help to reduce client anxiety and allow the client to feel more comfortable in the professional setting. The following problem illustrates many of the issues involved in the introductory ice-breaking period.

≣≣≣ **PROBLEM 3** ≣≣≣
The Commercial Lender

Your secretary has made an appointment for you to interview John Vincent, vice president of the commercial loan division of the First National Bank. The secretary has prepared the following memo on the information given by Mr. Vincent:

> Vincent approved loans totaling $150,000 ($50,000 initially and five subsequent advances of $20,000 on the original loan during the past year or so) to the Chase Construction Company. The bank received a security interest (filed by the bank) in certain heavy construction equipment owned by Chase. Vincent just learned that Chase has sold or traded in all of this equipment to Western Machine Company. Western apparently has sold some of the equipment to its usual customers. Vincent is concerned about the potential loss to the bank.

You have prepared for the interview by reviewing the applicable provisions of Article 9 of the Uniform Commercial Code, particularly the 9-300 series. In addition, you have learned that Chase Construction Company may be on the verge of bankruptcy because it has been unable to sell many of the homes in its large new development due to the depressed housing market. Also, Western is the largest distributor of new and used heavy equipment in the area. Finally, you have learned from one of your partners that federal bank examiners have been "nosing around" First National, that many of the bank's loans have turned sour, and that Vincent, the commercial loan VP for the past two years, "is the man in the middle."

It is now fifteen minutes before Mr. Vincent is to arrive for his appointment. Consider how to respond to the following questions.

QUESTIONS

1. What do you anticipate will be Vincent's emotional state at the time of the interview?

2. After greeting Vincent and introducing yourself, what topic(s) will you use to initiate the conversation? Will you begin with an immediate reference to the client's problem or with some form of small talk? If you begin with small talk, what goals should you try to achieve? How long should small talk last and how will you know when to shift the subject to business?

3. When your secretary notifies you that your client has arrived and is in the waiting room, what will you do?

2. The Goals of Ice-Breaking

The ice-breaking part of the interview has both client-centered and lawyer-centered goals. The former focus on making the client comfortable while the latter involve expanding the lawyer's information base.

To appreciate the range of client reactions to the initial interview, picture yourself about to visit a doctor with whom you have never consulted. Compare how you would feel if your visit were occasioned by your discovery of two or three of the classic warning signals of heart disease or cancer with how you would feel if, instead, you were going for an annual checkup. Though your anxiety would be higher in the first situation, both occasions are likely to produce tension. If you are like most people, you would appreciate the opportunity to adjust to your surroundings and to get comfortable before the doctor begins testing and probing. It is unlikely to relax you if you are coldly escorted to a small, sterile examining room, left alone for some time, and then immediately upon the doctor's arrival subjected to questioning about your physical condition.

While the foregoing analogy is far from perfect, your reaction to the visit with the doctor in either situation is not much different from the feelings of many clients, regardless of their level of experience with lawyers. Clients at any level are usually interested in getting comfortable in the setting before beginning a serious discussion of their problem.

Helping the client feel comfortable in your office should be a natural process similar to welcoming an acquaintance into one's home. An appropriate first step is to go to the waiting room to greet the client and then usher the client into your private office. This personal touch communicates that you consider the client important and avoids the formality attending a secretary bringing the client to your office or (what would be worse) the coldness involved in having the receptionist direct the client to your door. Escorting the client to the office allows you to engage in small talk about common, unchallenging topics and thus overcome that brief awkwardness most people experience when meeting someone for the first time. Topics that can be used at this stage, or when the lawyer and client are seated in the office, include the weather, any difficulty the client might have had in traveling to the lawyer's office or in parking, the decorative scheme or physical arrangement of the firm's offices, casual inquiry as to how the client was referred to the firm, a shared common experience or acquaintance, or a noncontroversial, current issue in the news.

Having taken steps earlier to reduce or eliminate interruptions and to arrange the furniture in a manner that enhances the information flow, you can seat the client directly without the need to bustle about tidying up the office. When the client is comfortably seated, you may wish to continue the graciousness by offering the client refreshments such as coffee, tea, or soda. Once these preliminaries have been accomplished, you may choose to continue in the ice-breaking mode or move directly to the important legal business at hand. In our experience, many lawyers, particularly younger ones, seem to err on the side of choosing the "business" topic. This choice appears to be dictated in many instances by the attorneys' discomfort with informality, by a need to appear very professional, and by a feeling that when "time is money" the parties ought to be anxious to get down to business. These concerns on the part of attorneys who decide to focus quickly on the problem are, for the most part, lawyer-centered rather than client-centered. It is inappropriate, we suggest, to base such an important early decision on the needs of the lawyer.

What factors should influence your choice? The primary barometer should be the client: Is the client ready to proceed to the task at hand or can more time profitably be spent on getting acquainted? Certainly, as soon as the client appears comfortable, you may safely begin the business phase of the interview. It is unlikely, however, that the client will say, "OK, I'm relaxed enough and now I'm ready to start discussing the problem that brought me to your office." You should therefore watch for the client's implicit messages to that same effect. Reaching for a briefcase or shuffling through papers are common signals by clients that they are prepared to begin a substantive discussion. Likewise, a continued relaxed and comfortable demeanor or signals of impatience communicate that the client has reached the end of the ice-breaking stage. In sum, take your cue from the client and gauge the length of this introductory phase by his or her needs.

For the attorney who has had little client interviewing experience, this advice may appear too vague. If one is unsure about the client's signals, is there a set time after which it is appropriate to move on to the next part of the interviewing process? Most attorneys caution that ice-breaking should not last too long, but two to five minutes is clearly acceptable.

Thus far, the focus has been on the client-centered goals of the ice-breaking phase. There is, however, a lawyer-centered goal of this introductory period. Though it is unlikely that the lawyer needs ice-breaking to get comfortable, an attorney does require some time to begin assessing the client. To be sure, that can be accomplished during the substantive discussion of the client's problem. There are advantages, however, in using the ice-breaking stage to initiate this often critical analysis.

What items should interest you during this early assessment period? Certainly you will want to determine as quickly as possible what verbal skills the client possesses, whether the client has any physical impediments that affect communication, and how well the client responds to open-ended questions. In addition to communication factors, you should be curious about the client's personality type: Is the client aggressive or withdrawn, nervous or relaxed, sophisticated or unsophisticated? Not only will these and other issues affect the attorney-client relationship, but they may be critically important if the client is called on to testify at trial or to make an important business presentation.

There are a number of advantages to beginning the process of client assessment during the ice-breaking stage. Because your small-talk topics are neither controversial nor factually critical, you should have a greater opportunity to concentrate on evaluating the client rather than on the substantive content of the client's response. Moreover, gaining information that allows an assessment of the client early in the interview permits you to make appropriate and necessary adjustments to the interviewing plan.

Returning to the commercial lender problem to apply some of these ice-breaking principles, assume that you have prepared your office for Mr. Vincent. When your secretary called, you went to greet your client, introduced yourself, and led him back to your office. While en route, the two of you chatted about the weather and an item of local interest in the morning news. Consider the following two examples of conversation you could have with your client upon arriving at your office. Keeping in mind the earlier comments in this section, evaluate the two examples.

Example 1

Attorney: Well, here we are. Won't you take a seat here, Mr. Vincent.
Client: Thank you very much.
Attorney: May I offer you some refreshments, coffee perhaps?
Client: No, thank you. I find I'm drinking too much coffee lately.
Attorney: OK. My secretary tells me the bank is having some problem with a substantial loan made to the Chase Construction Company. Why don't you tell me something about it.
Client: Yes. Well, about a year and a half ago . . .

Example 2

Attorney: Well, here we are. Won't you take a seat here, Mr. Vincent.
Client: Thank you very much.
Attorney: May I offer you some refreshments, coffee perhaps?

Client: No, thank you. I find I'm drinking too much coffee lately.

Attorney: To tell the truth, so am I. Actually, I've stopped having any after my cup at lunch because I find it's keeping me awake at night.

Client: Thankfully, I haven't experienced that problem. But I'm sure it can't be doing me much good.

Attorney: Along with too many other things we used to enjoy, I'm afraid. I understand you're in charge of First National's commercial loans?

Client: That's right, and a real headache it's become lately!

Attorney: That must force you to keep on top of current economic conditions, both nationally and locally.

Client: Yes, I do. Actually, it's easier to get a grasp of the national picture, what with all the data in the general news as well as in the trade journals. The local picture is much more difficult to read, trying to predict changes in employment patterns, how local consumers are reacting, and how the business community is responding to shifting conditions and the like. It's a very risky process.

Attorney: I assume—and here I'm just guessing—that the policies adopted by you and by other banks in the area can have a significant impact on the local business scene.

Client: Although we like to think that's the case, I'm not sure that's true, at least in today's economy. I have the sense the banking community is simply reacting to rapidly changing conditions rather than setting policies that have a true planning function. On the one hand, if we don't make capital available, the local businesses will dry up; inventory won't be restocked, building and expansion will be nonexistent. On the other hand, it's risky to make loans; it's harder and harder to predict who's going to be in good condition down the line.

Attorney: How does First National go about setting its loan policies? Is it a board decision or does everything rest with you?

Client: Oh no, no. It's never one person. Instead it involves . . . [Client goes on to explain the bank's loan policy, investigation process, and so on, emphasizing that general policies are made at a higher level and that he merely implements them in particular cases.] So you can see I'm just one cog in a much larger wheel.

Attorney: I see. I understand from my secretary that you've experienced some difficulties with a loan to the Chase Construction Company. Why don't you tell me something about that matter?

Client: Yes. Well, about a year and a half ago . . .

In the first example, the conversation turned directly to the problem that brought the client to the office. Such action may be acceptable, particularly if the client nonverbally indicated his willingness to begin discussing business, because attorney and client had a chance to engage in small talk during the walk from the waiting room to the office. There are some risks, however, when the lawyer ends the ice-breaking phase as abruptly as occurred in the first example. For example, the lawyer's "OK" in response to the client's comment about the consumption of coffee can be interpreted by the client to mean that the lawyer's apparently gracious offer was not genuine or sincere in the first place. Take care during the ice-breaking stage that your attempts at small talk are not done by rote but are sincere efforts to engage in comfortable conversation. For example, the follow-up by the lawyer in the second illustration appears to be a natural response to the client's comment, the type of response one might expect in a conversation with friends or associates.

Another risk inherent in the first example is that the lawyer has not exploited the information opportunities sufficiently to make the appropriate judgments about this new client. Although the small talk on the way to the office may have been enough to provide the lawyer with data to evaluate the client's verbal skills, it is not likely that the lawyer was able to gain insight into the client's emotional condition. In the second example, the lawyer pursued ice-breaking naturally and to advantage by raising questions about the general economic conditions and the role of banks. The lawyer learned that the client felt his job as the bank's chief loan officer was a "headache"; that making loans to local businesses was "risky" yet essential; that banks are in less control of economic policy today and were "simply reacting to rapidly changing conditions"; and that the client viewed himself as "just one cog" in the bank's loan policy wheels. Hearing these comments by this client, the lawyer would be justified in developing a tentative hypothesis that the client was being protective about himself and might be defensive when the time came to discuss the client's role in the Chase Construction loan. Realizing this, the lawyer would be in a better position to reconsider and perhaps alter the interviewing plan prepared for this client.

We emphasize that our concern here is on the formation of "tentative hypotheses." Information is received from a client in fractional amounts, in bits and pieces that eventually make a coherent whole on which critical judgments rest. Some early conclusions will be modified as more information becomes available. In the commercial lender problem, for example, the attorney may learn later that the client is neither defensive nor protective but open, candid, and honest. This does not mean, however, that you should pass up the opportunity to gain information or be afraid to develop tentative judgments about the client's emotional condition or personality type.

Finally, note that the lawyer in the second commercial lender example was able to obtain legally relevant facts about the bank's lending policies and procedures outside of the context of the particular problem that provoked the client to consult counsel. The ice-breaking period is well suited for learning such general information, and the knowledge gained can prove valuable. In addition to its obvious utility as background, such information can be used to structure specific questions later in the interview. Also, because the information is given when the client is not "on guard," the answers may be more candid and less factually selective.

In summary, ice-breaking is an important part of the interviewing process. Use it to relax clients and get them comfortable in the professional environment. To avoid intimidating clients, choose questions they can answer and topics that are not unduly challenging. While the principal goal of ice-breaking is client-centered, there are lawyer-centered aspects of the process. You should seek answers to questions about the client's emotional state and personality, as well as general information that can be useful later in the interview. Because ice-breaking is such an informative part of the process, you should not leave it to chance; prepare for small talk as well as for the more substantive portions of the initial interview.

D. PROBLEM IDENTIFICATION

At the close of ice-breaking, most initial interviews move into the problem identification stage, when the client reveals the basic outline of the problem that prompted the interview. How should you make the transition to problem identification? What types of questions should you use to get clients to articulate their problem as they perceive and understand it? What kind of response can you expect from clients?

≡≡≡ PROBLEM 4 ≡≡≡
The International Joint Venture[2]

A short time ago, you received a call from a former client who has recently assumed the position of CEO of Bazilian Enterprises, Inc. (BE), a U.S. corporation manufacturing a well-known make of office furniture. The CEO asked for your assistance in reviewing the legal implications and the feasibility of BE setting up a joint venture company in Mexico with a Mexican partner. Following are your notes of the telephone conversation with the CEO:

To: BE File

From: Lawyer

Re: Joint Venture in Mexico

BE's VP for International Development, Charlene Rogovin, is prime proponent of the joint venture. Some opposition within company because joint ventures by BE that predated CEO's and Rogovin's association with company were financial failures. CEO would like to expand BE's market beyond U.S. if there is no substantial risk. Potential Mexican partner, Antonio Bocchino, has no manufacturing experience but has substantial financial resources and extensive contacts within Mexican business circles. Mexican law has a "49% rule" which limits a foreign investor to 49% of the ownership and control of a Mexican business. Thus, Bocchino would own at least 51% of the Mexican joint venture company. Exporting to Mexico not feasible because of 100% duty on imported office furniture. Set up interview with Rogovin to get details of potential joint venture.

---

2. This problem is depicted in Harbaugh, *Bazilian and Bocchino* (negotiation problem videotape, Practising Law Institute 1986).

Before meeting with Charlene Rogovin, you reviewed Mexican law, confirming the 49 percent corporate structure rule and the 100 percent duty on imported goods. You also learned that BE's prior joint ventures were in Canada and Spain and they "failed" because BE did not assert sufficient quality control over the manufacturing of the goods or financial review of sales. Finally, you heard rumors that the BE board of directors brought in the new CEO because it felt the prior leadership was too conservative.

During the ice-breaking stage of your interview with Rogovin, you learned that she has been with BE for a little more than one year, during which she has increased the percentage of gross sales attributable to the International Division from 3 percent to 7 percent. Your impression of Rogovin during the five or six minutes of "small talk" is that she is a competent, articulate, and aggressive businesswoman, proud of her achievements, and determined to expand her role and position in BE's corporate structure.

At this point in the interview, Rogovin opened her briefcase, removed some papers, leaned back comfortably in her chair, and looked expectantly at you.

QUESTIONS

1. How much, if any, of the information you have gained from the CEO and from your independent factual and legal research will you communicate to Rogovin before asking her to identify the problem?

2. What question or statement will you pose to trigger a problem identification response from your client?

3. What type of response do you anticipate from Rogovin? Will you interject questions or comments before she completes her narrative?

Your goal during the problem identification stage of the initial interview is to obtain the client's perception of the problem without imposing your own structure on the client. To achieve this goal, begin with an open-ended question or statement that calls for a narrative response from the client and that contains only general guidance on the direction his or her response should take.

This goal is usually easier to achieve in those interviews where you know little or nothing about the client's legal problem. When the client has made an appointment, but has not said anything about the nature of the problem, you can make the transition easily from ice-breaking to problem identification by asking, "How can I help you?" or by stating, "Tell me about the problem that brought you here, how it began, and what you'd like to see done about it."

In those cases in which the client has indicated only the bare bones of the problem when the appointment was made, such as the minority stock-holder problem mentioned earlier in this chapter, your job is only slightly more difficult. In such a situation, you might use the following approach: "I understand you would like advice as to your right as a minority shareholder to block action by the company that may injure the business and your reputation. Why don't you start at the beginning and tell me about the problems you are having with this company, and how you'd like to see those problems resolved?"

In cases where you have a significant amount of pre-interview information, such as in the international joint venture problem, the task of initiating problem identification is most difficult. On the one hand, you should indicate an awareness of key facts involved in the client's problem. On the other hand, communication of all the information you know is likely to influence the client's response and force the client to adhere to your outline of the problem by simply filling in the gaps. Interviewing a client like Ms. Rogovin forces you to balance such competing demands. You might accommodate the competing considerations by making the following statement in transition: "I understand from the CEO that you are suggesting that BE engage in a joint venture in Mexico with a fellow named Bocchino, but there is some concern at BE about the risks involved in such a move, particularly in light of BE's joint venture history. Why don't you begin at the beginning and tell me how this opportunity presented itself, the problems you or others see, and how BE would like to see those problems overcome."

These three examples of initiating the problem identification stage illustrate the three important elements of the lawyer's transition statement. First, the client is asked to identify the problem in his or her own terms. Even where you communicate prior knowledge, as in the joint venture example, only a limited amount of the available information should be revealed to the client and then that information should be communicated in language that is as value-neutral as possible. In this way, any coloration of the facts or the issues will be painted by the client, not by you. Second, by suggesting there is a beginning of the problem, the client is reminded of the importance of chronological order. At the same time, however, you should refrain, as much as possible, from suggesting the starting point of the client's narrative. By allowing the client to decide where along the time continuum to begin, you are more apt to get the client's uninfluenced view of which facts are critical. Third, the client should be told to isolate his or her preferred solutions to the identified problems. In this way, you obtain valuable information about the client's goals and are in a position to evaluate whether the client's expectations are realistic or unrealistic. Inclusion of these three elements in your opening statement in the problem identification stage should assist you in obtaining legally relevant information from the client.

The client's response to an open-ended statement or question containing these three elements usually will fall into one of two categories. In the "short paragraph" response, the client will tersely signal the core of the problem as he or she sees it. The joint venture client who responds with a "short paragraph" might say:

"The Mexican market is booming and BE needs to take advantage of the opportunity. Because of Mexico's protective tariffs, the only feasible option is to form a company in Mexico. But Mexico's prohibition against wholly owned foreign subsidiaries means BE needs a local partner and Bocchino is the right guy—plenty of capital and contacts. Despite BE's earlier foreign misadventures, I know we can work with Bocchino to overcome any concerns about quality control and effective distribution. What we need from you is some legal device to spell out how BE can maintain control over manufacturing and sales."

The alternative to the "short paragraph" response is the "short story" answer. If this option is selected by the client, you will hear an expanded version of the issues, including a broad range of facts and feelings that surround the problem as the client perceives it. The joint venture client who decides to answer with a "short story" might sound something like this:

"The Mexican market is booming, especially in the Monterey area where I think we should locate the new plant. New high-rise office complexes are springing up everywhere and BE needs to grab this chance to expand its international base. [Client goes on to talk about possible sales growth in the rest of Mexico and in South America.] But the only way to tap into this growth market is to form a company in Mexico. [Client expands on the 100 percent tariff and the practical inability of BE exporting its U.S. products.] But the thing that's got a lot of people at BE hung up is Mexico's prohibition about wholly owned foreign subsidiaries and their 49 percent rule. [Client adds details explaining what practical impact these Mexican laws will have on BE's plans.] So, we need a Mexican partner and Bocchino is the guy. Actually, he's an Italian national who has been in Mexico in various distribution businesses for the last twenty years or so. He's 'cash rich' with plenty of key contacts and he's just itching to do a deal with us. I met him during one of my many trips to . . . [client gives more information on the suitability of the potential partner]. The real problem is that many of the key BE staff are too cautious and scared to take a chance in the international market because the company got burned before. Well, I know the international field and they don't, and it's my responsibility to boost BE abroad. There are some, particularly Ron Beal, the VP for Research and Development, who would love to see me fall on my face, but . . . [client goes on to talk about her expertise and to belittle the concerns of those opposed to the joint venture]. So, what I need is the right legal language that will calm the fears of those in the company who are saying 'slow down,' and let me get on with doing my job."

Clients, from the most sophisticated businessperson with extensive experience with lawyers to the most naive layperson with no prior legal contacts, usually have prepared for their initial encounter with counsel. Consciously or unconsciously, most clients review and organize the facts of their problems, think through their goals and options, and even select the words they will use in telling the lawyer about their problems and solutions. You can expect, therefore, to hear what the client believes to be the most favorable and effective presentation of the issues. In a litigation problem, you should anticipate that the client will respond in terms that tend to justify his or her position. In a transactional matter, such as the joint venture situation, you are likely to hear a presentation that makes the client's desired outcome relatively easy to achieve.

Given these likelihoods, you should listen carefully to the client's response to the initial open-ended question. In that first substantive statement, the client may be most revealing, both factually and emotionally. It is not uncommon for the client to touch on a high percentage of the legally relevant facts, using powerful descriptive language about parties and events, in the answer to your opening query. During your clients' narratives, you should encourage their elaboration with body language (maintaining eye contact, leaning forward slightly, holding your arms in an open position, and nodding) and positive oral signals (e.g., "uh-huh" and "I see").

Lawyers often err in interviews by failing to allow the clients to complete their description of the problem, their perceptions, and their proposed solutions. Two reasons explain this common failure: premature diagnosis and fear of wasted time. A "time is money" attitude seems to haunt lawyers and, as a result, they are concerned that the client will produce a long, unproductive answer to the problem identification probe. Most people, however, can handle topic control and generally confine their responses to relevant information. If, by chance, you are visited by a client who is clearly headed toward a never-ending answer, full of rambling superfluities, then you may exercise the authority provided by your professional position, interrupt the client's soliloquy, and assert control over the process. But you should hesitate to use this power unless it is absolutely necessary. The original problem identification by the client is so informationally valuable that the patience to hear the client out is a virtue to be developed.

While the fear of wasting time can be overcome by experience and the exercise of patience, premature diagnosis is a more difficult problem. Indeed, experience may be counterproductive to the avoidance of premature diagnosis. With experience, the lawyer begins to see patterns in the problems of clients. When patterns develop, the lawyer may think, "Oh, this is a run-of-the-mill [fill in the blank] case." If the attorney focuses too early on what appears to be the crux of the client's problem, the lawyer may impose this snap judgment on the rest of the interview. If this occurs, subtle facts can be missed, important emotions can be ignored, and unique solutions can be discarded. Premature diagnosis may taint indelibly the rest of the case; at the very least, it can be a frustrating waste of time, forcing attorney and client to follow unproductive paths before both can return to the appropriate route toward the solution of the client's problem.

The first step in avoiding these interviewing errors is simple: Do not interrupt the client's rendition of the problem. By letting the client come to a natural conclusion of the problem identification narrative, you are assured of receiving the information the client perceives and is willing to communicate. A complete problem identification also establishes an initial agenda of topics for you to follow in the next stage of the interview, the problem overview.

E. PROBLEM OVERVIEW

1. *Generally*

Once you gain an understanding of the problem as the client sees it and of the solution the client wants, you are ready to move to the heart of the interview: the overview. Do not be misled by the phrase we have selected to describe this stage of the interviewing process. While one might infer from the term "overview" that this stage involves a cursory and superficial examination of the client's problem, such interpretation would be far from our intention and from what should occur during this phase of an effective legal interview. By overview, we mean you should carefully scrutinize the whole of the client's problem during this stage. To do that—to conduct an effective problem overview—you must be aware of critical interpersonal communication issues and the techniques available to diagnose and overcome common impediments to complete and accurate communication.

≡ PROBLEM 5 ≡
The All-American Criminal Defendant

Your firm represents Veritex, Inc., a rapidly growing, sophisticated microcomputer software company, and its founder and CEO, Frank Reed. Reed phoned you a few days ago, distraught because his 22-year-old son, Tom, had just been arrested and charged with two serious felonies, possession of cocaine and statutory rape. You agreed to represent Tom and set an appointment for an initial interview, cautioning the father that neither he nor Tom should discuss the matter with anyone. Because of your close professional association with Frank Reed over the past five or six years, you have a significant amount of information about young Tom. The classic "All-American" kid, Tom was a two-letter athlete, member of the National Honor Society, and president of the Student Chamber of Commerce during high school. Tom has compiled an even more outstanding record as a student at St. Brendan's College, an excellent small school about 75 miles from your office. Now a senior, Tom was captain of the championship football team, an NCAA Division III first team All-American, and president of the student government. He is expected to graduate summa cum laude and he is a finalist for a Rhodes Scholarship. He has also been accepted at a prestigious law school. Both of those last two honors, you suspect, may be jeopardized by the pending criminal charges.

Prior to your interview with Tom, you have done some preliminary factual investigation. Though unable to obtain copies of the police reports because you have not formally filed an appearance in the case, you were able to informally obtain limited information from an acquaintance in the Detective division of the state police. You have learned that Tom was arrested in a motor home at a highway rest stop in one of the northern counties of the state, close to many of the state's ski resorts. The cocaine was found during a search of the motor home. Tom was accosted pursuant to an arrest warrant charging him with the statutory rape of one Bonnie Kreider, a 17-year-old runaway.

Your preliminary legal research has been limited to a review of the state's statutory rape law (which forbids "sexual conduct with another . . . if the complainant is at least 15 but less than 18 years of age and the actor is more than 48 months older than the complainant . . ."), the only state appellate case on the subject (a fifty-year-old per curiam decision of the intermediate appellate court holding without explanation or analysis that statutory rape is "a strict liability offense"), and some recent cases on arrest in and search of vehicles. Although Tom appeared nervous at the outset of your interview, your small talk about his college achievements and his pending matriculation in law school seemed to relax him. You moved to the problem identification stage as follows:

Attorney: All right, Tom, let's talk about your problem. I've obtained some bare-bones information from the state police and I know you're charged with a narcotics offense and statutory rape; that you were arrested in your motor home up north; that the police found some controlled substance in the vehicle; and that the young lady's name was Bonnie Kreider. Why don't you start at the beginning and tell me what led up to your arrest on these charges.

Client: Well, I guess it began a lot earlier, when I took a quick trip to the ski resorts at Thanksgiving to interview prospects for my Dad's business. But the most important thing is I didn't have anything to do with the cocaine found in the motor home. There were dozens of people in and out of that motor home while I was doing the interviewing. And it could've belonged to any of the people from Dad's company who used it before I picked it up. I don't do drugs of any kind, particularly cocaine! I'm an athlete and drugs will kill you! Anyway, it was on that first trip that I met Bonnie, but I thought her name was Krystal, and we kinda hit it off right away. So, I called her when I got back to school and, when I went back up there over the break to do the traveling office for my Dad, you know, interviewing computer hacks who were vacationing at the various ski resorts, well, we just took up together. But, see, I thought she was 20 or 21; she told me she had gone to college and she was taking some time off from school and working at the resort. So we were, uh, well, you know, intimate and all, you see, but I thought she was older. Stupid, I guess. But I'm not stupid enough to ever use or get caught with any hard drugs! Do you think you can do something to help me? If you can't get these charges dropped, I guess my career is ruined. That would just destroy my parents!

Attorney: I'll try my best to help you. I've now got a better idea of what happened and what you'd like to have done about it, but I'll need a lot more details in order to be of assistance. Let's start with . . .

QUESTIONS

1. What topic will you select to begin your overview of Tom Reed's legal problem? Why?

2. What type of question will you use to initiate the problem overview? What technique would you use to exhaust the topic you select to initiate the overview?

3. Make a list of the second and subsequent topics you will inquire about during the problem overview stage of this interview.

You must determine three important issues during the problem overview portion of the initial client interview: (1) the sequencing of topics; (2) the nature of the questions put to the client; and (3) the techniques of following up initial topic questions. Subsequent chapters consider these topics in depth; we introduce them here to meet the stated goals of this chapter.

2. *Sequencing of Topics*

The client's problem identification response creates an initial agenda for the overview stage of the interview. Crammed into most clients' "short paragraph" or "short story" answers are many of the key topics you will want to pursue during the primary information-producing portion of the interview. You must first identify the primary topics contained in the client's answer and place them in an order likely to maximize efficient and complete communication of legally relevant information.

The process of topic identification involves determining which events mentioned by the client are significant to the solution of the client's problem. Once you have scanned the client's problem identification response and isolated the significant events, you must place them in the order they are to be pursued. Usually, the most efficient sequence for the topics is chronological. Such an order facilitates lawyer understanding and aids the client's memory. Sometimes, however, the client may signal that a particular topic is so important to his or her perception of the problem that it deserves to be taken out of order. On other occasions, some organization other than chronological may be more appropriate and useful.

When deciding on the sequence of topics to be pursued, you should avoid starting the inquiry too far into the client's chronology of events. A common interviewing error is zeroing in on some "crucial" sequence of events and, therefore, overlooking less critical but still valuable information. Remember there are three levels of facts involved in any legally significant event: facts leading up to the event; facts immediately surrounding the event; and facts following the event. Thus, you should begin the inquiry earlier in time and space, lead gradually up to the event itself, exhaust the surrounding details, and then pursue the client beyond the event to be sure of getting all the relevant information known to the client.

We now apply these topic-sequencing principles to the problem identification response of the client in the All-American defendant problem. Following is our list of the legally significant events contained in Tom Reed's answer. As signified by the numbers to the left of each item, the events are listed in the order they were raised by the client. The numbers in brackets to the right of the events signify the order we would follow in discussing these topics with the client during the problem overview phase of the interview. Review this list and compare it with the one you made earlier.

1. Traveled to ski resort area at Thanksgiving [1]
2. Checked out "interviewing prospects" for Dad [2]
3. Cocaine in motor home [14]
4. People in motor home during interviewing [12]
5. People from company who used motor home previously [13]
6. Doesn't use drugs; athlete [15]
7. Met Bonnie during first trip [3]
8. Thought her name was Krystal [4]
9. "Hit it off right away" [5]
10. Called Bonnie from school [6]
11. Returned to ski resorts "over break" [7]
12. Traveling office; interviewing "computer hacks" [8]
13. Took up with Bonnie; "intimate" [9]
14. Thought she was 20 or 21 [10]
15. College back East; time off to work at resort [11]
16. Charges dropped or career ruined, parents destroyed [16]

We suspect that any differences between your list and ours relate to detail and order. Too often, lawyers lump legally significant events together, limiting the number of primary topics they are willing to pursue during the overview stage of the interview. Such an approach risks losing critical facts. For example, item 10, the call to Bonnie from school, may be missed unless the topic list is created with an eye toward detail. Failure to pursue this legally relevant event may mean that the lawyer will not obtain all available facts about the relationship between the parties. Because a reasonable mistake about the age of the victim of a statutory rape may be a defense to the charge, every contact between the defendant and the alleged victim must be scrutinized for information that may support or defeat such defense.

Many lawyers might disagree with the order we selected for the All-American defendant interview. Some lawyers could argue that the first two topics to be addressed should be the motor home and the fact that others had access to the vehicle and could be responsible for the cocaine found by the police. These issues, of course, are critical to the defense of the narcotics charge; for example, the search of a motor home may be governed by more stringent constitutional principles than the search of an ordinary vehicle. Other lawyers may contend that the order adopted by the client should determine the order followed by the attorney, while still others will say that the attorney should address first the client's emotional cry for help and his concerns for his career and his parents. We do not suggest that these are irrelevant concerns. In some interviews, the order should be dictated by the existence of a crucial legal fact or by the focal point of the client's emotions or by the topical order chosen by the client. But in most interviews, in the absence of unusual circumstances, the problem should be pursued in chronological order to assist the client's recall and maximize the lawyer's understanding.

Although the client's problem identification response should be the primary basis for the lawyer's sequencing of topics during the overview stage, it is unlikely to provide the complete agenda. Clients omit critical facts from their initial answers; they may not understand the legal significance of certain facts, or they may not recall the facts at that time. Thus, you must add topics to the agenda to be sure that all-important issues are addressed during the overview phase. For example, in the All-American defendant problem, the client omitted reference to a number of key topics in his initial statement of the problem. He never mentioned how the police approached his vehicle, under what authority they claimed to search, where in the vehicle the cocaine was found, or a host of other topics. When establishing the overview agenda, you must be conscious of what the client failed to say and where the unmentioned items will be placed in the sequence of topics.

3. The Nature of Questions

The primary means of obtaining information during the overview phase of the interview is the posing of a series of questions to the client. Questions, however, can be of various types, each type having different goals. Your inquiries can be broad or narrow, leading or nonleading. In this stage of the interview, you should prefer broad questions to narrow ones, nonleading questions to leading ones. Since your goal in the initial client interview (and many follow-up interviews) is to obtain information from the client's perspective, complete with the client's priorities and mental associations, you should avoid tainting the product with narrow, leading questions. Thus, you will normally use a funnel technique for the formation of questions. Having selected a topic for inquiry, start at the wide end of the funnel with the broadest question about the issue. As the client responds, move down the funnel toward the narrow end by gradually closing the questions to focus on the specifics of the problem. Each topic and subtopic can be handled by applying the funnel technique. (This technique is more fully described in Chapter 7.)

An inverted funnel approach begins with specific, narrow questions and leads toward inquiries of a broad, general nature. This technique is particularly useful when you address topics that may threaten the client. (For example, where the issue involves whether the client engaged in inappropriate conduct or the topic touches on the client's personal life.) And, when you encounter an unresponsive client, narrow and directive questions calling for short, precise answers are preferred. Individuals reluctant to speak do not respond well to open-ended questions, which may challenge and intimidate them. To reduce the client's tension and engender trust, begin with narrow, easy questions and gradually lead up to broad, general inquiries. (Again, see Chapter 7.)

To get an idea of how these principles can be applied, consider the following excerpts from the interview of the All-American defendant. The attorney and client are addressing Tom's telephone call to Bonnie from school and the "intimacy" between the client and Bonnie.

Excerpt 1

Lawyer: OK, Tom. You mentioned you phoned Bonnie from school. Why don't you tell me about that.

Client: Actually, I called her a couple of times. Like I said, we seemed to get along just great and I knew I was going to be back up there over Christmas break to do the interviewing for my Dad, so I wanted to see if we'd be able to see more of each other. Anyway, I called first when I got back to school, then during the middle of exams, and finally a couple of days before I drove back up to the resort. We didn't have that much to say to each other; you know, small talk about how things were going, me with exams, her with work. The most important thing was we talked about how much we enjoyed each other and agreed we'd see one another when I got back.

Lawyer: I see. Did Bonnie have any reason to expect a call from you?

Client: Oh, yeah. Before I left at Thanksgiving, I asked if I could give her a call to let her know my plans. She said, "Great!" I got her phone number and her work schedule for the next week so I'd know when to call her.

Lawyer: Give me the details of your first telephone conversation.

Client: It wasn't much, really. I told her that Dad had worked out a deal with the manager of Snow Top Lodge, you know, the one where Bonnie worked, for me to park the motor home in their back lot and to hook it up for electricity and sanitation. That way I could live and work out of it and still travel to the other lodges in the area to interview job applicants for Veritex. That meant I'd be up with her for almost a month. She was real excited about that and that made me feel real good.

Lawyer: Did you have anything else to say during that first call?

Client: Well, yeah, but nothing important. I told her I was kind of bummed out being back at school and I wasn't looking forward to exams. She said she'd been transferred from the main dining room to the cocktail lounge. That was good and bad. Good because tips were better there, but bad because she had to work most evenings. She laughed and said it might interfere with our social life.

Lawyer: Did Bonnie say what kind of work she'd be doing in the cocktail lounge?

Client: Sure, the same thing, you know, cocktail waitress, serving drinks to customers, that kind of thing.

Lawyer: Can you remember anything else you talked about during that first call?

Client: Nothing I can recall.

Lawyer: Was anything said about other calls in the future?

Client: Oh, yeah. She asked if I'd call again and I told her I would when I got a break in my exam schedule.

Lawyer: OK, let's turn to the second call . . .

Excerpt 2

Lawyer: You mentioned earlier that you and Bonnie were "intimate." By that do you mean you had sexual intercourse?

Client: Yeah, that's what I meant.

Lawyer: Did this occur on more than one occasion?

Client: Yes.

Lawyer: Where did this take place?

Client: In the motor home mostly. A couple of times in her room in the employees' quarters. That was before she kind of moved in with me in the motor home.

Lawyer: How many times did this occur?

Client: I don't know exactly. Ten, twelve. Something like that.

Lawyer: Did anyone else know about your relationship with Bonnie?

Client: Her best friend there, Janet Wertz. Others must have guessed once she moved into the motor home.

Lawyer: OK, let's back up a bit and tell me what led up to the first time you and Bonnie were intimate . . .

The preceding two excerpts of dialogue between attorney and client should give you a sense of the nature of the questions used in the overview portion of the client interview. In the first excerpt, the lawyer begins with a completely open-ended question after briefly identifying the topic. To be sure facts have not been omitted, the lawyer next asks the client in an open fashion if anything led up to the legally significant event, the telephone conversations between the client and the alleged victim. Having learned from the client that there were multiple phone calls, the lawyer identifies a subtopic (the first call) and in an open-ended fashion asks for details. After probing the client's further knowledge about the event with another open-ended question, the attorney narrows the form of the question. Based on a fact revealed by the client (Bonnie's reassignment), the lawyer formulates a focused question. To be sure that the client's recall has been exhausted, the lawyer uses a directed but open question, and then concludes the inquiry with a narrow and directive question, calling for specific information before making the transition to the next subtopic.

The second conversation between the lawyer and client provides an example of the inverted funnel technique. The client's original problem identification response ("So we were, uh, well, you know, intimate and all, you see, but I thought she was older") suggested that the client was reluctant or embarrassed about discussing his intimate relationship with the alleged victim. To overcome the client's hesitancy, the lawyer identifies the topic with the word used by the client and then asks a narrow, almost leading question. The next four questions posed by the attorney follow this narrow, directive pattern. By asking such focused questions in a neutral tone, the lawyer communicates a nonjudgmental reaction to the situation, indicates he or she has some understanding of the situation, and obtains relevant information without forcing the client to engage in long, narrative answers. This technique allowed the client to get into a potentially sensitive discussion with his lawyer with a minimum of discomfort. Once the lawyer senses the client's resistance has been diminished, the lawyer returns to the traditional funnel technique with a broad, open-ended question to ensure that the client's perceptions and feelings will be revealed.

4. Follow-Up Questions

Even if you have mastered and employ an effective questioning technique during the overview portion of the interview, there is no guarantee each of the client's responses will satisfy your request for information. From time to time, an appropriate question produces an inadequate answer by the client. To avoid being frustrated in the search for relevant facts, you must learn to overcome these inadequate client responses through effective follow-up questions. To decide what type of follow-up question is likely to be effective in a particular situation, you must have the diagnostic skills to classify the various inadequate responses. The following exchange between a lawyer and the All-American defendant provides examples of inadequate answers by the client:

(#1)   *Lawyer:* Let's switch to Bonnie's age. You said you thought she was 20 or 21. What led you to that conclusion?
        Client: Well, she sure looked and acted older than 17!

(#2)   *Lawyer:* Did she ever say she was that old, did she ever mention her age?
        Client: It was her obligation! I mean, she knew what was happening and what could happen to me. Any trouble she could've had wouldn't have involved criminal charges!

(#3)   *Lawyer:* Did you ever ask Bonnie how old she was?
        Client: [Shrugs.]

(#4)   *Lawyer:* Did she ever tell you anything about her friends, her family, about being a runaway?
        Client: Her friends? I don't think Janet or the other people at Snow Top had any better idea than I did. I got to know Janet

pretty well and I think she would've said something, warn me, you know. They had her working in the bar and you have to be more than 17 to serve drinks in this state. They must have thought she was older, just like I did. I bet she lied to them, produced a false ID or something.

(#5)   *Lawyer:*   Did you ever let her drive the motor home?
       Client: Oh, sure. She drove it a couple of times.

(#6)   *Lawyer:*   Well, did you ever get a look at her driver's license to see what name was listed or her age?
       Client: I'm not sure. There was one time at the store when she was paying for something . . . It had to do with her picture . . . I don't remember right now.

Five of the client's six answers in the preceding example can be classified as inadequate. By "inadequate," we do not mean that the answers are completely barren of information useful to the lawyer. Rather, we mean that the answers are not appropriately responsive to the attorney's questions; the responses fail to provide the precise information sought by the lawyer. The client's first answer can be categorized as a partial response, one in which the client produced information relevant to the question but incomplete in its scope. The client's answer to the second question is inaccurate, meaning the answer appears superficially relevant and complete, but the attorney is aware that either the answer is not in accord with other facts or, as here, it presents the client's distorted view. In reply to the third question, the client is nonresponsive; he has ignored the attorney's inquiry. In his fourth answer, the client produces an irrelevant response. The information supplied by the client is adequate, but the focus of the answer misses the mark. The lawyer's last question seeks information that the client has either forgotten or never had, and the client's response thus blocks the lawyer's attempt to obtain information. Of the client's six answers, then, the only one that qualifies as adequate was that made in reply to the fifth question.

There is no formula for selecting the right follow-up to each inadequate response by the client. There is, however, an assortment of probes available to the skilled interviewer. These probes, which vary from neutral and nondirective to controlling and very directive, are discussed in Chapter 7. For now, in this survey of the initial client interview, we need only suggest that you should set your strategy for countering an inadequate response according to what you perceive to be its cause. In addition, keep in mind your overall goal of trying to get clients to respond on their own terms and in their own way. Unless otherwise dictated by your analysis of the cause of the client's unsatisfactory answer, resist the urge to use a narrow, controlling, and directive follow-up. A more neutral and open-ended comeback may yet produce the specific details sought by the initial question. Of course, if the client persists in giving inadequate responses to the more neutral probes, you must resort to more directive methods.

Success at the problem overview stage of the interview is essential if you are to achieve the objective of gathering as much relevant information as possible. Mastering the identification and sequencing of topics and the formulation of effective probes is critical to success during the overview phase of the process. Succeeding chapters will expand on the techniques available to skillfully execute this part of the client interview.

F. VERIFICATION

As the interview progresses, particularly during the later stages of the problem overview, you develop some tentative hypotheses about how the client's problem may be resolved. As these alternative solutions evolve in your mind, you encounter a growing need to confirm pivotal facts, corroborate the important feelings of the client, and clarify the client's real goals. In short, you must verify those factors upon which identification of likely alternatives will depend.

Because the information goals in verification are more narrow and specific, the nature of questioning is different. In this phase of the interview, the questions become more focused and directive. At times, they may even take the form, though not the style, of cross-examination. For example, to determine whether three separate facts, related by the client at various points of the interview, create a particular legal conclusion, you might ask: "You did tell me Fact A, Fact B, and Fact C, didn't you?" Without an intimidating or threatening tone, you verify the information by leading the client. Or you may draw inferences from the information provided and engage in summarization: "From all that you've told me, it seems your real goal is X. Is that a fair statement?" Or the lawyer may verify facts or feelings through an explanation technique: "One of the areas we probably should concentrate on is Y because you've told me. . . ." Or speculation could be used to confirm information provided by the client: "Given what you've told me about your plans and goals, I wonder if you've considered Z?"

Although verification is aimed at supporting potential solutions to the client's problem, it does not necessarily follow that you reveal these possible outcomes to the client. In situations where the solution is obvious, is almost certain to be obtained (or denied), or requires immediate action, you generally disclose and discuss the options. You should, however, refrain from detailing predictions about possible outcomes to the client. Most potential alternatives developed during the interview are likely to require further research, further fact investigation, and further thought. Predicting solutions prematurely may create in the client's mind an overly optimistic or pessimistic picture as to the final outcome. Moreover, you may be forced to reverse yourself and redraw the picture after legal research or investigation of the facts has disproved the initial projection. Therefore, if you do discuss potential solutions in the initial interview, you should proceed cautiously while bracketing the discussion with qualifiers.

During the early stages of the interview, the client should be talking much more than the attorney. While you engage in attentive and active listening, the client is stimulated to speak at some length. During verification, however, you may talk almost as much as the client. The process undergoes a subtle change as you become more than a receiver of information.

During verification, you begin to assume the role of giver of information. Verification, then, marks the beginning of your role as counselor, a role we consider in detail in later chapters of this book.

Detailed verification plays a critical role in the representation of a client. Confirmation of facts concerning various legal options is essential to effectively execute the post-interview agenda of research, investigation, and analysis, as well as to properly close the interview.

G. CLOSURE

You should complete at least two important functions during the closing stage of the initial interview: responsibilities should be assigned and a future appointment or deadline should be set. Implicit in the assignment of duties is a statement of what has been achieved; implicit in setting a date for future interaction is a commitment to achieve specific goals in the future. If these two tasks are accomplished, the initial interview has reached its natural conclusion.

Assignment of responsibilities meets important needs of both your client and you. You reassure your clients when you tell them what specific steps you will take to further the resolution of their problems. Clients want to know, and are entitled to know, what they are paying for and what tasks the attorney has agreed to undertake. In this context, you finalize, or at least discuss, contractual arrangements. If possible, tasks should be assigned to the client as well. For example, you can direct the client to assemble relevant documents or locate important individuals. By assigning specific tasks to clients, you emphasize that solving their problems will be a joint enterprise involving both lawyer and client. This "team" approach to the resolution of the problem fosters a good attorney-client relationship, an important element as the parties move toward achievement of their goals. (Recall discussion of the above points in Chapter 3, Sections C-2 and D.)

Establishing a precise occasion for further discussion or a progress report is critical. No client likes to be told, "I'll get back to you as soon as I can." Clients are almost always irritated by attorney indefiniteness. As some doctors become insensitive to the pain and suffering of their patients, some lawyers become immune to the feelings of clients with legal problems. Attorneys too often forget the importance of even simple legal problems to the individuals involved. A specific appointment time or a deadline for an opinion letter assures the client that you are concerned about resolution of the problem, and are committed to action within the near future.

H. SUMMARY

This chapter provided an overview of the legal interviewing process. Breaking down the initial interview into component parts allows an examination of the steps that you and a client are likely to go through during your first encounter with each other. The parts, however, blend together to achieve the three goals set forth in the preceding chapter—gather the facts, establish rapport, and explore contractual understandings.

While the chapter may succeed in giving an overall sense of the first interview, it does not provide all the information needed by the skilled interviewer. In succeeding chapters, some of the elements that make up the component parts of the interview will be examined in greater detail. Only study of the principles contained in those chapters will provide the foundation for a career as an effective legal interviewer.

Chapter 5

Fundamentals of a Helping Relationship

A. INTRODUCTION

This chapter describes the essential "helping" skills and attitudes you need to effectively interview and counsel clients. "Helping" here refers to a theory of professional relations in which the professional (the "helper") respects the individuality and personal worth of each client, cares about each client, and provides each with expert guidance and support. The helping relationship requires you to master four interdependent fundamentals: empathy, genuineness, concreteness, and respect. Each includes a subset of skills, values, and attitudes. The following sections of this chapter develop, in the above order, those fundamentals.

The chapter concentrates on the early stages of the lawyer-client relationship—what we have somewhat arbitrarily labeled the "interviewing" stage. In practice, of course, interviewing and the concepts developed in this chapter continue to be important throughout the relationship and, consequently, this text. In particular, Chapter 11's discussion of advanced helping skills builds on the basics discussed here, just as this chapter elaborates on the philosophy and approaches described in Chapters 1 and 3.

While our focus is clearly on lawyer-client relations, you will find the principles of this chapter useful in any interpersonal context.[1]

≡ PROBLEM 1 ≡
Legal Malpractice: The Plaintiffs

John and Kathy Faust are in their late thirties and have been married fifteen years. John teaches in the music department at a university and Kathy is a top journalist for their city's leading newspaper. They have arranged to see an attorney, Dennis Leahy, who practices in one of the city's most reputable litigation firms. In making their appointment, the Fausts told the firm's secretary that they believe they have been cheated by another lawyer. Excerpts from Leahy's interview of the Fausts follow:

Leahy: My secretary informs me you are concerned about some problems you had with an attorney. Could you tell me what happened?

Ms. Faust: Well, I'll start at the beginning. About two years ago, John and I were involved in a serious accident. We were traveling down Cathedral Boulevard [a four-lane city street] when we were hit in the right rear portion of our car by a tractor trailer from Dorais Transports. Our car was spun around and we crashed into a street light on the corner. We were both banged up pretty bad. A short while later we went to see this lawyer, David Devine, to find out if we could get something from the trucking company for our injuries, expenses, lost work, and so on. We had heard from one of our friends he was pretty good, and we really didn't know any better. He agreed to represent us and said he thought we should be able to get a pretty sizeable judgment from the company. He wanted 40 percent of anything we recovered if it went to court and 33 percent of any settlement. He said that was the going rate. We thought about it, and checked around to see if it was typical, and then decided to go with him. So he filed a lawsuit for us, and then there were some, what do you call them, where their lawyers ask you questions in front of a reporter?

Leahy: Depositions.

Ms. Faust: Yes, depositions. Anyhow, they took a deposition of John and of me, and we deposed their driver. Then, shortly after that Devine called us to come in to meet with him. He said he had an offer from Dorais, or rather from its insurance company. When we met with him, he said they had made an offer to settle the whole case for $80,000. He said he thought that was not unreasonable. Well, we did. From what he had told us, and from what we'd been able to learn from looking at what other people got in accident cases, we thought we could get

---

1. The substance of this chapter has been well developed by others. In particular, we have drawn heavily on the following works: A. Benjamin, *The Helping Interview* (2d ed. 1974); R. Carkhuff, *The Art of Helping* (1972); R. Carkhuff, *Helping and Human Relations* (1969); W. Cormier & L. S. Cormier, *Interviewing Strategies for Helpers* (2d ed. 1985); G. Egan, *The Skilled Helper* (3d ed. 1986); C. Rogers, *On Becoming a Person* (1961); C. Rogers, *Client-Centered Therapy* (1951).

around $300,000. We told him we wanted at least $200,000 to settle. He said he'd go back to the insurance company, but said we could expect to litigate the case. We didn't hear from him then for about another six weeks, when we got another call to come in. He said he had done some more negotiating with the insurance company and it had upped its offer to $100,000. He told us he felt this would be their final offer, at least before the eve of trial. He also said he thought it was a real good offer because we would have to spend a lot of money on experts and go through two more years of litigation and physical examinations, and we could end up with nothing at trial. According to him, it was possible a jury could have found me negligent—I was driving at the time of the accident—and we'd have all these bills to pay with nothing to show for it. I didn't see how, but he was the expert. At first, we rejected the offer, but he kept pressing us, and we finally concluded, reluctantly, that we should take the money and run.

That was about six months ago. Last week, then, we learned from a secretary at the trucking company—we met her at a party, and she sort of let it slip out—that the truck that ran into us had failed an inspection a few days before the accident for having faulty brakes, and the company kept right on using it, bad brakes and all. She was also certain our lawyer knew about it because she remembered her boss muttering something about the trouble they were going to get in over using that truck. Well, we almost hit the ceiling. We didn't let on at the party, but we could hardly control ourselves. We *never* would have settled for $100,000 had we known then about the brakes and the failed inspection; we're sure a jury wouldn't let them get away cheap with something like that. But Devine never said anything at all about any inspection or bad brakes. We've been hoodwinked.

Leahy: You feel Mr. Devine betrayed you. You're angry about it, and want to do something, if you can, to correct matters.

Ms. Faust: Exactly.

Leahy: Let me get some more information about the accident before we analyze Mr. Devine. Can you describe how it happened?

Ms. Faust: Yes. I was driving north on Cathedral, well within the speed limit, and as I went through the intersection at Walnut Street, this tractor trailer came barreling through and hit the right rear panel of our car. The collision spun us around and we then crashed into the light pole on the northeast corner, I guess it was, of the intersection.

Leahy: There's a traffic light at that intersection, isn't there?

Ms. Faust: Yes. It was green, of course, although the truck driver insisted it was yellow in his direction. He said it turned yellow on him right as he reached the intersection and his only choice was to keep on going through. There were no witnesses, at least none who saw what the light was at the crucial time.

Leahy: What about you, Mr. Faust, did you see the light?

Mr. Faust: No, I was talking to Kathy at the time and was looking at her. I really wasn't paying attention to the road.

Leahy: [to Ms. Faust] You're confident, though, that you had the green light.

Ms. Faust: Yes.

Leahy: What was the nature of your injuries?

Ms. Faust: I had a concussion and several serious cuts and bruises, while John ended up with a compound fracture of his lower leg and serious back and neck injuries. I was in the hospital for three days and had headaches for a week after the accident. I missed about a week's worth of work. But John has had a whole series of repercussions. He's had surgery on his leg twice, was in the hospital for three weeks the first time and another ten days or so the second time. He also has been away from work a lot and has been seeing a physical therapist twice a week ever since the accident. Plus we were both pretty shook up; we were nervous and jumpy for some period of time after that.

Leahy: So the accident left you both with physical problems and discomfort, and just experiencing that kind of trauma had an unsettling effect on you.

Mr. Faust: Yes, very much so. I teach in the music department at the university, and a great deal of my work requires either intense concentration or creativity. But I just haven't been up to the task the last two years. I've not been able to produce either the academic writing or creative compositions as I had been able to before the accident. I sort of feel like my career, which had always meant a lot to me, has been put on hold for the duration.

Leahy: That sense of suspension is frustrating; it perhaps reinforces your nervousness, which then, in turn, makes working more difficult.

Mr. Faust: Yes, I believe you're right. It is like a vicious cycle.

Leahy: Do you recall what your out-of-pocket losses were?

Ms. Faust: Well, let's see. The medical bills for the two of us, including John's physical therapy treatments, have amounted to about $30,000. Our car was totaled. It was an almost brand-new Volvo, worth about another $20,000. Of course, our insurance covered those items. And we lost another $5,000 or so in income.

* * *

Leahy: Could you now describe just what Devine told you when you discussed the $100,000 offer?

Mr. Faust: He said he had spent a lot of time negotiating with the insurance company's lawyers, they had a lot of experience in these kind of cases, they knew what we would likely end up with at trial, and they just weren't going to budge any further without a lot more evidence from us on the traffic light's readings. He said we stood about a 50-50 chance of losing and getting nothing, and that would be after we spent several thousand dollars and another year and a half trying to put together expert proof on our injuries. He thought we might have difficulty proving some of our damages, especially on the back and neck pains I've had. Plus he said there were advantages to having the cash in hand. Of course, he neglected to remind us that after we paid him $33,000, repaid our insurance companies $50,000, and paid him for his expenses and the depositions, we would only be left with a little over

$10,000. Had we figured that out at the time, that alone would have been enough to dissuade us from settling there. That hardly seems worth the effort we put into the suit. We only got a couple thousand over what our lost earnings were, after all we went through after the accident and when it was clearly the other guy's fault.

Leahy: You feel you were in the right, have suffered a lot, and deserve to be compensated accordingly. You resent the fact you didn't get a more appropriate settlement.

Mr. Faust: Right. It's especially galling, too, that he got a pretty nice fee, for what he did, out of our suffering. And then when we learned about the defective brakes on that truck, we just couldn't believe it. I don't understand how he could do that to us. I mean we trusted this guy, and then he turns around and does that to us. No offense, but we're not very high on lawyers at this point in time. We don't want to get stung again.

Leahy: You feel betrayed; you put your faith in Devine as your advocate and he let you down. That hurts. And now you're much more cautious.

Ms. Faust: Yes, I think that's fair to say.

* * *

Leahy: To summarize, you've both been through a lot; you experienced a frightening and debilitating accident, suffered serious physical and emotional setbacks, and yet were not able to obtain a satisfactory compensation for your injuries. And now you feel your lawyer betrayed your trust in him. From what you've told me, I think the facts warrant going forward, at least to do some additional investigation and research. I cannot, at this time, give you any advice on what your alternatives or your chances are. I can tell you that I see some problem spots; I cannot be confident without further digging that he gave you bad advice, or that his failure to disclose the information about the truck's brakes can be grounds for recovering from Mr. Devine. I must also research inadequate counseling as a basis for a malpractice suit before I can properly advise you. I can only tell you now there is cause for proceeding to the next steps, and I would like to help you—if you want me to.

≡ PROBLEM 2 ≡
Legal Malpractice: The Defendant

The Fausts, represented by Dennis Leahy, have sued David Devine for malpractice, claiming he withheld important information from them, misled them, and incompetently counseled them on whether to accept the settlement offer. The plaintiffs seek what they feel they would have been entitled to with reasonable representation in their claim against Dorais Transport and additional damages for the emotional distress Mr. Devine allegedly caused them. Upon service on him, Devine notified his malpractice carrier, which then contracted the case to Cecil Brennan, a senior lawyer at a top insurance-defense firm. After studying the file, Mr. Brennan decides to interview Devine. Excerpts from that interview follow:

Brennan: I have reviewed the Fausts' pleadings, Mr. Devine, and also your file from the Dorais case. I think we should begin with the discussions you had with the Fausts concerning the $100,000 offer from Dorais. Tell me about them.

Devine: Well, after I filed the lawsuit against Dorais, we did some initial discovery, maybe three or four depositions and a round of interrogatories.

Brennan: Yes, I saw them in the file.

Devine: OK. So I early on raised settlement as a possibility, and the defendant's lawyers seemed interested. We did some negotiating, and they made an offer of $80,000. I thought that sounded reasonable, so I took it back to my clients. They flat out rejected it and said they wouldn't settle for anything less than $200,000. Well, that stopped negotiations for a while. A couple months later, in a phone conversation on some other subject, I prodded one of the defense lawyers again to see if she might come up with something more for the Fausts. That started some additional negotiations. I didn't at the time go below my authority, but I did get the settlement offer up to $100,000. Defendants convinced me they were not going to go any higher, at least not till the eve of trial. I wasn't sure spending another year and a half litigating the case would be worth it for the Fausts or for me. There was too much question on liability. The truck driver had a twenty-year record of perfect driving, and much of that had been inner-city driving. He made a pretty believable witness. So did Mrs. Faust, but we had the burden of proof and would lose on a tie. The Fausts' car was hit in the rear panel, so even if the light had turned green just before she got to the intersection, a jury could conclude she had either failed to slow down when the light had been red or should have seen the truck. And Mr. Faust's injuries, at least those involving his neck and back, were somewhat speculative and hard to prove. Her injuries weren't that serious. And then neither one of them was wearing a seat belt at the time, so there was a possibility that the defense could use that as contributing to their injuries. Taking all those things into consideration, I advised the Fausts to accept the offer. I conceded they could do a lot better at trial, but they could also end up with nothing, or the jury could decide to discount the case because of its ambiguities, and then they'd wind up with something near $100,000 anyhow, only that would be after eighteen months and considerable expense.

Brennan: So you felt you were giving them some pretty good advice?

Devine: Yeah, I think so.

Brennan: What about their claim that you kept information from them about the inspection of the truck and its faulty brakes?

Devine: I do recall learning about that. I think I got it somewhere in a response to one of the interrogatories. But I didn't give it much thought because I didn't think it was that relevant. The issue was who had the green light, not whether the driver could have stopped the truck in time if he had seen a red light. I just didn't consider the fact about the brakes to be important. If I had, I surely would have told the Fausts about it. I'm at a loss now trying to figure out what all the fuss is about.

Brennan: You feel inadequate on this occasion.

Devine: No, not inadequate. Perplexed, maybe.

Brennan: Did the Fausts ever call you and talk to you about this information they got concerning the truck inspection?

Devine: No, they didn't. I wish they would have. Maybe I could have explained things to them. It's all very upsetting to me. I thought we had a pretty good rapport and, if they had any questions about the way I handled their case, they would have come to me first, rather than go see another lawyer and sue me. You think you know someone, and have a relationship of trust, and then they more or less stab you in the back.

Brennan: I understand how you feel. You feel they stabbed you in the back.

Devine: Yeah.

Brennan: And you're confused about why they're pursuing this case.

Devine: Yeah.

Brennan: Have you ever been sued for malpractice before?

Devine: No, I haven't. I've never had clients this dissatisfied or accuse me of such incompetence. I've always maintained a lot of pride in my work; I liked to think I was doing a good job. I thought I did good work for the Fausts. They had a hard case, and I got them a decent settlement—in spite of the difficulties. It really hurts when something like this comes back at you. You're not as anxious to go into the office in the morning, you don't feel good about yourself, and it affects your relationships with other clients. That trust, that feeling of confidence, isn't there.

Brennan: I suppose you feel a blow to your self-esteem. When a client, or anyone with whom you've had a close professional relationship, accuses you of incompetence, it drains you, ruins your perspective on your work. A person needs to feel as if he is doing something of value, and that he is appreciated for doing it. And so when you're deprived of those elements, you get depressed, lack incentive, and maybe wonder why you're in the business in the first place, let alone why you're killing yourself for people who don't appreciate it. You don't enjoy the same degree of satisfaction from your work, from helping your clients, as you did before. And that can be very disheartening.

Devine: I don't know. Maybe the Fausts are right. Maybe I shouldn't be in this profession.

Brennan: Ach, you shouldn't let this suit bother you. I get these cases all the time. It can happen to anyone. You'll get over it.

QUESTIONS

Compare the performance of lawyers Leahy and Brennan in the above interviews. Consider (at least) the following questions in your comparison:

1. What were the lawyers trying to accomplish in these excerpts?

2. How successful were they in accomplishing their goals? Was one more successful than the other? Why?

3. What would you have done differently?

4. How would you react to each of the lawyers if you were the client?

5. What factual and legal issues do the lawyers face in their respective cases?

B. EMPATHY

Robert Carkhuff, the noted therapist and author, has said, "Without empathy there is no basis for helping."[2] Empathy is the sine qua non for effective interviewing and counseling. Through empathy, you show your concern and respect for the client, raise the client's level of self-exploration, encourage concreteness and genuineness, facilitate the process of choosing and executing action steps, and aid in dealing with the consequences (good or bad) of those action steps. Each phase of the lawyer-client relationship demands from you some level of empathic understanding.

Empathy, or empathic reflection, requires you to learn two subskills: "understanding" the client, and communicating, or reflecting, that understanding back to the client. We place "understanding" in quotation marks here to denote a very special use of the word. To "understand" empathically, you must get inside the client to perceive how the client feels. As an empathic lawyer, you must look at the case through the client's eyes.

Empathy is not sympathy, nor is it compassion, reassurance, or denial. Such reactions from a lawyer may (or may not) be appropriate in relations with a client, but they assuredly are not empathy. The sympathetic lawyer shares the client's values or feelings; the empathic lawyer understands them. Cecil Brennan may share the view of his doctor clients that malpractice law and judgments have gotten out of hand, but he may not understand how that perception has affected their feelings about their work and their relationships with patients—feelings similar to those expressed by David Devine. Brennan may also feel compassion for a client like Devine, feel pity for someone who is depressed and hurt, but still not understand why the client feels that way. Similarly, reassuring Devine that he is a good lawyer and that clients will trust him in the future, or denying that he has seriously erred in his representation of the Fausts, may allow Devine to feel better (on a superficial level, anyhow), but such reassurance and denial do not evidence real understanding of Devine's feelings and do not facilitate meaningful exploration of the issues in his case.

In his book, *The Helping Interview,* Alfred Benjamin illustrates empathy with a story about Schlomo the donkey, a favorite pet among the children

---

2. R. Carkhuff, *Helping and Human Relations* 83 (1969).

at an Israeli kibbutz. Schlomo was missing one day, which caused considerable distress in the community. Search parties spread out to find him, but with no luck. Finally, one of the village's elders walked home with Schlomo in tow. When the surprised residents asked the old man how it was that he had come to find the donkey when no one else could, he replied: "It was simple. I just asked myself, '[Now,] if you were Schlomo, the donkey, where would you go off to?' So I went there and found him and brought him back."[3] The old man was successful in finding the donkey because he was able to view things from the donkey's perspective. "If I were that donkey, given what I know about him, where would I go?" The counselor/helper, too, must try to get inside the client, must try to determine, "If I were this client, given what the client has told me, how would I feel?"

Once you "understand" the client, then you must exercise the second empathic skill and communicate that understanding back to the client by articulating the client's feelings. When you empathize successfully—that is, both accurately and appropriately—the client will know that you have listened, you understand, and you care. That, in turn, encourages greater concreteness and elaboration from the client. Respect and trust also follow empathy. Thus, the justification for describing empathy as the sine qua non of interpersonal skills is apparent.

Effective empathic reflection is a difficult skill to master and requires substantial practice. Fortunately, it is a skill that can be practiced in an endless number of settings. Empathy is the cornerstone of not only professional interpersonal relations, but also any meaningful human relationship. Parent-child, husband-wife, teacher-student, student-student, and employer-employee communications all need some level of empathy. (The only difference in the professional counselor's situation is that the empathy need not be, and usually is not, mutual. The empathy flows only from counselor to client, and not vice versa.) Because we all participate in some interpersonal relations, we all have the opportunity to practice empathic reflection.

To respond empathically, you must first listen carefully. That seems obvious enough, but the number of truly poor listeners among lawyers is shocking. Too many lawyers interrupt, fail to allow the client to finish a thought (or even, sometimes, a sentence), and fail to carefully observe the client's nonverbal modes of communication. These lawyers are so busy formulating their questions or their answers to the client's problem that they simply miss what the client says. Listening, then, is not a skill that can be taken for granted; it requires intense concentration and discipline.

To aid in listening and in formulating empathic responses, you must properly pace the interview. Reject the common perception that each second of the interview should be filled with chatter. By pausing after the client speaks, you can ensure that the client has finished his or her train of thought and also allow for the time needed to frame an empathic response or probe.

---

3. A. Benjamin, *The Helping Interview* 46-47 (2d ed. 1974).

Once you comprehend the client's statement, then you must analyze what the client has said and what feeling(s) the client has expressed. The question posited above following the story of the old man and the donkey is a good starting place: If I were in this client's position—given this client's own values and worldview—how would I feel? This question must be addressed to fully understand and appreciate the client's concerns.

To articulate empathic understanding, you describe, in your own words, the client's feelings and the experience that produced them. Thus, when a client says that he is in the dumps and his business is on the brink of bankruptcy, you could properly respond:

Attorney: You're really dejected. You've worked so hard on the business and now you could lose it.

The first sentence of this accurately empathic response captures the client's feeling, and the second sentence describes the experience producing that feeling. Through that response, the lawyer has communicated that she understands the client and his predicament.

This feelings-experience response can be reduced to a "You feel . . . because . . ." formula. (For example, "You feel dejected because you worked so hard and now you could lose your business" or "You feel apprehensive because of what might happen in the bankruptcy court.") The formula helps to focus your analysis and reflection. Of course, the effective counselor does not persistently repeat the "You feel . . . because" words. Such repetition would sound mechanical and rather unfeeling, and there is often a better form of expression. (For example, compare "You feel apprehensive because of what might happen in the bankruptcy court" with "You're apprehensive about the bankruptcy proceedings.") The feelings-experience formula is not a rigid frame to be imposed unthinkingly. You must adapt and respond as is most appropriate under the circumstances. When, for example, the client's statements concern only his feelings or only his experience, then your empathic response should correspondingly reflect only that which is expressed.

The latter point also illustrates the principle that the empathic response should cut to the core of the client's statements. The response must be succinct, yet fully capture the essence of the client's experience. The process, then, is like smelting gold from its diluted form as ore to a concentrated, precious purity. The empathic reflection must show you understand precisely how the client feels.

Of course, to be effective the recharacterizations must be accurate and appropriate. When your effort is inaccurate, the client may perceive that you do not understand, may take the response as a cue to go into some other subject (the one wrongly identified by the inaccurate response), or may correct you. The first two of those possibilities have negative impacts, though the third can have a positive effect if the client clarifies the feelings and the experience. Nevertheless, you must concentrate to achieve maximum accuracy in communicating empathy.

Consider, for example, the alternative responses to the client's statements in the following two examples:

Example 1

[A husband and wife visit their lawyer about a possible medical malpractice case.]

Client: After the accident, we did all that was medically possible to save our daughter. Or at least we thought we had. Now, we've learned there was a procedure that might have saved her, but the doctors, for some damn reason, didn't use it. To think that our Jean could still be alive today if those doctors had only known their business.

Attorney A: You're very sad that your daughter died.

Attorney B: That the doctors could have saved Jean's life, but didn't, makes you very angry.

Attorney A here has made an inaccurate and inappropriate response. The couple has not focused on the sadness of their daughter's death, though surely that was a sad experience for them. The core of this passage is, instead, their anger and frustration provoked by their perception that the doctors could have saved their daughter. Thus, that should form the basis of the attorney's response, as it did for Attorney B above.

Example 2

[The client has come to see an attorney about the validity of her father's will.]

Client: Andrea, my sister, was always the favored one. And now this is the last straw. You don't know what it's like to go through life being ranked second by your own parents.

Attorney A: You're mad at Andrea because she has always been favored by your parents.

Client: Well, there was one occasion I remember when she took my favorite dress back to school with her. My parents let her keep it and didn't do anything about it.

* * *

Attorney B: Your parents' treatment of you and their preference for your sister have caused you a lot of pain.

Client: Yes, it sure has. Sometimes I just feel like crying. I guess, too, I always hoped it was all my imagination, but my Dad's will seems to prove it wasn't.

In the first exchange, Attorney A inaccurately reflected the client's remarks, and the client's response shows the effects. The client has deviated from the focus of her concerns by following the lawyer's misstatement. The client apparently believes that is the direction she is to take. Thus, the inaccurate stab at empathy not only fails to reflect understanding, but it also deflects the topic away from the client's real concerns and disrupts her narrative. In contrast, Attorney B's accurate reflection evokes an emphatic response affirming the lawyer's accuracy and an elaboration that is relevant to the matter at hand.

To enhance the chances for responding accurately to the client, you should prepare. With foreknowledge of some facts, you can anticipate the client's feelings from how others have reacted in similar circumstances. Many clients also share certain feelings, such as anxiety and nervousness, in merely going to see an attorney. There is, however, a caveat to this approach: You can wrongly stereotype the client as a "typical" case. The risk of variations from the "typical case" is particularly high in dealing with human emotions set in a legal context. Thus, preparation can aid accurate empathy, but only if you sustain careful listening and concentration during the interview.

To communicate the empathy commonly appropriate for early interviews of clients, you should reflect only what the clients have actually expressed, what they have generally understood to be their emotions and experience. You operate here at "primary level empathy." If you go beyond what the client has stated, add information accumulated elsewhere, or delve into the client's subconscious, then you will have drifted into "advanced empathy." While good counselors use advanced empathy after establishing themselves with clients and learning the facts well, they avoid it in the early interviews. Assume, for example, that a client says that he has been depressed and his marriage is on the rocks. After hearing that the client's wife has obtained employment, her first real job and a well-paying one at that, the lawyer suggests to the client that his troubles flow from his dissatisfaction with his wife working. That is advanced empathy; the lawyer has stated a problem that the client has not (yet) articulated. When you venture prematurely into the client's unexpressed feelings and experience, you run a substantial risk of an inaccurate or threatening remark. Such exploration should await development of the facts and of attorney-client rapport. (See Chapter 11 for a full treatment of advanced empathy.)

You should deliver empathic responses with meaning; that is, for your empathic remarks to be effective, you must use a pace, pitch, tone, volume, and posture that communicates warmth and regard. Slow pace, low pitch, moderate volume, and appropriate emphasis are the key traits of an empathic response. An open, forward-leaning posture best reinforces the response. (See Chapter 6 on nonverbal communication and paralinguistics).

Finally, the timing and frequency of empathic reflection affect the interview. If the responses are too frequent, they may sound redundant and mechanical (and therefore insincere). Overuse can also unduly interrupt the client's narrative and thus inhibit communication. If reflection is used too sparsely, you forfeit the goals of empathic communication; rapport is sacrificed, information flow is reduced, and factual analysis fails to get beyond a superficial level. The proper medium and timing for reflection are largely determined by the substance and flow of the client's remarks. You should empathically reflect, without interrupting the client, important feelings and experiences described by the client. But to avoid client detours into irrelevant topics, you generally want to minimize empathic responses to client statements unrelated to the interview's purpose. Remember, empathy encourages the client to elaborate on the reflected subject.

The excerpts from the interviews of John and Kathy Faust and of their former lawyer, David Devine, illustrate the major points of the preceding discussion.

First, we consider Dennis Leahy's interview of the Fausts. Upon finishing the long narrative in which she generally describes the facts of the case to Mr. Leahy, Ms. Faust describes what happened when she and her husband learned about the defective brakes on the truck and about Devine's failure to disclose that information. We pick up the dialogue there:

Ms. Faust: Well, we almost hit the ceiling. We didn't let on at the party, but we could hardly control ourselves. We *never* would have settled for $100,000 had we known then about the brakes and the failed inspection; we're sure a jury wouldn't let them get away cheap with something like that. But Devine never said anything at all about any inspection or bad brakes. We've been hoodwinked.

Leahy: You believe Mr. Devine betrayed you. You're angry about it, and want to do something, if you can, to correct matters.

Ms. Faust: Exactly.

Here Leahy accurately empathizes. He has taken what the client has expressed, condensed it to its essence, and succinctly reflected it back in his own words. Note that his words do not mimic the feelings-experience formula, but the substance is there: experience (betrayal) and resultant emotion (anger). Leahy adds, then, speaking to both clients, "you . . . want to do something, if you can, to correct matters." That is not something the clients have necessarily articulated, although it is a conclusion that may be obvious from their expressed anger and their presence in Leahy's office. In any event, Ms. Faust's response ("Exactly") indicates that Leahy has effectively communicated his understanding and his clients now know that their lawyer is with them.

Leahy succeeds again at empathy in his discussion with the Fausts about their injuries, and this time his reflection also encourages some additional and valuable fact-gathering:

Leahy: What was the nature of your injuries?

Ms. Faust: I had a concussion and several serious cuts and bruises, while John ended up with a compound fracture of his lower leg and serious back and neck injuries. I was in the hospital for three days and had headaches for a week after the accident. I missed about a week's worth of work. But John has had a whole series of repercussions. He's had surgery on his leg twice, was in the hospital for three weeks the first time and another ten days or so the second time. He also has been away from work a lot and has been seeing a physical therapist twice a week ever since the accident. Plus we were both pretty shook up; we were nervous and jumpy for some period of time after that.

Leahy: So the accident left you both with physical problems and discomfort, and just experiencing that kind of trauma had an unsettling effect on you.

Mr. Faust: Yes, very much so. I teach in the music department at the university, and a great deal of my work requires either intense concentration or creativity. But I just haven't been up to the task the last two years. I've not been able to produce either the academic writing or creative compositions as I had been able to before the accident. I sort of feel like my career, which had always meant a lot to me, has been put on hold for the duration.

Leahy: That sense of suspension is frustrating; it perhaps reinforces your nervousness, which then, in turn, makes working more difficult.

Mr. Faust: Yes, I believe you're right. It is like a vicious cycle.

In these two reflections, Leahy again capsulizes what the client has expressed, and each of his recharacterizations pushes the clients to a deeper level of awareness. Identifying their experience as "traumatic" helps the clients to perceive what has happened to them, and it encourages Mr. Faust to expand on the emotional impact the accident has had on him. In the process, Leahy gains valuable information; Mr. Faust's discussion of the accident's effects on his work and his mental state is highly relevant in determining, and enlarging, his damages. In his second reflection in this excerpt, Leahy articulates for Mr. Faust the relationship between his emotional distress and his inability to work at his accustomed level: Each makes the other worse. Leahy's reflection here borders on advanced empathy— Faust had not expressly described the cyclical nature of the afflictions—but it is nevertheless a risk-free conclusion he ventures and he could be confident about its accuracy. Given those conditions, the minimal extension Leahy makes beyond pure reflection is appropriate. And with Faust's enhanced understanding of his predicament, he can now begin to cope better with his situation. Thus, Leahy's empathy in these exchanges serves its purposes of facilitating information flow, client self-awareness, and attorney-client rapport.

Leahy's final two reflections, those regarding Devine's counseling on the settlement offer, also illustrate accurate empathy. The lawyer's response to Mr. Faust's description of his and his wife's dissatisfaction with the settlement succinctly states the clients' articulated experience and feelings:

Leahy: You feel you were in the right, have suffered a lot, and deserve to be compensated accordingly. You resent the fact you didn't get a more appropriate settlement.

That reflection prompts from Mr. Faust further important "facts" for Leahy: (1) a possible litigation theme for the Fausts—Devine got $33,000-plus for his minimal efforts, while the injured parties ended up with little more than their out-of-pocket losses; and (2) the Fausts now harbor a general mistrust of lawyers. Recall the exchange:

Mr. Faust: Right. It's especially galling, too, that he got a pretty nice fee, for what he did, out of our suffering. And then when we learned about the defective brakes on that truck, we just couldn't believe it. I don't understand how he could do that to us. I mean we trusted this guy, and then he turns around and does that to us. No offense, but we're not very high on lawyers at this point in time. We don't want to get stung again.

Leahy: You feel betrayed; you put your faith in Devine as your advocate, and he let you down. That hurts. And now you're much more cautious.

This last reflection really goes to the heart of the Fausts' perception of their case. They feel betrayal; they trusted someone, and he let them down. And, as Leahy notes, that hurts. Whether the Fausts' perception is an *accurate* one is beside the point at this stage of the interview and of the attorney-client relationship. The crucial factor is that Leahy has proved to his clients that he understands their case and how they feel. Because of that proof, Leahy has a foundation upon which he can build rapport and trust—and overcome the Fausts' low regard for lawyers. If further investigation into the facts reveals that there is no basis for obtaining relief (as might well happen), then Leahy will have in place the lawyer-client relationship needed to deal with that eventuality. The Fausts might not be satisfied with the result, but at least they will be properly satisfied with their lawyer. More important, if Leahy's other lawyering skills match his interviewing skills, the Fausts' interests will have been effectively represented.

In contrast, Cecil Brennan's efforts at empathy were less skillful and less successful. Consider, for example, his exchange with Devine regarding the nondisclosure of the truck's inspection failure:

Brennan: What about their claim that you kept information from them about the inspection of the truck and its faulty brakes?

Devine: I do recall learning about that. I think I got it somewhere in a response to one of the interrogatories. But I didn't give it much thought because I didn't think it was that relevant. The issue was who had the green light, not whether the driver could have stopped the truck in time if he had seen a red light. I just didn't consider the fact about the brakes to be important. If I had, I surely would have told the Fausts about it. I'm at a loss now trying to figure out what all the fuss is about.

Brennan: You feel inadequate on this occasion.

Devine: No, not inadequate. Perplexed, maybe.

As is obvious from Devine's response here, Brennan's stab at empathy missed the mark. He does not reflect the essence of what Devine has said. Perhaps Brennan has not listened well. Whatever the reason for his failure, it is clear that the essence of Devine's statements is not inadequacy; indeed, he communicates that he has analyzed the accident case correctly and the Fausts are mistaken in their concern about the truck brakes. The feelings he expresses are those of frustration, confusion, or, as he characterizes them, perplexity.

Brennan's next efforts may be accurate, but they are nevertheless ineffective:

Brennan: Did the Fausts ever call you and talk to you about this information they got concerning the truck inspection?

Devine: No, they didn't. I wish they would have. Maybe I could have explained things to them. It's all very upsetting to me. I thought we had a pretty good rapport and, if they had any questions about the way I handled their case, they would have come to me first, rather than go see another lawyer and sue me. You think you know someone, and have a relationship of trust, and then they more or less stab you in the back.

Brennan: I understand how you feel. You feel they stabbed you in the back.

Devine: Yeah.

Brennan: And you're confused about why they're pursuing this case.

Devine: Yeah.

Brennan's statement, "I understand how you feel," adds nothing. Understanding is not communicated by such claims. Indeed, when those statements are made, it usually means that the counselor is unable to put into words the meaning of what the client has expressed. Until the lawyer can do just that, any understanding the lawyer might have remains uncommunicated to the client.

Brennan's "back-stab" response illustrates parroting. He has not restated in his own words Devine's meaning, but has, instead, simply repeated Devine's words. Parroting, especially when committed frequently, generates three problems. First, although indicating that the client has been heard, the response does not reflect that the client has been understood—the major premise of empathy. The client hears only his words being recited back and does not hear a reformulation that shows you understand. Second, when your reformulation is missing, and the client gets back only his own description, the client is not pushed forward into further self-exploration. He is not forced to examine what you have said, and he is not asked to analyze his own descriptions. Parroting, then, is a much more passive response than an empathic reformulation. Third, when you persistently repeat the client's words, you appear as if you are just going through the motions and not fully concentrating on the client.

Brennan thus misses an opportunity at this point to empathize with Devine about the sense of betrayal and hurt he feels from the Fausts' actions—that is, to empathize with Devine regarding the same feelings and in the same manner as Leahy had done with the Fausts. That coincidence is not uncommon; opposing parties often have similar feelings of unjust treatment (e.g., litigants in a divorce action or in a case where each side insists the other is lying). Moreover, the juxtaposition of the Faust and Devine interviews demonstrates the typical situation in which both sides have strong feelings that call for empathic reflection.

In Brennan's last response in the above excerpt, he attempts to empathize concerning Devine's confusion about the Fausts' motives. That effort is also inappropriate—at least at this point in the discussion. That remark is the one Brennan should have made earlier when he ventured that Devine felt inadequate. It seems Brennan is trying to compensate for the earlier, muffed opportunity he had to empathize. To be most effective, the empathic reflection should be immediate; it should respond directly to what the client has just said.[4] If a client sends inconsistent signals, thus leaving you confused and uncertain about how to respond, then you should confess that perplexity.

Brennan does finally achieve a timely and accurate empathic reflection, but, once he gets started, he doesn't know when to stop:

Brennan: Have you ever been sued for malpractice before?

Devine: No, I haven't. I've never had clients this dissatisfied or accuse me of such incompetence. I've always maintained a lot of pride in my work; I liked to think I was doing a good job. I thought I did good work for the Fausts. They had a hard case, and I got them a decent settlement—in spite of the difficulties. It really hurts when something like this comes back at you. You're not as anxious to go into the office in the morning, you don't feel good about yourself, and it affects your relationships with other clients. That trust, that feeling of confidence, isn't there.

Brennan: I suppose you feel a blow to your self-esteem. When a client, or anyone with whom you've had a close professional relationship, accuses you of incompetence, it drains you, ruins your perspective on your work. A person needs to feel as if he is doing something of value, and that he is appreciated for doing it. And so when you're deprived of those elements, you get depressed, lack incentive, and maybe wonder why you're in the business in the first place, let alone why you're killing yourself for people who don't appreciate it. You don't enjoy the same degree of satisfaction from your work, from helping your clients, as you did before. And that can be very disheartening.

Everything Brennan says here is all right, but it is not all right to say everything he has said. The response is too long; it deflects the focus away from the client and onto the attorney's own groping or, as here, pontificating. And the more the lawyer talks, the less the client is so inclined. A crisp, concentrated reflection communicates the same degree of empathy, without taking over the interview and frustrating the client. Brennan could have said, for example, "Your self-esteem has been damaged, and that has made your work less enjoyable."

Now consider the next Brennan-Devine exchange:

Devine: I don't know. Maybe the Fausts are right. Maybe I shouldn't be in this profession.

Brennan: Ach, you shouldn't let this bother you. I get these cases all the time. It can happen to anyone. You'll get over it.

This is *not* empathy. Apparently, Brennan is trying to console but, as emphasized above, sympathy and pity do not equal empathic understand-

---

4. Delayed empathy can be effective, however, when used in the context of summary or recapitulation. Leahy's closing demonstrates such use of empathy. The technique is further explored in Chapter 11's discussion of advanced empathy.

ing. Moreover, Brennan does a poor job of consolation. He insults Devine by implying he has overstated the problem. Brennan's condescension toward Devine's predicament makes him feel like an unduly emotional child. Brennan also reduces Devine and his problem to a stereotype: "I get these cases all the time." Lawyers, of course, do get cases involving unpleasant events "all the time," but to the clients who experience those events they are significant—and disturbing.[5]

A more appropriate response in this instance would have been for Brennan to reflect on Devine's discouraged state. Note, though, that the attorney should not, at this stage of the relationship, propose that Devine is letting self-pity get the best of him. That might be accurate, but it might not be. The lawyer at this point does not have sufficient information with which to make that judgment, and the client has certainly not expressed it. Such speculation would engage the attorney in premature advanced empathy of a risky and threatening nature. Besides, the Fausts (for all we know) may indeed be right; maybe Devine should not be practicing law.

C. GENUINENESS

Genuineness means that you are at all times yourself. At a minimum, you must shed the professional mystique, authority, and technical language that go with being "the lawyer."[6] To be genuine, you must be aware of your own feelings and experiences, be adjusted to them, and, if appropriate, communicate them. You must also recognize your own capability, responsibilities, and limits.[7] You are, therefore, nondefensive. Dennis Leahy, for example, was able to understand and empathically reflect the Fausts' mistrust of lawyers without feeling the need to except himself from their generalization. He knew he could earn their trust.

This genuineness embraces honesty. As used here, honesty has a dual significance. First, as a "genuine" lawyer, you are candid with the client and recognize the client's right to be informed. Second, you are sincere and thus mean what you say. The performances by the Fausts' two lawyers, David Devine and Dennis Leahy, contrast in their apparent ability to meet those prerequisites. The information about the truck inspection was important enough that Devine should have informed his clients. Moreover, the facts as they appear at least suggest that Devine may have understated the Fausts' chances for success in order to persuade them to settle. If he did, then either he allowed his own needs (ego or financial) to unconsciously

---

5. It is not inappropriate for a lawyer to inform a client that she has previously handled cases similar to the client's. Such a disclosure advances the client's confidence in the lawyer. In addition, the lawyer may—indeed should—draw on other cases for instructive experience with which to help the client during counseling. Neither of those purposes, however, seemed to be advanced by Brennan in this case.

6. Recall Chapter 1's "Parable from a Patient's Mother" (pages 15-16) and that same chapter's discussion of Professor Elkins' article on the "legal persona" (pages 9-12).

7. See also Chapter 12 on lawyer self-awareness—particularly as it relates to personality needs and motivation.

manipulate his counseling presentation or he consciously misled the Fausts. On the other hand, Leahy showed some degree of genuineness in his closing summary to the Fausts:

Leahy: To summarize, you've both been through a lot; you experienced a frightening and debilitating accident, suffered serious physical and emotional setbacks, and yet were not able to obtain a satisfactory compensation for your injuries. And now you feel your lawyer betrayed your trust in him. From what you've told me, I think the facts warrant going forward, at least to do some additional investigation and research. I cannot, at this time, give you any advice on what your alternatives or your chances are. I can tell you that I see some problem spots; I cannot be confident without further digging that he gave you bad advice, or that his failure to disclose the information about the truck's brakes can be grounds for recovering from Mr. Devine. I must also research inadequate counseling as a basis for a malpractice suit before I can properly advise you. I can only tell you now there is cause for proceeding to the next steps, and I would like to help you—if you want me to.

In this passage, Leahy communicates not only his empathic understanding, but also his honest—albeit very tentative—appraisal of the case and his identification with his clients' central cause. (We assume that his identification is "honest"; only Leahy knows for sure, of course.) Other lawyers might respond differently, yet still genuinely. Many attorneys, for example, are reluctant to take on malpractice claims against fellow members of the bar. They fear intrusions on professional collegiality or, more likely, sense that "there, but for the grace of God, go I." Others may be reluctant to push malpractice law to new levels of rigor. Genuineness dictates that those feelings be communicated as well to the client. You must remain consistent (or, in Rogerian terms, "congruent") in your feelings and your communications with clients.

Of course, tact and good sense must qualify candor. Bluntness, crudeness, and indiscretion cannot be justified by simply labeling them honesty. Out of respect for clients, you will not (at least early in the relationship) comment on a client's poor taste in dress, body odor, sexual attractiveness, or grammar, no matter how distracting the client's particular trait is. Moreover, you may form early impressions about the client or her case that are better left unsaid until the relationship is more solid. Robert Carkhuff has made the point well:

> [I]t is quite natural to employ tentatively some techniques or stereotyped modes of responding during early phases of all significant human interactions—indeed, it would be quite unnatural to be fully oneself with someone one does not yet know or respect; conversely, to attempt to remain completely unknown while attempting to come to understand and know someone else is also quite unnatural.[8]

---

8. R. Carkhuff, *Helping and Human Relations* 91 (1969).

Thus, your genuineness will progress with the relationship. As the client feels more secure with you and, as the rapport grows, you learn more about the client and the client's case, you can be more at ease in venturing opinions and in probing sensitive subjects. In addition, your genuineness in the advanced stages can include disclosures from your own experience that can help clients deal with their problems. (Early self-disclosure, however, may deflect attention away from the client and toward the attorney. The client may also become impatient with the lawyer's apparent self-centeredness. See Chapter 11 for a discussion on the effective use of attorney self-disclosure.)

D. CONCRETENESS

The effective lawyer-counselor fosters concreteness in the lawyer-client relationship. Concreteness means specificity and clarity in description and narrative. You need concreteness from clients when they discuss the facts of the case and their feelings. Without that concreteness, your ability to represent clients will be impaired. In turn, clients need concreteness from you—for example, during your explanations of the law and of alternative action steps. Moreover, lawyer concreteness acts as an encouragement and a model for client concreteness.

Several factors threaten concreteness. Language presents particular problems. Generalities and vague expressions can quickly reduce an interview to inane chatter. For example, the client says, "Things are lousy." "Things?" "Lousy?" What do those words mean? The lawyer probes, "Can you tell me about it?" The client responds:

> "I don't know. Things just haven't been going well. You know, you can really get down on yourself when things are going bad, and that makes them worse."

This client needs to be pushed to greater concreteness both as to what those "things" are and what feelings he has experienced in response to the "things." Recall as another illustration the language in the Fausts' description to Leahy of the accident's impact: "serious back and neck injuries"; "pretty shook up"; "nervous and jumpy." The clients' use of such vague terms inadequately informs the lawyer.

The client in the above example has also taken advantage of another avoidance tact by switching from the first person to the second person. (See Chapter 7 on "language within language," pages 148-151.) David Devine did much the same thing when asked whether he had previously been sued for malpractice. Devine switched from the first to the second person as he moved from his past experiences to the more sensitive subject of his present emotional responses to the malpractice suit (see page 115). When a person makes that switch, he distances himself from his description and signals he is not yet prepared to confront himself about it.

Client run-on can also damage concreteness. The client may want to avoid a sensitive subject, or remain on a safe one, and will thus ramble to satisfy those desires. Other clients may simply be inclined to run on because of senility, scatterbrains, nervousness, or some other trait. Lawyer rambling can severely damage an interview, too.

A third obstacle to achieving concreteness is client evasion—when the client answers a question other than the one asked by the attorney. Such nonresponsiveness is compounded when the client then rambles to steer discussion away from the topic you have identified. Unless you concentrate and follow up on your original question, evasive responses can be truly debilitating. (Of course, that the client has evaded a probe can, in itself, give you important information.)

So, what means are available to you for dealing with these problems and achieving concreteness?

First, accurate empathy helps. Recall that after Ms. Faust gave her vague descriptions of her and her husband's injuries to Leahy, he followed with an empathic reflection on their nervousness. That then evoked a meaningful elaboration from Mr. Faust about the emotional impact the accident and subsequent events had on him. Leahy certainly had significant fact-gathering left to do, but, just as certainly, his empathic remarks significantly advanced his fact-gathering.

With empathic reflection, you force greater articulation and specificity in describing feelings and experiences. The substance of the empathic responses not only pushes the discussion in that direction, but it also provides an instructional model for the client. In a sense, you can, by your own performance, teach the client to be concrete.

Second, effective probing addresses many of the problems of inadequate concreteness. Problems in language, rambling, and evasion can all be dealt with by good listening techniques and follow-up probes seeking clarification, explanation, or topic control. These techniques form the substance of Chapter 7 and will be fully developed there.

Third, you can confront the client about the lack of concreteness, particularly if the client has been evasive or nonresponsive. Cecil Brennan, for example, might comment to an evasive David Devine:

Brennan: You seem to be avoiding discussion of your counseling session with the Fausts. Is there a reason?

The lawyer should then move toward a frank exchange on the client's evasiveness. By such a technique, you can deal with the evasiveness problem and can also, perhaps, gain some valuable information. Obviously, though, confrontation can be threatening to the client. For example, Brennan's question implied that Devine might have something to hide and has not been fully forthcoming. To avoid being too confrontational too early in the relationship, use discretion and consider the nature of the threat posed, the availability of alternative techniques, and the need for immediate clarification.

E. RESPECT

The respect referred to here as a basic ingredient of the helping relationship is a function of the mutual trust described in Chapter 3. Here, the focus will be on the need for you as a helper to maintain and show respect for the client.

The first step in bringing respect to the lawyer-client relationship is to, in fact, respect the client. You do that by genuinely valuing the client as a person, viewing him or her as a person who exists beyond the legal context with which you deal. Maintaining that kind of respect for the client is a prerequisite to being a helper.

Your respect for clients also includes a genuine regard for them. Once you take a case, this regard is given freely. Unless the client urges means or seeks ends that offend your values, the regard should be unconditional and nonjudgmental. If value conflicts arise, then they should be aired. (See Chapter 13.) For the lawyer-client relationship to be effective, it must allow for open discussions of values or differences between you and the client. That openness naturally facilitates mutual respect.

Communicate your respect to the client. Obviously, you do not tell the client, "I respect you." That would be embarrassing for the client and meaningless as well. The client will perceive your respect only after you have demonstrated it through your actions and responses.

You communicate respect through (again) accurate empathy; your understanding of the client's feelings and experiences necessarily implies that the client has acted, or reacted, in a way that is natural and appropriate. That is, the client's feelings and experiences are "understandable."

You also communicate respect when you join with the client in a partnership, as discussed in Chapter 3. You treat the client as an equal, request the client to perform certain tasks, explain the case to the client, and keep the client fully informed. You reinforce the partnership and show respect by relating to the client that ultimate decision-making rests with the client. Decisions must then be reached accordingly, after full and frank discussion with clients. When you ensure that clients retain self-determination, they feel the respect flowing from you to them.

Thus, Leahy's accurate reflections, plus his closing's straightforwardness and stated desire to help, communicated respect to the Fausts. Brennan, on the other hand, often failed to accurately reflect, seemed mechanical at times—thus implying his participation was just business—and concluded by suggesting that Devine's case was just like all the other malpractice cases. He did not, then, deal with Devine as a worthy, unique person. Devine, as well, failed to maintain his respect for the Fausts if, as they alleged, he deceived and manipulated to displace their decision-making. The Brennan/Devine inability to accord essential respect severely strains a lawyer's relationships with clients and impairs effectiveness. That inability can also, as Devine learned, lead to an unwanted lawsuit.

Chapter

6

Nonverbal Communication and Techniques

A. INTRODUCTION

In fulfilling the information-gathering and relationship-building goals of interviewing, lawyers tend to concentrate almost exclusively on the actual words exchanged between themselves and clients. Many lawyers believe that what is said during an interview is vastly more important than how it is said. It is not surprising that lawyers rely to such a degree on the choice and meaning of words used in an interview and correspondingly de-emphasize the nonverbal elements accompanying the delivery of those words. From the outset of their legal careers, lawyers are drilled on the need for precision in the selection and use of words. In their earliest days of law school, lawyers experienced directly or vicariously the results of using loosely such terms such as "intended," "caused," "delivered," or "agreed." Lawyers are the products of a learning environment that ignored the nonverbal circumstances that can surround speech while stressing that the language used by the parties to a legal dispute is at the heart of law and lawyering; as a result, attorneys understandably focus on the verbal aspects of interviewing.

While word choice is critical in the communication between parties to an interview, other helping professions have discovered that various forms of nonverbal communication play a central role in the information exchange and in the creation of an appropriate relationship between the parties. Indeed, several experiments have shown that nonverbal channels of communication have a greater impact on clients' impressions of counselors than do their verbal expressions. There is no reason to believe that nonverbal communication is of less importance in the attorney-client relationship.

Nonverbal communication affects the interviewing process through three primary channels of expression, each of which will be discussed in detail later in the chapter:

1. proxemics—the importance of spatial relationships to communications;
2. kinesics—body movements (or the failure to move) as a communications device;
3. paralinguistics—vocal phenomena (pace, pitch, tone, and volume) other than the actual content of speech.

The cumulative effect of the operation of these various channels by a "speaker" creates a "global" impression upon the "listener" of nonverbal communication. No one level of communication is preemptive of the others (though they do vary in importance), so it is the global impression with which you are primarily concerned. But to adequately send and receive global nonverbal impressions, you must first be able to break down the composite into its components and to appreciate their significance.

Most individuals' nonverbal channels operate at an involuntary, subconscious level. Thus, paying close attention to a client's nonverbal communication channels may provide valuable information that supplements, supports, or contradicts the client's conscious verbal communications. At the same time, you should be aware and in control of your own nonverbal communication. Your communicative effectiveness is greatest when the nonverbal messages to the client are congruent with (rather than contradictory to) your spoken words.

Though all forms of information flow through the nonverbal channels, feelings and attitudes, particularly negative ones, are especially likely to be imparted in nonverbal communication. In our society, individuals typically suppress negative feelings, or at least censor their verbal channels. Proper etiquette frowns on the verbalization of insulting thoughts. But people are not as selective with their nonverbal messages because most nonverbal information is released unconsciously. Thus clients' negative impressions may be obtainable only through observation of their nonverbal behavior. Similarly, inconsistencies between the verbal and nonverbal signals of a client may warrant probing or skepticism. The unconscious source of most nonverbal messages gives them a measure of reliability that verbal statements lack. Mastery of nonverbal communication therefore allows you to better express yourself, to better understand the client and the client's case, and to enhance the lawyer-client relationship.

No foolproof system exists, however, for interpreting nonverbal messages. Nonverbal channels are especially subjective and susceptible to distortion by variations in individuals. Some individuals, for example, are naturally bland in appearance and delivery while others are hyperactive and frenetic. Such idiosyncrasies must be taken into account. While the following sections generalize about the meaning of assorted nonverbal actions, and empirical evidence supports those generalities, you must remain sensitive to individual variations. Nonverbally communicated information, like any other information, should be considered as evidence leading toward a given conclusion, but not necessarily as unimpeachable proof.[1]

B. PROXEMICS

≡ PROBLEM 1 ≡
Setting Up the Office

You have just accepted an offer to join a medium-sized firm (six partners, eleven associates) in a suburban area. The firm's offices occupy half of a floor in a ten-story, modern office building located just off a busy highway and close to a new shopping mall. Given your junior status, you have been assigned an interior office without windows. Though of reasonable size (15′ × 15′), in its unfurnished form the office can be best described as "antiseptic": white walls and "institutional tan" wall-to-wall carpeting. You have learned from the firm's managing partner that you are entitled to an allowance of $3,000 to furnish the room in any manner and style you wish. You have examined the other lawyers' offices and found furniture styles from modern to traditional to Early American.

(a) Keeping in mind the message you want to send to your clients, select the furniture, wall and floor treatment, and accessories for your new office.

---

1. Before turning to specifics, two points of semantics need to be made. First, even though this chapter is titled "nonverbal" communication, some of the included expressions are closely related to verbal forms—particularly those under "paralinguistic" effects (pace, pitch, tone, and volume). In response to that ambiguity, a researcher and leading scholar on nonverbal communication, Albert Mehrabian, contends that the term "implicit communication" would be more accurate. A. Mehrabian, *Nonverbal Communication* 1-2 (1972). Such a term would unambiguously embrace all communications not expressly articulated, including vocal intonations. Although conceding the correctness of Professor Mehrabian's position, we have opted to stay with the "nonverbal" heading in the belief that its wide acceptance as an all-inclusive term overrides the argument for change.

The second point concerns the chapter's classification scheme. Some of the issues could easily fit into more than one subgroup. For example, some writers have listed eye contact and trunk lean as features of proxemics, while we have placed them under kinesics. There are other examples, and we admit placement under one heading or another is somewhat arbitrary. But, then, most efforts at classifying share such problems. Cf. West's Key Number System. Moreover, we do not find it terribly significant which label you stick on eye contact and trunk lean—as long as you understand their communicative value.

(b) Draw a diagram of your new office indicating the position of the furniture and other items you have selected and where you and your clients will be seated during interviews.

———————————————

The arrangement and appearance of your law office can affect your interpersonal relations. Consider, for example, the following description of a lawyer's office.

"As I entered, the lawyer stood up from behind his large walnut desk and asked me to please come in, motioning me to one of the overstuffed leather chairs several feet in front of his desk. His half of the room—including desk, chair, and credenza—was positioned atop a six-inch platform framed in wood. When I sat on the chair he had indicated for me, I had a sprawling sensation, as if my bottom were headed for the floor and my chin was going to bounce off my knees. The cushion, though, gave just enough resistance to prevent such an embarrassment.

"I then looked up (my chair seat seemed to leave me only inches from the floor) and beheld the lawyer's presence looming above his desk and me. He sat down on his high-back swivel chair, leaned back, and touched together the tips of his fingers from each hand, as if to form a steeple."

Though not atypical, this scene is deadly from an interpersonal perspective. The lawyer has exaggerated his built-in authority and dominance over the client. First, the client has seemingly been ushered into the lawyer's inner sanctum rather than been greeted by the attorney in the more neutral reception area. Next, the desk's placement on the platform implies a regal—even a deified—presence. That impression is reinforced by the client's sinking seat, which leaves the client literally gazing at the heavens to find the lawyer. Finally, by positioning himself across his desk from the client, the lawyer uses the desk as an additional crutch for his authority. The larger and more imposing the desk is, the greater the impression of authority.

Most law office settings raise problems more subtle than those sketched above, but all lawyers share important concerns expressed by the vignette, one of which is presented specifically in the "Setting Up the Office" problem. What chair-and-desk arrangement should you use when interviewing a client? What message do you send to the client by each chair/desk alternative? The diagrams on page 135 depict five possibilities:

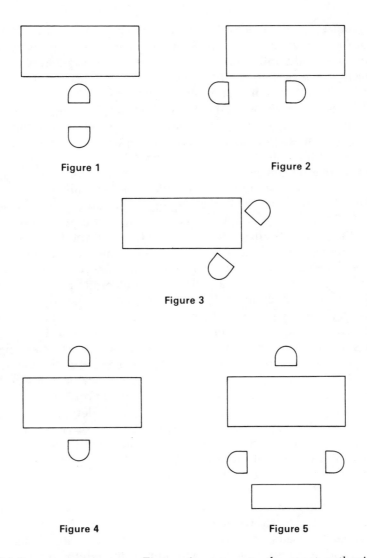

Figure 1

Figure 2

Figure 3

Figure 4

Figure 5

Of these arrangements, Figure 4 represents the most authoritative. The desk acts as a barrier, a protective device for the lawyer. It reinforces your professionalism and control and reminds the visitor that this is your turf. Of course, in a negotiation or a witness interview, you may want to achieve those effects but, in interviewing or counseling a client, they inhibit communication and rapport.

Among the other possibilities, some authorities prefer Figure 3, which shows the parties positioned across the corner of the desk. Such an arrangement reduces the interference created by the desk in Figure 4, while still providing you with some support and convenience from the desk. Figure 2 accomplishes much the same purpose, except that it creates a more open impression. The desk is not a barrier, yet you can still use it for writing or keeping reference and other materials handy and organized. Figure 1 further emphasizes openness while still permitting you to keep materials in a convenient place.

Of course, if you can afford a larger office and the extra furniture, you can opt for a couch and two chairs (perhaps with a coffee table in the middle) on the side of the room opposite the desk, as in Figure 5. An arrangement in which you adjourn the discussion to a place away from the desk is the least threatening and intimidating and the most intimate. It is especially good for accommodating conversations among three to five people. That office arrangement also leaves you the option of staying at the desk when seeking additional authority or control, as in a discussion or negotiation with another lawyer.

Furniture arrangement in the office is not the only proxemics issue for you to consider. Other trappings in the office can send important signals to the client. For example, displaying diplomas, bar and court admissions, and professional awards on the walls of the office underscores the competence of the lawyer. Younger attorneys who have not yet developed a professional reputation or widespread experience may opt to display the evidence of their achievements, while more senior lawyers may be comfortable replacing the narrow framed diplomas and certificates with works of art and personal photographs. If a bookcase forms a part of the furnishings, this too can be used to send messages to the client. A lawyer who has embarked upon a specialty practice may wish to include books whose bindings prominently display the specialty area. Another lawyer, engaged in a general local practice, may wish to fill the shelves with titles from a broad range of legal subjects, including selected local statutes and rule books—and perhaps some texts on interviewing and counseling.[2]

The relatively large but drab, windowless office depicted in the problem presents other proxemics issues. You must give the room a sense of life, warmth, and comfort. Care should be taken with office lighting to avoid a somber effect while avoiding the glare of a stage set. A modest display of plants and color can also help to enliven the room and relax the client.

Office maintenance contributes to the message you send clients. If your office has papers strewn across the desk, books piled on the floor, and files stacked on chairs, you communicate poor organization, lack of expertness, and perhaps even a failure to care.[3] Although the place need not be empty of evidence of other legal work, it should be neat enough to indicate that the client's problem will receive your careful attention.

Finally, proxemics involves the physical distance that should be maintained between you and the client during the interview. The appropriate distance for conducting interviews varies between cultures. American custom generally prefers some intermediate range. In the lawyer-client setting, clients construe an extended distance as a negative sign, indicating your

---

2. Recall, for example, the scene from *Play It Again, Sam,* in which Woody Allen, in anticipation of his blind date's arrival, scatters intellectual magazines and literature about his apartment in an effort to impress her.

3. Recall the impression made in the film, *The Fortune Cookie,* by Walter Matthau's character, whose closet-like law office filled from floor to ceiling with legal debris reinforced his role as the ambulance-chasing "Slip and Fall Willy." Compare "Karenin Visits a Lawyer" in Chapter 4, Section A.

aloofness, authority, or dislike for them. Thus, the closer the space—to a point—between lawyer and client, the more intimate and positive the effect. But unlike people in some other cultures, Americans insist on a "personal space" surrounding them that is not to be trespassed on. When you invade that space in a client interview, the client feels threatened, perhaps even offended.

C. KINESICS

≡ **PROBLEM 2** ≡
The Multiple Client Interview

An attorney is set to interview a husband and wife whose infant daughter was injured in a fall in a hotel when she was in the company of the wife. The interview opens with "small talk" about the weather and the husband's trick knee that forecasts the weather. The clients decline the lawyer's offer of refreshment. During this introductory phase, the husband does virtually all the talking. The wife sits with her head down, feet together, and her hands folded in her lap. The following partial transcript of the interview is accompanied by a description of the parties' physical movements.

Transcript

Lawyer: Well, my secretary told me your daughter was injured in a fall when she was with you, Mrs. Milam. How is she now?

Wife: Well, she's . . .

Husband: Oh, she's much better now. See, this all happened six months ago but my wife wouldn't do anything till now. The important thing is to see if we can get any help to pay all the medical bills.

Physical Activity

Lawyer straightens up in chair, leans slightly forward, shifting eyes from husband to wife and nods. Husband leans back in chair. Wife picks head up briefly to look at lawyer, glances at husband, lowers her head again. Wife looks up quickly at husband and frowns. Husband leans forward, holding up palm of one hand to lawyer and then pointing his finger. Husband does not look at wife. Lawyer moves eyes from wife to look at husband.

* * *

Lawyer: Mr. Milam, since you weren't there when your daughter was injured, why don't we let your wife tell us what happened. OK?

Husband: Well, I don't see why . . .

Lawyer: Mrs. Milam, can you tell me what happened?

Lawyer looks sternly at husband and nods toward wife. Wife lifts head and a brief smile appears. Husband looks confused, lifts both hands with palms upward and then leans back with arms folded. Lawyer smiles at wife and nods.

* * *

Wife: . . . and I did the best I could; you know, without a crib all I could do was push the bed over. The radiator wasn't hot when I did it.

Wife, looking directly at lawyer, shakes head and touches one hand to her chest. Husband, with arms folded, looks up to ceiling and shakes head. Lawyer nods to wife.

* * *

Husband: . . . the manager said it wasn't the hotel's fault, that she should've put the baby . . . well, anyway, he said they wouldn't pay.

Lawyer: I see.

Husband is looking down and then shrugs shoulders. Wife looks at husband with eyes squinting and mouth opens briefly. She then looks quickly to the other side of the room. Lawyer looks from husband to wife and then back again.

QUESTIONS

Based on the partial transcript and the action annotations, can you describe the feelings and attitudes of the husband and wife? What nonverbal "messages" were sent by the husband, the wife, and the lawyer? How did you "get the message"?

Dancers and mimes communicate with their audiences entirely through kinesics or "body language." Actors use movements to enhance the playwright's lines, to fill out the meaning of the script. We all routinely communicate with body language; hailing a taxi, thumbing a nose, or doffing a cap are typical of such expressions. These are examples of intended, explicit, and planned communication through body movements. At other times, however, our words are accompanied by body movement (or the failure to move) that is not planned as an explicit form of communication but, nevertheless, is capable of interpretation as a "message."

Clients in interviewing and counseling situations, and attorneys in negotiation settings, constantly communicate through body language. Body movements of parties in such stressful situations communicate anger, pleasure, confidence, distrust, evasiveness, and a host of other feelings and attitudes. The spoken words, however, may simultaneously send a distinctly different message.

Facial expressions are the most important communicative body movements. We depend on facial expressions for transmitting so much of our feelings and substance. A simple wink or wry smile can completely change the meaning of spoken words. Photographers and artists have long concentrated on capturing just the right facial expression either to convey a particular message or to mystify us (e.g., Mona Lisa's smile). The eyes and eye movement send the most telling facial expressions. Phrases such as "wild-eyed," "starry-eyed," "watery-eyed," and "bleary-eyed" (among others) describe very different looks sending out very different messages.

Eye contact is both a prerequisite to receiving most nonverbal information and a means for transmitting valuable information. Excessive concern with notetaking or ignorance of eye contact's importance will cause you to miss much of the client's nonverbal expressions. Because the face is the chief transmitter of such cues, concentrate on the client's face and establish eye contact. You also want to maintain eye contact to send messages to the client. Through eye contact, you show an attentive and caring attitude toward the client. Conversely, the absence of eye contact conveys a negative attitude, ranging from indifference to dislike toward the other person in a conversation.

An inability by the client to sustain eye contact for more than a second or two at a time can also be informative. Client persistence in glancing away from you immediately after making eye contact evidences nervousness or, possibly, deceit (hence, the term "shifty-eyed"). A client who never, or almost never, looks at you indicates a severe state—perhaps a total breakdown in trust, an intense dislike, extreme nervousness, psychiatric or physical illness, or some combination of these.

In the preceding problem, facial expressions and eye movements played a major role in the communications between the clients and the attorney. In the first exchange, the lawyer made eye contact with both clients, ended with the wife, and nodded his head toward her. In so doing, the lawyer indicated it was the wife who was expected to respond to the question. On the other hand, the wife's head and eye movement suggested a reluctance on her part to respond. In the next sequence, the wife's head movement and her frown communicated her annoyance with her husband either because he spoke or because of what he said. Later in the interview, when the lawyer asks that the wife be allowed to tell what happened, the husband's facial expression communicates that he is unsure why he is being scolded by the lawyer. The wife's smile suggests she is pleased the lawyer put her husband in his place. In the final segment, the wife, through her eyes and head movement, concentrates on the husband's words, appears about to interrupt him, and then seems to withdraw from the conversation by looking away from the scene. A lawyer who was not attending to eye contact would have missed these important nonverbal facial messages.

Messages from body movements and positions, other than facial expressions, are more subtle and normally operate out of the person's unconscious. Nevertheless, there is agreement about the significance of some body expressions. First, by adopting a posture with a slightly forward trunk lean (about 75 percent) toward the client, you communicate attentiveness and regard. Conversely, a backward trunk lean implies indifference toward, or even rejection of, the client or the verbal information the client is communicating. Second, by holding your arms in open, natural, and (when not in use) symmetrical positions, you communicate acceptance of and comfort with the client. You should gesticulate in a normal manner, so long as it is not distracting. Arms-folded or other closed positions are disfavored; they connote rejection or, perhaps, a sense of being threatened. At the other extreme, do not sit in a spread position; that is perceived as a little too relaxed, possibly even exhibitionist.

The nonfacial body movements of the parties in the preceding problem are important forms of communication. In the first exchange, the lawyer indicates a change in topic from small talk by shifting in the chair and leaning forward in an expectant way. Later, the husband inserts himself back into the conversation by leaning forward to speak. The husband's use of his hand is supportive of his claim that the important issue is not the present condition of his daughter. He then points his finger to emphasize that money for medical expenses is critical. In another part of the interview, the wife, by shaking her head and gesturing to herself, underscores her insistence that she had done all she could to protect her daughter from injury. The husband's body movements suggest he has some doubts about his wife's assertions. The various body actions of the clients and the lawyer in the problem provide powerful messages that an alert attorney should understand.

Body language, particularly facial expression, accompanies all verbal communication. You must make a conscious effort to "read" the body movements of clients and others to expand your information base. Just as important, you should be conscious that your own body language does not send messages inconsistent with your verbal expressions.

D. PARALINGUISTICS

≡ PROBLEM 3 ≡
The Commercial Lease

Two years ago, a lawyer wrote a five-year percentage lease for his client, John Whitmore, the landlord of a small commercial property. Whitmore agreed to this form of lease to assist the tenant, Robert Rice, the son of Whitmore's best friend, to get started in business. Under the agreement, Whitmore is entitled to a percentage of Rice's gross sales, with a monthly minimum rent of 75 percent of the fair rental value. Whitmore is back now to see the lawyer because Rice has informed him of an intention to vacate the property and move to a new location. Rice claims he is presently paying, under the percentage lease terms, far more than the building's fair rental value.

The following partial transcript includes bracketed descriptions of the manner of speech of the client, Whitmore, and the attorney:

Client: This is a tough issue for me [moderate pace and volume; even pitch and tone]. On the one hand, Bob Rice is right; his business "took off" and, because he's making a lot of money now, I'm getting far more than a fair rent. But on the other hand [pitch and volume emphasis on "other"], I took a real chance, too [pitch emphasis on "I" and "too"]. Who would guess in this economy that his business would be such a success [pace speeds up; volume increases]? I was a heckuva lot more than just a landlord; I was more like a partner in the beginning [pitch, tone, and volume emphasis on "heckuva," "just a landlord," and "partner"; marked increase in pace]. Without me "investing" in his business by discounting the rent, he would never have gotten started [tone harsh; volume remains higher than normal].

Lawyer: I can see how difficult this is for you. Are you willing to modify the original agreement, even let Rice out of the contract entirely, or do you want to enforce the lease agreement [pace slower and volume lower than normal; pitch and tone even except at end of statement where they rise slightly]?

Client: Well, one thing's for sure [pace quick] [pause of two seconds], I don't want to lose a good deal that I bargained for [pace quite slow; tone and volume drop]. But [pitch and tone emphasis on "But"], then again [pause], I don't want to foul up these personal ties with the family [pace quick; volume, pitch, and tone low]. He's almost been like a son to me [pace remains quick; volume, pitch, and tone emphasis on "son"] [pause of three seconds]. I guess I want to keep him in the building and get as much as I can [pitch and tone firm; volume normal and pace even].

Lawyer: Does that mean you'd be willing to take Rice to court to get him to live up to the agreement [all elements normal]?

Client: [Pause with sigh] If that's the only way [pause; pitch and tone emphasis on "only"], then, I [hesitation], I'll take him to court [pace slow; volume drops as sentence concludes].

QUESTIONS

Describe the client's attitude toward Rice. Does the client value the benefit of the bargain more than he values the personal relationship with Rice's family? Are you confident the client is willing to initiate a lawsuit against Rice? What factors have influenced your decisions on these questions?

Paralinguistics, the study of vocal phenomena aside from the actual content of speech, includes the speaker's pace, pitch, tone, and volume. Use of these variations has a dramatic effect on perceptions. For example, by inflection a speaker can sarcastically make words mean the exact opposite of their literal content. Actors and speechmakers flourish or perish according to their abilities in inflection and delivery. You need to be conscious of both your own and the client's speech patterns to communicate as effectively as possible.

Pace, the speed at which people speak, is particularly important in the conduct of interviews and counseling sessions. As the interviewer, you should set the pace and, ordinarily, should strive for a somewhat slow pace to maximize possibilities for thoughtful, relaxed discussions. A fast-paced interview can create or heighten anxiety while inhibiting information flow and rapport-building. But a slow pace allows clients to relax and encourages them to think about their statements. You set the contemplative pace through the use of a purposeful speech pattern and by using silent probes. (The latter are discussed in Chapter 7, pages 164-165.) Pace can also send messages independent of the verbal content of speech. If, for example, a client's pace seems unnaturally fast, then he or she is probably nervous or anxious, and you should counter with a slow pace or should discuss with the client the apparent anxiety. If the pace seems unduly slow, perhaps the client is tired, ill, uncertain, or depressed. After you accumulate other evidence, you may decide to make the client's state of mind a topic for inquiry.

Pitch in speech patterns is closely related to pace; frequently, high pitch and fast pace go together, as do low pitch and slow pace. Thus, a client's high pitch indicates nervousness and anxiety, and your use of low pitch will have a calming, contemplative effect. Of course, judgments made on the basis of such indicators need to take account of the speaker's natural voice pitch.

Tone is used here in a broad sense to include word emphasis and voice quality. Strive for a varied tonal pattern; it connotes interest and enthusiasm, while a monotone implies lack of interest or boredom. Stress patterns vary meaning. For example, the classic Abbott and Costello "Who's on first?" routine is premised on the comedians' failures to pick up the stress patterns that change questions into statements and vice versa. The audience is not similarly fooled—and is therefore amused by (among other things) both Abbott's and Costello's frustrations caused by their inability to recognize the stress distinctions. Quality of voice includes those accents and deliveries that shade meaning. Speakers can create different impressions according to whether they use a gruff, growly, breathy, or bland delivery.

The volume of the speaker's voice also affects meaning in a variety of ways. The volume with which the question "What?" is expressed can vary the meaning from outrage or surprise to a mere request that the speaker repeat a statement. Whispers and murmurings denote a desire to speak confidentially. When a speaker's voice trails off—that is, loses volume—at the end of sentences, it indicates uncertainty about the statement. The speaker unconsciously lowers his or her voice so that any misstatement might pass unheard.

Applying these paralinguistic principles to the Whitmore problem helps to explain the "messages" sent by client and lawyer to each other in that situation. As Whitmore begins an analysis of the competing equities in the matter, his paralinguistic channels are normal. As he moves, however, to a discussion of his own rights, the client communicates by pitch and volume the risks he took. By pace and volume, the client emphasizes his perception of his role in a joint venture. His tone dramatically reinforces the point that Rice could not have started the business without him.

The lawyer recognizes the paralinguistic signals signifying that the client is disturbed, even angry, at the way he has been treated by Rice, and responds by using a slow pace and low volume to calm the client and direct him toward an articulation of his goals. By initially answering quickly, the client appears to know what he wants. But the subsequent slow pace and long pauses, general drop in tone and volume, and the tonal highlighting of "but" and "son" suggest doubt in the client's mind about his precise goal. A return to a firm pitch and tone and normal volume and pace signifies that the client has resolved that doubt. The client's final comment, dominated by slow, irregular pace and a concluding trail-off in volume, is evidence that the client may be unwilling to implement the steps necessary to achieve his stated goal.

Pace, pitch, tone, and volume add much to the meaning of words. You must be sensitive to fluctuations in clients' paralinguistic messages or run the substantial risk of misinterpreting clients. At the same time, you should control your own pace, pitch, tone, and volume to achieve desired effects and to avoid sending mixed messages.

E. CONCLUSION

The combination of the three primary channels[4] of nonverbal communication results in an extraordinarily rich information source. Because it is the total effect of all nonverbal channels that is significant, listeners tend to absorb such effects without dismantling them into component parts. The

---

4. There are two other nonverbal channels identified by scholars. First, "chronemics" refers to the effects of time and timing on communications. Time, from promptness or tardiness in keeping an appointment to the duration of an interviewing, counseling, or negotiating session, sends messages or places limitations on communications. Moreover, time affects perceptions through ranking and ordering. Under the principles of "primacy" and "recency," individuals remember best those things that occur or are said first and last. For example, in drafting a political speech, a closing argument to a jury, or a presentation in a negotiation session, the wise speaker puts forth the strongest points at the beginning and at the end: "Open with a bang and close with a flourish." Similarly, the first item in a list assumes a certain importance, and ranking subjects in ascending order of importance highlights the last named. Finally, in assessing a client's response, you pay particular attention to what is said first.

Second, personal appearance of attorney and client is also important. You should appear reasonably neat and respectful of clients to facilitate relationship-building and promote client confidence. The client's appearance can send important messages that may affect the interview procedure or add to your information base. For example, in interviewing an elderly client, you might notice a hearing aid and a disheveled appearance. The hearing aid indicates a hearing deficiency and tells you to face the client when talking, enunciate clearly, and keep your hands away from your mouth when speaking. The disheveled look is evidence—though certainly not proof—that the client may have difficulty taking care of herself.

variations blend together as they reach the eye and the ear, combine with the meaning of the words used by the speaker, and produce a composite message. The listener thinks, "this person appears nervous," not "this person is speaking in a fast-paced, high-pitched, loud voice and is averting his eyes, drumming his fingers, and squirming in his seat and, therefore, may be nervous." Although global impressions are valuable, awareness of each component heightens sensitivity to cues—consistent and inconsistent—and better prepares you to recognize and use nonverbal communication techniques in probes and responses.

7

Verbal Techniques and Probing Skills

A. INTRODUCTION

Although the importance of verbal skills in interviewing is apparent, gaining proficiency in them is not easy. You must simultaneously probe for information and advance your relationship with the interviewee. Achieving those goals requires intense concentration and ability. Along the way, misstatements and misspoken words can cause serious setbacks. Missed cues can stall the interview and thwart meaningful information-gathering, and inadequate responses left unprobed can defeat the interview's purposes.

This chapter describes verbal techniques you can use to further your interviewing goals. Our primary focus is on the means of information-gathering. The chapter thus complements the preceding two chapters, which described the (mostly) verbal techniques for communicating empathy and the various nonverbal techniques for advancing both the informational and relationship goals of interviewing.

The first three sections of this chapter address three general aspects of verbal techniques: learning the role and subtleties of language in interviewing (Section B); formulating objectives for probing (Section C); and understanding the functions of probing (Section D). The concluding three sections discuss specific aspects of probing. Section E describes topic control and its relationship to the breadth of your questions. Section F delineates the various probes and their uses. Finally, Section G explains how to use topic control and probes to structure the interview.

B. THE ROLE AND SIGNIFICANCE OF LANGUAGE

≡≡≡ PROBLEM 1 ≡≡≡
Doris Thompson v. Jesse Thompson

The following dialogue contains excerpts from a second interview of a divorce client, Doris Thompson, in a jurisdiction with a fault divorce system.

Attorney: As you know, Ms. Thompson, we filed the divorce papers you signed and they were served on your husband. Since then, Jesse has seen an attorney and served on us an answer and a notice that he intends to contest the divorce. Last time you informed me that you and your husband have not lived together for four years. Is that right?

Ms. Thompson: Yes. I haven't even seen him in two years.

Attorney: Can you tell me, then, why would he contest the divorce?

Thompson: I don't know. I haven't seen him since . . . I'm sure he don't care about me anymore.

Attorney: Why are you sure?

Thompson: The way he treated me and the kids when he was home, always drunk, always screaming at us, then not giving us any support for four years. Man, he don't care about me.

Attorney: I see. [Silence.]

Thompson: I've had to hide from him ever since . . . the last two years. He kept threatening me and saying he was going to kill me.

Attorney: So you think he is contesting out of spite?

Thompson: I don't know. I guess so.

Attorney: Well, let's go back and discuss the circumstances that led to the break-up of your marriage. Now that your husband has contested your suit, I will need a complete description. Under our state's law, your conduct as well as his is relevant in the court's decisions about alimony, support, custody, and whether to grant the divorce. So start anywhere and tell me what happened to your marriage.

Thompson: [Narrative omitted.]

Attorney: Did Jesse have steady employment?

Thompson: Mostly he'd go out drinking with his buddies. He'd come home all drunked up, meaner 'n hell. He'd start screaming. The kids would hide from him, and I'd be afraid too. He never hit us much, but he seemed so angry; it frightened us. Like he was a bomb ready to explode.

Attorney: Well, you were married, prior to your separation, for five years. Did he hold any jobs during that period?

Thompson: Yeah, he had worked on a street crew for the city for about a year and a half, but then they had cutbacks and he got laid off.

Attorney: Anything else?

Thompson: A few odd jobs, now and then. You know, a construction job here and there. Sometimes he'd work moving furniture. But nothing steady.

Attorney: Where did your family income come from?

Thompson: What do you need to know this stuff for?

Attorney: Well, I think the judge would want to know whether Jesse supported his family. It's relevant to deciding if you have grounds and also in determining any award for support or alimony.

Thompson: Oh. We got money from different places. He drew unemployment for awhile, and then we got the welfare. My daddy helped us some, too. And I'd occasionally sneak in some ironing and cleaning for money.

Attorney: You stated earlier that you found out Jesse had an affair. Did you confront him about it?

Thompson: Yeah. That's when he left. He took off and moved in with that woman.

Attorney: That was December, four years ago?

Thompson: Yes.

Attorney: What did you do?

Thompson: We stayed on 19th Street until January two years ago when . . . when we had to move because he started threatening me all the time.

Attorney: You've mentioned several times now that you haven't seen Jesse since he began threatening you. Did something happen between you and him at that time that made things worse?

Thompson: Well, us, we, that is to say me and the kids and James.

Attorney: Who's James?

Thompson: He, he was my boyfriend back then. He was living with us.

Attorney: I see. Does he still live with you?

Thompson: No. No. [Silence.]

Attorney: OK. Did Jesse and James have a run-in or something?

Thompson: No.

Attorney: Did anything in particular bring about Jesse's threats and your move?

Thompson: Well, uh, our son . . .

Attorney: You mean yours and Jesse's?

Thompson: Yes. [Pause.]

Attorney: Go on.

Thompson: Junior, he died from abdominal injuries when, uh . . . . He hurt himself playing when he and some other boys were jumping on the bed.

Attorney: I'm sorry to hear that. That's tragic. Did Jesse blame you?

Thompson: James was arrested for child abuse and then, when Junior died, he was convicted of a homicide. But that was later thrown out 'cause the cops had beat the confession out of him. Then that's when we had to move 'cause of the threats; he said he'd get even with me for Junior's death.

Attorney: Jesse said that to you?
Thompson: Yeah.

QUESTIONS

What problems in information-gathering did the lawyer have to deal with in this interview?

1. How did he handle those problems?
2. Could some of the difficulties have been prevented? How?
3. What verbal "cues" did Ms. Thompson give the attorney?
4. What various probing techniques did the attorney use?
5. What would you have done differently? Why?

───────────

Subtleties in language affect all communications, but they are especially critical in the often emotionally charged, always sensitive legal interview. The significance of language asserts itself at both conscious and unconscious levels and on both your client's remarks and your own.

Clients respond to the shades of meaning in your probes and statements, thus making your word selection an important interviewing skill. A divorce client is sure to be insulted by the question, "When did you desert your wife and children?" but not by "When did you and your wife separate?" The judgment implicit in the former would obviously inhibit the client's willingness to talk. Clients, too, communicate messages through their word selection.

In choosing your words, you should adjust your vocabulary to fit the client. If the client has a limited education, then you should select words of common understanding. In speaking with any lay person, you should avoid legalese. If you must use legal terms (e.g., "summary judgment," "preliminary injunction," or "directed verdict"), then you should explain them carefully. You want to talk at the client's level, but not in a manner that makes you appear insincere or mocking. For example, a white, well-educated lawyer interviewing a poor, black youth would come off badly using ghetto slang or jive talk.

You should strive to achieve "immediacy" in your communications with clients, encourage it in clients, and be aware of its absence. Particular verbal forms connote different levels of immediacy; the more immediate the form the more positive the message. Your statements about persons you like have more immediacy than your statements about those you dislike. Similarly, immediacy communicates positive speaker feelings. The level of immediacy in a particular communication derives from "language within language"[1] and depends on a number of variables. We canvass six of them here.

─────────────────

1. The phrase and most of the following analysis are derived from A. Mehrabian & M. Wiener, *Language Within Language: Immediacy, A Channel in Verbal Communication* (1968), and A. Mehrabian, *Nonverbal Communication* 31-53 (1972).

First, the medium of communication is important. Face-to-face communication is the most immediate. Telephone conversation is less so, but is more immediate than a letter, which, of course, involves only the "cold" written medium. Generally, a communicator will choose a less immediate medium to send unpleasant information. The "Dear John" letter and the "pink slip" are classic examples.

Second, spatio-temporal indicators give evidence of the speaker's attitude toward the subject of her conversation. (The subject can be a person, place, thing, or event.) Selection of a particular demonstrative—for example, "this," "that," "here," and "there"—is significant when its use is incongruous with the actual fact. For example, a comment from an observer at a party referring to a raucous group within the same room as "those people" indicates disapproval and the speaker's desire to set herself apart from them. In addition, unnecessary phrases convey a negative attitude when they emphasize space or time differences between the speaker and her subject. Ms. Thompson's statement that James "was my boyfriend back then" is less immediate than the simple statement "he was my boyfriend." The distancing Ms. Thompson adds says something concerning her feelings about that period of time and about James. Finally, levels of immediacy are reflected in the choice of verb tense when the context allows some variation in usage. For example, a former member of the Democratic Party might confess, "I have been a member," or "I was a member," or "I had been a member." The successive examples show diminishing levels of immediacy between the speaker and his political affiliation and, thus, increasing levels of negative feelings.

Third, a descriptive term's relative ambiguity, what Mehrabian labels "denotative specificity," implicitly alters meaning. When specific references are possible, increases in ambiguity will create correspondingly negative impressions. "For instance," states Mehrabian, "parents referring to their son's fiancée might say, 'our daughter-to-be,' 'our son's fiancée,' 'his fiancée,' 'his lady friend,' 'his friend,' 'she,' 'the person,' or 'that thing.' These examples show decreasing degrees of denotative specificity and are interpreted as expressing decreasing degrees of liking."[2] In similar fashion, Ms. Thompson referred to Jesse's lover as "that woman" and consistently referred to Jesse as "he" or "him"—even when the impersonal reference created some ambiguity, as in the final exchanges.

Personal pronoun usage has additional relevance under denotative specificity when the speaker describes his or her own feelings and experiences. Use of pronouns other than first person-singular distance the speaker from the subject. The following statements reflect decreasing levels of identification: "I support abortion-on-demand," "We support abortion-on-demand," "People support abortion-on-demand," "One supports abortion-on-demand," "You [meaning "I"] support abortion-on-demand," "There is support for abortion-on-demand."

The fourth verbal variant implicitly affecting speech content is "selective emphasis." When speakers focus on specific objects out of a group of

---

2. A. Mehrabian, *Nonverbal Communication* 35 (1972).

objects—be they persons, places, events, or characteristics—they empha-size selectively. A speaker can focus by sequencing, by omitting, by high-lighting, and by isolating a particular aspect of a complex subject. The sequencing of objects has effects resembling those of chronemics, the non-verbal channel referred to on page 143 note 4. For example, each of the ways to describe a married couple connotes something different. "Let's go see John and Mary" as opposed to "Let's go see Mary and John" indicates the primacy of the first named. "Let's go see John" or "Let's go see Mary" is an even more emphatic statement that one of the spouses—the named one—has a primary importance in the speaker's mind. Similarly, a speak-er's omission of one person from a list or group communicates a negative inference about the person or thing being omitted. And if the speaker's suggestion is stated as "Let's go see the Smiths," then she has emphasized the unity or nonseparateness of the pair. Conversely, when the couple is identified as "Mary and John" or "John and Mary," the speaker focuses on the individuals' separateness and implies a different attitude toward each spouse.

The speaker's highlighting of certain attributes from a complex subject or event naturally gives those attributes a greater importance than the omitted attributes. Thus, if a man responds to a question about his mar-riage by saying, "Well, my wife's a good housekeeper," he has revealed something important about his own values and about the nature of his marital relationship. Similarly, a speaker bestows a special significance on a subject by "isolating" it from a group, collection, or list. For example, a teacher may recall a graduated class as "Jane Smith's class," thus giving ob-vious prominence to Ms. Smith. Or a speaker might expose his own views, as well as draw attention to the isolated subject, by remarking, "Thurgood Marshall and his buddies on the Supreme Court are ruining this country."

Fifth, the speaker's agent-action-object relationships can be signifi-cant. (A person initiating an action is the "agent," and the recipient of the action is the "object.") Assume a collision of two moving vehicles could be accurately described in any one of the following ways: "John ran into Mary," "Mary ran into John," "They collided," or "They ran into each other." Each of the descriptions carries a different impression about who was at fault. The speaker's selection of which of the drivers was the agent and which was the object made the difference. Similarly, you can find im-plicit information in speaker attribution of the action to a source other than the ostensible agent. Mehrabian illustrates by contrasting "I should go, " "I have to go," "I must go," "I am compelled (or driven) to go," with "I want to go," "I would like to go," or "I will go." The latter formulations dilute the speaker's responsibility for the decision "to go."

Whether the passive or active voice is used also affects the meaning of an agent-action-object statement. For example, "I drove the car" is a clearer articulation of the agent's/speaker's responsibility for the action than "The car was being driven by me." The implications of Patty Hearst's description "I was taken to the bank by the Harrises" certainly differ from those im-plicit in the statement "I went to the bank with the Harrises." (Or compare "I went to the cleaners with my bookie" with "I was taken to the cleaners by my bookie"!)

"Automatic phrasing," the final language variant discussed here, includes words and phrases used out of habit rather than with an intent to affect content. These utterances can nevertheless have meaning. Use of words like "just" or "simply" indicates the speaker's desire to minimize his association with, or responsibility for, the described subject or action. "I just wanted to see if it was real or artificial" and "It's only minor damage" illustrate. These forms signify the speaker's negative attitude toward the object or event referred to in his message. In addition, expressions such as "you know," "all right?" or "right?" implicitly seek confirmation from the listener that she understands. In immediate conversations, the speaker generally takes for granted the listener's understanding. "Thus," says Mehrabian, "phrases like 'you know' or 'I mean' show that the speaker regards himself as separate or different (nonimmediate) from the listener, and therefore imply negative affect."[3]

Automatic phrasing also occurs through speech fragments, sounds, pauses, slips, and false starts. "Well," "uh," and "that is" are examples. These forms, according to Mehrabian, can reflect inconsistent experiences, ambivalence toward the event being described, or ambivalence toward the particular addressee. For example, in the question "How did you like the party?" and the reply "Well, ah, [or uh] [pause] it was fine," uncertainty or ambivalence is conveyed by the use of automatic phrases ("well") and by the pause. Temporal delay in these instances is considered a prime index of separation or nonimmediacy between a speaker and his message.[4] Ms. Thompson's sputtering whenever she came close to references to the circumstance of her son's death indicated ambivalence (to understate the matter) toward that subject.

As with nonverbal communication, you need to learn the "language within language" both to better understand interviewees and to be more conscious of your own communications. Like many nonverbal forms, the verbal variants described here cannot be perfectly translated, yet they are significant evidence of an individual's thoughts and feelings. Certainly, you can expect that others will form impressions, consciously or unconsciously, from your use of the variants.

C. DEVELOPING OBJECTIVES AND PLANNING THE INTERVIEW

≡ PROBLEM 2 ≡
The "As Is" Motor Home Sale

Charles Dorsey is an experienced attorney and a partner in a small firm. He has served as David Johnson's lawyer for the past 15 years. Johnson runs an auto parts store and maintains several investment proper-

---

3. Id. at 39.
4. Id.

ties. He recently came by Dorsey's office bearing a summons, a complaint, and a copy of a contract for the sale of a mobile home. He had just been sued by a purchaser of a used trailer. Dorsey was not then available to talk with Johnson, so they set up an appointment for a later date. Meanwhile, Dorsey would have an opportunity to review the complaint and contract.

Upon reading the documents, Dorsey discovered Johnson had been sued by Betty Field, d/b/a Carrot Enterprises, who claimed Johnson had sold her a trailer with a defective axle. She sought $500 from him for the down payment she had made and $600 for the cost of repairing the axle. The contract, which was a form document supplemented by typed and handwritten terms, specified the property was sold "as is." The sale price was $3,000, to be paid with a $500 down payment and 24 monthly payments at 10 percent interest.

QUESTIONS

1. What are Dorsey's objectives in his interview with Johnson? What preparation does Dorsey need to do?

2. What subjects should Dorsey pursue with Johnson? How should Dorsey accomplish them?

3. What, if any, problems might Dorsey anticipate in interviewing Johnson?

To be most effective, you must clearly identify your objectives for an interview and then plan accordingly. Without established objectives, you are more likely to lose your sense of direction, miss important information, and even damage your relationship with the client. While planning may not always be feasible—especially for initial client interviews (see Chapter 4)—it is certainly always desirable.

Formulating objectives requires you to identify why you are conducting the interview—what you hope to derive from the interview (both in terms of information-gathering and other goals) and what you hope the interviewee will derive from it. Once you have ascertained your general purposes, plan your conduct of the interview; to do that, you isolate topics for probing and then consider how those can best be explored. As will be developed below, the appropriateness of a given probing technique depends on a variety of factors, including the nature of the subject matter and the relationship between you and the client. You must also anticipate potential problems and likely inhibitors to communication, such as ego threat, forgetfulness, peer pressure, and fear. (See Chapter 8, Section B, pages 178-184.) By anticipating difficulties, you can better develop strategies to deal with them. In addition, you may in particular cases want to draft some of your questions in advance. Certain kinds of fact-gathering even lend themselves to a prepared questionnaire (e.g., group surveys, compilation of assets and debts for a bankruptcy, employment history). Finally, interview preparation should include consideration of appropriate empathic responses.

According to R. L. Kahn and C. F. Cannell, the development of specific objectives depends "upon the ingenuity, insight, and experience of the interviewer. The determination of interview objectives is primarily a matter of getting insights and hunches as to what things may be important in explaining the problem to be solved, or what factors may be related to the broad question which constitutes the purpose of the interview."[5] Those authors suggest that the sources of the objectives can be derived from the interviewer's personal experience, the experience of others, specialized training, and professional and psychological literature. Lawyers should add their legal research to this list.

For example, Charles Dorsey's informational objectives in his interview with David Johnson will revolve around whether Ms. Field can prove a claim against him. Dorsey knows the "as is" clause protects Johnson from liability for defects in the trailer he did not fraudulently conceal. Dorsey can therefore identify the following as subjects for probing: Betty Field and Carrot Enterprises; the degree of Field's familiarity with mobile homes; the circumstances surrounding the contract negotiation; Johnson's knowledge, at the time of the sale and now, about the damaged axle; Field's performance under the contract; and, possibly, options for resolving the dispute without further litigation. Dorsey can effectively cover those topics by eliciting a detailed chronological narrative and supplementing it with follow-up probes. He should also consider how he might handle two potential problems: Johnson's reluctance to be forthright about his concealment of the broken axle (if it is broken and if he knew about it) and his embarrassment as an experienced businessman upon finding himself in this position.

In another example, Attorney Nancy Brown is retained by a real estate development company that is contemplating buying an apartment building and converting it to condominiums. The company's executives are concerned about the building's condition, about the soundness of such an investment, and about whether its residents will fight the conversion. Naturally, the executives also want to know if the residents have any legal basis for a challenge. Research instructs Ms. Brown that the conversion is arguably open to attack, but the transaction would probably be sustained by a court. She discusses the matter with the developers and, upon her suggestion, they decide she and her staff should interview some of the tenants to find out more about the building and assess the potential for a lawsuit by the residents. Those two points produce Ms. Brown's general purposes; she wants to (1) find out as much as possible about the building and (2) determine the risk of extended litigation or other resistance from the current tenants.

In achieving the first purpose, Ms. Brown identifies several specific subjects for probing: the reliability and cost of the heating and air conditioning, problems with plumbing and wiring, the security system and its effectiveness, the present and past owner's maintenance performance, neighborhood problems, and noise problems. Toward her second purpose, Ms. Brown frames several additional topics: the tenants' desire to stay,

---

5. *The Dynamics of Interviewing: Theory, Technique and Cases* 98 (1957).

their interest in buying, their ability to buy, their attitudes toward conversion, their attitudes toward moving, and their attitudes about litigation.

Next Ms. Brown considers tactics. Her experience tells her that the tenants will probably talk freely about the building's conditions, but might find the conversion issue to be threatening or inflammatory. Thus, she decides to pursue the safer purpose first, get the residents talking, empathize with their problems, and hope to establish some minimal rapport. She plans to then move into the more controversial questioning about conversion. She also decides to tell the tenants she is an attorney and that her clients are considering a purchase of the building. At the end of the questions on the building's condition, she will inform the residents that her clients are considering conversion, that their decision will depend—in part—on how the tenants feel, and that she is interviewing them to assess those feelings.

Ms. Brown next determines that in ordering her questions for the first purpose, she will pursue the specific topics first, before asking the residents about their general attitudes on living there. That way, the interviewees will not color their responses to more specific probes by a need to justify an initial, unthinking reaction. For her second purpose, she determines that it would be best to ask about general attitudes on buying and on conversions before addressing the more sensitive subjects of moving or litigation. She decides to finish with an explanation of her client's desires to accommodate the residents, to consider their feelings on conversion, to give them first options at buying if the building is converted, and to facilitate schedules in moving, if that became necessary. In so doing, she will begin and finish on relatively positive notes (considering the circumstances), and the more threatening discussion will be sandwiched between. (Recall the description of the concepts of primacy and recency in Chapter 6 at page 143 note 4.) Finally, she reviews the format with her paralegals, who are to help with the interviews. Together they discuss possible inhibitors to communication and how to deal with them.

By planning her interviews carefully, Ms. Brown maximizes her information-gathering without unduly antagonizing the residents. Her client and the residents should both benefit.

D. PROBING IN CONTEXT: DEALING WITH INADEQUATE RESPONSES

Before you can move into the techniques of probing (covered in the sections that follow), you must understand the context, or conceptual background, in which probing is used.[6] As we have already seen, your basic interviewing goals are to acquire information while furthering, or at least not damaging, the relationship between you and the interviewee. With

---

6. The analysis in this section is drawn from K. Kahn & C. Cannell, *The Dynamics of Interviewing* (1957).

each interview, you identify certain informational objectives. In the specialized world of legal interviews, the person interviewed will not be able to provide *all* the relevant information and *only* relevant information without guidance from you, the expert. You need to provide the interviewee with directions on where to start, where to go, how to stay on course, and when to stop—and you must do so in a manner that promotes your relationship goal as well. The techniques you use to give that guidance are your probing techniques.

The broad subject headings identified in your informational objectives for the interview provide the starting places for probing. Most of your probing efforts, however, concentrate on the follow-ups that keep the client on course toward complete coverage of the desired information. To put it another way, your probing techniques are devices for shaping inadequate client responses into a final product that meets your informational objectives. In the excerpts from the Thompson divorce interview, for example, the lawyer's apparent objective was to determine why the husband was contesting the divorce, given that the couple had not lived together for four years. The probing, after considerable maneuvering, eventually led the client to provide the sought-for information.

Your first task in this probing process is to identify the inadequacy of any response. Inadequate responses come in several forms, including those described in the following paragraphs.

1. Partial responses are the most common. They provide some relevant information, but not all of what is needed. Their frequency should not be surprising; clients cannot be expected to recall everything at once or know precisely what information is legally relevant. In the Thompson interview (see page 146), the lawyer's question near the beginning as to why the client was sure the husband did not care about her anymore could have elicited the entire story, yet Ms. Thompson chose to mention only some of the reasons. Those were very good reasons to support the conclusion he did not care, but we eventually learn there were additional and important facts to explain the situation. Several other questions put to Ms. Thompson could also have elicited the information about her son's death and its repercussions, but she chose not to elaborate until the lawyer began to hone in on the problem.

Partial responses can present difficult problems because you cannot always tell that full information has not been provided. The causes of partial responses can also vary widely, from instances of limited client recall to uncertainty about what is relevant to (as in Ms. Thompson's case) a conscious or unconscious desire to avoid certain topics.

2. Nonresponses occur when the client either remains silent after being asked a question or refuses to answer, as Ms. Thompson did initially to the lawyer's question about where her family income came from while Jesse was living with her. Your decision on how to probe after a nonresponse depends on your analysis of its causes. Once Ms. Thompson's lawyer explained the relevance of the query, of course, she then responded adequately.

3. With irrelevant responses, the client responds with information, but it is not pertinent to the question that has been asked. Ms. Thompson did

just that when she responded to the question about her husband's employment. She lost her focus and veered off to describe his drinking habits and their effects. Such responses can derive from a misunderstanding about what has been asked, a failure of concentration, or a conscious or unconscious desire to avoid the subject raised by the question.

4. Inaccurate responses can present the most difficult inadequacies for you to correct. You must first recognize the inaccuracy, which can be difficult if your only or primary source of information on the subject is the person you are interviewing. After identifying the inaccuracy, you must then determine whether it is a result of a misunderstanding, lack of knowledge, client misperceptions, or deliberate falsehood. If either of the latter two is responsible, you then face the touchy task of confronting the client.

As should be clear, your challenge once you have recognized the inadequate response is to determine the cause of the inadequacy. Only then can you decide what type of probe is most appropriate. The causes of inadequate responses include the following:

1. The client fails to understand the question. That can result from the client's failure to hear the question, from an inability to understand terms or concepts in the question, or from a misperception about what information is requested. Such inadequacies are the most easily corrected; you simply repeat or rephrase the question to ensure it is understood by the client.

2. The client does not realize the full breadth of information requested, which typically results in a partial response. You cure this deficiency through follow-up probes that guide the client to the additional relevant facts.

3. The client lacks the ability to articulate a complete response. The client may not have the necessary vocabulary if the sought-for information is complex or technical. Many clients, too, experience difficulty articulating their feelings. To combat inadequacies caused by inarticulateness, your probes must do the articulating for the client, either by explaining the meaning of possible responses or by suggesting answers.

4. The client cannot maintain focus and thus loses grasp of what is relevant. Rambling clients make for very difficult interviews. Your probing strategy should call for more topic control, more directive questions, more guidance, and lots of patience.

5. The client does not remember the requested information. Effective probing can sometimes overcome memory lapses, particularly by making mental associations with facts that have been remembered or with events that occurred, or were likely to have occurred, contemporaneously with the events that are the topic of discussion.

6. The client consciously conceals, distorts, or fabricates information. Such deceit must be confronted.

7. Unconscious psychological factors limit the client's ability to recall or discuss the information sought. Overcoming such factors requires intensive, empathic probing and maybe even referral for expert psychological counseling.

Sections E through G of this chapter describe the fundamentals and techniques of probing to address inadequate responses. In addition,

Chapter 8's section on "Inhibitors of Communication" (pages 178-184) elaborates on some of the above causes of inadequate responses and on appropriate treatments.

E. TOPIC CONTROL
AND BREADTH OF QUESTIONS

"Topic control" refers to the control of conversation in the interview: what topics are discussed for how long and in what manner. The amount of an interviewer's topic control can range from almost none (as in counseling by a Rogerian psychotherapist) to near total control (as in a lawyer's cross-examination of an adverse trial witness). Several factors determine topic control in an interview. Your nonverbal communication, for example, has a substantial impact, including the way you arrange your office, your general demeanor, and the signals you give. (Recall from "The Multiple Client Interview" in Chapter 6 (pages 137-138) how the lawyer used head and eye movement to direct the interview.) The clients, too, may have their own agenda and can take charge of the interview.

For the most part, however, topic control in the legal interview is a function of the kind of probes you use to develop the facts. As explained in the next section, there is a range of verbal formulations available to probe for information. Here, however, we address only the matter of the question's breadth and its corresponding effect on topic control. To do that, we classify probes into two general categories: open-ended (or broad) questions and close-ended (or narrow) questions.[7]

An open-ended question asks for an elaborative response; it leaves to the interviewee the responsibility for structuring the answer and setting its bounds. For example, in interviewing a car accident client, you might ask, "Tell me about your accident." You identify the topic generally but do so without imposing any particular structure or emphasis. Similarly, follow-ups such as "Tell me more about . . . " and "What happened next?" are open-ended, even if narrower in scope than the original question. (There are different degrees of breadth within the category.) These broad formulations turn over most of the topic control to the client.

The narrow question seeks specific information and asks for only a short, nonelaborative response. In the auto accident interview, you might use such narrow questions as "How fast were you going?" or "Was it raining?" or "Who was in your car?" or "Had you been drinking?" With these probes, you maintain tight topic control.

Your judgment about the appropriate breadth of questions and how much topic control to exercise or surrender turns primarily on: (1) the objectives of the interview; (2) the subject of the interview and type of information sought; (3) the type of motivation sought; (4) the identity of

---

7. The discussion in this section relies on, and expands on, the principles stated in R. Gorden, *Interviewing: Strategy, Tactics, and Techniques* 323-328, 423-439 (4th ed. 1987).

the interviewee; and (5) competing time demands. The following discussion describes the principal considerations for evaluating each of those elements.

(1) Objectives of the Interview. Developing a strategy for probing should always be done in light of your objectives for the interview. There is a strong correlation between certain objectives and the breadth of questions you should be using. If you have identified the gathering of facts from the client's frame of reference and learning about the client as a person as major goals, you should use open-ended probes as much as possible. The broad questions allow clients to emphasize what they see as important, to rank order, and to better express their feelings. Narrow questions tend to impose your own perspectives and judgments on the informational content of the interview.

On the other hand, when your informational goals are very specific, or establishing rapport and continuing your relationship with the interviewee are not a high priority, narrowly focused questions may better suit your objectives. For example, the survey information collected by Nancy Brown and her paralegals in interviewing the apartment building tenants would, at least in part, be collected by narrow questions. Although she may want to remain cordial with the tenants, her primary objectives—assessing tenant resistance as well as learning about the condition of the building—lend themselves to substantial use of direct questions.

Cross-examination of witnesses at trial presents an exaggerated example of use of close-ended probes. In that context, your objective is to totally control the topic and the information elicited; you want the jury to hear only certain facts described in specific terms (by you). Thus, you use narrow and leading questions.

Other witness interviews involve special problems in topic control and question formulation. Those problems and their possible resolutions are dealt with in Chapter 9.

(2) Subject of the Interview. The interview's subject directly affects topic control in three ways: (a) the type of factual information to be gathered; (b) your familiarity with the subject; and (c) the relative sensitivity or threatening nature of the subject.

Facts that lend themselves to narrative or chronological development are generally best gathered by giving considerable topic control to the interviewee. Open-ended probes allow you to obtain facts you might not think to ask about and could elicit answers to several narrow questions without your having to ask them. In addition, narrow questions would interrupt the client's natural paths of association and reduce your fact-gathering effectiveness.

If detailed or technical information is sought, however, then you may need to assume greater control. If you want to know the age, residence, and phone number of the client, it would be silly for you to say to the client, "Tell me about yourself." (But if you want to learn general information about clients, including their self-perceptions and values, then leading with such a probe would be appropriate.)

Typically, your expertise and knowledge of the law enable you to identify the questions needed to gather essential data. Thus, in an interview on the drafting of a contract, you should know what provisions, in addition to those reached by the working agreement, are needed to protect the client. You take charge to gather the information on those specific provisions. In a bankruptcy case, you need all sorts of detailed information that is not of the sort subject to general recall. The same is often true for will interviews; the disposition of sizeable property holdings may require you to probe specifics to adequately assess tax ramifications and to satisfactorily execute clients' desires about which beneficiaries should receive what. Even in an interview about a tort suit, you will typically have to fill in omitted details after the client has provided a narrative description.

Your familiarity with the subject of the interview also influences your decisions on topic control. When you are not familiar with the facts or the context of a client's problem, narrow questions will poorly serve you. Your probes will be hit-or-miss stabs at the substance of the case. We have already seen in Chapter 4 that initial client interviews are best conducted with prominent use of open-ended probes. In that context, you are not only unfamiliar with the facts, but you also do not know the needs, vocabulary, and abilities of your client. By allowing new clients to talk freely in response to broad questions, you can better learn about both the clients and their cases. You can also more easily avoid posing your direct questions in forms too sophisticated or abstract for the client to understand.

In the Dorsey interview of David Johnson, the lawyer already knows the client well, knows his abilities and limits, and has an established rapport with him. In addition, Dorsey has some knowledge of the client's case. Nevertheless, Dorsey should still lead with open-ended questions. He has read the contract and complaint, but he lacks his client's side of the story as well as crucial information about circumstances surrounding the agreement and its alleged breach. The lawyer may know enough to identify general topics for open-ended probes, but he could more effectively obtain a full set of facts by allowing Johnson to develop the topics on his own.

Sensitive and other threatening subjects can inhibit the interviewee's willingness to talk. Full treatment of such problems and of your alternative resolutions must await Chapter 8. For now, we note only that topic control figures prominently in the analysis. If you opt to deal with the causes of the reluctance, you will necessarily assume a greater degree of topic control. Or you can use close-ended questioning to help the interviewee along, to provide support by reducing pressure, and just to get the interviewee talking. In the Thompson interview, for example, the lawyer had to resort to narrow questions to focus the client and force her to talk about a subject she obviously found threatening and painful, but which was crucial to the lawyer's understanding of the case.

On the other hand, broad questions can sometimes avert the ego threat that would result from the personal judgments you reveal to the client through direct questions. The mere asking of particular questions highlights the significance, and thus often the threatening nature, of the response. Broad questions do not hint at what conduct is illegal or might offend you. For example, a union's attorney interviewing workers charged with committing unfair labor practices while on a picket line would probe with "What happened?" and "Then what happened?" rather than identify (at least initially) forbidden activities with pointed questions.

(3) Type of Motivation Sought. The relative breadth of your questions can affect the respondent's ability and willingness to give relevant information. Both categories of questions have certain values that must be appreciated.

There are several ways in which open-ended probes act as motivators. You communicate respect when you merely introduce broad topics and let the clients tell their stories in their own way. You also show respect through the implied message in broad questions that you are more interested in the client as a unique person than as a source of information reducible to standardized questions. The client perceives you are interested in his or her priorities. (Narrow questions tend to shift the focus away from the client's unique concerns.) And the nonrestrictive probes also allow clients to include positive, but not directly relevant, information about themselves that direct questions would not have elicited. Finally, the freedom that open-ended questioning gives to clients can provide them with an opportunity for catharsis, a release that many individuals with legal problems find valuable. These forms of recognition and sympathy encourage clients, motivate them to talk, and advance rapport.

In certain circumstances, narrow questions can motivate the client to provide relevant information. We have already mentioned the situation, illustrated by the Thompson interview, in which the client avoids or blocks a subject because it is threatening or painful. Broad questions will not penetrate the client's defense systems, so you must assume topic control. (See Chapter 8, pages 193-196, on defense mechanisms.) In addition, clients may sometimes be unable to grasp the relevance or meaning in the broader, and necessarily more abstract, open-ended questions. Narrow probes can counter that by pointing the clients to the needed information and relieving them of any embarrassment or frustration that they might feel from their failure to grasp what is relevant. Finally, and especially in the counseling stage of client relationships, you may find direct and pointed questions useful to position clients to see perspectives on issues or recall facts that they have previously overlooked.

(4) Identity of the Interviewee. The interviewee's faculties and sympathies affect your decisions on topic control in a number of ways. The age (especially if very young or very old), intelligence, education, and personality of respondents contribute to their ability to handle topic control. For example, a loquacious, often lonely, and perhaps slightly senile client will take the opportunity of an interview to talk about anything and everything, if left free to do so. Or, if the interviewee is a reticent adolescent, you may have to assume greater topic control just to get the interviewee to talk. The less intelligent and less sophisticated interviewee presents similar problems. Even when dealing with a relatively intelligent person, you may have to adjust topic control to account for personality variants. A client may be excited, nervous, or strung out; in order to slow the client down and make sense of the interview, you need to assert yourself and take control. Every-

one is familiar, too, with scatterbrained individuals who have difficulty remaining on relevant topics and thus require you to exercise greater control. On the other hand, most clients can effectively handle a topic-control assignment to clearly and completely describe the facts. Certainly, the businessman David Johnson—although, as we will see, not one to challenge Alistair Cooke for eloquence—should be able to field open-ended questions to best develop his particular case.

In all of these instances, the interviewees' personal traits affect their ability to discern the relevant from the irrelevant and to articulate the problem and the facts. The greater the client's abilities are in making judgments and in articulation, the less you need to take control.

As we have already noted in the discussion on motivation, the interviewee's willingness to talk affects your tactics. Reluctant and adverse witnesses can be most uncooperative and resistant to open-ended questions. Interviewees may feel their own interests threatened or feel confined by some inhibitor. Chapters 8 and 9 explore your alternatives for addressing these special-case interviewees.

(5) Competing Time Demands. As a general rule, efficiency in fact-gathering is a function of the preceding criteria affecting topic control. Sometimes, however, time constraints force you to adjust your tactics. If you have a very limited amount of time to obtain certain essential facts, then you must impose your informational priorities on the interview. That, of course, means you assert a greater degree of topic control than you might otherwise. You may find this greater control necessary, for example, if you have scheduling limitations or if you are interviewing someone you fear might end the interview at any time. In addition, considerations of time at some point offset the rapport gains to be made by allowing client catharsis or rambling. Again, you remedy the problem by taking control.

Incidentally, when the time constraints are generated by the interviewee, your maintenance of topic control has the effect of stretching out the interview; the greater your control of the topic, the harder it is for the interviewee to terminate the conversation.

To see the degrees of breadth in different question forms, review the following chart, which moves from narrow to broader questions. The chart, which was adapted from one developed by Raymond Gorden,[8] also serves as a bridge to the next section on formulating probes.

BREADTH OF QUESTIONS

Request for Specified Information	*The Facts*	*Interpretation/ Explanation*	*Request for Unspecified Information*
Did . . . ?	Who . . . ?	Why . . . ?	What happened?
Was . . . ?	When . . . ?	How . . . ?	Tell me about it.
Will . . . ?	Where . . . ?		
Has . . . ?	How much . . . ?		
	How many . . . ?		

8. Id. at 324.

F. PROBES

≣ **PROBLEM 3** ≣
Interview of David Johnson

After reviewing the documents David Johnson delivered to him, Charles Dorsey set up an interview with Johnson. Excerpts of that interview follow.

[Small talk omitted.]

Dorsey: I've read the complaint and the contract. Please just start at the beginning and tell me about this problem you've run into.

Johnson: Well, I had rented this trailer, a 1970 Nakima, for the past ten years—I bought it used right before that—and the tenant recently moved out. The trailer was in pretty bad shape, so I was in the process of fixing it up. I had advertised it for sale in the paper for $4,500. Then this lady comes by while we were there working and says she's in the business of trading on mobile homes and wants to take a look at mine. So I showed her around; I told her it was in a bit of a mess and needed some serious work. She asked how much and I quoted her the $4,500 figure, like was in the paper. So then she says, "I'll give you $3,000 for it as is." She said she had men working for her who could do the work on it. She said she could give me $500 down and spread the rest out over two years, with interest.

Dorsey: Uh-huh.

Johnson: So, I figured, "What the hell?" The trailer was going to be tying me up for several days, I wasn't going to make much on it no how, and $3,000 allowed me to do a little better than break even. Frankly, I wasn't sure I'd be able to sell it because it really was beat up. So I accepted.

Dorsey: Then what happened?

Johnson: Then she said she'd draw up the contract and we set a time for her to come by, pay me the down payment, and sign the contract. About a week later, we met, she gave me a check for $500, and we signed the agreement you have there. A couple days after that, she and her crew came by and hauled the trailer out. And that's the last I ever heard from Betty Field till I got served with these papers.

Dorsey: I see.

Johnson: I never did get any payments from her. She basically got the trailer for $500, and now she wants that back.

Dorsey: So, if I've got it right, you were renting this trailer and you decided to sell it. It was in pretty bad shape, and you were in the process of fixing it up when Mrs. Field came by and offered to purchase it as is, but for less money than you'd previously asked. Figuring you would save a lot of time—and maybe some money, as well—you accepted.

Johnson: That's right. And I have clippings of my want ads, too, showing what I was originally asking for the trailer.

* * *

Dorsey: Earlier you mentioned the trailer was in bad shape and you were making repairs. Can you tell me about them?

Johnson: I was going to put in a new bathroom, fix the plumbing, paint the inside, and replace the floor boards.

Dorsey: Where's the trailer now?

Johnson: I have no idea.

Dorsey: What can you tell me about Betty Field?

Johnson: Not much, other than I think she's a little crazy. She said she was in the business and put herself out as knowledgeable about mobile homes. But I never heard of her. I don't even know where she's from, other than she has a post office box downtown.

Dorsey: You didn't check that out before you sold her the trailer?

Johnson: Well, uh, no. She said she was in the business, she had her own form contract, and had men working for her. And to tell you the truth, I was so glad to get rid of that trailer without having to fix it up, and to get $3,000 to boot, that I was afraid I'd blow it if I didn't just go right along with her.

Dorsey: I see. What about the broken axle?

Johnson: I really don't know anything about that.

Dorsey: You weren't aware of it when you sold her the trailer?

Johnson: Nope. And I still don't know.

Dorsey: Tell me about the trailer and its history.

Johnson: Well, it's a Nakima, three-bedroom. My brother-in-law bought it when it was new, while he was finishing his degree, and we allowed him this plot of land I own to put it on. When he graduated, I just bought it from him. He needed the money, and this way we could help him out. The trailer was about three years old then. After that, I advertised it for rent, and that's when I rented it to this family with three kids. They're the ones who beat it up. They lived there for ten years, until a couple months ago. When they told me they were moving out, I figured I'd get rid of the thing; it was a nuisance, and I had been thinking about some other things I wanted to do with that property.

Dorsey: Did you ever move the trailer?

Johnson: As far as I know, the trailer was never moved from the time it was delivered new till the time Betty Field's crew hauled it away.

Dorsey: So if the axle was broken, you would have had no way of knowing about it?

Johnson: That's right.

Dorsey: Is it possible the axle could be broken?

Johnson: Yeah, it's possible. It could have been broken when they delivered it new—I never had any occasion to crawl under and check it out. Or her crew could have damaged it when they moved it. Seeing as how everything else on it was falling apart, I don't know why the axle would be any different.

Dorsey: OK. Tell me what happened when you met to sign the contract.

Johnson: We met in my office, about a week after she had come by. She gave me a copy of the contract, which she had drawn up, and she showed me where it said the trailer was being sold "as is" and that I was warranting I had good title to the trailer. I reminded her I wanted the trailer moved—I guess I forgot to mention that. Moving the trailer was part of our agreement. That didn't seem to bother her, though, because she said she would want to move it to her trailer park in any case. Anyhow, she gave me a check for $500 and I signed over and handed her the title.

Dorsey: You gave her the title?

Johnson: Yeah. Dumb, huh?

Dorsey: When did the exchange occur?

Johnson: It was on May 7th. I have the date on my canceled check.

Dorsey: How soon after that did she get the trailer?

Johnson: Just a couple of days.

Dorsey: And she never made any of the monthly payments on it, right?

Johnson: Right.

Dorsey: Earlier you said Mrs. Field came by while "we" were working on the trailer. Was there someone else there at the time?

Johnson: Yeah, my brother-in-law, Ray, was helping me.

Dorsey: What's his full name and address?

Johnson: Raymond Dean, South Hills Drive, here in town.

Dorsey: Did he hear your conversation with Mrs. Field?

Johnson: Yeah, he was right there with me the whole time.

QUESTIONS

1. What kind of probes did Dorsey use to gather the facts? Why do you think he selected those probes?

2. How effective were Dorsey's probes in pursuing the inadequate responses and in acquiring the essential facts?

3. What would you recommend that the lawyer do differently, if anything?

You use probes to follow up primary questions and to remedy inadequate responses. This section describes the various probes. The labels affixed by us and others[9] to the probes have no independent significance other than for use in identification and discussion. The important lessons are that you have an assortment of tools available and that each of them has its own utility and limitations.

Silent Probe. Although infrequently used by beginning interviewers, silence can be an effective probe. It is the most neutral of probes; it makes no effort to steer the client in any direction, though generally the interviewee will respond by elaborating on his or her previously stated point. You must realize that silence in an interview is not necessarily deadly but can serve important purposes. By using silence as a probe, you slow down

---

9. The classification scheme used here was developed by R. Gorden, id. at 423-439. We have expanded on Gorden's list of probes as well as his analysis and application of them.

the interview's pace and ensure that you are not interrupting the client. Silence works as a probe because clients respond to it by assuming that they should fill the time and that you want them to elaborate.

Thus, silence is particularly effective when you want to gain the interviewee's perspectives and minimize your professional authority. The silence encourages clients to open up and adds to the policy of shared control in the relationship. Silence is ineffective with interviewees who are hostile or who tend to ramble.

To be used properly, silence must be accompanied by proper nonverbal communications. You should be in a forward position with an expectant, interested look. If you are slumped back and yawning, then the silence conveys lack of interest, even boredom.

Encouragement. Encouragement probes include the array of common sounds that we use to indicate attention. They include, among others, "hmmm," "I see," "uh huh," and "really." They do not ordinarily have independent meaning other than to convey that you are listening and that the client should proceed. Encouragements, like silence, are largely neutral, except that they tend to elicit elaboration of the topic under discussion. Clients generally respond positively to encouragement probes, especially when the probes are accompanied by sincere nonverbal expressions. The danger with the encouragement probes is that you can become too dependent on them, will overuse them, and will use them when empathic reflection is needed. Overuse of encouragements sounds mechanical and reduces their effectiveness.

Immediate Elaboration. Immediate elaborations are open-ended questions that ask the client to further describe (to elaborate on) the topic under discussion. Thus, this probe is also neutral, as it pushes the client on, rather than changing subjects or focusing the interviewee on a particular point. Examples of immediate elaborations are "Then what happened?" or "Tell me more about that" or "What happened next?"

Retrospective Elaboration. Retrospective elaborations are open-ended probes that refer back to some subject previously raised by the interviewee. In his interview of David Johnson, Charles Dorsey used several retrospective elaborations. For example, he inquired of Johnson, "Earlier you mentioned the trailer was in bad shape and you were making repairs. Can you tell me about them?" Such probes are neutral to the extent they allow the interviewee freedom to structure and develop the response. Yet you do exert greater topic control than with immediate elaborations because the retrospective probe changes (or reverts) the subject. The basic principles of open-ended questioning, however, embrace both immediate and retrospective elaborations.

The encouragement and elaboration probes—the neutral probes—tell the respondent you are listening and you want to hear more. They permit the client maximum freedom while still providing support and guidance. They are useful in following up the very broad open-ended, topic-setting question; they probe for full elaboration without disrupting the respondent's priorities and perspectives on the facts. Finally, the encouragement and elaboration probes minimize the risk that you will seriously err through an imprudent or offensive remark or question.

Clarification. Clarification probes seek additional information about specific points in preceding answers. As with elaboration probes, clarifications may be immediate and relate to the topic under discussion or retrospective and refer to statements the client made earlier in the interview. Several clarification probes appear in the Dorsey-Johnson interview. Dorsey's immediate clarifications included: "Where's the trailer now?" and "When did the exchange [of money for title] occur?" and "How soon after that did she get the trailer?" Dorsey also used a retrospective clarification when he asked: "Earlier you said Mrs. Field came by while 'we' were working. . . . Was there someone else there at the time?"

Clarification probes, which focus the client on particular points, obviously impose considerably more interviewer topic control than do elaborations, which merely introduce a topic in a general way or bid the client to continue on the current subject. Thus, choosing between elaboration and clarification requires you to consider the substance of the preceding section, which compared broad versus narrow forms of questions (pages 157-161).

Your decision between seeking elaboration or clarification immediately and postponing the probes until later in the interview also involves significant tactical concerns. Immediate probes risk disrupting the client's momentum and train of thought, yet, by sticking to the subject at hand, they impose less topic control than retrospective probes, which direct the client back to discarded topics. Thus, when you probe retrospectively, you exchange less topic control early in the interview for more topic control later.

So, when should you postpone probing and when should you probe immediately? Gorden suggests you should probably postpone if:

1. the objectives of the interview call for a wealth of detail, including some "unanticipated" information you would not think to ask for specifically;
2. topics, subtopics, or questions are so interrelated that there are opportunities for the respondent to give several needed specifics in response to subsequent general questions;
3. the topic is one in which you can motivate the respondent to talk fairly spontaneously in response to broad questions; or
4. there is a danger that too many interruptions for needed clarifications might inhibit the respondent's spontaneity, as is often the case early in an interview.[10]

Gorden explains, "Conditions 1 and 2 depend mainly upon the nature of the problem and are, therefore, more constant throughout the whole interview. Conditions 3 and 4 tend to fluctuate from moment to moment and therefore require the interviewer to vary the amount of topic control he uses."[11]

---

10. Id. at 429.
11. Id.

Recapitulation. After the client has described the subject, you can facilitate further fact-gathering by accurate, clear, and brief recapitulation. Your effort can organize your perceptions and give the interview's subject some structure. In so doing, you can better identify additional areas for probing and better formulate legal theories and solutions. In addition, you provide the client with the opportunity to correct any misunderstandings you might have, and the recounting may also strike associations previously forgotten by the client. Thus, recapitulation is helpful both to organize and to probe. In the Dorsey-Johnson interview, the lawyer's recap (beginning "So, if I've got it right") elicits a previously omitted, yet potentially important recollection about classified ads the client had placed regarding the trailer.

You should, however, be sensitive about potential problems with recapitulation. If you err in your statement of the facts or make unwarranted inferences, the client may be reluctant to correct you (the authority figure) or may feel you are signaling what you want to hear.

Empathic Reflection. As should be obvious from earlier chapters, empathic reflection includes probing among its functions. By reflecting clients' feelings and experiences, you extend the clients' self-awareness and push them to further introspection and elaboration. For full discussion of empathic reflection, refer back to Chapter 5, Section B (pages 116-126).

Speculation. You can, at times, use speculation to prod the client into matters of a sensitive nature. For example, the lawyer in the Doris Thompson interview (Problem 1, page 147) may have said to the client, "I wonder if Jesse is contesting your divorce out of spite. Is there something you're reluctant to tell me?" Or consider the interview of a divorce client who tells her lawyer about marital tension and arguments, while also disclosing her husband has lost his job and creditors have been hounding them about overdue bills. Assuming additional facts lend support, that lawyer may have speculated, "I'm just thinking out loud, but maybe the problems in your marriage stem from your husband's unemployment and all the financial difficulties you two have had." In these instances, speculation is a means for confronting clients with a point or an idea that may not have occurred to them but is implicit in what they have stated. When properly executed, the speculation pushes clients into areas they have not yet entered, but should.

There are difficulties in the use of speculation. When the speculation includes confrontation or advanced empathy, the client may feel threatened unless you have already established a firm relationship. The speculative form of the question, though, helps to reduce its threatening nature. With interviewees other than clients, you may feel the risk of threat is worthwhile if the information to be gained is valuable enough and if you have already obtained other essential information. (Confrontation and advanced empathy are further developed below in Chapter 11.)

Mutation. A mutation changes the subject to a topic different from those previously discussed. You may want to ease the transition with an introduction: "The information that you've given me on the accident is very helpful, but I also need to know about your prior driving record. Can you tell me about that?"

Ineffective interviewers tend to resort too quickly to mutations. The tendency is especially debilitating in client interviews, which generally call for more restrained interviewer topic control. Before using a mutation, be sure you have adequately covered the topic then under consideration. Review your probe notes and perhaps ask the interviewee if he or she has anything to add to the discussion of that topic. You can also use a silence probe before a mutation to ensure that you do not interrupt the interviewee's train of thought and cut off valuable associations.

Leading Questions. Leading questions ask for a "yes" or "no" answer and typically suggest what the appropriate choice is. "Isn't it true that you drank six beers before you left the bar to drive home?" and "You go to church every Sunday, don't you?" are examples. Leading questions obviously exert the most stringent interviewer topic control. They, therefore, are most useful when you seek to maintain the maximum amount of control over what is said. The classic example, of course, is trial cross-examination; there, attorneys use leading questions to convey information through their own words and inflections—instead of through the witness's—and to ensure only certain information is communicated. You may also ask leading questions in a deposition to make a particular point or to lock in the witness. On the other hand, leading question forms are often used to convey empathy (recall "you feel . . . because . . . ," pages 118-119) and sympathy or to seek confirmation of particular facts—much like clarification probes. Dorsey used leading questions in that manner in his fact-gathering with Johnson.

Interviews with reluctant witnesses may provide another occasion for use of leading questions. When a witness does not want to talk, the only way for you to get any information may be for you to do the talking and to try to force the respondent to confirm or deny. Perhaps the ultimate example is the following scene from *All The President's Men*. Washington Post reporter Carl Bernstein needed an additional confirmation that Bob Haldeman was one of five people with authority over disbursements from a slush fund and that he had been so identified before a grand jury by Hugh Sloan, former treasurer of the Committee to Reelect the President. Bernstein's source was unwilling to discuss Haldeman. The scene begins as the reporters leave a conference in which their editors have expressed reservations about implicating a White House official so close to the President without adequate substantiation.

> On the way out, Simons [the Post's managing editor] told the reporters he would feel more comfortable if they had a fourth source. It was past 7:30; the story could not hold beyond 7:50. Bernstein said there was one other possibility, a lawyer in the Justice Department who might be willing to confirm. He went to a phone near Rosenfeld's office and called him. Woodward, Simons and Sussman were going over the story a final time.
>
> Bernstein asked the lawyer point-blank if Haldeman was the fifth person in control of the secret fund, the name missing from Hugh Sloan's list. He would not say.

Bernstein told him that they were going with the story. They already had it from three sources, he said; they knew Sloan had told the grand jury. All we're asking of you is to warn us if there is any reason to hold off on the story.

"I'd like to help you, I really would," said the lawyer. "But I just can't say anything."

Bernstein thought for a moment and told the man they understood why he couldn't say anything. So they would do it another way: Bernstein would count to 10. If there was any reason for the reporters to hold back on the story, the lawyer should hang up before 10. If he was on the line after 10, it would mean the story was okay.

"Hang up, right?" the lawyer asked.

That was right, Bernstein instructed, and he started counting. He got to 10. Okay, Bernstein said, and thanked him effusively.

"You've got it straight now?" the lawyer asked. Right, Bernstein thanked him again and hung up. He told the editors and Woodward that he now had a fourth confirmation, and thought himself quite clever.[12]

It should be added that this sequence backfired on Bernstein, and it backfired for reasons related to the limitations of leading questions. Because the source could, in effect, respond only "yes" or "no," and because there was no opportunity for elaboration or explanation, Bernstein's formulation of the question became critical. Bernstein framed the question in the form of whether Haldeman was one of five people responsible for slush fund disbursements, but the Post's story also stated that Haldeman had been named by Sloan in grand jury testimony. The latter fact was not true. That is, Haldeman was one of the five, but he was not identified before the grand jury. The distinction proved to be significant.

In addition, the question form did not leave room for the witness to reveal if he misunderstood what was asked of him. Open-ended questioning (had it been available to the reporter) would have been more likely to uncover the distinction.

Except to empathize or clarify, your use of leading questions with clients should be rare. As a rule, you do not want to restrict clients' abilities to respond and elaborate. Not only do leading questions confine the client, they also retard development of the lawyer-client relationship. Your authority and aggressiveness are dramatized and the client feels threatened and defensive. Obviously, such conditions are not conducive to information flow and rapport-building.

≡ PROBLEM 4 ≡
Interview of David Johnson Revisited

Return to the excerpts from the Dorsey-Johnson interview at the beginning of this section. Examine each of the lawyer's probes to identify its category and, more important, to assess its purposes and its effectiveness in accomplishing them. Consider what alternatives could have been used and what issues (factual, legal, and interpersonal) remain after the inter-

---

12. C. Bernstein & R. Woodward, *All the President's Men* 180 (1974).

view. How would you resolve them? Finally, as an introduction to the next section, see if you can identify any structure to the sequencing of Dorsey's probes of Johnson.

G. SEQUENCING OF PROBES

Careful sequencing of probes significantly advances clarity and thoroughness in fact-gathering. Although there are many means available for organizing an interview, the following suggestions are the most useful in law-related interviewing:

Chronological Structure. One of the simpler means of structuring the interview is to proceed chronologically. For that method to be effective, of course, the subject of the interview must lend itself to a time narrative. In a tort case or in a breach-of-contract suit, the facts can typically be structured into a chronological review. The format provides the client (or witness) with an easy-to-grasp organization while assisting your understanding. Moreover, in many instances, the precise chronology of events is crucial to the determination of liability issues.

On the other hand, some cases resist a time-sequenced development. Will interviews to discuss disposition of property, for example, have little to do with chronology. Similarly, discussions about the antitrust implications of a proposed contract might be best developed under a topical approach (e.g., effects on the market, restraint on competition, increased efficiency).

Your role in a chronologically structured interview is an easy one. Just pose an open-ended query with the structure implicit: "Please start at the beginning and tell me all about it." Then probe with immediate elaborations—for example, "What happened after that?" or "Then what?" or "Tell me what happened next." The interview can be rounded out with clarification probes and recapitulation.

Chronological structure is also frequently used in combination with other formats. The interviewee's narrative recall can, for example, form one of the topics identified for discussion in a funnel sequence, which is described next.

Funnel Sequence. The funnel sequence uses another common organizational method for achieving clarity. The sequence begins with the broadest statement of the case and gradually narrows to the specific. It is effective in cases that lend themselves to topical breakdowns or when the interviewee's perspectives and priorities are important. The initial client interview is one example. (As will be recalled, the funnel sequence was discussed in that context in Chapter 4, pages 101, 103-104.)

Your directions can be easily summarized: Ask the general, initial question; identify the topics to be probed; lead into each with an open-ended question; follow that with elaboration probes; and finish with clarification probes or recapitulation. Thus the entire interview resembles a funnel (broad to specific), and the development within each topic and subtopic also resembles a funnel.

An illustration will help. Our attorney, Ruth Ames, opens her initial interview of the client, Rachel Booth, with the question, "How can I help you?" Booth responds: "I've been subjected to sex harassment on my job and my bosses won't do anything about it."

From the client's overview, the lawyer can isolate several topics to develop with the funnel sequence. Ames should probe the nature of the harassment, the nature of Ms. Booth's job and workplace, what she has said to her bosses, and how they responded. The opening topic might proceed (in abbreviated form) as follows:

(#1)   *Ames:*   I see. Can you tell me about the harassment?
       Booth: Well, my co-workers are all men, and they are constantly touching me and making these remarks that are, you know, suggestive, insulting.

(#2)   *Ames:*   I realize this may be embarrassing for you to talk about, but can you tell me about the touching they've been doing?
       Booth: Oh, a guy will walk past me and will slide his hand across my butt. And this other guy keeps pinching me in the breasts, says OSHA sent him to inspect my chest protector.

(#3)   *Ames:*   That is offensive. What other incidents can you describe?

                     *   *   *

(#4)   *Ames:*   How often do these incidents occur?
       Booth: Somebody puts his hands on me at least once a day, and some days there are two or three incidents.

(#5)   *Ames:*   That must be a very unpleasant situation for you. [Pause.] You mentioned earlier that your co-workers had also made harassing remarks. Can you tell me more about that?

                     *   *   *

(#6)   *Ames:*   How many of your co-workers have been involved?
       Booth: There are about 20 guys in my section and at least 15 of them have said or done something at one time or another. I sorta' feel like I'm the fish in the tank everybody's grabbing at.
       Ames: You feel overwhelmed and exposed working in that environment.
       Booth: Yes, exactly.

(#7)   *Ames:*   How long has this been going on?
       Booth: It started about a week after I was assigned to that section, and that was about four months ago.

Here the lawyer has identified the topic for probing, pursued it with a general open-ended question (#1), immediate elaborations (## 2 and 3), and a retrospective elaboration (#5). She pursues those subtopics until she gathers the necessary details (## 4, 6, and 7). Next, Ames can pursue her other topics in similar fashion, leading into them with probes like these:

(#8) *Ames:* You mentioned at the beginning of the interview that you've complained to your bosses but they won't do anything about your situation. Can you tell me about the complaints, to whom they were made, and when?

*   *   *

(#9) *Ames:* What responses, if any, have you received from your employers about your complaints?

*   *   *

(#10) *Ames:* You've done well in describing what must be a very difficult situation for you. Now, though, I need to know more about your department and your job at the plant. Will you describe them?

Thus, when the attorney has finished, her interview could be diagrammed as a funnel or inverted triangle:

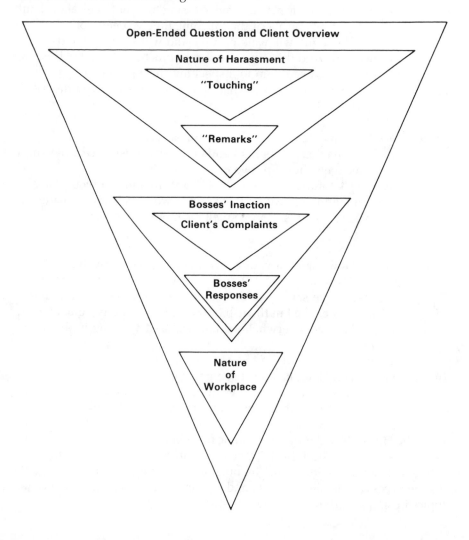

Inverted Funnel Sequence. The inverted funnel sequence begins with specific questions and builds on them toward an ultimate conclusion.

You can use this method when you want to avoid locking an interviewee into a conclusion before the latter has carefully considered the supporting facts. Recall, for example, the discussion at pages 153-154 concerning Attorney Brown's tactics for interviewing apartment building tenants on their opinions about the building and about conversion to condominiums. Because she was concerned the tenants might give a knee-jerk reaction to a general question about living in the building, and might therefore color their responses to the follow-up questions, Ms. Brown decided to lead with specific questions about plumbing, utilities, security, and noise, and then ask the general question.

Second, the inverted funnel sequence can be used as a back-door approach to sensitive subjects. An interviewee may be quite threatened (especially if his relationship with you is not well established) by a broad, open-ended question on a matter that, for example, implicates the interviewee in wrongdoing or concerns an intimate subject. Your decision about which technique to use turns on your judgment about the respondent's maturity and ability to handle broad probes on that topic. (Recall the lawyer's questioning in Chapter 4, pages 103-104, of the All-American defendant's "intimacy" with his 17-year-old friend.)

Third, you will find the inverted funnel useful when interviewing individuals who are reluctant to talk, such as a witness in sympathy with an opposing party. By beginning with narrow questions, you will be more likely to get at least some answers. Individuals reluctant to talk do not respond meaningfully to open-ended questions, but they will respond to questions calling for short answers. With the latter questions, you can try to wedge yourself through to the information you need. (See Chapter 9.)

Fourth, the inverted funnel sequence can be used in counseling to discuss and decide on action steps. Rather than present the alternative action steps first, you may begin by probing the client's feelings about key issues that must be explored before a decision is made. By proceeding in that manner, the client will not jump on a particular alternative and block out the others. Instead, the client will have articulated her priorities first and will have that as background at decision time. (See Chapter 10.)

Psychosocial Influences on Communications

A. INTRODUCTION

At the end of *Annie Hall*, Woody Allen reminds us of the man who complained to a psychiatrist, "Doc, my brother's crazy; he thinks he's a chicken." When asked why he didn't turn the brother in, the man replied, "I would, but I need the eggs."

Obviously, this man—let alone his brother—would be a tough interview. This chapter will not help you to "treat" that level of disability, but it should help you to identify and, as much as possible, cope with psychological and socially imposed obstructions to communication and intelligent decision-making. These barriers to communication are at once more complex and more subtle than the physical factors discussed in the preceding materials. The psychosocial forces are particularly difficult to recognize and deal with because they operate primarily on an unconscious level and are inherently subjective. Yet they persist to some extent and in some form in all interpersonal relations, and they affect both lawyers and clients.

These psychosocial influences often overlap and resist simple categorization. In practice, they appear as a bundle of multiple, complex forces.

Nevertheless, we feel compelled to classify them here to facilitate discussion and analysis.

So, in this chapter, we aim to raise consciousness, show the importance and nature of psychosocial influences, and teach how they affect others and ourselves. Awareness is the key. The chapter also notes some of the means you can use either to enhance positive influences or remove negative ones. (Chapters 10 through 12 add substantially to that discussion). We fully acknowledge that treatment of some of the negative effects described here extend beyond the lawyer's expertise. Their presence requires you to seek the help of experts from other fields, such as psychiatry or psychology. You must, however, be aware of the presence and possible effects of unconscious forces.

Sections B and C[1] build directly on the preceding materials about interviewing while providing a basis for further development in the counseling chapters. Section B describes the inhibitors of communication and Section C describes the facilitators. The sections are not exhaustive in their listings of such factors, but they concentrate on those that most commonly affect law office relationships. Several of the inhibitors and facilitators have been discussed in preceding materials, but are included again here to provide a comprehensive perspective.

Sections D and E delineate deep-seated psychological forces that affect individuals in their interpersonal relations. Section D describes the phenomenon of transference, which has formed such a major part of Freudian psychotherapy and which can substantially affect extended lawyer-client relationships. Section E lists and defines ego defenses. Together, Sections D and E provide information you need to evaluate both others and yourself. (See also Chapter 12 on personality needs and conflicts, which is primarily concerned with lawyer self-awareness—how your own traits, desires, and goals can affect your relationships with others.)

B. INHIBITORS OF COMMUNICATION

An inhibitor is "any social-psychological barrier which impedes the flow of *relevant* information by making the respondent *unable* or *unwilling* to give it to the interviewer at the moment."[2] The influences affecting a person's *willingness* to talk can originate from forces that are either external to the interview or that are internal to the interview. Most, however, are internally generated. (Admittedly, the line between external and internal causes is not always clearly drawn.) Influences affecting the interviewee's *ability* to communicate stem from external causes.

---

1. Some of the terminology and analysis in those sections has been previously developed in D. Binder & S. Price, *Legal Interviewing and Counseling* 8-20 (1977), and R. Gorden, *Interviewing: Strategy, Techniques, and Tactics* 119-135 (4th ed. 1987). See also M. Schoenfeld & B. Schoenfeld, *Interviewing and Counseling* 10-16 (1981).

2. R. Gorden, *Interviewing: Strategy, Techniques, and Tactics* 122 (4th ed. 1987) (emphasis in original).

You must first recognize the inhibitors and then devise strategies to alleviate their effects. Naturally, you can more easily deal with the internal causes. With skill, you can remove them entirely, although some are much more difficult than others.

(1) Ego Threat. Ego threat restricts information flow when the subject of discussion threatens the interviewee's self-esteem. For example, an accident witness resists discussing the accident if it occurred as he emerged from a peep show in a notorious red-light district. Similarly, a prominent trial lawyer may grow reticent when the discussion turns to one of her cases in which she made a tactical blunder. She tries to avoid the topic and block it from her mind. You may frequently encounter ego threat in interviews about incidents in which the interviewee's conduct indicated fright or panic. In fraud cases, clients may be reluctant to open up if they were suckered into a bad investment by a smooth-talking con man.

Ego threat can manifest itself not only by clients' reticence but also by attempts to sound out your attitude toward their conduct. Thus, a client who has had an adulterous affair may try to test your attitudes on extramarital sex before admitting to the affair.

To counter ego threat, you should assure the interviewee of confidentiality. Persons affected by the inhibitor are most concerned about exposure; if they can be assured their conduct will not be revealed, then the threat will be reduced. In addition, maintenance of a nonjudgmental attitude also helps; if you show disapproval of the morality, intelligence, or rationality of the interviewee's conduct, you exacerbate the threat. Empathic understanding of the interviewee's predicament also mitigates the threat.

Ego threat can occur in varying degrees. It can be so severe that it amounts to repression, which passes the line from the speaker's willingness to recall to his or her ability to do so. The intense pain and threat associated with the event pushes its recollection beyond the individual's consciousness. Extracting information from the unconscious normally requires expert psychiatric help. (Repression is further discussed below in Section E's treatment of "ego defenses").

(2) Case Threat. "Case threat"[3] can overlap with ego threat, but there are differences. Case threat occurs when the clients perceive that disclosure of certain information will harm their case. The disclosure, however, may or may not threaten the clients' self-esteem. Conversely, ego threat can operate independently of case threat.

For example, in a fraud case, a businessman who prides himself on his professional acumen may experience ego threat and thus be reluctant to admit that he had been fooled, even though the admission would help his case. The same is true for the "macho" man who, to be entitled to insurance proceeds, must describe how a woman knocked him down and

---

3. The term is taken from D. Binder & S. Price, *Legal Interviewing and Counseling* 10-11 (1977).

then damaged his property. Ego threat operates there, but not case threat. They coincide when a professional discusses a matter that raises questions about the ethics of her conduct in a particular case. The subject threatens both her self-perception about her own honesty and her estimate of which facts would best prevent her liability. Case threat, but not ego threat, affects the accused criminal defendant who is asked to describe a barroom brawl. He may be very proud of his aggressive conduct but nevertheless reticent because he fears a full rendering of the facts could convict him of a crime.

Case threat can be countered by empathic understanding and by explanation of your need for full information. That is, you must show clients it is in their best interests to be open and candid. The consequences of building litigation (civil or criminal) or planning a will or negotiating a contract on incomplete or false information can be disastrous. You can demonstrate that by playing out what happens when the client is caught being less than candid. In a trial or hearing, a party's dishonesty will cost that party dearly when the judge or jury decides on the facts. Even outside the litigation context, the client's credibility will be impugned, and his or her ability to achieve desired goals will be impaired. If such explanation proves unproductive, and you continue to find the client reticent or evasive in talking about important issues, confront the client with the contradictory information and ask for an explanation. (Confrontation is further discussed in Chapter 11.)

(3) Conformance to Social Norms.   Communications can also be substantially affected by certain preconceived notions that clients bring to the law office.

Clients have expectations about appropriate roles. Generally, clients anticipate an interview and a relationship in which the lawyer will dominate. Your professionalism and expertise about the legal implications of the subject give you an elevated stature. Clients—particularly if they perceive themselves to be of a lower professional status than you—feel restrained by your dominance and may even be submissive. The anticipation of the unknown, or of the possible necessity of dealing with an unpleasant subject, can create anxiety that inhibits clients' willingness to talk.

Chapters 3 through 6 offered many techniques for overcoming role expectations. Empathy, open-ended questions, and explanation of the interview's goals are the primary means for dealing with that inhibitor. In effect, you must teach the client—through both explanation and your own conduct—that the interview is a cooperative, equally participatory undertaking.

Social norms also restrict information flow through common conceptions of etiquette. Etiquette barriers affect individuals' comfort in discussing certain subjects with certain individuals. For example, many persons resist talking about intimate matters (especially sex) with the opposite sex. A molested woman typically finds it easier to talk about the incident with another woman than with a man. Men, too, have less difficulty in discussing personal matters with other men than with women. Many men retain certain chivalrous notions about the impropriety of describing sexual or gruesome subjects to women. Even if individuals do not experience total blockage on a subject, they will adjust their language according to the listener's identity and thereby restrict their descriptive abilities. Similar restraints affect interviewees who differ significantly in age or social status from the interviewer. A college student's description of a party to a friend is likely to be quite different from his description of the same scene to his parents or teachers.

To deal with etiquette barriers, you can use empathy and explanation. Communicate that you understand the interviewee's hesitance to discuss a subject; reflect on both the sensitivity of the subject and the differences between yourself and the interviewee. Explanation of those circumstances and of the need for candor helps to overcome the inhibitor. Switching to direct questions may also help the interviewee to feel at ease and to gradually open up. If these techniques fail, consider using someone who does not present identity differences to gather the necessary information.

Social norms and etiquette can, at times, facilitate communication. For example, it is poor manners to terminate conversations abruptly. Thus, people generally are reluctant to eject (by verbal demand or physical force) an interviewer from their homes, to abruptly hang up during a telephone conversation, or to suddenly walk out of an interview. Moreover, etiquette says individuals should be polite and should answer questions directed at them. Although etiquette does not require a respondent to elaborate, it can at least give you an opportunity to use other facilitators and to probe.

(4) Bias. Occasionally, interviewees' prejudices impede communications. Strong racist or sexist stereotypes, for example, may inhibit their willingness to respond to a black lawyer or a woman lawyer. (Such interviewees might think black lawyers are not as capable as white ones and women belong in the home.) More typically (and less offensively), interviewees may be biased because they identify strongly with an individual or cause in opposition to you or your client. (See Chapter 9, Section D, pages 213-218 below.) For example, assume that a newly arrived legal services lawyer represents Vietnamese immigrant fishermen whom the community perceives as threatening jobs and profits. When the attorney interviews local officials about various issues affecting the immigrants, he may encounter several biases. First, the officials might resent "outsiders" like the lawyer interfering in local decision-making. Second, the officials may have outsider and racial biases against the lawyer's clients. Third, the officials may have political or philosophical predispositions against legal services lawyers and their reputed leftist leanings. Fourth, the officials may resent the federal government's policies that brought the lawyer's clients to that locale. A white lawyer from a large utility company would encounter similar levels of hostilities if she interviewed poor black residents who were about to be displaced from their community by the utility's exercise of eminent domain.

Thus, bias that inhibits information flow can be based on any number of factors—racial, social, economic, political, philosophical, religious, and moral factors, to name a few. Many of these are so deep-rooted and substantial that overcoming them cannot be accomplished quickly, easily, or with simple techniques. Strongly held biases can be dealt with (if at all) only by exposing them and proving their premises inapplicable or wrong. That takes time, patience, and perseverance.

(5) Competing Time Demands. Obviously, interviewees concerned about other pressing matters, or about rushing to meet other commitments, may be distracted, may hurry to finish, or both. Similarly, if you show (by either verbal or nonverbal signals) that you have competing time demands, then the client will be likely to hurry. In either event, information flow is reduced.

(6) Environment. We include environment here only for emphasis and completeness. Chapters 4 (pages 82-86) and 6 (pages 134-137) have amply described how the interview's setting can affect the interviewee's comfort and willingness to talk. An environment that is stuffy, oppressive, dank, or malodorous diminishes the interviewee's desire to open up. The setting may be so forbidding that he wants to withdraw into himself (and thus say little) or tries to finish the interview as quickly as possible (and thus talk quickly and superficially).

Consider, for example, the procedure once used by a metropolitan public defender in running criminal defendants through their preliminary hearings. At the beginning of the court's day, the police put all the defendants in one 20' x 20' cell, appropriately called the "bullpen," and left them there until they were called for their hearings. The public defender's office, which represented most of the arrestees at the hearings, conducted its initial interviews in the bullpen. At times, there could be 15 individuals in the cell. The room was dark (there was one light bulb in the ceiling and no windows) and very warm. In such an environment, the public defenders should have been little surprised that their clients were reticent and the interviews were ineffective. The environmental factors and the lack of confidentiality stifled meaningful information-gathering and rapport-building.

(7) Perceived Irrelevance and Greater Need. Binder and Price[4] have identified two more inhibitors that interfere with clients' concentration. First, "perceived irrelevance" distracts clients when they are unable to see the connection between their case and your questions. The clients may simmer with impatience or hostility as they wonder about your lack of insight or competence. In addition, the clients' attention may be diverted to figuring out why you have focused on a particular subject. In legal interviews, such client perceptions can be quite common, as clients often do not know what is relevant under the law. (That is why they go to lawyers.) For example, a client who has been injured in an automobile accident by a milk-truck driver may not understand why the lawyer is curious about the circum-

---

4. Id. at 13-14.

stances that brought the truck driver to the scene. (Was he on a delivery route? What time of day was it? Did he have milk on the truck?) The lawyer, of course, wants to know if the truck driver was acting as an employee of a milk company at the time of the incident or if he was on his own. The answer to that may determine whom to sue and whether there will be a "deep pocket" to pay damages. Determination of those issues can seriously affect litigation and negotiation tactics, yet the significance may not be readily understood by the client. You can counter this perceived irrelevance with a brief explanation of your purpose. You can also do much to avoid the inhibitor by remaining sensitive to the lay perspective.

Second, the clients may become impatient when you focus on a matter they perceive to be less important than other issues. That is, clients are distracted when they perceive a "greater need." Thus, in a case involving the intrusion by an obnoxious industry into a residential community, the lawyer may focus on what damages the clients have suffered while the clients want to know how to stop construction. Even though damages are not perceived by the clients as either irrelevant or threatening, their preoccupation with injunctive relief may prevent them from concentrating on the lawyer's probes about damages. Similarly, a client who has been fired may have difficulty concentrating on the facts surrounding his discharge when he is most concerned about how he will be able to pay the next month's rent and food bills.

(8) Trauma.   Individuals who have suffered a traumatic experience frequently have a difficult time discussing the episode and their reactions. These individuals assume that talking about the experience will reopen their wounds and that reticence helps to block recollection. With trauma, interviewees fear neither damaging their self-esteem nor offending the interviewer, but they do fear reawakening the emotions associated with the events.

Trauma can occur in varying intensities. The death of an immediate family member, a serious automobile accident, or a violent crime[5] can each cause psychological pain and traumatic aftershock. On a less severe level, the break-up of a romance can result in at least a temporary reluctance in some people to talk about the experience.

At the most intense end of the spectrum, catastrophe survivors endure a complex of traumatic aftershocks. Studies of survivors from, for example, earthquakes, airplane crashes, and wars have revealed lingering and deep wounds quite apart from the physical injuries suffered during the tragedy. In the most extensive study of post-catastrophe effects on survivors, researchers identified a pattern of psychological reactions among those who lived through the Buffalo Creek Disaster in southern West Virginia. In that tragedy, a huge coal "slag" dam collapsed and released a tide of black water on the valley below. Within 15 minutes, 14 villages were damaged or obliterated, 125 individuals were dead, and thousands were homeless. The

---

5. See, e.g., Sutherland & Scherl, Patterns of Response Among Victims of Rape, 40 Am. J. of Orthopsychiatry 503 (1970).

latter group then had to endure a persistent syndrome, described by two psychiatrists as follows:

> The disaster activated intense affects, including fear, rage, and helplessness. The waves of external and internal over stimulation overran the stimulus barrier and the ego's capacity to integrate the traumatic experience and control and discharge the affects. There was a temporary ego collapse and the ego was damaged.[6]

Disaster survivors may suffer intense guilt and ego threat (for having survived and for their feelings and conduct during the event) that can further complicate the interpersonal process.

If confronted by such severe trauma, you must call on all of your patience and understanding and call in expert psychiatric help.

(9) Memory Failure. An obvious and potent inhibitor to communication, memory failure is a pervasive problem in any interview that delves into facts or past events. Unlike the previously discussed inhibitors, memory failure affects the interviewees' ability to communicate, not their willingness.[7] Although effective interviewing and probing techniques can often treat memory failure, the shifting and often self-serving content of memory nevertheless qualifies any interview, litigation, or other fact-finding that relies on personal recollections.

Memory failure is a function of the shortcomings of the human mind. We forget. In fact, we forget an incredibly high percentage of the facts and experiences we encounter. Try to recall, for example, who said what in the last movie you saw or novel you read. Certain persons and remarks might stand out, but most of the discussion has been forgotten. Our brains do not (as a rule) retain details. While memory fades with time, we also lose our grasp on a vast majority of facts within a very short time after exposure to them. (For example, you may have played a party game as a youth in which—if you can remember—you were asked to look at a tray or table of ordinary items and, after going to another room, write down as many objects as you could. You did well to recall more than 50 percent of the items.)

Although memory failure can be total, the more common problem is an inability to maintain accurate and complete recall. Generally our memories filter what has occurred. We remember bits and pieces, and we often unconsciously sift through the images and facts so that our recollections approximate the way we would like things to have occurred rather than the way they were. "Swearing contests" in litigation can involve two sides with contrasting stories, yet each honestly believing it is telling the truth. Similarly, during the Watergate affair, various officials trying to recall the same

---

6. J. Titchener & F. Kapp, Family and Character Change at Buffalo Creek, 13 Am. J. of Psychiatry 299 (1976). See also K. Erikson, *Everything in Its Path* (1976), and G. Stern, *The Buffalo Creek Disaster* (1976).

7. The statement in the text oversimplifies somewhat. Trauma and ego threat can be so severe that they leave the interviewee unable to discuss the causative experience. See also Section E, below, on "repression" (pages 193-194). Similarly, a person's willingness to recall can substantially affect the reach and accuracy of her memory.

conversation often had very different but sincerely held recollections. Moreover, memory has a tendency to emphasize the pleasant and de-emphasize the unpleasant. Thus we have nostalgia for the "good old days."

As time fades on events and experiences, confusion about their chronology grows. Looking back, we often forget just when an event occurred; we forget not only its approximate date, but also its relative position in a series of events. Chronological confusion (the term is Gorden's) occurs, too, when an individual recalls an experience while attributing his present beliefs and hindsight to the earlier date. For example, when reflecting on the sixties' antiwar movement on a college campus, a former student from that era may recollect that he supported the various protests. In fact, he may not have formed his opposition to the war until several years later.

You can treat memory failure. When you encounter the problem, you want to jog the interviewee's memory and trigger associations. Take available information and pursue logically connected possibilities. For example, assume the interviewee has forgotten who was present when she signed a contract, but has previously stated she executed the agreement on a Friday afternoon. You could try to jog her memory by asking how the interviewee knew it was a Friday (that might trigger some remembrance of a special event that day) or by asking about Friday work schedules and habits. Your general knowledge and experience offer additional sources for memory associations. If interviewing a client who is trying to qualify for a pension and who must prove—but cannot recall—where he worked during 1947 to 1949, you could relate the time frame to events of national or local significance: "Remember Thomas Dewey? . . . Where were you living when Truman beat him? . . . Where did you work when you lived there?" or "Where were you when the '47 flood came through?" Facts contributed from other sources may also be used to trigger the interviewee's memory. A client who cannot recall the name of a former doctor could be prodded, "Your son couldn't remember his name, either. But he thought it sounded Italian. Does that help?" "Italian, huh? Oh yeah! His name was Romanoffsky." (Well, we never said associations were always logical.)

The goal in such efforts is to provide the interviewee's memory with some clues to give it momentum. The memory works in remarkable ways; things seemingly long and irrevocably forgotten can be called forth through a chain of associations. The process, though, requires a patient and understanding interviewer who prods, pushes, and challenges the interviewee's memory.

(10) Unconscious Behavior. Gorden[8] identifies three types of unconscious behavior that interviewees are unable to describe. The most common is custom or habit—that behavior engaged in repeatedly and unthinkingly. For example: "Do you maintain eye contact with people you dislike the same as with people you like?" or "Do you use the active or passive voice more in your speech?"

Second, unconscious behavior includes reactions to many subliminal,

---

8. R. Gorden, *Interviewing: Strategy, Techniques, and Tactics* 134-135 (4th ed. 1987).

nonverbal cues. If a client says she just didn't like the way an individual acted or looked, her reasons for feeling that way may be based on her global response to particular mannerisms and demeanors. An exaggerated example of this occurs when films include suggestive frames that flicker by so fast that we do not consciously perceive them, yet they act on our subconscious. Thus a movie theater could insert frames of popcorn that will suggest hunger or thirst (you cannot eat popcorn without getting thirsty) to customers to help concession sales. Television and magazine ad people have been accused of using subliminal sexual images to sell their products. The viewer may be moved by such tactics, but wholly unable to explain why.

The third category of unconscious behavior comprises reactions taken under acute emotional distress. Thus, an individual in a serious automobile accident may not recall what he did immediately after the collision. The severe physical shock of the incident blocks the victim's awareness.

≡ PROBLEM ≡
The Tax Shelter

In this problem the client is consulting counsel to determine if he is liable to make continued payments to a race horse investment/tax shelter group. As you will learn from the transcript, the client agreed to join the group and is now dissatisfied with the investment prospects.

To test your understanding of inhibitors to communication, review the following conversation between an attorney and the client. See if you can identify the barriers that restrict the flow of relevant information from the client to the lawyer. When you identify an inhibitor, try to develop a strategy you would employ to overcome the information block if you were in this attorney's position.

Client: And so I found myself in the position of having too much earned income and in the need of a tax shelter that could provide some long-term growth potential. I had reached the 50 percent bracket so that half of each dollar was ending up in the hands of the IRS. I had invested the limit in IRAs and the other usual dodges. And tax-free bonds didn't seem to have much growth potential. Besides, there was all the talk at the time about the new tax reform package, so I knew I better do something quick.

Lawyer: What did you do?

Client: Well, I talked to my accountant but she's too damn conservative for my tastes. Then I started sending in those coupons you see in the newspaper and in those airline magazines. You know, "Great investment opportunity! No salesperson will call!" Those kind of things. Well, I got on everybody's list, I guess, because I was getting phone calls and brochures from all kinds of outfits. From diamonds to Swiss francs to rare coins to real estate limited partnerships and to I don't know what all. And each one of them said I would be virtually guaranteed a phenomenal return and, at the same time, I could shelter huge sums of money from the feds.

Lawyer: How did you decide on the Breeders Investment Group?

Client: I was debating what to do, considering the options. Then I talked with Ray Brady, one of the guys who rides the commuter train with me. He told me about the Breeders Group. Said he'd put in a big chunk of excess cash and had saved thousands in taxes. At the same time he claimed his original investment had quadrupled or something and that when he cashed in he'd be taxed at the more favorable capital gains rate. He said he'd have his agent, that sweet-talking Brookie Ann Spalding, call me about it.

Lawyer: What did this Ms. Spalding say when she called you?

Client: Well, we sure didn't cover all the details that are listed in that agreement thing I gave you! She cited all the growth and tax advantages. For example, she said there weren't enough thoroughbred race horses to fill up the entry slots at the tracks all over the country. Therefore, there was an incredible demand for horses, even ones that wouldn't win the big stakes races. She also emphasized that all the cost of maintaining these horses could be written off my taxes as a legitimate business expense and, in the early years, I could generate sizeable paper losses. In the long run, however, I was going to make a bundle.

Lawyer: Uh-huh.

Client: And, you know, as a kid I was really into horses and I really like going to the track. So, this seemed to be a far more enjoyable way to make and save money than some foreign currency futures or something like that. Hell, someday I could end up in the winner's circle! I pored over that glossy brochure she sent me and the excerpts of articles from a couple of business magazines that she included. But I didn't jump right in, you know. I asked for references and I called the Better Business Bureau down there in Florida. Then I had my bank contact their bank. Everything seemed OK to me. Their trainer who bought the horses at the various annual sales checked out as qualified. So, I decided to get in.

Lawyer: What did you do?

Client: Well, as it says there in the agreement, I decided to put up $10,000 for a one-tenth interest in four horses, two mares and two stallions. The primary money would be made in breeding the horses. I was to get a portion of all the stud fees from the stallions and a percentage interest in all the foals of the fillies. In addition, I had to put up $1,200 for the first year's maintenance fee.

Lawyer: What do you see as the problem with the deal?

Client: Oh, everything was great at the beginning. I deducted the maintenance fee and depreciated something or other and it was all fine. Then, the maintenance fee got bigger and the horses wouldn't be ready for breeding until much later. Then there was trouble finding the "perfect matches" with the horses we owned. Then I found out I couldn't sell my interest without giving the Group the right of first refusal at a ridiculously low price. And all this time I kept putting out more and more money for maintenance. I sure had tax losses! And they kept having income from me and the other suckers!

Lawyer: OK, I've got the basic picture. Let me try to get some of the details. Tell me some more about your conversations with Ray Brady.

Client: What does Brady have to do with it? It's Spalding and the Breeders Group that's got me tied up.

Lawyer: I need to understand the entire transaction from beginning to end. For example, what did you tell Brady about your financial situation and what did he tell you about his?

Client: It was all kind of general. You know, "I'm looking for some tax breaks" and "I've found a foolproof shelter." Just that kind of stuff.

Lawyer: OK. Now you said you checked with the BBB and the Breeders Group's bank. Can you be more precise about what you learned?

Client: You know, they gave Breeders Group a clean bill of health, so to speak. How much can you learn from sources like that?

Lawyer: Did you investigate them any further? Did you, for example, ask for any other references or for the names of investors other than Brady?

Client: What good would that stuff have done? These outfits only provide you with the names of folks who will tell you they're an A-1 operation. Nobody's dumb enough to refer you to people who think they got a raw deal or to creditors who are pounding on their door.

Lawyer: Let's focus on your conversations with Ms. Spalding. What did she say to you about the investment program?

Client: Looking back on it now, it's easy to see how I got taken. First, she's a woman. Second, she's Southern. The combination is overpowering. You know, one of those Dixie belles with double names and honey just dripping off her tongue? She came on so open and honest and enthusiastic. Every time I asked a tough question or raised a potential objection she seemed to agree with me and then would turn some cute phrase or something and sort of brush by it. In the end, she promised me the moon but never really got around to telling me how dangerous the trip was going to be.

Lawyer: Well, did she ever inform you that there was a time lag between the purchase of the horses and the initial breeding period and that you would be responsible for maintenance costs in the interim?

Client: I can't recall. We talked about a lot of things but I'm not sure about some of the details.

Lawyer: Those facts are mentioned, however, in this written agreement that you signed.

Client: Look, I got all that stuff from them right around the time we learned that my mother had terminal cancer. I was so upset over her illness that I don't remember much else that was going on just then. I don't remember if I read about the time lag and the maintenance costs or not.

A number of communication inhibitors are contained in the preceding interchange between the attorney and the client. Some are difficult to spot. Some are difficult to classify once they have been identified. In deciding which strategies to pursue in overcoming these barriers to complete information, you will find all your skills as a lawyer challenged.

If you had difficulties spotting and classifying the inhibitors or in developing an approach to bypass them, perhaps some additional information about this client will make your task somewhat easier. Before reading through the following material, however, be sure to attempt to identify the inhibitors present in the transcript.

Now that you have created your list of inhibitors and developed a compensating strategy, let's assume the following additional facts. The client is shocked and bitter at the amount of federal taxes he has been required to pay now that his income has risen sharply. He was bewildered by the array of tax shelter choices available. Although he will not readily admit it, the client did not completely understand how the various programs operated or the economic and monetary principles on which they were based. In his conversation with his fellow commuter, the client said he now understood why so many successful people become white-collar criminals and resorted to cheating on their taxes. In response to that statement, Brady told the client that the Breeders Group was a "foolproof way to cheat on your taxes."

Although the client did call the BBB, he did not have someone at his bank speak with someone at the Breeders Group's Florida bank. Instead, he spoke to an assistant vice president at his local bank. The VP told the client he would not be able to learn anything of value in evaluating the Breeders Group as an investment opportunity through a phone call to the Group's bank. Upon receiving this information, the client decided against making the call. It was only after he committed himself to the Breeders Group that the client learned the Group had been in operation for less than one year. It was also only later that he learned Brady had received a bonus for referring him to the Group.

When he was younger, the client had been stationed at an armed forces base located in the deep South. Although he was aware of how gracious and open the people in the local community appeared, he distrusted them, believing them to be disingenuous. While there, however, he fell in love with a local woman (Laurie Ann Harper) who seemingly returned his affections. When he proposed marriage, he was shocked and devastated by her refusal. Moreover, he was resentful of her statement that, although she enjoyed his company, she hoped to marry a local man and remain in her own community.

The client feels guilty about his mother's illness and death. Although he knew that she was not herself, he did not know the extent of her sickness. As an only child, however, he had often thought about what he would be able to do with his inheritance from her.

With the added information, the inhibitors become more apparent and the strategies to overcome them are easier to develop. The very fact that the additional information makes it simpler for you to identify and attack the inhibitors of communication should emphasize for you how important it is to develop your communication skills. Only by recognizing the barriers to complete transmittal of relevant information will you be able to take the appropriate steps to surmount them. The failure to surmount such inhibitors will mean that you will receive less than full information from your client.

C. FACILITATORS OF COMMUNICATION

This section overviews those psychosocial influences that facilitate fact-gathering and rapport-building. The listing does not include all varieties, but only those most important to lawyers.

(1) Helping Relationship. As explained in Chapter 5, the ingredients of a "helping relationship" facilitate information flow through several means. First, empathy encourages the interviewee to open up. People feel more like talking when they know their listener appreciates their circumstances or troubles.

Second, nonjudgmental acceptance facilitates communications from the interviewee. Acceptance is particularly important when the topic of discussion may threaten the respondent's self-esteem. Clients must realize that you will still respect them and regard them as worthy persons, regardless of what disclosures are made. Thus, both your language and nonverbal reactions must convey acceptance.

Third, a solid, positive relationship with clients creates global impressions conducive to full and honest information flow. When clients feel comfortable with you and sense your commitment, understanding, and esteem, the *combined* effect optimizes the chances for meaningful dialogue. The relationship then takes on the characteristics of a precision team effort, with each element working together toward mutually identified goals. (For further elaboration on the facilitative effects of the helping relationship, refer back to Chapter 5.)

(2) Recognition. All individuals need and thrive on "recognition," meaning esteem as distinct from affection. In effect, the recognition facilitator is the opposite of the ego threat inhibitor. Just as individuals are inhibited when they fear that certain revelations will damage both their self-perception and how others perceive them, they also respond positively when their self-esteem is bolstered by (verbal and nonverbal) expressions of admiration from others. Recognition, then, means more than acceptance; it includes the additional element of approval. Of course, if recognition is to be a facilitator, it must be sincerely felt and conveyed.

You can use recognition on two levels. First, your specific statement of praise or appreciation to the client will spur communication. For example, "Your description of the accident was very good and helpful. Now tell me about your injuries." Second, your overall esteem for the client can be communicated through the various forms of nonverbal expressions and general statements of sincere regard.

Be very cautious, however, in your expressions of approval as they relate to the "merits" of a client's problem. Generally, you should maintain a neutral, nonjudgmental attitude on the issues in a case. Statements of attorney approval can distort the client's thinking on ultimate issues as much as attorney disapproval. Thus recognition should be confined to reinforcement of the client's cooperation with you or of general character traits. Examples include "Your records and notes are excellent; they are very helpful to me" and "I commend your concern for achieving justice."

(3) Extrinsic Rewards. Your relations with clients typically include a motivator that is external to the interview. The "extrinsic reward" is that which brought the client to your office—to seek a tort judgment, to defend against a lawsuit, to get a contract drafted. Clients want something and in order to get it they must communicate with you. Thus, there is an extrinsic reward for them to talk.

When interviewing nonclients, however, extrinsic rewards are not so common. For example, your interview of witnesses will often lack any incentive for them to get involved; indeed, witnesses often perceive their best interests are served by staying out of the case. (Competing time demands might inhibit communication if the witnesses think that being interviewed and possibly testifying later would be a drain on their time). Nevertheless, you should give extrinsic reward considerable forethought as a facilitator for witness and other nonclient interviews; you need to explain to the interviewees why their best interests would be served by talking. (See Chapter 9.) Of course, when obtaining information from experts on a matter within their field, you can provide an extrinsic reward—the expert's fee. There may also be other occasions in which paying for information (not to be confused with paying for testimony) is appropriate.

(4) Catharsis. Gorden defines "catharsis" as the "process by which one person obtains a release from unpleasant emotional tensions by talking about the source of these tensions and expressing his feelings."[9] Put colloquially, the individual feels better when he gets something that has bothered him "off his chest"; he experiences an emotional release when he talks about a troublesome subject. Confessionals, for example, often serve that purpose.

Lawyers, too, frequently provide cathartic opportunities to clients in emotionally charged cases, such as those involving domestic troubles, serious accidents, or death. For you to fill that role, you must first provide understanding. The understanding will encourage the client to talk and, once the client begins to open up, the cathartic release will further facilitate information release.

(5) Fulfilling Expectations. Interviewees respond positively when you articulate your expectations. You should brief clients on three levels. First, you need to clearly explain at the outset of the relationship that the client

---

9. Id. at 145.

should work with you as a partner. Clients must know that they share responsibility in the relationship—for decision-making and fact-gathering—and that they are expected to actively participate. Second, you should inform clients with each interview and counseling session what agenda and expectations you have set for that day. That helps to structure the session and to clarify issues for the clients. It also pushes them to satisfy their responsibilities in the meeting. Third, you need to assert your expectations as you and the client discuss facts and issues, and you should reflect confidence that your expectations will be met. If, for example, the client too easily quits in efforts to remember facts, or if he procrastinates in making decisions, you should first empathize and then remind the client that he has responsibilities to meet:[10]

"The accident was a harrowing experience for you, and talking about it is difficult. But I think that if you concentrate, you will find that the details we need will occur to you. Can you give it some thought?"

You can also use in nonclient interviews the second and third techniques mentioned above; set the agenda and gently but confidently prod the interviewee (through verbal and nonverbal means) to meet expectations.

(6) *Altruistic Appeals.* Some interviewees may be moved to communicate by a desire to further values they consider to be important. Witnesses, for example, can be moved by appeals to help you find the truth and seek justice. In interviewing witnesses to an automobile accident, you might appeal both to their sense of duty as citizens to provide essential information and to their sense of justice in seeing that adequate compensation is given to a person injured by a reckless driver. When representing a particular "cause" (as well as a client) you may find that appeals to the values implicit in the cause will sway witnesses and experts to communicate freely. Of course, for altruistic appeals to have a facilitative effect, the interviewee must agree with the values identified in the appeal and must be a person to whom values are meaningful.

(7) *Environment and Conformance to Social Norms.* As noted and discussed above in Section B, environment and conformance to norms each have facilitative as well as inhibitive effects. For elaboration, see Section B (pages 179-180) and Chapter 6, Section B (pages 134-137).

D. TRANSFERENCE

Psychological phenomena affect your professional relations and practice in many ways. Although their subtleties and complexities are beyond the scope of this book, some familiarity with the more important principles

---

10. See D. Binder & S. Price, *Legal Interviewing and Counseling* 16 (1977).

enhances your effectiveness as a lawyer. This and the following section sketch those principles to put you on notice of their existence and potential consequences. You might find them crucial both in analysis of others and in self-analysis. In some of your work, further study may be needed.

This section addresses the phenomenon of transference, which has been so critical in psychoanalytic theory and practice. (Recall the discussion in Chapter 2, Section B-3, page 25.)

≡ A. WATSON, PSYCHIATRY FOR LAWYERS
3-8 (rev. ed. 1978) [11]

Transference has been variously defined as the concept developed. We will define it as the fusion of unreal attributes which the observer believes to be present in the observed, with those which in fact are present. The unreal attributes consist of "projections," which derive from some superficial likeness to an important person from the past, such as a parent. The observer then treats the new person as if [the person] were the original model. The part qualities are seen as the whole.

What is the importance of the concept of transference to the law? Fortas states that "Lawyers have been increasingly aware of the fact that their interrelationships with clients, witnesses, judges and jurors are at least as important as their mastering of the statutes in precedence." The concepts of transference and countertransference describe the nature of these interrelationships. . . .

[T]oday the term transference has been broadened to include all of the reactions which the patient has to the physician—not only the unconscious projected images from the past, but also reactions related to the physician's personality as it is correctly and appropriately perceived by the patient. It is, however, the irrational, projected elements in the relationship which provide the physician with the most potentially beneficial means for understanding his patient, for here he has the opportunity to compare the real with the unreal, provided he has some awareness of his own personality attributes. What could be a major barrier to therapy is turned to enormous therapeutic advantage.

Whenever one makes an acquaintance, there is an immediate flood of perceptions about the newly encountered person. This includes such things as physical characteristics, interests, estimates of various personality traits, and other impressions about this nature. These new, mainly unconscious impressions are associated with many past personal encounters, especially with members of one's immediate family. There is a powerful unconscious tendency to generalize the nature of the new acquaintance so that instead of perceiving a face which is reminiscent of father's face, or a manner of speech which is like brother's, there is the feeling that this new person is *like* father or *like* brother. In other words, from the similarity of a part, the new person is given the whole characteristic of the past figure. Thus, at best, part of the reaction to the new person is inappropriate. While

---

11. References in the original are omitted.

this distortion may be helpful in establishing a close relationship with great rapidity, it can just as likely cause coolness and withdrawal, depending on the nature of the past relationships from which the transference is made. At any rate, the reaction is not based on a realistic appraisal of the nature of the new person, and the way is laid open for future problems which can be formidable and difficult to untangle. We must regard this kind of projection as universal and hold it responsible for at least some difficulty in all interpersonal relationships.

Let us consider a simple illustration of this phenomenon in a legal setting. A young lawyer starts to work for a law firm shortly after his graduation from law school. His superior is a forceful, direct, and forthright person who makes judgments swiftly and tends to stick to them. In reality, this man is remarkably skillful in making good decisions rapidly. However, the young lawyer, whose father had been dogmatic and impulsive in his judgments, immediately and unconsciously identifies this new person with his father. He "transfers" his attitudes toward his father into this new relationship; he reacts to his superiors in terms of his earlier relations to his father. Father had been autocratic and belittling and had never shown respect for his son's capacity for independent thinking and good judgment. The young lawyer projects this expectation onto his new boss.

Unfortunately, he was wrong, since his superior desired and encouraged independent thought and action from his subordinates. The "transference" inhibited the young lawyer's ability to act decisively and, in this way, to gain the respect which he so strongly desired. Instead of taking appropriate action, he was made hesitant and defensive by his expectations. His superior could hardly be expected to be impressed favorably and, after a few efforts at encouragement or challenge, he wrote off the younger man as hopelessly lacking in initiative. This is not an unusual example. Irrational reactions such as this one occur in everyone to some degree. . . .

Once the idea is accepted that the emotions aroused in a relationship always have specific unconscious meanings for the participants, these very emotions can become useful. It is this fact which permits the analyst to penetrate unconscious aspects of his relationship to his patients. The young man already mentioned obviously has problems with authority figures. In the analytic situations, he would have the same reactions to the analyst as to his superior in the law office. This would be seen as hesitance to express himself, reluctance to take issue with anything that the analyst said, and other evidences that authority, in this case the analyst, causes him to withdraw. The patient would be all too ready to agree with everything that was said, and yet it would be clear that there was no real acceptance. Persons who need to acquiesce in this manner generally resent intensely having to do so. Sooner or later this resentment would be manifested in subtle ways which the analyst would feel, even before they became visible. Against the relatively neutral ground of the analytic situation, the patient demonstrates the way he deals with authority, and his feelings and methods of dealing with anger. Through interpreting this behavior and demonstrating it over and over again, the psychiatrist slowly helps the patient toward an understanding of himself.

While the lawyer will never use the transference phenomenon in this same way, he can at least learn that emotional responses to his client may be due to hidden provocations of which his client is unaware. With practice, this insight will help him immensely in dealing with his clients. For example, he will encounter clients who come into the office, ask for advice, and then progressively provoke him to anger until he is inclined to drop his contact with the client altogether. Early in the game, it would be well for the lawyer to ask himself, "Why should a person ask me for help and then make me want to withdraw?" While answers to such questions are not always forthcoming, especially in the lawyer-client relationship, such questioning lends a perspective to the relationship which was previously absent and raises the possibility that some of the transactions between the lawyer and his client are based on irrationality, not on logic. This kind of diagnostic mind-set is similar to that of the physician, who is taught to forestall treatment until he knows why certain symptoms have occurred. Most legal problems are also best resolved when the dramatis personae are understood as fully as possible. The lawyer who can learn to do this (many do it intuitively) is in a better position to help his clients and accomplish his professional goals.

Countertransference, or the counselor's projections onto the client of attitudes associated with a significant figure in the counselor's past, can also have a substantial impact on lawyer-client communications. The concept could logically be discussed at this point, but we have opted to include it in Chapter 12 (Section C, pages 296-297) along with consideration of other conflicts that affect lawyers in their relationships with clients.

E. EGO DEFENSES

H. FREEMAN & H. WEIHOFEN, CLINICAL LAW TRAINING: INTERVIEWING AND COUNSELING
64-67 (1972)

We all need to have a healthy self-image, a good, reasonably self-satisfied feeling about ourselves. If our idea of self is attacked, we are hurt and we tend to react defensively. Beset by the buffetings and stresses of daily living, the ego may call up one or more defense mechanisms. These defenses against anxiety operate largely on the unconscious level, and may grossly distort the person's perception of reality.

The concept was originally developed by Freud. Today, at least a score of these defenses are generally recognized among psychologists and psychiatrists. Lawyers are likely on occasion to encounter clients exhibiting the following:

Repression. Unconscious purposeful forgetting of internal or external influences that would be painful at the conscious level. This was the defense that Freud concentrated on, and it is perhaps found in all others.

Repressions may be temporary, until one can face the reality. But if some neurotic need prevents reassessing some gross distortions of the past, and keeps the repressions intact, the anxiety-provoking truth will remain permanently buried in the unconscious.

Every lawyer, whether he knows the term or not, has come across the phenomenon in the client who in telling his story omits certain facts unfavorable to his cause. The lawyer who does not understand may consider this simply lying, but the client may indeed have "forgotten" the unpleasant fact, and may be less to blame when the truth is disastrously revealed than the lawyer who failed to draw it out during their interviews.

Rationalization. Reinterpreting our behavior so as to make it seem reasonable; substituting acceptable for unacceptable reasons for our actions. From a complex of mixed motives, we select the most acceptable and repress the less acceptable. Rationalization is easy and potent, because it has the strength of truth, even though only a half-truth or less.

Clients will use rationalization, and we must cut through it. But we lawyers use it too, for it enables us to avoid the guilt or shame of facing openly the unworthy nature of our real motivation. A lawyer may hold strong moral, political, or religious views. At the same time, he may also feel that professional ethics impose a duty not to reject a client because he disapproves of his conduct or his objective. So instead of admitting that he doesn't want to defend the man's freedom to distribute "disloyal" literature, or help him get a divorce or avoid paying alimony, he manages to find reasons why the proposed action cannot succeed or why the client should not retain him. These "reasons" are mere rationalizations.

It takes a degree of sophistication to recognize when we are rationalizing our behavior. Most people either fail to recognize they are doing so or become angry if told. But this anger itself is a symptom that deep in their unconscious they do know it, and are upset at being exposed.

Projection. Turning onto outside persons or things painful emotions or ideas so that the projector feels they are outside himself.

Freud postulated the theory that the ego is much more able to screen and deal with stimuli from outside the body than internal ones. The man who hates someone he knows he ought to love (his mother, his brother, his wife) may refuse consciously to recognize his feeling; it is easier to project it on the other person: "I don't hate her; that would be wicked. She hates me."

This is an infantile and dangerous defense, because it grossly distorts reality. The paranoid person may in all sincerity tell of persecutions he has suffered or evil plots against him. The projection is usually built on some kernel of reality, which, however, is then embroidered and invested with high emotion. A lawyer needs to be aware of such possible distortions or overreacting to a fairly minor incident. Even normal, healthy people may resort to projection when they find themselves in a situation that is anxiety-producing or that places them in an embarrassing or discreditable light.

Introjection. This is the opposite of projection, the process by which one incorporates into himself some human trait or force from outside, for the purpose of using it (if desired) or destroying it (if feared). The child incorporates the characteristics of the emotionally important persons in his life. An adult who loses a loved one may feel "a part of me has died," or if the deceased was not loved but hated or feared, may have strong guilt feelings and may make irrational or unwise dispositions of property or take other legal action, prompted by such feelings.

Conversion. Translating a threatening impulse into a symbolic expression of pain or functional disorder. All of us, when under stress, have felt "butterflies in the stomach" or even nausea. More serious are the "traumatic neuroses" following accidents.

Displacement. A mechanism by which an idea or a feeling about one object is moved or displaced to another less obvious one. Thus a woman without her husband may transfer her love to her boss or her cats; a man who has been "bawled out" by his boss may unleash his pent-up anger against his wife or children after he gets home.[12]

Denial. Treating realities as though they never happened or didn't exist. The person who refuses to believe that a loved one is dead; the man who, shaking with fear, dashes into the fray with reckless abandon; the lady who tries to blot out an unpleasant altercation by suggesting that "we forget the whole thing"; all these are using denial to exorcise painful thoughts.

Reaction Formation. A means to prevent eruption of an unacceptable instinctual impulse by substituting an overemphasis of the opposite. Lawyers need to understand this defense if they are to appreciate the motivations that often lie behind our legal rules and our law-enforcement methods—why the sadist may become a law-enforcement officer, and the person who cannot tolerate temptation an axe-wielding saloon destroyer.

Regression. The abandonment, temporary or permanent, of a more mature level of adjustment to return to a more infantile one. Old men who indulge in exhibitionism or other sexual acts with children provide a prime example. Such conduct is often a function of increasing loss of ability to adjust to circumstances, loss of old friends and familiars, and a developing senility that is indeed a kind of "second childhood," in which they feel a true relationship with children. Less extreme are the various forms of escapism—into alcoholism, drug use, religiosity, or increasing dependence on a father figure.

Sleep is in a sense regression, a biologically necessary withdrawal from the tensions of life, to allow recharging of our physiological batteries.

Isolation. The thought or act is allowed into the conscious but without normal emotional elaboration. The murderer or sex pervert may wall off this act or activity from the rest of himself. Young adults who fail to develop warm relationships with family and friends may withdraw more and more into themselves. Or, to avoid such desolating isolation, they may join some group that is essentially antisocial.

Undoing or Nullifying. A kind of negative magic, doing a second act to abrogate or neutralize a first act, believing that thereby neither has oc-

---

12. We acknowledge these examples could be seen as building on sexual stereotypes. Nevertheless, when read in a gender-neutral light, the examples illustrate well the authors' points. We suggest, too, that developing an awareness of the use of stereotyping would greatly enhance your interpersonal skills.—EDS.

curred. This usually happens on the unconscious level. Compulsion to turn off the gas to undo a suicide fantasy—having first turned it on; token throwing of salt over the left shoulder to annul spilling—these are examples of a ritual of undoing. False confessions that so often occur following a sensational crime come from persons with feelings of guilt about some "crime" they feel they have committed, and for which they feel a need to be punished.

Sublimation. The unconscious redirecting of emotions or drives to socially approved ends. Of all the ego defenses, this is the most normal and most socially esteemed. Thus the woman who needs to exhibit herself becomes an actress; the verbally aggressive man driven by a need to prove that he is eternally right and the other fellow wrong may become a lawyer.

Turning Against the Self. Directing inward against the self feelings of anger aroused by some outside object. Although this may seem an odd reaction, it is more common than we might think. Death wishes, and the urge to seek punishment that we sometimes find underlying antisocial behavior, may be manifestations.

Ego defenses should not be regarded as wholly negative. We may at times need them to maintain ourselves and to buffer the forces beleaguering us. Nevertheless, most of these defenses are relatively inefficient, and some of them—regression, for example—downright childish. They are therefore regarded as more or less pathological.

Chapter
9

Witness Interviews

A. INTRODUCTION

For the most part, interviewing witnesses or other nonclients involves application of the principles learned in the preceding chapters. You must still use helping and probing techniques, remain sensitive to nonverbal signals, and contend with the inhibitors and facilitators of communication. Indeed, in considering those aspects of interviewing in the lawyer-client context, we have encountered examples of how nonclient interviews illustrate the basic principles. (For example, recall from Chapter 7 the attorney's preparation for interviews with tenants of an apartment building that is being considered for condominium conversion.)

Yet witness interviews do present distinguishing features that affect your preparation and execution. Quite obviously, such interviews are not part of a special professional or fiduciary relationship, so your responsibilities to the interviewees are less substantial than, as well as manifestly different from, those owed to clients. The absence of that close, ongoing professional relationship, however, deprives you of a major resource for encouraging open discussion and places greater pressure on your probing skills. Simultaneously, helping skills, though still useful, are not always as crucial in the nonclient context as they are when dealing with clients.

Moreover, the motivations of nonclient interviewees present special problems. Unlike clients, witnesses ordinarily have no perceived self-interest in talking with, let alone opening up to, a lawyer investigating a case. In fact, many witnesses perceive your inquiries as intrusive and as posing a potential for future time-consuming and threatening duties.

Those witnesses will be reluctant to talk. Other witnesses may identify with parties in opposition to your client and will be downright hostile toward you. As we will see in this chapter, the attitudes and motivations of the witness substantially affect interviewing tactics and choices.

Finally, your role as a lawyer in our legal system may affect your role in the interpersonal process with witnesses. In your interviewing of witnesses—unlike your dealings with clients—the interviewee is not the primary object of your concern. Rather, you continue to seek advancement of the client's interests. Many lawyers, when questioning witnesses, thus feel free to purposefully design their tactics to manipulate the interviewees. Perhaps the manipulative methods are justified. In any event, such interviews present both tactical and ethical issues not encountered in dealing with clients.

The materials below first offer some general guidelines to witness interviewing (Section B) before turning to specific issues and tactics as they relate to three groupings of witnesses—disinterested, hostile, and friendly (Sections C-E). The chapter concludes (in Section F) with a consideration of the ethical and personal questions raised throughout the chapter.

≡≡≡ PROBLEM 1 ≡≡≡
The Restaurant Review

A lawyer, Jane Bowers, represents Paul Sneed, who has been sued by the "Dutch Country Kitchen" for libel. The lawsuit derives from a restaurant review Mr. Sneed wrote for the Lux County Times, which he owns and manages. In the review, Sneed described the ambience, service, and fare of the Kitchen in uncomplimentary terms. His title was, "T'ain't Dutch, T'ain't Country, T'ain't American, T'ain't Good." The review then detailed his evening at the restaurant:

> "Our party of four arrived at the restaurant at 8:00 on a Saturday night. We had no difficulty, however, finding a table among the six other patrons daring enough to battle through the entanglement of cobwebs and potted corn plants in the restaurant's anteroom. Apparently the cocktail special of the evening was soot and beer because each of our bottles of imported beer came accompanied by a dirty glass. (We decided drinking straight from the bottle would be the better part of wisdom.) Our salads of limp lettuce drenched in a rancid sweet-sour dressing arrived promptly. The efficient service ended there, however. The unusually long wait for our entrees was punctuated only by the entertainment provided by cockroaches dancing crisscross over the floor. Our meals were not worth the wait. And one of our group's members had to accept a last-minute change in his order from medium-rare prime rib to well-done—the kitchen was 'all out of' medium-rare meat, we were told."

The review continued on to describe the food in a similar, less than laudatory, fashion.

The restaurant in its complaint charged that Mr. Sneed maliciously fabricated the entire review in order to entertain, rather than inform, his readers, all to the ruination and eventual dissolution of the Kitchen's business. Mr. Sneed admits to some hyperbole (he says the cockroaches did not dance), but insists the thrust of the review was accurate.

During an interview by Ms. Bowers, Mr. Sneed recalled that one of the "daring" patrons eating at the Kitchen the evening Sneed was there was a local businessman, Edwin Trumble. According to Sneed, Trumble could verify some of the details about the restaurant's poor service and spotty record in maintaining clean facilities. Trumble is approximately 50, married, has two children in college, sells insurance, and has lived in Lux County all his life. Sneed and Trumble are casual acquaintances. On occasion, Trumble buys advertising space in the Lux County Times.

QUESTIONS

Ms. Bowers has decided to interview Mr. Trumble. How and what should she prepare? What problems and issues might she anticipate? When, where, and how should she interview Trumble?

B. BASIC PRINCIPLES

1. Interview Witnesses Pursuant to a Theory of the Case and a Fact-Gathering Plan

After you have thoroughly interviewed your client, you should develop a theory (or theories) of the case and a plan for gathering the facts. To do that properly, you engage in a thought process akin to a computer search. A computer operator plugs a request into the computer; the computer scans its information bank and selects entries that satisfy the request; the operator then pursues the computer's responses to determine which best fits the immediate needs. Similarly, you begin with a set of facts provided by the client; you then plug that information into your bank of legal and nonlegal knowledge and scan all potential theories; after identifying the possible theories, you pursue additional information to either confirm or reject their application. That pursuit of information should follow a fact-gathering plan, which includes identification of facts to be proved and the means and sources for acquiring the information. The plan requires consideration of the full range of discovery and investigative tools targeting at least four sets of facts:

(1) facts establishing the existence or nonexistence of the substantive elements entitling the plaintiff to relief;

(2) facts corroborating the client's version of the case;

     (3)   facts constituting the adversary's version of the case; and

     (4)   facts contradicting the adversary's version of the case.[1]

In litigation, you seek information that is admissible as evidence, will lead to such evidence, or provides leverage in negotiation. In addition, you want evidence or testimony that logically supports your theories and that juries find persuasive. You aim to make your client's story more believable than the adversary's. Therefore, you take into account that articulate grandmotherly types are more persuasive than hippies; police officers more than convicts; and visual and documentary evidence more than descriptive testimony.

Two cases demonstrate the above points. In the first, your client is a rape defendant who was arrested following an eyeball identification. The defendant informs you he was nowhere near the scene of the crime at the time of the incident. Your scanning in this case should produce not only the obvious defense theories of alibi and misidentification, but also the possibility that there was no crime at all. Upon ascertaining those potential theories, you then investigate the facts. In pursuing an alibi defense, you would interview persons the client says were with him at the time of the crime and seek other forms of corroboration. If, for example, the client states he was alone shopping for clothes at that time, you should ask yourself, "What facts would likely follow from a shopping venture that would logically support the alibi?"[2] Did the defendant charge any purchases? If he did, then he and the store should have dated receipts of the purchase. If he paid by check, then his canceled check would provide similar evidence. Even if his purchase was with cash, many stores give handwritten receipts with dates and descriptions of all purchases and maintain those records for some period of time. By identifying which clerk's handwriting was on the receipt and when the clerk worked that day, you might confine the defendant's visit to the store to a particular time period. Perhaps a clerk remembers the defendant being there and at what time. (The client might recall something unusual that happened or was said while he was in the store and that could jog the clerk's memory.) If the client parked his car in a nearby lot or garage, then he may have a stub showing the date and the time. If he bought gas with a credit card, his receipt should show the date and place of purchase. Perhaps he recognized some individuals while he was shopping. (The client could state where he saw whom when, and the identified persons could confirm they were at a given place at a given time.)

To develop the misidentification defense, you should visit the scene of the crime at the time of day on which the crime allegedly occurred. Check there for environmental factors that might have impaired the ability of the victim or any eyewitness to observe people and events. The quality of the lighting would be particularly important in that context, as would the proximity and angle between the assailant and the person who made the identification. You also want to learn about the length of time the witness or

---

1. D. Binder & S. Price, *Legal Interviewing and Counseling: A Client-Centered Approach* 124 (1977).

2. See id. at 125-126.

victim was able to observe the assailant, the speed with which events unfolded, and distractions created by simultaneous occurrences. (In a rape case, though, the likelihood of a distracting occurrence would be small.) Finally, you probe factors within the observer that could impair his or her ability to make an accurate identification. Those would include sensual acuity (e.g., vision, hearing), other physical factors (e.g., age, drug or alcohol consumption, fatigue, degree of stress, intelligence), attention paid to the event, and biases.

In pursuing the theory that there was no crime, you would focus on whether the alleged victim has bruises, cuts, torn clothes, or other evidence to show she had been in a struggle. Were any tests conducted by a doctor or the police in the course of their investigation? If so, what were the results? You would also investigate whether there could be an explanation for fabricating the crime. Did the woman have a motive to hurt the accused? Is she, for example, an ex-lover the client jilted? Does she have a history of psychological problems?

Once you fully investigate the facts, then you must identify which theories are sufficiently supported by your findings to justify presentation to a judge or jury. The fact-gathering stage emphasizes inclusion of theories—to ensure no arguments are overlooked—but trial preparation emphasizes trimming and paring. At that stage, you marshal the evidence to present, as simply as possible, a coherent and understandable case. In our hypothetical, as in most instances, there may be more than one viable theory. For example, if the defendant has an alibi, then one of the other two defenses must also apply.[3]

For the second illustration, we refer back to the restaurant libel problem. In developing a theory of the case, Attorney Bowers' scan would produce several potential defenses: truth; fair comment privilege; or a qualified First Amendment privilege requiring the plaintiff to prove either actual malice or negligence by the newspaper. With those theories in mind, Ms. Bowers would seek evidence bearing on the truth of the story, the "public" character of the restaurant and its owners, and Sneed's view of the facts at the time of publication. (This discussion focuses only the question of liability. Ms. Bowers could also pursue procedural defenses and arguments to reduce an award of damages.)

In her fact-gathering on the truth defense, Bowers would interview the persons who accompanied Sneed to the restaurant as well as other patrons there that night. Those customers not in Sneed's party would be more likely to be perceived as disinterested. The restaurant's employees might also produce relevant and convincing information in interviews or depositions. In addition, Ms. Bowers should investigate if other publications or media had reviewed the restaurant, what other patrons thought of it, what its reputation was, and what health inspectors and their reports said about the cleanliness of the restaurant. The restaurant's business records might

---

3. In practice, this process of theory evaluation should never really stop during a case. And development of a case does not always proceed through a neat chronology—as might be implied by the text's summary. The text also confines its discussion of theory development to the litigation context, but the principles advanced are just as applicable to transactional cases handled by a lawyer.

reveal its level of popularity; the relative briskness of the business would indicate the restaurant's quality and would be highly relevant in calculating damages. The more evidence Bowers can produce to substantiate the truth of Sneed's review, the more likely she can establish he had a reasonable basis for believing it was true (even if it was not). Naturally, Sneed would testify on his "state of mind" in publishing the article. He may be able to corroborate an absence of actual malice or negligence through his notes and rough drafts.

So, you need to map out your theories of the case, identify their elements, determine how those elements can be proved, and then proceed with fact-gathering. Theories and plans can, and should, be subject to constant reevaluation and modification, but you must maintain a "big picture," that is, a grid for constructing your case and for interviewing witnesses.

2. Interview Witnesses as Soon as Possible

Swiftness in interviewing witnesses is important for several reasons. First, the sooner you can interview a witness, the better the witness's recollection of the facts will be. Second, people's perceptions of events can become colored by their attitudes and by subsequent developments. Thus, the earlier you can talk with witnesses, the better are your chances for minimizing distortion in their recollections. The need to move quickly is particularly acute when you desire to "lock in" a witness to a favorable version of the relevant events. Third, there can be advantages to beating the other side to a witness. Skillful interviewing can, in some cases, move the witness to identify with the interviewer's client. That is, you can help to shape the witness's perceptions. Conversely, as the first lawyer there, you have an advantage because opposing counsel has not influenced the witness. Ethical considerations can limit ability to shape testimony, but the adversarial system does permit you to take advantage of the play in a witness's perceptions of events. (See Section F, below, on the ethical considerations. For a discussion on the malleability of memory, see Chapter 8, pages 182-183.)

3. Prepare as Much as Possible
for Each Witness Interview

Perhaps the most important element in effective witness interviewing is preparation. The need to prepare can be even more critical with witness interviews than with client interviews. When talking to witnesses, you face greater pressure to thoroughly gather the facts in one session. You can always go back to clients for further discussion without interfering with the case, but most witnesses resent multiple interruptions. Such witnesses may vent their resentment of the lawyer by unconsciously (or consciously) adjusting their recollections to punish the client. Careful forethought and anticipation of contingencies also enhance your use of the facilitators of communications and your ability to deal with the inhibitors.

We see adequate preparation as including six tasks, which need not be completed one at a time or in any particular order. Those tasks, discussed below, are: (1) set informational goals and agenda; (2) identify other goals; (3) gather information on the interviewee; (4) learn about the subjects to be discussed; (5) plan tactics; and (6) anticipate problems.

First, to *set information goals and the agenda*, you review the theories of the case and accumulated facts to produce a list of subjects for probing. The subjects normally comprise both information that is directly admissible as evidence and information that could lead to admissible evidence or leverage for negotiation. So, planning takes into account hearsay and references to other informational sources. Then analyze and outline each of the subjects to ensure you cover them effectively during the interview.

Thus, in preparing to interview Mr. Trumble, Ms. Bowers would identify a range of general topics:

- background on Trumble
- his recollections of the night upon which the review was based
- his knowledge about specific statements made in the review
- his experiences, if any, at the restaurant before and after the night Sneed was there
- his knowledge, personal or second-hand, of the restaurant's operations
- his knowledge of others who had eaten or worked at the restaurant and who might be amenable to talking about their experiences
- his general opinion of the food, service, and atmosphere at the restaurant

Bowers could also identify subtopics within several of those categories. With the topic, "knowledge about specific statements made in the review," Bowers could go through the article and plan questions on each potentially libelous statement. For quizzing Trumble on his experiences at the restaurant, Bowers could break the discussion down into: (1) food—what did he order and how would he describe it? (2) service—how was he treated by the staff and how efficient were they? (3) cleanliness—were there noticeable problems in the dining area, in the restrooms, with the service settings or glasses? (4) other supportive information—were there any other revealing or unusual occurrences? Of course, during the interview, Ms. Bowers would pursue each of these areas in detail using the skills discussed in Chapter 7.

In the course of planning the agenda, you must also decide the sequence for discussing the identified topics. That decision, which is particularly important in witness interviews, normally turns on the degree of cooperation you expect to find in the witness. We therefore defer specifics on sequencing to Sections C and E, below, which address variations in tactics according to the witness's level of responsiveness. In addition, the discussion in Chapter 7, Sections F and G (pages 162-173), should prove helpful at this point.

Second, you must *determine what other goals you might have* for the interview. You will normally want to establish some level of rapport with the witness, especially when the interviewee is a potential witness for a trial.

Rapport facilitates communications in any context; the better your rapport with witnesses, the more they open up, the more they cooperate, and the more likely they will sympathize with your client. Of course, when you interview witnesses whom you expect to identify with an opposing party, your "rapport goal" may simply be to avoid antagonizing them.

At times, procuring a written statement from the witness is a crucial goal that requires forethought to be achieved. You may also find persuasion an important witness interview goal; the interview allows you an opportunity to enlighten the witness on the validity of your client's position.

In our restaurant review case, depending on what could be learned about Mr. Trumble, the lawyer might pursue a number of these goals. Certainly she would want to cultivate some rapport with Trumble; that goal would call for preparation on small talk, ordering of probes, possible empathic responses to align Trumble with Sneed, and other techniques for promoting rapport. If Ms. Bowers feels Trumble is nonaligned, then she could note her goal of persuasion and plan how to effect that goal. She could, for example, begin her interview by posturing the case as an incompetent business trying to collect a windfall at the expense of a journalist who has honestly reported what he observed. (See Section F, below.)

The third and fourth steps cannot always be fully executed prior to the interview because they may require facts that become available only in the interview itself.

In the third step, you should *learn as much as you reasonably can about the interviewee*. Such information can aid you in rapport-building with the witness, in deciding on tactics, and in anticipating problems that could develop. In the Kitchen Restaurant case, Ms. Bowers could use the knowledge she has about Mr. Trumble. That he is an established businessman himself provides a possible wedge for developing some rapport; Bowers could use that to more readily bring Trumble to identify with Sneed, while emphasizing the differences between those two and the plaintiffs. That Trumble has two children in college gives a starter for small talk along the way (e.g., "What colleges do they attend?" or "Putting two children through college at the same time is an impressive feat these days."). From the thumbnail information she has on Trumble, Bowers could also anticipate that he is a relatively conservative individual, and she would therefore want to adjust her dress and manner to avoid creating an unnecessary barrier to communication and rapport.

Fourth, you should *learn as much as possible about the subjects to be discussed* during the interview. Obviously, the major purpose of the interview is to learn about those subjects, but any foreknowledge that can be acquired will aid probing. Well-informed interviewers can probe deeper and more meaningfully than poorly informed ones. Preparation on the subject is especially critical when interviewing individuals in a technical field or those unlikely to be elaborative. Moreover, an interviewer who comes across as knowledgeable will be more likely to receive honest responses; people are more reluctant to deceive someone whom they believe would be aware of their dishonesty than one who they feel would not readily detect deception.

Fifth, you must *prepare your tactics.* Specifically, you must decide on the nature and order of your questions, on possible techniques for bringing the witness to your side, and on arguments or leverage points that can be used if the witness is unwilling to talk. Your decisions on these matters depend on the degree of cooperation and responsiveness you anticipate receiving from the witness. Accordingly, we defer discussion of the possibilities to Sections C-E. In addition, Section F elaborates on ethical considerations relevant to tactics.

Sixth, you must *carefully anticipate problems* you might encounter in the interview and devise strategies for dealing with them. Naturally, not all problems can be foreseen, but at least some of them recur with sufficient frequency to permit planning. (Eventually, experience in confronting and dealing with recurrent problems enables you to respond effectively and diminishes the need to repeat preparations.) Again, many of the difficulties that arise frequently are related to the receptivity of the interviewee. Therefore, see Sections C-E, below. If you cannot learn about the degree of responsiveness you will likely encounter, then you must anticipate any possibility. Thus, in the restaurant hypothetical, Ms. Bowers would have to think through what she should do if Mr. Trumble proves to be a close friend of the restaurateur or particularly recalcitrant in discussing the matter.

Other barriers can also be identified prior to the interview. If the interview concerns an incident that occurred well in the past, then you must devise means for jogging the interviewee's memory. An interviewee who is very old, very young, or dull-witted presents special probing difficulties that can be minimized by preparation. Language difficulties, differences in economic and social status, and ego-threatening subject matters illustrate other potential problems. For discussion of dealing with such inhibitors to communication, see Chapter 8.

C. INDIFFERENT WITNESSES

≡ PROBLEM 2 ≡
The Restaurant Review and the Neutral Patron

The scene is Ms. Bowers' interview of Edwin Trumble at his office. Excerpts of their dialogue follow:

Bowers: Good afternoon, Mr. Trumble. I'm sorry to bother you. You have quite an operation here. I hadn't realized your business was so big. How many employees do you have?

Trumble: We have ten full-time and two more who work for us when we get behind.

Bowers: Tremendous. Do you have other ventures besides insurance?

Trumble: Yeah. We do some investing, land speculation and the like. Nothing too risky, though. I like to stick with what I know best.

Bowers: Well, I can see you're busy, so I won't keep you long. As you may know, I represent Paul Sneed in this libel case he has against him, on that restaurant review he wrote on the Dutch Country Kitchen. Have you heard about it?

Trumble: Yeah. But I really don't know what that has to do with me.

Bowers: Well, I'd like to ask you just a few questions if I could. Do you know the restaurant's owners?

Trumble: No, I don't.

Bowers: Did you eat at the restaurant often?

Trumble: Maybe three, four times, counting lunches.

Bowers: I see. Can you tell me about those occasions?

Trumble: Uh, look. I know you have your job to do, but so do I. I really don't have anything to tell you, and I don't want to get involved in any lawsuit. I've got far too much to do. So . . .

Bowers: Yes, of course. I am imposing, and your time is valuable. But your perspective could prove to be very helpful to us in sorting this case out. I'll only be a few minutes. In your trips to the restaurant, were you able to form some opinion of the place?

Trumble: [Makes no response.]

Bowers: Mr. Trumble, if you can talk to me now, I may not have to bother you again. I may be able to take what you tell me, and whatever else I can find out, and settle this case. But if you don't talk to me now, then I'll surely have to intrude on your time later, in much more significant ways. I can't guarantee you that you won't have to participate after today, but I can guarantee that if you don't talk with me today, you will have to later. I know you're very busy and I was hoping I could save you, and me, some time down the road. Can you take just a few minutes now?

Trumble: What could you do?

Bowers: I'd have to subpoena you to a deposition. That would involve me directing questions at you, which you'd have to answer, and having a court reporter take it all down. I have to be honest with you and tell you a deposition might be necessary anyhow, but at least I can try to avoid it if you'll give me a few minutes now.

Trumble: Well, I've got to leave soon for the Coast, so you'd better get on with it.

Bowers: Yes, of course. You mentioned you'd been to the restaurant several times. What convinced you to go back there after the first time?

Trumble: No special reason. It was convenient, I guess.

Bowers: Did the Kitchen have efficient service at lunch?

Trumble: It wasn't too bad. Of course the most people I ever saw in there for lunch was about fifteen. It wouldn't be too hard to serve a soup, or salad, or sandwich, or the special to that number of people.

* * *

Bowers: About dinners there—how was the service in the evening?

Trumble: Now that was pretty awful. I think Sneed probably exaggerated some in his article, but I do know we waited a long while each time we ate dinner there, which was twice, I guess. And it wasn't crowded either time.

Bowers: What about the service in terms of friendliness and manners?

*   *   *

Bowers: What did you order when you ate dinner there?

*   *   *

Bowers: How was the prime rib?

*   *   *

Bowers: And the strip steak?

*   *   *

Bowers: What about the cleanliness of the restaurant?

*   *   *

Bowers: What was your general opinion of the place, then?

Trumble: I would say it was ordinary, at best. Maybe they never had a chance to get the kinks out of the operation, or maybe they just weren't very competent. For the reasons we talked about, it wasn't a very pleasant place to eat, and whenever they tried to serve something a little different, they failed. Maybe what they needed was a real, down-home country cook. I know I simply stopped going there; the food wasn't worth what I paid for it.

Bowers: Do you recall the night Sneed was there?

Trumble: Yeah.

Bowers: I have just a few questions about some of Sneed's specific statements in his article. [Bowers proceeds through the article inquiring about the accuracy of key passages.]

*   *   *

Bowers: Are there other people you know who ate there frequently?

*   *   *

Bowers: Do you know any of the employees who worked at the Kitchen?

Trumble: Let's see. I knew the cashier-hostess, Karen Owen, and one of the waiters was Ed Farese's boy—Joe, I believe, is his first name. [Bowers follows Trumble's response with queries on who the employees are, what they did at the Kitchen, what they did before working there, and what their opinion of the restaurant was.]

*   *   *

Bowers: Well, this has been very helpful, Mr. Trumble. Let me see if I can just wrap this up with a brief summary. You ate at the Kitchen on about four occasions. You found the service to be slow, inefficient, and unfriendly. Your dinners were OK; basically, you ordered a well-done steak or prime rib with potato each time and that's what you got. Your wife, though, found the "Dutch Country"-style dinners she ordered to be bland and not well prepared. And you didn't see any significant problems with the restaurant's maintenance of sanitary conditions. As to the night Sneed was there [this part of the summary is omitted.]

OK, Mr. Trumble, I must let you get back to your work. I really do appreciate your talking to me. I think you must realize, as a proven businessman yourself, what a frivolous suit like this can mean to someone like Mr. Sneed. The Kitchen's owners are trying to make him pay for their incompetence, and we need to see that the responsibility for the restaurant's failure rests where it belongs—on the owners. I'm going to leave you my business card, so if you think of anything else you feel I should know, please call me. I've written my home phone on the back, and I don't mind being called there.

Trumble: Well, I doubt I'll think of anything.

Bowers: That's fine, but you have my numbers just in case. Enjoy your trip to the Coast. Is it business or pleasure or both?

Trumble: Both. At least, I hope it will be both. You can't always be guaranteed pleasure on any trip, you know. Of course, the success I find on the business end will directly affect whether it will also be a pleasurable trip.

Bowers: Yes, I'm sure that's true. I know, at least, our conversation has been both productive and pleasurable for me. It was good talking with you. Have a nice day.

Trumble: You too. Good-bye.

---

1. Introduction

Indifferent witnesses are neutral third parties with no stake in the case and no ax to grind. The degree of responsiveness can nevertheless vary substantially among such individuals. At one end rest the cooperative witnesses who are eager to perform their duty as citizens, to display their knowledge on a matter of apparent importance, or to be significant participants in an interesting proceeding. At the other end sit the individuals who do not want to get involved, who resent the intrusion on their time, or who have some other reason for wanting to remain aloof from the case. In between these poles are those witnesses who do not necessarily resist involvement, but who submit to it with apathy, reluctance, or some notable lack of enthusiasm. Within that range, certain generalities apply. The following discussion considers the issues in an order roughly similar to their appearance in the above dialogue between Bowers and Trumble.

2. Location and Time

Your location for the witness interview should be convenient to the witness and afford sufficient privacy to allow for a thorough and candid discussion. Allocate enough time for an unrushed and careful exchange. Practicalities may preclude such arrangements, but the effort should be made to attain them.

Ms. Bowers had several choices about where to conduct her interview of Trumble.[4] They included her office, Mr. Trumble's office, his home, a restaurant, or a club. She could also have questioned him over the phone. For in-person interviews of neutral witnesses, you should generally travel to them, especially when you are not certain of finding an amenable respondent. Your office is not necessarily inappropriate, but the need to strike a good relationship with the witness reduces the desirability of that site. Unless the witness is eager to cooperate, rapport-building requires that you accommodate the witness. In addition, reluctant or uncertain witnesses can simply refuse to show up at your office but would be much less likely to refuse you the opportunity to travel to them for a talk. In deciding between the interviewee's home or place of occupation, you should opt for the one the witness is most likely to deem the least intrusive. That, in turn, often depends on the job held by the witness. Many employers, for example, would be upset by their employees talking on the job for any length of time. On the other hand, many people feel their home life belongs to them and their families and deeply resent any intrusions into it. For interviews of such persons, restaurants, public parks or buildings, or similar semi-social settings might be more accommodating. Of course, when you arrange public or semi-public meetings, you risk sacrificing the privacy you may need for full, candid discussion. At any rate, we suggest that you determine the time and place of witness interviews by, whenever possible, asking the interviewees what they prefer.

3. Opening

The attorney's opening of the Trumble interview applies basic interviewing techniques. Ms. Bowers initiates the conversation with an apology for the intrusion—she has aptly anticipated Trumble's resentment of her consumption of his time—and then engages in agreeable, if abbreviated, small talk. The chatter about his business relates to a subject in which Trumble is surely interested. Such conversation helps to establish friendly terms and set the tone for the interview. Because Trumble is concerned about his time, Bowers does well here to keep the small talk short and move quickly to substantive topics.

The utility of small talk in the witness interview is the same as in client interviews. You use it to assess the interviewee's ability to understand and describe events. By steering discussion to particular topics, you also gain helpful information about the witness's background and perspectives. As noted above, the low-keyed conversation also works toward creating

---

4. In addition to settling on a location, Ms. Bowers also had to make two threshold determinations: (1) Should she interview the witness herself or use an investigator? and (2) If she decided against the investigator, should she interview the witness alone or with an accompanying person? What are the arguments regarding the advisability of using another person either to do the interview or to accompany the lawyer? Would those arguments apply as well to hostile or friendly witnesses? See Section F-3, pages 230-232.

friendly relations between you and the witness and helps both of you to relax. Indeed, effective small talk may be of even greater significance with witnesses than with clients because you have a more limited opportunity to learn about witnesses and to establish a congenial relationship with them. Moreover, you are more likely to need small talk to put yourself at ease with witnesses than you would with clients.

4. Probing

In interviewing witnesses, as with clients, you want a full rendering of the facts from the interviewee's perspective. The optimum method for accomplishing that is typically through a wedge of open-ended questions and use of the funnel sequence, which are discussed in Chapter 7 (pages 157-161, 170-172). That approach best enables you to seek the truth and to determine what the interviewees would say if called as witnesses, what prejudices they might have, and what kind of witnesses they would make. Can they articulate well? Do they speak convincingly? The free association encouraged by an open-ended question should also help interviewees to recall items they might otherwise overlook in responding to more directive probes. (See Chapter 7, pages 157-161.)

In the interview of Mr. Trumble, Ms. Bowers does attempt to lead with elaboration probes. After verifying that Trumble was not a close friend of the restaurant's owners (an important preliminary point) and that he had eaten there several times, Bowers asks, "Can you tell me about those occasions?" Then, after wrestling with Trumble over whether he should talk with her, Bowers tries again, "What convinced you to go back there after the first time?" The question could elicit an elaboration from Trumble about his opinion of the restaurant. His answer this time is responsive, though still not elaborative. Bowers then shifts to topical probes—still open-ended but narrowed to focus on a particular topic within the general subject matter of the interview. In that manner, Bowers hits each of the criteria a customer would normally consider in judging a restaurant. In omitted portions of the interview, she pursues in funnel-sequence fashion Trumble's responses to the topical probes.

Bowers pursues her fact-gathering goals, then, largely through a set of probes calling for elaboration, yet narrow enough to deal with Trumble's reluctance. More radical shifts in probing tactics may be necessary, however, as the degree of interviewee reluctance increases. Open-ended probes generally elicit only superficial and uninformative responses from reluctant witnesses, who thus force you to use more directive probing. The elaboration probes make it too easy for the interviewee to dodge the question. They can also exasperate an already irritated respondent because they require more thought and effort. By contrast, direct questions confine the witness, make it more difficult to be evasive, and, when asked quickly, give the appearance of a rapid pace. The latter is particularly important with persons who are reluctant because of competing time demands. Obviously, your use of narrow questions means you cannot fully achieve some interviewing goals; you will not acquire as accurate a picture of the witness's story or verbal skills. On the other hand, those goals escape you just as well when a witness replies tersely or not at all to open-ended questions.

After identifying and probing each of the restaurant review criteria, Bowers restates the broad, open-ended question about Trumble's general opinion. By this time, however, Trumble has already described the bases for forming that opinion and a response now follows more easily. In fact, Trumble offers an impression that could prove helpful in assembling Sneed's defense. Thus, Bowers used—albeit in a limited fashion—an inverted funnel sequence; she probed the subtopics and then restated the general question. That sequencing was necessary given Trumble's initial refusal to respond to the broader elaboration probes. The more direct questions helped to get him talking and to provide a ready justification for his opinion when it was offered.

That inverted approach can also be helpful when the interviewer fears the interviewee may have preconceptions that could affect his response to the broad question.[5] The prejudice might dissipate if probing on the bases for the opinion occurs first. For example, when a pollster inquires among voters about a president's job performance, many respondents indicate a positive opinion, and then, to justify that opinion, adjust their responses to follow-up probes. But if the more specific probes about different aspects of the president's performance are addressed first, the voters are more likely to respond objectively, and those responses could, in turn, affect the objectivity of the overall performance rating.

Bowers concludes her probing with inquiries into two very important subject matter areas. First, she reviews the specific statements made by Sneed in his article. Given the litigation's focus on the truth or falsity of those statements, the importance of such a line of questioning is apparent. Their placement in the interview following the more general discussion can be explained, again, by a desire on the lawyer's part to force Trumble to think through and reveal his opinions of the restaurant before getting to the ultimate issues. On the other hand, had Trumble displayed more reluctance, Bowers would have been well advised to go immediately to Sneed's article because of its obvious importance to the case.

Second, Bowers attempts to learn from Trumble the names of other potential witnesses or sources of information. That is one probing topic you should pursue with virtually every witness interviewed. Note especially that Bowers asks Trumble about the restaurant's employees. Former or disgruntled employees can provide a particularly fertile source of information.

5. Dealing with Inhibitors

Shortly into her interview of Trumble, Bowers encounters real resistance. Trumble telegraphs that message as soon as Bowers first raises the subject of Sneed's article about the Kitchen. Trumble responds, "I really don't know what that has to do with me." After some efforts at probing, a prom-

---

5. See D. Binder & S. Price, *Legal Interviewing and Counseling: A Client-Centered Approach* 133-134 (1977).

ise to keep the interview short, and a statement of Trumble's importance to her assessing the case, Bowers then stops her questioning to confront the reluctance. Trumble has indicated the source of his resistance to be the intrusions into his time and the disruption they would cause to his schedule. Bowers therefore attempts to counter his concerns by explaining that he can best minimize the potential intrusion by talking now:

> "Mr. Trumble, if you can talk to me now, I may not have to bother you again. I may be able to take what you tell me, and whatever else I can find out, and settle this case. But if you don't talk to me now, then I'll surely have to intrude on your time later, in much more significant ways. I can't guarantee you that you won't have to participate after today, but I can guarantee that if you don't talk with me today, you will have to later. I know you're very busy and I was hoping I could save you, and me, some time down the road. Can you take just a few minutes now?"

Trumble, apparently skeptical, challenges Bowers about what she could do, to which she responds that she can subpoena him to a deposition.

Bowers thus tries to overcome the inhibitors on communication—time and inconvenience—by meeting them head-on and showing Trumble that talking now is in his best interests as he has defined them. If time and disruption are his major concerns, then he may find cooperation will mean less intrusion.

Unfortunately, not all interviewees can be satisfied, or will capitulate, as easily as Trumble. Nevertheless, the excerpts reveal some worthwhile techniques. When Bowers meets resistance, she probes the interviewee's reasons for resisting. After all, an interviewer cannot deal with inhibitors if she does not know what they are. An empathic remark followed by a probe is appropriate. For example, "You appear reluctant to talk, Mrs. Jones. Is there some reason for that?" Or, "I sense you don't feel like talking, Mr. Jones. Is that right? Can you tell me about it?"

With Mr. Trumble, Ms. Bowers has no need to probe for his inhibitors; he freely volunteers that he has competing demands and is unwilling to get involved. Had she met with additional resistance after discussing that inhibitor, however, she may have appropriately inquired whether there were other factors limiting his willingness to talk.

Competing time demands and a general mistrust of lawyers and the legal system are probably the most common inhibitors encountered in interviews of "neutral" witnesses. Expressions of concern for the witnesses' time and efforts to accommodate them help to alleviate their worries about intrusions. Typically, the lawyer seeing a witness for the first time can use the approach Ms. Bowers used with Trumble. She convinced him that talking with the lawyer might alleviate the need for later intrusions. But decency—as well as long-term goals—requires you to be honest about what might be expected from the witness. If the witness has pertinent and helpful information and if the case proceeds to trial, then you will probably want to use that witness at trial. If you unthinkingly promise not to bother the witness again, you may aggravate the inconvenience and the discomfort felt by the witness when subsequently called upon to testify at a deposition, a trial, or both.

To combat the witness's mistrust of lawyers and the legal system, use empathy and explanation. Empathy about the problems of dealing with lawyers exposes the issue, reveals your understanding, and thus facilitates dealing with the inhibitor. Empathy enhances rapport between you and the witness, which in turn helps to align the witness with your client and encourages information flow. Explanation about the process can alleviate the witness's mistrust, which is often based on ignorance about what is required of a witness in our adversarial system. Witnesses can better deal with their apprehensions when they know what to expect.

The list of potential inhibitors for witnesses includes those applicable to clients, as discussed in Chapter 8, pages 176-184. Similarly, your tools for overcoming a witness's inhibitors include those used for clients. Hostile and friendly witnesses present special inhibitors, and those are addressed in Sections D and E.

D. HOSTILE WITNESSES

≡≡ PROBLEM 3 ≡≡
The Restaurant Review and the Former Employee

In preparing her defense of Mr. Sneed, Ms. Bowers decides to interview some of the restaurant's former employees.[6] One of them, Betty Henson, worked as a cook at the Kitchen and had previously worked ten years for its owners, Guy and Jean Yoder, when they ran a small grocery store. Bowers learns that Henson has been a close friend and loyal employee of the Yoders. She has not found other work since the Kitchen shut down when the Yoders declared bankruptcy. Bowers stops by Henson's home unannounced one afternoon. Excerpts from that interview follow:

Attorney: Ms. Henson? Hi. I'm sorry to disturb you. My name is Jane Bowers and I represent Paul Sneed. You might know that he's been

---

6. If the restaurant were still operating, could Ms. Bowers interview *current* employees of the restaurant without violating Rule 4.2 of the Model Rules of Professional Conduct? That provision prohibits a lawyer representing a client from "communicat[ing] about the subject of the representation with a party the lawyer knows to be represented by another lawyer in the matter, unless the lawyer has the consent of the other lawyer or is authorized by law to do so."

The Comment to Rule 4.2 holds that the prohibition applies to a lawyer's communications with employees within an organization's "control group" and "with any other person whose act or omission in connection with the matter may be imputed to the organization for the purposes of civil or criminal liability or whose statement may constitute an admission on the part of the organization."

The rule does not attach to a lawyer's interview of a lower level *former* employee. See G. Hazard & W. Hodes, 1 *The Law of Lawyering: A Handbook on the Model Rules of Professional Conduct* 436-436.1 (1989 Supp.).

sued by Guy and Jean Yoder. If you wouldn't mind, I'd like to ask you a few questions.

Henson: I would mind very much, thank you. [Starts to close the door.]

Attorney: I'll only be a minute; if you talk to me now perhaps I can save us both the trouble of requiring you to attend a deposition. That would be much more burdensome for you and more expensive for the Yoders, because depositions cost money. And I can be brief. You worked at the Kitchen the whole time it was open—is that right?

Henson: Yes.

Attorney: And before that you worked for the Yoders in their grocery store—right?

Henson: Yes.

Attorney: How long did you do that?

Henson: About ten years.

Attorney: You must have found them good people to work for.

Henson: I did. They're nice folks and they took good care of me.

Attorney: I'm sure. You worked as a cook at the restaurant, I believe.

Henson: Yeah. I helped Mrs. Kline. She was the chief cook.

Attorney: I see. What did you do?

Henson: I chopped vegetables, fried burgers, made the broths, pie dough, cleaned up, did dishes sometimes, and whatever Mrs. Kline or the Yoders told me to do.

Attorney: Do you know if Mrs. Kline worked in any restaurant before?

Henson: I don't think so. She was a cook at the high school cafeteria though.

Attorney: OK. You mentioned pie dough. Did you bake your own pies at the Kitchen?

* * *

Attorney: Did the Yoders have a janitor for the restaurant?

Henson: Yes. Not a regular employee. They paid Thompson's Janitorial Service to come in three times a week and give the place a real good cleaning. And then Mr. Yoder himself would sweep up the nights the janitors didn't come. The place was always real clean. I don't understand how Mr. Sneed could say the things he did.

Attorney: I only have a couple more questions for you. Who else did any cooking?

Henson: Well, besides Mrs. Kline, Guy and Jean would help out sometimes. And then we had a college student work part-time for a while, but he quit.

Attorney: What was his name?

Henson: Jim. Jim Campbell.

Attorney: How long did he work there?

Henson: Oh, about six months.

Attorney: Why did he quit?

Henson: I don't know. You'll have to ask him. He was sort of surly. Mouthed off a lot to Guy and Jean.

Attorney: Did he go to school here?

Henson: Yeah.

Attorney: Were you responsible for getting the dishes washed?

Henson: Not ordinarily. Only when the regular fellow was out.

Attorney: Who was that?

Henson: Joe Mining. Nice man; but dumb.

Attorney: So he worked five nights a week and you did them the other two?

Henson: The other one. We were only open six days a week. We were closed on Mondays.

Attorney: Did anyone else work in the Kitchen?

Henson: No. That was it.

Attorney: Did you or Mrs. Kline have any training for cooking or working in a restaurant?

Henson: Well, we both been cooking since we were 17. I'd say that was pretty good training. And, of course, Mrs. Kline worked at the school all those years.

Attorney: Yes, of course. But you had no special or formal training. Right?

Henson: Right. Look, I have to go pick up my son, so . . .

Attorney: OK. I have just one more question for you. Did the Yoders have any special restaurant training?

Henson: You'll have to ask them that.

Attorney: Were you at the restaurant the night Mr. Sneed and his party ate there?

Henson: I couldn't tell you. I've got to go. Good day, ma'am.

Attorney: Good day, Mrs. Henson. Thank you for your time. I hope I won't need to bother you again.

1. Tactics

To effectively interview hostile witnesses, you must carefully prepare. To do that, you must first recognize the potential for hostility in the witness. With Ms. Henson, that recognition should come easily. She was a long-time employee of the Yoders, thus indicating loyalty to them. Moreover, Sneed's article at least contributed to the Kitchen's demise, and that demise cost Ms. Henson her job.

Once you anticipate the hostility, you must develop strategies to deal with it. Your alternatives focus on devising means for persuading or coaxing the witness to talk. Identify reasons—if possible—why talking promotes the witness's interests. That strategy could include the use of threats or accommodations you could make in exchange for information.[7] You should also explore how empathy and other helping techniques could mitigate the hostility. The process of extracting information from a hostile witness thus operates much like a negotiation; you anticipate the other side's

---

7. That is not to suggest you should "buy" the witness. There are accommodations you can make without threatening unethical conduct. For example, you could urge a witness to talk by promising to try to avoid disclosure of his identity or of particularly personal information.

position and interests and then devise means to convince that side that its interests are best served by conceding.

In the interview of Ms. Henson, Ms. Bowers combines several strategies. She urges that Ms. Henson would be better off responding in the interview because that would be less intrusive than submitting to a deposition. In effect, Ms. Bowers injects a threat: Talk to me now or I'll force you to talk in a deposition. The attorney then adds that the Yoders' interests would also be better served if Ms. Henson agreed to answer questions informally; otherwise, the Yoders would have to spend money on a deposition.[8] Because Ms. Henson's hostility is a function of her concern for the Yoders, the lawyer's argument meets head-on Ms. Henson's interests in not talking. Bowers also steamrolls the interview by forging ahead with questions without providing Henson an opportunity to mount a defense.

Ms. Bowers could also use empathy. Expressions of understanding about Ms. Henson's feelings for the Yoders and about losing her job might generate some rapport that would aid information flow. If Henson finds the lawyer to be fair and understanding, then she might conclude her information would further some resolution of the conflict. Bowers could effectively couch her persuasion in those terms. For example, she could have said to Ms. Henson:

> "You resent Mr. Sneed and his paper. You're angry because of what he said about the Yoders and the restaurant and because you've lost your job. So your reluctance to talk with me is understandable. You might have information, though, that could convince me that Mr. Sneed should settle the case, which would, of course, benefit your friends—and maybe you if the Yoders start a new business."

The use of empathy in this context, however, does present a higher risk of inaccurate reflection than in client interviews. Because a hostile witness is unlikely to elaborate on anything, including the reasons for his or her refusal to elaborate, you are left to guess about underlying feelings and motivations. Moreover, an inaccurate empathic remark could cause a particularly troublesome backfire.

Use of these persuasive tactics can raise perplexing personal issues for the lawyer. Can you identify them? They are discussed in Section F, below.

2. *Information-Gathering*

In addition to planning tactics, you must prepare informational goals. For hostile witnesses, the goals must be specific and prioritized. Individuals antagonistic to your client or your cause are likely to be brief in answering your questions and liable to end the discussion at any time. You cannot loft open-ended probes to a hostile witness and expect expansive responses. Thus, your preparation should identify precisely the facts needed and as-

---

8. Frequently, of course, a deposition is the only means available to you to get information from a hostile witness. You may also prefer a deposition to have a record of the witness's responses.

sess which of them are most important. You can anticipate that narrow questions requiring only brief responses will be most effective. They call for less effort from the witness, less opportunity for digression, and greater efficiency in getting directly to the most important points. Advance formulation of questions would be appropriate in such cases.

To plan the order of your probes, consider three primary criteria: (1) the degree of threat posed to the client by the questions; (2) the importance of the sought-for information; and (3) organizational clarity.

Hostile witness interviews typically involve sensitive subjects that, when broached, risk antagonizing the witness to the point that the witness refuses to continue. If you decide the questions need to be asked despite the risks, plan them for a later stage in the interview. By beginning with material having a low level of threat to the witness, you may accustom the witness to answering questions, thus increasing the potential that he or she will later respond to the more difficult probes. Moreover, by deferring the sensitive material until later in the interview, you can better ensure acquisition of at least *some* information before the witness terminates the discussion. The more neutral subjects may also have the effect of desensitizing, to some extent, the more threatening inquiries.

Second, in devising your fact-gathering plan, you should consider the relative significance of the probing topics. Because hostile witnesses do not ordinarily permit extended interviews, you want to probe the most important subjects early in the interview. Ideally, application of this criterion blends with use of the first, but in practice the two criteria frequently cause a conflict; the most important information may also be the most sensitive. In that case, leading with the important topics means opening with the sensitive material and endangering the rest of the interview. In instances of such conflict, the first criterion controls. You will get nowhere initiating a hostile witness interview with threatening questions.

The third consideration—organizational clarity—simply calls for application of basic interviewing strategy. For example, the attorney can better probe when he has first gained an understanding of the "big picture" and essential background facts. Some subjects, too, may be better understood when they are developed in a chronological sequence. With hostile witnesses, however, the concern for clarity can often conflict with the other, above-mentioned criteria. When that happens, the considerations of sensitivity and importance take precedence. Thus, you need to gather as much of the background information as you can *before* talking to a hostile witness.

In the interview of Ms. Henson, Bowers primarily sought information that would aid use of formal discovery methods against the Yoders or that would instruct on maintenance and food preparation at the Kitchen. Bowers also sought to learn whatever she could about other Kitchen employees present the night Sneed was there.

To accomplish her informational goals, Ms. Bowers opened with a series of nonthreatening, almost casual, queries seeking confirmation of background facts about Ms. Henson. These probes achieved clarity without disrupting her pursuit of other goals. Framing the probes as leading questions, the lawyer wedged her way into the conversation. From that opening, Bowers moved into relatively easy questions about food preparation and personnel and learned some worthwhile pieces of information: The chief cook's name was Mary Kline; the Yoders occasionally helped in food preparation; they had employed a janitorial crew that worked three nights a week; none of the cooks had formal training; and there was a possibility of finding a disgruntled former employee who might be antagonistic to the Yoders. The interview could help Bowers in her discovery and trial preparation by identifying new leads and acquiring needed background. That was all accomplished before Ms. Bowers turned the discussion to the more threatening subject of Sneed's visit, which finally stretched Ms. Henson's resilience beyond its limit.

E. FRIENDLY WITNESSES

The friendly witness does not ordinarily present interviewing problems significantly different from those covered in the preceding chapters on client interviewing. You seek to gather information and establish rapport, just as with clients. And, like clients, the friendly witness generally is self-motivated to talk. If anything, friendly witnesses present fewer communication problems than clients because the clients' greater personal involvement leaves them more likely than witnesses to be susceptible to conflicts and emotional distortions.

To meet your goals in interviewing a friendly witness, use open-ended questions, empathic reflection, and other probing techniques designed to elicit the facts as perceived and framed by the witness. That affords the best opportunity to hear the facts as they are most likely to be delivered by the witness at trial or in a deposition. In addition, open-ended questions and minimal topic control, supplemented by clarification probes, best achieve comprehensive and accurate fact-gathering. (See Chapter 7 at pages 157-161.)

Friendly witnesses can present a problem, however, if they are *too* friendly. That is, they may seek to conform their recollections to what they perceive to be most advantageous to the client's interests. You must resist witnesses' efforts to distort the facts. Outright deception, at least, is ethically unacceptable. Moreover, the client would be ill-served by witnesses who fabricate or conceal; such individuals create serious risks of providing litigation opponents with impeachment ammunition that could jeopardize the believability of the client's case. The exposure of a party's witness as a liar impugns the integrity of that party's entire case. Finally, you need accurate information—even information damaging to your case—if you are to prepare adequately for a negotiation, trial, hearing, or presentation of any sort. You must be ready to rebut opponents' theories and to reduce as much as possible the potential for unwanted surprises.

To counteract a friendly witness's desire to reconstruct the facts, you must explain the consequences. As with reluctant witnesses, you should extend reasons why it is in the witness's best interests to be candid as well as open. You have several arguments to use with a less-than-candid supporter. By definition, the friendly witness identifies with, and wants to help, your client. Thus, you can describe your need for accurate information and demonstrate the damage an impeached witness can inflict on a case. If helping the client is indeed the witness's goal, then such arguments should have some persuasive force. For serious instances of deception, you could detail the consequences of a perjury conviction. Finally, you can explain that you cannot ethically purvey information of questionable validity in testimony, discovery, negotiation, or any other context.

F. ETHICAL AND PERSONAL CONSIDERATIONS

Assess the ethical issues presented by the lawyer's conduct in the following cases. What would you do if you were the lawyer?

≡ PROBLEM 4 ≡
The Discriminatory Landlord

Julius Oates is a young black professional looking for a new apartment. He recently learned the Village Green Apartments had vacancies. He called the apartment's manager, David Cooper, to ask about renting a suite and was told to come by the office and fill out an application. When Oates did so, Cooper informed him there were no vacancies then available and none was anticipated in the next several months. Oates was also told, however, that his application would be kept on file. If an apartment came open, Cooper would contact him when his turn on the waiting list came up.

Oates was certain, however, that the Village had an opening. A good friend from Oates's office lived there and personally knew of several unoccupied apartments. The friend, who is white, said that during the three years he had lived there he had not noticed any black residents in the complex, and he had also heard of other blacks being wait-listed when apartments were apparently sitting empty.

Oates had visited the friend's apartment on several occasions and found the Village Green offered considerably more in aesthetics, convenience, and special features than Oates's current apartment. He therefore believed the Village would be a major, yet affordable, improvement in his life-style and he wanted very much to live there. Oates was insulted by what he perceived to be the discrimination practiced by the Village management. Oates thus decided to see a lawyer, John Bellefleur, to determine if the village had unlawfully discriminated and could be forced to rent an apartment to Oates. Bellefleur agreed to research the law and investigate the facts. He subsequently telephoned the Village and asked if the complex had any apartments available. Mr. Cooper said there were none, but he invited Bellefleur to come by and complete an application. The next day Bellefleur visited the Village's office and said he wanted to rent an apartment. In response to Cooper's questions, Bellefleur used an alias and gave phony information about his job, background, and reasons for his interest in the Village.

Was Bellefleur's conduct here proper? ethical? advisable? Why or why not? Should Bellefleur have sent someone else to try to rent the Village apartment rather than go there himself and alone? Would his sending someone else change your analysis of the ethical considerations?

≡ PROBLEM 5 ≡
The Restaurant Review: The Cook

Assume that the Dutch Country Kitchen is still operating when Jane Bowers decides to interview the restaurant's cook. To get a more cooperative witness, Bowers decides to appear as a person collecting information from the Chamber of Commerce for a brochure on local restaurants and entertainment spots.

Is Bowers' tactic here legitimate? ethical? Why or why not?

≡ PROBLEM 6 ≡
The Reneging Borrower

One year ago the Wolfe Finance Company loaned $6,000 to Ken Kerouac to help him get over the hump in his business venture of buying and selling used school buses for private use. Alas, the loan was not enough to salvage Kerouac's dreams for financial prosperity, and the business went under. Because Kerouac had never incorporated, and had inadequate inventory to cover the outstanding amount on the loan, Wolfe had to pursue Kerouac personally. Wolfe contacted its attorney, Janice Kesey, to file a civil action and recoup the full amount owed on the loan. Ms. Kesey first sought to talk to Kerouac to determine if there was a possibility for imminent payment or if there might be some possible defense to an action on the loan. Kerouac, however, was not at his old address and did not leave a forwarding address. Phone records showed no listing for him.

In an effort to locate Kerouac, Ms. Kesey calls Kerouac's sister and tells her she is from the Readers' Digest Sweepstakes and has exciting news, which must be personally delivered, for Mr. Kenneth Kerouac.

What is your opinion of the propriety of the lawyer's tactic here? Would your opinion change if the debt were only $1,000 and investigative costs for locating an individual average $1,200?

≡ PROBLEM 7 ≡
The Kidnapping Parent

Truman Breckinridge is a lawyer who represented Myra Kerouac in her divorce from Ken two years ago. After extended litigation, the court awarded Myra custody of the couple's two young children and gave Ken reasonable visitation. Breckinridge has now received a call from a nearly hysterical Myra, who said Ken did not return the children after his weekend visitation. She had also received in her Monday morning mail a letter from Ken saying he was leaving the area and taking the children with him. She had been to his apartment and he had indeed moved out without leaving a forwarding address.

In an effort to locate Kerouac, Breckinridge calls Kerouac's sister and tells her he is from the Readers' Digest Sweepstakes and has exciting news, which must be personally delivered, for Mr. Kenneth Kerouac.

Is your opinion of Breckinridge's use of this tactic any different from your assessment of its use by the attorney for Wolfe Finance? If so, why?

≡ **PROBLEM 8** ≡
The Stonewalling Witness

Attorney David Wade represents Harley Wise, who has been indicted for the armed robbery of a liquor store and the slaying of its owner. The prosecution's case rests almost entirely on an identification made by a witness to the crime. The witness, Arthur Stone, was sitting in a car across the street from the store when the crime occurred. Stone was in the car with his mother, Mrs. Anita Stone, waiting for Arthur's daughter to return from a drugstore purchase. Both Stone and his mother observed the assailant as he emerged from the liquor store following the shooting. They immediately ducked down. Apparently, the felon did not see them as he made his escape.

Anita Stone is 86 years old and extremely frail. She has a bad heart condition and cannot take much excitement. In fact, Stone had to take her to the doctor's office immediately after the liquor store incident.

To evaluate his case and prepare a defense for Wise, Wade decided he had to interview Arthur Stone. When Wade called on Stone at his office, Stone refused to discuss the case with Wade. Expressions of empathy from Wade and appeals to Stone's sense of fairness failed to persuade Stone to discuss the case. Wade then said to Stone, "Look, if you don't talk to me now, I will be forced to put your mother on the witness stand and subject her to some pretty rough examination."

Do you see any ethical problems in Wade's threat to Stone? Would it make a difference to you if the threat was an empty one? (It probably was; "rough examination" of a frail, 86-year-old woman susceptible to having a heart attack on the stand would generally be ill advised.) What would your reaction be if, instead of his above threat, Wade had said to Stone, "Look, if you talk to me now, I'll do everything I possibly can to keep your mother out of the case"?

≡ **PROBLEM 9** ≡
The Alcoholic Husband

John Smith has been charged with inflicting a serious blow to the head of his 7-year-old daughter, Amy. John admits responsibility for the injury, but maintains it was an accident. He says he had been drinking heavily the day of the incident, and around midnight became embroiled in a nasty verbal battle with his wife, Mary. John picked up a rifle butt he had under the bed and threatened Mary with it. In a fit of rage, he then flung the butt across the room. Unbeknownst to him, Amy had heard the commotion and had walked into her parent's bedroom to see what was going on. She stepped into the doorway just as John threw the rifle butt and she was struck on the head with it. Mary insisted to the police, however, that when Amy came into the room, John walked over and purposely hit her with the rifle butt.

John has a long history of alcoholism and alcohol-related belligerence, including a couple of assaults on Mary. The Smiths are quite poor; their only income comes from John's sporadic work as a construction laborer. In addition to Amy, the Smiths have a 14-year-old retarded son.

Diane Zimmerman is a public defender who has been assigned to represent John Smith regarding the injury to Amy. In preparing to interview Mary Smith, Zimmerman devises as her main strategy a plan to persuade Mrs. Smith to ask the prosecution to join with the defendant in having John assigned to an alcohol rehabilitation program. To accomplish that goal, Zimmerman intends to convince Mrs. Smith that it is in the best interests of her family to have John out of prison, sober, and bringing home money on a regular basis to support her and the children.

What opinion do you have about the propriety of Ms. Zimmerman's tactic in her interview of Mrs. Smith?

═══════════════════════════════

1. The Issues and Their Regulatory Background

The foregoing problems, as well as the preceding sections in this chapter, present some very nasty ethical and personal issues for you as a lawyer. Do you, or should you, owe anything to the witness? Do you have any responsibility to consider the feelings or interests of the witness? Or does your duty run solely to the client? If you do have restrictions on your treatment of a witness, what are they? What *should* they be?

Throughout this chapter, we have referred to devices and techniques that enable a lawyer to secure a witness's information and support. They include several categories.

First, as illustrated in Problems 4 through 9 at the beginning of this section, lawyers could deceive witnesses into talking or taking positions against their will or against their interest. Is use of deception by a lawyer in dealing with witnesses justified? What if you have no other means of obtaining the evidence? What if deception affords a means for acquiring evidence that is far less expensive than the alternatives? What if the expense of alternatives makes securing the client's rights prohibitive? And how is "deception" defined? For example, what if the lawyer in the fair housing case in Problem 4 was fully honest about his name and position, and asked the apartment complex manager only whether he had any apartments available for rent—would that at all lessen the deception? (That is, the lawyer would at no time give the manager false information, but he would conceal from him the fact that he is not really interested in renting an apartment or that his real motive is entrapment. Is that concealment unethical?)

The second category comprises a variety of measures designed to persuade a witness to cooperate, to identify with the client's cause, or to give more favorable testimony. The most extreme of these are coercive tactics. For example, Problem 8 presented a situation in which the lawyer attempted to coerce a witness to talk by threatening a vulnerable relative. (See also page 215 and note 7.) In such a case, a question could be raised about whether at some point an attorney's conduct toward a witness becomes ruthless and unjustified by countervailing considerations, even though that conduct may not be technically illegal.

This chapter has also been laced with suggestions of more subtle forms of persuasion that you can use on witnesses. Pages 212-213 and 215-216 discuss prodding witnesses to talk by convincing them that it is in their best interests to do so. "Talk now and save yourself the trouble of testifying in a deposition or hearing later," you say. But what about arguments suggesting that the witness should not talk to the lawyer? Do you have a duty to identify those concerns for the witness? Page 204 lists persuading the witness about the rightfulness of the client's case as an important goal in interviewing and urges you to "posture" the facts to win the witness over to your client's side. On page 202, the text advises you to move as quickly as possible to be the first to interview potential witnesses. Being first would lock the witness into his story and would enhance your prospects for instilling sympathy in the witness for the client's case. Through measures suggested in the text, then, you seek to shape the witness's perception of the facts and eventually, perhaps, his testimony.

Finally, the text repeatedly counsels you to use empathy and sympathy—much as you would with a client—to gain the witness's favor and trust. For example, Jane Bowers, as shown on page 216, could have empathized with Ms. Henson, the cook, about her anger regarding the published article critical of the restaurant and sympathized with her on losing her job and her income. Bowers would have been motivated by the goals of representing her client and of presenting a case that Ms. Henson would no doubt find inconsistent with her own views and interests. Moreover, lawyers frequently engage these techniques fully aware that they may eventually want to use the information from the witness to impeach that same witness at trial.

The preceding chapters in this book are premised on the primacy of the individual, on his or her self-worth, on the lawyer's concession of control to the client, and on the lawyer's role as helper and adviser. Accordingly, the materials teach skills and techniques that are designed to implement those goals and a person-centered theory of interpersonal relations. Yet this chapter advocates use of those same techniques and skills to *manipulate* someone else to do something she might otherwise not want to do. Does that not contradict the theories underlying this book?[9]

---

9. However one might respond to that question, recognition of the issue is at least instructive with regards to the use of any set of techniques and skills; they are all subject to the motives, desires, and needs—conscious or unconscious—of the person using them. Thus, to be fully committed to the theories in this book, you must not only use the skills and techniques taught in these chapters, but must also engage in a constant self-scrutiny to prevent unwanted dominance over the client by subtle as well as overt means. See Chapter 12, which explores the need for and methods of self-scrutiny.

As noted at the beginning of this section, the various tactics for witness interviewing raise a number of issues relating directly to some general definition of your professional duties and responsibilities. You certainly owe a duty to your clients to represent their interests. But it is also clear that your conduct can affect the witness, who is typically only a bystander to the client's controversy. Do you owe anything to the witness, or does your responsibility run solely to the client? If you do have legal or moral restraints concerning your treatment of a witness, what are they?

The provisions regulating lawyers' professional behavior do not provide clear answers. Both DR 1-102(A)(4) of the Code of Professional Responsibility ("the Code") and Rule 8.4(c) of the Model Rules of Professional Conduct ("the Model Rules") hold that a lawyer may not "engage in conduct involving dishonesty, fraud, deceit or misrepresentation." In addition, the Code's DR 7-102(A)(5) and Model Rule 4.1 prescribe that, in representing a client, a lawyer should not knowingly make a false statement of material fact or law to a third person. And Model Rule 4.4 proscribes a lawyer representing a client from using "means that have no substantial purpose other than to embarrass, delay, or burden a third person, or us[ing] methods of obtaining evidence that violate the legal rights of such a person." Do these provisions preclude your use of deception in interviewing witnesses? It is clear that the above-cited provisions preclude use of deception in witness interviews when such deception also violates other, more specific, provisions. For example, use of subterfuge to gain an interview with witnesses known to be represented by an attorney in the matter under discussion violates DR 7-104(A) and Model Rule 4.2. Similarly, taking on the guise of a law enforcement official or other public official to coerce a witness's cooperation would, in all likelihood, be a criminal act and thus violate both DR 1-102(A)(3) and Model Rule 8.4(b). And creating circumstances in order to threaten a witness with criminal prosecution would violate DR 7-105 as well as the general prohibition on deception.

The language in DR 7-102(A)(5) and Model Rule 4.1 forbidding misrepresentations to third parties could arguably apply to lawyers' witness interviews. Those provisions, however, have generally been read as governing lawyers in their role as advocate or in advancing their clients' interests, as in negotiations, contract administration, lobbying, and litigation. Under that construction, the provisions would not cover witness interviews, at least when the witness is not in an adversarial relationship with the client.

Read literally, the general proscriptions on misrepresentation in DR 1-102 and Rule 8.4 proscribe any knowing deceptions in witness interviews—as in any other context. On the other hand, arguments have been made that the lawyer's duty to the client and to the system of justice to fully develop the facts qualifies the general language. The Code's edict to the lawyer (in Canon 7) to "represent a client zealously within the bounds of the law" could be said to authorize the use of subterfuges involving nonparty witnesses, at least when no other specific provision is violated. Professor (now Judge) Robert Keeton has concluded that the use of subterfuge in investigation "probably" does not constitute "deceit" or "misrepresentation" within the meaning of DR 1-102. According to Keeton's reasoning:

> The Code of Professional Responsibility does not deal specifically with the use of subterfuge in investigation. It is generally considered a permissible practice within reasonable limits, and it is often justified on the basis that it is a practical necessity in discovering falsification by the adverse party or his witnesses.   Doubtlessly, the spirit of the Code may be violated by some uses of subterfuge in interviewing [nonparty] witnesses, but the absence of an absolute prohibition leaves some area, not clearly defined, in which the use of subterfuge to interview persons other than the adverse party is proper.[10]

To be sure, few reported cases address the Code's application to witness interviewing. The dearth of cases may derive, in part, from the practical effects of DR 5-101 and 5-102 and Model Rule 3.7, which limit lawyers' ability to testify in cases in which they are an advocate. If lawyers cannot testify later at trial about a witness's falsehoods, or in the alternative must give up their representation to do so, then they are likely to either avoid entirely any tactic involving subterfuge or hire an investigator to do it. Lawyers may fear, too, the risk that the deception might backfire on the client when a jury learns about it. It is also possible that the absence of cases simply reflects acceptance of the practice as unobjectionable.

In any event, neither the Code nor the Model Rules regulate your efforts to persuade witnesses as to the justice of your client's cause or to shape the witnesses' perceptions of the facts. Nor does any provision restrain your use of empathy or sympathy with a witness.

Thus, as a practical matter, any meaningful restrictions on your conduct with witnesses must come from your personal code of morality. But if your personal code does limit your dealings with witnesses, might you then risk violating the Canon 7 duty to zealously represent your clients' interests?

2. Possible Resolutions

We offer this subsection with some trepidation. We fear its inclusion will block your own thinking about the professional issues raised in this chapter and thereby thwart one of our major purposes. We must confess, too, our fallibility; we offer merely our perceptions and they have no special ties to omniscience. Nevertheless, we persist here to provide a starting point for your analysis. We also feel morally compelled not to "cop out" on the tough questions. At any rate, we urge you read this subsection with a skeptical eye.

The search for answers to the questions raised above is primarily an analysis of appropriate means to a legitimate end. What means can you use, and what means should you reject, to effectively gather information

---

10. R. Keeton, *Trial Tactics and Methods* 326-327 (2d ed. 1973).

and represent your client's interests? We suggest these criteria control: You should zealously represent your clients, but in doing so should use means that evidence respect for the worth of each involved person; accordingly, you should deal with witnesses honestly and in a manner consistent with how you would want to be treated as a witness.

Proceeding from that basis, the deductions described in the following discussion can be reached. The discussion tracks the three categories identified in the preceding subsection of how to secure a witness's information and support.

a. Deception

At least two feasible analyses apply to the question of whether you, as a lawyer, should use deception in interviewing witnesses or in investigating a case. Under one approach, you balance: You should not deceive witnesses unless compelled to do so by a countervailing need. Within that general standard, however, lies a spectrum of possible rationales about what constitutes a "countervailing need." Some might argue that your duty to represent the client's interests justifies any tactic not prohibited by law or the Code. Because the bounds of the law do not reach most forms of deception in a lawyer's investigative and interviewing work, the lawyer would not be significantly inhibited in the use of deceptive tactics. This seems to be the message from Canon 7 and EC 7-3 of the ABA Code of Professional Responsibility.

"Countervailing need" could also be defined in terms of the importance of the client's rights or interests at stake. For example, the lawyer in Problem 7 uses deception in an effort to locate his client's children, who are being held by her ex-husband (their father) in violation of a custody order. Such a compelling set of facts could coax a lawyer to use any lawful means to advance his client's interests. The importance of the client's interests, though, is a tough standard to apply. Would the personal and societal interests in rooting out race discrimination justify the deception used by the lawyer Bellefleur in Problem 4? What about Wolfe Finance's interests in Problem 3 in retrieving its $6,000? What if Wolfe were chasing Kerouac for $600,000?

At the end of the "countervailing need" spectrum rests the argument that deception can be justified only by necessity. That is, if you cannot obtain the information by any means other than deception, then you may use such tactics. For example, Bellefleur might argue that, without a trap, he could never catch the apartment complex in the act of discrimination; therefore, setting the manager up was a morally justifiable act—much like the law condones the use of undercover operations in law enforcement. (Bellefleur could also contend that deception is less problematic when deployed against a tortfeasor than when used in an interview of a third party.)

But a "necessity" standard has a fudge-like consistency, too. How is "necessity" to be defined? In practical terms or in absolute terms? If in practical terms, the key question may be posed as whether "reasonable" alternatives are "readily" available. For example, in the follow-up questions to Problem 6, the Wolfe Finance Company facts are juggled so that the cost of the alternative to deception exceeds the amount owed on the outstanding loan. If the alternative is prohibitively expensive, grossly ineffective, unduly time-consuming, or otherwise unrealistic, then, in practical terms, there is no alternative. The deception would therefore be reasonably necessary and justified. At least, that is the argument.

If, however, "necessity" was used in absolute terms, the instances in which deception could be justified would be extremely rare. Indeed, the occasions in which you could not identify *some* means to obtain the information without deception—no matter the cost, the time, or relative effectiveness—may be so rare that an absolute necessity standard would be tantamount to an absolute prohibition.

That brings us to a second, and we think better, analysis of lawyer's deception: You categorically should not use deception in witness interviewing—including when clients' interests could not be otherwise satisfied. Such an approach avoids the slippery slope presented by the utilitarian balancing analyses and thus prevents the possibility that rationalization would make the exception the rule. Preventing that possibility, and ensuring honest dealings with witnesses, honors some very basic points about interpersonal relations. First, the categorical negative recognizes that your conduct toward witnesses can seriously affect the interests of these persons who typically are merely observers of—not participants in—the clients' conflicts. The intrusion from lawyers and litigants into witnesses' lives can cause disruption, inconvenience, embarrassment, loss of friends or even jobs, and so on along a lengthy list of various injuries.

Second, an absolute approach resolves the means-end problem embedded in the balancing approaches described above. Regardless of the criteria used to balance, the bottom line is always that in some instances the end of representing the client's interests justifies the use of a means ordinarily considered to be improper. That pushes you onto a very slippery moral slope.

Third, an absolute approach reflects a respect for the individual consistent with the theories about human worth and values espoused throughout these chapters. Witnesses, no less than clients, are individuals worthy of honest treatment. The categorical negative is a function of the Judeo-Christian and humanistic emphasis on the philosophy of the Golden Rule.

Finally, utilitarians themselves can offer two arguments for an absolute standard. First, witnesses over the long term will cooperate more with, and respond better to, a lawyer who has dealt honestly with them than one who has resorted to subterfuge. Second, whatever you do contributes to your reputation as a lawyer. Your use of deception therefore risks your developing a reputation of one who cannot be trusted. Conversely, if you are straight in your dealings with all individuals, you build a positive reputation that would encourage people to cooperate with you. Thus, the long-term benefits of straightforwardness outweigh any short-term gains paid by a deceptive tactic.

b. Persuasion

The discussion in Section B noted several kinds of persuasion you could use in dealing with witnesses. As a general rule, your efforts to persuade witnesses to cooperate or to sympathize with your clients are ethically proper. Everyone knows attorneys are advocates for their clients and must represent their interests. Thus, a witness who talks with you, knowing you are a lawyer representing a particular client, will be on notice about where you are coming from and what your goals are. Under such circumstances, your efforts at persuasion are appropriate and essential in the adversarial system.

There are limits, however, because the propriety of persuasion rests, in part, on the fact that the witnesses will be aware of your motives. That rationale vanishes if the witnesses do not know they are being interviewed by a lawyer. Thus, you should provide notice of who you are and whom you represent. You should also avoid using disingenuous or deceptive arguments and threats.[11]

Coercive tactics should be used with great care, but they can, at times, be justified. Use of subpoena power, for example, is a coercive tactic. Use of leverage on recalcitrant witnesses can be legitimate because witnesses generally have no moral or legal claim to keep nonprivileged, relevant information to themselves and from litigants and others. As with any tactic, however, you should retain regard for the individual with whom you are dealing.[12] Similarly, appeals to the witnesses' altruism, arguments convincing them about their best interests, or other arguments intended to induce cooperation are appropriate when done honestly and with due regard for the individual witness.

Finally, your efforts to shape witnesses' perceptions through use of measures suggested in this chapter do not necessarily breach ethical standards. As trial lawyers learn, the "facts" always have a certain amount of play in them. That persistent degree of looseness necessarily follows from the imperfection of human recollection and from personal, social, or political predispositions. Moreover, the vagueness in many legal standards means that the facts can be interpreted in more than one way. Manipulation of facts or law cannot be avoided in any disputed case; if both sides shared the same perception, there would be no dispute. Your role as an advocate is to shape and present the facts in a manner most advantageous to your client. Your efforts to interview witnesses first, to move them to

---

11. Model Rule 4.3 requires disclosure:

> In dealing on behalf of a client with a person who is not represented by counsel, a lawyer shall not state or imply that the lawyer is disinterested. When the lawyer knows or reasonably should know that the unrepresented person misunderstands the lawyer's role in the matter, the lawyer shall make reasonable efforts to correct the misunderstanding.

See also Code of Professional Responsibility DR 7-104(A)(2).

12. Certainly, any tactic you use should comport with Model Rule 4.4:

> In representing a client, a lawyer shall not use means that have no substantial purpose other than to embarrass, delay, or burden a third person, or use methods of obtaining evidence that violate the legal rights of such a person.

empathize with your client's case, and to "see" the facts as your client does are therefore legitimate functions of the lawyer-as-advocate. You do not breach an ethical standard so long as you believe in your client's cause and stay within the natural "play" inherent in the presentation and interpretation of facts.

c. Use of Person-Centered Techniques

Use of person-centered techniques to manipulate witnesses into cooperation seems, at first blush, to contradict the assumptions underlying the development of those techniques. They are used in client interviewing and counseling to most effectively gather the facts while sustaining the client's control of decision-making. The techniques are used to help instill client trust and confidence in the lawyer. Yet in interviewing witnesses, you engage those same skills to try to retain control yourself of the decision-making and to help your client—not the witness. Deeper analysis, however, suggests the techniques are not used inappropriately in witness interviewing—just differently.

The skills of probing, empathy, and so on, are all fundamental to all forms of professional fact-gathering and consultation. Research interviewers, pollsters, and salespersons, for example, may all put these skills to good and proper advantage. Lawyers conducting witness interviewers—just as researchers—are entitled to use those techniques that best encourage the interviewee to open up and provide information.

As we noted above, when you honestly interview a witness, your goal is on the table: You want to gather the facts to enable you to best represent your client. That is indisputably a legitimate goal. Indeed, if you did not pursue fact-gathering, you would breach a moral and professional duty. Because both your goals and motives are open and known to the witness, any "manipulation" that occurs is done with the tacit (or explicit) consent of the witness. After all, witnesses can refuse to talk to you, at least until served with a subpoena. At the same time, witnesses have no moral entitlement—barring privilege—to keep the facts to themselves.

The question thus focuses on whether there is something inappropriate about your means when you use the helping skills.

Use of helping skills in witness interviewing is perfectly consistent with the criteria we have set out to assess the propriety of the means used by lawyers to reach their interviewing ends. Empathic reflection, expressions of concern, and statements of sympathy certainly evince a respect for the individual witness. That you are not in a helping relationship with the witness does not necessarily mean your expressions of empathy or concern must lack genuineness. Nothing precludes you from being concerned about your interviewees as persons just because the extent of your relationship is limited. In fact, empathy and genuineness are difficult to separate. Certainly, the witnesses themselves, if given the choice, would prefer to be interviewed by someone who strives to understand what they are experiencing.

Your fact-gathering efforts are practical and moral necessities. You can neither represent your client nor discern the truth without them. Witness interviews, while not always pleasant for the witnesses, play an essential role in fact-gathering and are, in themselves, morally justified. But you have choices about how you go about the interviews, and those choices are subject to scrutiny. Choosing to use helping skills in interviewing witnesses allows you to complete the task in a fashion that is the least offensive, most understanding, and most preferred by witnesses.

3. Use of Investigators and Observers

In addition to those issues explored thus far in Section F, other practical and ethical concerns affect your fact-gathering strategies. This subsection focuses on those concerns that inform your judgment on whether and how to use support personnel for witness interviews.

As previously noted, a lawyer who has offered testimony as a trial witness cannot ordinarily continue to serve as an advocate in that proceeding. Thus, if you represent a client whose interests would be best served by your testimony about a solo interview you conducted of a now unavailable witness, you would probably have to relinquish your role as trial counsel.[13] More commonly, you might want to impeach a witness with statements made to you when you and the witness were alone. Assuming that you did not tape the conversation or get a signed statement (measures that could alleviate the problem) and further assuming that the witness does not admit to the prior inconsistent statement, your alternatives would be either to leave the witness unimpeached or to request the court's permission not only to testify on the prior conversations but also to remain as counsel. The court has the discretion to grant your request, but you can anticipate that it would ordinarily be denied.[14] If it is, then you and your client are left to choose between the value of your testimony and the value of your services.

To avoid these dilemmas, you have the obvious option of hiring an investigator (or a paralegal or some other assistant) to interview witnesses. Then you could call on the investigator to provide the needed testimony. If you are being paid by the hour, an investigator would also save money for your client, since investigators' rates run appreciably lower than lawyers'.

---

13. Model Rule 3.7(a) recognizes only the following exceptions to the rule against allowing a lawyer to be both advocate and witness in the same trial:

(1) The testimony relates to an uncontested issue;
(2) The testimony relates to the nature and value of legal services rendered in the case; or
(3) Disqualification of the lawyer would work substantial hardship on the client.

See also ABA Code of Professional Responsibility DR 5-101 and 5-102, EC 5-9.

14. See M. Graham, *Handbook of Federal Evidence* §606.3, at 406 (1981):

[T]he court has wide discretion to refuse a lawyer to testify in favor of his client. Discretion will often be exercised to prevent such testimony where other sources of evidence as to the fact of consequence are available or where the necessity for testimony by the lawyer could have been avoided.

The author adds in a footnote, "One situation that can usually be avoided is the offering of lawyer testimony as to the existence of an alleged inconsistent statement of a witness."

Alternatively, you could have a person accompany you to a witness interview. That person could then take notes and serve as a trial witness about the conversation should the need arise. Indeed, at least for criminal cases, American Bar Association standards advise you to customarily have a third person with you for witness interviews.[15] Moreover, the presence of a third person could help to protect you against unfounded charges of harassment or other misdeeds under Model Rule 4.4.

Problems can arise, however, with either alternative. Using an investigator means, of course, that you sacrifice control over the interviewing. Because you will not be there to ask the questions, the fact-gathering may not be what you want; leads might be missed and issues left unexplored, especially if the interviewer is not well versed in the relevant law. In addition, when you assign the job to an investigator, you can no longer be certain which interviewing strategies will be used. That could be troublesome because charges of ethical violations could be leveled against you if your agent does employ questionable tactics. These problems, however, can be alleviated if you carefully select, and then properly prepare and supervise, the investigator.

In fact, the Model Rules require you to supervise nonlawyers under your direction to ensure that their conduct is "compatible with the professional obligations of the lawyer."[16] Model Rule 5.3(c) holds a lawyer responsible for the actions of nonlawyer personnel if the lawyer ordered, ratified, or—knowing of the misconduct at a time when its consequences could be avoided or mitigated—failed to take reasonable remedial action.

Consider the illustration offered by Hazard and Hodes[17] in which lawyers in a law firm learn of a plan concocted by an investigator working for the firm. The investigator had been maintaining surveillance of a client's husband, hoping to catch him in an adulterous act. Having failed to do so, the investigator arranged to hire a woman to approach the husband and entice him into a liaison. Hazard and Hodes conclude that the lawyers would have violated the standard of Model Rule 4.4 had they themselves designed and executed the plan. Therefore, even though they had no initial or active involvement in the plot, the firm's partners and any of its lawyers with "direct supervisory authority" over the investigator violated Rule 5.3 if they knew of the scheme and failed to invoke reasonable preventive measures.[18]

Taking a third person to a witness interview with you also has its downside. First, it is more expensive; regardless of whether the person is

---

15. ABA Standards Relating to the Administration of Criminal Justice, Standard 4-4.3(d):

> Unless the lawyer for the accused is prepared to forgo impeachment of a witness by the lawyer's own testimony as to what the witness stated in an interview or to seek leave to withdraw from the case in order to present such impeaching testimony, the lawyer should avoid interviewing a prospective witness except in the presence of a third person.

16. Model Rule 5.3(a). See also ABA Model Code EC-3-6, DR 4-101-(D), and DR 7-107(J).
17. G. Hazard & W. Hodes, 1 *The Law of Lawyering: A Handbook on the Model Rules of Professional Conduct* 466-467 (1989 Supp.).
18. Id. at 467.

engaged hourly or is on your payroll, there are going to be added costs involved. Second, the presence of another person can increase the intimidation level and possibly discourage a witness from opening up to you. Third, if you are interviewing an employee of a corporate or other organizational client, the third person's presence could jeopardize the privilege of confidentiality that your conversation might otherwise enjoy.[19] To prevent loss of the privilege, use as the observer someone who is your agent—such as secretary, clerk, or paralegal—and take steps to ensure that you properly protect the client information handled by your nonlawyer personnel.[20]

In sum, you can use investigators and support staff to good advantage in your fact-gathering, but you must supervise and prepare them with care and vigilance.

---

19. Application of the attorney-client privilege to communications between an attorney and employees of a corporate client is not easily summarized. Federal law, as established by *Upjohn Co. v. United States*, 449 U.S. 383 (1981), extends the privilege to at least those communications between corporate employees and the corporation's lawyer in which the following conditions are met: (1) the lawyer conversed with the employee in the lawyer's capacity as counsel to the client; (2) the lawyer acted at the direction of corporate superiors who were seeking legal advice from counsel; (3) the communications concerned matters within the scope of the employee's corporate duties; and (4) the employee knew the interview was for the purpose of allowing the corporation to obtain legal advice. The *Upjohn* Court, however, strictly limited its decision to the facts before it and declined to set forth rules for general application. Rather, the scope of the privilege is to be determined on a case-by-case basis. State courts have not uniformly followed *Upjohn*, but have pursued various alternative approaches to defining the scope of the attorney/corporate client privilege. See generally Freedman, Corporate Attorney-Client Privilege Since *Upjohn*, 9 U. Dayton L. Rev. 425 (1984); Waldman, Beyond *Upjohn*: The Attorney-Client Privilege in the Corporate Context, 28 Wm. & M. L. Rev. 473 (1987).

20. See Restatement (Third) of the Law Governing Lawyers §120 (Tent. Draft No. 2, 1989).

PART III COUNSELING

Planning and Structuring the Counseling Session

A. INTRODUCTION

Counseling is a highly complex and challenging process. You must continue to engage all of the interviewing skills while adding more advanced skills. In interviewing, you gather facts and build rapport; in counseling, you gather facts, build rapport, and help the client to reach decisions and select action steps. To attain those additional goals in counseling, you must command a range of lawyering skills—analytical, verbal, and interpersonal. To complicate the process, counseling must often be done in emotionally charged circumstances, thus requiring you to sort through your own and the client's emotional needs while maintaining your objectivity. Except in simple cases, effective legal counseling requires a solid lawyer-client relationship. Thus, the nature of that relationship and the respective roles of its participants are important concerns in the following materials.

The theory of counseling set forth continues with and builds on the partnership model of the lawyer-client relationship established above. The

features of that model are even more important in counseling than in interviewing. You and your client work together to identify priorities, alternatives, consequences, and action steps. You contribute an array of helping
skills, expertise (in the law), experience (legal and nonlegal), and objectivity (emotional detachment, but not emotional insensitivity). Your helping role means more than just laying the case and its alternatives before the
clients; it means clarifying issues and forcing the clients to undertake introspection and to articulate their feelings and priorities. These are no mean
tasks, and the first lesson toward becoming an effective counselor may well
be an appreciation of their difficulty.

The client's input is not only to continue providing information, but
also to make the ultimate decisions. The client decides. That is a simple
enough proposition, and has even been codified by the Bar.[1] In practice,
though, adhering to the principle is quite difficult; it requires you to exercise extraordinary self-awareness and self-discipline.

As we have previously explained (see Chapters 1 and 2), the lawyer's counseling function differs from that done by counselors in the fields
of psychology and psychotherapy. Unlike the specialists in those areas,
you are not primarily concerned with personality growth and change or
with "curing" emotional disorders. Rather, you generally counsel clients
on what alternatives are available to achieve some identified goals. The
skills needed to help clients identify the goals and choose among the alternatives overlap significantly with counseling skills in other fields, but the
fit is not a perfect one. Your special responsibilities (to the law, to society,
and to self) and limitations (in training and in knowledge) dictate a specialized counseling role.

To teach the skills and substance of counseling, this and the following
chapters first offer an essentially chronological consideration of what you
should think about and do in counseling a client. Thus, this chapter discusses how to prepare for and structure a counseling session, and Chapter
11 describes the intrasession techniques and skills you need to help the
client make the best decision possible. The remaining two chapters on
counseling shift the focus to the conflicts and personal tensions you will
confront as a lawyer-counselor. Chapter 12 explores personality needs
commonly experienced by lawyers and the ways in which those needs can
disrupt the principle of client autonomy. Chapter 13 concludes Part III by
returning to questions raised in Chapter 1 regarding the moral responsibility of lawyers in their partnerships with clients.

————————————

You have completed your interview of two women who operate an increasingly lucrative crafts business. They want to determine the form of
business organization best suited to maximize their profits while protecting them from personal liability and undue tax burdens. They are considering a formal partnership, a joint venture, and a corporation. You have

————————————

1. ABA Code of Professional Responsibility EC 7-7, 7-8, 7-11, 7-12. See Chapter 12,
below.

scheduled an appointment for next week to counsel the clients. What do you do now?

You will find the answer in this chapter's discussion of the essential steps to counseling any client. Section B describes the step-by-step preparation necessary for effective counseling. You will realize that you have much to do between the interview and the counseling session, and that the latter's success will largely depend on the intervening work. Section C then discusses development of a language of prediction to aid the client's deliberations. Basically, the chapter offers the nuts and bolts of counseling; it builds the basic framework to support the more advanced techniques of Chapter 11 and to address the more sophisticated issues and problems of Chapters 12 and 13.

B. PREPARATION FOR A COUNSELING SESSION

Preparation for counseling is essential. Without adequate preparation, you cannot effectively develop the full range of alternatives open to the client or effectively use your helping skills during the counseling session.

The following is a step-by-step model you can use to plan a counseling session.

Step 1. Research the law and investigate the facts.   In the litigation context, for example, the research should be done before the issue of whether to file the lawsuit is decided, not on the eve of drafting the pleadings or going to trial. Factual digging should also be completed as much as possible *before* decisions are made. Obviously, when your clients choose among alternatives, they should have the most complete information feasible. After learning the law and facts, you must plan how to explain the findings to the client.

Step 2. Clarify your goals for the counseling session.   What needs to be accomplished? What decisions need to be made? Detailed preparation can proceed only after you have articulated your goals.

Step 3. Scan your research, investigation, and experience to identify alternatives for the client.   Consider both legal and nonlegal avenues for resolving problems.

Sometimes your clients may have already identified alternatives before consulting you. For example, a businessperson may say to you, "I want to contract with the XYZ Corporation for exclusive distribution rights to our brass widgets. Can I force XYZ to also take our plastic widgets?" The alternatives identified by the client are to contract or not to contract. Yet, in this circumstance, you should consider what other alternatives you can suggest to the client. The tying arrangement proposed by the client could risk violating antitrust laws, but there may be variations available that would accomplish some or most of the client's purposes without risking liability or offending basic antitrust policies. You must explore those possibilities.

Step 4. Note the positive and negative consequences of each alternative to ensure that the client fully considers the total impact of his or her decision. Your explanation should include legal and nonlegal consequences. Moreover, you should be sensitive to potential consequences that can be fully described only after consultation with the client (see Step 5) or after additional investigation. Finally, your preparation on alternatives should include calculations about the probabilities of success accorded by each action step. (See Section C, below, on developing a language of prediction.)

Step 5. Plan for in-session probing to accomplish three interrelated objectives. During the consultation, (a) you clarify the client's priorities, (b) ascertain the client's reactions to the possible consequences of the identified alternatives, and (c) cure informational gaps and ambiguities. Each of those in-session tasks requires forethought about the specific topics to be probed, the probes to be used, and the counseling techniques that will be helpful. (See also Step 7.)

Step 6. Plan the format for the counseling session. That is, you must plan the order in which you want to treat the above-identified subjects—the alternatives, the consequences, and the three probing areas. The order you select will vary with the particular circumstances of the case. Several considerations are worth highlighting.

You may, for example, decide to lead with a description of your research findings. By doing so, you ease the client's curiosity at the outset (thus reducing distractions hindering the client's concentration) while clarifying the issues for the client (thus encouraging relevant discussion and additional client recall of important information). There is, however, a risk to beginning with the legal discussion. On occasion, the client may adjust his or her facts to fit the law. The famous novel and movie *Anatomy of a Murder* offers an example. Paul Biegler, the lawyer, has researched the law and tells Lieutenant Manion, the client and a murder defendant, that there are several possible defenses to murder. Biegler then describes them one by one and explains that each is wholly inapplicable—until he reaches the insanity defense. Next, he states which facts establish "temporary" insanity. Not surprisingly, Manion responds with facts conveniently sustaining the elements of that defense.[2] Subsequently, the plot reveals what the reader/viewer suspected from the beginning—that the story supporting the defense was fabricated. Biegler's conduct was extreme and probably violated the Code of Professional Responsibility.[3] Nevertheless, the scene illustrates the risks of detailing law before completion of fact-gathering. Those risks require you to consider—in advance of counseling—the character of the client, the likelihood that the client would distort the facts, the extent to which the facts are already known, and the nature of the subject matter. In addition, you should avoid suggestive delivery or description during the counseling session.

In planning format, you also consider when and how the client's priori-

---

2. R. Traver, *Anatomy of a Murder* 51-52 (1958).
3. See EC 7-26 and DR 7-102(A)(4), (6), and (7).

ties should be identified and when and how the alternatives should be discussed. The resolution of those questions depends primarily on whether the client's feelings and priorities should be probed before, during, or after discussing alternatives. Though seemingly innocuous, the choice can substantially influence the effectiveness of the counseling session.

When you begin by probing the client's priorities and feelings, you risk inhibiting communications. Without the background on alternatives, your client may not perceive the relevance of the discussion and may feel frustrated discussing conflicts in the abstract. Moreover, in many cases, the client cannot meaningfully assess the priorities without putting them in a specific context or comparing them to other priorities. For example, most clients could cite saving or obtaining money as a priority, but that priority usually acquires meaning only when it is discussed in terms of how much some other priority is "worth" in dollars to the client.[4]

To avoid the above problems, you can probe for priorities and additional facts as each of the alternatives is discussed. If one alternative is litigation, you can take time immediately after presenting the option to discuss (among other things) the client's ability to afford litigation and his feelings about getting involved in formal legal proceedings, about making public accusations against the potential defendants, and about subjecting himself to discovery and cross-examination.

On the other hand, probing feelings and priorities before you have summarized the alternatives and consequences may encourage a more thoughtful self-examination by the client. That sequencing of the discussion is more open-ended and puts greater pressure on the client to articulate feelings and values. Probing priorities first also avoids the possibility that your client will jump on one of the alternatives without adequate deliberation and then subconsciously edit responses to probes to justify the jump. In addition, it is the *impact* on the priorities that changes from one alternative to the next, not the priorities. That is, each alternative affects the same set of priorities. Therefore, running through the priorities with each alternative can get redundant.

By ascertaining feelings and priorities first, you essentially use the inverse funnel sequence described in Chapter 7, Section G (page 173). The client's rendering of his or her primary concerns will be more in the abstract, but it will also be untainted by any prejudgments. Thus, you can lead into discussion with such questions as, "How do you feel about suing your employer (or your union)?" or "How important to you is establishing the legal principle in this case?" Those questions force clients to articulate their feelings and determine how their priorities stack up when the one "perfect solution" is unavailable.

The selection of the appropriate agenda for discussing alternatives, consequences, priorities, and facts thus depends on several variables.

---

4. To be sure, though, money is not always a priority nor is it always something that cannot be discussed separately. Some clients may be so determined to establish a legal principle that they are willing to spend whatever it takes. Other clients may be so poor that they have none to lose or so wealthy that money is no object. Then, too, the client may have as a priority a specific amount of money, but beyond that point money is irrelevant. In that latter case, the client could discuss the money priority separately from the other alternatives.

First, you have to decide whether it is more important in a particular consultation to avoid the risk that the client will become impatient from the delay in discussing alternatives or the risk that the client will make a premature selection. Second, you should consider your client's facility to discuss issues in the abstract. Such discussion can be more difficult and generally places greater demands on the client's abilities to analyze and articulate. Third, look at the kinds of issues and the way they relate to the alternatives. You may see a particular need to have structure and deal with issues in concrete form, which would suggest that you summarize alternatives first. Or you might find the issues recur in similar fashion through each alternative. In that case, efficiency would be better served by probing priorities first. Finally, you can factor in your personal concerns. For example, most people find working in the abstract to be more difficult. Thus, inexperienced counselors, especially, might be more comfortable organizing the counseling session around a step-by-step presentation of the alternatives. On the other hand, you may be one who takes naturally to free-form discussion. If so, then that could be decisive in deciding to explore priorities first.

Step 7. Think through what helping techniques might be appropriate during the counseling session.   Chapter 11 fully describes those techniques, thus preempting discussion of them here. Present purposes are satisfied by noting that selection of the appropriate techniques requires you to analyze the conflicts and emotions the case holds for your client. The techniques then provide the means to help your client deal with those conflicts and emotions. For example, empathy is a helping technique. As noted in Chapter 5, forethought by the attorney can help to identify what will likely be accurate empathic reflections during an interview or counseling session. As we will see in Chapter 11, such forethought is especially critical in use of the more advanced techniques in counseling. Effective legal counselors clarify—they explain, restate facts, identify issues, juxtapose conflicts, and reflect expressed and implied feelings. These clarifying functions demand considered, deep analysis. You must think out in advance when and how to empathize, to disclose analogous experiences of your own, or to confront the client.

Step 8. Prepare visual aids for the client.   They can range from a written agenda to a chart or a blackboard. (The latter allows you to write as you go, thus preventing the client from reading ahead. But unless you prepare a written outline as well, use of a blackboard also means the client does not have a permanent reference.) Such materials and displays are every bit as clarifying to a client in a counseling session as they are to students in a class or to a jury during a trial. (They are like the anatomical model that a doctor would use to explain a surgery.) The aids should organize the substance for the client to allow quick and easy conceptualization of the consultation's issues and goals. That assistance is particularly crucial when the issues are complex and there is much ground to cover.

These preparation steps will assume more meaning with some illustration. Two hypothetical problems follow. In the first one, we offer a sample preparation. In the second, the factual background is provided, but we leave to you the identification of alternatives, consequences, and issues. (Although both of the problems are set in the context of potential litigation, the preparation will not vary in form when the counseling has a nonlitigation setting, as with the drafting of a trust or a contract.)

≡ PROBLEM 1 ≡

Interview and Fact-Gathering

The client is Anthony Selin. Mr. Selin owns a home in a quiet but modest residential section of Snydertown. His long-time close friend and neighbor, Ralph Kratzer, retired a year ago from his job at a nearby auto plant. Shortly thereafter, Ralph's wife died, and he quickly grew restless with his uneventful, solitary routine. To combat his boredom, Kratzer remodeled his ranch-style home and converted the first floor of his house into a bar—"Ralph's Place," naturally—and moved his living quarters downstairs to his basement. His front yard was graveled into a parking lot. Ralph did inform his neighbors what he was doing, but no one in the neighborhood wanted to complain and upset him.

The bar opened six months ago and the neighborhood has never been the same. Ralph hires a local rock group three nights a week and they play raucous music until 2:00 A.M. Loud, drunken shouts emanate from the parking lot even past that time. Beer cans have collected on and around Ralph's property, and the parking lot is inadequate to handle the number of customers. Local residents have frequently lost their on-street parking and some have even complained that their driveways have been used or blocked. There have also been complaints that customers have been relieving themselves of their overconsumption of liquids at assorted outside locations in full public view. Mr. Selin and his neighbors have thus lost sleep, parking, and the general enjoyment of their property. The community's parents are also concerned about the impact that the bar and its associated revelries may have on the moral development of the children.

Although the neighborhood is largely residential, there is a gas station and a small quick-service grocery store within two blocks of the bar. A commercial district featuring a variety of retail stores and banks is about one mile away.

Mr. Selin wants to know if there is anything that can be done about the bar.

Preparation for Counseling

Step 1. Research into the state code reveals no applicable statute. There are, however, many cases on nuisance law. The precedents evince a balancing approach that weighs the character of the community; the length of time that the offending establishment has been in operation; the notice to neighbors (including whether the establishment predated or postdated the residential development); the degree of intrusion into residential life; the effects on the health, safety, and morals of the community; and the availability of less restrictive alternatives. Upon balancing those factors, the courts have recognized a range of appropriate results, including complete and permanent injunctions, compromise or partial injunctions limiting the operations of the establishment, damages (either in addition to or instead of injunctive relief), and no relief. From the facts of the precedents, the lawyer can deduce that Mr. Selin would be entitled to at least a partial injunction and perhaps even a total injunction and damages.

Research into Snydertown's municipal code discloses the bar is in compliance with the rather loosely drawn zoning ordinances. Although it is possible to petition the Zoning Board to change the laws and zone out the bar, such a change could raise serious constitutional questions about its effects on preexisting uses.

Finally, research into the state's liquor laws instructs that a liquor licensee must, to retain his license, maintain his establishment in a clean, unobtrusive manner. Neighbors of liquor establishments have been accorded standing to challenge license renewals (which come up every two years) for failure to meet that duty. In practice, though, the Liquor Board has been reluctant to revoke licenses and put operators out of business. Typically, the Board had imposed small fines and, occasionally, a short probationary period. A bar can generally clean up its act for the two or three months of the probation and then continue business as usual.

Step 2. With research and investigation sufficiently completed, the lawyer is ready to counsel the client. The session's goals will be to fully inform the client of his rights and to identify what, if any, action steps he wants to take. If the latter goal cannot be reached during this particular consultation, then the client should at least leave with the relevant and competing considerations clearly articulated; he should have isolated precisely those issues that he must then contemplate. Finally, unless the client decides to drop the matter entirely, some timetable should be developed as a target for either implementing specific action steps or for making some decision on action steps.

Step 3. In scanning the law and facts, the following alternatives can be identified:

1. file a civil action for injunctive relief and/or damages
2. press Zoning Board to change zoning laws
3. challenge liquor license renewal

These are the potential legal remedies, but that does not end the matter. As a lawyer, you should not be so funneled in your thinking. Experience and common sense also suggest the following:

4. negotiate with Kratzer toward some compromise
5. organize the community and put pressure on Kratzer and on local officials

6. buy out Kratzer
7. move
8. do nothing

Selection of one alternative does not necessarily exclude pursuit of another; in fact, Selin could decide to pursue all of the alternatives 1 through 7 until one or more of them satisfy him.

Step 4.   The consequences of the various alternatives are manifold. In identifying them, the lawyer must again draw on professional expertise (to predict probabilities of success), experience, and common sense. The following chart outlines the major consequences for Mr. Selin:

Alternative	Consequences for Client
1. File Civil Action	Strain on relationship with Kratzer Time and effort required Money to pay for fees and expenses Exposure to deposition and trial examination Need to take public stance and be "up front" Excellent (90%) chance for some success Good (60%) chance for some damages to offset costs
2. Press Zoning Board	Time (though not clearly as great as litigation) Money for attorney's fees (less than litigation) Strain on relationship with Kratzer Fair (50%) possibility of effecting ordinance change Possibility of extended litigation on legitimacy of applying ordinance to Kratzer (with attendant delays and costs)
3. Challenge Liquor License	Time (less than litigation) Money for attorney's fees and expenses (less than litigation) Strain on relationship with Kratzer Must wait at least one year for any relief Poor (33%) probability for meaningful relief
4. Negotiate with Kratzer	Time (less than litigation) Money for attorney's fees (less than litigation) Good probability of preserving friendship with Kratzer Probability of meaningful success (depends in part on client's judgment about Kratzer's willingness to cooperate) Total relief unlikely The negotiated agreement could adversely affect ability to seek total relief from court at a later date
5. Organize Community	Time (probably greater than in other alternatives) Money (minimal expenses required; much less than litigation) Strain on relationship with Kratzer Poor to fair (20%-50%) probability of success (depends, in part, on client's judgments about community's reaction and response of Kratzer) Need to take leadership role and be "out in front"
6. Buy Out Kratzer	Money (need large amount up front, though partially recoverable later)

Money (need to make payments while in possession)

Possibility of taking a loss on resale (because purchase price would have to be enough to persuade Kratzer to sell, yet resale of a house converted into a bar would not bring top dollar)

Imposition of restrictive covenants on resale to prevent a recurrence

Time in buying and reselling (but less than litigation)

Preserves relationship with Kratzer—but Kratzer moves away

Total relief (if Kratzer will agree)

Probability of success (depends on client's judgment of Kratzer agreeing to sell)

7. Move

Time (looking for new home)

Money (costs of moving; likely loss on sale of house located next to noisy bar; down payment on new house; higher interest rate—possibility reduced by benefits of buying nicer home and by potential tax advantages)

Hassle of moving

Preserves relationship with Kratzer

Effects on family

Effects of leaving neighborhood

8. Do Nothing

No time commitment

No expenses or fees

Money—loss of property value

Loss of enjoyment of home (noise; nighttime disturbances; litter; parking)

Aggravation

Effects on family

Adverse effect on probability of success in civil action if the client sues later

Preserves relationship with Kratzer

Further thinking may render additional potential consequences, but this chart should provide some idea of the process of identifying consequences. That process requires evaluation of probabilities of legal steps, considerations personal to the client, and incidental (though not necessarily insignificant) effects.

The lawyer must be prepared to project for the client both probabilities of success and the costs of his identified alternatives. These also require the lawyer to make use of expertise and experience. In this case, the consequences listed on the table include references to probabilities. The costs of litigation and administrative remedies can be projected by predicting the amount of investigation, discovery, and attorney's hours that will be needed to pursue each action step. (In addition, the attorney must judge whether a contingency fee arrangement is practical.) The costs to the client of either buying out or moving can be ascertained by consultation with a local realtor. It may well be, for example, that the client could most cheaply shut down the bar by buying out Kratzer and then reselling the property with restrictive covenants. If so, the client should be informed of that before he makes his decision.

Step 5. The lawyer needs an update on the bar's operations and their effects and on any other relevant developments in the neighborhood. The analysis of alternatives and consequences also indicated several nonlegal subjects to be developed. Those include the client's attitudes and priorities. Continuing with the chart begun on pages 243-244, the probing subjects could be identified, as listed in the expanded chart on pages 246-248.

The list of probing subjects reveals several pervasive and determinative issues for discussion in the counseling session. These must be clarified for the client's consideration and disposition. The issues can be synthesized as follows:

- How much is the client willing to spend to shut down or control the bar? And how much can he afford?
- How important to the client is his friendship with Kratzer?
- How acceptable would a more controlled operation of the bar be to the client?

These last two issues can be further reduced to what may well be the central conflict in the case:

- Is shutting down the bar, or substantially controlling its operation, important enough to the client to risk losing his friendship with Kratzer?

Step 6. Planning the format for the Selin counseling session should not be difficult once the foregoing analysis has been completed. An appropriate place to begin is with a fact-gathering update on the bar and its patrons. After that, the relative placement of presenting alternatives and of probing priorities must be set. Here, the substantial number of alternatives (eight) and the overlapping issues counsel against a thorough review and probing of the alternatives one at a time. That would be inefficient and somewhat confusing, as the discussion would continually rehash the same ground and would do so without adequately confronting the competing priorities and dilemmas that the client faces (maintaining friendship vs. maintaining enjoyment of home vs. expending large sums of money). Thus, the format choice reduces to (1) establishing an overview of alternatives first and then discerning priorities or (2) discerning priorities and then applying them to the alternatives. In this case, the client may find it particularly difficult to articulate and rank in order his priorities in the abstract. Thus, the first choice above—reviewing alternatives and consequences and then probing—seems the more appropriate. The probing should focus the client's attention on the key issues stated at the end of Step 5. Those general issues could then be supplemented by probing the more specific subjects identified on the above chart for each alternative action step.

The session's planning must also include consideration of the relationships between different priorities and the action steps. If, for example, the client expresses that he wants the bar out of the neighborhood at all costs— in terms of money and of the friendship with Kratzer—then "Do Nothing"

Alternative	Consequences for Client	Probing Subjects
1. File Civil Action	Strain on relationship with Kratzer Time and effort required Money to pay for fees and expenses Exposure to deposition and trial examination Need to take public stance and be "up front" Excellent (90%) chance for some success Good (60%) chance for some damages to offset costs	How important to the client is his friendship with Kratzer? How does the client feel about litigation? about being out front as a plaintiff? about being deposed and cross-examined? How much time and money will the client commit to seeking relief? Will the client's neighbors join in a court action—both to defray costs and to bolster the case? How important are damages? If partial relief is granted, what conditions would the client want imposed?
2. Press Zoning Board	Time (though not nearly as great as litigation) Money for attorney's fees (less than litigation) Strain on relationship with Kratzer Fair (50%) possibility of effecting ordinance change Possibility of extended litigation on legitimacy of applying ordinance to Kratzer (with attendant delays and costs)	How important are the time and money factors? Does the client know the Zoning Board members? What are his impressions of the members? Are any of the members friends of the client or of Kratzer? How does the client feel about appearing personally before the Board? How does the client feel about the possibility of litigation over the constitutional questions? How important to the client is his friendship with Kratzer?
3. Challenge Liquor License	Time (less than litigation) Money for attorney's fees and expenses (less than litigation) Strain on relationship with Kratzer Must wait at least one year for any relief Poor (33%) probability for meaningful relief	How does the client feel about appearing before the Liquor Board? How important are time and money considerations? What does the client know about the Liquor Board? How does the client feel about waiting one year for relief from the Liquor Board—especially given the lower probability of success?

4. Negotiate with Kratzer	Time (less than litigation) Money for attorney's fees (less than litigation) Good probability of preserving friendship with Kratzer Probability of meaningful success (depends in part on client's judgment about Kratzer's willingness to cooperate) Total relief unlikely The negotiated agreement could adversely affect ability to seek total relief from court at a later date	How receptive is Kratzer likely to be? Would Kratzer respond better to the lawyer or to Selin? How important is it to the client to get complete relief? How does the client feel about having the bar continue to operate under more controlled conditions? What sort of conditions would the client want imposed?
5. Organize Community	Time (probably greater than in other alternatives) Money (minimal expenses required; much less than litigation) Strain on relationship with Kratzer Poor to fair (20-50%) probability of success (depends, in part, on client's judgments about community's reaction and response of Kratzer) Need to take leadership role and be "out in front"	How does the client feel about being out front as a leader? Is there a neighbor who might accept the leadership role (if the client does not want it)? How responsive will the community be to such efforts? How is Kratzer likely to react to such pressures?
6. Buy Out Kratzer	Money (need large amount up front, though partially recoverable later) Money (need to make payments while in possession) Possibility of taking a loss on resale (because purchase price would have to be enough to persuade Kratzer to sell, yet resale of a house converted into a bar would not bring top dollar) Imposition of restrictive covenants on resale to prevent a recurrence Time in buying and reselling (but less than litigation)	Does the client have the money or can he get the credit? Will any of the client's neighbors (Kratzer excluded, of course) join with the client in making the purchase? Can the client afford to take the possible loss when reselling the Kratzer property? How receptive is Kratzer likely to be to such an offer? How important to the client is his friendship with Kratzer?—Does it matter to the client that Kratzer would move?

Alternative	Consequences for Client	Probing Subjects
7. Move	Preserves relationship with Kratzer—but Kratzer moves away Total relief (if Kratzer will agree) Probability of success (depends on client's judgment of Kratzer agreeing to sell) Time (looking for new home) Money (costs of moving; likely loss on sale of house located next to noisy bar; down payment on new house; higher interest rate—possibility reduced by benefits of buying nicer home and by potential tax advantages) Hassle of moving Preserves relationship with Kratzer Effects on family Effects of leaving neighborhood	How important is the total relief offered by this alternative? What are the client's feelings about the neighborhood? How would he feel if he had to leave the neighborhood? How would his family feel? Can the client afford to sell at a deflated value (because of the bar next door)? Can he afford to buy another house at this time?
8. Do Nothing	No time commitment No expenses or fees Money—loss of property value Loss of enjoyment of home (noise; nighttime disturbances; litter; parking) Aggravation Effects on family Adverse effect on probability of success in civil action if the client sues later Preserves relationship with Kratzer	How important to the client is his friendship with Kratzer? How disturbing is the bar's operation to the client's enjoyment of his home? How would the client's family feel about the bar's continued operation? Will other neighbors be likely to pick up the responsibility for fighting the bar?

can be ruled out and the lawyer can proceed to implement each action step that could lead to complete relief (i.e., file a lawsuit, seek zoning change, seek liquor license revocation, organize the community, and try to buy out Kratzer). If the client wants to be rid of the bar, but is concerned about costs, then the client would be wise to rule out at least those alternatives with low probabilities of success (Zoning and Liquor Boards). If the client does not have the money to spend, is squeamish about litigation, or highly values the Kratzer friendship, then the alternatives of negotiating with Kratzer and doing nothing surface as Selin's most likely choices. (That would, of course, leave open the possibility of taking other action steps at a later date, if conditions deteriorate even more.)

Step 7. To meet his responsibilities, the attorney must clarify issues and help the client to isolate his priorities and to match them with the appropriate action steps. Adequate preparation for accomplishing those goals requires thoughtful consideration of the various helping techniques, such as primary and advanced empathy, confrontation, genuineness, or self-disclosure. Although significant exploration of these techniques must be postponed until Chapter 11's complete discussion, we can note now that Selin's lawyer should analyze the client and his case to identify his expressed feelings, his implied or suppressed feelings and motives, any inconsistencies, and any conflicts. For example, Selin's prior talks with his lawyer may have indicated Selin's reluctance to take a leadership role. In planning for the counseling session, the lawyer can prepare a timely expression of advanced empathy about Selin's misgivings. Perhaps the lawyer's experience includes an instance in which he had to choose between satisfying his own or his family's best interests and preserving a friendship. A timely disclosure of how the lawyer approached the problem could help Mr. Selin resolve his dilemma. A case of this complexity would present plenty of opportunities for such helping techniques. The point is that the lawyer should, as much as possible, prepare both the substance and form of his helping remarks.

Step 8. The attorney-client consultation in the Selin case would be substantially aided by a chart, similar to that shown at pages 243-244, which details the available alternatives and their consequences. The chart provides the client with a means for following and understanding the lawyer's overview and with a sense of structure. The chart, though, should not include the subjects for probing; such detail could distract and confuse.

≡ PROBLEM 2 ≡
The College Newspaper Editor

Your client is Josh Reade, a senior at State University and editor-in-chief of the school's newspaper, "The Weekly Crier." He is a conscientious, self-motivated youth who has been forced pretty much to make his own way through college. During Josh's last year of high school, his father was killed when his tractor-trailer rig jackknifed on a wet road into a head-on collision. Reade's mother has since experienced serious emotional problems while trying to cope with the tragedy. Despite these personal trials, Reade has done well at school. He has regularly qualified for the Dean's List, been selected to the School of Journalism's honorary society, and held a series of positions with progressively increasing responsibilities on the Crier staff. At the end of the last academic year, the staff chose him to serve as editor-in-chief.

Josh's present problems stem from a two-part article prepared by members of the Crier's staff about dating among the school's most "desirable" students. The reporters interviewed friends and former dates of selected students and gathered generally available information regarding background and campus activities. The article then described and rated the quality of an evening with each of these "Big Persons on Campus," using the criteria of wit, charm, looks, thoughtfulness, sincerity, humility, and sexual performance. Some of the descriptions were rather personal and explicit. (For example, the story included "how far" the students would try to go on the first date and how well they did what they did.) The article did not give the subjects' names, but most of them could be identified by the summaries of their activities and campus status. The reporters wrote the article, they said, to see if there were good reasons why these individuals were the most desired on campus, if expectations met reality, and if "life at the top" was any better than what most of the student body experienced. The article was seen as part of an ongoing series by the Crier dealing with students' social lives, sex lives, and status on campus.

Publication of the first installment (it dealt with the male elite) provoked considerable reaction. The university's president, William Hoover, was furious. He immediately called a press conference and denounced the article as an offense to all members of the community, an embarrassment to the university, and an inexcusable invasion of the privacy of the student subjects. He also blasted Reade as irresponsible, incompetent, and unfit to manage any newspaper. (The president and Reade had clashed previously; a number of articles with Josh's byline during the preceding year had described problems at the university, and several of his recent editorials had been critical of administration policies.) Hoover then ordered Reade to cancel the rest of the article (that portion dealing with the female elite) and threatened to remove him as editor-in-chief and as a Crier staff member if he refused. Hoover stated that the administration had a responsibility to prevent the use of state funds and student fees to propagate such scandalous material. The school therefore needed a person as editor-in-chief who could be counted on to uphold decency. Hoover also informed Reade that, if he were removed as editor, he would lose the remainder of the tuition waiver he was receiving for his work as editor-in-chief.

Reade did not personally review the article in dispute prior to its partial publication, although he did approve the concept of the article. When it was submitted, Reade was out of town attending a statewide conference of college newspaper editors. He thinks the reporters should have done more to protect the students' privacy, but otherwise finds the article unobjectionable yet provocative and informative.

The university has no rules or standards governing administration of the Crier or the president's ability to discipline or remove any Crier staff member. The paper has a faculty adviser, but she has never exerted any control over the paper's content other than to advise students who come to her for help. She has not taken a position regarding President Hoover's actions or allegations.

Reade has come to see you to determine what his alternatives are before he has to decide whether to publish the second installment, which is currently due to go to press in three days. He is concerned about the Crier's integrity and future; he believes the president's actions violate the students' freedom of the press, imperil the paper's ability to deliver the news, and damage the staff's morale and incentive. Reade fears Hoover may try to interfere in the upcoming selection of next year's editor-in-chief or possibly cut into the paper's funding.

Reade also has several personal concerns. He has only two months remaining as editor-in-chief, but losing the tuition waiver will still cost him almost $4,000, which he does not have and would have trouble borrowing at this stage of the semester. In addition, he is worried about how his removal would affect his career opportunities. Good journalism positions are extremely competitive, and Reade thinks being "fired" as an editor and staff member could exclude him from consideration for those jobs. (He is currently in the middle of the job-hunting process.) He also thinks he is a good editor, will miss working on the paper, and feels personally insulted and enraged by Hoover's actions and statements. Josh suspects, too, that Hoover may have seized this opportunity to retaliate against him for his critical reporting and editorials during the past two years. That suspicion further infuriates him.

Finally, Reade is sincerely concerned about the university and about the substance of what the paper is trying to do. He thinks Hoover has exaggerated and exacerbated any problems the publication might have presented. Hoover's handling of the affair, says Josh, will damage the school far more than anything the paper has done. Although he would have gone about writing the article differently than the reporters did, Reade firmly believes they have contributed to an important public dialogue about life at the school by exposing certain stereotypes, misguided expectations, and social stratification. Reade was responsible for initiating the Crier's series about campus society and considers the sociological, psychological, and health issues associated with the social and sexual environment on campuses to be among the most important facing colleges today. The schools' responses to those issues will have a continuing impact on the institutions themselves and on their students, both before and after they graduate.

Using the model provided in this section, prepare to meet with Reade to address the concerns he identified and to help him decide what he should do. You can assume that you have gathered the above information in an initial interview and you have now had time to prepare to counsel him.

Regarding the freedom of the press issues, see, e.g., *Hazelwood School Dist. v. Kuhlmeier*, 108 S. Ct. 562 (1988); *Papish v. University of Missouri Bd. of Curators*, 410 U.S. 667 (1973); *Healy v. James*, 408 U.S. 169 (1972); *Stanley v.*

Magrath, 719 F.2d 279 (8th Cir. 1983); *Mississippi Gay Alliance v. Goudelock,* 536 F.2d 1073 (5th Cir. 1976); *Joyner v. Whiting,* 477 F.2d 456 (4th Cir. 1973); *Swope v. Lubbers,* 560 F. Supp. 1328 (W.D. Mich. 1983). Reade's facts may also suggest to you other issues that are worth researching.

C. DEVELOPING A LANGUAGE OF PREDICTION

As we have noted, part of your responsibility in the counseling process is to predict the probable consequences for each proposed action step. If the action step contemplated is litigation, what are the probabilities of success and what will those probabilities turn on? If, in representing a city, the action step is the drafting and enactment of a municipal ordinance, what are the probabilities that it could be successfully attacked as unconstitutional? Would a partnership, a joint venture, or a corporation be most likely to offer the clients with the crafts business their most advantageous tax status? If the issue is whether to accept a negotiation offer, what is the likelihood the other side will make additional concessions? Your client needs such information to decide; thus, you must include those calculations in preparing to counsel your client and must then communicate them to your client.

To meet that responsibility, you need to develop a language of prediction. The language must be clear and accurate. The description should include estimates of probabilities and factors affecting the probabilities and must account for the client's ability to comprehend.

Clarity is crucial; misunderstood prognoses can do the client more disservice than service. To achieve clarity, you reduce the case to some quantitative description through use of verbal or numerical indicators. You can use adjectives along a continuum; for example, the range could include "certain," "excellent," "very good," "good," "fair," "poor," "very poor," and "impossible." Alternatively, you can use percentage descriptions (100 percent to 0 percent) or mathematical odds (e.g., 50-50, 10 to 1, 2 to 1). The numerical indicators seem to provide greater clarity to clients.

An explanation to the client of how you arrived at your prediction also aids clarity. Thus, the lawyer in the Selin case could remark:

"If we go to trial on the issue of the bar's nuisance, I think we would have a very good chance of winning. The cases have emphasized the character of the neighborhood and have been protective of residential communities. And the court here will be particularly impressed by these offensive activities going around the bar. On the other hand, we could draw old Judge Crotchety; he's very capricious. He may decide the whole free enterprise system is threatened by your claim. So, while I think your chances are very good, there is some element of uncertainty involved."

In addition to clarity, your predictions must be as accurate as possible. You can be as clear as glass, but if the prediction defies the law, the facts, or logic, the client would be better off without it.

The need for accuracy is, of course, obvious, as is the fact that there is little this book can do to teach accuracy. Three years of training in substantive law, plus experience, diligence, and honesty, provide the necessary ingredients. We can, however, identify here a couple of cautionary points to help achieve accuracy in prediction.

First, many lawyers experience a temptation to provide emotional support for clients by unduly reassuring them about the merits of their cases. A new client, for example, says she has been gravely wronged by a disreputable company that keeps claiming her back forty as its own. The lawyer, feeling sympathy, responds with a first-year property analysis, "Well, they can't do that. We'll stop them." But the lawyer does not yet have the facts and providing emotional support through such remarks can backfire later when the lawyer finds the company has a viable claim. Just as commonly, the lawyer may have a client who feels legitimately wronged in a case where relief is either unavailable or hard to get because of some technical defense (such as immunities or the Statute of Frauds). Again, the attorney may be tempted to give the client support by overstating the potential for recovery. When reality eventually catches up with lawyer and client, the client will feel cheated not only by the law but also by the lawyer. Attorneys in such cases disserve their clients by deluding them and providing them with inaccurate information upon which to base their decisions.

On the other hand, many lawyers understate a client's case to assure themselves of success and happy clients. If the clients' prospects are very good, and the lawyer characterizes them as "fair," then when the clients are successful, they will naturally believe their lawyer has done exceptional work. Similarly, a lawyer may understate the case in hopes of prodding a quicker settlement, and thus an easier and quicker fee. Here, too, the lawyer disserves clients by giving them inaccurate information upon which to base their decisions. (The clients might agree to a settlement less favorable than that they would insist on if they had an accurate analysis.) Lawyers can practice client-centered techniques and preach client autonomy and decision-making, but when they understate the case they really manipulate, and thereby preempt, client decision-making. They also skirt the rules governing professional responsibility.[5]

In addition, you and your clients must recognize the vagaries of making predictions. A lawyer's prognoses often change during the course of representation. As new factual discoveries are made, as new law develops, or as other contingencies arise, you must constantly reevaluate the case. Such possibilities must be communicated to the client. Consider, for example, the qualification made in the above illustration from the Selin case by the lawyer cautioning the client that referral of his action to Judge Crotchety could adversely affect the chances for success. You will often need to hedge the degree of precision until such time as full investigation and research are completed. For example, you might inform the client his chances for success are "not good" or are "less than 50-50," rather than

---

5. ABA Code of Professional Responsibility EC 7-7 and 7-8; Model Rules of Professional Conduct 1.4 and 2.1. See also Chapter 12, Section B (pages 285-295), and Chapter 13 (particularly pages 319-323).

using more precise descriptions such as "very poor" or "35 percent." Or, when dealing with dollars or other fungible damages, you might forecast a range of possibilities rather than focusing on specific amounts. Thus, you might advise a client on her chances for recovering from $10,000 to $40,000. Finally, you must account for varied probabilities regarding multiple claims or remedies. Selin, for example, might have a 60 percent chance to recover for damages to his property, but only a 30 percent chance for an injunction and a 10 percent chance for emotional distress damages. If he waits another six months, then he might also encounter a 50 percent probability of losing it all on laches. Whatever the variables, you must clearly and accurately describe them and their interrelationships to the client.

Chapter

11

Helping the Client
Reach a Decision

You have a responsibility not only to identify alternatives for your clients, but also to help the clients analyze their situations, search within themselves, and reach decisions. This chapter describes the resources you need to completely discharge those counseling responsibilities. Section A discusses decision-making models for clarifying and structuring issues. Section B delineates several advanced skills you will use to help your client analyze the issues and priorities to reach the best decision.

A. LAWYER'S ROLE IN DECISION-MAKING

In counseling clients, you convey and clarify information, exercise judgment, give guidance, provide emotional support, and steer the client to enhanced self-understanding. You convey and clarify through substitution of lay terminology for legal terminology and through development of a language of prediction, as described in the preceding chapter (pages 252-254). You also clarify through appropriate structuring of the session and by reducing the case to understandable issues. You exercise judgment in both your preparation for counseling (through use of experience and legal expertise) and your analysis of clients' responses during counseling sessions.

You give guidance through your ability to predict consequences, reflect and clarify clients' concerns, and ensure that all the consequences for each alternative are considered. You guide the clients through discussion and analysis of the alternatives and their consequences. Emotional support develops from your use of the helping skills described in Chapter 5 and of the more advanced skills described in Section B, below. Your exercise of those skills helps your clients to achieve self-understanding. Your understanding of and respect for clients also help them to cope with emotional strain.

To fulfill your counseling responsibilities, you must realize that reaching a decision—selecting an appropriate action step or alternative—is a cooperative venture between you and the client. That imposes several obligations on you. First, you must remain mindful that the clients, not you, make the decisions and that you must filter out your own needs from the decisional process. (See Chapters 12-13 for discussion of, and limits on, those notions.)

Second, you must execute *both* of counseling's two major tasks: You not only present alternatives to the clients; you also help them to decide which selection best meets their needs and priorities. You do that by probing the clients on those needs and priorities and on how they feel about the consequences of the alternatives. Your probing includes subjects in which the client has the greater knowledge and experience. A businessperson, for example, would normally be better informed than you in evaluating the commercial impact of alternative contract provisions. It is nevertheless your responsibility to push the client to analyze that impact. Clients are also typically the experts on their own feelings. The exploration of the client's feelings and needs requires use of the advanced skills described below in Section B. When appropriate, you offer advice to the client on matters within your expertise or experience.

Finally, you must give your clients a structure they can use to assess the information and reach decisions. For example, if you and your client confront a range of alternatives, you can use a process of elimination either to select the most desirable action or to simplify the selection. In the preceding chapter's case concerning the neighborhood bar, if the client says he wants to be rid of the bar and does not care about sustaining his friendship with the saloonkeeper-neighbor, then the lawyer and client can strike the "do-nothing" alternative. Next, suppose that the client says he has limited funds and could not afford to finance efforts that do not stand a good chance of success. Two more alternatives (challenging the zoning and liquor permits) could then be struck. This process could continue until the lawyer and client have whittled the alternatives down to an appropriate course of action.

Now assume that the client wants both to preserve his friendship and to get rid of the bar's offensive activities, while remaining within a fairly tight budget. In such a case of conflicting priorities, the lawyer could aid decision-making by breaking the action steps down and, with the client, ranking each alternative according to how it furthers each goal. In the Selin case, the action step of a lawsuit may get a number 1 or 2 ranking in furthering the goal of toning down the bar, but would be dead last in preserving friendship. It could also be expensive. The do-nothing alternative would rank highest in maintaining friendship and minimizing costs, but hold the bottom slot in dealing with the bar's offensive character. The lawyer and client might then find an alternative—say, negotiating or buying out Kratzer—that would not be the best as to any one particular goal, but would rank high under each priority. Such an analysis could provide the client with a basis upon which to reach a final decision.

Some choices can be reduced to a quantitative analysis. For example, assume that you represent a plaintiff who, you project, has a 50 percent chance of winning a $90,000 verdict at trial. Midway through discovery, the defendant offers $30,000. First, subtract from the potential judgment your contingency fee ($30,000) and then discount the difference ($60,000) by multiplying it times the probability of success ($60,000 × 50% = $30,000). Next, subtract $5,000 for the costs needed to complete discovery and try the case. You arrive at $25,000. Finally, you figure in inflation and lost interest to appraise the lawsuit's current "value" at $22,500.[1] That figure must then be compared to the $30,000 offer less your contingency fee for settlements ($30,000 × 25% = $7,500), or $22,500. The defendant's offer thus appears to be a reasonable one. You can then pose to the client that he can go for the $90,000 by, in effect, gambling $30,000 at even odds that he will win.

Your valuing of the case may also include calculations and probabilities on the worst and best outcomes that are reasonably possible. The quantitative analysis, although not conclusive, should help to illuminate the client's decision-making. You would also want to probe other factors affecting the decision, such as the client's immediate need for cash, his long-term need for the full $90,000, his feelings about litigation, or the importance of the principle at issue.

The above-described methods for reaching a decision have no particular magic about them. The variety of different models you can use is limited only by your creativity. The important lesson to learn is that *some* structure is required. The models described here work because they clarify the issues and choices for the client. That must be your objective in devising decision-making models. They should highlight how the alternatives relate to the critical issues; the models should focus and juxtapose priorities, action steps, and consequences in some clear and meaningful arrangement.

B. COUNSELOR HELPING SKILLS

1. Introduction

This section describes special skills you can use to help your client reach a decision. These skills focus on the human relations aspects of the decision-making process and build directly on the basic interviewing skills described

---

1. For more complete discussions of case valuations, see G. Bellow & B. Moulton, *The Lawyering Process* 479-495, 501-503 (1978); Sindell, Formula for Estimating Value of a Case, in *Negotiating Settlements in Personal Injury Actions* (Practising Law Institute 1956).

in Chapter 5. The skills described in this chapter are more advanced than the basic interviewing skills on several levels. First, the helping skills of interviewing are necessary for, and are included within, the counselor skills; that is, the interviewing skills are prerequisites for this chapter's skills. Second, the counseling techniques are more difficult; they are more subtle, require you to go beneath the surface, and demand more of you. Third, persistently effective use of the counseling skills requires a firmly established lawyer-client relationship; the greater complexity and sensitivity inherent in use of the advanced skills demand a healthy rapport with your clients and substantial knowledge of their situation.

The skills described here include advanced empathy, self-disclosure, and confrontation. While the selection is not exhaustive, it does illustrate the kind of skills essential for effective counseling. The skills of this section form a core of resources available to you to sharpen the decision-making process through increased client self-awareness. These skills also force the lawyer-client relationship into a level of mutuality not present in earlier stages. That is, the flow of information, regard, and understanding should run in both directions, thus reinforcing the partnership arrangement in the decisional process.

2. Advanced Empathy

a. The Substance of Advanced Empathy

Advanced empathy in legal counseling can take several forms. You may, for example, articulate that which the client has left implicit; summarize key elements of what the client has given you; or synthesize the client's information and feelings to identify major themes.[2] The discussion below elaborates on each of these forms of advanced empathy and illustrates their utility through application to the following problem.

≡ **PROBLEM 1** ≡
The Lakeside Development

Joan Martin is a 52-year-old businesswoman with diverse financial interests. Her primary holdings are in commercial real estate and in apartment house rentals. Her lawyer of twenty years is David Rowe.

A local developer, George Stevens, recently approached Martin to enlist her as an investor in a lakeside beach and resort Stevens has planned. The property sits on the edge of Blue Lake, a mountain lake used for swimming, boating, and fishing. Small, privately owned cabins dot its perimeter. Recently, several new and more exclusive residential communities have developed near the lake. In addition, the Lake Overlook, a modest yet

---

2. The examples are, with some changes, appropriated from G. Egan, *The Skilled Helper* 212-219 (3d ed. 1986).

fashionable resort hotel with a tournament-quality golf course, sits nearby on a ridge overlooking the lake. Despite the lake's recreational potential, it has but one small beach for swimming. Until recently, that area was owned by the state, but its Parks Department announced last month that it had sold the beach and 40 adjoining acres to Stevens. The additional acreage includes an attractive, chateau-like office building. Stevens now plans to develop the entire property into a resort complex by enlarging the beach, installing a boat dock, converting the office building into a hotel, and adding other recreational facilities. If his plans proceed as contemplated, the beach, which is now free to the general public, would be restricted to the resort's patrons. Stevens needs financial backing for his ambitious project and that provoked his solicitation of Martin for help.

When the state Parks Department announced the sale of the lake property to Stevens, local residents complained loudly. They objected to the procedures used by the Department in making the sale and to the substance of Stevens' plans. The Department had not given any public notice that the property was for sale and had not allowed any opportunity for public comment or input from other government agencies on the sale to Stevens. Rumors of resulting financial gain for Department officials from land deals in the lake vicinity have further inflamed the protests. The protestors include two state legislators who live near the project site and several prominent lawyers and business leaders who own summer cottages on the lake. They and the other local residents fear the project will deprive them and the public of the only decent swimming area on the lake, increase congestion around the lake, and thereby ruin the area's bucolic character. The protesting residents have formed a group and are contemplating legal action. The two legislators have already requested the state Attorney General to determine if the Department's procedures (or lack of them) rendered the property transfer a nullity. He has not yet responded. Some residents have talked of calling for an official investigation of the sale.

Ms. Martin has consulted her lawyer for help in deciding whether to invest in Stevens' project. She is concerned about the legality of the sale to Stevens. If there is a serious question about its validity, she could have her investment tied up in litigation for years. Given the amount of money she and Stevens have been discussing, Martin cannot afford to lose the income on it for any substantial period of time. Indeed, to get her investment together, she must liquidate some other income-producing property. Martin has also mentioned that she counts several good friends among the lake area's residents and property owners, and those relationships now appear to be giving her some pause. In addition, she is reluctant to antagonize the two local legislators.

Martin and Rowe have known each other since their school days at the local high school. Rowe has served as Martin's lawyer since her divorce from her first husband twenty years ago and through numerous business ventures following that initial representation. The two have a sound working relationship, developed through mutual trust and respect.

Martin and Stevens have also known each other a long time. They have gone to the same church since childhood and are both active in an alumni support group for the university they attended together. While they have always been friends, Martin does not completely trust Stevens; he has a reputation for bending the rules to suit his needs and his honesty is not above questioning. His current project, though, has struck Martin as a sound business idea. The recreational potential for Blue Lake has never been fully developed. The lake sits half-way between two large urban areas and could, with proper management and advertising, easily draw large numbers of weekenders and vacationers from those cities. Stevens also plans to set up some cooperative arrangement with the nearby Lake Overlook resort. Its patrons could use his beach and dock facilities, while his customers would receive reduced rates at the Overlook's golf course. If these projections go as well as Stevens and Martin anticipate they will, then Stevens and his backers should receive a handsome return on their investment. Stevens' ultimate idea, and his long-term project for huge profits, is to establish casino gambling at his and the Overlook resorts. Those plans are strictly confidential at the moment. If they become public, Stevens is sure the local residents will pursue every legal avenue to stop him.

Articulating the Implicit. When you accurately describe significant points your client has only implied, increased understanding ensues. You push the client toward enhanced self-awareness and more enlightened decision-making. Consider the following dialogue between attorney and client in the Martin hypothetical:

Martin: Stevens has always been a shrewd businessman. He's made a lot of money and, of course, there were those land deals he made a killing on when they finished the interstate over by Johnsville. He was just as secretive about those ventures as he is about this one. That's his way, I guess. I've known George a long time, and he's always been a friend. If he's putting his money into this project, I guess there are profits to be made. I could stand some of those, no question about that.

Rowe: You're enticed by a venture that could be lucrative for you. But, maybe, at the same time you're apprehensive because you're not sure you can trust George.

Martin: Yeah, I hate to say that about a person, especially if he's a friend. But I do know George can be pretty ruthless when it comes to money. And there's this casino gambling idea he's got. I don't know if I want to get into that business. It's so offensive to some people—and addictive for others.

Rowe: So the gambling also troubles you. You think it might be wrong to make money off of it?

Martin: I guess I don't care if other people want to gamble, but I'm not sure I want to be the one who makes it possible for them. It can ruin lives, you know.

Rowe has first empathized at the primary level; he has reflected back the core of what the client has said, as we described in Chapter 5. Yet Rowe has also gone beyond what Martin has said and has expressed the unexpressed. The lawyer's responses here also reveal why advanced empathy must usually await an advanced stage of the lawyer-client relationship. Each response, but especially the second, could offend Martin if Rowe did not already have a solid rapport with his client. Moreover, Rowe could not have confidently empathized with accuracy at an advanced level in the above exchanges if he did not already have substantial knowledge about Martin. Rowe's empathic statements illustrate how a client can be pushed into areas that she has either failed to recognize or has been reluctant to admit and articulate.

Summarizing Core Material. You can achieve advanced empathy through summaries of the essential matter revealed by your client. The summary is most useful when the client's discussion has been rambling, fragmentary, or confused. The empathic summary pulls together the fragments scattered about by the client and puts them into some coherent pattern that can lead to meaningful analysis. You must compensate for the client's inability to organize. The structuring should help the client to focus and thus to better explore the issues.

To effectively summarize for advanced empathy, gather the information provided by the client, select the relevant items, and then systematically organize them. The following summary of information from the Martin case illustrates those tasks:

Rowe: Before you can decide what to do, it seems to me we have to put all these different considerations into some order. On one hand, you've got an opportunity to invest in a project you believe could bring you a very substantial return. It meets a perceived need, is close by, and could be fun for you. On the other hand, you are talking about a lot of money, there is some financial risk in it, and you're concerned the whole thing could be tied up in litigation for a long time. And you also seem to me to be concerned about whether your involvement could risk your friendships with some of the people who live there and your standing with some powerful people. Those concerns are intensified because you know Stevens is contemplating a casino, and you're uncertain how people will respond to that. And you have your own personal misgivings about supporting gambling. Finally, you're not sure you trust Stevens, and you therefore have reservations about getting involved with him.

Now, my research tells me the community, at present, has no basis for voiding the property sale to Stevens or stopping the development. [Explanation of the law is omitted.] So I doubt there will be long delays from litigation. But I've also learned Stevens cannot start a casino without a change in state law, which would not seem likely to develop if those two legislators who live at the lake would be opposed to it. What we need to explore further, then, are your feelings about Stevens and what sort of impact you think his project will have on your friends at the lake.

Rowe's remarks here summarize the core of the client's situation, crystallize the issues, and nudge the client to deal with important but previously unarticulated matters. The lawyer thus goes beyond mere restatement, since he includes organization, analysis, and probing.

Note, too, that Rowe's summary here would serve as an excellent opener for a counseling session. Summary can be a useful technique at any point in a consultation, but it has special utility at the outset. You have substantial time, prior to the consultation, to think about the client's case, break it down, and consider its meaning. A summary at the outset refreshes the clients' recollections of the issues and of prior discussion and directs clients to the issues to be discussed during the session. Visual aids could be prepared for additional clarity. Rowe also used the opportunity to weave in new information discovered during his research.

Synthesis.   You also use advanced empathy when you identify overriding themes or patterns from the sum of the client's discussions. (Synthesis is related to summary, but the focus in synthesis on theme identification warrants a separate discussion.) Clients often see only the isolated impact of their various experiences, thus leaving to you the task of determining whether there may be overarching issues whose resolution could lead to dissipation of the individual problems. Consider the case of a young mother of two small children who arrives at a legal aid office seeking a divorce. Her husband has been out of work for 16 months, his unemployment is about to expire, and there are no jobs in sight. She tells the lawyer her husband has been irritable and short-tempered the past year, and he constantly berates her. She also refers to several specific financial problems, some of which the attorney may be able to address: The client and her husband bought into a "freezer plan" that has failed to deliver edible meats and vegetables; they defaulted on a payment plan for aluminum siding after it began to crack and peel within a month of installation; their youngest son needs medical attention; and they have run into difficulties with the welfare office. Upon scrutiny, the assorted financial troubles appear at least partially attributable to the couple's naiveté and mismanagement of family resources. The marital problems, in turn, stem from the husband's unemployment and the financial distress. Assuming the accuracy of that analysis, the attorney could appropriately counsel the client:

Attorney: It seems to me there may be a persistent problem that lies at the bottom of much of your trouble. That is, you appear to need help in managing your money, so you don't get trapped into these bad, even fraudulent, contracts, and so you can squeeze the most out of what you do have. Do you think your marital situation might improve if we got your finances straightened out, got you some help in budgeting your resources, and got your husband a job?

Through this advanced empathy, the attorney has identified for the client a pattern she was not conscious of and has suggested a beginning point for easing her predicament.

Similarly, in counseling Joan Martin, David Rowe could synthesize her situation as follows:

Rowe: Correct me if I'm wrong, but from what you've told me, your decision really boils down to how much you're willing to risk to make a killing on this investment. Do you want to risk your security, possibly risk some personal relationships, and risk working with someone you don't fully trust, for a shot at the big money? To focus some more, you need to assess how substantial those risks are and whether they're counterbalanced by the gain you anticipate.

Theme identification requires a synthesis not unlike synthesis in legal analysis. In legal analysis, you align all of the precedents relating to the issue. Then you dissect them and analyze how important the presence or absence of each element was to the courts' rationales and conclusions. Once the significant elements have been isolated, then you shape them into a legal rule or standard. Similarly, as a counselor, you dissect your client's problems into their components and isolate those components that pervade all of the problems. Then you further analyze the facts to assess causal relationships. If possible, the client's problems should be compared to similar experiences that did not produce negative consequences. Were there factors present in the positive instances but absent in the negative? Or vice versa? Once the operative components have been isolated and analyzed, you shape them into some coherent, understandable theory for your client to consider. (The process could also be compared to what bridge (or hearts or pinochle) players do: After they are dealt their cards, the players sort the cards into organized units, consider alternatives, and then select the most viable strategy(ies).)

Just as in your legal analysis, you do not unquestioningly accept the clients' construction of their situation as the only possible one. You should independently assess and synthesize the facts to determine if there are no alternative conclusions available. For example, a client may have concluded that her boss discriminates against and mistreats her on the job because she is a woman, citing several incidents in which she and her boss have had disagreements. There may be, however, other possible interpretations of the facts. Perhaps the client was unreasonable or oversensitive, or perhaps she performed her work poorly. Other theories may also apply. You must do your own scanning and analysis, and not rely on the client's. This principle applies in any counseling context.

To summarize your function in advanced empathy, we quote Gerard Egan:

> Through advanced accurate empathy, what is said confusedly by the client is stated clearly by the helper; what is said half-heartedly is stated cogently; what is said vaguely is stated specifically and concretely; and what the client presents at a superficial level is represented by the helper at a deeper level. In a sense, the helper interprets the behavior of the client, but his interpretations are based on what the client reveals about his own feelings, experiences, and behavior and how the client acts during the counseling sessions

themselves—not on abstract psycho-dynamics. Neither does the . . . helper lay his interpretations on his client like so many laws; he suggests them and invites the client's response so that they can collaborate in trying to understand.[3]

b. Verbal Techniques for Communicating Advanced Empathy

Skillful use of advanced empathy requires not only insight but also caution. Because advanced empathy moves clients into awareness of matters they have previously suppressed, either consciously or unconsciously, your statements of advanced empathy frequently strike chords of a sensitive or threatening nature for the client. Your effectiveness thus requires a well-established lawyer-client relationship. Premature use of advanced empathy increases the risks of inaccuracy, both in the sense that the difficulty and subjectivity of the skill make an erroneous judgment more likely and that the stakes are much higher than with primary-level empathy. Your thorough knowledge of the client's facts is generally a prerequisite to a successful effort at going beneath the surface of your client's statements, and such knowledge cannot normally be acquired in one interview. Clients are also more likely to respond positively to an attorney whom they trust and with whom they share a rapport rather than one they have just met.

In addition, you should frame your advanced empathy in tentative language. In so doing, you reduce both the risk that you will offend or threaten your client and the risk that the client will take your analysis as "the answer." Advanced empathy should not be the end of the discussion; rather, it should provoke the client not only to consider the lawyer's analysis but also to move toward a deeper self-understanding.

This necessary tentativeness can be communicated through words and phrases that dilute or qualify an otherwise concrete statement. They include certain auxiliary verbs ("may," "can," "could," "might"), qualifying adverbs ("perhaps," "maybe," "possibly"), and a variety of introductory phrases, clauses, and sentences. Some examples of the latter group are:

"Let me see if I can summarize what you've told me, and perhaps put it in some perspective."

"I wonder if . . ."

"If I understand what you've told me . . ."

Review the examples given earlier in this section; each of them uses expressions indicating caution and tentativeness. Next, compare the following advanced empathy efforts and gauge the differences in impact on the

---

3. *The Skilled Helper* 147-148 (1st ed. 1975).

client between those with tentative language (italicized portions) and those without:

Attorney A: Your problems with your wife stem from your unwillingness to accept her as an equal and from your resentment that she has gone back to a job that pays more than yours.

Attorney B: *From what you've told me, and correct me if I'm off base*, but *it appears that* your marital problems *may* stem from your unwillingness to accept your wife as an equal and your resentment that she has returned to work in a well-paying job.

Attorney A: Your insistence in refusing their offer and in forcing a lawsuit is motivated by a desire to get even. Is that correct?

Attorney B: *I wonder, and maybe you should consider this, whether* your rejections of their offers *may* be based on revenge. *What do you think?*

The major shifts accomplished by tentativeness in these examples changed the counselor's expression from an inquisitorial cross-examination style to that of a joint, cooperative undertaking. Note, however, that the tentative language in the above examples does not diminish the clarity of the empathy. The lawyer should not soften the effects of advanced empathy by sacrificing concreteness.

In addition to using tentative language, you can guard against an adverse client reaction to advanced empathy by introducing it with primary-level empathy. The latter communicates that you continue to listen and understand, and it helps the client to see the relationships between the articulated facts and your forthcoming analysis. For example, in the dialogue on page 260 both of David Rowe's responses to Joan Martin include a primary-level empathy followed by advanced empathy. And in each instance, the primary-level empathy not only demonstrates Rowe's accurate listening but also provides an explanatory basis for the deeper analysis that follows. The client then follows the attorney's lead and tries to sort out what in fact are her feelings at that moment. Once she gains a firm understanding of those feelings, she is better prepared to assess and decide among her alternative courses of action.

3. Counselor Self-Disclosure

a. Introduction

When you self-disclose, you describe feelings or experiences you have had that are analogous to your client's. Although certain side-effects restrict its use, self-disclosure can provide the client with helpful insight and support. After the following discussion problem, this section explains how self-disclosure contributes to client decision-making, how its misuse can cause unwanted effects, and then how you can achieve the technique's desired results while avoiding its disadvantages.

≡ **PROBLEM 2** ≡
Trouble in the Lakeside Development

After much deliberating, Joan Martin decided to invest in Stevens' lakefront project. He began construction to enlarge the beach area and add a new building to serve as a bath-house, boat facility, snack bar, and an open-air cocktail lounge extending over the water. Stevens contracted with the Stone Mountain Construction Company (SMC) to do the needed excavation work and to provide high quality sand for the beach expansion. The plans provided for the beach to be trebled in size, so the SMC contract amounted to over a million dollars, including a couple hundred thousand just for the sand. After on-site excavation was completed, but before delivery of the sand, Stevens sent a pair of experts out to SMC to make a surprise inspection of the sand that had been designated for use at the lake. The experts declared the sand unfit for an exclusive beach. Stevens then abruptly canceled the unexecuted portions of the SMC contract and within days had a new contract with the Lost Creek Quarry for the needed sand. Lost Creek sold its sand to Stevens for considerably less than the SMC contract price. SMC officials were furious and contended the allegation about the quality of their sand was ludicrous. Their outrage found expression in a lawsuit after they accidentally learned that Stevens' "experts" were actually Lost Creek employees. As the facts developed, it became obvious that midway through his contract with SMC, Stevens received a much better price for the sand from Lost Creek. Stevens and Lost Creek officials then concocted a scheme to save Stevens from having to pay breach of contract damages.

In its complaint, SMC accused Stevens and his group of intentionally breaking the contract. Other counts accused Lost Creek and Stevens' group with conspiring to defraud SMC and to violate antitrust laws. SMC also threw in allegations of kickbacks and sweetheart arrangements. Given the nature of its claims, SMC sued not only Lost Creek and the entity Stevens had formed for his project, but also joined Stevens and his partners—including Joan Martin—and Lost Creek's officers in their individual capacities. Martin, however, had not been involved in any of the above transactions and was totally ignorant of Stevens' maneuverings.

Service of SMC's complaint on Ms. Martin brought her back to her lawyer's office. During the course of their meeting, the following exchange occurred:

Martin: What a mess! I didn't do anything wrong, so I'm not worried about any liability—or at least I don't think I should be—but when you're even associated with a situation like this, people think you're as responsible for it as anyone else. I've worked hard to build up my reputation and these stupid shenanigans of Stevens are ruining it in one fell swoop. You just can't function in business if people don't trust your word on a contract.

Rowe: It really is infuriating, I know. I experienced something like that after I'd been in practice for about three years. I was working in a small firm, and one of the partners was found to have falsified some impor-

tant evidence. He did it on his own, but he still managed to soil everyone in the firm. I'd been trying so hard to establish a decent reputation
for myself, and, like you, took a lot of pride in maintaining my integrity. Then it seemed it would take me forever to restore my reputation
and feel good again about my job. I was surprised to learn that the
clients I personally worked with continued to trust me.

Martin: Well, that's reassuring. Still, I feel so drained having to go about
the rebuilding task. And I don't know what to do, either, about the
lakefront project. The money certainly isn't worth my going along with
lies and contract breaches and sacrificing my reputation, and I don't
give two bananas anymore about Stevens, but I do feel some loyalty to
the other partners. They were duped, too, and I'm not sure I should
bail out on them when things are rough. God, this whole project has
been tiresome.

Rowe: So you have still another dilemma. You're torn now between escaping from the whole mess and trying to help your partners salvage
something from it. I know I thought seriously about leaving my firm
when our partner was exposed. I felt, at times, I just didn't want to
have anything to do with an organization where such dealings went
on. But I thought about it, and I factored in the close friendship and
the loyalties I had at the firm, the alternatives I had available to me,
whether I was really condoning improper tactics if I remained, and
whether my reputation would be enhanced or impaired by either leaving or staying. After weighing all those concerns, I decided the best
thing for me at the time was to stay on a while. And I did stay there
another two or three years. Of course, if you consider those same criteria to be determinative, you could apply them to your situation and
find they tell you to do something quite different.

b. Utility

Appropriate counselor self-disclosure can enhance the counseling
process by providing clients with a disclosing and coping model and by
positively affecting the clients' perception of themselves, of you, and of
the lawyer-client relationship. Through self-disclosure you demonstrate
the nature and depth of the disclosure expected from your clients. In effect, your illustration enhances the clients' understanding of the counseling process. Similarly, when you disclose problems analogous to the
clients' problems, they can observe someone who has confronted and dealt
with problems like their own.

Effective lawyer self-disclosure can benefit clients' perceptions and attitudes within the professional relationship. Your self-disclosure strength-
ens the participatory model of attorney-client problem-solving. By *sharing*
your experiences and feelings, and by confirming that you are a person
with problems like the clients', you reduce the level of your control and
professional superiority. Through the shared experiences, you establish a

common bond between yourself and your clients; you thereby build a better rapport and enhance the lawyer-client relationship.

Attorney self-disclosure can improve clients' perceptions about you. Because your self-disclosure deprofessionalizes you, you appear warmer, more human, and more friendly. When you reveal that you have experienced what a client is experiencing, you impress the client as one more likely to be empathetic and understanding. Because the disclosure is revealing, you appear more honest. These factors all work together to create a positive attitude in your clients toward you and their professional relationship. That in turn helps clients to fully disclose, to be open, and to be willing to engage in deeper and more meaningful self-analysis.

Lawyer self-disclosure can also add valuable information to the counseling process. Your clients benefit from knowledge about your experience and the relative effectiveness of the action steps you pursued. Clients should not be encouraged either to select or reject the course you have chosen, but they should be apprised of the consequences (good and bad) of your choice.

Finally, your articulation of your experience, feelings, and coping can help clients to better understand and analyze their own situation. If you properly analogize your situation to the clients' situations, then you provide them with a frame of reference and assist them in sorting out their feelings and alternatives. Your articulation helps clients to find their own words and to move forward to greater elaboration, either through recognition that they have shared your experience and reaction or through perceiving differences between their cases and yours. Thus, the self-disclosure advances the primary counseling goals of achieving client self-understanding and of making good decisions.

The exchange between Martin and Rowe illustrates several of the above observations. Rowe responds to Martin's feelings about the predicament her association with Stevens has caused her by describing the turmoil he had once endured when a law partner had breached the law. Rowe's self-disclosure demonstrates he understands what Martin feels at the moment: embarrassment, guilt by association, anger at Stevens, hurt from the damage to her pride and reputation, and exasperation over the anticipated time needed to repair the damage. By articulating those feelings, Rowe enhanced Martin's understanding of her own situation and provided her with support through their common experiences. He was also able to give an extra measure of encouragement and support in this instance because Rowe had found the recovery period was neither as long nor as difficult as Martin was anticipating. So Martin has a helpful coping model.

With the reassurance from Rowe, Martin then moves on to her dilemma: whether she should withdraw from the project or stick with it to aid her co-investors. Rowe's next self-disclosure adds valuable information to the counseling by offering the criteria he used to make a similar decision (whether to leave his law firm after the partner's crime was unveiled). Rowe identifies for consideration: friendships and loyalties, professional career alternatives, propriety, and effects on reputation. Those criteria should provide a basis upon which the client can begin her decision-making. Rowe discloses that when he applied the criteria to his situation, he concluded he should stay in the firm. But, as he indicates, application of the same criteria to Martin's situation may produce a very different conclusion. The loyalties in a loose business arrangement are not nearly as strong as those in a law firm, and Martin's career probably allows her greater flexibility than that enjoyed by a new attorney at the bottom rung of a law firm. Identifying those distinctions can lead to important insights, and Martin may have her own criteria to add to the discussion. Thus, while much counseling remains to be done, Rowe's self-disclosure effectively served its purpose.

c. Disadvantages

The preceding subsection described the contributions of appropriate and properly delivered counselor self-disclosure. Yet the technique of helper self-disclosure also entails significant risks. There are potential disadvantages involved even when it is skillfully used, and the risks escalate dramatically when disclosures are made carelessly.

First, your self-disclosure can make you seem self-centered. Given many clients' expectations or impressions about lawyers as egotistical, the connection between your self-disclosure and perceived self-importance can be easy for clients to draw. Lawyers who see everything in relation to themselves have limited vision. When a client seeks an attorney's help, and the lawyer immediately uses his or her own experience to minimize or define the client's problem, the client perceives the lawyer as incapable of seeing things from the client's perspective. The self-centered lawyer appears to disparage the significance of the client's problem. These consequences are more likely to occur when the disclosures are made frequently or early in the relationship.

Second, your self-disclosure—especially if you urge a particular solution or make one appear obvious—can come across as very patronizing. "Listen to your lawyer, 'the voice of experience,'" is the message if you presume that your treatment of an analogous situation provides the inevitable solution or that your solution in itself is so simple as to reduce the problem to insignificance. For example, most everyone can recall experiencing some doctor, teacher, coach, or parent who dismissed a problem with a self-adulatory reference: "I went through that when I was your age, but I learned how to deal with it and so can you." Rowe faced these risks in his self-disclosures to Joan Martin, but he avoided the negative consequences because he braced his disclosures with empathic reflections and a recognition that Martin must assess and decide her own case.

Third, your self-disclosure can deflect the focus away from the client and onto you. Some clients may feel more comfortable talking about you and may seize on your self-disclosure to avoid discussing their problems. You may dominate the relationship to such an extent that your disclosures will appear more important or more likely to reveal truth and wisdom than anything your client could say. In addition, your self-disclosure normally requires you to talk more, which in turn means the client will talk less. If you self-disclose early in the relationship—before the client has learned to engage in open give-and-take—then your assumption of topic control for a self-disclosure can have consequences beyond the immediate issue. The client may acquire the wrong perception of who controls and who talks.

Fourth, your self-disclosure pulls the discussion and thinking toward past experiences rather than present perceptions. In counseling, the focus should be on present reactions and planning for action steps that are either ongoing or soon to be implemented. Thus, self-disclosure risks detouring you and your client to topics of lesser significance. To use the technique effectively, you must ensure that the clients perceive the immediate relevance of the self-disclosure and use it toward the ends of better understanding their present circumstances and of plotting the most advantageous action steps.

Fifth, extended lawyer self-disclosure may make you appear loose in revealing confidences and, thus, less trustworthy. If you expose your own intimate experiences to strangers with little provocation, then it follows (in your client's view) that you will also be more likely to expose the client's intimacies to others. That, in turn, will chill the client's willingness to open up and be fully candid about sensitive topics.

These risks of attorney self-disclosure do not preclude its use. But they do call for caution in its application, sensitivity to the disadvantages, and efforts to minimize the technique's negative potential. The following section offers some suggestions on how to accomplish the positive effects of self-disclosure while reducing its risks.

d. Variables Determining Effectiveness

As with other counseling functions, several factors typically blend together to produce a global impression that ultimately determines the success or failure of self-disclosure. The skilled counselor manipulates the variables to achieve the desired effect. Of course, self-disclosure's impact will also be colored by the quality of your rapport with the client and by your use of other skills, most particularly the assorted elements of nonverbal communication. As those matters have been amply treated elsewhere in this book, they will not be enlarged on here.

The following discussion examines other key variables affecting self-disclosure in four categories: (1) content, (2) timing, (3) frequency, and (4) duration.

(1) Content

The most telling test in determining self-disclosure's effectiveness is the degree to which you *accurately* analogize to a *significant* issue. To reach an acceptable degree, you must first have developed your empathic skills. Once you perceive the issues as the client perceives them, then you can venture into your own experiences for an analogous situation whose disclosure will contribute to furthering your client's self-understanding and decision-making. The analogy need not be perfect, but it should reveal an instance in which you have encountered a dilemma or feelings similar to the client's. If you miss the mark with your disclosure, the negative consequences typically follow. Clients could construe a faulty analogy as a lack of understanding and possibly even as an insult. Rather than push clients to greater self-awareness, you could alienate them. They will not only be frustrated by your failure to understand, but they may also be angered by your failed attempt to try to climb or descend socioeconomic or professional barriers to reach their level. Slight distinctions between your narrative and a client's problem will not detract from the disclosure. (Indeed, they can have a positive effect by prodding clients to articulate the distinction and thus to better articulate their cases.) Once you cross into substantial discrepancy, however, the dangers of damaging rapport are greater than any likely gain. The relationship may thus be seen as a sliding scale: "[A]s the counselor's disclosure becomes more discrepant from the client's experience, the perceptions of that disclosure will likely become progressively less favorable."[4]

An example will illustrate. The scene is a public meeting concerning the construction of a coke plant—a particularly noxious industry—in a modest residential community in a rural county. The meeting is populated by community residents and the speakers are representatives from the plant builder and from government agencies. The residents are quite upset about several matters related to the company's plans and several times during the meeting the crowd vents its anger through sarcastic remarks, caustic questions, and jeering. After one particularly angry outburst the company vice president, who is a lawyer, responds, "Look, I know how you feel. I own a home in a suburb near Washington. Not long ago our town put in a public park near our house; you can even see the baseball diamond from our front doorstep."

This example, of course, does not involve an attorney-client relationship, but it certainly illustrates gross discrepancy in a self-disclosure. The two situations (the coke plant and the park) are loosely analogous; they both involve the intrusion of some activity into a residential community. But the differences are so compelling that they override the similarities and actually diminish rather than further the establishment of a cooperative relationship. The vice president's story emphasizes his big-city, probably exclusive background, which the rural, middle-class residents will resent. More important, the differences in the intrusive qualities of a coke plant and of a baseball diamond on the health and quiet of the communities are so dramatic as not to require elaboration. (Most of the community would, in fact, probably welcome the easy availability of a recreational park.) The vice president thus seemed to prove the insensitivity his company was being accused of.

(2) Timing

During the early stages of a relationship, counselor self-disclosure should be used sparingly. A disclosure early in an initial interview greatly increases the risk that you will appear egotistical and preoccupied with yourself. By disclosing early, you imply you are unable to perceive problems except in the context of your own experience. Premature disclosures

---

4. Nilsson, Strassberg & Bannon, Perception of Counselor Self-Disclosure: An Analogue Study, 26 J. of Counseling Psychology 399, 403 (1979).

also exacerbate the potential that your clients will perceive you as unable to empathize, to step into their world, because you are trapped in your own. The early stages of the relationship should concentrate on fact-gathering and establishing rapport, so you want to focus as much as possible on the clients and their problems. You thus want to avoid the risk your self-disclosure presents for deflecting focus. Self-disclosure should also be limited early in the relationship because the facts are not then fully developed and you are therefore less likely to analogize accurately. If you do disclose early in the relationship, the disclosure should be brief.

Self-disclosure is most effective when you and your client reach the stage of searching for client self-understanding and for action steps. The precise moments for the most propitious application arrive when the client is groping, when he or she feels frustrated by the difficulty of the issues and a seeming inability to cope. At that juncture, your self-disclosure has the most potential to seal the partnership concept, to show the client that coping is possible, to suggest starting points for identifying alternatives, and to move the client into more substantial and meaningful self-understanding.

(3) Frequency

Counselor self-disclosure and helping effectiveness share a curvilinear relationship. Overuse of the disclosure occasions its ill effects: The client perceives you as preoccupied with yourself and less concerned with helping; the disclosures maneuver the discussion away from the client's problems and into your realm; you assume greater control and power; and you appear to lack discretion and, thus, to be less trustworthy. At the other end, failure to disclose when appropriate forfeits opportunities to advance client self-understanding and to enlighten the selection of alternatives; meanwhile, the client may perceive you as aloof and trapped in your professional role.

The more severe consequences, though, fall upon those counselors who overindulge in self-disclosure. The negative effects of too frequent use are extremely difficult to counteract, while other techniques are at least available to achieve counseling goals without significant self-disclosure. (Indeed, you may not have experienced events or feelings sufficiently analogous to the client's to allow for a meaningful disclosure.) Moreover, undesirable consequences are more likely to follow overuse than underuse.

To reach an effective middle position, be certain the timing of your self-disclosures is appropriate. That will at least reduce the potential for overuse of disclosure. Also, remain aware of the frequency of your disclosures, and be sure they have a purpose.

(4) Duration

Your self-disclosures should take only so long as is necessary to establish the analogy, express understanding, and suggest discussion points for analyzing the client's problem or alternatives. The longer the self-disclosure is, the more likely that the discussion will veer away from the client and that your power and ego will intrude on the counseling process.[5]

4. Confrontation

a. Generally

The utility of confrontation as a counseling technique has been somewhat controversial among psychotherapists. Certain programs for peer self-help (such as Alcoholics Anonymous) and encounter groups have depended on confrontation for much of their development. Some of the research supports these uses and theories for counselor confrontation, while other studies have found such confrontation to be ineffectual.[6] The discussion in this section (as well as references in some earlier sections) should reveal our view that confrontation is a useful and essential—but difficult—skill for the legal counselor.

As used here, confrontation means the counselor's presentation to the client of some apparent or implied conflict.[7] The conflict may relate, for example, to a factual discrepancy or to some inconsistency between the client's articulated priorities and his or her conduct. Confrontation does not, however, signify a frontal attack on the client. The technique, when properly used and timed, appears as a normal, nondisruptive element in your discussion with a client.

Ineffective counselors generally follow one of three patterns on confrontation: they avoid it entirely; they confine it to nonthreatening and neutral topics; or they confront the client only in an aggressive, attacking manner. The latter approach obstructs development of the lawyer-client relationship, of client self-understanding, and of action steps. In the first two patterns, the lawyer risks breaching a duty owed to clients to help them fully understand their situation and a duty owed to the legal system to ac-

---

5. You may decide, though, to fully discuss the client's problem through a self-disclosure or through an analogy to some set of facts besides those actually presented by the client. After exhausting the analogy, steer discussion back to the client's case. This tactic is appropriate when the client's ego is so involved or threatened that he experiences difficulty in analyzing the issues in his own case. By first diverting the topic to a "neutral" fact situation, you may provoke a meaningful discussion before the client's ego can interfere.

6. Compare R. Carkhuff & B. Berenson, *Beyond Counseling and Therapy* 172 (1967); Berenson, Mitchell & Laney, Level of Therapist Functioning, Types of Confrontation and Type of Patient, 24 J. of Clinical Psychology 111 (1968); Berenson, Mitchell & Moravec, Level of Therapist Functioning, Patient Depth of Self-Exploration and Type of Confrontation, 15 J. of Counseling Psychology 136 (1968), with Kaul, Kaul & Bednar, Counselor Confrontation and Depth of Self-Exploration, 20 J. of Counseling Psychology 132 (1973). See generally B. Berenson & K. Mitchell, *Confrontation: For Better or Worse* (1974).

7. We have already dealt with aspects of confrontation in our consideration of advanced empathy. When you articulate explicit and implicit information in advanced empathy, you frequently identify inconsistencies in the client's facts and priorities. In a divorce case, for example, a client may send mixed signals about whether termination of the marriage is really the desired end. And Ms. Martin, deciding what she wanted to do about investing in the lakeside project, implied discordant emotions about her goals. In such cases, you must identify these conflicts and "confront" the client with them.

curately represent clients' cases to others. Yet confrontation can often be threatening to the client. Many lawyers, therefore, hesitate to confront clients for fear of offending them or creating an uncomfortable scene. That fear must be neutralized by the development of appropriate skills and sound lawyer-client relationships. Working with those assets, you can effectively confront a client whenever appropriate.

The following problem provides illustration for the discussion in the remainder of this section on how you can effectively use confrontation in counseling clients.

≡ PROBLEM 3 ≡
The Female Executive

Alice Wagner is a 32-year-old executive with the Vortex Corporation, a mid-sized manufacturer of parts for car and truck brakes with six regional operations across the country. She began her work at Vortex eight years ago, following her magna cum laude completion of the M.B.A. program at a prominent school of management. She quickly earned two promotions to become a regional sales supervisor. But her ascendancy stopped there despite her exemplary job performance. Although Vortex has several female executives, they are all in low-level positions. The women are, however, relatively young and inexperienced compared to most of the company's top executives. Vortex cites experience as an important criterion in its promotion decisions.

Vortex promotes from within the company as much as possible. In its normal promotion routine, Vortex does not advertise openings, but canvasses its employees to determine whether any are qualified. If any are, then it selects the most qualified. That was the procedure used for both of Wagner's earlier promotions. Even though the company does not ordinarily solicit applications, it tells its employees they can inform their supervisor they are interested in an open position, and they are then considered. Vortex goes outside its own ranks only when it concludes none of its employees qualifies for the job in question.

About a year ago, Ms. Wagner learned the regional vice president's job was about to become vacant. Believing she was ready for the increased responsibilities, Wagner notified the appropriate people that she was interested in the promotion. After several weeks, however, Vortex advertised the position and eventually hired a man, Jay Buchanan, from outside the company.

Wagner felt she had been the victim of sex discrimination, and was enraged at the disrespect shown women by top management. She therefore consulted an attorney, Karen Goodman, concerning a possible sex discrimination claim against Vortex. Upon the advice of counsel, Wagner filed a complaint with the state fair-employment agency. After the statutory period for administrative investigation and conciliation lapsed, she received a right-to-sue letter initiating a 90-day period during which she could pursue the claim with a civil action. That time has now almost expired as Wagner and Goodman meet to decide whether to pursue the matter with a lawsuit. Excerpts of their discussion follow:

Wagner: I must admit I'm not sure I want to go ahead with a lawsuit. It seems like it would be a lot of hassle and expense, and I don't know if I'm up for it either.

Goodman: It would be a lot of hassle and expense, and you do need to factor that in. [Pause.] I wonder, though, how you balance that against what you told me when we first talked, that your main goal was to make a point about rampant sex discrimination in hiring and promotion into top management, especially at Vortex. What do you think?

Wagner: Well, I guess the principle is still important to me, but I'm not really sure a lawsuit will get me anywhere. I mean, I know they didn't give me fair consideration because I'm a woman, but on the other hand I don't know if I could handle the job if they had promoted me. It is an awfully demanding position and I'm not sure I'm up to it. And the guy they did hire has experience over me. He may be better qualified than I, and so even without the discrimination, he would have gotten the job.

Goodman: You're uncertain about how you would function in that position. Of course, you know you graduated near the top of your class in management school, as you did in every other school you've been in. More important, you've done extremely well, I know, in your present job. You're very bright and energetic, and you work hard. It seems the skills and aptitude are certainly there.

Wagner: Well, I appreciate that. I guess it's a question I have in my mind about my capacity, since I never had that much responsibility. And I suppose, too, there are some reservations that I have about whether I could function in their all-male environment, and whether I could emotionally handle supervising a lot of men with more experience than I in that field.

* * *

Goodman: You mentioned earlier you were sure you were a victim of discrimination, yet you also said you thought Buchanan might have been better qualified than you and might have been hired even without the discrimination. I'm not sure what you meant by those two statements.

Wagner: I guess what I was saying was that I'm sure they do not want a woman in a responsible position—they don't think one can handle the job and they don't want a woman ruining their male preserve. So I'm sure they did not seriously consider me. But even if they had seriously considered me, they still might have hired Buchanan since he has a lot more experience.

Goodman: I see. I wonder, though, if you can look at what happened a little differently. If you were a man, they would have seriously considered you. And if they had, they would have been satisfied with you. What do you think?

b. Functions

You can use confrontation to: (1) enhance client self-exploration and self-understanding; (2) spur the client to action; and (3) ensure accuracy or lawyer understanding. These are discussed below, in turn.

(1) Enhance Client Self-Exploration and Self-Understanding

Properly executed confrontation of your clients can help them to better explore and understand their priorities, needs, and feelings. The confrontation juxtaposes before clients conflicting information, values, statements, beliefs, or relationships, forcing the clients to explain the conflict. When it directly concerns matters within your clients' own experience, they must then explore their feelings, recollections, or priorities. That, in turn, brings the clients to a better self-understanding and facilitates the selection and implementation of alternatives. The dialogue in the Wagner case illustrates how the process works. First, Goodman identifies a potential conflict between Wagner's previously expressed goal of attacking rampant sex discrimination in top management, as well as her articulated anger about the situation, and her recently developed concern about the hassle and expense of litigation. When Wagner is so confronted, she looks deeper (past her rationalization?) and finds anxiety about her ability to handle the job. Goodman then pushes for further clarification by confronting Wagner with an inconsistency between her anxiety and her (past and present) demonstrations of ability and aptitude. The client is forced to delve deeper into herself to explain the contradiction. She is then able to articulate that her reservations are generated by the discomforting prospect of functioning in a male environment and supervising more experienced men. The counseling cannot end there; there is still much to consider about how those feelings should affect her selection of an appropriate course of action. Clearly, though, her new understanding is crucial to her decision. Perhaps she will want to overcome those insecurities, or perhaps she will prefer to remain in her present position with the security it offers and to seek only the additional money she would have earned with the promotion. At least those are alternatives the client should consider before deciding what she should do. Whatever conclusion the extended discussion leads to, the client will at least have made her decision with full awareness of how it interacts with and affects her professed values and goals.

(2) Spur Action

Through counseling, clients gain personal insights, express values, and identify goals. The process ideally should result in some action that gives effect to those insights, values, and goals. You help your clients to move toward that end when you position them to recognize their conflicts and, after clarification of the competing factors, to resolve the conflicts.

You lay the basic issues before the clients in such a way that they must choose and act on their choices.

Confrontation has special utility in working with indecisive clients. When clients have articulated their goals, yet procrastinate in deciding (or claim an inability to decide) which action plan to implement, you must force a decision if the vacillation could prevent attainment of the identified goals. Self-exploration and self-understanding are of little value if your clients are unable to convert the introspection into a decision and appropriate action. Conflict results between the clients' stated insights, values, and goals on the one hand, and their inaction on the other.

To force a decision, confront such clients with the mutual exclusivity between reaching the identified goals and inaction. You thus help the clients to see the necessity for action. If a decision is still not forthcoming, then perhaps the clients have identified the wrong goals (in terms of their own feelings and values) or are psychologically incapable of a decision. In the latter case, consider referral to an appropriate expert.

In Ms. Wagner's case, the client articulated during an early discussion that her goals were to vindicate the policies of the civil rights statute and to secure the job she was denied. When she then displays reluctance to initiate a civil action, an apparent conflict arises between the client's goals and her conduct. By confronting the client with the conflict, Goodman dramatizes the necessity for reaching a decision, any decision. If Wagner fails to act and pursue her sex discrimination claim, her inaction combined with the statute of limitations will defeat her previously identified goals. Her lawyer, in effect, creates a crisis that the client must resolve. The resolution moves the client toward her identified (or restated) goals.

The process, then, steadily progresses from client self-exploration, through self-understanding, to action. This process not only works to contend with your clients' legal problems, but it also serves as a general problem-solving model for the clients. They learn about self-analysis, conflict recognition, and conflict resolution.

(3) Ensure Accuracy

You confront clients to clarify and correct conflicts in information and signals. This use of confrontation serves both practical and ethical purposes.

Obviously, if factual conflicts occur, you must resolve them. Legal tactics alone require resolution; you would be foolish to blindly proceed in a case in which evidence contradicts your client's story, or in which your client's statements are self-contradictory. If no attempt is made at resolution, then you and your client will be certain to face undesired consequences when the action step is implemented, be it a trial, negotiation, contract, will, or whatever. Moreover, you have an obligation to yourself, your clients, the legal system, and society generally to ensure you do not endorse falsehoods.

Your goals in confronting clients in the context of this section are to accurately understand them and their cases and to bring the clients to the same understanding. Impeaching clients is not a goal. The need to confront clients to ensure accuracy arises not only when you suspect them of lying, but whenever an inconsistency appears. For example, the facts may admit two disparate interpretations, or a client's emotions (identified by collected data from the client's verbal and nonverbal communications and from outside sources of information) may appear to run counter to his or her self-descriptions or to typical reactions. In Goodman's discussion with Ms. Wagner, the lawyer confronts the client with seemingly inconsistent conclusions the latter has reached: (1) she was a victim of discrimination, but (2) Buchanan probably would have been hired in any event. Wagner's response provides Goodman with a better understanding of the case, but it also suggests two interpretations of the facts with potentially diverse legal consequences. On one hand, the facts disclose Buchanan was perhaps better qualified and would have been the employer's choice even without the discrimination. On the other hand, the facts could also be construed to show that, had the employer followed its normal promotion policies in a nondiscriminatory manner, Wagner would have been hired. Goodman then presents these disparate conclusions to Wagner for her reaction. The exchange should lead to a better understanding of the case by both the lawyer and the client and, therefore, to better decision-making.

c. Content

The substance of effective counselor confrontation varies considerably. Yet certain types of client behavior are both common and especially appropriate for a confrontation response. This section assesses those situations to provide a better sense of when you will find confrontation to be a helpful technique.[8]

First, you can appropriately confront your clients when you detect discrepancies between apparent reality and your clients' expressions or feelings. Individuals' self-perceptions often differ from how others perceive them. Clients in the process of a criminal defense, a libel trial, a divorce, or some other ego-threatening experience will often suffer an unjustifiably diminished perception of self; they feel less worthy than they really are. Alice Wagner, for example, had an opinion of her abilities that was apparently inconsistent with what she had demonstrated in school and in work. On other occasions, the self-impression can be inflated and you may be justified in confronting the client with facts that bring the client down to reality. You help the client reach a better self-understanding by pointing out the discrepancy.

---

8. G. Egan, *The Skilled Helper* 219-227 (3d ed. 1986), provides the basis for much of the following discussion on the content of confrontation. See also Berensen, Mitchell & Laney, Level of Therapist Functioning, Types of Confrontation and Type of Patient, 24 J. of Clinical Psychology 111 (1968); Berensen, Mitchell & Moravec, Level of Therapist Functioning, Patient Depth of Self-Exploration, and Type of Confrontation, 15 J. of Counseling Psychology 136 (1968).

Consider the following excerpt from a counseling session of an abused wife:

Attorney: You said you and your husband are getting along fine now. But you still seem to be very much afraid of him—as when he was in here earlier, you avoided looking at him and seemed to shrink into your seat.

Client: Well, Jim hasn't hurt me, lately—not since that night I called you. I guess, though, there's always some concern in my mind that he'll blow up again.

Attorney: I wonder if those kinds of feelings can coexist with a happy marriage.

Here, the attorney's confrontations (there are two of them) identify one discrepancy between the client's verbal statements and her nonverbal conduct and a second discrepancy between the client's fears of her husband and her desire for a healthy marriage. In confronting the client on each discrepancy, the counselor disdained attack and encouraged the client to explore and understand her feelings.

Second, you should be especially sensitive to discrepancies between your clients' articulated values and the clients' behavior. You owe clients a duty to expose any such conflict to be certain they are moving in the direction they want. Assume, for example, a client who is a divorced father claims that his children's well-being is a very high priority, yet refuses to increase their support payments while maintaining a lavish personal lifestyle. In such a circumstance, the lawyer should indicate to the client that his actions conflict with his expressed values. The conflict resolution there may be a redefinition of the client's values, or it may be a recalculation of the client's financial needs. In either event, the lawyer has fulfilled his obligation of ensuring that the action step best accomplishes the client's real priorities. Goodman accomplished much the same purpose when she confronted Wagner about the conflict between her new-found reluctance to initiate litigation and her previously stated goal of fighting sex discrimination at Vortex.

You have a responsibility to confront apparent discrepancies between values and behavior because such conflicts go to the very core of counseling's function of identifying priorities. If the inconsistencies cannot be explained, then you must work with the client to redefine and clarify priorities toward a more meaningful analysis of appropriate action steps. You do not usurp your clients' values, but you do ensure that the clients' actions are consistent with their articulated values.

Third, you may confront clients when they rationalize. Clients may distort reality, conjure excuses, or engage in some game or charade to obscure reality. In distortion, for example, clients might confuse their stubbornness in a negotiation with adherence to a principle, or might perceive their resentment of authority as an expression of independence. Their impressions may, in fact, be accurate, but you cannot ignore confronting your clients with the possibility that they have rationalized an unjustifiable position.

Clients may conceive excuses to rationalize their behavior. If, for example, a client persistently misses work for apparently flimsy reasons (at least when viewed cumulatively), then you should ask whether there may be other explanations for the absenteeism. In Wagner's case, she presented an "excuse"—that she may not have been qualified for the job in question—to avoid dealing with her insecurity about supervising more experienced men. Again, the confrontation technique allows you to force the client into meaningful introspection.

Clients might extend rationalization to construct complex games and smoke screens. The clients may, for example, be unwilling to take responsibility for decisions; they may want the insulation provided by the explanation that they were just acting on their lawyer's orders. Clients might present themselves as helpless and weak and inject obsequious and flattering remarks about your superior position and insight. By goading you into making the decisions, such clients figure to relieve themselves (or so they think) of the responsibility for any actions you take on their behalf. You must avoid participating in or condoning such rationalizations. Thus, you will find it necessary to confront these clients about the fictions, to discern their motives, and then to work toward elimination of the games and smoke screens.

Fourth, you must be vigilant to detect and to confront a client's evasion of issues and challenges. A typical problem arises from a client's inclination to blame others for the consequences of his or her own conduct. The client may also evade by deflecting the issue to avoid facing difficult, underlying questions.

Assume, for example, that a client illustrates his claim of job harassment from his supervisor by describing a series of incidents in which the supervisor scathingly berated him for being late, for haphazard work, and for failing to wear safety gear. When the incidents are viewed separately, the supervisor did seem to overreact, but when viewed cumulatively, the question arises whether the client provoked such vehemence. Consider the lawyer's presentation of that issue to the client in the following exchange:[9]

Attorney: How does this supervisor treat the other workers?
Client: He gets along fine with them. It just seems that he's picked me out.
Attorney: I see. Do you think you've done anything that called for the special treatment?
Client: No. I just mind my own business.
Attorney: Well, suppose I ask you this: What do you think he believes is the reason you are singled out? How would he respond if I asked him why he has berated you?
Client: He'd probably say I was late a lot and didn't do my work very well.

Here, the client has avoided considering the real issue, even when he is asked if he has provoked the special treatment. Thus, the lawyer was forced to reformulate the question to compel the client to face the issue. The attorney did not take sides, but pushed the client to a level of analysis that he was incapable of on his own.

---

9. This illustration is adapted from G. Egan, *The Skilled Helper* 163 (1st ed. 1975).

Finally, you confront clients on their strengths as well as their weaknesses. Indeed, research has revealed that effective counselors confront clients on their positive characteristics more often than on their negative ones. Thus, Goodman placed before Wagner her academic and professional successes to force her to consider other explanations for her reluctance to seek the job she had been denied. Clients frequently overlook or underestimate their own capacities and you should see that these are accurately assessed in deciding on appropriate action steps. When you identify overlooked strengths, you often provide emotional reassurance, another important counseling function. Of course, relevant weaknesses cannot be ignored either.

d. Methods and Limitations

The methods you use to confront clients substantially influence your effectiveness. Confrontation can be abused and cause undesired client reactions. You must therefore use it with discretion and skill. That requires cognizance of the following points.

First, confrontation—unless it relates to clarification of factual inconsistencies—should not ordinarily be used in the early stages of the lawyer-client relationship. The typically threatening nature of confrontation can damage and stunt an undeveloped relationship. In addition, you need an established lawyer-client partnership to ensure that the client views a confrontation as an invitation to a dialogue and not as a personal attack. If the equal status between you and your client has not been established, then your confrontation seriously risks leaving the client overly defensive or, worse, overwhelmed. The position of superiority you normally hold early in the relationship will give your confrontations a potency you do not want.

Second, you should use the verbal tentativeness techniques described in the discussion of advanced empathy in Section B, above (pages 264-265). By making the confrontation more tentative and less immediate, you reduce its threatening quality. You aim for tentativeness when you put the confrontation as a question or a speculation probe. Such forms imply a greater degree of give-and-take than direct statements. Confrontation is, after all, only the presentation of a conflict to clients for their explanation and discussion.

Third, the nonverbal accompaniment to confrontation must be consistent with caring, empathic, respectful, and genuine counseling. Of particular importance to confrontation are the paralinguistic effects—pace, pitch, tone, and volume. By voice inflection, you can transform a confrontation from an invitation to a cooperative discussion into an all-out attack on the client—and vice versa. Thus, you should be soothing and slow-paced in voice quality and delivery.

If you fail to deliver your confrontation properly, your client will likely construe it as an attempt by you to judge and persuade. For example, one can easily foresee that premature or careless confrontation in the child support hypothetical (see page 279) could make the lawyer sound judgmental. Rather than accomplishing the positive goals of confrontation, a bungling attorney in that instance could totally preempt client decision-making. A client might also react to ineffective confrontation by arguing with you. The open discussion then turns into an open debate. You must use proper timing, nonverbal communication, tentativeness, and explanation to communicate that your confrontations are necessary for full and effective consideration of the relevant issues.

Would you ever be justified in using confrontation to "attack" the client? Perhaps. Two extreme possibilities come to mind. First, if the client has resisted all lesser measures to force a decision—any decision—then you may consider an aggressive approach, or even anger, to cajole action (or a final decision not to act) from the client. You must assess the effectiveness of that approach compared with your alternatives. You could also: (1) refer the client to an expert for therapy; (2) make the decision for the client based on the client's descriptions of his or her priorities and your common sense; (3) withdraw from representation.

Second, you may find that the facts apparently contradict the client's statements, yet the client stubbornly adheres to his or her version without offering adequate explanation for the contradictions. To avoid catastrophe in pursuing an action step, you might conclude that cross-examination or other aggressive techniques are necessary to expose falsehoods, discern some rationale for the inconsistencies, or at least relieve your mistrust of the client. Again, you must consider the alternatives. Here, they would be referral and withdrawal.

Chapter 12

Conflicts in the Attorney-Client Relationship

A. INTRODUCTION

You have learned thus far that your role as a counseling lawyer requires you to structure, probe, empathize, confront, and advise, while remaining nonjudgmental. Your clients contribute information, priorities, and—most important—decisions. For this model of the lawyer-client relationship to work, each participant must both fulfill and stay within his or her role. That, however, is a precarious contingency, as the relationship necessarily renders the client susceptible to manipulation by the lawyer. Any time that one party in a relationship controls the structure and agenda and unilaterally maintains knowledge about the external standards affecting decisions—as lawyers do with their monopoly on the law—then domination and manipulation can only be avoided by persistent and conscientious self-control by the more powerful party. More than containing one's conscious motivations is required to meet that condition.

The realities of human relations and limitations supply an incalculable number of possibilities for conflict between an attorney's own needs and the client's priorities and for disruption of the model lawyer-client relationship. Some of those possibilities are obvious: The attorney wants money and therefore uses a client's trust funds for personal use or charges the client an exorbitant fee for a mechanical task. Even the culpable attorney can at least recognize such conflicts. Thus, while fraud and intentional deception are certainly offensive and must be avoided, their precondition—intentional and conscious wrongdoing—means they require no elaboration in this text.

We focus here on more subtle motivations, on how personality needs, desires, values, likes, and dislikes manipulate unwitting lawyers into manipulating their clients. Lawyers know full well that their inherent advantage in knowledge and expertise gives them power over almost any client and enables them to convince the client of the desirability (or undesirability) of any action step. For example, in a decision on whether to accept a settlement offer, the lawyer possesses such discretion in describing the impact of the law on the client's facts that the lawyer can literally dictate the client's decision. Even without a desire to "cheat" the client, the lawyer may feel the need to work the client to a particular result. The lawyer may need money immediately, may dislike the client and seek to get rid of him or her as soon as possible, may not have time for a trial, or may believe acceptance of the offer would be advantageous to the client. In such instances, the lawyer is tempted to agitate for, or even coerce, settlement. On the other hand, the attorney might want the opportunity for a jury trial to satisfy competitive urges or to gain personally from the anticipated publicity. These feelings move the attorney to manipulate rejection of the settlement offer. If you are caught in such circumstances, you may be unaware of the impact these motivations have on you, your counseling, and your "expert" advice. The conduct that results from unconscious motivation may not be as reprehensible as intentional wrongs, but its disruption of your partnerships with clients can nevertheless be substantial.

Your manipulative capability draws support from perceptions held by most laypersons (and many lawyers) that law is an objective, predictable, discernible set of rules easily applied to any factual situation. You can always rationalize your insistence on a given course of action by simply declaring that "the law" requires its selection. Your informational advantages over your client on other issues—such as jury reactions or the practicalities of trust or estate administration—add to this position of power. At times, of course, the law may be both clear and unbending, and the alternatives reducible to only one. But you must address the degree to which your legal and factual analyses are influenced by your own needs, values, and motives.

Attorney personality needs and attributes that interfere with client decision-making appear in varied forms and degrees. They range from deep-seated personality disorders, to ego defenses, to less serious but still debilitating personality conflicts. The recognition and remediation of severe psychiatric problems are beyond this text, but we can, and must, examine those more typical motivators having special relevance for lawyers. This chapter tries to meet that goal by describing the most common sources of conflict. Section B analyzes attorney personality needs in terms of the needs for power, achievement, association, and order. Next, Section C sketches the phenomenon of countertransference and its relevance for lawyers. The chapter then turns to Section D's discussion of value clarification. Chapter 13 considers whether there might not be some conflicts or countervailing concerns that require exceptions to the principle of client autonomy.

B. ATTORNEY PERSONALITY NEEDS

1. Generally

The human personality is an extremely complex subject. Witness, for example, the libraries full of volumes of psychology and literature trying to explain or illustrate human nature. Our effort here is decidedly more modest. We briefly describe a general framework for examining the personality of lawyers and then focus on their motivational needs. The discussion provides you with an understanding of how your own personality makeup can affect the way in which you practice law and relate to clients.

The great humanistic psychologist, Abraham Maslow, developed a hierarchy of needs to describe human motivation.[1] The hierarchy includes five general classifications of needs: physiological, safety, belonging and love, esteem, and self-actualization. These are ranked from the "lowest" human needs to the "highest." At the lowest end, physiological needs include the basic physical needs of food, shelter, clothes, and sex. The safety needs require multiple levels of security. Individuals seek physical safety; they need to be free of fear from bodily harm. They also seek routine, predictability, and order in their world. Moreover, persons require some level of job or financial security, as is expressed in the common desires for tenure, seniority, savings accounts, and various insurance measures. Belonging and love needs reflect individuals' desire for close and meaningful human relationships. A person "will hunger for affectionate relations with people in general, namely, for a place in his group, and will strive with great intensity to achieve this goal."[2] The esteem needs may be classified into two subsets. "These are, first, the desire for strength, for achievement, for adequacy, for mastery and competence, for confidence in the face of the world, and for independence and freedom. Second, we have what we may call the desire for reputation or prestige (defining it as respect or esteem from other people), status, dominance, recognition, attention, importance,

---

1. Maslow developed his theories in a number of works. See especially *The Farther Reaches of Human Nature* (1971); *Toward a Psychology of Being* (1968); and *Motivation and Personality* (1954). Our text's summary of Maslow's theory is largely derived from the latter work at 80-106.

We recognize, of course, that there are many different theories of human psychology that you can use to enhance self-understanding. Chapter 2 presented a sampling of those theories in the context of their use by schools of psychotherapy. We have selected Maslow's work for discussion here because we think it is the most consistent with, and informative on, the interviewing and counseling model we construct in this book and because we find Maslow's structure is particularly useful and easy to apply. We take comfort, too, in the number of commentators (cited in note 10, below) who have seen the utility for lawyers of needs analysis similar to that we describe in this text.

2. A. Maslow, *Motivation and Personality* 89 (1954).

or appreciation."[3] Finally, self-actualization refers to an advanced state of personality development in which individuals seek self-fulfillment and accomplishment through personal growth. Self-actualized persons desire "to become everything that [they are] capable of becoming."[4]

Maslow saw these needs as hierarchical in the sense that the needs at one level must be fairly well satisfied before the individual develops substantial needs at the next, higher, level. Thus an individual who confronts hunger or a lack of shelter does not develop strong safety or social needs.[5] But if the physiological needs are met, then

> [a]t once other (and higher) needs emerge and these, rather than physiological hungers, dominate the organism. And when these in turn are satisfied, again new (and still higher) needs emerge, and so on. This is what we mean by saying that the basic human needs are organized into a hierarchy of relative prepotency.[6]

The hierarchical structure of the needs, though, is neither a rigid nor an all-or-nothing configuration. Some people, for example, may develop esteem needs in advance of love needs. In addition, there may seem to be a hierarchical reversal when a need has been satisfied on such a long and sustained basis that it is undervalued. (Thus, people who have never experienced hunger or a lack of shelter are prone to underestimate the psychological significance of adequate food and housing.) Finally, a need does not have to be 100 percent gratified before the next need emerges. Most normal persons in our society are partially satisfied in all their basic needs. "A more realistic description of the hierarchy would be in terms of decreasing percentages of satisfaction as we go up the hierarchy of prepotency."[7] Physiological needs may be 100 percent satisfied, safety needs 80 percent, love 60 percent, esteem 30 percent, and self-actualization 10 percent. The new need emerges by gradual degrees. Although more than one level can be simultaneously operative, the lower prepotent need still takes precedence.

In the United States, the physiological needs of practically all lawyers

---

3. Id. at 90.

4. Id. at 92. Self-actualization is discussed further in Chapter 13, in the excerpt from Bastress, Client-Centered Counseling and Moral Accountability, 10 J. of the Legal Profession 97 (1985).

The portion of that article reprinted in this text at pages 312-315 elaborates on the model for self-analysis described in this chapter. We must emphasize the modest treatment provided in these materials cannot be the final word on self-analysis.

We also admit that self-awareness and self-development are very personal undertakings. While we believe the models described in this section (which have a heavy emphasis on humanistic psychology and cognitive development theories) can be of immense value to attorneys, we also believe they can be best used, along with the discussions in Chapter 2, as a starting point for further study and for the construction of personalized models for self-development. Perhaps, then, the most important point to be learned is that there is a critical need for introspection and for a worldview that will produce self-control and growth as a person and as a lawyer.

5. "Hunger" should be distinguished from "appetite": "The average American Citizen is experiencing appetite rather than hunger when he says 'I am hungry.' He is apt to experience sheer life-and-death hunger only by accident and then only a few times [at most] through his entire life." Maslow, *Motivation and Personality* 83 (1954).

6. Id. at 83 (emphasis deleted).

7. Id. at 100.

are adequately satisfied. Lawyers can thus function at higher levels; their needs satisfaction is focused on financial security, love, esteem, and self-actualization.[8] To this list, certain of Maslow's followers have added an autonomy need, which describes individuals' desire to make decisions on their own and to enjoy a measure of independence.[9] These higher needs operate in complex ways and, as indicated above, have a complex configuration. In lawyers, the higher needs manifest themselves most significantly through the needs for power (safety and esteem), achievement (esteem and autonomy), association (love and esteem), and order (safety).[10]

We isolate those traits because of their recurrent predominance in lawyers' personalities and because of their interrelationship with legal counseling issues. Individuals choose a profession (when social forces and personal abilities permit a choice) that will satisfy their most prominent personality needs.[11] Law practice feeds—even rewards—the desires for power, achievement, association, and order. Thus, practitioners as a group possess unusually high satisfaction levels for those needs. As we shall observe, the needs are both essential to and potentially disruptive of your work and relationships. The distribution of the needs within your personality has a profound effect on your interpersonal and professional functioning. We now address each of them more fully.

2. *Need for Power*

The need for power compels the individual toward acquisition, possession, and control. The individual may seek fulfillment through material or financial wealth, assiduous retention of it upon acquisition, positions of importance or leadership, and domination of relationships.

Law practice can gratify such desires. Many see law as a lucrative en-

---

8. Leete, Francia & Strawser, A Look at Lawyers' Need Satisfaction, 57 A.B.A.J. 1193 (1971).

9. Porter, A Study of Perceived Need Satisfaction in Bottom and Middle Management Jobs, 45 J. of Applied Psychology 1 (1961). See also Leete, Francia & Strawser, A Look at Lawyers' Need Satisfaction, 57 A.B.A.J. 1193 (1971). Maslow's description of the esteem needs could well embrace Porter's autonomy classification. A. Maslow, *Motivation and Personality* 90 (1954).

10. Other commentators have also perceived these needs as predominant in attorneys' personalities, although the terminology used to describe the needs has varied somewhat. See, e.g., Greening & Zielonka, Special Applications of Humanistic Learning: A Workshop on Attorney-Client Relationships, 2 Interpersonal Dev. 194 (1971-1972); Leete, Francia & Strawser, A Look at Lawyers' Need Satisfaction, 57 A.B.A.J. 1193 (1971); Redmount, Attorney Personalities and Some Psychological Aspects of Legal Consultation, 109 U. Pa. L. Rev. 972 (1961); Watson, The Lawyer as Counselor, 5 J. Fam. L. 7 (1965); Watson, The Quest for Professional Competence: Psychological Aspects of Legal Education, 37 U. Cin. L. Rev. 93 (1968). See also W. Cormier & L. S. Cormier, *Interviewing Strategies for Helpers* 11-21 (2d ed. 1985).

11. See, e.g., Watson, The Quest for Professional Competence: Psychological Aspects of Legal Education, 37 U. Cin. L. Rev. 93, 99 (1968): "When a decision is made in career choice, it will reflect among other things the patterns of need gratification, which may be best satisfied in a certain occupational area." See also LaRussa, Portia's Decision: Women's Motives for Studying Law and Their Later Career Satisfaction as Attorneys, 1 Psychology of Women Q. 350 (1977); Redmount, Attorney Personalities and Some Psychological Aspects of Legal Consultation, 109 U. Pa. L. Rev. 972 (1961); Stone, Legal Education on the Couch, 85 Harv. L. Rev. 392 (1971).

deavor, as a means to earn and accumulate wealth. Lawyering also provides a measure of social status and esteem, which can enhance the sensation of "dominance." In addition, law practice affords the easiest access to political office with its attendant power, and lawyer-client relationships give lawyers the opportunity to control important aspects of people's lives. Finally, the legal system is saturated by the concerns of power, thus providing a steady lure to those tracking it. Robert Redmount has described this phenomenon:

> Law has so much to do with the definition and protection of property rights, with the benefits and safeguards of status, and with protection and freedom for a variety of profit and gain motives. It promotes these ends by means of a highly conspicuous adversary process. It is stubborn and self-protective in the way in which it guards its power through the zealous operation and use of statutes, rules of procedure, and similar standards. These are all circumstances that allow possessiveness of various kinds to flourish.[12]

The power need has positive attributes. It moves the individual to assume essential leadership roles, and (God knows!) we do need leaders. Lawyers with a healthy dose of the power need typically attempt to influence the law, the bar, or society to ends they find just. Such efforts are time-honored and desirable activities for the lawyer. Moreover, an undersized need for power can debilitate the personality; the individual can be an unblinking follower, susceptible to the power manipulations of others. In lawyers, a vulnerability to intimidation can damage their clients' interests. Lawyers with a low power need are ineffective in counseling, negotiation, and litigation. In counseling, they tend to avoid appropriate confrontation of the client and are unwilling to analyze and go beneath the surface of the client's statements. They may also manipulate their clients to pursue nonconfrontational alternatives. In negotiation and litigation, lawyers lacking in the need for power capitulate too quickly and unnecessarily avoid high-intensity measures to reach the clients' goals.

On the other hand, the need for power can be destructive if it predominates the lawyer's personality. The need to acquire and possess material wealth can frequently conflict with client priorities. The natural inclination of a lawyer with a high power need to dominate and control undermines the basic premises of the lawyer-client partnership. Such attorneys often view their role as gathering facts and applying law toward their selection of the most advantageous course of action. Typically, that course of action reflects the alternative that best enhances the lawyer's status and profit. That criterion sometimes produces a strategy or result that concurs

---

12. Redmount, Attorney Personalities and Some Psychological Aspects of Legal Consultation, 109 U. Pa. L. Rev. 972, 975 (1961). See also Watson, The Quest for Professional Competence: Psychological Aspects of Legal Education, 37 U. Cin. L. Rev. 93, 95 (1968):

> Law provides a means for advancing one's social position by virtue of the prestige which favors a professional person. There can be little doubt that lawyers are a very powerful group, and may well be the most important group in American society with respect to crucial decision-making. The legal profession may also be utilized as a stepping-stone to social status and to the intra-psychic reality of being "somebody important."

with the client's priorities (as in a personal injury case when the client wants as large a settlement as possible, or in a spectacular criminal case of a wealthy defendant who insists on a trial), but an unacceptably high potential for conflict persists.

Most persons perceive the dominant attorney to be the norm, and that is probably an accurate assumption; because of the capacity of law practice to satisfy the power need, the profession attracts many with high satisfaction levels for power. The media reinforces such perceptions of the lawyer's role. Perry Mason frequently bullied his clients and was saved only by his omniscience. High-profile lawyers are often flamboyant, status-seeking, or in pursuit of the world's record for a money judgment. That is not to say such individuals are ineffective lawyers, but the prominence and visibility of their images reflect perceptions about "successful" lawyers. Notions of status, wealth, and power are frequently ingrained in those perceptions. The risk is that public notions about lawyers creep into their offices and their interpersonal dealings. That invasion in turn effects a domineering approach to lawyering.

The need for power can be consuming and disruptive. Consider the case of a sole practitioner disbarred for borrowing from several of his clients' trust accounts. He had also, on occasion, assessed exorbitant fees and pursued other questionable strategies for profit. Upon public revelation of his misdeeds, the lawyer was contrite, acknowledged his wrongdoing, and said he had intended to, and did in fact, repay the borrowed money. He explained that he had appropriated it because he needed it to support his desire to gain public office (the state legislature). He had always wanted to be a public official; he had entered law for that reason; and he needed money both to "look successful" and to finance his campaign. In the end, though, he had seen that he had allowed his goal of holding political office to obscure his better judgment.

But why did he want public office? Here the lawyer did not seek wealth as an end in itself, but as a means to another goal—political success. The motivation is much the same. The lawyer sought power and status, and he compromised his clients' interests to attain it. As the evidence revealed, not all of his compromises were technically "unethical" (meaning in violation of the Code). Yet one could certainly assume that if he was juggling accounts to satisfy his needs, then he was also engaging in related but lesser evils, such as manipulating client decisions for self-gain. The story reveals the degree to which attorney motivations can interfere with the proper functioning of the lawyer-client relationship.

Finally, lawyers' confusion about their ability to exert power can cause them serious interpersonal difficulties. Consider the following:

> Unresolved feelings about oneself in relation to power and control may include impotence, passivity, dependence. There are several ways that power can be misused in counseling. First, a counselor who fears being impotent or weak or who is afraid to give up control may try to be omnipotent. For this person, counseling is manageable only when it is controllable. Such a counselor may use a variety of maneuvers to stay in control, including persuading the client to do what the counselor wants, getting upset or defensive if a client is resistant or hesitant, and dominating the content and direction of the

interview. The counselor who needs to control the interview may be more likely to engage in a power struggle with a client.

In contrast, a counselor may be afraid of power and control. This counselor may attempt to escape from as much responsibility and participation in counseling as possible. Such a counselor avoids taking control by giving too much direction to the client and by not expressing opinions. In other words, risks are avoided or ignored.[13]

3. Need for Achievement

The personality's achievement need manifests itself through competitiveness, aggressiveness, independence, and persistence. The need often finds fulfillment in the struggle for individual freedom within a society. High-achievers push themselves, work hard, seek to win. They take games seriously; they are the type of people who turn a friendly game of Monopoly, Scrabble, or tennis into a seemingly high-stakes test of wits, will, and ego.

The practice of law, with its emphasis on the adversarial process, with its opportunities for championing clients and causes, and with its perpetual schedule of contests, offers an ideal playing field for those with high satisfaction levels for achievement. For such individuals, "law is an accommodating and sometimes over-powering mistress."[14] Litigation, negotiation, and representing individuals in pursuit of justice clearly satiate this compelling need.

Naturally, there is much that is positive about the achievement need. The adversarial process depends on effective champions, and clients can benefit from having attorneys who fight hard to secure favorable outcomes. The need pushes individuals to make the best of their abilities, which is the most clients or society can ask from their lawyers. Generally, though not always, clients are better off when their lawyer "wins" their cases for them. Moreover, a low satisfaction level for the achievement need denotes a serious personality problem for lawyers. They must, after all, be motivated to work on behalf of clients. An individual short on competitive drive would make a lousy litigator. Of course, there are noncompetitive areas of law practice, but some achievement need is always desirable to move the lawyer to accomplish clients' goals, to *achieve* in the legal profession.

On the other hand, a surfeit of the need for achievement can be disruptive of the proper lawyer-client relationship. Supercompetitors, while desirable in professional sports, can let their drive to win override their clients' feelings. Such lawyers may push for trial to sate their need or may pursue belligerent—and ultimately counterproductive—tactics in negotiations in order to "win" them. Typically, the supercompetitor lacks the patience and tolerance required for optimum effectiveness in counseling and in many negotiations. The desire to engage in combat and to win can sub-

---

13. W. Cormier & L. S. Cormier, *Interviewing Strategies for Helpers* 14-15 (2d ed. 1985).

14. Redmount, Attorney Personalities and Some Psychological Aspects of Legal Consultation, 10 U. Pa. L. Rev. 972, 976 (1961).

tly, but officiously, override client concerns and dictate outcomes in the counseling process.

Thomas Shaffer recounts a story[15] that illustrates well the mischief of overexuberant lawyer competitiveness. As a young attorney, Shaffer's research in Indiana law revealed to him that a surprisingly large number of appeals in the 1890s were taken from one small Indiana county. When he mentioned that observation to a senior partner from that county, the partner explained there were then only two active trial lawyers in the county and they had a fierce competition. They opposed each other in nearly all the trials, which naturally made one or the other of them a loser. "And there was bound to be an appeal if the client would stand still long enough."[16]

Quite obviously, the lawyers here were calling the shots, not the clients. They had permitted their personal war to preempt client decision-making on whether to appeal.

The lawyer's achievement need creates potential for conflict beyond just personal competitions. The need for achievement often produces a fierce independence that, in turn, renders a deep concern for protecting individual rights against social and majoritarian injustices. Thus many "public interest" lawyers (from across the political spectrum) possess high thresholds for satisfaction of their achievement need. Such attorneys often encounter a conflict between the goals of a particular client and the desire to establish a principle or precedent that will (in the lawyers' view) further a cause and benefit individuals generally. For example, a client might seek help from an ACLU attorney to distribute leaflets at a shopping mall. The lawyer may see the case as an opportunity to establish malls as "public forums" under the state's constitution and be personally unreceptive to an offer by the mall owner to allow limited access to this client only. The offer might meet the client's needs, but would preempt the lawyer's ability to establish the important point of law. The conflict is thus set and challenges the lawyer to restrain his or her need for achievement.

4. Need for Association

The need for association comprises the individual's requirements for meaningful involvement with others. The person experiences a need to be with others, to like (love) others, to be liked (loved) by others, to belong. The need expresses itself through empathic communication and through conciliatory and cooperative attitudes. Robert Redmount has written of this personality aspect:

> In the reciprocity and mutuality of human relations, the person is assured of acceptance, belonging, and support that make his contact with reality very real, gratifying, and reassuring. On a plane of practical evidence this means establishing affable and affectionate relationships, cooperative enter-

---

15. T. Shaffer, *Legal Interviewing and Counseling in a Nutshell* 4-5 (1st ed. 1976).
16. Id. at 5.

prises based on mutual consent, and mutual dependence and loyalties. In these there is the touchstone for political and social groupings, and for the survival and promotion of the human species itself.

The principal behavior that sustains human relations is empathic communication. It is friendly and conciliatory behavior and may be marked by concern, helpfulness, and possibly affection.[17]

Many phases of law practice offer substantial fulfillment for the association need. Lawyers help people in need, and in meeting that duty can develop meaningful relationships with those they help. The relationships can be rewarding both for the satisfaction to be derived from helping others and for the intrinsic value inherent in human relations. Lawyers' interviewing and counseling tasks provide them with the opportunity to deal with people at a complex level about important problems in their lives. Effective counseling requires empathic understanding and communication. Negotiation, too, can benefit from a conciliatory attitude, and work as a mediator compels lawyers to call forth all of those attributes. We quote Redmount:

> Once again, the offices and traditions of law and the character of some social problems with which it is involved are the means for reinforcing predispositions in human relations. The attorney may negotiate and conciliate, ostensibly for "practical" reasons of maneuver and advantage, but quite possibly for the personal gratification of resolving problems of relationship in this manner.[18]

As Redmount suggests, relationships with clients are not the only source for fulfillment of association needs. Most lawyers work in some cooperative arrangement with other lawyers. Such peer interaction can be a source not only of professional accomplishment, but also of meaningful relations and enjoyment. Working with lawyers for other parties to reach agreement or to prevent or resolve conflicts can also help to satisfy association needs.

Particular subject matters or specialties in law practice are especially suited to meeting association needs. Much of domestic relations law and estates and trusts law, for example, concerns personal issues that can only be resolved by understanding of, sensitivity to, and reliance on basic human interaction. Such practice areas are people-focused.

A low satisfaction level for the association need indicates a substantial disability in practicing law and conducting interpersonal relations generally. An individual with a depressed association need has little use for empathic understanding and communications, which provide the basis for productive human relationships. Gruffness, insensitivity, impatience, and intolerance characterize such a person.

Yet the need for association can also become too dominant. The need to be conciliatory, to be liked, to avoid conflict can seriously diminish a

---

17. Attorney Personalities and Some Psychological Aspects of Legal Consultation, 109 U. Pa. L. Rev. 972, 976 (1961).
    18. Id. at 976.

lawyer's effectiveness. In the litigation context, the need can lead law-yers into forced settlement, even when trial is the more salient alternative. Lawyers who earn a reputation for avoiding trial impair their negotiation ability because they remove the threat of going to trial. Moreover, a concil-iatory attitude can, when standing alone, produce a poor negotiator. The lawyer-negotiator needs other qualities and must be prepared to advance and defend the client's interests to achieve a fair agreement. That may re-quire toughness on the issues and an ability to withstand and repel difficult and even devious tactics from opposing negotiators. An unduly concil-iatory negotiator pitted against an effective hard bargainer produces an unfair or undesirable settlement. And, once in a trial, the lawyer with an oversized need for association may encounter difficulty in cross-examining witnesses and forcefully presenting the client's case.

An overabundance of the need for association can also disrupt the counseling process. Lawyers who feel compelled to avoid trial in favor of settlement are likely to influence clients to settle. Moreover, an exaggerated need to be liked and to avoid conflict discourages the lawyer from confront-ing clients. As we saw in Chapter 11, confrontation can be a valuable—and at times essential—counseling technique. Lawyers dominated by the asso-ciation need may also show indecision—for fear their decisions will offend someone—and that wishy-washiness can infect clients. Finally, the need to be liked affects lawyers' genuineness and concreteness in their expressions to clients about the law or about the clients themselves. People frequently dislike those who bear bad news, and high-association-need attorneys, be-ing aware of that, do not like to bear bad news. Such lawyers compromise and qualify their language, resulting in a lack of clarity in lawyer-client dis-cussions and a failure to force the client into deeper understanding.[19]

5. Need for Order

Individuals seek order in their lives. Neatness, routine, normalcy, and or-ganization provide security and facilitate efficiency. People vary in the degree to which they need order; they range between the extremes of Neil Simon's "odd couple"—from the Felix Ungers (high need) to the Oscar Madisons (low need).

Law presents an alluring profession for those who seek order in their

---

19. See W. Cormier & L. S. Cormier, *Interviewing Strategies for Helpers* 15 (2d ed. 1985):

A counselor's unresolved intimacy needs also can significantly alter the direction and course of counseling. Generally, a counselor who has trouble with intimacy may fear rejection or be threatened by closeness and affection. A counselor who is afraid of rejection may behave in ways that meet the need to be accepted and liked by the client. For example the counselor may avoid challenging or confronting the client for fear the client may be "turned off." Or the counselor may subtly seek positive client feedback as a reassurance of being valued and liked. Negative client clues also may be ignored be-cause the counselor does not want to hear expressions of client dissatisfaction.

A counselor who is afraid of intimacy and affection may create excessive distance in the relationship. The counselor may avoid emotional intimacy in the relationship by ignoring expressions of positive feelings from the client or by behaving in a gruff, dis-tant, or aloof manner and relating to the client through the "professional" role.

lives and their world. The allure, however, can be misleading. Andrew Watson has described this human need and its relationship to law:

> All human beings, as they grow toward maturity, have a biological necessity and a psychological desire to control their environment. . . . However, for a variety of reasons in individual cases, some persons come into adulthood with a greater than average need to have the specific patterns of their life space fully defined. Some professions more visibly fulfill this need for mastery than others. For example, bookkeepers, accountants, and engineers not only have the need, but they may readily fulfill it in their respective professions. Law too, at least before you understand it, seems to offer this possibility. It was well stated by Sir Edward Coke when he said, "The knowne certaintie of the law, is the safetie of all." This venerable statement aptly sets forth what most people believe the law to be. It takes considerable sophistication before one comes to know that this is a slight oversimplification. Similarly, the limited reality of the concept of stare decisis plays into this need. The gross frustration of these expectations for explicitness will be extremely important in shaping the behavior of lawyers.[20]

A need for order can benefit the lawyer. The need calls for the attorney to organize, and organization is essential to an effective, productive law practice. Management of time, preparation for and conduct of trials, preparation for and conduct of interpersonal endeavors (interviews, consultations, and negotiations), document drafting, and billing procedures all require organization for the lawyer to achieve peak proficiency. Order and neatness in the law office and the lawyer also facilitate communications. See Chapters 6 (on nonverbal communication) and 8 (on facilitators of communications).

As with the other needs, however, an exaggerated need for order can be counterproductive. Lawyers so afflicted experience frustration when they encounter uncertainties in the law and may therefore tend to oversimplify and pigeonhole to avoid personal discomfort. Those lawyers thus deny to their clients the benefits of effective legal analysis and advocacy. Lawyers who overvalue order also tend to be reluctant to disrupt their routine to provide immediate or emergency assistance to a client. For example, the clients who are concerned about an obnoxious enterprise coming into their residential community (see Problem 1 in Chapter 10, page 241) had an alternative of seeking an immediate temporary injunction. That relief, however, would require the lawyer to disrupt routine, rearrange the week's schedule, and cram to prepare for a quick hearing. The lawyer with a high

---

20. The Quest for Professional Competence: Psychological Aspects of Legal Education, 37 U. Cin. L. Rev. 93, 101 (1968). See also Redmount, Attorney Personalities and Some Psychological Aspects of Legal Consultation, 10 U. Pa. L. Rev. 972, 974 n.2 (1961):

[T]he late Jerome Frank had a good deal of acerbic comment about the impact of attorney personality. Opportunely using tenets from Freudian psychology, but without accepting or developing any systematic attorney personality, Judge Frank noted the attorney's delusive "quest for certainty," his continuing dependency on a kind of paternal authority, and his childish conception of words as magic. These, in his view, have contributed to and supported a largely inflexible, overly-absolute, and insensitive process of judicial decision-making. [See J. Frank, *Law and the Modern Mind* 57-92, 243-253 (1930).]

need for order would be tempted to dissuade the clients from choosing that alternative, or simply fail to advise them of its availability, because it would upset an orderly, planned law practice. Once again, the lawyer would effectively preempt client decision-making.

6. Postscript on Needs

Three general points should emerge from this section. First, personality needs overlap and interact. At times, a combination of needs may move a person in a particular direction. At other times, the needs may compete with each other. You can see this interplay in the litigation-settlement process, which we have invoked repeatedly in this section to illustrate how needs work. In a given case, the lawyer's power and achievement needs might combine to push the lawyer to assert leverage on the client to reject a settlement offer and go to trial. That would be particularly true for a plaintiff's lawyer in a high-stakes, high-publicity litigation. In contrast, the power and achievement needs may also clash when considering a settlement offer; the achievement need could, for example, push for "winning the big one" at trial, while the power need pulled for settlement to gain the good graces of a prominent opposing counsel.

The second general point teaches that, to be most effective, you must have a blend of each of the needs and must have them in moderate doses.

The third point is the one that justifies an extended discussion in this book of the various personality needs: To be an effective counselor, you must maintain a close vigilance over your own needs. The needs for power, achievement, association, and order are those most likely to motivate lawyers, compromise their objectivity and neutrality, and create a potential for conflict in the lawyer-client relationship. By learning how these needs operate on individuals generally, and on lawyers in particular, you acquire a framework for analyzing your own needs. Through enhanced self-awareness, you can better check those needs and prevent them from interfering with client decision-making.

≡ **PROBLEM 1** ≡
A Needs Quiz

Assess the power, achievement, association, and order needs of the following people and describe how you think their needs configurations have affected their relationships with other persons:

1. the president
2. the protagonist in the novel or biography that you most recently read
3. an (unnamed) employer or supervisor for whom you have worked
4. a current or former (unnamed) teacher
5. yourself

C. COUNTERTRANSFERENCE

The preceding discussion in Chapters 2 and 8 has described transference as the client's irrational projections onto the counselor of attitudes and associations derived from the client's emotionally significant past relationships. Countertransference, then, refers to the counselor's irrational projections onto the client. The term is also used to encompass all of the counselor's feelings and reactions toward the client.[21] The reaction typically originates in the counselor's subconscious and finds expression in the counselor's attitudes and behavior toward the client.

Consider, for example, the case of Frank Adams and his representation of a prominent businessman, Sherm Clayton. At the time of their professional relationship, Adams was in his late thirties (five years Clayton's junior) and recently named a partner in a locally prominent law firm. Clayton was the All-American type; he was tall, handsome, athletic looking, self-assured, fashionably dressed, and very successful in his real estate and investment enterprises. Good fortune seemed to come naturally to him. By contrast, Adams was slightly built, nasal, and rather dull. He was more of a plodder than a dynamo and had worked very hard to achieve some status as an attorney.

As their professional relationship developed, Adams grew increasingly irritated with Clayton. Although the lawyer was superficially cooperative, he avoided extended discussions with Clayton and never challenged or pushed the client in their consultations. Adams grew to resent each direction he received from Clayton and each decision the client made. Clayton, however, was always cordial and receptive to criticism and discussion from any of his advisers. He was therefore baffled by his lawyer's reticence and increasing gruffness. After substantial efforts to establish some rapport with Adams and gain some mutual confidence, Clayton concluded he did not need such unpleasantness but did need a legal counselor with whom he could more openly discuss complex decisions. Rather than continue or confront the situation, Clayton finally opted to switch his business to another attorney.

Adams' irrational behavior derived from his subconscious association of Clayton with Adams' older brother, Scott. Throughout their youth, Scott had always been the fair-haired boy and Frank was the runt. Scott succeeded in athletics, in school, and with girls, while Frank tagged along, seemingly unable to match his brother's prowess in any significant way. Frank perceived that his parents doted on his brother while only grudgingly giving him attention. Scott treated Frank as little more than a pest and totally dominated him. Naturally, Frank deeply resented all this—the unlucky cards dealt him (compared to his brother's), his parents' prejudice, and Scott's domination. So when Clayton's appearance and success sprung a subconscious association in Frank's mind with his brother, Frank also transferred his fraternal resentment to Clayton, which eventually destroyed the attorney-client relationship.

But was that destruction preventable? If transference and counter-

---

21. A. Watson, *Psychiatry for Lawyers* 6 (rev. ed. 1978).

transference occur at a subconscious level, can the lawyer do anything about it? According to Watson,

> the answer is something of a paradox. The mere acknowledgment of the possibility of such unconscious reactions permits the participants to look more objectively at their relationships and to question causes. The capacity to accept the possibility that one's feelings about another may be due to unconscious and unrealistic coloring rather than to the other's real traits is a major step toward understanding. Without awareness of transference phenomena, people are over- or under-convinced by their own emotional responses and have no opportunity to work out any understanding of them.[22]

You thus benefit from an awareness that some of your reactions to clients derive from subconscious sources and not rational thought. To become sensitive to manifestations of countertransference, ask yourself such questions as the following:[23]

1. How do I feel about the client?
2. Do I anticipate seeing the client?
3. Do I overidentify with, or feel sorry for, the client?
4. Do I feel any resentment or jealousy toward the client?
5. Do I get extreme pleasure out of seeing the client?
6. Do I feel bored with the client?
7. Am I fearful of the client?
8. Do I want to protect, reject, or punish the client?
9. Am I impressed by the client?

Should answers to any of the above point to problems, then ask why such attitudes and feelings exist. Is the client doing anything to provoke such feelings? Does the client resemble anybody you know or have known, and, if so, are any attitudes being transferred to the client that are related to another person? What other impulses are being mobilized in you that account for your feelings? What role do you want to play with the client? Mere verbalization to yourself of answers to these queries permits a better control of unreasonable feelings. An awareness that you feel angry, displeased, disgusted, irritated, provoked, uninterested, unduly attentive, upset, or overly attracted may suffice to bring these emotions under control. In the event untoward attitudes continue, more self-searching is indicated.

The ability to maintain an objective attitude toward the client does not mean that you will not, on occasion, temporarily dislike many of the things the client does or says. Indeed, you may become somewhat irritated with any client on certain occasions, especially if the client subjects you to unjust criticisms or demands. But your capacity to understand your feelings helps you to be more tolerant of the client and to maintain a better working relationship.

---

22. Id. at 7.
23. The questions and the two paragraphs that follow are adapted from L. Wolberg, 2 *The Technique of Psychotherapy* 799-800 (4th ed. 1988).

D. VALUE IDENTIFICATION
AND VALUE CONFLICT

In addition to your needs and psychological makeup, your values can significantly affect your relationships with clients.[24] For example, in counseling a client about a possible divorce, you might be morally offended by the client's satyric tendencies or his irresponsibility toward his children. Or consider the conflict of values one of the authors experienced when, as a legal services attorney, he represented a recent college graduate who wanted to blow off his government loans through bankruptcy. The client was not in hardship, but merely thought it would be a good way to get rid of his financial burden and knew the law then permitted him to do it. The lawyer stuck the case in the back of his drawer, intending to reopen the file only when every other case was cleared away—which, of course, he knew would never happen. (Was that an appropriate response?) In such cases, your values can obviously impede your ability to empathize with the client, to fully discuss the issues, and to vigorously pursue the client's goals. The conflict of values may also cause you to suffer emotional distress. You must, therefore, remain sensitive to the presence of, and the degree of strain between, your values and the client's. To do that, you must analyze what your beliefs and values are, whether your professional conduct is consistent with your beliefs, and what values you actually effect.

Defining the term "value" is in itself an imposing task. As we use the term here, a value is a considered belief held and acted upon by an individual. Values are necessarily judgmental; they reflect perceptions about the desirability and propriety of means and ends. Leading texts have identified and classified seven constituent criteria for values. The criteria add to definitional clarity, and, collectively, they measure whether a person actually maintains a particular value:

CHOOSING: 1. freely
2. from alternatives
3. after thoughtful consideration of the consequences of each alternative

PRIZING: 4. cherishing, being happy with the choice
5. willing to affirm the choice publicly

ACTING: 6. doing something with the choice
7. repeatedly, in some pattern of life[25]

Using such definitional guides, you should assess your own values. That self-analysis produces two significant benefits. First, you personally gain from the enhanced self-awareness; you learn whether your actions

---

24. See Greenebaum, Lawyers' Relationship to Their Work: The Importance of Understanding Attorneys' Behavior, 53 N.Y.U. L. Rev. 651 (1978); Watson, The Lawyer as Counselor, 5 J. Fam. L. 7 (1965). Your decision about what to do once you recognize a value conflict between yourself and your client is considered in Chapter 13.

25. L. Raths, M. Harmin & S. Simon, *Values and Teaching* 28 (2d ed. 1978). Smith adds an eighth criterion: A value enhances the person's total growth. M. Smith, *A Practical Guide to Value Clarification* 13-14 (1977).

match your beliefs, and you force deeper scrutiny of your values and possible alternatives. Presumably, such heightened scrutiny will render a more complete, more consistent, and more positive value system. Those results will, in turn, spawn personal growth and a healthier psyche. Second, the value clarification aids in your conduct of lawyer-client relationships; you can better recognize and deal with value conflicts between yourself and your clients.

We therefore offer the following selection to elaborate on the criteria listed above and to promote a better understanding of values clarification.

≣ M. SMITH, A PRACTICAL GUIDE TO VALUE CLARIFICATION
7-14, 62-63 (1977)

FIRST CRITERION: A VALUE MUST BE CHOSEN FREELY

A full value is a guide, a norm, a principle by which a person lives. The values that a person chooses freely are the ones that he will internalize, cherish, and allow to guide his life. Free choice excludes overt coercion by tyrants and subtle, or gentle, coercion by loved ones. Introjected values from childhood are not full values. Physical or environmental circumstances and societal laws may impose a value on a person that he does not espouse—to that degree it is not his value.

SECOND CRITERION: A VALUE MUST BE CHOSEN FROM ALTERNATIVES

That a value must be chosen from alternatives follows from the first criterion that a value must be freely chosen. If there are no alternatives, there is no freedom of choice. In many situations, it may initially seem that there are alternatives when, in fact, subsequent evaluation shows that there are no alternatives. A thief demanding your money or your life is not really extending alternatives; nor is a parent who demands that a child eat his spinach or go straight to bed. . . .

At work, a person may be offered a choice between a number of undesirable tasks (according to that person's appraisal) and choose one of them only because he values supporting his family, not because he values that task above the others. On more important levels: a man may stay married, not because he values his wife, but because he values the institution of marriage; a woman may choose a particular career, not because she values that kind of work, but because she values the status and financial rewards that go along with it. . . .

THIRD CRITERION: A VALUE MUST BE CHOSEN AFTER CONSIDERING THE CONSEQUENCES

More precisely, a value must be freely chosen after careful study of the consequences of each alternative. That is, the consequences must be known. If a person does not realize the consequences of a particular alternative, he does not know what is going to happen; he has therefore not freely chosen that consequence. . . .

Many times, of course, the consequences of one's choices cannot be known in advance. This fact does not necessarily mean that a free choice has not been made; it does mean, however, that once the consequences are understood the person must re-evaluate his choice in light of the new information.

FOURTH CRITERION: A VALUE MUST BE PERFORMED

A value is acted upon, performed, carried out: it influences a person's behavior in some way. Thus, what a person does reflects his values. We tend to read literature that supports our values; we join clubs or informal groups whose members share our values and whose goals correspond to our values; and we even use money according to our values—for instance, if we value thrift, we save money; if we value travel, fine food, or private education, we spend a good deal of it.

The importance of a particular value may be judged in terms of how much time we spend on it. If a person professes a high value for political awareness, for example, but never reads a newspaper or magazine, and never votes or attends political meetings, it might be said that political awareness is not really his value. . . .

Because people act according to their values, their values give direction to their lives. If a person does not act on his proclaimed values, then what he is talking about may be a desire, a feeling, or an idea; it is not a value. Many of the activities and experiences that are part of the value-clarification process are designed to help people discover what things they act on, as opposed to what they simply desire, feel, or think. It is common for persons who are well educated to believe that they have many values that in reality they do not. . . .

FIFTH CRITERION: A VALUE BECOMES A PATTERN OF LIFE

Values are acted on repeatedly and become life patterns. And the stronger the value, the more it influences one's life. For example, a person who strongly values service to others may choose to become a social worker. He may spend a great deal of time, energy, and money earning the necessary credentials, and he may even move his home to a remote area of the world where his service is most needed. His whole life becomes ordered around service to others. Although this example may be somewhat extreme, it is useful for understanding the extent to which a strongly held value can influence one's life. It also helps explain the motivation behind certain extreme actions. In the context of this criterion for a full value, it is worthwhile to look at the value of work in contemporary American society. The motivation for this value lies in the Protestant work ethic, which maintains that work brings salvation—union with God. People who hold this value get up early to go to work; because they abhor wasting time, relaxation breaks are short and meals are strictly functional (as opposed to other societies in which meals are long and provide an opportunity to relate to others). Work is valued over family life; many people bring work home and continue working during what is family time in other societies. This "homework" may be actual work or it may be time spent worrying about work and about whether one is advancing quickly enough. Work is valued over recreation, so additional work is done during what could be a time of leisure; often it is rationalized that this is a "different kind" of work, so it is "really" recreation. . . .

A value that becomes a pattern of life manifests itself in all aspects of one's existence: in dress, in friends selected, in the place one lives, in recreation time, in what one reads, in one's career, in the selection of a spouse, and in the way one relates to one's relatives.

Because the nature of the valuing process is dynamic, frequently a person will think that he still has a value that, in reality, he no longer holds. He assumes that because he once held a particular value he continues to hold it, and it may come as a great surprise when he finds it is no longer a value. For instance, a person may have once valued reading and spent several hours a day engrossed in books and magazines. If he is asked when was the last time he read a book and his response is "Three years ago," reading is obviously no longer a value in this person's life. In brief, a value tends to permeate and influence all aspects of one's life.

SIXTH CRITERION: A VALUE IS CHERISHED

A value is something a person feels positive about; he prizes it, cherishes it, respects it, rejoices in it, and celebrates it. As the individual grows toward full development of his values, he derives increasingly greater contentment, satisfaction, fulfillment, and joy from the act of choosing his own destiny.

Once a choice has been experienced as worthwhile and happy, it may be an indication of a value. If a person is not happy with the consequences of his choice, or if in the experience of the choice the person discovers that this is the wrong choice for him, it is not a full value. For example, a woman may hold a particular job, do well at it, and spend a great deal of time and energy on her work. But if the only reason she maintains the job is because it is the best she can do to support her family, and if she is not really happy with that particular work, then the job does not represent a value for her. The value is supporting her family, not the work she is doing to accomplish the value. . . .

SEVENTH CRITERION: A VALUE IS PUBLICLY AFFIRMED

This criterion is directly related to the preceding criterion—that a value is cherished. When we have good news, we like to share it. When we discover a value that is freely chosen, the consequences of which we know, and that makes us happy, we want to tell others about it. In fact, if the value is a full value, we may even crusade for it. If we value a particular political ideology, we may campaign for the politician who holds the same value. . . .

In fact, the danger is that the person may be so enthusiastic about his value that he imposes it on other persons—causing them to "adopt" his value only as a matter of expediency. At the other extreme is the unfortunate person who is so apathetic about his life that he has few or even no values that he is willing to publicly affirm.

A possible exception to this criterion, however, might be a situation in which one's value conflicts with the norms of the society in which one lives. In this case, to publicly affirm his value, the person might be putting himself in jeopardy. . . .

Publicly affirming one's value has direct bearing on an eighth criterion, enhancement of the person's total growth. Generally, values help us to grow toward becoming what we consider a "good" person. If something moves us toward what we consider "bad," or unhealthy, we tend to hide it. If we are not growing by what we are doing, and therefore unwilling to make our position or activity known, then what we are doing is not really a value for us.

EIGHTH CRITERION: A VALUE ENHANCES THE PERSON'S TOTAL GROWTH

This final criterion is not so much a separate measurement of a full value as it is a natural outgrowth of the preceding criteria. In other words, if a value has been affirmed as a full value by having met the seven preceding criteria, it follows as a matter of course that that value will contribute to and enhance the person's total growth toward the goals and ideals that he has chosen for himself.

The prizing criteria (cherishing, affirming, enhancing) emphasize the emotional component of the process of valuing. We may choose and act, but if we do not also prize something, then it is not a full value. We are more apt to continue a full value as a pattern of life and act on it repeatedly when we prize it and find that doing it helps us to grow as a total person. People who dedicate themselves to their values experience joy regardless of the problems, difficulties, or sacrifices they may have to make. People who lack the quality of prizing in their lives lack vitality, tend to be apathetic, find life meaningless, and often suffer chronic depression.

Values are, by their nature, goal directed. As mentioned earlier, we tend to choose activities that relate to the values that we have selected as goals or even as ideals. In turn, our activities support or, in some cases, undermine our values. Value clarification does not attempt to advocate a particular direction for growth, it merely is a process by which a person can discover meaning and direction for his life through recognition of his values. Thus, if a value does not enhance the person, it is lacking one of the above criteria and is not a full value.

[By thoughtfully responding to the questions Smith lists below, you should gain a clearer understanding of your values:]

Questions for a Values Autobiography

1. What are some major decisions you have made that have had happy consequences for you?

2. What is the ideal version of what you are going to do with your life?
3. What would you be willing to die for?
4. List the kinds of activities on which you have spent a considerable amount of time.
5. What have you spent most of your money on?
6. If you could be doing anything you wanted, what would you be doing?
7. What is your favorite activity?
8. Give the history of your favorite hobby or leisure-time activity.
9. What has been your plan of life?
10. What goals do you set for your life?
11. List and describe the important people in your life.
12. Describe your philosophy of life.
13. List things, ideas, and people you like and describe what you like about them.
14. Of the values that you received from your family, which have you accepted and which have been rejected?
15. What do you consider to be your potential in life?
16. What kind of person will you be ten years from now?
17. What would be an ideal vacation for you?

E. SUMMARY

We conclude this chapter with Andrew Watson's "Psychological Taxonomy of Lawyer Conflicts," which structures the range of personal conflicts you might encounter in law practice. We recommend you study the taxonomy carefully. This chapter, of course, has addressed many of the conflicts Watson identifies. Others, those dealing with the lawyer's moral conflicts, are treated in the next chapter.

≡ A. WATSON, THE LAWYER IN THE INTERVIEWING AND COUNSELING PROCESS
93-100 (1976) [26]

There are several reasons why it is worthwhile to conceptualize [the conflicts that lawyers encounter], even though there are a few risks. . . . Human beings need to "master" their environment, to be and feel safe. One technique used to accomplish mastery is to apply a concept-label to the situation, and then it can be "understood" and controlled. If we could clearly visualize the conflicts which a working lawyer will encounter during his career, it might be possible to learn in advance of the encounters how to handle them appropriately. In a very real sense this is the only way in which such subtle and fragile behaviors as "ethicalness" may be approached educationally. Otherwise we are left with the necessity to rely on

---

26. Footnotes in the original are omitted.

whatever effects the individual's childhood upbringing has left on his behavior. To identify these role conflicts and to "worry" about them in advance will facilitate (what might be called) an anticipatory rehearsal for subsequent professional activity.

A possible negative effect of this identification process is to inappropriately stereotype behavior in ways which make recognition artificial and "intellectualized." Then instead of seeing a client in a highly personalized way, the client is promptly cast in an image that may be grossly incorrect.

. . . The [following] taxonomy is divided into three major categories. The first, "Problems of Conscience Conflict," involves the internalized values which are derived from one's upbringing, around such issues as "Good" and "Bad." The second category, "Problems of Self-Image Conflict," relates to issues of "identity" or "self-image." They cover a whole gamut of questions about how the lawyer thinks he should appear in order to be all right in the eyes of others. The last category, "Problems of Mastery and Control in Case Management," is related to ego skills which will emerge in the lawyer's ways of doing things. An examination of the taxonomy makes it clear that there are flaws in the ways these categories are divided, and no doubt they will have to be changed. This will occur as the taxonomy is used and as efforts are made to relate behaviors to the taxonomy. In the meantime, the taxonomy can serve as a way to begin to tease out and understand some of the explicit problem areas which attorneys encounter in their work.

A Psychological Taxonomy of Lawyer Conflicts[27]

I. Problems of Conscience Conflict: Hierarchies of Values.
   A. Issues of Truthfulness.
      1. Defense of "guilty" client.
      2. Use of nonverbal signals for legally nonpermissible messages—e.g., judge shrugging shoulders to imply untruth in witness, which he could not lawfully say.
      3. The truth-justice tension in a trial.
   B. Use of Case or Client for Personal or Self-Aggrandizement (Narcissistic) Purposes.
   C. The Use/Misuse of Power and Coercion.
      1. "Informing" client of lawyer's acts/intentions without coercion—e.g., client need for lawyer facilitates possibility of "coerced" agreement.
      2. Lawyer conflict over issue of leading/being led.
      3. Conflicts over use/misuse of economic power in fee, litigation costs, etc.—e.g., the client needs a lawyer but the lawyer "needs" a fee.

---

27. Dr. Watson published earlier versions of this taxonomy in Lawyers and Professionalism: A Further Psychiatric Perspective on Legal Education, 8 U. Mich. J. of L. Reform 248, 253-259 (1975), and in M. Bloom, J. Fellers, M. Kayne, B. Rogow, H. Hacks & A. Watson, *Lawyers, Clients and Ethics* 119 (1973). For an analysis and application of Watson's classification scheme with regard to the professional relationship created by the Code of Professional Responsibility, see Kelso & Kelso, Conflict, Emotion, and Legal Ethics, 10 Pac. L.J. 69 (1978).

D. Temptations and Misuse of Sexual Opportunity.
   1. Client need/distress may lead to sexual proffer.
E. Conflict and Reticence over Peer Discipline—"There but for the grace of God. . . . "

II. Problems of Self-Image Conflict: Apprehensions About Lawyer Roles.
   A. Concern About Lawyers' Negative Public Image.
      1. Lawyer as "shyster"/immoralist.
      2. Lawyer as manipulator/"mouthpiece."
         a. Conflicts re: right to counsel.
         b. Right to not serve as counsel.
      3. Lawyer as scapegoat for public ills or concerns—e.g., during post-Revolutionary War and Jacksonian periods; the current crime-wave due to lawyers "getting criminals off"; causing social problems through nuisance class-actions on behalf of poor.
      4. Lawyer as representative for "Fat-Cats"—e.g., tension caused by representing those who have wealth or "too vigorously" seek it.
   B. Concerns Raised When Acting as Champion of Justice.
      1. Aggressiveness versus acquiescence.
         a. "Am I being aggressive (masculine) enough?"
         b. "Can I be a 'good' (aggressive) advocate and still be a woman?"
         c. Does need to organize case to "win" threaten attitudes toward "passivity"?
      2. Conflicts over "showing off" while advocating a cause—e.g., "Am I serving this client (cause) because of professional role requirements or just in order to show off?"
      3. Conflicts over caring about justice.
         a. "Lawyers who care about 'justice' are bleeding hearts or soft-heads."
         b. "Technique without ideals is a menace: and that all men know and laymen fear." Similarly, ideals without technique are also to be feared as ineffectiveness.
      4. Conflict issues involving value-judgment about race, ethnicity, gender.
   C. Concerns and Conflicts About One's Adequacy and Competence.
      1. Law generalist v. law specialist tensions: "Can I handle this patent case or should I refer it to a specialist?"
      2. Inexperienced v. veteran tensions.
         a. "How am I as a relative neophyte and should my client know?"
         b. "I certainly feel stupid as compared with my mentor/supervisor."

III. Problems of Mastery and Control in Case Management.
   A. Tension Regarding Certainty/Uncertainty.
      1. Over-simplification and premature closure of conceptualization and/or exploration to give pseudo-control.

        a.   Do not look for more information about facts or law; might upset theory of case.

        b.   Possession of a limited set of conceptual choices into which must fit all issues.

    2.   The utilization of words and definitions as if they exist in the real world—e.g., affix the label of "sexual psychopath" and then "understand" what to do with a given person who committed a "sexual crime."

    3.   A reluctance to be creative with law because it might generate uncertainty.

        a.   The tension in judge between stare decisis concepts and his impulses to make new law.

        b.   Lawyer writing brief to help court reach a new kind of decision and avoid the stare decisis conflict.

        c.   The need to adapt rules to a hard case in order to solve problems.

    4.   A reluctance to think through from affirmative standpoint the other side of the case because it might make one's own case seem/be less solid.

    5.   A fear of accepting/developing new lawyer roles because "I don't know how to do them"—e.g., how does a lawyer function as a "Child Advocate" in juvenile court?

B.   Conflicts in Management of Interpersonal Transactions.

    1.   Tensions in interviewing process.

        a.   The lawyer as listener—e.g., conflict over passive-active issues: "Am I a good lawyer if I just listen?"

        b.   The lawyer as reactor.

            (1)   Conflict over what the client expresses: too disturbing, or too seductive, or too "crazy."

            (2)   Conflict over whether I should hide the emotion which client stimulates: "Should I be angry?"

            (3)   Conflict of over-identification with client's feelings and ideas (i.e., problems of "empathic distance").

                (a)   embarrassment.

                (b)   pain.

                (c)   avarice.

                (d)   guilt.

                (e)   above may be felt as "invasions" of client privacy.

        c.   Lawyer discomfort as judge of another's credibility—e.g., "They won't like me/approve of me if they know I don't believe them."

        d.   Lawyer distress caused by clients' psychological defenses—e.g., "Why do they come for help from me when they don't trust me and don't use it?"

    2.   Psychological problems caused by incompetence.

        a.   Of supervisors or senior colleague—e.g., senior partner "permits" one to make serious and self-defeating error in direct examination of a witness.

        b.   In a colleague—e.g., causes serious loss to client through sloppy handling of case. What should I do when the client asks me what to do about it?

        c.   In client—e.g., client fails to provide you with adequate information about his case, making your work difficult or impossible. How do you understand and handle it?

        d.   In self—e.g., you discover during trial that you have seriously botched up client's case due to your own ignorance. How do you handle the situation?

   3.   Tensions caused by need to manage own time, psychic and physical energy, and private life.

        a.   Conflict between client's needs and own needs.

        b.   Need to maintain one's own private life in psychological security and stability in order to be able to attend to professional work.

        c.   Need to deal with conflicts between father-husband roles and professional role demands.

        d.   Need to deal with role conflicts between wife-mother and professional woman.

           (1)   Conflicts between child-rearing necessities and demands of profession.

           (2)   Conflicts between wife-professional and husband vocational goals.

               (a)   Where work? How balance the competing and possibly conflicting interests?

               (b)   Work schedule conflicts. Who should be home and when?

           (3)   Who does what work around the house?

C.   Conflicts Caused by Losing a Case.

   1.   Loss of case you expected to win (and should have won?).

   2.   Handling case you expect(ed) to lose.

        a.   Do you turn off your interest and thus underprepare?

        b.   Is your expectation accurate or is it a defense against risk to your self-esteem?

        c.   Could other counsel with greater skill win the case?

        d.   Does your desire to win a losing case cause you to do unlawful or unethical things?

        e.   How do you handle the client's feelings and ideas (rational and nonrational) about you?

           (1)   Did you accurately inform him of what he should expect?

           (2)   Does his feeling stir discomfort in you? Why?

When a lawyer is learning how to cope with the many emotional reactions stimulated by the interview situation, the knowledge that he is not the first one to encounter these problems can be helpful in dealing with them. When human beings struggle with intrapsychic conflicts they have a strong tendency to believe that they are going it alone. This tends to create a sense of isolation with the progressive feeling of despair, an attitude which does not lead to proficiency in resolving emotional problems. Perhaps some familiarity with this taxonomy can help alleviate this inclination. . . .

≡≡≡ **PROBLEM 2** ≡≡≡
The Student's Crisis

You are an associate in a six-person law firm. You have just interviewed Ruth Nielson, a 19-year-old student at Central University, which is located in your city. You and all of the members of your firm have received one or more degrees from the university and have supported various programs at the school.

Ms. Nielson informed you that ten days ago she was forced against her will to have sex with the school's star basketball player, Rick Weiss. She claims that Weiss visited her at her off-campus apartment on a recent weekend night while her roommate was out of town. The client and Weiss had been casual friends for nearly a year; they shared the same major and had attended several classes together. According to Nielson, Weiss had been drinking. When he arrived, he said he was upset about something and needed to talk. He made other intentions known very quickly, however, and overpowered Nielson, forcing her into intercourse. He then left abruptly. She did not know what to do; she felt angry, betrayed, humiliated, and confused. After thinking about it overnight, she reported the incident to the police, but the investigating officers seemed to discourage her from going forward. They emphasized the unpleasantness she would encounter, how exposed she would be, and how much people around the city respected Weiss. She has not yet decided whether to file a formal complaint. Nielson also contacted the basketball coach. He questioned Weiss about the charge and then reported back to Nielson that the athlete claims she had consented to the sex. The coach said he did not know whom to believe or what else he could do. After that, Nielson went to see a counselor, who suggested to her that she contact you to discuss her legal rights and alternatives.

Central University has always maintained a strong academic reputation and boasts about its ability to keep its standards while also fielding successful sports teams. For example, it consistently ranks among the nation's leaders in the graduation rate of its student athletes, and many of them go on to graduate-level education. Moreover, the football and basketball revenues finance all of the university's sports programs, and there is usually enough money left over to lend support to special scholarship and research projects. This year looks particularly promising; the football team is headed for a bowl and the basketball team has placed in the top ten in all of the preseason rankings.

Weiss led last year's team in scoring and figures to be considered for All-American honors and a lucrative professional contract at the end of this season. He has a squeaky clean reputation; he is a solid student, this year's team captain, and the son of a wealthy financier. The father is a leading figure in the state and has been a strong supporter of the university over the years. Ms. Nielson has a modest background, but has built an enviable academic record.

During your interview, Nielson continued to express confusion about what, if anything, she wanted to do. She remains very hurt, angry, and distraught from the incident, but she is not sure she wants to endure the trauma of legal proceedings or public scrutiny (and, possibly, vilification). She also told you that she has heard there have been several other occasions of improper conduct by Central athletes in recent years that city and school officials have either ignored or managed to resolve quietly.

What feelings would you have in representing Ms. Nielson? How might different turns of events in her case satisfy, or conflict with, any of your personal needs, values, or concerns?

13

Counselor Self-
Development
and Autonomy

A. PERSONAL GROWTH
FOR THE LAWYER-COUNSELOR

The preceding chapter emphasized your need for self-analysis to avoid preempting your clients' autonomy and to sustain effective professional relations. The text described various dimensions of one's personality that provide common sources for conflict in attorney-client relations. But Chapter 12 stopped there, with analysis. It did not address what direction you could take after, or with, your self-analysis. Nor did it consider what you should do when a conflict arises between your discovered values and those implicated by your representation of a particular client. This chapter takes you to those next steps. In the process, it manifests the essential premises of the model for the lawyer-client relationship developed in this text.

Self-understanding and personal development have a symbiotic relationship. That is, knowledge of self is essential for personal growth; correspondingly, as you mature and realize your potential, you reach increasingly higher levels of self-understanding. Moreover, a thorough self-awareness is a prerequisite to becoming self-actualized. These processes that lead to self-knowledge and self-development also share a foundation of mutually supportive psychological and philosophical concepts.

The interrelation of those concepts can be seen in the writings of two preeminent theorists, Abraham Maslow and Lawrence Kohlberg. We have already sketched the basic model of Maslow's needs hierarchy (see pages 285-287), but have deferred until here discussion of his final stage, self-actualism. To Maslow's theory of personality, we now add Kohlberg's theory of developmental moral psychology, which divides the individual's moral progress into six stages. The following excerpt briefly describes Maslow's notion of self-actualism and Kohlberg's view of moral development before explaining their relationship and how they can help us to be better counselors.[1]

≡ R. M. BASTRESS, CLIENT-CENTERED COUNSELING AND MORAL ACCOUNTABILITY FOR LAWYERS
10 J. Legal Prof. 97, 119-125 (1985)[2]

Maslow described personality development in terms of a "hierarchy of needs," in which the individual is preoccupied with satisfaction of a progression of basic needs. [See Chapter 12, pages 285-287.] He strives to sate—in order—his physiological, safety, and love needs. Once those are largely filled, then he can move on to deal with a new discontent and restlessness, what Maslow termed the need for self-actualization. "This tendency might be phrased as the desire to become more and more what one is, to become everything that one is capable of becoming." The aspirations can find expression in any field—music, art, athletics, teaching, carpentry, and so on. Those who experience a high need for self-actualization, which necessarily means their lower needs are largely satisfied, are the most psychologically healthy people. They are growth-motivated, not deficiency-motivated, as are those dominated by the lower needs of physiology, safety, and love. . . .

Self-actualized persons are accepting of themselves, of others, and of nature. They accept their own frailties and their discrepancies from the ideal without disruptive concern. That is not to say they are self-satisfied; rather, they acknowledge the inevitability of weakness and human frailty without undue fret or psychological disturbance. They accept the imperfections of nature and humans. The psychologically healthy lack defensiveness and abhor posturing and artificiality.

Self-actualizing persons focus more on external problems than on themselves. That is, they perceive "some mission in life, some task to

---

1. The article draws heavily from L. Kohlberg, *The Psychology of Moral Development* (1983); L. Kohlberg, *The Philosophy of Moral Development* (1981); A. Maslow, *The Farther Reaches of Human Nature* (1971); A. Maslow, *Toward a Psychology of Being* (1968); and A. Maslow, *Motivation and Personality* (1954).

2. Footnotes in the original are omitted.

fulfill, some problem outside themselves which enlists much of their energies." They are typically concerned about the basic and persistent issues of philosophy and ethics. They rarely get so close to the trees that they fail to see the forest. They lack pettiness and generally look past the trivial. Yet, while maintaining an external focus, the self-actualizing also make use of solitude and privacy to a much greater degree than the average person. Such comfort with solitude follows, perhaps, from their contemplative nature, their knowledge and acceptance of self, and their independence.

That independence or autonomy crosscuts through much of the self-actualized's makeup. "Since they are propelled by growth motivation rather than by deficiency motivation, self-actualizing people are not dependent for their main satisfactions on the real world, or other people or culture or means to ends or, in general, on extrinsic satisfactions. Rather, they are dependent for their own development and continued growth on their own potentialities and latent resources."

At the same time—and this is crucial to client-centered helping—the interpersonal relations of the self-actualizing are marked by deep feelings of identification, sympathy, empathy, and affection for fellow human beings. Self-actualizing persons accept and respect the autonomy of others, although they can also be impatient with, and disgusted by, stupidity. They generally maintain deeper and more profound interpersonal relations than do other adults. The interpersonal relations of the self-actualizing also reveal a true democratic character; they are open-minded, egalitarian, and free of stereotypical thinking. Thus, in the most profound implication of this attribute, the growth-motivated "give a certain quantum of respect to any human being just because he is a human individual." Self-actualizing individuals also value and effect honesty and genuineness in their relations with others.

Finally, self-actualizing individuals are distinctly aware of the value dimension in their life. They have an acute awareness of what values they, in fact, hold; "these individuals are strongly ethical, they have definite moral standards. . . . " They independently arrive at their views of right and wrong, which follows naturally from their autonomy and independence of thought. Thus, the self-actualizing do not accept without scrutiny the moral edicts of religion, law, or other individuals.

Maslow's progression to self-actualization parallels Lawrence Kohlberg's theories on developmental moral psychology. Building on the theories of Jean Piaget, Kohlberg has identified three levels of moral development that individuals experience in six stages from childhood into adulthood. The levels comprise the premoral (or preconventional), conventional role conformity (conventional), and self-accepted moral principles (postconventional). Each of the levels has two stages.

The premoral level is that of the child and is premised on consequences rather than intent. "I can fudge, or even cheat, on my income taxes because the chances of the I.R.S. discovering me are very small." Thus, good and bad depend on the probability of punishment, and "moral" decisions are reached without considering others.

The second level reveals a quantum leap forward in moral development as morality shifts away from egocentrism to societal expectation. Right and wrong are defined by peer group or external authority. Loyalty, duty, and obedience surface as the key virtues. This conventional morality is exemplified by strict adherence to law (i.e., legalism), religious dogma (e.g., the Bible or the Koran), or politico-social doctrine (e.g., Das Kapital, the Sayings of Chairman Mao). Most lawyers function at this level, an unsurprising consequence of legal education's methods and substance and the adversarial system's ethics. Lawyers measure their "ethics" by adherence to the Code of Professional Responsibility, even though that Code is as much concerned with business regulation as morality and even though the Code encourages lawyers to assign most of their moral decisions to clients. Clients and their views, then, supplement the Code and, in practical effect, constitute lawyers' most common "external authority." This system of "vicarious responsibility" in moral decision-making is particularly troublesome because clients—unlike most other external authorities—do not prescribe moral choices according to some world view that takes into account competing values. The problem is compounded when lawyers do not at least confront clients with moral and social considerations relevant to clients' alternatives.

In the third level of Kohlberg's structure, representing another quantum leap in moral development, the person's own conscience emerges as the moral arbiter:

> The moral focus shifts again, this time away from group expectations and back to the self. But this is not return to the selfishness of level one. Not egotism but autonomy is the rule—the self as autonomous. I'm less concerned about how others see me, and more concerned about how I see myself. Ethical decision-making at this level submits even laws and moral convictions to the test of universal moral principle to which the autonomous self is committed. Ethical principles appeal to comprehensiveness and logical consistency. [E. Stevens, *Business Ethics* 17 (1959).]

Thus, Level III individuals may look to an external authority for moral guidance, but they will adhere to the authority only if, after evaluation and thought, it satisfies their own perceptions of right. . . .

The descriptions here of Maslow and Kohlberg should reveal a great deal of similarity between the characteristics of Maslow's self-actualizing people and Kohlberg's Level III persons. While Maslow was primarily concerned with personality growth, moral development plays an integral role in his theories about psychological health. Indeed, Maslow referred to his need hierarchy as encompassing a value order. And Kohlberg, although concentrating on moral development, nevertheless recognized the interrelationship of values and personality. The Maslow and Kohlberg theories thus share certain basic assumptions and the characteristics rendered by the advanced categories of both Maslow and Kohlberg overlap in many critical ways. Those shared assumptions and characteristics create a distinct model for functioning and growth as a lawyer-counselor.

Maslow and Kohlberg constructed their theories on the keystone of individual autonomy. That autonomy embraces both the individual's own independence—in thought, self-determination, and responsibility—and a sincere and abiding respect for the independence of others. For Kohlberg's Level III, respect for the individual is the universal value, and Maslow's self-actualizing persons reserve that "certain quantum of respect [for] *any* human being just because he is a human individual." The respect extends to a genuine regard for and acceptance of others. Through that regard and acceptance, relations with others achieve the highest level of honesty and clarity, and therefore, mutual benefit. That regard for others also forms the moral foundation for the mature person. Because the morality of decisions is based on their impact on others, the advanced individual therefore has the capacity to understand the needs of others, to put himself in their shoes, to empathize.

The Maslow and Kohlberg theories[3] provide psychological and moral foundations for the counseling approach and skills described throughout the preceding chapters. That is, the Maslow self-actualizing model and Kohlberg's third level of moral development enlist the personal attributes and values that are essential to lawyer-client partnerships. As such, the theories provide a ready model to study (we hope you will pursue them in greater depth than described here) and to strive for.

Through such study and striving, we can also experience real personal growth. We can develop a comprehensive, consistent morality, can move toward achievement of our full potential, and become all that we are capable of. Such growth makes us not only better counselors, but also better and healthier persons.

---

3. We acknowledge the recent critiques of Kohlberg's work from feminist theorists who have identified a morality based on caring and connections with others (largely associated with women's moral vision), as opposed to moral decisions reached through deductions from principles (the Piaget-Kohlberg "male" morality). C. Gilligan, *In a Different Voice* (1982); N. Noddings, *Caring* (1984). See also N. Chodorow, *The Reproduction of Mothering* (1978). These critiques strike us as warranting serious consideration, but they do not cause us to question our reliance on that aspect of Kohlberg's analysis that sees the higher stages of moral development as requiring the individual to exercise an independent judgment about moral issues. Indeed, we read Gilligan as endorsing that concept:

> [B]ecause women's sense of integrity appears to be entwined with an ethic of care, so that to see themselves as women is to see themselves in a relationship of connection, the major transitions in women's lives would seem to involve changes in the understanding and activities of care. Certainly the shift from childhood to adulthood witnesses a major redefinition of care. When the distinction between helping and pleasing frees the activity of taking care from the wish for approval by others, the ethic of responsibility can become a self-chosen anchor of personal integrity and strength.

Gilligan, above, at 171. See also Prose, Confident at 11, Confused at 16, The New York Times Magazine 22, 40 (Jan. 7, 1990). In other words, what Gilligan and her colleagues have contended is that morally developed women, in particular, base their moral decisions on criteria different from those applied by the morally developed men described by Kohlberg. Our use of Kohlberg focuses not on the criteria to be applied in the higher stages, but on the fact that the decisions are made by the individual after independent (or collaborative) analysis of the issues and in reliance on some comprehensive morality.

Certainly, the respect and regard for others that we see as essential attributes in our counseling model are substantively consistent with the perspective described by the above authors.

B. LIMITS ON CLIENT DECISION-MAKING

≡≡≡ PROBLEM 1 ≡≡≡
Estelle Crum

Richard Hart is a member of a three-person firm in a small city. He has represented the Crum family on personal and business matters for many years. The family business, Crum Plastics, is a prosperous, closely held corporation. Founded by Emil Crum in 1946, it now employs over 250 people. Mr. Crum died three years ago leaving ownership of the business to his widow, Estelle. Mrs. Crum, though, has little to do with the corporation, as the Crums' only child, Harper, has managed it since his father's death. Mr. Hart has entered the following memo into Mrs. Crum's file.

MEMO TO THE FILE OF ESTELLE CRUM

10/19—Mrs. Estelle Crum called today to say that she is coming in tomorrow to sign a revised draft of her will. She wants her son Harper deleted as a beneficiary and his entire share given to the Fairfax Charity Fund. (Fairfax Charity Fund collects and distributes money for the preservation of "cultured" life-styles.) Mrs. Crum is apparently very irate (she always did have a quick temper) with Harper because he's moved in with his girlfriend. As far as I know, however, Harper is still running the family business in capable fashion.

I guess Fairfax finally got to Estelle; I know it's been after her money for some time.

QUESTIONS

How would you handle the counseling session with Mrs. Crum? Why? What additional information would you seek? Do you have an opinion about the wisdom or propriety of Mrs. Crum's decision to disinherit Harper? Will you communicate that decision to Harper?

Now consider the following alternative approaches to counseling Mrs. Crum:

MEMO TO THE FILE OF ESTELLE CRUM
(Alternative A)

10/20—Mrs. Crum is coming in this afternoon to sign the will, but I think it will be better if I point out to her how foolishly she is acting.

My strategy is to tell her that I will not, for her own good, redraft her will. I will explain to her that she is acting irrationally and without sufficient reflection, that her exclusion of Harper will exacerbate (if not obliterate) her apparently already deteriorating relationship with

Harper, and that the exclusion could substantially jeopardize the stability of the family business. If need be, I'll have to inform her what shysters they are at Fairfax Charity.

I will demand that she at least postpone her decision and think about it for a few days. Let her cool off. I think Estelle's long-standing trust in me will help her to see the light.

MEMO TO THE FILE OF ESTELLE CRUM
(Alternative B)

10/20—Mrs. Crum is coming in this afternoon, but I believe a counseling session is appropriate before she signs the will. I should explore with her the possible repercussions (personal and legal) from disinheriting Harper.

By questioning her, and forcing her to think through the situation, I believe Mrs. Crum will realize the following points:

1. She will doubtlessly alienate her son, perhaps beyond repair.
2. She will jeopardize the stability of the family business, which is now providing her with financial security and which her husband worked so diligently to build.
3. She is perhaps acting hastily and should give the matter further thought.
4. She should know that Fairfax has a very questionable reputation and should be investigated further.

After we discuss these matters, I will then give her the opportunity to reconsider her decision to exclude Harper. I'm sure that my explanation and her long-standing trust in me will help her to see the light.

QUESTIONS

Evaluate and compare the two alternative approaches. Are they different in approach? In effect? In result? In purpose? If yes, how? What should the lawyer's role be in counseling Mrs. Crum? How would you present to Mrs. Crum the factors listed in the attorney's memorandum? What, if any, conflicts does the Crum lawyer face?

≡ PROBLEM 2 ≡
Frank Colon

As a sole practitioner in the county seat of a rural county, you are contacted for an appointment by Mr. Frank Colon, about whom you know nothing. You set a time for him to come in.

When he arrives, he is wearing a swastika armband. He wants to hold a rally on Patriots Day for his branch of the American Nazi Party, but city officials have refused to issue a permit to him. They told Colon they did not allow fascists in this town. You believe that, despite Colon's intent to use the rally to insult Jews and blacks and to attack racial integration, the city officials' action violates the First Amendment rights of Colon and his associates.

QUESTIONS

Do you represent Colon in his effort to get a permit for a rally? Why or why not? Would your answer change if Colon told you that no other attorney in the county would take his case? Would attendant publicity that would follow the case affect your decision? What, if anything, do the Model Rules or the Code of Professional Responsibility say about your decision?

≡ **PROBLEM 3** ≡
Moore Industries

You are an associate in a medium-sized firm in a large city. One of the firm's most important clients is Moore Industries, a chemical manufacturer. An executive from Moore informs you that an OSHA inspector recently cited one of the company's five plants for failing to have railings to protect employees from falls off a four-feet-high walkway. The railing will cost $10,000 to install. Moore has decided to put in the railing. The executive wants to know, however, if Moore should also install railings at its other plants, each of which has a similar walkway. (The other plants are located in different sections of the country.) That is, what effect does the citation at one plant have on the company's responsibilities at the other plants? The Moore executive wants to know if the company's potential liability for failure to install the railings would be greater than the costs of installing the railings.

Your research leads you to the Occupational Safety and Health Act at 29 U.S.C. §666, which you summarize as follows:

(a) Willful or repeated violations—up to $10,000 for each violation;

(b) "Serious" violations—up to $1,000 for each violation; . . .

(d) "Failure to correct" a cited violation—up to $1,000 for each failure;

(e) "Willful" violation that causes death to an employee—up to $10,000 and/or six months imprisonment for first violations and up to $20,000 and/or one year imprisonment for subsequent violations.

Research into administrative regulations and decisions reveals that failure to correct a hazard, cited in similar facilities, can result in a finding of a "willful" violation. The agency, however, has been inconsistent in its citation and enforcement practices on this point.

QUESTIONS

How would you counsel the Moore executive? What pieces of additional information will you want? Suppose that the client, against your advice, decides not to install the railings and is subsequently assessed a penalty; would you represent the company in resisting any penalties?

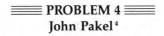

PROBLEM 4
John Pakel[4]

You represent the Chicago Savings and Loan and its president, John Pakel. Indeed, they are your most important clients. Mr. Pakel was recently sued for repayment of a debt. Mr. Pakel incurred the debt 23 years ago, when he borrowed $10,000 from an employee-carpenter, Joseph Zabella. Shortly after that, Pakel declared bankruptcy and listed his debt to Zabella in the petition. Subsequently, Pakel rose to the successful and lucrative position as Savings and Loan president. Zabella's complaint alleges that two years ago Pakel had orally promised to repay the loan. The applicable state law allows the subsequent promise to block the bankruptcy defense, but, because the new promise was oral, the cause of action would fail because of the statute of limitations. (Written promises have a ten-year life, oral promises only two.) Pakel concedes that he borrowed the money from Zabella and did not repay it.

QUESTIONS

Would you assert the statute of limitations defense on behalf of Mr. Pakel? If no, why not? What would you do? Would it matter to you if Pakel admits to having made the oral promise? What additional facts, if any, would you want to learn?

PROBLEM 5
Generally

Do you recognize issues the above problems share? What are those issues? How do you resolve them?

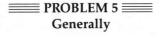

In the preceding chapter, we discussed the development of a sensitivity to personality and value conflicts between you and your client. That sensitivity is essential to a client-centered model; without an acute awareness of self, your needs, motives, and beliefs can cause you to manipulate a client and destroy in a subtle—often undetected—way the relationship's

---

4. Cf. *Zabella v. Pakel*, 242 F.2d 452 (7th Cir. 1957).

sharing of trust and concern and (most important) the principle of client decision-making.

This section assumes that you have recognized a conflict between yourself and your client and you know the source of that conflict. The questions now to be addressed are: What should you do about it? Do you suppress your needs or values and always accede to the client? Or are there limits to client autonomy and decision-making? If so, what are they?

Obviously, there are *some* limits. You clearly cannot participate in the client's direct violations of the law. If a client tells you the contract you are about to negotiate is a sham and a fraud on the contracting party, then you should preempt client decision-making or, at least, disassociate yourself from the client's schemes. But those are the easy cases. What about representing Frank Colon? Or executing a client's irrational desire to disinherit a faithful son? What if you are offended by a client's insistence on a technical defense to relieve him from a clear obligation? What do you do if you conclude that your corporate client is violating the spirit, if not the letter, of an important regulatory law? On another level, what if the client insists on making tactical decisions and directing the conduct of your representation?[5] Suppose a client desires a course of action you believe to be frivolous

---

5. EC 7-7 of the Code of Professional Responsibility offers the following, not terribly enlightening, guideline:

> In certain areas of legal representation not affecting the merits of the cause or substantially prejudicing the rights of a client, a lawyer is entitled to make decisions on his own. But otherwise the authority is exclusively that of the client and, if made within the framework of the law, such decisions are binding on his lawyer.

Just about anything, of course, can "affect the merits of the cause." (Why else do it?) Decisions such as whether to accept a settlement offer, file a lawsuit, or invoke a constitutional right are obviously the client's to make. But what about tactical decisions such as choosing between federal and state forums, determining a witness list, calling witnesses, or selecting a negotiation strategy?

We suggest that in selecting tactics and planning representation you should remain sensitive to the client's role as a partner in decision-making. Although clients will normally defer to your judgment on tactical issues, many of your decisions in a case can benefit from full and open discussion with the client. See Rule 1.2(a) of the Model Rules of Professional Conduct ("A lawyer shall abide by a client's decisions concerning the objectives of representation . . . and shall consult with the client as to the means by which they are to be pursued"). Indeed, to be effective, the process should often amount to joint decision-making. The client knows the facts, the witnesses, what she wants, and what she can afford. Frequently, the client can gauge better than you the reactions of opposing parties in a negotiation or litigation. Moreover, many decisions carry such importance that the client has a "right" (in a moral sense) to participate in the decision-making.

But what do you do if, after full discussion, you and the client disagree about whether to use a particular tactic or means? What if you perceive the client as officious, and confronting him about it does not alleviate the problem? You have several choices. You can submit to the client's wishes; override the client, thus leaving him with the choice of going along or finding a new attorney; or you can withdraw from the case. (Keep in mind that the Code of Professional Responsibility limits your discretion to opt out, depending on the nature and status of the case.) Your decision should turn on the importance and content of the issue, the client's rationale, the importance of the client and the case to you, and—if the issue arises in litigation—the extent to which the lawsuit has progressed.

For a different point of view, see Goldberg, On Trial in Foley Square, 74 A.B.A.J. 42, 45 (Jan. 1988), describing F. Lee Bailey: "At one lunch, he tells of the mafioso who wanted to control his defense—a decision Bailey didn't care for. 'I told him that I'm an ex-Marine and that it wouldn't bother me to put a bullet between his eyes and eat spaghetti off his face.' The client backed off."

or seriously detrimental. Do you still defer to client decision-making?[6] Do you adjust the level of your deference if the client is uneducated? Of borderline intelligence or competence?[7]

This text has advocated a model of the lawyer-client relationship that requires you to be empathic, nonjudgmental, and solicitous of client decision-making. This model, however, if stretched to an apparently logical extreme, could render you totally amoral in your professional relations with clients, bound only by your client's desires and the limits of the law. Can you as a counselor be accepting and nonjudgmental yet still adhere to your own moral code? Should you assert your moral views? When? An amoral approach to lawyering sustains the traditional perception of the lawyer's role. It has also been a ground for criticism of client-centered models.[8] How you

---

6. Rule 3.1 of the Model Rules and EC 7-4 of the Code prohibit you from asserting frivolous positions in litigation (see also Fed. R. Civ. P. 11), but that standard covers only a narrow range of decisions made by lawyers and clients. Certainly, when confronted with a client who is about to make, or has made, a frivolous decision, you should inform the client of your opinion. (Indeed, to hold back your advice could leave you open to a malpractice charge.) You should be sure to fully discuss the issues with the client. If you remain unconvinced, and the client persists in pursuing the apparently frivolous course of action, then you must decide if you want to execute the client's desires despite your reservations. In representing Mrs. Crum, for example, if she cannot explain why she wants to cut off her son, then you could tell her she must find another lawyer. As alternatives, you could probe to determine the cause of the irrational behavior or enlist the help of others (family, friends, a counseling expert). If you decide to accede to the client's wishes, be sure you are not in violation of the Code and your backside is covered.

7. See the Code of Professional Responsibility:

EC 7-11—The responsibilities of a lawyer may vary according to the intelligence, experience, mental condition or age of a client. . . . Examples include the representation of an illiterate or an incompetent. . . .

EC 7-12—Any mental or physical condition of a client that renders him incapable of making a considered judgment on his own behalf casts additional responsibilities upon his lawyer. Where an incompetent is acting through a guardian or other legal representative, a lawyer must look to such representative for those decisions which are normally the prerogative of the client to make. If a client under disability has no legal representative, his lawyer may be compelled in court proceedings to make decisions on behalf of the client. If the client is capable of understanding the matter in question or of contributing to the advancement of his interests, regardless of whether he is legally disqualified from performing certain acts, the lawyer should obtain from him all possible aid. If the disability of a client and the lack of a legal representative compel the lawyer to make decisions for his client, the lawyer should consider all circumstances then prevailing and act with care to safeguard and advance the interest of his client. But obviously a lawyer cannot perform any act or make any decision which the law requires his client to perform or make, either acting for himself if competent, or by a duly constituted representative if legally incompetent.

The Model Rules, however, place a greater responsibility on the lawyer to maintain the normal lines of decision-making. Rule 1.14 prescribes:

(a) When a client's ability to make adequately considered decisions in connection with the representation is impaired, whether because of minority, mental disability or for some other reason, the lawyer shall, as far as reasonably possible, maintain a normal client-lawyer relationship with the client.

(b) A lawyer may seek the appointment of a guardian or take other protective action with respect to a client, only when the lawyer reasonably believes that the client cannot adequately act in the client's own interest.

8. See, e.g., Simon, Homo Psychologicus: Notes on a New Legal Formalism, 32 Stan. L. Rev. 487 (1980).

perceive your moral accountability in your professional work critically affects the counseling process; at issue is the allocation of decision-making between you and your clients.

Under traditional perceptions, which extend back to the English system and predominate today, lawyers are not to be identified with their clients or the arguments made on behalf of clients. During his 1820 defense of Queen Caroline, Lord Brougham proclaimed the following oft-cited view of the lawyer's role:

> An advocate, by the sacred duty which he owes his client, knows, in the discharge of that office, but one person in the world, THAT CLIENT AND NONE OTHER. To save that client by all expedient means, to protect that client at all hazards and costs to all others, and among others to himself, is the highest and most unquestioned of his duties: and he must not regard the alarm, the suffering, the torment, the destruction which he may bring on any other. Nay, separating even the duties of a patriot from those of an advocate, and casting them, if need be, to the wind, he must go on reckless of the consequences, if his fate it should unhappily be to involve his country in confusion for his client's sake.[9]

The Code of Professional Responsibility, as well as tradition, holds that lawyers must zealously represent their clients, limited only by the bounds of the law.[10] Whom lawyers represent and what they advocate impose no responsibility—they are not held accountable for the causes they advocate. The legal system's truth-finding (or at least decision-making) process depends on the competing sides in a dispute presenting their cases to a neutral judge or jury. The litigants, to have their positions adequately and fairly argued, are entitled to be represented by skillful advocates, well-schooled in the procedures and quirks of the system. Indeed, traditionalists contend that the process can work only if each side is technically proficient and "blindly zealous."[11] Thus, to ensure that each party will receive a fair hearing, the lawyers are insulated from accountability for the position they advocate, even though a client's position is ultimately found to be unlawful, unjust, or immoral. In the nonlitigation context as well, lawyers work without accountability for the propriety of their lawful acts because tradition holds that everyone is entitled to the advice and counsel of a lawyer. Scrutiny of attorneys for their negotiation, drafting, or advice for clients could leave many persons without needed representation.

---

9. Quoted in Schudson, Public, Private and Professional Lives: The Correspondence of David Dudley Field and Samuel Bowles, 21 Am. J. of Legal History 191, 205-206 (1977).

10. ABA Code of Professional Responsibility, Canon 7 and EC 7-19. Samuel Johnson's view on the subject has often been cited in support of the traditional model and illustrates the depth of its roots. He stated, "[A] lawyer has no business with the justice or injustice of the cause which he undertakes, unless his client asks his opinion, and then he is bound to give it honestly. The justice or injustice of the cause is to be decided by the Judge." Quoted in Postema, Moral Responsibility in Professional Ethics, 55 N.Y.U. L. Rev. 63, 73-74, n.28 (1980).

11. See, e.g., Fortas, Thurman Arnold and the Theatre of the Law, 79 Yale L.J. 988, 1002 (1970); Landsman, The Decline of the Adversary System and the Changing Role of the Advocate in That System, 18 San Diego L. Rev. 251 (1981).

The traditional conception, then, is marked by two central themes:

(i) Partisanship: the lawyer's sole allegiance is to the client; the lawyer is the partisan of the client. Within, but all the way up to, the limits of the law, the lawyer is committed to the aggressive and single-minded pursuit of the client's objectives.

(ii) Neutrality: once he has accepted the client's case, the lawyer must represent the client, or pursue the client's objectives, regardless of the lawyer's opinion of the client's character and reputation, and the moral merits of the client's objectives. On this conception, the lawyer need not consider, nor may he be held responsible for, the consequences of his professional activities as long as he stays within the law and acts in pursuit of the client's legitimate aims. Thus, the proper range of the lawyer's concern—the boundaries of the lawyer's "moral universe"—is defined by two parameters: the law and the client's interests and objectives. These factors are the exclusive points of reference for professional deliberation and practical judgment.[12]

To deal with this approach, lawyers typically compartmentalize their moral spheres by separating their personal and professional lives. According to Montaigne, "There's no reason why a lawyer . . . should not recognize the Knavery that is part of his vocation. . . . An honest man is not responsible for the vices or the stupidity of his calling."[13] To maintain his personal integrity, despite the necessary indulgences in "Knavery," Montaigne divided his personality: "I have been able to concern myself with public affairs without moving the length of my nail from myself. . . . The mayor and Montaigne have always been two people, clearly separated."[14]

The traditional perception has recently, however, come under attack, as commentators have urged some degree of moral independence and attendant accountability for lawyers in their advocacy.[15] This moral responsibility extends beyond the rigid confines of the law and requires lawyers to reach their own moral judgments about the substance of their advocacy.

We offer below three selections to enlighten your decision about the morality of your role as a lawyer. The first is a sophisticated defense of the traditional model. The second selection argues for a revisionist approach. The third deals specifically with the lawyer's moral accountability in the client-centered model of the lawyer-client relationship.

---

12. Postema, Moral Responsibility in Professional Ethics, 55 N.Y.U. L. Rev. 63, 73-74 (1980).

13. Quoted in id. at 63, and in Curtis, The Ethics of Advocacy, 4 Stan. L. Rev. 3, 20 (1951).

14. Quoted in Postema, Moral Responsibility in Professional Ethics, 55 N.Y.U. L. Rev. 63, 64 (1980), and in Curtis, The Ethics of Advocacy, 4 Stan L. Rev. 3, 20 (1951). See also Shaffer, The Legal Ethics of the Two Kingdoms, 17 Val. U.L. Rev. 3 (1983).

15. See, e.g., Kennedy, The Responsibility of Lawyers for the Justice of Their Causes, 18 Tex. Tech. L. Rev. 1157 (1987); Bastress, Client-Centered Counseling and Moral Accountability for Lawyers, 10 J. of the Legal Prof. 97 (1985); Noonan, Other People's Morals: The Lawyer's Conscience, 48 Tenn. L. Rev. 227 (1981); Flynn, Professional Ethics and the Lawyer's Duty to Self, 1976 Wash. U.L.Q. 429; Wasserstrom, Lawyers as Professionals: Some Moral Issues, 5 Human Rights L. Rev. 1 (1975); Symposium, The Lawyer's Amoral Ethical Role, 1986 Am. B. Found. Res. J. 613.

≣ C. FRIED, THE LAWYER AS FRIEND: THE MORAL FOUNDATIONS OF THE LAWYER-CLIENT RELATION
85 Yale L.J. 1060, 1060-1061, 1065-1067, 1071-1089 (1976) [16]

Can a good lawyer be a good person? The question troubles lawyers and law students alike. They are troubled by the demands of loyalty to one's client and by the fact that one can win approval as a good, maybe even great, lawyer even though that loyalty is engrossed by over-privileged or positively distasteful clients. How, they ask, is such loyalty compatible with that devotion to the common good characteristic of high moral principles? And whatever their views of the common good, they are troubled because the willingness of lawyers to help their clients use the law to the prejudice of the weak or the innocent seems morally corrupt. The lawyer is conventionally seen as a professional devoted to his client's interests and as authorized, if not in fact required, to do some things (though not anything) for that client which he would not do for himself. In this essay I consider the compatibility between this traditional conception of the lawyer's role and the ideal of moral purity—the ideal that one's life should be lived in fulfillment of the most demanding moral principles, and not just barely within the law. So I shall not be particularly concerned with the precise limits imposed on the lawyer's conduct by positive rules of law and by the American Bar Association's Code of Professional Responsibility except as these provide a background. I assume that the lawyer observes these scrupulously. My inquiry is one of morals: Does the lawyer whose conduct and choices are governed only by the traditional conception of the lawyer's role, which these positive rules reflect, lead a professional life worthy of moral approbation, worthy of respect—ours and his own?

I. THE CHALLENGE TO THE TRADITIONAL CONCEPTION

[Professor Fried notes two criticisms of the traditional perception: (1) "the ideal of professional loyalty to one's client permits, even demands, an allocation of the lawyer's time, passion, and resources in ways that are not always maximally conducive to the greatest good of the greatest number"; and (2) "this loyalty appears to authorize tactics which procure advantages for the client at the direct expense of some identified opposing party."]

II. THE LAWYER AS FRIEND

THE THESIS

In this essay I will consider the moral status of the traditional conception of the professional. The two criticisms of this traditional conception, if left unanswered, will not put the lawyer in jail, but they will leave him without a moral basis for his acts. The real question is whether, in the face of these two criticisms, a decent and morally sensitive person can conduct

---

16. Footnotes in the original are omitted.

himself according to the traditional conception of professional loyalty and still believe that what he is doing is morally worthwhile. . . .

I will argue in this essay that it is not only legally but also morally right that a lawyer adopt as his dominant purpose the furthering of his client's interests—that it is right that a professional put the interests of his client above some idea, however valid, of the collective interest. I maintain that the traditional conception of the professional role expresses a morally valid conception of human conduct and human relationships, that one who acts according to that conception is to that extent a good person. Indeed, it is my view that, far from being a mere creature of positive law, the traditional conception is so far mandated by moral right that any advanced legal system which did not sanction this conception would be unjust.

The general problem raised by the two criticisms is this: How can it be that it is not only permissible, but indeed morally right, to favor the interests of a particular person in a way which we can be fairly sure is either harmful to another particular individual or not maximally conducive to the welfare of society as a whole?

The resolution of this problem is aided, I think, if set in a larger perspective. Charles Curtis made the perspicacious remark that a lawyer may be privileged to lie for his client in a way that one might lie to save one's friends or close relatives. I do not want to underwrite the notion that it is justifiable to lie even in those situations, but there is a great deal to the point that in those relations—friendship, kinship—we recognize an authorization to take the interests of particular concrete persons more seriously and to give them priority over the interests of the wider collectivity. One who provides an expensive education for his own children surely cannot be blamed because he does not use these resources to alleviate famine or to save lives in some distant land. Nor does he blame himself. Indeed, our intuition that an individual is authorized to prefer identified persons standing close to him over the abstract interests of humanity finds its sharpest expression in our sense that an individual is entitled to act with something less than impartiality to that person who stands closest to him—the person that he is. There is such a thing as selfishness to be sure, yet no reasonable morality asks us to look upon ourselves as merely plausible candidates for the distribution of the attention and resources which we command, plausible candidates whose entitlement to our own concern is no greater in principle than that of any other human being. Such a doctrine may seem edifying, but on reflection it strikes us as merely fanatical. . . .

In explicating the lawyer's relation to his client, my analogy shall be to friendship, where the freedom to choose and to be chosen expresses our freedom to hold something of ourselves in reserve, in reserve even from the universalizing claims of morality. These personal ties and the claims they engender may be all-consuming, as with a close friend or family member, or they may be limited, special-purpose claims, as in the case of the client or patient. The special-purpose claim is one in which the beneficiary, the client, is entitled to all the special consideration within the limits of the relationship which we accord to a friend or a loved one. It is not that the claims of the client are less intense or demanding; they are only more limited in their scope. After all, the ordinary concept of friendship provides only an analogy, and it is to the development of that analogy that I turn.

SPECIAL-PURPOSE FRIENDS

How does a professional fit into the concept of personal relations at all? He is, I have suggested, a limited-purpose friend. A lawyer is a friend in regard to the legal system. He is someone who enters into a personal relation with you—not an abstract relation as under the concept of justice. That means that like a friend he acts in your interests, not his own; or rather he adopts your interests as his own. I would call that the classic definition of friendship. To be sure, the lawyer's range of concern is sharply limited. But within that limited domain the intensity of identification with the client's interests is the same. It is not the specialized focus of the relationship which may make the metaphor inapposite, but the way in which the relation of legal friendship comes about and the one-sided nature of the ensuing "friendship." But I do insist upon the analogy, for in overcoming the arguments that the analogy is false, I think the true moral foundations of the lawyer's special role are illuminated and the utilitarian objections to the traditional conception of that role overthrown.

THE PROFESSIONAL ROLE AS SOCIALLY DEFINED:
THE CONTENT OF THE RELATION

The claims that are made on the doctor or lawyer are made within a social context and are defined, at least in part, by social expectations. Most strikingly, in talking about friendship the focus of the inquiry is quite naturally upon the free gift of the donor; yet in professional relationships it is the recipient's need for medical or legal aid which defines the relationship. So the source of the relationship seems to be located at the other end, that of the recipient. To put this disquiet another way, we might ask how recognizing the special claims of friendship in any way compels society to allow the doctor or the lawyer to define his role on the analogy of those claims. Why are these people not like other social actors designated to purvey certain, perhaps necessary, goods? Would we say that one's grocer, tailor, or landlord should be viewed as a limited-purpose friend? Special considerations must be brought forward for doctors and lawyers.

A special argument is at hand in both cases. The doctor does not minister just to any need, but to health. He helps maintain the very physical integrity which is the concrete substrate of individuality. To be sure, so does a grocer or landlord. But illness wears a special guise: it appears as a critical assault on one's person. The needs to which the doctor ministers usually are implicated in crises going to one's concreteness and individuality, and therefore what one looks for is a kind of ministration which is particularly concrete, personal, individualized. Thus, it is not difficult to see why I claim that a doctor is a friend, though a special-purpose friend, the purpose being defined by the special needs of illness and crisis to which he tends.

But what, then, of the lawyer? Friendship and kinship are natural relations existing within, but not defined by, complex social institutions. Illness too is more a natural than social phenomenon. The response here requires an additional step. True, the special situations—legal relations or disputes—in which the lawyer acts as a limited-purpose friend are themselves a product of social institutions. But it does not follow that the role of the lawyer, which is created to help us deal with those social institutions, is defined by and is wholly at the mercy of the social good. We need only concede that at the very least the law must leave us a measure of autonomy, whether or not it is in the social interest to do so. Individuals have rights over and against the collectivity. The moral capital arising out of individuals' concrete situations is one way of expressing that structure of rights, or at least part of it. It is because the law must respect the rights of individuals that the law must also create and support the specific role of legal friend. For the social nexus—the web of perhaps entirely just institutions—has become so complex that without the assistance of an expert adviser an ordinary layman cannot exercise that autonomy which the system must allow him. Without such an adviser, the law would impose constraints on the lay citizen (unequally at that) which it is not entitled to impose explicitly. Thus, the need which the lawyer serves in his special-purpose friendship may not be, as in the case of the doctor, natural, presocial. Yet it is a need which has a moral grounding analogous to the need which the physician serves: the need to maintain one's integrity as a person. When I say the lawyer is his client's legal friend, I mean the lawyer makes his client's interests his own insofar as this is necessary to preserve and foster the client's autonomy within the law. This argument does not require us to assume that the law is hostile to the client's rights. All we need to assume is that even a system of law which is perfectly sensitive to personal rights would not work fairly unless the client could claim a professional's assistance in realizing that autonomy which the law recognizes. . . .

CONCLUSION

. . . The notion of the lawyer as the client's legal friend, whatever its limitations and difficulties, does account for a kind of callousness toward society and exclusivity in the service of the client which otherwise seem quite mysterious. It justifies a kind of scheming which we would deplore on the part of a lay person dealing with another lay person—even if he were acting on behalf of a friend.

But these special indulgences apply only as a lawyer assists his client in his legal business. I do not owe my client my political assistance. I do not have to espouse his cause when I act as a citizen. Indeed, it is one of the most repellent features of the American legal profession—one against which the barrister-solicitor split has to some extent guarded the English profession—that many lawyers really feel that they are totally bought by their clients, that they must identify with their clients' interests far beyond the special purpose of advising them and operating the legal system for them. The defendants' antitrust lawyer or defendants' food and drug lawyer who writes articles, gives speeches, and pontificates generally about the evils of regulation may believe these things, but too often he does so because it is good for business or because he thinks that such conduct is what good representation requires. In general, I think it deplorable that lawyers have specialized not only in terms of subject matter—that may or may not be a good thing—but in terms of plaintiffs or defendants, in terms of the position that they represent.

There is a related point which cuts very much in the opposite direction. It is no part of my thesis that the *client* is not morally bound to avoid lying to the court, to pay a just debt even though it is barred by the statute of limitations, to treat an opposite party in a negotiation with humanity and consideration for his needs and vulnerability, or to help the effectuation of policies aimed at the common good. Further, it is no part of my argument to hold that a lawyer must assume that the client is not a decent, moral person, has no desire to fulfill his moral obligations, and is asking only what is the minimum that he must do to stay within the law. On the contrary, to assume this about anyone is itself a form of immorality because it is a form of disrespect between persons. Thus in very many situations a lawyer will be advising a client who wants to effectuate his purposes within the law, to be sure, but who also wants to behave as a decent, moral person. It would be absurd to contend that the lawyer must abstain from giving advice that takes account of the client's moral duties and his presumed desire to fulfill them. Indeed, in these situations the lawyer experiences the very special satisfaction of assisting the client not only to realize his autonomy within the law, but also to realize his status as a moral being. I want to make very clear that my conception of the lawyer's role in no way disentitles the lawyer from experiencing this satisfaction. Rather, it has been my purpose to explicate the less obvious point that there is a vocation and a satisfaction even in helping Shylock obtain his pound of flesh or in bringing about the acquittal of a guilty man.

Finally, I would like to return to the charge that the morality of role and personal relationship I offer here is almost certain to lead to the diversion of legal services from areas of greatest need. It is just my point, of course, that when we fulfill the office of friend—legal, medical, or friend *tout court*—we do right, and thus it would be a great wrong to place us under a general regime of always doing what will "do the most good." What I affirm, therefore, is the moral liberty of a lawyer to make his life out of what personal scraps and shards of motivation his inclination and character suggest: idealism, greed, curiosity, love of luxury, love of travel, a need for adventure or repose; only so long as these lead him to give wise and faithful counsel. It is the task of the social system as a whole, and of all its citizens, to work for the conditions under which everyone will benefit in fair measure from the performance of doctors, lawyers, teachers, and musicians. But I would not see the integrity of these roles undermined in order that the millennium might come sooner. After all, it may never come, and then what would we be left with?

≣ G. J. POSTEMA, MORAL RESPONSIBILITY IN PROFESSIONAL ETHICS
55 N.Y.U. L. Rev. 63, 75-83 (1980)[17]

III. RESPONSIBLE ACTION UNDER THE STANDARD CONCEPTION

. . . Psychological distance is especially characteristic of professional roles. . . . [O]ne can identify with, or distance oneself in varying degrees

---

17. Reprinted by permission of New York University Law Review. Copyright © 1980. Footnotes in the original are omitted.

from, this available self-image. The more closely one identifies with one's role, the more one's sense of self is likely to be shaped by the defining features of the role. At one extreme, maximal identification is characterized by an unquestioning acceptance of the duties and responsibilities of one's role. For the person who maximally identifies with his role, the response "because I am a lawyer," or more generally "because that's my job," suffices as a complete answer to the question "why do that?" One minimally identifies, on the other hand, when one conforms only to avoid the external consequences of failing to do so, in no way internalizing the role or its basic principles. Several possible intermediate states separate these extremes.

Thus, in addition to the dimension of moral distance between private and professional morality there is the dimension of psychological distance between oneself, or one's moral personality, and one's role. Furthermore, these two dimensions are interrelated: faculties will tend to shape one's moral personality and, thus, one's inclination to identify with the role. The problem of responsibility lies in the fact that as the moral distance between private and professional moralities increases, the temptation to adopt one or the other extreme strategy of identification also increases; one either increasingly identifies with the role or seeks resolutely to detach oneself from it. Under either extreme, however, one's practical judgment and sense of responsibility are cut off from their sources in ordinary moral experience.

The problem of responsibility is especially troubling for the legal profession. The risk of severing professional judgment from its moral and psychological sources is particularly strong in a profession that serves a system of institutionalized justice. As a result, the problem of developing a sense of personal responsibility is critical for the legal profession. First, the factors inducing maximal psychological identification are strong. Publicly dedicated to serving socially valued institutions, the lawyer occupies a key role in society, enjoying considerable social status. His claim to specialized knowledge and skill puts the lawyer in a position of power relative to his client. These facts, in addition to the important intrinsic satisfaction of exercising his special skills, encourage a high degree of role identification. As a result, principles of professional responsibility, originally justified on functional grounds, take on independent value and significance for lawyers. Professional integrity becomes a mark, often the most significant mark, of personal integrity.

Second, the characteristic activities of lawyering often require the lawyer to act in the place of the client, and thus require the direct involvement of the lawyer's moral faculties—i.e., his capacities to deliberate, reason, argue, and act in the public arena. All professionals, and many persons in service-oriented occupations, do things for a client that the client is unable or unwilling to do for himself. But, unlike the lawyer, the physician or auto mechanic acts only to provide services for the client. The lawyer also acts as the client's *agent*. Although an individual may employ a physician or mechanic to operate on his body or his automobile, the work of these professionals is in no sense attributable to the patient or customer. When the lawyer acts to secure the client's interests, however, he often acts, speaks, and argues in the place of the client. He enters into relationships with others in the name of the client. When he argues in his client's behalf, he often presents his client's arguments; when he acts he is often said to be "exercising his client's rights." And what he does is typically attributable to the client. Thus, at the invitation of the client, the lawyer becomes an extension of the legal, and to an extent the moral, personality of the client.

Since the lawyer often acts as an extension of the legal and moral personality of the client, the lawyer is under great temptation to refuse to accept responsibility for his professional actions and their consequences. Moreover, except when his beliefs coincide with those of his client, he lives with a recurring dilemma: he must engage in activities, make arguments, and present positions which he himself does not endorse or embrace. The lawyer's integrity is put into question by the mere exercise of the duties of his profession.

To preserve his integrity, the lawyer must carefully distance himself from his activities. Publicly, he may sharply distinguish statements or arguments he makes for the client and statements on which he stakes his professional honor. The danger in this strategy is that a curious two-stage distancing may result. First, the lawyer distances himself from the argument: it is not his argument, but that of his client. His job is to construct the arguments; the task of evaluating and believing them is left to others. Second, after detaching himself from the argument, he is increasingly tempted to identify with this stance of detachment. What first offers itself as a device for distancing oneself from personally unacceptable positions becomes a defining feature of one's professional self-concept. This, in turn, encourages an uncritical, uncommitted state of mind, or worse, a deep moral skepticism. When such detachment is defined as a professional ideal, as it is by the standard conception, the lawyer is even more apt to adopt these attitudes.

The foregoing tensions and pressures have sources deep in the nature of the lawyer's characteristic activities. To eradicate them entirely would be to eliminate much of what is distinctive and socially valuable in these activities. Nevertheless, these tensions can be eased, and the most destructive tendencies avoided, if lawyers have a framework within which they can obtain an integrated view of their activities both within the role and outside it. The framework must provide the resources for responsible resolution of the conflicts that inevitably arise. The standard conception of the lawyer's role, however, fails notably on this score. Clearly, the standard conception calls for a sharp separation of private and professional morality in which, to quote Bellow and Kettleson, "the lawyer is asked to do 'as a professional what he or she would not do' as a person." The conception requires a public endorsement, as well as private adoption, of the extreme strategy of detachment. The good lawyer is one who is capable of drawing a tight circle around himself and his client, allowing no other considerations to interfere with his zealous and scrupulously loyal pursuit of the client's objectives. The good lawyer leaves behind his own family, religious, political, and moral concerns, and devotes himself entirely to the client. But since professional integrity is often taken to be the most important mark of personal integrity, a very likely result is often that a successful lawyer is one who can strictly identify with this professional strategy of detachment. That is, the standard conception both directly and indirectly *encourages* adoption of one or the other of the extreme strategies of identification. But, as we have seen, both strategies have in common the unwanted consequence that practical deliberation, judgment, and action within the *role* are effectively cut off from ordinary moral beliefs, attitudes, feelings, and relationships—resources on which responsible judgment and action depend. This consequence is very costly in both personal and social terms.

Consider first the personal costs the lawyer must pay to act in this detached manner. The maximal strategy yields a severe impoverishment of moral experience. The lawyer's moral experience is sharply constrained by the boundaries of the moral universe of the role. But the minimal strategy involves perhaps even higher personal costs. Since the characteristic activities of the lawyer require a large investment of his moral faculties, the lawyer must reconcile himself to a kind of moral prostitution. In a large portion of his daily experience, in which he is acting regularly in the moral arena, he is alienated from his own moral feelings and attitudes and indeed from his moral personality as a whole. Moreover, in light of the strong pressures for role identification, it is not unlikely that the explicit and conscious adoption of the minimal identification strategy involves a substantial element of self-deception.

The social costs of cutting off professional deliberation and action from their sources in ordinary moral experience are even more troubling. First, cut off from sound moral judgment, the lawyer's ability to do his job well—to determine the applicable law and effectively advise his clients—is likely to be seriously affected. Both positivist and natural law theorists agree that moral arguments have an important place in the determination of much of modern law. But the lawyer who must detach professional judgment from his own moral judgment is deprived of the resources from which arguments regarding his client's legal rights and duties can be fashioned. In effect, the ideal of neutrality and detachment wars against its companion ideal of zealous pursuit of client interests.

Second, the lawyer's practical judgment, in the Aristotelian sense, is rendered ineffective and unreliable. . . . [B]ecause human values are diverse and complex, one is sometimes thrown back on the faculty of practical judgment to resolve moral dilemmas. This is as true within the professional context as outside of it. To cut off professional decisionmaking from the values and concerns which structure the moral situation, thereby blocking appeal to a more comprehensive point of view from which to weigh the validity of role morality, is to risk undermining practical judgment entirely.

Third, and most importantly, when professional action is estranged from ordinary moral experience, the lawyer's sensitivity to the moral costs in both ordinary and extraordinary situations tends to atrophy. The ideal of neutrality permits, indeed requires, that the lawyer regard his professional activities and their consequences from the point of view of the uninvolved spectator. One may abstractly regret that the injury is done, but this regret is analogous to the regret one feels as a spectator to [a traffic accident]; one is in no way personally implicated. The responses likely from a mature sense of responsibility appear morally fastidious and unprofessional from the perspective of the present Code. This has troubling consequences: without a proper appreciation of the moral costs of one's actions one cannot make effective use of the faculty of practical judgment. In fact, a proper perspective of the moral costs of one's action has both intrinsic and instrumental value. The instrumental value lies in the added safeguard that important moral dilemmas will receive appropriate reflection. As Bernard Williams argued, "only those who are [by practice] reluctant or disinclined to do the morally disagreeable when it is really necessary have much chance of not doing it when it is not necessary. . . . [A] habit of reluctance is an essential obstacle against the happy acceptance of the intolerance."

But this appreciation is also important for its own sake. To experience sincere reluctance, to feel the need to make restitution, to seek the other's pardon—these simply are appropriate responses to the actual feature of the moral situation. In this way, the status and integrity of important moral principles are maintained in compromising circumstances, and the moral relations between persons are respected or restored.

Finally, the moral detachment of the lawyer adversely affects the quality of the lawyer-client relationship. Unable to draw from the responses and relations of ordinary experience, the lawyer is capable of relating to the client only as a client. He puts his moral faculties of reason, argument, and persuasion wholly at the service of the client, but simultaneously disengages his moral personality. He views himself not as a moral actor but as a legal technician. In addition, he is barred from recognizing the client's moral personality. The moral responsibilities of the client are simply of no interest to him. Thus, paradoxically, the combination of partisanship and neutrality jeopardizes client autonomy and mutual respect (two publicly stated objectives of the standard conception), and yields instead a curious kind of *impersonal* relationship.

It is especially striking, then, that Charles Fried, the most sophisticated defender of these central ideals of the standard conception, should describe the lawyer as a "special purpose" friend. Indeed, it is the contrast between the standard conception of the lawyer-client relationship and the characteristics of a relationship between friends which, on reflection, is likely to make the deepest impression. The impersonalism and moral detachment characteristic of the lawyer's role under the standard conception are not found in relations between friends. Loyalty to one's friend does not call for disengagement of one's moral personality. When in nonprofessional contexts we enter special relationships and undertake special obligations which create duties of loyalty or special concern, these special considerations must nevertheless be integrated into a coherent picture of the moral life as a whole. Often we must view our moral world from more than one perspective simultaneously. . . . [R]oles are often structured with the recognition that persons occupying the role fill other roles which are also important to them. Room is left for the agent to integrate his responsibilities from each role into a more or less coherent scheme encompassing his entire moral life.

But it is precisely this integrated conception of the moral personality that is unavailable to the professional who adopts either the minimal or the maximal identification strategy. Either the moral personality is entirely fragmented or compartmentalized, or it is shrunk to fit the moral universe defined by the role. Neither result is desirable.

IV. TOWARD AN ALTERNATIVE CONCEPTION: THE RECOURSE ROLE

The unavoidable social costs of the standard conception of professional legal behavior argue strongly for a radical rethinking of the lawyer's role. One alternative is a "deprofessionalization" of legal practice so as to eliminate the distance between private and professional morality. Deprofessionalization, however, would involve a radical restructuring of the entire legal system, reducing the complexity of the law as it currently exists so that individuals could exercise their rights without the assistance of highly specialized legal technicians. But, setting aside obvious questions of feasibility, to discredit this proposal we need only recall that deprofessionalization ignores the significant social value in a division of moral and social labor produced by the variety of public and professional roles.

A second, more plausible alternative is to recognize the unavoidable discontinuities in the moral landscape and to bridge them with a unified conception of moral personality. Achieving any sort of bridge, however, requires that lawyers significantly alter the way they view their own activities. Each lawyer must have a conception of the role that allows him to serve the important functions of that role in the legal and political system while integrating his own sense of moral responsibility into the role itself. Such a conception must improve upon the current one by allowing a broader scope for engaged moral judgment in day-to-day professional activities while encouraging a keener sense of personal responsibility for the consequences of these activities.

The task of forging a concrete alternative conception is a formidable one. To begin, however, it may be useful to contrast two conceptions of social roles: the fixed role and the recourse role. In a fixed role, the professional perceives the defining characteristics of the role—its basic rules, duties, and responsibilities—as entirely predetermined. The characteristics may be altered gradually through social evolution or more quickly by profession-wide regulatory legislation, but as far as the individual practitioner is concerned, the moral universe of his role is an objective fact, to be reckoned with, but not for him to alter. Sartre, proponents of the standard conception, and advocates of deprofessionalization all rest their positions on the assumption that the defining features of each role remain fixed. But this assumption fits only some social roles. A bank clerk, for example, must follow set routines; little judgment is required, and he has no authority to set aside the rules under which he acts or alter these rules to fit new occasions. This is not troubling because the sorts of situations one is likely to face in such a job lend themselves to routine treatment.

In contrast, in a recourse role, one's duties and responsibilities are not fixed, but may expand or contract depending on the institutional objectives the role is designed to serve. The recourse role requires the agent not only to act according to what he perceives to be the explicit duties of the role in a narrow sense, but also to carry out those duties in keeping with the functional objectives of the role. The agent can meet these requirements only if he possesses a comprehensive and integrated concept of his activities both within and outside the role. Role morality, then, within a recourse role is not properly served by maximal identification with one's role. Nor can the role agent minimally identify with his role so as to abandon or disengage his personal morality or basic sense of responsibility. Indeed, responsible professional judgment will rely heavily on a sense of responsibility.

If we perceive the role of the lawyer in our legal system as a recourse role, a viable solution to the problem of responsibility may be available. A recourse role conception forces the lawyer to recognize that the exercise of his role duties must fully engage his rational and critical powers, and his sense of moral responsibility as well. Although not intended to obliterate the moral distance between professional and private moralities, a recourse role conception bridges that gap by integrating to a significant degree the moral personality of the individual with the performance of role responsibilities. Most significantly, this conception prevents the lawyer from escaping responsibility by relying on his status as an agent of the client or an instrument of the system. He cannot consider himself simply a legal technician, since his role essentially involves the exercise of his *engaged* moral judgment.

≡ R. M. BASTRESS, CLIENT-CENTERED COUNSELING AND MORAL ACCOUNTABILITY FOR LAWYERS
10 J. Legal Prof. 97, 112-113, 117-119, 125-127 (1985) [18]

III. A PROPOSAL—A DUTY FOR LAWYERS
TO EXERCISE INDEPENDENT MORAL JUDGMENT

The amoral adversarial model should be replaced by one that requires a lawyer to exercise independent judgment. This section proposes such an alternative model and explains its basic features, difficulties, and advantages.

A. OVERVIEW

The alternative model calls for the lawyer to gain an understanding of the client's facts, following [a client-centered approach]. That is, the lawyer should be open and accepting, and gathering the "facts" should include an awareness of the client's feelings and motives. The lawyer should then independently assess the case to determine if she has any moral or social objections, both in terms of the consequences to the immediate parties and of the effects on broader policy implications. If so, then she should carefully prepare for a most sensitive counseling session and proceed to fully dis-

---

18. Footnotes in the original are omitted.

cuss the issue with the client. The client may satisfy the lawyer's reservations and the representation can then continue. If, however, the client cannot meet the lawyer's objections, then the lawyer should explore possible alternatives with the client. If that fails, then the lawyer should again exercise her independent judgment and, if the concern persists and is serious, should refuse to proceed with the case. The judgment should be based on the lawyer's personal sense of right and justice and not, as presently exists under the adversarial standard, focused on the client's interest in being adequately represented. . . .

Scrutiny of the lawyer's moral judgments should focus on what he advocates and how, not on whom he represents. The distinction has practical significance for the lawyer; it means the lawyer should not judge the client's morality in matters unrelated to the position advocated. Thus, for example, an attorney may find adultery immoral, but can nevertheless nonjudgmentally and unequivocally counsel an adulterer-divorce client. The lawyer has no business morally judging clients on personal or other matters when they are not essential to the result sought; in the divorce case, the attorney need assert only that the marriage is irretrievably broken and need not argue that adultery should be condoned. . . .

B. ADVANTAGES

The advantages of moral independence and accountability for each lawyer are manifold and weighty. The benefits will further the needs of the legal system, of society generally, of the organized bar, and of individual lawyers as well.

One of the approach's major benefits should be a fairer and more just legal system. After all, lawyers and their clients are continuously making "legal" decisions in law offices and board rooms. Imposing a duty on lawyers to assert themselves morally would help assure full consideration of societal implications. Thus, when a cereal company decides whether to fight a federal ruling on sugar-coated cereals, when a steel company (or steelworkers' union) looks for loopholes in fair employment laws, when a solvent debtor seeks to invoke a statute of limitations to avoid repayment of a loan, or when a bank fires an employee for insisting on compliance with credit reporting statutes, the lawyers representing these clients should confront them about the moral and socio-economic consequences of their conduct. Such confrontations should occur as soon as the lawyer has the facts. (Ideally, that would be before the conduct is initiated, but unfortunately clients do not always consult their attorney before acting.) In any event, this fuller, more balanced process will produce better decisions. . . .

Finally, and perhaps most significantly, this model of the morally independent lawyer makes for happier, healthier, more productive lawyers and lawyer-client relationships. Attorneys who believe in their advocacy and in their clients enjoy their work, while those who toil in conflict with their beliefs can experience inner turmoil, self-doubt, and constant struggles with rationalization. A person who works against his beliefs, or who delegates to others (such as clients) his moral choices, is unable to achieve self-actualization. That is, he cannot develop his full potential as a person, and he flounders in frustration. The lawyer's contradiction of values and work also damages relationships with those clients whose cases occasion the conflict. The lawyer's deception of self and others inhibits communication and deprives the relationship of the genuineness it needs to be fully effective. In contrast, a lawyer who acts consistently with his values and uses the [client-centered model of the lawyer-counselor] clears the way to fully develop both himself and his relationships with clients. That theme pervades the following [sections] as they explain the seeming paradox of how an accepting, client-centered lawyer not only *can* be morally independent in his work, but *must* be.

IV. Relationship of Moral Accountability for Lawyers to Client-Centered Counseling

How can a lawyer/counselor be open and accepting with clients while still insisting on his own moral code? The response is that a counselor cannot be open and accepting unless he is honest with himself and with his client. A counseling relationship based on falsehoods is doomed to failure. An "open and accepting" approach requires respect for the client and a willingness to listen; it does not mean that the counselor surrenders all his social, political, and moral commitments to each client. The relationship can best be described as a partnership between equals who share both common goals and responsibility. Thus, as this section explains, client-centered and morally independent counseling are interdependent and both demand "honest" counselors.

The concept of the lawyer as a morally independent counselor follows naturally from the philosophical, psychological, and psychotherapeutic premises of client-centered lawyering. These premises can be traced to humanist, existential, Taoist, and Judeo-Christian thinkers, such as Abraham Maslow, Soren Kierkegaard, Martin Buber, and Carl Rogers. [The article here summarizes the relevant theories of Abraham Maslow in humanistic psychology and of Lawrence Kohlberg on moral development. That summary is included in Section A of this chapter, pages 312-315.]

The client-centered psychotherapeutic theories of Carl Rogers also emphasize self-awareness; knowledge of self and a corresponding honesty with clients combine to provide a cornerstone for effective counseling. The self-understanding allows the counselor—including the lawyer-counselor—to experience personal growth while his frankness fosters healthier relations with his clients and facilitates resolution of moral issues that arise during the relationship. The results reflect what the philosopher Martin Buber called "I-Thou" relationships; they are based on felt experiences between persons who bring their whole, genuine selves into the relationship. (These contrast with "I-It" relationships, which would portray the lawyer as a distant professional dealing with the client in a depersonalized manner.)

Rogers sees self-awareness, self-acceptance, and genuineness as the ingredients of "congruence." The congruent counselor operates "without front or facade, openly being the feelings and attributes which at that moment are flowing in him." He is "able to live these feelings, be them, and able to communicate them if appropriate." For Rogers, genuineness in the counseling relationship is crucial:

I have found that the more that I can be genuine in the relationship, the more helpful it will be. This means that I need to be aware of my own feelings in so far as possible, rather than presenting an outward facade of one attitude, while actually holding another attitude at a deeper or unconscious level. Being genuine also involves the willingness to be and to express, in my words, and my behavior, the various feelings and attitudes which exist in me. It is only in this way that the relationship can have reality, and reality seems deeply important as a first condition. It is only by providing the genuine reality which is in me, that the other person can successfully seek for the reality in him. [C. Rogers, *On Becoming a Person* 33 (1961).]

These varied client-centered sources reveal recurring themes of large importance to the lawyer-counselor. They first recognize an individual cannot reach his full potential unless he is honest with himself and acts consistently with his values. A failure to look inward and follow conscience prevents psychological healthiness and stunts personal development. Second, the mature, actualized person reaches his own moral conclusions based upon a set of self-developed and thoughtful values. Third, a relationship between two (or more) persons cannot reach its potential unless those persons consider each other as equals and are honest with each other. So in counseling, the individual respect a counselor must maintain for the client demands the counselor be forthright.

Lawyers have no claim to an exception from these fundamental precepts. The lawyer must communicate to, and discuss with, his clients the moral issues. He must resolve for himself the moral conflicts by applying and following his own moral standards. The lawyer's personal and professional development and the effectiveness of his relationships with clients depend on adherence to that code of conduct. Thus, by being honest with himself and with his client, the lawyer experiences personal maturity and solidifies his relationship with his client. If he merely cedes the moral decisions to his clients, then his relationships with clients are deprived of mutuality; the lawyer is no longer an equal and his very identity is threatened.

The technical and adversarial nature of the legal process, however, can easily interfere with lawyers' candor in client relations. The process tempts lawyers to don a "professional mask" to conceal (from their clients and themselves) their feelings, insecurities, and reservations. That is, lawyers will often use the law and its jargon to maintain a distance from their clients and to erect security barriers between themselves and their clients. Further, the traditional adversarial model provides lawyers with an easy excuse for role-playing and for suppressing their convictions; they hide behind their adversarial mask to legitimate stifling their own feelings and mores. When a lawyer submits to these temptations, the lawyer's psyche becomes confused; he loses touch with his moral standards; he increasingly loses his ability to remove his "mask" when leaving the adversarial setting. The professional mask chills the lawyer-client relationship. The lawyer acts out a role and cordons himself off from his and the client's feelings.

Self-awareness and self-honesty help the lawyer to overcome these difficulties. He does not deceive himself or his client. When he achieves congruence, the lawyer is more at ease with himself and with others; he loses his need for the professional mask. He avoids the inner-conflict that results from the clash between his professional model and his feelings as a human being. . . .

The gains from self-awareness and candor carry over to the lawyer's relationship with his clients. When he expresses himself honestly with acceptance and respect for the client, he fosters similar responses from the client. Mutual respect and candor result. The lawyer thus disserves himself and his clients when he submerges matters he finds morally or socially significant.

Thus, while the lawyer should express to his clients his support and positive regard for them, he must also be open enough to discuss with them the moral and social implications of their cases. The discussion should be full, frank, and [cordial]. A client may or may not satisfy the attorney's concerns. Only through frank discussion, however, can the lawyer reconcile his roles as counselor and as an independent citizen, and only in that way can the advocate maintain touch with his own identity and keep his cases in perspective.

If the lawyer becomes convinced that serious moral or social problems are raised, and the client fails to resolve the doubts, then the honesty and integrity of the lawyer require him to sever the relationship (or at least his work on that case). The lawyer should not advocate that which he believes to be morally or socially wrong. If he does, he loses his identity and self-respect.

When the lawyer assumes an adversarial role, he is espousing his client's cause; he is not a counselor attempting to help a client mature and reach contentment. Though some might conclude that, therefore, the client-centered model breaks down at this point, the discussion in this section shows that the model requires the lawyer to be honest and independent at all times—for independent thought is a key to self-actualization. The counselor who advocates a cause contrary to his values serves neither his client nor himself.

PART
IV

NEGOTIATING

14

Introduction to Negotiation

A. OVERVIEW

Lawyers use interviewing and counseling skills with each client they agree to represent. While negotiation skills are not required in every legal matter, most of the average lawyer's cases include negotiation as an important, if not the only, "action step" taken to achieve the client's goals and to fulfill the client's needs. Indeed, it is probably accurate to state that as much as 90 percent of the legal matters dealt with by lawyers eventually involves the negotiation process.

Recent annual reports of the Administrative Office of United States Courts reveal that more than nine of ten civil cases filed in the federal district courts are disposed of without trial. Similar statistics on the resolution of civil matters appear to prevail in our state courts.[1] Although a larger number of criminal cases result in a trial, it is safe to say that more than two-thirds are concluded without a binding evidentiary hearing on the defendant's guilt or innocence. Thus, the overwhelming number of apparently pure conflict matters that typify litigation cases are settled by the parties out of court. (One could also intuit that many cases that do result in a trial have been negotiated at some point, albeit unsuccessfully.) Lawyers

---

1. Perschbacher, Regulating Lawyers' Negotiations, 27 Arizona L. Rev. 75, 75 (1985).

and clients have learned that the trial model is expensive (in terms of lawyer time and client financial resources), traumatic (in terms of client and witness emotional resources), and risky (in terms of predicting the final decisions of judges and juries).

Most persons who seek a lawyer's counsel, however, do not do so for help in resolving a dispute. Rather, most clients present their lawyers with transactional or planning problems. These clients may want legal assistance in establishing a joint venture or in concluding another business deal; in purchasing a home or in planning an estate; in complying with government regulations or in understanding the tax implications of a particular investment. In the majority of such matters, the client needs to reach an agreement or understanding with some other person or legal entity. To assist the client in achieving that type of goal, the lawyer most often will negotiate with the representative of the other person or entity to arrive at a mutually satisfactory outcome.

For you to act effectively on behalf of clients whose needs and goals you have carefully learned through client-centered interviewing and counseling, you will have to master the additional skill of negotiation. While there are important differences between the skills of effective negotiation and of interviewing and counseling, there is a remarkable overlap in essential skills.

B. SIMILARITIES BETWEEN NEGOTIATION AND INTERVIEWING AND COUNSELING

Clients often bring mixed motivations to the attorney-client relationship. On the one hand, clients perceive a need to seek the assistance of a lawyer in resolving a conflict or concluding a transaction. This perceived need motivates them to be open, candid, and complete in disclosing information and sorting out goals. On the other hand, clients may be sensitive about a past event or a particular goal and worry that the lawyer will find the disclosed matter inappropriate or damaging to the case. Such feelings motivate clients to be selective in revealing facts and cautious about articulating real needs.

Negotiation between a lawyer and another party or the representative of that other party is another classic mixed-motive situation. Whether the issues involve conflict resolution or a transactional matter, each party to the negotiation has motives that tend to bring them together and motives that tend to drive them apart. Examine for a moment the situation that exists between negotiators for a buyer and a seller of a commodity. The seller is anxious to deliver the goods to a ready buyer; the buyer is eager to obtain the goods from a willing seller. Such motivations on the part of the principals tend to bring the negotiators together and encourage them to reach an accord. At the same time, however, the seller knows there are other potential purchasers of the commodity and, if the price or other terms are not acceptable, negotiations with other buyers could be initiated.

Likewise, the buyer is aware that there are other sellers of similar items, and unacceptable demands made by this seller will not preclude purchase of the product elsewhere. The motivation to agree only to those terms defined as acceptable according to the self-interest of each party tends to keep the negotiators apart.

To overcome client motivations that pull in different directions, you have learned to use helping and probing techniques, to remain attuned to nonverbal signals, and to be conscious of the inhibitors and facilitators of communication. You will use these same skills in the negotiation process. To be a successful negotiator, you must stimulate the other party's motivations that move the sides together and suppress or otherwise deal with those motivations that keep the sides apart. The techniques, for example, of active listening and empathy, so important to effective interviewing and counseling, must be employed by you during negotiations with other parties if you hope to resolve conflicts or conclude transactions on behalf of your client. Information-gathering is important in all phases of interpersonal relations, but its difficulty is greatest in negotiation. Because the other side has such strong incentives to keep information from you and maintain (or gain) an informational advantage, negotiation severely tests your probing and listening skills. Information in a negotiation often comes to you *only* obliquely or nonverbally. Therefore, what you learned in the preceding chapters on attentiveness to verbal and nonverbal cues and on the need to control your own communication must be used with special adeptness in negotiations.

Empathy and active listening skills assume additional importance in negotiations in order to identify the goals of the respective parties and isolate both mutual interests and direct conflicts. As you will learn, good negotiators must often place themselves in the other party's shoes and understand that party's positions and needs. When you do that, you can more effectively present your own client's position and, just as important, better develop creative solutions that will benefit both sides. You are most persuasive in negotiation when you can convince the other side that more concessions are dictated by its own priorities. To do that, however, you must first be able to accurately identify what those priorities are. And that requires use of empathy skills. Moreover, in negotiation, as in interviewing and counseling, empathy acts as a facilitator of communication, thus enhancing the flow of information and creating a relationship conducive to settlement.

Other aspects of the interviewing and counseling process are likewise applicable to negotiation. You have learned, among other things, that the sequencing of topics and the ordering of questions within a topic can have a dramatic impact on the quality and quantity of information that you receive from a client. So, too, in negotiation can the sequencing of topics (usually referred to as agenda control in negotiation) and the ordering of questions (an important part of information-bargaining during the assessment phase) influence the outcome in negotiation. You have studied how valuable appropriate planning for interviewing and counseling sessions can be, even for the initial interview with a new client, and you have developed strategies for effective planning for these client encounters. You will find that planning is equally valuable in negotiation and that there are planning strategies and techniques that will enhance your negotiating abilities.

The message should be clear. Many of the analytical, verbal, and interpersonal skills learned in connection with interviewing and counseling are similar to those you need in legal negotiation. You can transfer some of the interviewing and counseling skills, such as active listening and rapport-building, directly to the negotiation process with little or no modification in substance or style. The basic principles of other skills, such as sequencing of topics and planning, will be useful in negotiation when modified to account for the differences between negotiation and the other two interpersonal skills. (For example, dealing with a person who is not a client calls for significant adjustments. Recall Chapter 9 on witness interviewing.) Thus, as we proceed through our discussion of lawyer negotiation, you must remain aware of the skills you learned through the interviewing and counseling chapters.

C. DIFFERENCES BETWEEN NEGOTIATION AND INTERVIEWING AND COUNSELING

Even though negotiation requires use of many of the same skills and much of the same knowledge as used in interviewing and counseling, it also diverges substantially from the latter two activities. Shared skills must be modified, new skills learned, and theories on bargaining mastered. The divergence results from both the obvious changes in the purposes for which the activities are undertaken and the equally obvious changes in the identity of the party with whom you are communicating and the corresponding changes in the nature of your relationship with that party. This section elaborates briefly on those points.

We have articulated throughout this book the need for you and your client to unite in pursuit of a client-defined goal. Once you accomplish that, you are empowered to act as the client's representative to achieve the client's goal. Now enters another party who presumably has gone through the same goal-defining process with his or her lawyer. When you meet with that lawyer to negotiate on behalf of your principals, it is unlikely you will have been given identically conditioned, client-defined goals to achieve.

Consider again the negotiation between the lawyers representing the buyer and seller of a commodity. No matter how eager the seller and how anxious the buyer are to consummate a transfer of the goods, it is likely both have defined their needs to their lawyer in somewhat different terms. The seller may have instructed the lawyer about needs as to price, payment schedule, and a security interest in the goods. The buyer's attorney probably has been told of the client's requirements concerning the same issues, as well as such matters as delivery times and warranty provisions. If each attorney-client relationship has attained the level of communication noted in the earlier sections of this book, then each client has disclosed to his or her lawyer how much the deal means, what risks are associated with making this particular sale or purchase, and the consequences of not reaching agreement. Thus, while the principals to this friendly transaction have the same ultimate purpose—a purchase and sale of the commodity—they probably have quite different conditions that control the achievement of that mutual purpose.

As a lawyer-negotiator on behalf of the buyer or the seller, you have the duty to protect your client's interests and to obtain for the client all that to which the client is legally entitled. Thus, even though it may be "fairer" in some objective sense to have your client pay more or get less, or to demand fewer legal devices to protect the client's interests, or to reveal to the other side all the constraints under which the client is operating, your primary obligation is to your client. Because you do not have a similar obligation to the other party, you may be required to demand that which is less than "fair" to the other side and more than "fair" to your client.

The term "arm's-length" is often used to describe the relationship between the lawyers negotiating on behalf of their clients. That description accurately contrasts the relationship between these legal representatives and the "special" relationship each has with his or her principal. The "special" relationship is designed to foster open, candid, and complete communication between attorney and client. The "arm's-length" relationship between lawyer negotiators requires communication which is more guarded, selective, and limited. While many of the communication skills applicable to interviewing and counseling are useful in negotiation, how, when, and for what purpose those skills are employed are often quite different in the negotiation process.

Lawyers typically negotiate with other lawyers, which further explains the divergence of negotiation from interviewing and counseling. The lawyers with whom you negotiate will undoubtedly share with you the same duty to zealously represent clients and the same training and expertise. Unlike interviewing and counseling, negotiation requires you to be demanding, persuasive, and critical in your communication with others. You need additional skills to meet this requirement. Because you negotiate with persons who are familiar with the specialized language of the law, the techniques you developed to explain probabilities and consequences to your lay client may be inappropriate. Certainly, to be persuasive and critical when negotiating with a lawyer, you must be technically precise and detailed in stating legal positions and forecasting outcomes.

These and other differences between the communication skills of interviewing and counseling and those of negotiation will become apparent in the succeeding chapters. While many of the skills explained in earlier portions of this book will continue to be useful to you as a legal negotiator, new ones must be learned if you are to represent your clients effectively. We encourage you, throughout your study of the negotiation process, to turn back to earlier chapters, to reflect on your own whether our previous suggestions are applicable to negotiation, and to practice employing those strategies and tactics that are appropriate in this new lawyer setting.

D. THE EGO INVOLVEMENT
OF THE LAWYER-NEGOTIATOR

One noncommunication distinction between interviewing and counseling and negotiation must be discussed before closing this introductory chapter. Negotiation is an "action" stage in your representation of a client, a stage in which you take an "active" part and are required to deal with those who are "outside" of the attorney-client relationship. You "act" simultaneously as a detached representative of a principal and as a personally involved participant. In both capacities, but particularly in the latter capacity, your ego is drawn into the process. Your individual fears, needs, ambitions, risk-taking traits, and other emotional factors are on the line. For the first time in the tripartite interpersonal process we have been discussing, you are subject to a win-lose evaluation. You are likely to perceive yourself, and be perceived by others, as engaged in a competition with the lawyer representing the other side in the negotiation.

What impact does the contest-like nature of negotiation have on you as a person and as a lawyer? What ego risks do you face in lawyer bargaining? Naturally, the answers to these questions vary with the respondent. We suggest, however, that you consider the following general concerns in making your responses.

At the outset, ask yourself how you should measure whether you have been successful in negotiating an agreement. You are likely to respond that your client is the best appraiser of your efforts. If the client accepts the negotiated accord, the client has affirmed your "winning" effort. The problem with that answer, of course, is that there never can be a negotiated settlement unless the client approves of the compact. Thus, if the client's assent is the measure of success, all parties to a negotiated agreement are, by definition, "winners."

We concede there is some merit to the proposition that all negotiations ending in consensus should be considered "win/win" encounters. When parties accept an accord following the bargaining of a dispute or a transaction, they communicate they have obtained the best outcome possible, at least when that outcome is measured against all the risks and ramifications of the available alternatives. On the other hand, many negotiated agreements unravel following the euphoria of resolution; disputes flare up again and transactions disintegrate. In many of these cases, the settlement collapses because one or more parties did not obtain the best possible outcome under the circumstances and have come to realize and resent that fact.

The danger of the client as the sole arbiter of negotiation success is that, consciously or unconsciously, an attorney can manipulate the client's expectations, thereby virtually guaranteeing that any bargaining outcome presented by the lawyer will be approved. Lawyers with both low and high risk-taking traits can play the manipulation game to meet their own rather than the client's needs. Thus, an attorney with an above-average fear of failure may lower a client's sights by offering information that the expected settlement will be less than the attorney actually anticipates. In that way, the low risk-taking lawyer ensures success as measured by client approval.

On the other hand, an attorney with high risk-taking traits may raise client expectations by ratcheting the expected settlement a notch or two higher. This approach fulfills the lawyer's ambitious ego needs, but it also increases the danger of deadlock and exposes the client to added emotional trauma.

Attorney risk-taking traits are not the only ego factors that can intrude on a negotiation on behalf of a client. A lawyer's anger with opposing counsel for conduct in this or another context may cause the attorney to be less willing to compromise or less enthusiastic about offers from the other side. A lawyer facing a cash-flow problem and resulting economic fears may be too eager to accept a low offer from the opponent or, alternatively, may demand an unrealistic concession in order to calm his or her own anxieties, meanwhile jeopardizing the client's needs.

Unlike most sporting events, the stock market, or even the outcome after trial, there are seldom objective criteria available to measure the success of lawyer-negotiators. The best measure of achievement is what could have been accomplished under the circumstances. As we will learn in succeeding chapters, the level of possible accomplishment is often more sophisticated than the simple totaling of the money or units received by the parties to the bargain. The relationship of the parties in the aftermath of settlement, the achievement of mutual gains without the imposition of mutual costs, and the distribution of nonfinancial and nonfungible items are among the many matters that must be considered when evaluating the success or failure of a particular negotiation.

Because client satisfaction can be a misleading barometer of negotiation accomplishment and fails to account for lawyer ego issues, we suggest an alternative model for gauging your bargaining success. First, be sure to engage in client-centered counseling that isolates goals and needs and communicates your candid appraisal of potential outcomes. Second, engage your client in a discussion of possible negotiation strategies and tactics, seeking client input and understanding of the bargaining options. Third, persistently assess your own feelings about the case (e.g.: Do I want to get rid of this case? Do I think this client's a turkey? Am I intimidated by the other party's lawyer?) and question whether they are affecting your counseling or negotiation. Fourth, applying the principles, concepts, and theories set forth in subsequent chapters, plan in detail for the negotiation process. Fifth, after completion of the negotiation, stand back and objectively analyze the planning and action steps leading to agreement or deadlock, questioning whether your ego intruded on the process and asking yourself if more could have been achieved. Finally, based on such critical self-analysis, modify your preparation and execution in your next negotiation.

By following this guide, you are apt to reduce your ego involvement in the negotiation and any resulting interference in the outcome. In this way, you will enhance your role as a counselor to and representative of your client.

E. OUTLINE OF THE CHAPTERS ON NEGOTIATION

In the chapters that follow, we discuss the lawyer negotiation process in a way that is consistent with our earlier practice. In the next chapter, we begin with an examination of negotiation theories developed and advanced by other disciplines, suggesting how those theories can be applied by lawyers on behalf of clients. That discussion is followed by an explanation of effective lawyer negotiation models available to you and the criteria you might use in selecting a model for a particular negotiation. Later chapters break down lawyer negotiation into its three primary phases: assessment, persuasion, and exchange. Each of these phases is dissected to give you an appreciation of underlying negotiation principles and an introduction to tactics and techniques that can be used to implement those principles. As in earlier parts of the book, examples and problems are included to ensure that you understand the matter being discussed and can test yourself on your comprehension.

Chapter

15

Theories of Negotiation

A. INTRODUCTION

Until quite recently,[1] there has not been a significant body of literature for lawyers on the bargaining process. As a result, lawyers have been forced to develop their negotiating skills through the trial-and-error method, observing others, listening to the oral history transmitted by senior practitioners, relying on particular tactical tricks of the trade, and guessing about the effectiveness of various strategies. While generally increasing an individual lawyer's negotiating skills over a period of time, the learning approaches are unlikely to produce coherent and identifiable theories of lawyer negotiating. Although, as a group, lawyers are consummate and careful planners, they have been remarkably shortsighted in failing to approach negotiating from a conceptual perspective.

Lawyers, of course, are not alone in their use of the bargaining arts.

---

1. See, e.g., G. Bellow & B. Moulton, *The Lawyering Process: Negotiation* (1981); C. Craver, *Effective Legal Negotiation and Settlement* (1986); R. Fisher & W. Ury, *Getting to Yes* (1981); D. Gifford, *Legal Negotiation: Theory and Applications* (1989); H. Edwards & J. White, *The Lawyer as Negotiator* (1977); M. Schoenfield & R. Schoenfield, *Legal Negotiations: Getting Maximum Results* (1988); G. Williams, *Effective Legal Negotiation* (1979); G. Williams, *Legal Negotiation and Settlement* (1983); R. Condlin, "Cases on Both Sides": The Role of Argument in Legal Dispute-Negotiation, 44 Md. L. Rev. 65 (1985); G. Lowenthal, A General Theory of Negotiation Process, Strategy and Behavior, 31 U. Kan. L. Rev. 69 (1982); C. Menkel-Meadow, Toward Another View of Legal Negotiation: The Structure of Problem Solving, 31 U.C.L.A. L. Rev. 754 (1984).

Diplomats engaged in complex international negotiations, politicians seeking compromise on the budget allocations of government, business people striking bargains with venture partners and attempting to gain advantage over marketplace competitors, labor unions hammering out wages, benefits, and working conditions with management, teachers threatening students with extra homework for misbehavior, family members arguing over which program to watch on television, and bridge players trying to ruff a losing card are all engaged in forms of bargaining.

Theoreticians have examined these intricate human negotiating activities from mathematical, economic, psychological, sociological, and other points of view and have developed a variety of bargaining models. Although none of these theories is transferable in its entirety to the negotiating process employed in the legal system, aspects of some theories prove useful in developing a basic model of negotiating for lawyers. The remainder of this chapter is devoted to a description of various negotiating theories. The theories selected for discussion include cooperative and competitive models, as well as adversarial and problem-solving strategies. To demonstrate how these theories might be applied in the lawyering process, typical lawyer negotiating problems will be presented. Answers to some problems will be given, while others will be left to you to interpret and apply an appropriate negotiating theory.

B. GAME THEORY:
A MODEL OF PURE CONFLICT

▤ PROBLEM 1 ▤
The Defendant's Dilemma

You have been retained by the co-owner of a business who has been charged with a RICO white-collar crime of defrauding customers. Your client's partner is charged as a co-defendant in the case but is represented by another lawyer. Prior to trial, the prosecutor calls you and counsel for the co-defendant together to inform you of the government's plea-bargaining posture. You are told that if either defendant confesses and agrees to be a witness against the other, the government will recommend a fine and probation for the one turning state's evidence. For the one who fails to admit guilt, the recommendation will be five years imprisonment upon conviction. If neither defendant confesses, the prosecutor will proceed to trial and, if defendants are convicted, will request a minimum three-year prison term for each. If both are willing to plead guilty, the prosecutor will recommend a six-month jail term for each defendant. The prosecutor informs you and counsel for the co-defendant that the offer will remain open until the conclusion of the business day. At the expiration of this time, the prosecutor intends to withdraw all offers and proceed to trial.

As you leave the prosecutor's office, you attempt to question counsel for the co-defendant about the advice that will be delivered to your client's partner and about the possibility of a joint defense negotiating strategy.

When the other attorney parries your inquiries, you disengage, refusing to comment on the advice you intend to give to your client. You believe that the evidence now available to the government will probably, but not necessarily, result in the conviction of both defendants. If either defendant turns state's evidence, however, the government will be virtually guaranteed a guilty verdict against the other. You are convinced further that the trial judge will honor any sentencing recommendation made by the prosecutor. Based on your earlier conversations, it is very likely counsel for the co-defendant shares your assessment of the situation.

In conjunction with your client, you must develop a response to the government's plea-bargaining offer that takes into account the possible independent actions of the co-defendant. How do you go about constructing the choices? Can you create a framework that aids you in predicting which alternative will be selected by the co-defendant? Resolution of these questions is critical to you as a lawyer called upon to create a negotiating strategy on behalf of your client. The use of game theory, the first bargaining model presented, will help you sort out the negotiating moves open to your client and to the co-defendant.

1. Overview of Game Theory

The strictest and most precise of negotiating theories is the mathematically expressed game theory of von Neumann and Morgenstern.[2] Having conceived a method for the study of rational decision-making in situations of conflict, von Neumann and Morgenstern stated their purpose as "find[ing] the mathematically complete principles which define 'rational behavior' for the participants in a social economy, and to derive from them the general characteristics of that behavior. . . . The immediate concept of a solution is plausibly a set of rules for each participant which tell him how to behave in every situation which may conceivably arise."[3] With that most lofty goal in place, mathematical game theory provides "a language for the description of conscious decision-making processes involving more than one individual . . . [and] a means to make certain relatively subtle concepts operational, such as the state of information, choice, move, strategy, outcome [and] payoff. . . . "[4]

At the outset of this description of the theory, an understanding of the meaning of a "game" and its component parts is necessary. Any situation in which two or more people compete is a "game." Poker and racquetball are obvious examples. Union and management negotiations and the independent but intersecting actions of competing firms bidding on a state contract are less clearly "games" but are included within the theory's definition.

---

2. J. von Neumann & O. Morgenstern, *Theory of Games and Economic Behavior* (1944).

3. Id. at 31.

4. M. Shubik, *Games for Society* 14 (1975).

The elements of a game are *players, rules, strategy,* and *payoff,* each of which deserves further explanation. According to one leading game theorist:

> A *player* in a game is an autonomous decision-making unit . . . [though] not necessarily a single person. He may be a country, . . . a politician, a firm, or a group of individuals. The distinguishing feature of a player is that he or it has an objective in the game and operates under its own orders in the selection of its actions . . . [while] in control of some set of resources.[5]

Based on this definition, all parties to a legal negotiation qualify as players.

The *rules of the game* include all the initially available data that specify how the players may use the resources under their command. In the previously mentioned examples of games, the rules include the ranking of poker hands, the size of the racquet and composition of the ball, the limitations imposed by the National Labor Relations Act, and the statutes regulating the offering of state contracts.

The *strategy* of game theory can be explained as the moves available to a player during the course of the game:

> In a game one assumes that all possible courses of action for each player are known. Each particular course of action is called a "strategy" which, by definition, is a complete specification of the action to be taken by a player under every possible contingency in the playing of the game.[6]

An examination of the strategic moves available to the person showing the high card after the first round in a five card stud poker game will illustrate this principle. The poker player may fold, pass, or bet. By folding, the player withdraws from the conflict, allowing an opponent to win the ante pot. If the player passes, the opponent then has the three strategic moves (fold, pass, or bet) as options. By betting, the player denies the opponent one of those strategic options (passing), dictates the limits on another (calling the amount bet by the player), and creates a new option for the opponent (raising the player's original bet).

The outcome of any game, or the *payoff,* will depend on the strategies or moves employed by each and every player. The establishment of an overall game strategy by a player first entails the advance determination of all possible situations that may arise during the game and all the moves the game's players might make in response to the various situations. The payoff of the game depends on what is produced by the interactive strategies of the players. Thus, for every possible outcome of the game (i.e., the result of any set of moves by the players), each player must assign a value (in terms of money, units of production, points, and so on). By assigning a value, a player can weigh and evaluate the various outcomes or payoffs from playing the game.

A labor-management dispute exemplifies how the valuation process creates a method for determining payoffs. Suppose, in a particular situa-

---

5. M. Shubik, *Game Theory and Related Approaches to Social Behavior* 12 (1964).
6. C. E. Ferguson & J. P. Gould, *Microeconomic Theory* 327 (5th ed. 1980).

tion, that management has three options or strategic moves: (A) acceding to the union's demand, (B) laying off 10 percent of the workers, or (C) cutting salaries by 10 percent. Assume further that the strategic moves of the union are limited to (a) accepting management's action, (b) going to arbitration, or (c) striking. If management lays off workers (B) and the union accepts this (a), it will produce a very different result or payoff than if management cuts salaries (C) and labor reacts by striking (c). The difference in result must be measured in terms of values (money, power, status, etc.), and which player (management or union) will gain the advantage. Thus, a player must create a "method of valuation, preferences, or utility which enables him to decide whether one outcome is preferred to another."[7] Equally important, a game theory player must understand the valuation system of the opponent in order to produce a mathematical matrix of possible payoffs.

2. *Game Theory and the Defendant's Dilemma*

Applying game theory to the "defendant's dilemma" problem, the *players* obviously are your client and the co-defendant. The *rules of the game* are those set by the prosecutor in outlining the government's plea-bargaining position plus the assessment by each attorney of the likelihood of conviction and the reaction of the judge to the government's sentencing recommendations. The *strategies* of this game are the limited moves (confess or not confess) available to each player. The *payoff* is the nature of the sentence (time) each defendant will receive, which, in turn, depends on the combination of strategic actions taken by each player. According to game theory, the payoff in this classic defendant's (or "prisoner's") dilemma problem can be expressed in the mathematical matrix that appears at the top of page 354.

The payoff is expressed in the chart in terms of years sentenced to prison. Of the two numbers appearing in each cell, the italicized number is the sentence of the co-defendant and the nonitalicized number is your client's term.

The payoff matrix reveals that your client has two strategic moves (rows A and B), and the co-defendant also has two strategic moves (columns a and b). The payoff amount expressed in the number of years each player must serve in prison is set out in each of the intersecting cells. For example, if your client continues to maintain innocence (row A) and the co-defendant decides to confess (column b), your client will serve five years in jail while the co-defendant is placed on probation.

Game theory asserts that in this type of situation,[8] the appropriate strategy for each player becomes obvious. The theory dictates that the most

---

7. M. Shubik, *Game Theory and Related Approaches to Social Behavior* 14 (1964).

8. The "prisoner's dilemma" problem, in various combinations of punishments and rewards, is a classic example of the operation of game theory. See A. Rapport & A. Chammah, *Prisoner's Dilemma* (1965). This variation is selected to illustrate how the mathematical model can assist you in identifying the consequences of choice in a bargaining situation. The outcome of the game is more difficult to predict if certain variables are changed. For example, what changes would you have to make in the mathematical model if, at trial, the prosecutor

Payoff Matrix for Two-Person, Defendant's Dilemma Problem

Co-Defendant's Strategies

		(a) Does not confess	(b) Confesses
	(A) Does not Confess	3, 3	5, 0
Client's Strategies	(B) Confesses	0, 5	.5, .5

"rational behavior" on the part of each player would be to minimax, that is to minimize loss and maximize gain. Thus, in this instance, each defendant should confess (row B, column b) to limit the time served in jail to six months, and, in the event the other fails to minimax, avoid incarceration altogether. In this perfectly informed situation, each player should maximize preference by behaving rationally. And for each, "the opponent's strategy becomes more and more apparent and the play tends towards the minimax solution predicated by game theory. . . . The minimax game determines, independently, the best strategies for each player under certain assumptions."[9]

═══ PROBLEM 2 ═══
The Teachers' Contract Dispute

Although the "defendant's dilemma" was a simple problem, easily worked out without resorting to a mathematical matrix, it served to illustrate some of the important operating principles of game theory. Using these game theory concepts, try to work out the options for your client in a somewhat more complicated setting.

Expanding on the labor problem mentioned earlier in connection with the explanation of payoff (see page 353), assume you are counsel to a teachers' union local of 1,000 members, all of whom are employed by a single school district. The recently elected president of the local comes to you with the first crisis since his election. The union is in the midst of the first year of a two-year contract. The agreement contains provisions for no layoffs, a 10 percent raise of the average $28,000 salary of members in the

---

could only reasonably expect conviction on a lesser included offense that carries a maximum sentence of six months *and,* if both defendants confessed to the original charge, the government threatened to recommend a three-year sentence?

Timing is another variable that can impact on the play of the game. Consider whether the outcome would be different if your client were required to select an option before the co-defendant expressed his choice. Would the payoff change if your client could not choose until the co-defendant decided? What would happen if both defendants were incarcerated and not allowed to speak with each other or counsel before choosing? Does it matter if the players are allowed to communicate before selecting their option or are forced to remain incommunicado? Manipulation of the *rules of the game* affects the *strategies* of the *players* and, thus, the eventual *payoff.* If all the factors are known and values can be assigned, however, changing the rules does not affect the usefulness of the model.

9. O. Young, *Bargaining: Formal Theories of Negotiation* 36 (1975).

second year, and a no-strike, mandatory arbitration clause in the event of a dispute between the parties. The union president tells you the school district has just projected a two to three million dollar shortfall due to a sharp drop in federal and state government subsidies following massive budget cutbacks and an unexpected decrease in the number of enrolled students. Because of higher than politically acceptable interest rates, the general unavailability of money for government units, and statutory restrictions, borrowing is not an option the school board will pursue. The school district has strongly hinted that economies in other areas will not make up the losses and that it may be forced to lay off 10 percent of the teachers, to refuse to give the promised raise in the second year of the contract, or to take both of these actions.

As a labor lawyer experienced in the education field, you are aware arbitration usually results in a "splitting of the differences" between the parties. The history of this particular school district suggests, in the event of a strike, that the district probably will delay settlement for up to 10 percent of the school year in order to make up the cost of acceding to union demands. Assume, therefore, for the purpose of this example that the only options open to the union are acceptance of the school district's actions, demand for arbitration, or going out on strike. Your client asks you what negotiating position the union should take in this conflict situation.

In this problem each *player* understands completely the *rules of the game*, is fully aware of the *strategic moves* available to self and opponent, and can identify each other's value according to a common *payoff* term (money). In creating your mathematical matrix, you should be aware that this is what game theorists denote as a zero-sum game. Zero-sum means that one player's gain is equal to the other player's loss. In this example, your matrix should reflect the school district's losses in wages paid as equal to the union's gain in money received by its members. Thus, unlike the prisoner's dilemma matrix, only one number will appear in each of the cells.

3. Advantages of the Game Theory Model

If you developed a matrix that predicted the school district should lay off 10 percent of the teachers and reduce salaries by 10 percent, and decided that the union's most rational response to such a move should be to demand arbitration, then you have isolated some of the advantages of the game theory model. Negotiating in a conflict-ridden, competitive environment is a process of interdependent decision-making between parties exercising free will and having multiple options. In such a complex setting, negotiators must acquire information to structure the dispute and predict the direction the conflict may take. Game theory assists the lawyer in performing both of these essential functions.

Information about the rules, options, and payoffs available to you and your opponent is critical. Using game theory, the lawyer is able to structure the conflict in precise terms and discover where information gaps exist. Indeed, the technique may result in demonstrating that the needed information is available but in unusable or unclear form until reduced to the matrix model. As one writer has noted, "the language of game theory permits the formulation of sharp definitions of important problems that tend to remain ambiguous within other conceptual frameworks."[10] To structure a legal conflict situation, you must be perceptive in identifying the choices available to each of the parties and in assigning values to those choices. Game theory should help you decide if the information necessary for these tasks is available and, if not, what information is needed.

Predicting where the conflict may be going is a precondition to influencing its direction and outcome. Because game theory can help you identify the decisions the client and the opponent should (but not necessarily will) make, it aids you in your predictive task. The game approach is particularly helpful because the strict precision of the theory forces you to analyze the dispute so as to facilitate efforts to evaluate the choices available to your client and to the opponent.

4. Disadvantages of the Game Theory Model

The elegant precision of game theory is at once its greatest strength and its most serious weakness. While game theory can help you identify options and predict outcomes, it may compel you to prematurely speculate as to an opponent's values, or to collapse choices available to your client and reduce the alternatives open to the other side. To construct a true game theory mathematical matrix, you may force facts or feelings in an attempt to reach a state of perfect information, a premise on which game theory rests but a state that seldom if ever occurs in the real world of lawyer negotiations.

The exactness of the minimax model is another flaw in the transportability of game theory to the real world of lawyer bargaining. The minimax theory postulates that negotiation decision-makers are always rational. Thus, according to game theory, your clients always will evaluate alternatives on the basis of carefully arranged, internally consistent, and sequenced preferences. Moreover, game theory postulates that, once decided, your clients' preferences will remain fixed and, most important, that clients always will choose as the preferred alternative the most logical choice. But we know human nature is not always logical, that individual preferences change over time, and that clients are often willing to risk a minimized loss in the hopes of increasing their gains.

The most serious disadvantage of game theory, however, is that it is static while real-life lawyer negotiations are dynamic. Basically, game theory postulates an interaction involving two moves, one by your client and one by the opponent. In fact, most legal negotiations comprise a series of moves by each party, many of which involve positioning oneself appropriately to create the very conditions game theory assumes by the development of its matrix. Typically, the parties make intermediate moves before eventually reaching settlement or deadlock. Because negotiation usually involves a series of interdependent moves by each party that are communicated to the other party by word and deed, game theory analysis would have to be continuous and a matrix created following each move. Not only

---

10. Id. at 23.

would this be cumbersome, but it would fail to account for the process of convergence toward settlement or deadlock that is an important aspect of the typical adversarial negotiation. Game theory's focus on outcomes diverts attention away from the natural movement that occurs in bargaining. Let's turn to a problem where the dynamic aspects of negotiating are apparent and then to a bargaining theory that can aid you in structuring these active features of negotiation.

C. ECONOMIC MODEL OF BARGAINING

≡≡ PROBLEM 3 ≡≡
Selling the Business

Your client has been engaged in a business for 25 years and has decided to retire. He has been approached by a potential buyer, a national firm operating the same type of business in localities all across the country. While your client is agreeable to dealing with this firm, he wants to maximize the amount of money he receives. He estimates the business (including real estate, equipment, accounts receivable, "goodwill," a covenant not to compete, etc.) is worth "somewhere between $750,000 and a million dollars." Your client sees advantages in selling to the prospective buyer (a quick sale for cash without the problems of advertising and buyer financing issues), but is willing to seek a purchaser in the open market if he does not get the "right price."

You and your client have researched the previous five purchases of similar firms by the prospective buyer. The sales prices have ranged from $500,000 to $1.25 million, with the median price at $750,000. Your client has given you authority to negotiate with the prospective buyer and to consummate a deal at "as much as you can get over $750,000."

Before you engage in face-to-face negotiations with the attorney for the prospective buyer, can you think of a way to structure the upcoming bargaining process? Will it assist you in deciding the amount of your initial demand? Will it help you to anticipate your opponent's opening offer? Can you plan what your concession steps will be and predict the moves the other side will take? If you cannot answer most of these questions before you reach the negotiating table, you will probably be doing your client a disservice. An economic model of bargaining can assist you in structuring the dynamic processes of adversarial negotiating in which you will be engaged.

1. Overview of the Economic Model

Much of lawyer negotiating occurs in the context of what economists describe as a "bilateral monopoly," that is, a situation involving a seller and a buyer who must come to the specific terms of exchange between themselves or fail to execute an exchange at all. Most nonlitigation negotiations, including property agreements, contracts for the sale of goods, and corporate mergers, involve two parties who wish to exchange commodities or divide resources. Even litigation cases, where the court or arbitration panel could ultimately decide the final division between the parties, have the aspects of "bilateral monopoly." In many tort cases, the parties would rather work out an agreement instead of leaving the matter in the hands of judge or jury. In many will disputes, the competing beneficiaries would like to divide the estate rather than take their chances with the judicial process. Thus, these situations, too, take on the attributes of an "isolated exchange" where the inability of the parties to agree is tantamount to ultimate failure. In these matters lawyers would benefit from models of bargaining derived from the field of economics.

While game theory flourishes in the context of pure competition, economic models of negotiating apply only in mixed-motive situations involving neither pure conflict nor pure cooperation. The economic approach to negotiating addresses conflicts where the parties understand there is a range of possible outcomes and where each would prefer to reach an agreement rather than accept a deadlock, despite differing views on the precise terms of the final agreement. There are other important differences between game theory and economic models of negotiating:

> The economic models treat bargaining as a process of convergence over time involving a sequence of offers and counteroffers on the part of the participants. Consequently, the economic models are dynamic models which focus on the bargaining process as well as on the ultimate outcome of bargaining, whereas the game-theoretic models are predominantly static models which concentrate on the ultimate distribution of payoffs among the participants. Finally, the economic models tend to emphasize the formation of expectations about the behavior of the relevant other(s) in contrast to the models of game theory which stress . . . conditions that allow each player to make accurate predictions concerning the behavior of the relevant other(s). . . . Although the results are somewhat similar with respect to the problem of coping with strategic interaction and specifying the ultimate distribution of payoffs, the emphasis on the formation of expectations in the economic models leads to an interest in dynamic adjustment processes which fits well with the underlying conception of bargaining as a process of convergence over time.[11]

The various economic models, which we have collapsed into a unified theory for purposes of applying it to the lawyering process, are built on the following premises. First, the models envision two parties whose values and goals (utilities) remain stable over time. Thus, at any given point in the negotiation process the payoff possibilities of each party can be identified. Second, these models assume that a settlement zone exists within which each party is willing to agree. This settlement zone must be susceptible to relatively precise identification and should remain more or less stable during the negotiation process. Third, economic models deal primarily with single-issue negotiation involving a continuously divisible commodity

---

11. Id. at 131-132.

such as money. Thus, multiple-issue negotiations over competing legal rights and obligations are outside the scope of these models. Finally, economic bargaining theories, as convergence models, assume that the initial demands of the parties are incompatible and are likely to fall outside of the settlement zone.

Based on these operating conditions, the economic models create a method for analyzing the process of the offers and counteroffers made by the parties, from the initial demands of each side through the steps of convergence over time toward some specific point on the settlement curve within a settlement zone where they either agree or the negotiation breaks down. "[T]he key element in each of these models is the development of a specific concession mechanism that permits the positions of the parties to converge in the course of a series of offers and counteroffers."[12] One of the most helpful features of the economic models is the creation of a graphic method of examining the settlement curve from initial offers through agreement to display the concession pattern of the parties. At the top of page 360 is an economic bargaining graph that will help us visualize the negotiation process in the sale-of-the-business problem.

The graph represents a negotiation process of the sale of the business at a price of $890,000. The line (A)-(B) is the settlement curve. Point (A) represents the Seller's ultimate utility (receiving $1.35 million for the business), while point (B) equals Buyer's outside goal (purchasing the business for $450,000). The triangle formed by (X), (Y), and (Z) represents the settlement zone formed by each party's resistance level ($750,000 for Seller; $970,000 for Buyer). The dotted lines represent the concessions (offers and counteroffers) of each party leading to an agreement.

Use of this type of graph or some other model[13] is important in the planning of a successful adversarial negotiation and in plotting the bargaining process. In addition to providing lawyers with a general framework to plan and plot a legal negotiation, the economic bargaining theorists have developed some concepts about opening positions and concessions that may aid attorneys engaged in the dynamic process of negotiation.

Though the classical economic bargaining theorists[14] would not agree on all that follows, we have combined their independent analyses into a set of principles that could influence how lawyers negotiate. Prior to negotiating, the individual bargainer should calculate specifically (1) a rank ordering of preferences among payoff outcomes; (2) a schedule of costs during the time when the parties are bargaining and agreement or deadlock is in suspension; and (3) an estimate of the opponent's concession pattern over the course of negotiations.[15] When this information is combined with a fundamental premise of the economic theorists, it helps the negotiator to develop the most efficient opening position. The premise is that a tough

---

12. Id. at 134.

13. See Section D-2, page 370, on bargaining theory for a linear model, which portrays the same process.

14. J. Cross, *Economics of Bargaining* 17-36 (1969); J. Pen, A General Theory of Bargaining, 42 American Economic Review 24 (1952); F. Zeuthen, *Problems of Monopoly and Economic Warfare* 104-135 (1930).

15. O. Young, *Bargaining: Formal Theories of Negotiation* 138 (1975).

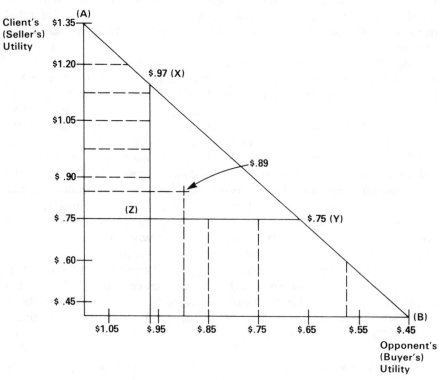

Economic Model of the Sale of the Business
(Dollar Amounts in Millions)

opening position will produce a better outcome for the tough bargainer's side. The initial demand or offer is actually obtained by scaling any potential gain in outcome attributable to a tougher opening stance against any increase in costs associated with a resulting delay in settlement caused by the hard opening.

After creating a model for structuring a negotiator's opening bid, the economic bargaining theorists turn their attention to an analysis of a concession strategy. The concession mechanism they advance embraces the doctrine of "convergence to settlement," a process that operates as follows:

> After stating his initial demand, each bargainer observes the behavior of the other side. If the other side acts in the expected fashion, the bargainer concludes that his estimate of the other's concession rate was correct and retains his initial bargaining plan in the next phase or round of the interaction. If the other party fails to respond in the expected fashion, on the other hand, the bargainer adjusts his expectations concerning the other's concession rate and formulates a new demand on the basis of his revised expectations. In general, if the other side concedes more slowly than he initially expected, the bargainer makes a concession[;] if the other concedes more rapidly than he expected, [then the bargainer remains firm.][16]

---

16. Id.

The adjustment process that produces counteroffers to initial demands leading to settlement is a process of learning within the negotiation framework. Each bargainer begins with a set of *confident expectations* about the opponent that may be (and often are) inaccurate and that the bargainer learns to correct on the basis of the interactive experience.

In addition to learning about the opponent and the opponent's concession patterns, economic bargaining theorists suggest that the individual negotiator evaluates the gains and losses associated with accepting or rejecting a particular offer on an *expected utility* basis. Given specific values for the bargainer's own preferred outcome, the opponent's current offer, and the costs of deadlock (a crucial calculation), the negotiator develops an expected utility by estimating the maximum risk of deadlock at which it is still advantageous to hold out for the preferred outcome. To determine the maximum risk of deadlock, the adversarial negotiator's risk willingness, or "propensity to fight," is compared to an estimation of the actual risk of deadlock if the negotiator refuses to make another concession. One economic bargaining theorist[17] argues that each party will continue to negotiate so long as the "propensity to fight" exceeds the estimate of the actual risk of deadlock. A settlement occurs when the estimate of the actual risk of deadlock equals the "propensity to fight" for both sides. Another theorist[18] posits that the next concession will always be made by the side less willing to accept the risk of deadlock at any given moment in the negotiation. To accommodate that risk analysis, the negotiator must "reduce his own demand (that is, alter his current offer) to the point where he is willing to accept a greater risk of [deadlock] than the other bargainer."[19]

2. *Advantages of the Economic Model*

The economic model of bargaining adds much to our understanding of negotiation. First, its focus on the dynamic process more resembles actual lawyer negotiating than does game theory's static approach. It permits conceptualizing negotiation as a series of moves and countermoves that occurs between negotiating attorneys rather than as a two-move game. Second, the economic model replaces game theory's unreasonable demand for perfect information by substituting the attorney's capacity for developing confident expectations. Thus, where the lawyer has less than complete information concerning an opponent's goals, the techniques of economic theory remain applicable. Because the theory anticipates that the negotiator will likely miscalculate an opponent's demand and concession strategy, it builds in a dynamic for adjusting the previously developed "confident expectations." Third, although there is some ambiguity among the theorists, economic bargaining principles do not assume absolute rationality on the

---

17. J. Pen, A General Theory of Bargaining, 42 American Economic Review 24, 35-36 (1952). Pen's work is summarized in O. Young, *Bargaining: Formal Theories of Negotiation* 135-136 (1975).

18. F. Zeuthen, *Problems of Monopoly and Economic Warfare* (1930).

19. O. Young, *Bargaining: Formal Theories of Negotiation* 134 (1975) (discussing Zeuthen's writings).

part of negotiators. Recognizing that goals may change during the course of negotiation, the principle of expected utility creates a mechanism for measuring and modifying preferred outcomes during bargaining. This introduces an appropriate flexibility missing in game theory and should help the lawyer avoid unnecessary deadlocks due to a rigidity of goals.

The advantages of the economic model can be illustrated by the sale-of-the-business problem. The dynamic aspects of the model are apparent in the graph on page 360. The Buyer and Seller began with widely divergent offers or demands and proceeded to converge on settlement through a series of counteroffers. Unlike game theory, which envisions but two moves, economic theory realizes each party to a negotiation may, and probably will, have a number of fallback positions.

Confident expectations about an opponent's various offers and counteroffers is all an attorney can anticipate. A lawyer in a bargaining situation, however, can plan the moves an opponent is expected to make and can design in advance responses to those moves. Moreover, using the learning devices of the economic model, a lawyer can modify these confident expectations by measuring them against the opponent's performance within the negotiation. For example, assume that Seller in the problem had a confident expectation that Buyer would make an opening offer of $500,000. When Buyer opened the bid at $50,000 below Seller's estimate, Seller "learned" in an economic modeling sense and was in a position to modify that particular confident expectation.

Finally, the doctrine of expected utility allows the bargainer to estimate the risk of maintaining a demand when faced with apparent intransigence on the part of opponent. Suppose that Seller's lawyer, for example, had decided $950,000 was the preferred outcome. Buyer, on the other hand, began lower and the counteroffers were smaller than Seller's confident expectations anticipated. Seller's lawyer, applying the expected utility analysis, could conclude that the "propensity to fight" did not exceed the risk of deadlock, or "no sale," and could adjust the Seller's preferred outcome downward. When Seller's risk willingness equaled the actual risk of "no sale," Seller was able to conclude a deal at $890,000.

Economic modeling of negotiation emphasizes the importance of planning and information in the bargaining process. Lawyers must plan their negotiating moves in advance and anticipate the reactions of their opponents. As with game theory, the economic model places a premium on information. Without information, the negotiator's confident expectations about the process are of limited value and may force the bargainer to make concessions when they are unwarranted.

3. Disadvantages of the Economic Model

Despite its recognition that adversarial negotiation is a dynamic process of multiple moves, too much of economic bargaining's attention is devoted to *what* occurs during bargaining and too little time is spent explaining *why* it happens. Thus, economic bargaining can help lawyers to plan their own concession strategy and anticipate their opponent's. But it adds little to our understanding of the causes of an opponent's concession. In particular, economic theory too often ignores the influence bargainers have on each other. In fact, one of the leading theorists claims "[a party] does not think of [his estimate of the opponent's concession rate] as a function of his own behavior." [20] This attitude assumes that each negotiator has a set of expectations and goals that are not susceptible to manipulation by the other.

Yet actions of one party in a negotiating session do influence opponents. For example, in a draw poker game a player who has opened with a high pair may keep a third card "kicker" to influence the other players' belief he is holding three of a kind. The opening player's "bluff" may affect opponents' subsequent betting and the final outcome of the hand if others *believe* the opening player has three of a kind.

To be more specific about the impact of strategic actions in lawyer negotiations, reexamine the economic model graph of the sale-of-the-business problem. Assume that the diagram accurately charts the course of bargaining between the Seller and Buyer from opening demands, through various concessions, to agreement of sale at $890,000. Assume that Buyer made the first concession, altering its initial offer upward to $570,000. Why did Buyer increase its first bid by $120,000, an increase of more than 25 percent? Economic theory would have us believe that Buyer, upon hearing Seller's opening demand, checked this against its confident expectations, calculated its expected utility, decided it was less willing to risk deadlock than was Seller, and conceded accordingly. This is simply too sterile an analytic process to be "real." Why did Buyer believe Seller had a greater willingness to risk breakdown in negotiations? What did Seller say or do to make Buyer believe it should make the first concession? Are there techniques or tactics one party can employ to influence opponent's belief concerning the risk allocation?

In the highly competitive conflict situation of adversarial negotiation, there are some definitive techniques one may employ to manipulate an opponent's attitude toward the conflict. Scholars who have studied strategic interaction in such conflict settings have developed theories of bargaining to account for this modification process. The next section examines those theories. After introducing another lawyer negotiation problem, we will review the approaches taken by adherents of the "bargaining" and the "social-psychological" schools to help explain the actions of the parties.

D. SOCIAL-PSYCHOLOGICAL BARGAINING THEORIES

≡ PROBLEM 4 ≡
The Medical Malpractice Case

Plaintiff, a 38-year-old printer, is married with two teenaged children and lives in a small town in a rural county. Four years ago he noticed that a mole on his back had changed in size and bled occasionally. Plaintiff visited

---

20. J. Cross, *Economics of Bargaining* 46 (1969). J. Pen, on the other hand, recognizes that strategic interaction between the parties influences bargaining, and his analysis assumes negotiators will use techniques such as promise, threat, and commitment. J. Pen, A General Theory of Bargaining, 42 American Economic Review 39-42 (1952).

defendant, a 71-year-old physician, the senior practitioner of three in the town, who had served the community for 40 years and the plaintiff since childhood. Defendant examined the mole and then "tied it off," a procedure involving wrapping surgical thread around the mole so it would fall off within a short time. Within a few days the plaintiff found the mole had disappeared, leaving a small scar. Defendant doctor claims he observed nothing unusual about the mole when he examined it and has no recollection of plaintiff telling him about it bleeding or changing in size.

About one year later, in response to classic symptoms, plaintiff went to a hospital in a larger town nearby where a biopsy disclosed he was suffering from an advanced stage of malignant melanoma (a serious form of skin cancer). Referred to an eminent surgeon in a large city, plaintiff submitted to extensive back surgery to remove the malignancy and a surgical excision of the lymph nodes under his right arm, which had been invaded by the disease. Following surgery, plaintiff began an 18-month chemotherapy regime, suffering the accompanying nausea and vomiting, which lasted one to three days per month.

Tests identified the mole earlier removed by the defendant as the primary lesion and the source of the disease. If a biopsy had been conducted on the removed mole, plaintiff would have had a 95 percent chance of total remission. His chances for complete remission are now only one in three. Plaintiff has $35,000 in medical expenses and $5,000 in lost wages. He seeks a total of $790,000 in damages in his suit. Defendant has been sued rarely and has increased his malpractice coverage only through the inflationary clause in his policy; he has just $150,000 in insurance.

Both sides are aware of the preceding facts. Plaintiff's counsel, a young partner in a prestigious litigation firm from the city, is also aware of the following information. Plaintiff and his wife are reluctant litigants, having been pushed by a relative to file suit. After consulting counsel but before agreeing to the filing of the complaint, plaintiff and his wife consulted their clergyman to determine if "it was all right to do this and it wouldn't offend God." They are thankful plaintiff has survived (and pleased the doctors predict complete recovery), and do "not want to test God." Moreover, though angry at defendant for his "mistreatment of [plaintiff] that almost cost him his life," they are afraid their friends in town will be "disgusted" with them if they "go after poor old Doc who has served us as best he could all these years." Counsel is concerned, therefore, that plaintiff will refuse to go through the "ordeal" of trial, a fact more than hinted at a number of times.

The treating chemotherapy oncologist and another expert will testify that the failure to diagnose the condition of the mole through common and accepted testing caused the spread of the disease, the massive surgery, and the resulting chemotherapy. Proper diagnosis would have occasioned a relatively minor surgical "coring" of the mole and a significant decrease of risk to plaintiff's life. The surgeon, on the other hand, who opposed any legal action ("we all make mistakes sometime"), will be a grudging witness at best, testifying that early diagnosis and surgery could not have guaranteed that the disease would not later spread.

Counsel has researched jury verdicts in the rural county and was shocked to learn they averaged less than half of those returned in the city.

She just learned, for example, that a jury awarded only $100,000 in a recent death case involving a 48-year-old plaintiff who lingered in a coma for a few days.

Defendant's counsel, an older "down-home" but quite shrewd local lawyer, has access to the following facts. His client simply has not kept up with the changes in medical practice over the years. Aware of his lack of knowledge, the defendant usually refers any serious matters to the other two "young hotshot" doctors in town or to a staff physician at the nearby hospital. Defendant did not believe plaintiff's mole was serious and treated it in the same way he had done for "the thousands [he'd] seen in 45 years of practice with nary a problem." Defendant does not have significant financial resources, having spent his professional career in the same, relatively poor, town. Defendant is quite proud, however, of his position within the community and does not want to "jeopardize" his good name. He has been thinking about retirement and would be willing to do so within a year if that would "satisfy" the plaintiff.

Counsel has found it very difficult to locate an expert who would approve of defendant's treatment of plaintiff. The best he could do was to get one who would testify that "tying off" a common mole (that is, one not changed in size, color, shape, or texture) has been an accepted method for years. If pressed, however, the expert would testify that he personally would recommend removal by incision followed by a biopsy in any instance "where there is a shadow of doubt."

During the two years since the complaint was filed, the lawyers have had sporadic discussions on the case. Both sides have moved slowly, the plaintiff's lawyer gradually reducing her settlement demand to $550,000 based on her city verdict experience, and defendant's counsel finally offering $50,000, "something more than specials and way more than it's worth as a nuisance case." Trial has been set for next week and both lawyers are at the local courthouse for a final pretrial conference with the judge. While waiting for the judge, the two lawyers "chat" about the case. The following excerpt is from their conversation:

Plaintiff's Counsel: Your offer is viewed by my client as an insult after what your guy caused him to go through. And he still might die, you know. How would she be able to take care of those kids without him?

Defendant's Counsel: My client was not negligent. He did what he should've done, and it was just bad luck your fella came down with more serious cancer. I think even some of your experts will have to admit that, won't they?

Plaintiff's Counsel: Tying it off! My God, they even biopsy when they remove a hangnail these days! Your client is going to look like a doctor from the Dark Ages using witchcraft and potions. Our experts will say it was plain malpractice, and it caused the plaintiff's subsequent massive surgery and treatment and dramatically increased the risk to his life.

Defendant's Counsel: Be that as it may, you can't get blood from a stone. My client is a poor country doctor and hasn't got the assets to come close to what you're asking.

Plaintiff's Counsel: My client and I couldn't justify less than a return of a quarter-million on this. If you won't be reasonable, we'll simply have to go to trial.

Defendant's Counsel: You can't believe a jury from this area will ever give you anything like what you're demanding. Why, everybody up this way knows and loves Doc. This isn't the city, you know, young lady.

Plaintiff's Counsel: I understand that, but no jury in the world will fail to find your client is incompetent. When they do, well, we'll just have to take our chances they'll look at his pain and suffering and understand he could still die. I bet all the folks around here believe your client, a doctor, has plenty of money.

Defendant's Counsel: Look here, if you're willing to be realistic and drop way down to a reasonable amount, I'll go back to the insurance company and see if they'll increase the ante a bit.

Plaintiff's Counsel: If the carrier is willing to put everything into the pot and your client will add something to it, then maybe we can avoid trial. If not, my clients are determined to go ahead.

Before considering the following questions, assume that you represent either one of the parties and try to determine your bargaining range and that of your opponent. Set it out in such a way that you are able to plot any moves by you and the other side.

In addition to charting the negotiation, can you identify the initial positions of the two parties during the dialogue? Did either make any concessions or indicate possible fallback positions? If so, why did their attitudes apparently change? Can you categorize the tactics employed by both lawyers and construct a method for examining the process in which they engaged? The advocates of the social-psychological and the bargaining theories should provide some answers to these questions and suggestions for employing various negotiation maneuvers and for recognizing the tactics when they are used by your opponent.

1. Introduction

We have combined two closely related schools of negotiation—the social-psychological and the bargaining schools—into a single theoretical description because both groups concentrate on examining the manipulative aspects of the process. Bargaining theory is the more refined and complete of the two models, in part because it is an outgrowth of a critical analysis of the more established game theory approach to negotiations.[21] Finding game theory static and its progeny, economic theory, dynamic but merely descriptive of the negotiating process, bargaining theory scholars posit an alternative approach for analyzing negotiations, an approach that addresses *why* decision-makers change their positions during the process.

---

21. The preeminent scholars in this field are Thomas C. Schelling and Daniel Ellsberg. See T. Schelling, *The Strategy of Conflict* (1960); Schelling, An Essay on Bargaining, 46 American Economic Review 281 (1956); Ellsberg, The Theory and Practice of Blackmail, 46 American Economic Review 909 (1956).

Social-psychological researchers of the negotiation process are loosely grouped around psychology and related disciplines. These students of bargaining explore dispute and transactional negotiations to determine how and why parties give, take, and perform. In hundreds of experiments and observations, these researchers have examined the manipulative nature of bargaining, the environmental constraints, the influences of personality, the impact of tactics, and other issues.[22] The social-psychologists have yet to produce a whole, complete, and coherent theory of negotiation. Instead, these scholars are still in the theory-building stage or, as one commentator has termed it, the social-psychologists are now discovering "islands of theory" about the bargaining process.[23]

Bargaining theorists and social-psychologists look at negotiation from the same perspective but see somewhat different things. Nevertheless, a review of the analytical framework of each of these schools will assist you in your understanding of the adversarial bargaining process as it is employed by lawyers.

2. *An Overview of Bargaining Theory*

Bargaining theory is premised on the existence of imperfect information and strategic interaction between or among the parties to the negotiation. While information gaps may be filled in and strategic interplay between the parties may be reduced as the negotiation progresses toward resolution, the existence of these conditions at the outset of the process is essential. In addition, bargaining theory requires considerable and continuous communication between the parties. The theory then focuses on manipulation by the parties of their opponent's understanding of the facts and on the range of the parties' behavior. One writer, Oran Young, has compared these perspectives to the assumptions of game and economic theory:

> By contrast with the game-theoretic conception of bargaining, this means that bargainers will attempt to manipulate the understanding of the other side both about their approach to the presence of strategic interaction and about the content of the payoff matrix itself. And by contrast with the economic models, it means that bargainers will try to manipulate each other's perceptions of such things as their "risk-willingness," utility functions, and learning behavior. . . . [T]he combination of opportunities for communication with the presence of strategic interaction . . . paves the way for the manipulative activities that constitute the core of bargaining. . . . [Thus,] bargaining is the manipulation of the information of others in the interests of improving the outcome for one's self under conditions of strategic interaction.[24]

Young suggests when the manipulative aspects of bargaining theory will be applicable. Negotiators acting to maximize their own gain (or the gain of those they represent) are the most likely users of bargaining theory. Although bargaining theory is applicable to negotiations that run along the

---

22. J. Rubin & B. Brown, *The Social Psychology of Bargaining and Negotiation* 2-3 (1975).
23. D. Druckman, *Negotiations: Social-Psychological Perspectives* 15 (1977).
24. O. Young, *Bargaining: Formal Theories of Negotiation* 303-304 (1975).

full spectrum of purely competitive to purely cooperative, it dominates competitive, adversarial negotiations. On the other hand, the manipulative aspects of bargaining theory may also be present in negotiations where the achievement of the common interests of the parties is a goal. Bargaining theory is also most often viewed as applying to

> roughly symmetrical [negotiating] activities on the part of two or more pur-
> posive actors. . . . [P]erfectly symmetrical bargaining is the . . . case in which
> the players engage in equal or identical efforts to manipulate the informa-
> tion conditions of each other. And perfectly asymmetrical bargaining is the
> [opposite] case in which only one of the players makes any effort at all to ma-
> nipulate the information conditions of the other(s). . . . It seems reasonable
> to conclude . . . that perfectly symmetrical bargaining will seldom appear in
> the real world, if only because the resources and personal attributes of the
> players are unlikely to be identical.[25]

The applicability of bargaining theory to lawyer negotiations should be clear. Much of lawyer bargaining is quite adversarial and often highly competitive, though far from the purest form of competitive adversarial negotiating. Moreover, adversarial negotiation by lawyers usually is "roughly symmetrical" in that each party is attempting to manipulate the information of other parties.

Bargaining theory involves efforts by one or more parties to manipulate the information communicated to others within the negotiation framework. The type of information supplied by the negotiator to the opponent may relate to matters previously unknown to the other side or to matters earlier assumed to be known by the opponent, but which the negotiator now claims to be inaccurate:

> It does not follow from this, however, that the information supplied by a bar-
> gainer must be true or accurate in any sense of those terms. In fact, the bar-
> gainer has a range of options along these lines. He may supply information
> that is true and complete or information that is correct as far as it goes but
> carefully selected to create a desired impression. By the same token, he may
> supply information whose truth or falsity is deliberately left indeterminate. A
> bargainer may communicate a contingent threat to another individual, for ex-
> ample, in the hope that the other will capitulate to his demand without forc-
> ing him to decide whether or not to carry through on his threat. In general,
> bargainers will make their decisions concerning the type(s) of information
> to supply on the basis of a cost-benefit calculation dealing with the specific
> situation at hand.[26]

The effectiveness of bargaining theory ultimately depends on the negotiator's ability to manipulate the perception and expectations of others. But how does one party convince another person to believe something?

---

25. Id. at 307.
26. Id. at 305-306. The ethical issues arising from the use of untruthful information by lawyers in a negotiating session to influence the actions of an opponent will be dealt with in a subsequent chapter. At this stage it is important only to understand that information, irrespective of its inherent truth or falsity, must be communicated by one party to another to influence the other's bargaining actions.

Schelling asserts "[i]t is easier to prove the truth of something that is true than something that is false."[27] For example, if your client does not have the financial resources to pay the claim demanded by an opponent, communicating a certified audit of your client's books is strong evidence of the truth of your assertion. On the other hand, if your client has the funds available to meet the opponent's demand but refuses to do so because your client views the claim as unfair or wrong, it is more difficult to "prove" to your opponent that your client is impecunious. Notwithstanding that truth usually is more effective than falsehood in manipulating your opponent, "success in [adversarial] bargaining ultimately goes to the player who can manipulate the information conditions of others regardless of the techniques he employs to accomplish this objective."[28]

Now that we understand the conditions under which bargaining theory operates and better realize how the theory might be employed by adversarial lawyer negotiators, we will apply some of the principles and guide you through the use of tactics derived from bargaining theory. The principles and tactics will be discussed in the context of attempting to resolve some of the questions raised by the medical malpractice problem. The chart on page 370 will assist in plotting the bargaining moves of the parties in that problem.

The chart, based on a model suggested by the bargaining theorists, Ikle and Leites,[29] is an effective method for analyzing the moves within an adversarial negotiation. The primary line reveals that the two parties in this tort case are in conflict over a set of mutually exclusive alternatives (money), with the defendant always preferring the lower options ($25,000 to $50,000, $50,000 to $75,000, and so on), and the plaintiff's preferences in reverse order. Plaintiff's *Minimum Disposition* ($100,000, or 2.5 times specials) is that point (A) where client would prefer no agreement (that is, trial) to an agreement for less money. Plaintiff estimates defendant's *Minimum Disposition* (that is, point (B), where the defendant would prefer no agreement to paying more than this amount) at $200,000 (the full amount of the insurance plus a $50,000 contribution by the doctor). Plaintiff's attorney estimates the *Probable Outcome* at trial will range from $100,000 to $150,000 (range (E)), depending on comparative lawyer skills, the performance of witnesses, the eventual makeup of the jury, and related factors. The remaining letters on the diagram (points C, D, and F) represent defendant's analysis of these same issues.

Based on each party's judgments, plaintiff's *Estimated Bargaining Range* runs from $100,000 (plaintiff's *Minimum Disposition*) to $200,000 (plaintiff's estimate of defendant's *Minimum Disposition*), while defendant's *Estimated Bargaining Range* is between $75,000 and $150,000. This does not prevent the plaintiff from demanding more or the defendant from offering less. When plaintiff demands $550,000 and defendant offers $50,000, both pretending these are serious positions, the parties are within their *Sham Bar-*

27. Schelling, An Essay on Bargaining, 46 American Economic Review 281, 283 (1956).
28. O. Young, *Bargaining: Formal Theories of Negotiation* 305 (1975).
29. F. Ikle & N. Leites, Negotiation: A Device for Modifying Utilities, in *Game Theory and Related Approaches to Social Behavior* 245, 247 (M. Shubik ed. 1964).

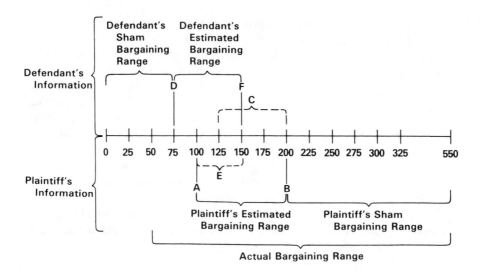

gaining Range. When either party offers a concession, therefore, it is either a *Sham Concession* or a *Genuine Concession* depending on its location along the continuum of mutually exclusive alternatives.[30]

Bargaining theorists conclude that an opponent will move from its Sham Bargaining Range and into its Genuine Bargaining Range, first making Sham and then Genuine Concessions, based on how successful the negotiator has been in manipulating the opponent's perception of the information and the actions the negotiator will take if the opponent does not move into the negotiator's bargaining range. Negotiators will use a variety of techniques to manipulate the opponent's perception. Dire threats and enticing promises, factual arguments and blatant appeals, bluffs, misrepresentations, and evasions—all of these and more may be used by a negotiator to manipulate the other side. A bargaining theorist will review the interaction of the parties to a negotiation, such as that portrayed in the transcript excerpt of the medical malpractice problem (pages 365-366), identifying and categorizing the tactics used to manipulate the other side's perceptions and beliefs. By concentrating on the interaction of the parties, the advocate of bargaining theory is able to explain results and develop predictions about the outcome of future negotiations where similar tactics are employed.

---

30. Ikle and Leites explain the importance of the difference between the two types of concessions:

> We can now define concessions. Hitherto discussions of negotiations usually failed to distinguish between a negotiator who makes a "concession" by dropping a demand he never expected the other side to accept, and one who thinks his concession increases the attractiveness of a proposal that the other side might have accepted prior to the concession. Based on our model, we may call a negotiator's change in bargaining positions from one he prefers more to one he prefers less a Sham Concession if these two positions lie in his Sham Bargaining Range, and a Genuine Concession if they fall within his Genuine Bargaining Range. A concession moving from the "sham" into the "genuine range" would combine both a "sham" and a "genuine" part.

Id. at 246-247.

3. An Overview of Social-Psychological Theories

Bargaining theory provides us with an excellent framework for planning and analyzing the exchange process in adversarial negotiations. Social-psychological theorists add more to our understanding of the power of the lawyer-negotiator to maneuver the bargaining and direct the process toward the client's ends. The social-psychological researchers accomplish this by breaking down the negotiation into a variety of components and then studying those components intently. Using social science research techniques in both laboratory and field settings, the theorists have discovered how these aspects of bargaining influence both the process and outcome of bargaining.

The social-psychologists begin with the premise that almost everything related to negotiation can have an impact on it, can manipulate the perceptions of the parties. Thus, their studies have ranged from the personalities of negotiators to the role of third parties, from the cognitive abilities of bargainers to the effect of argument and debate. The research includes a review of offers and concessions; threats and promises; the race, religion, and age of bargainers; and a multitude of other factors that the social-psychologists believe can and do influence negotiation procedure and outcome. We cannot repeat here the results of all these studies or the contents of dozens of publications that chronicle the work of these researchers.[31] We can give you, however, some feel for their work and suggest how it may bear on lawyer bargaining.

Social-psychologists have reviewed the effect audiences have on negotiation. The use of audience here does not necessarily mean observation of the process by the public. Instead, it refers to parties being represented by negotiators (e.g., labor unions or lawyers' clients). The research suggests that, whether absent or present at the bargaining table, represented parties significantly influence specific negotiator tactics as well as overall bargaining goals. Indeed, the social-psychologists conclude that negotiators tend to behave according to standards set by the audience. Thus, attorney tactics are likely to be influenced by client attitudes as to what is and is not appropriate conduct.

In a similar vein, researchers submit that the presence of third parties (e.g., judges at settlement conferences) generates pressure on negotiators to reach agreement. The pressure exerted by third parties appears to increase based on one's perception of the personality and reputation of the outsider. For example, the more the third party is perceived to be trustworthy and fair, the greater the impetus to agree.

Social-psychologists have analyzed many aspects of the negotiation setting. For example, they have studied the time and location of the bar-

---

31. Lawyers would do well to acquaint themselves with the growing body of social-psychological literature on negotiation. Two books that will provide an overview of the research and a sense of the breadth of topics covered, are D. Druckman, *Negotiations: Social-Psychological Perspectives* (1977), and J. Rubin & B. Brown, *The Social Psychology of Bargaining and Negotiation* (1975). See also the authorities collected by Menkel-Meadow, Toward Another View of Legal Negotiation: The Structure of Problem Solving, 31 U.C.L.A. L. Rev. 754, 757 n.5 (1984).

gaining. As time pressures increase, negotiators will reduce their aspirations, modify their demands, and moderate their tactics (e.g., avoid bluffs and threats). Negotiators who visit another's office are likely to behave less assertively, to the point, social-psychologists have found, of sometimes becoming positively deferential.

Researchers have examined the nature of the issues being negotiated in a number of ways. For instance, the more issues involved in a negotiation, the longer the time needed to complete the bargaining. While that result may not be surprising, it is interesting to learn that a greater number of issues produces more choices for the negotiators, and more choices combined with the availability of intermediate and tentative agreements lead to greater cooperation and settlements. On the other hand, the social-psychological theorists have found the data inconclusive on the question of whether it is better to begin the negotiation with the more important or the less important issues.

Intangible issues also have been the subject of study. The studies indicate that if a party makes excessive demands, allows insufficient concessions, or acts to punish the opponent (e.g., uses or implements threats), such actions are likely to cause the opponent to interject intangible issues involving such things as honor, public image, face, and self-esteem. When these intangibles are superimposed on the real issues being negotiated, the opponent is apt to take steps to prevent a repetition of the unwanted conduct and repair the damage. These steps may be taken even though the opponent must pay a heavy penalty in terms of losses on the real issues.

As final examples of the work of the social-psychologists, consider their findings that more cooperative bargaining occurs when people of the same race negotiate with each other as opposed to negotiating with people of another race. Blacks, it was found, are more cooperative in negotiations than are whites. A bargainer with a high tolerance for ambiguity is more prone to present a cooperative style than one who is only happy with a definitive answer. And, researchers have concluded, there appears to be no relationship between intelligence (assuming a minimal level) and negotiating ability or bargaining behavior.

The reach of the social-psychologists' research on the negotiation process is impressive. Some of the results fit well with our intuition. Other outcomes are remarkably counterintuitive. Only by familiarizing oneself with the literature being produced by these theorists will lawyers be able to make informed judgments about the strategies and techniques to apply in particular bargaining situations.

4. Advantages of Social-Psychological Bargaining Theories

The principles presented by these two schools aid us in understanding how the negotiation process works, what happens between bargainers, and why negotiators do what they do. Bargaining theory provides a model for conceptualizing the exchange phase, for planning offers, for plotting demands, and for understanding concessions. The social-psychologists give us the information we need to make rational decisions about the tactics we will use in the negotiation. Without the proponents of social-psychological bargaining theories, we might not have an appropriate appreciation for the role of manipulation in adversarial negotiation.

Lawyers who select an adversarial bargaining strategy will have to plan for the manipulation of their opponents' perceptions. The bargaining chart developed by the bargaining theorists is a significant aid to the preparation for negotiation. Setting out your own moves on the bargaining continuum, visualizing the maneuvers of the other side, and verifying both with the client should make you a more effective adversarial negotiator. Using the chart as a device to review progress between rounds of the negotiation should help keep you on your bargaining track.

The more you become aware of what the social-psychologists have to offer, the greater will be the range of things you will be able to do comfortably in the negotiation setting to manipulate the other side to achieve your client's desired goals. Flexibility of approach to legal negotiation will allow you to respond to the many tactical choices you will confront in your negotiating career. The more you learn about how negotiators react, the better able you will be to counter your opponents' bargaining moves.

5. Disadvantages of Social-Psychological Bargaining Theories

One disadvantage to these combined negotiating theories is that there is no end to the factors that can influence this complex human activity known as negotiation. Once you realize that this interdependent, interpersonal activity of lawyers involves everything from criminal justice matters to business deals to family problems to social legislation, you confront the fact that everything is relevant to the process and the outcome of the negotiation. It is not surprising that there are some who are quite skeptical of social-psychological research, claiming that all the relevant variables have not and cannot be tested simultaneously and, therefore, results are either incomplete or contradictory. Indeed, lawyers will find the criticism familiar: Just as you can find a reported court decision to support any reasonable proposition, you can also find, say the critics, a social-psychological study of negotiation to bolster any conceivable bargaining strategy, tactic, or technique.

The most serious conceptual problem with relying too much on the teachings of these two schools of negotiation is that it pushes you toward adoption of an adversarial strategy. Because both focus on how negotiating parties manipulate each other, these theorists emphasize "winning" as an important goal. Of course, when "winning" becomes the negotiator's aspiration there is likely to be a "loser." This zero-sum approach ignores alternatives to the win-lose paradigm, alternatives that may produce more satisfying results for the parties to a legal dispute or transactional negotiation.

To this point in our discussion of negotiation theories, we have concentrated on the adversarial or zero-sum theories of bargaining. Although the tactics used to implement adversarial strategies can be cooperative as well as competitive, the zero-sum nature of the bargaining process dominates each of the negotiating forms thus far reviewed. We now turn your attention to another model of negotiation, a type known as integrative or problem-solving negotiation. In this paradigm of bargaining, the process is conceptualized as non-zero-sum.

You will note that we devote greater attention to this theory of negotiation than we have to any of the others. There are two reasons for this imbalance. The other three bargaining concepts are akin in their fundamental approach to the resolution of disputes and the completion of transactions. Thus, the theory explanations support and reinforce each other. Problem-solving, on the other hand, stands alone and has no companion theory that aids understanding. The second reason for the length of our outline follows from the first. Adversarial negotiation is the typical and traditional model, one that lawyers and others adopt instinctively. Therefore, an appreciation of the strategy does not require the same explication as problem-solving, an approach to negotiation that is counterintuitive for most lawyers.

E. PROBLEM-SOLVING NEGOTIATION

≡≡≡ PROBLEM 5 ≡≡≡
The Sale and Purchase of a "Lemon"[32]

Ms. Harris, a salesperson at Triangle Motors, Inc., sold a four-year-old used car to Mr. Collins. For about a month after the purchase, Collins was very pleased with the reliability and performance of the vehicle. Then began a series of problems with the automobile that led Collins to file a lawsuit. First, the fan continued to run when the ignition was turned off. Next, the car refused to start. Finally, the engine ceased running while the auto was being operated. Over the next three months, Collins returned the car to Triangle Motors for repairs on numerous occasions. The service department gave a variety of reasons for the difficulties Collins was experiencing: a faulty switch, an electrical malfunction, and, finally, a glitch in the auto's computer, one of the earliest models to be installed on board an American car. Each time Collins brought the car in to Triangle for service he was forced to miss or be late for work. Eventually, Collins lost his job because of repeated absences.

At this point, Collins sued Triangle for rescission of the sale of the car, claiming in the alternative that either Harris misrepresented the condition of the vehicle or that there was a breach of warranty. In addition, Collins

---

32. The problem is based on *Valley Marine Bank v. Terry James*, a simulated case file prepared by the Office of Program Support of the Legal Services Corporation (1975). The underlying problem also appears in Menkel-Meadow, Toward Another View of Legal Negotiation: The Structure of Problem Solving, 31 U.C.L.A. L. Rev. 754, 772 (1984). Students of many law school clinical programs will recognize the simulated case as one used in the teaching of a number of lawyering skills.

demanded consequential damages resulting from the loss of his job. Triangle Motors counterclaimed for the balance due on the car, asserting that its service department was not given sufficient opportunity to find and repair the defect and that the warranty period on the used car had expired.

Collins purchased the car for $5,900, putting down $1,200 in the form of a trade-in allowance for his old car ($800) and $400 in cash. Collins made a single payment of $189 on the car before the trouble began. He spent $500 on repairs to the car and calculates his job-related lost income at $3,500. On the other side of the case, based on the terms of the sales contract, Triangle Motors claims the unpaid balance on the car plus attorney's fees for the collection action required to recover the amount owed.

Assume that subsequent to the filing of the lawsuit the lawyers for the parties agree to meet in an attempt to resolve the dispute. Plan for a traditional adversarial negotiation using the theories previously examined in this chapter. What do you believe will be the most likely outcome of this negotiation if the parties follow an adversarial strategy? Once you have anticipated the result of an adversarial negotiation, attempt to formulate a bargaining strategy that rejects a zero-sum framework in favor of one that strives to satisfy the fundamental needs of the disputants. In developing this alternative approach to lawyer negotiation, what central principles of bargaining that we have learned thus far must be discarded? Are there any concepts we have studied that should be preserved?

1. Adversarial and Problem-Solving Solutions to the Lemon Problem

When you structured the "lemon" problem as an adversarial negotiation, you probably calculated each party's respective monetary claims and created a bargaining chart similar to the one set out in the section on economic theory or the model explained in the segment on social-psychological concepts. If so, your chart is apt to look something like this:

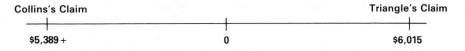

Collins's Claim   Triangle's Claim

    $5,389+   0 $6,015

The claim of Collins is made up of lost income, the cost of repairs to the car, the total value of the trade-in, the amount of the single monthly payment, and an unspecified amount for punitive damages for the allegedly fraudulent representations of the salesperson, Ms. Harris, concerning the condition of the vehicle. Triangle's claim consists of the contract price of the car less the combined total of the trade-in and the monthly payment plus an amount for attorney's fees (calculated above at one-third of the settlement).

In the traditional adversarial negotiation, the parties are likely to begin by discussing the validity of their respective legal claims. This discussion forms the foundation on which the disputants construct a model to designate the amount of money at stake in the negotiation and to decide who should pay how much to whom. Because the model is supported by references to criteria (i.e., legal rules governing contracts for the sale of chattels) that are external to the incident being negotiated, the parties are engaged in what has to be described as a principled negotiation. Once the negotiators have exhausted the process of persuading their opponent on the validity of their claims, they bargain along the monetary continuum on the basis of these principles or on the basis of compromise and concession or on the basis of a combination of these two settlement forms.

Seen in this light, you will not be surprised to learn that when lawyers and law students negotiate the lemon problem the dominant result is a wash-out, that is, the parties drop their claims against the other side, executing mutual releases and walking away from the table without exchanging any money. While many parties are likely to be frustrated by such a result because their "rights" have not been vindicated nor their real needs satisfied, they accept the consequences because of the inherent risks of a trial that must end in a winner-loser, zero-sum outcome. Adversarial negotiators are not at all discomforted with such an end product of bargaining. Target and resistance points along the bargaining continuum were adjusted realistically based on an assessment of the likelihood of success at trial and further discounted by a precise computation of the costs associated with a full and complete adjudication of the legal claims. Thus, the process produced a result based on careful reasoning and an analysis of costs and benefits, risks and rewards.

Problem-solving negotiators, on the other hand, are deeply troubled by this adversarial result. In the words of Carrie Menkel-Meadow, the most articulate spokesperson on problem-solving negotiation for lawyers:

> The difficulty with this solution is that the real goals or objectives sought by the parties might not be accomplished at all. [Collins] wants a reliable car to [get] to work and [Triangle Motors wants] a profitable sale and a satisfied customer who will make recommendations to . . . friends. If, however, the parties considered what they had initially desired from this transaction, they might arrive at other solutions. Alternatives could be found that would more completely and efficiently satisfy their needs, solutions not necessarily arising from compromise.[33]

Professor Menkel-Meadow suggests that there are relatively low-cost solutions to the lemon problem that would leave the parties in a state of greater satisfaction. Triangle should either repair the auto to an acceptable working condition, providing Collins with a "loaner" until servicing is concluded, or substitute another car from its inventory of used automobiles. In either event, Collins will be held to the earlier sales contract or the parties must negotiate a new agreement. If either solution is implemented, both parties satisfy their underlying needs at the minimum cost to each. Collins obtains dependable transportation and goes away with positive feelings

---

33. Id. at 774.

about Triangle and a willingness to encourage others to patronize the dealership. Triangle has a completed sale and a happy customer. Of the proposed solutions, the more expensive option for Triangle is apt to be providing Collins with another vehicle. Even so, the costs to Triangle are likely to be relatively low because it has a full service staff, the ability to resell a repaired vehicle, and a supply of used cars on which to draw. In calculating the costs of the deal, the parties should consider that the suggested problem-solving solution avoids the monetary and nonmonetary costs of litigation and minimizes the transaction costs of negotiation.

2. Assumptions of Adversarial Bargaining Theories

The problem-solving solution to the lemon problem is radically dissimilar from the outcomes expected from and achieved by most adversarial negotiations. Are there fundamental conceptual differences between the game theory, economic, and psychological bargaining models and the problem-solving model that explain outcomes so unlike one another? Are there process distinctions between adversarial and problem-solving negotiators that lead to such sharply divergent products? The simple answer to these questions is "yes" but we ought to spend some time accounting for the variations in result.[34]

Traditional adversarial negotiation theories proceed on the assumption that each party to a dispute or in a transaction desires to maximize the gain to itself. In adversarial bargaining, a maximized gain can be measured in at least two ways. First, a party determines whether it has "won" on an overall basis (a "majority" win) without regard to what the other side has gained. Thus, in a baseball game where the winning team has five runs, the winner does not care whether the opponent has three or one or no runs. As long as the winner has one more run, that team has maximized gain according to one form of assessment. Gain also can be gauged by accounting for the differences between the parties. In this approach to maximization, the goal is to increase your own return while precluding gains by the other side. Thus, in a baseball game that is part of an elimination tournament where ties are resolved by total run differentials, preventing the opponent from posting any runs and running up the score by your own team would be concurrent goals. No matter how gain is measured, the adversarial negotiator postulates that there will be a winner and a loser in the negotiation game and that winning (maximization) is the primary aim.

In addition to maximizing gain, adversarial theories assume that the parties to a negotiation want the same things and possess the same values. If the parties desire the identical objects, it follows for the adversarial negotiator that the sides to the dispute or transaction are in conflict over limited or fixed resources, most commonly money but also such items as units of

---

34. Professor Menkel-Meadow sets out the conceptual assumptions and the process tactics that underlie adversarial models. Id. at 765-767, 775-793. Other commentators also distinguish between the mind-set of the adversarial negotiator and the approach of the principled problem-solving negotiator. See R. Fisher & W. Ury, *Getting to Yes* 96-98 (1981).

production, measures of time, division of geographic territory, and the like. The finite resource that is valued equally by the parties becomes the subject matter of the negotiation. Thus, in a simple buy-sell case, the finite resource is money, a fungible, equally valued commodity that the seller wants more of and the buyer wants to keep. In an effort to accommodate such conflicting desires, adversarial negotiators keep constant the item being negotiated (money) and the parties shift and alter their outcome preferences (seller agrees to take a little less and buyer accedes to paying somewhat more) until a settlement zone is discovered or deadlock occurs.

A further assumption by lawyers who follow an adversarial strategy can exacerbate the differences between the solutions they develop and those constructed by problem solvers. Because lawyers "bargain in the shadow of the law,"[35] their view of the solutions that are available and the results that can be achieved may be warped. Lawyers involved in dispute negotiations where the matter is in or on the verge of litigation tend to view possible outcomes of the bargaining after an analysis of the legal remedies available to the court and the likelihood of each of those remedies being applied in their case. Attorneys involved in transactional negotiations where the parties are trying to buy, sell, create, modify, or destroy some legal thing tend to look to similar deals, industry standards, and boilerplate clauses that have withstood legal challenge. While there are advantages to such comparative analyses, the tendency of lawyers to examine normative solutions and results can inhibit, limit, and restrict their development of creative solutions that address the fundamental needs and desires of the parties. If a court is confined to designating a winner and a loser, if it is forced to convert rights into money, and if its "remedial imagination"[36] is constrained by narrowly drawn rules and procedures, this can and often does have a stultifying and suffocating effect on the crafting of alternative outcomes by litigator-negotiators. In the same vein, transactional lawyers can be and are constrained by what has been done in analogous settings with the result that their creativity is curtailed and their interest in fashioning unique answers is inhibited.

The underlying conceptual assumptions of adversarial bargainers lead to certain negotiation approaches that help account for differences in the nature and quality of the solutions achieved by negotiators of each school. The process that is produced by an adversarial strategy is indelibly marked by fierce competition over the equally valued limited resource the parties use as a real or substituted goal of the negotiation. Accordingly, the parties conceive of the bargaining linearly and establish their own and anticipate the opponent's positions along the resource continuum. They make plans for offers and responses, counteroffers and concessions. They work to conserve information about needs, goals, strengths, fears, and the like. They engage in a form of argumentative debate designed to manipulate, intimi-

---

35. A phrase first used by Mnookin & Kornhauser, Bargaining in the Shadow of the Law: The Case of Divorce, 88 Yale L.J. 950 (1979), and used again in Cooter, Marks & Mnookin, Bargaining in the Shadow of the Law: A Testable Model of Strategic Behavior, 11 J. Legal Stud. 225 (1982). See also Menkel-Meadow, Toward Another View of Legal Negotiation: The Structure of Problem Solving, 31 U.C.L.A. L. Rev. 754, 789 (1984).

36. Id. at 791.

date, cajole, and persuade the opponent to accept a solution in which their side maximizes gain. These and other adversarial tactics lead to a determinative and distributive model of bargaining in which the negotiators decide on the valued thing to be negotiated and then battle over the division of that limited, often fungible, always highly (and usually equally) valued commodity.

3. Underlying Principles of Problem-Solving Negotiation

According to advocates of problem-solving negotiation, adversarial bargaining leads to inefficient and ineffective results, outcomes that can sacrifice long-term consequences for short-term gains and agreements that are difficult to enforce because participants are often resentful and dissatisfied. If adversarial negotiation strategies can produce such distasteful negotiation results, what are the principles of problem-solving bargaining and how do they spawn more acceptable solutions?

The principles that underpin problem-solving negotiation are deceptively simple. Although the primary proponents of this approach to bargaining use somewhat different terminology, they agree on most of these principles. First and foremost, problem solvers seek to identify the real needs of the parties and try to ignore the bargaining positions that often mask those needs.[37] The importance of identifying the real needs of the parties is explained by Fisher and Ury and by Menkel-Meadow:

> Interests motivate people; they are the silent movers behind the hubbub of positions. Your position is something you have decided upon. Your interests are what caused you to so decide. . . .
>
> Reconciling interests rather than positions works for two reasons. First, for every interest there usually exist several possible positions that could satisfy it. All too often people simply adopt the most obvious position[.] . . . When you do look behind opposed positions for the motivating interests, you can often find an alternative position which meets [the interests of both parties]. . . . Reconciling interests rather than compromising between positions also works because behind opposed positions lie . . . shared and compatible interests, as well as conflicting ones.[38]

> Parties to a negotiation typically have underlying needs or objectives—what they hope to achieve, accomplish, and/or be compensated for as a result of the dispute or transaction. . . . By attempting to uncover those underlying needs, the problem-solving model presents opportunities for discovering greater numbers of and better quality solutions. It offers the possibility of meeting a greater variety of needs both directly and by trading off different needs, rather than forcing a zero-sum battle over a single issue. The principle

---

37. While Menkel-Meadow calls on negotiators to uncover the actual or underlying needs and objectives of the parties and Fisher and Ury urge bargainers to focus on interests and not positions, they are addressing the same principle.

38. R. Fisher & W. Ury, *Getting to Yes* 42, 43 (1981).

underlying such an approach is that unearthing a greater number of the actual needs of the parties will create more possible solutions because not all needs will be mutually exclusive. As a corollary, because not all individuals value the same things the same way, the exploitation of differential or complementary needs will produce a wider variety of solutions which more closely meet the parties' needs.[39]

To be an effective problem-solving negotiator, it seems obvious that a lawyer first must learn to be a client-centered interviewer and counselor. A client-centered attorney is in a position to discover the underlying needs, interests, and objectives of the client. When the client's needs are fully determined, the lawyer can then redirect attention to the opponent and, with the assistance of the client, may be able to anticipate some of the essential needs and objectives of the other side.

Consider this situation. Suppose you represent a young entrepreneur, Bob Rice, who wants to open a new type of convenience store where customers make all of their purchases from vending machines.[40] Rice realizes that the venture is risky and its success depends on almost immediate public acceptance of his unique marketing approach. He believes firmly that the concept will catch on with customers who will save time now spent in check-out lines. Unfortunately, Rice is short on capital. Although he has enough money to rent the vending machines, purchase sufficient inventory to keep the business going for a reasonable period, and pay for advertising and other essential activities, he does not have enough funding to assume the burden of a costly, long-term lease. On the other hand, Rice needs good space in a prime location if he is to give his novel, fledgling business a real chance to take off. Unless a landlord is willing to "work with" him, Rice will be unable to begin his new business. Rice tells you that a close family friend, John Whitmore, owns a prominent real estate business in the area and is heavily invested in commercial real estate. He wants to approach the family friend and suggest to Whitmore that the latter help him start the new venture.

What do you anticipate will be some of Whitmore's needs and objectives? Obviously, Whitmore wants to profit from leasing the commercial real estate he owns. How much profit? Will he accept nothing or less than the fair rental value (FRV) at the beginning of the lease in return for the opportunity to make considerably above FRV later on? How much is less than FRV? How much is considerably above FRV? What are the relevant time frames? Whitmore probably wants to rent to a profitable business that is likely to stay in the leased premises for a reasonably long period. But how long? How much does Whitmore value the security of a long-term lease? Whitmore may want to preserve or strengthen the relationship with the Rice family. If so, at what risk and at what possible cost? Is Whitmore interested in being associated with the successful development of a new

---

39. Menkel-Meadow, Toward Another View of Legal Negotiation: The Structure of Problem Solving, 31 U.C.L.A. L. Rev. 754, 795 (1984).

40. See the Whitmore and Rice commercial lease problem in J. Harbaugh, *Lawyer Negotiation Training Materials* (1988).

and innovative retail business? How much is that association worth in terms of the risk that the business will fail?

As Fisher and Ury point out, for problem-solving negotiators, the job of figuring out the needs, interests, and objectives of the other side is at least as important as figuring out the goals of your own client. But you can see from this example how getting answers to those questions about Whitmore's needs and interests may facilitate an agreement with Rice. The discovery of different or complementary needs increases the chances that a deal may be struck. For example, if Whitmore has an interest in taking part in the formation of a unique venture, he can satisfy that objective by working with Bob Rice. On the other hand, a demand by Whitmore for a five-year lease is a negotiation position about which Rice's lawyer must seek information concerning underlying needs. What interests caused Whitmore to demand such a long-term lease? Is there an alternative to the lengthy lease that will satisfy those interests of Whitmore instead of acceding to his positional demand? By learning what are the underlying needs, interests, and objectives of the client and the opponent, the problem solver has taken a major step toward an efficient and effective bargaining result.

Following a detailed needs analysis, the second principle supporting the problem-solving model is the development of solutions for mutual gain.[41] The goal of solution development must be to satisfy the parties' needs and interests, to achieve a result that the parties recognize as more advantageous to themselves and each other than the available alternatives. While it is easy to say that lawyers should develop solutions for mutual gain, this goal is exceedingly difficult to accomplish. As Fisher and Ury point out, inventing creative options to satisfy complementary and conflicting needs of parties to a dispute or transaction is not something that comes naturally to negotiators. At the same time, it is difficult, if not impossible, to teach creativity.

What then do the proponents of problem-solving suggest to lawyers who wish to follow the model? Fisher and Ury are quite prescriptive in laying out an approach to solution development. They begin by admonishing negotiators to avoid the four obstacles to invention of multiple options for mutual gain.[42] Premature judgment that stifles imagination, searching for a single solution, the assumption of a fixed resource pie, and thinking that opponents are responsible for solving their own problems all impede the development of solutions for mutual gain. After warning about the barriers to creative solutions, Fisher and Ury go on to suggest ways of facilitating new ideas.[43] The process they recommend revolves around brainstorming, an approach to negotiation solutions designed to produce as many ideas as possible to satisfy the interests of the parties. Brainstorming with partners, allies, or opponents demands adherence to one key rule: All criticism,

---

41. Again, there are slight variations in terminology. Menkel-Meadow talks about searching for and creating solutions to meet the parties' needs and expand the resources available to the parties. The phrases used by Fisher and Ury to describe the same principle of problem-solving include inventing creative options for mutual gain.

42. R. Fisher & W. Ury, *Getting to Yes* 59 (1981).

43. Id. at 62-83.

analysis, evaluation, and judgment of the ideas generated must be post-poned until all possible proposals have been articulated and listed for later consideration. To invent solutions, negotiators must be willing to voice wild ideas and crazy schemes without the risk of appearing ridiculous.

Menkel-Meadow is less specific in discussing the process of develop-ing creative solutions, relying more on a conceptual analysis of solution development. Instead, she notes the remarkable power of the parties' un-derlying needs to suggest appropriate solutions, thereby emphasizing that the effective problem solver must focus on the precise needs of the parties. Professor Menkel-Meadow also suggests that lawyer-negotiators seek at all times to expand the resources available for the parties to share. An ex-panded pie, even one distributed by division, provides greater means for bringing satisfaction to the parties. According to Menkel-Meadow, explor-ing who distributes and what, when, how, and how much is distributed promotes an expansion of the resource pie.

Applying Menkel-Meadow's needs-expansion approach to our earlier example, we can identify potential solutions that might satisfy possible needs of the parties to the new business problem. Rice's cash-flow crunch and fear of business failure fit nicely with Whitmore's interest in long-term tenancy. If Whitmore will agree to a percentage of gross sales rent provi-sion—meaning the rents would be lower at the front end of the lease but would increase as Rice's sales rise—it will meet the tenant's cash concerns. In return, Rice's agreement to a long-term lease will satisfy Whitmore's need for a long-term relationship with his tenants. Rice would be more willing to assume the obligation of a long lease if Whitmore will agree to an escape clause allowing Rice to abandon an unprofitable venture based on an agreed-upon financial formula. An expansion of the resource pie might include the suggestion that Whitmore accept a percentage of Rice's busi-ness in return for the infusion of cash and/or the provision of commercial space at reduced or no cost.

There are times, however, when the parties' needs do not fit together so neatly, thereby making for tidy trade-offs and organized options for mu-tual gains. Proponents of problem-solving recognize that on occasion nego-tiators are faced with demands by the parties for the same material item. Family disputes are a rich source of such demands that must be confronted by lawyers for the parties. Classic are the claims by divorcing spouses for the custody of the children. The substance of this dispute cannot be parti-tioned, sold, or divided. The parties have similar if not identical needs that must be satisfied. And the children themselves have extraordinarily im-portant interests that must be protected. The procedure known as joint or shared custody is a problem-solving solution designed to satisfy the com-peting needs of the principals in a family dispute. Because of the interests of the third parties (children), some settlements involve the children re-maining in the family home and the divorcing parents moving back and forth. While some things, in the end, may have to be split or divided among the parties, problem solvers resist doing so in the first instance, explor-ing sharing or substituting solutions before succumbing to the division compromise.

These approaches to solutions mark an important difference between adversarial and problem-solving negotiators. As noted earlier, adversarial negotiators keep constant the item being negotiated (e.g., money) and the parties shift and alter their outcome preferences along the bargaining continuum until a settlement zone is discovered or deadlock occurs. Problem solvers reverse the fixed and floating variables. In problem-solving negotiation, the bargainers keep the parties' value preferences constant and shift among and between proposed combinations of resources until a solution that satisfies mutual needs emerges.[44]

4. A Brief Comparison of the Process of Adversarial and Problem-Solving Negotiations

Although we already have identified some process differences between adversarial and problem-solving negotiation, it is important to review briefly and emphasize some of the important distinctions. Adversarials proceed linearly to develop their plans, concentrating on creating and defending positions along the bargaining continuum. Planning by problem solvers, on the other hand, focuses on identifying needs and brainstorming to develop solutions for mutual gains. Adversarials engage in positional argument while problem solvers tend to explore interests. Adversarials make offers to which they appear to be committed. Problem solvers advance proposals that invite opponents to accept, reject, or modify based on how the proposals intersect with their interests. Adversarials are more likely to restrict information flow, problem solvers more inclined to exchange data. Adversarials reject the opponents' offers summarily and make concessions along the continuum. Problem solvers explain why solutions are acceptable or unacceptable in whole or in part based on a needs analysis. They also seldom make concessions, as their adversarial colleagues do, but instead shift to another proposal that more completely addresses the parties' mutual problems.

This brief summary is designed to stress that adversarial and problem-solving negotiation differ significantly on both conceptual and process levels. While we have noted important distinctions among the adversarial theories, the adversarial negotiating processes have identifiable similarities. While the adversarial theories may be loosely described as the obverse

---

44. Although they agree on many things, the leading advocates of problem-solving negotiation do have some differences over the principles of this bargaining strategy. For example, Fisher and Ury advocate separating the people from the problem, dealing with their emotions and feelings independently of the substance. Menkel-Meadow asserts that often the people are the problem and they cannot be separated from the substance. Fisher and Ury urge problem solvers to insist that proposals be measured by objective criteria, standards that are external to the will of the parties and the peculiar circumstances of the dispute or transaction. Those authors view that as a fundamental precept of principled negotiation. Menkel-Meadow raises questions about the objective criteria requirement. She suggests it leads to sequential bargaining and compromise-like solutions. Thus, she notes, Fisher and Ury can be interpreted to mean that the parties first attempt to satisfy their underlying needs and interests. But, if that fails, then the parties negotiate based on objective criteria to reach a "fair" solution while avoiding adversarial, positional bargaining.

Whatever differences exist among these problem-solving proponents, those differences have not created schisms.

of the same coin, problem-solving involves another currency. In formulating a viable conceptual framework for lawyer negotiation, we will have to take into account the substantial differences between these two bargaining approaches.

5. *Advantages of Problem-Solving*

Consistent with our analysis of other negotiation models, we consider briefly some of the advantages of problem-solving as a negotiation strategy. The most obvious benefit of problem-solving is that solutions for mutual gain are likely to bring greater satisfaction to the parties. In a representative profession such as lawyering, client satisfaction is an important goal and one significant measure of our success. Thus, if we can better achieve our clients' goals and meet their underlying needs, we ought to do so. Fundamental to this advantage of the model is that we understand and appreciate the clients' interests and objectives. That, of course, depends on effective use of client-centered interviewing and counseling strategies.

A second important advantage of the model is that it is easier to implement. The preceding comparison of adversarial and problem-solving processes reveals that the former is tactically testing to the negotiator. In an adversarial negotiation, the lawyer must be ever alert, carefully avoiding unforced errors of omission and commission and sidestepping the traps set by an opponent. Effective problem-solving is less dependent on faultless execution and more related to careful attention to the needs and interests of the parties. On the other hand, planning for problem-solving may be more complex and demanding than adversarial preparation.

In addition to direct gains flowing from the successful execution of a problem-solving strategy, lawyer-negotiators can profit from a consideration of this bargaining model. For example, an indirect benefit of examining problem-solving is a greater appreciation of the role of information in the negotiation process. Game theory provided us evidence of the importance of information in the adversarial context. An understanding of problem-solving underscores that importance in all negotiation situations. An awareness of our clients' and our opponents' underlying needs, interests, and objectives is crucial to negotiation success. With such knowledge we can fashion adversarial offers that may be accepted as well as problem-solving proposals that meet underlying needs. If the dominant role of information in negotiation was not apparent before this review of problem-solving, it must be now.

6. *Disadvantages of Problem-Solving*

The most serious disadvantage of problem-solving negotiation is that it cannot be used in a setting where the parties are bargaining over a single fungible item such as money. Even the most ardent advocates of problem-solving must grudgingly admit that you cannot problem-solve a pure and simple division of a sum of money. If, for example, the seller of an item is interacting with a casual buyer who will never purchase from the seller again and there are no side issues (e.g., timing of delivery, quantity needs, or financing issues), problem-solving will not be helpful to the resolution of the deal. In this situation, the only goal of the seller is to complete a sale for the best possible price and the only goal of the buyer is to make the purchase for the lowest conceivable amount. It is impossible to construct multiple solutions for mutual gain in this setting. The parties are forced to battle over price by moving along the adversarial continuum until they reach accord or deadlock.

Proponents of problem-solving point out, however, that such pure conflict situations are exceedingly rare in the real world, particularly in legal dispute and transactional situations. Most matters involving lawyers, they claim, consist of multiple issues that are valued differently by the parties if underlying interests are exposed. If this is so, they note, the matters are ripe for problem-solving solutions. There is much to be said for their assertion about the complexity of most negotiations involving lawyers. On the other hand, the complexity of cases may make problem-solving less desirable than adversarial outcomes.

A downside to problem-solving is that it may take more time and thrust the parties into relationships that are discomforting. The effort required to identify underlying needs and interests, to brainstorm to develop potential solutions for mutual gain, and to sift through and evaluate possible results may be too great. It may be easier for the parties to use principled adversarial strategies to resolve the problem. Moreover, problem-solving solutions often force the parties into initiating, resuming, or continuing a relationship. On occasion the feelings of the parties are so strongly negative that the relationship is unacceptable even though the result is more efficient and effective when measured by other criteria. For example, Mr. Collins in the lemon problem may now be so distrustful of Ms. Harris and angry with the management of Triangle Motors that he would find it unacceptable to purchase another car from them.

Finally, there may be certain lawyer negotiation settings where problem-solving becomes difficult. The parties may be too wealthy, too powerful, or too set in their bargaining ways to consider seriously negotiating for mutual gain. In the first two situations, it can be frustrating trying to convince persons to negotiate in a problem-solving manner when they are resistant or oblivious to an analysis of mutual gains. If they perceive that the gain to them is minimal, it may not justify an alteration in approach. The more overriding problem involves the lawyer or client who enjoys, is comfortable with, and has been successful employing adversarial negotiation strategies. While perhaps interested in the model from a theoretical perspective, they do not perceive value in the approach. Indeed, many believe problem solvers are bargaining wimps who will be cleaned out by effective adversarials, although no credible evidence presently supports that belief.

Menkel-Meadow and Fisher and Ury both address the limits of problem-solving negotiation in the reality of a harsh and competitive bargaining world. Each has a series of suggestions on how to deal with an opponent who, for a variety of reasons, resists problem-solving. While the techniques are interesting and application of them often will lead to joint problem-solving bargaining, the bottom line is clear. If the other lawyer will not negotiate according to problem-solving principles, you will have to decide whether you and your client can afford to abandon the bargaining process. We cannot force an opponent to candidly discuss its needs and interests and then engage in a creative search for mutually satisfactory solutions.

≡ PROBLEM 6 ≡
The Wrongful Death Tragedy

Test your evolving problem-solving skills on the following problem. It is based on an actual case that was resolved because the parties ultimately focused on real needs, brainstormed together, and developed solutions for mutual gains. To help you avoid the temptation to use an adversarial strategy, the problem is set in the aftermath of failed traditional negotiation.

Although there are federal regulations that govern the number of hours a commercial airline pilot may work, there are no rules limiting the consecutive hours of the non-cockpit members of the crew. Because of this situation, the National Association of Flight Attendants (NAFA), a union representing airline employees, has lobbied Congress for legislation to control the hours and working conditions of flight staff other than pilots and engineers. NAFA argues that exhausted flight attendants will not be able to perform at expected safety levels during emergencies, thereby endangering all of the passengers. Congressional hearings on NAFA's proposed legislation are scheduled next month. The Association of United States Airlines (AUSA), a powerful industry group, is expected to oppose the new laws, claiming that there is no safety issue because airlines do not abuse flight staff, that legislation in this area is the first step away from deregulation, and that passengers will pay dearly due to increased labor costs.

About eight months ago, Pat Swisher, a flight attendant with Midwest Airlines, was forced to pull triple-up duty because of employee illness, schedule changes, and equipment problems. As a result, he worked 13 flight segments over 22 consecutive hours, 7 segments and 14 hours more than the usual assignment. Not surprisingly, extreme fatigue had set in by the time Swisher arrived at his base airport. Because he lived some distance from the field, Swisher had a 40-minute drive to his home. Unfortunately, he fell asleep at the wheel and his car crossed the median of a four-lane road and he crashed head-on into an oncoming vehicle at high speed. Luckily, Swisher survived the crash although he suffered very serious injuries. The driver of the other car, its sole occupant, was not so fortunate. She died after fading in and out of a coma over a six-day period.

Almost recovered physically, Swisher suffers from a combination of guilt, anger, and frustration. He blames himself for the death of the other person but he is bitter that the airline overworked him, exhausting him to the point that he dozed off while driving. He is discouraged by his slow recovery and the prognosis that he will not be able to return to work for another six months.

The victim of the accident was Denise Gibbs, a 19-year-old first-year student at the Jullian Academy of Music, a prestigious music school of national renown that accepts only gifted young musicians, each of whom receives a full scholarship. Ms. Gibbs was a cellist with a budding international reputation. In the two years before her death, Gibbs had won three major musical competitions, one a premier event held in Moscow. Gibbs is survived by her parents, the plaintiffs in the multimillion-dollar wrongful death action against Swisher and Midwest Airlines. The resentment and anger of the parents is almost without bound. They seem to want to punish both Swisher and the airline. Although they understand intellectually that it was an accident and that Swisher did not intend to injure their daughter, in their despair they can focus only on the fact that directly and indirectly Swisher and Midwest caused Denise's death. They watched their only child grow with the music she loved and are deeply depressed that neither they nor the world will ever again hear her play the cello. They want their daughter back with them, something they know they cannot have.

You are an associate in the firm representing the insurance carrier covering Swisher's interests. Your colleagues and senior company personnel evaluated the settlement of the case at a significant seven-figure level based on a comparison with jury verdicts in similar cases and with agreements reported by others in the insurance industry. The law firm employed a structured settlement expert to put together a package and the offer was extended to counsel for the Gibbs. The settlement proposal was rejected almost immediately, opposing counsel reporting that the offer was not sufficient to satisfy Mr. and Mrs. Gibbs. The plaintiffs demanded the full amount claimed in the complaint. Two more structured settlement plans were prepared, and they were refused with the same explanation and counterdemand.

Because your colleagues know you have an understanding of problem-solving negotiation, you have been asked to provide an objective analysis of the situation and suggest possible proposals to break the deadlock. The insurance carrier is unwilling to add more money to the offer because it fears that would set a dangerous precedent for it and the industry. Moreover, the company's offer and the plaintiffs' demand are so far apart that the gap cannot be closed in negotiation. Unless you can devise some alternatives, the client is resigned to a trial on the merits where it risks the full amount of the plaintiffs' claim and the parents of the girl will be forced to gamble that they will get more than the fair and generous offer presently on the table. Advise your colleagues.

Chapter

16

≡≡≡≡≡

Lawyer Negotiation Models

A. INTRODUCTION

In the previous chapter on negotiation theories, certain terms—"zero-sum," "non-zero-sum," "competitive," "cooperative," "adversarial," and "problem-solving"—were used in our attempt to describe some of the conceptual approaches to the negotiation process articulated by those writing in sister disciplines. Those terms will be used again in this chapter as we set out for you what we believe are models for effective legal bargaining and some criteria you may use in selecting a particular model in a specific situation.

First, recall that lawyers are involved in two basic types of cases on behalf of clients. One type of case involves disputes, situations where the client and others are in legal or factual conflict about rights or duties. In these matters, attorneys invoke or threaten to invoke the litigation process, which includes administrative proceedings and arbitration, as a means of resolving the dispute. If the litigation process is allowed to run its full course in a dispute matter, the trial will be a purely adversarial forum and the outcome is more than likely to be zero-sum or absolute win-lose. But most litigation cases are not allowed to run the full course and most legal disputes are not resolved by a zero-sum trial judgment. As mentioned ear-

lier, almost all of the civil suits filed in our state and federal courts are resolved without a trial. Most of these conflict matters are concluded by a
negotiated agreement between the parties.

The second type of matter lawyers handle on behalf of their clients can
be titled planning or transactional. Contrary to popular notions, most of
the legal work in this country does not involve dispute resolution; most attorneys spend their time planning for or implementing transactions on behalf of their principals. As the agents of their clients, lawyers are buying,
selling, creating, dissolving, or modifying some legal entity or other thing
in order that the client can reach some legitimate goal. Virtually all of this
transactional work involves private rule-making agreements between the
parties, agreements that are usually achieved by the voluntary negotiation
process. These transactional agreements are accomplished through a process that can be characterized in either zero-sum or non-zero-sum terms.

The models of effective lawyer negotiation we recommend in this
chapter can be used in either dispute or transactional matters. "Adversarial" and "competitive" are not model types reserved for dispute resolution matters, and "cooperative" and "problem-solving" approaches are not
the exclusive province of lawyers involved in transactional matters. Nor is
the reverse of those combinations a rule of legal negotiation. There are, as
we shall see, four combinations of negotiating style and strategy that mix
competitive, cooperative, adversarial, and problem-solving techniques.
The important thing to remember at this point is that as an independent
professional agent, you can and should select the bargaining model you
want to use in each case or setting.

B. NEGOTIATING STYLE:
COMPETITIVE AND COOPERATIVE

In this section we discuss negotiating styles. While it is difficult to
draw a bright line between bargaining style and negotiating strategy, the
distinction between these two aspects of the bargaining process is important. When discussing style we will focus on the interpersonal behavior of
the negotiator and identify how that behavior affects the negotiation process. By negotiating strategy, on the other hand, we mean the conceptual
approach adopted by the negotiator, from planning through implementation, to achieve the underlying goals of the client through bargaining.
When discussing strategy we will concentrate on both the theories and tactics of effective negotiation.

As just mentioned, the distinctions between style and strategy are
easily blurred. Indeed, many who have written about the negotiation process have ignored or confused the differences between style and strategy.
As a result, the fundamental choices available to negotiators have been reduced to two. Those choices usually have been labeled as competitive (or
adversarial) and cooperative (or problem-solving). As we shall see, our ap-

proach to legal negotiation will give lawyers the opportunity to select one of four basic models of bargaining.

In an extensive empirical study of lawyer-negotiators, Professor Gerald R. Williams identified two basic bargaining styles: the competitive negotiator and the cooperative negotiator.[1] Williams studied hundreds of lawyers in Denver and Phoenix to isolate the bargaining styles employed in legal negotiations. The study concluded that approximately 60 percent of the lawyers employed a cooperative style and about 40 percent used a competitive style. Within each basic style category, Williams went on to distinguish between effective, average, and ineffective negotiators as measured by results in real and simulated negotiations and by the perceptions of fellow lawyers. Among the attorneys who used a cooperative style, Williams found that more than half were identified as effective, while about one-third were average negotiators and the remainder (about 15 percent) were ineffective in their bargaining. Of the competitive negotiators, about one-quarter were discovered to be effective negotiators, one-half were identified as average bargainers, and the remaining one-fourth were tagged as ineffective.

In identifying the personality traits that make up a distinctive negotiating style, Williams found that effective competitive lawyers are dominating, forceful, attacking, aggressive, ambitious, clever, honest, perceptive, analytical, convincing, and self-controlled. Effective cooperative lawyer-negotiators, on the other hand, were found to be trustworthy, fair, honest, courteous, personable, tactful, sincere, perceptive, reasonable, convincing, and self-controlled.[2]

Williams' study of lawyer-negotiators appears consistent with studies of nonlawyer-negotiators. Nonlawyer-negotiators appear to fall into the same two style classifications. Cooperative nonlawyer-bargainers are reported as favoring abstract thinking, tolerating ambiguity, disliking authoritarianism, accepting ethical flexibility, having a positive view of self, and exhibiting trustfulness and trustworthiness. The same studies indicate that competitive negotiators tend to have Machiavellian attitudes, to be suspicious, and to hold negative views of self.

The observed negotiating behavior of lawyers with cooperative and competitive styles fits with the characteristics identified in the Williams study. Williams found that cooperative negotiators move psychologically

---

1. G. Williams, *Effective Negotiation and Settlement* (1981). In his report of the study, Williams uses the term "aggressive" rather than "competitive" as the primary category label. We have adopted the latter term because most negotiation researchers and writers seem to prefer "competitive" as the descriptive word. We note that Professor Williams is one of those who has ignored the distinctions between style and strategy. Throughout his book he interchanges the two words and quite often uses them in the disjunctive.

2. While ineffective lawyers of both styles possess some of the characteristics of their effective counterparts, they have some traits that set them apart and, presumably, account for the difference in classification as measured by outcome and perception by others. For example, the style of ineffective competitives includes the following traits: irritating, argumentative, quarrelsome, unreasonable, demanding, headstrong, rigid, arrogant, intolerant, and hostile. Ineffective cooperatives are trustful, sociable, friendly, obliging, gentle, and forgiving.

toward an opponent, trying to create a reasonable image of self and a strong image of the other party. Cooperative attorneys seek common ground and shared interests by establishing a positive atmosphere of understanding and creativity. The competitive attorney-negotiators, on the other hand, move psychologically *against* the other party with behavior designed to un-nerve opponents and to take advantage of them wherever possible. Com-petitive bargainers create a self-image of shrewdness and try to establish a tense, defensive, and conflictive negotiating atmosphere.

Competitive styles and cooperative styles both have strengths and weaknesses. For example, Williams found that in some cases, particularly complex ones, a competitive style results in more favorable outcomes than those produced by a cooperative strategy. Not surprisingly, that outcome advantage is maximized when the effective competitive is matched against an ineffective cooperative. Moreover, because competitives are suspicious of all opponents and are unlikely to be too "soft," they are less likely to give away too much of that which they have deemed to be important. There are, however, disadvantages that tend to accompany competitive style bargain-ing. As Williams discovered, the style generates tension and encourages negotiator distrust. As a result, opponents are induced to take retaliatory action, misunderstanding between the parties increases, and deadlock is more likely to occur.

The cooperative style, on the other hand, is not without its own weak-nesses. The natural tendency of the cooperative negotiator is to be tolerant even when being exploited by an opponent. Being too slow to respond to exploitation, Williams found, can lead to poorer outcomes for cooperative bargainers. The flipside of tolerance of an opponent is the tendency of co-operatives to be too generous, making concession after concession in an attempt to persuade an opponent to be morally or socially responsible. Fi-nally, according to Williams, when cooperatives eventually decide to act in the aftermath of exploitation and overgenerosity, they tend to overreact and to assume much more disagreement between the parties than actually exists.

There are clear advantages, however, to a cooperative style of negotiat-ing. As it encourages mutual understanding, a cooperative style reduces the risk of deadlock. Moreover, concluded Williams, the resulting agree-ments take less time to achieve than agreements produced by competitive means. Perhaps more important, Williams found that the effective use of a cooperative style regularly produced a higher joint outcome for the parties. Indeed, cooperation often produced a higher individual outcome even when only one party was using the cooperative approach.

The results of Professor Williams' study are not startling because they mirror other studies of negotiation. His work, however, is of great impor-tance to lawyer-negotiators. It confirms that there are at least two distinct negotiating styles available to attorneys. The study also highlights the ad-vantages and disadvantages of each bargaining style, thus alerting lawyers to factors that deserve emphasis or avoidance. Armed with this knowledge, you are in a better position to exercise your choice of negotiating style on a case-by-case basis.

C. NEGOTIATING STRATEGY: ADVERSARIAL AND PROBLEM-SOLVING

In her seminal article, Toward Another View of Legal Negotiation: The Structure of Problem Solving,[3] Professor Carrie Menkel-Meadow identified and developed fully the strategic choices that are presented here. Fundamental to choosing between the two options of adversarial or problem-solving is an understanding that strategy selection initially involves a planning process aimed at identifying the underlying goals of the bargaining process. In this sense, the choice of strategy is akin to the counseling process described extensively earlier in this book. Once the underlying goals of the negotiation are clear, the lawyer selects the fundamental bargaining model, either adversarial or problem-solving, as those strategies are described in this chapter. Finally, when the strategy has been selected, it is matched with one of the two negotiating styles described in the preceding section to form an integrated style and strategy approach to the negotiation. Thereafter, the attorney selects the tactics to implement the chosen style and strategy during the assessment, persuasion, and exchange stages of negotiation.

Professor Menkel-Meadow describes the adversarial strategy as the traditional or usual legal negotiation model. It is one that has as its goal the maximizing of gain by the party employing it. An adversarial strategy is truly a zero-sum game, one in which the gains of one party equal the losses of the other party and the resulting balance sheet always equals zero. In identifying the goals of an adversarial strategy, the entire negotiation—and, quite often, each issue in the negotiation—is conceived of as being a fungible item (such as money or units of production). Indeed, if an issue is not composed of fungible matter (e.g., the pain suffered by a plaintiff in a personal injury suit or a party's emotional distress resulting from action taken by another party), the lawyer adopting an adversarial strategy will convert that issue into a fungible commodity, usually money. Once negotiation issues are conceptualized as fungible items, the adversarial strategy dictates placing them along a continuum so that each dollar, unit of production, or other item is exactly like any other dollar, unit, or item. Having accomplished that, adversarial negotiators can engage in a process of movement along the continuum (generally called concessions), attempting to get as much money or as many units on their side of the bargaining table as possible. Of course, each dollar or unit that is gained by one negotiator is taken away from, and becomes a loss to, the other negotiator.

A problem-solving strategy involves substantially different goals than does the operative process of maximizing gain inherent in the adversarial strategy. Once having identified a client's underlying needs, the problem-solving negotiator candidly anticipates and itemizes the needs of the other party. Once the needs of both parties have been developed, the problem solver refuses to convert them into fungible commodities that inevitably

---

3. 31 U.C.L.A. L. Rev. 754 (1984).

will be divided through a zero-sum process. Instead, a problem-solving strategy forces the lawyer-negotiator to develop solutions that satisfy the client's needs and accommodate the needs of the other party. The process of meeting mutual needs may take a variety of forms. Professor Menkel-Meadow explains, for example, that the nonconflicting needs of the parties may be traded; that is, one party receives what it wants from the other side and, in return, that party provides the other side with what it needs. Or, where needs conflict directly and cannot be exchanged, the negotiators search for ways to expand the total resources available for exchange by the parties; that is, the game is converted from zero-sum to non-zero-sum where there is more for the parties to divide, increasing the likelihood that both will have their underlying needs satisfied.

D. STYLE AND STRATEGY COMBINATIONS

Now that you have an understanding of cooperative and competitive negotiating styles and have been introduced to the elements involved in adversarial and problem-solving strategies, you should not conclude that negotiators *always* match a competitive style with an adversarial strategy or that cooperative bargainers *always* adopt a problem-solving approach. A lawyer with a cooperative style, one who is courteous, personable, and friendly, may very effectively adopt an adversarial strategy designed to destroy an opponent's confidence and induce in the opponent a series of unilateral concessions of some fungible item, such as money. On the other hand, a competitive negotiator may use a dominating, forceful, and clever style to implement a limited problem-solving strategy where the opponent is convinced to accept a solution that meets some of the opponent's needs but also maximizes the competitive problem-solving negotiator's gain.

Professor Menkel-Meadow developed a two-by-two matrix similar to that at the top of page 395, which allows us to visualize the interplay between bargaining styles and negotiating strategies.[4]

What happens when you combine one of the bargaining styles with a negotiating strategy? What resulting conduct will you observe in a lawyer-negotiator who has adopted a particular combination? What behavior are you likely to exhibit if you opt for one as opposed to another match-up of

---

4. Id. at 818. We have adopted the graphic form used by Professor Menkel-Meadow to communicate the relationships between Competitive/Cooperative and Adversarial/Problem-Solving. We also have retained the essential meaning of the labels she has attached to each of the four cells. Professor Menkel-Meadow, however, does not identify her rows and columns as Style and Strategy, but as Ends and Means. Her conceptualization of the interchange of the two basic concepts is quite different than the one we present here. Indeed, Professor Menkel-Meadow apparently adheres to the view that style and strategy are interchangeable terms and are equivalent to that which she has identified as Means. See id. at 758. Her description of Ends as "goals of a particular negotiation" appears closer to our view of counseling and too narrow for our needs in describing the lawyer negotiation process. This is not to say that Professor Menkel-Meadow's conceptualization of problem-solving negotiation is any less a major breakthrough in the literature on lawyer bargaining.

STRATEGY

		Adversarial	*Problem-Solving*
	Competitive	Rigid positions, hard bargaining	Limit consideration of needs, solutions
BARGAINING STYLE			
	Cooperative	Concessions and compromise	Open consideration of needs, solutions

style and strategy? Try to describe the manner and tactics of each of the four combinations. Once you have done so, read the brief descriptions we give below and compare them with your specifications of negotiation tactics and demeanor.

1. Competitive Adversarials

When a competitive style is combined with an adversarial strategy, lawyer-negotiators adopt a total negotiating approach, which can only be described as very rigid and marked by hard bargaining. Competitive adversarials try to dominate any bargaining session by, among other things, controlling the agenda and defining the formulation of the issues. These negotiators attack aggressively any position advanced by an opponent and defend vigorously all claims asserted on behalf of their clients. The high aspirational levels of most competitive adversarials will be evidenced by unreasonably high/low opening demands/offers. Their ambitious opening is often followed by such hardball tactics as "take it or leave it" or few concessions grudgingly given, or bluffs, threats, personal characterizations, and other high-risk techniques that increase the likelihood of deadlock. The adversarial strategy of pursuing the maximum possible gain[5] is carried out in a tense, competitive atmosphere. If this strategy-style combination predominates in the negotiation, a zero-sum outcome is preordained.

2. Cooperative Adversarials

A subtle change can be observed when the adversarial strategy is merged with the cooperative style. While the fundamental strategy adopted by these negotiators is virtually indistinguishable from that used by their competitive colleagues, their demeanor appears quite different. Cooperative adversarials are friendly and courteous, not belligerent; are trustworthy

---

5. The competitive adversarial focuses on doing better than the opponent. Thus, the goal of the competitive adversarial appears to be to maximize the difference between the parties, attempting to accumulate as much of the resource in question as possible while allowing the opponent as little of it as possible.

and trustful, not suspicious; and are logical and tactful, not domineering. The change in style may mask the fact that negotiators incorporating this mixture strive for favorable zero-sum outcomes, trying to maximize the gain for their clients by increasing the amount of the limited available resources that end up on their side of the negotiation table.[6] Thus, these lawyer-bargainers, focused on the differences between the parties and following the linear distribution model, can be expected to open with a high/low demand/offer, but not a patently unreasonable one; to appear committed to positions; to try to induce unilateral concessions on the part of opponents but be willing to make a limited number of concessions "in the spirit of compromise"; and, when necessary, to use threats, but not deliver them in the quarrelsome manner of competitive negotiators.

3. Competitive Problem Solvers

Another dramatic change occurs in moving from cooperative adversarial to competitive problem-solving. The style reverts to the more harsh, competitive tones—the negotiators are demanding, forceful, and clever. But instead of characterizing the issues as fungible commodities cast along a continuum, these negotiators formulate the issues as problems that must be solved instead of resources that must be divided. In other words, competitive problem solvers will articulate the needs of their clients and seek to identify the needs of opponents. Competitive problem solvers are not likely, however, to be completely candid in itemizing the needs of the parties. Instead, the controlling, aggressive style of the competitive problem solvers is used to manipulate the statement of the underlying needs of the parties and to convince the opponent that only their formulation of the joint needs is acceptable. In doing so, competitive problem solvers may advance feigned needs and discount legitimate needs of their opponents. Once the needs acceptable to the competitive problem solvers are in the open, these negotiators attempt to use existing resources or create additional resources to meet all or most of the identified needs. At this stage, the competitive style of these negotiators emerges again as they attempt to limit the number of solutions to be applied to the problems articulated. Not surprisingly, most of the solutions favor their clients. Thus, the competitive problem solver will dismiss as inadequate certain apparent solutions because they do not provide the bargainer's client with a positive advantage.[7]

---

6. Negotiators with this combination have been labeled as individualistic negotiators by J. A. Rubin & B. R. Brown, *The Social Psychology of Bargaining and Negotiations* (1975). Thus, the cooperative adversarial tries to maximize the gain for its client without regard for whether that results in more or less for the opponent.

7. The competitive problem solver is similar to the cooperative adversarial in distributive goals. The competitive problem solver works to maximize the client's gains. Though this negotiator superficially may appear to be deeply concerned about the opponent's benefits, in reality the problem solver has little regard for the gains and losses of the other party. If the opponent prospers, so be it; if the opponent is unsuccessful, so be it.

4. *Cooperative Problem Solvers*

Cooperative problem solvers are the most open and candid of the four types of negotiator combinations. Even though these negotiators are appropriately reluctant to reveal sensitive information that an opponent could use as leverage against them (see the discussion in the next chapter), cooperative problem solvers are willing to volunteer more about their clients' real underlying needs than are competitive problem solvers. Also, unlike their competitive problem-solving colleagues, these bargainers do not attempt to discount or dismiss the legitimate needs of their opponents. Finally, cooperative problem solvers willingly discuss all potential solutions to the problems of the parties, even those solutions that, if values were totaled up, give more resources to the opponents and less to them.[8] Cooperative problem solvers create a positive atmosphere in the negotiation by looking honestly for the common ground and the shared interests of the parties instead of highlighting differences. The style of cooperative problem solvers communicates that they trust their opponents and that they, in turn, expect to be and are worthy of trust.

E. EXAMPLES OF THE STYLE-STRATEGY COMBINATIONS

This section provides additional insights into the differences among the various types of lawyer-negotiators, by presenting each of them "in action," so to speak. We reproduce here excerpts from two negotiations of "Wendy's Way and Robert Gordon,"[9] a combination dispute/transactional matter between a franchiser and a franchisee. The problem opens with background information, then two subsections recreate aspects of the negotiation by lawyers representing the parties. Each of the negotiation scenes depicts a different style-strategy combination and is based on an actual negotiation of the problem by lawyers or law students.

We realize that a transcript of an excerpt of a negotiation cannot communicate the breadth and depth of information available if one were to actually observe the bargaining session. The nonverbal communication and the pace, pitch, tone, and volume that add so much to our understanding is totally missing. Nonetheless, as you read the two transcripts, try to identify the style and strategy combinations depicted. Isolate what it is about each negotiation that leads to your conclusion. Further break down the factors that influence your identification by classifying them as either matters of style or strategy. Remember that the two lawyers within each negotia-

---

8. The cooperative problem solver is the negotiator who truly tries to maximize the joint and mutual gains of the parties to the bargaining.

9. J. Harbaugh, *Lawyer Negotiation Training Materials* 317-369 (1988). The negotiation transcripts that follow are from id. at 358-359, 363-365.

tion may not be using the same style-strategy combination. Be conscious of any differences between the attorneys.

☰ PROBLEM ☰
Wendy's Way and Robert Gordon

Wendy's Way, a relatively new entrant in the multibillion-dollar fast-food market, has grown to the point that it claims about 10 percent of the U.S. fast-food market. Recently, Wendy's Way embarked on an aggressive national advertising campaign with the goal of doubling its market share, thereby putting it in the number two position behind McDonald's. Prominently featured in most of the commercial messages is an explicit statement about the standard prices of Wendy's Way products.

Robert Gordon, an early purchaser of a Wendy's Way franchise, located his franchise on the ground floor of a new and attractive professional building in the center of the business and commercial district of a rapidly growing community. When Gordon began his business ten years ago, the rental cost for his 2,500 square feet was quite low. Two years ago, upon the expiration of the agreement, Gordon and his landlord negotiated a five-year renewal at four times the original rental price. Gordon acknowledges this is a fair and competitive price based on the existing and projected business growth in the area. Although reasonable under the circumstances, this increase in rental costs has altered significantly Gordon's profit calculations.

About fifteen months ago, Gordon began deviating from the Wendy's Way standard prices and balked at participating in the Wendy's Way promotional campaigns. Gordon tagged on an average of 10 percent to most of the standard prices of meals, desserts, and beverages. When Wendy's Way initiated an inquiry, Gordon replied that his adjustments were necessary to maintain a reasonable profit margin given increased rental costs. Shortly thereafter, Wendy's Way began receiving complaints from customers and other franchisees about Gordon's pricing policies and his refusal to honor coupons and nationally advertised price reductions that were part of various promotional programs associated with the advertising campaign.

During this same period, Wendy's Way has been investigating the feasibility of locating another franchise in the same business district, at a new mall within one and one-half miles of Gordon's outlet. When Gordon asked Wendy's Way if it intended to locate a new outlet within his exclusive territory under the franchise agreement, the company confirmed it was considering the matter.

In the last two months, Gordon declined to purchase from Wendy's Way the accessories necessary to operate his fast-food business (e.g., napkins, cups, and food containers bearing the distinctive Wendy's Way logo). Gordon insists he can purchase such items locally at significantly lower rates than those charged by the franchiser. Pursuant to a contract provision, Wendy's Way has refused to approve such purchases until it is convinced that there will be no deviations in the quality of the products and that its trademark is protected in an adequate manner.

Finally, Wendy's Way has also refused to approve Gordon's proposed local advertising because it conflicts with the franchiser's national campaign and it contains references to the higher prices charged by Gordon. While the contract between the two parties refers to the importance of uniformity and cooperation for success in the franchised fast food-business, the document is careful to avoid mandating concerted action because of the antitrust problems of vertical restraint of trade and tie-in agreements.

Gordon is worried that Wendy's Way will exercise its right to terminate him under the franchise agreement. On the other hand, Gordon will fight any termination attempt, including instituting an antitrust action. Moreover, he wants Wendy's Way to stay out of his territory or be prepared to compensate him handsomely for the invasion. On the other side, Wendy's Way wants Gordon, one of its best franchisees, to conform his conduct (pricing, advertising, and purchasing) to the group norm. Wendy's Way is willing to make some concessions to assist Gordon in realizing a reasonable profit. It will insist, however, on locating the new outlet within Gordon's zone. It is in this context that the following negotiation scenes are set.

First Negotiation Excerpt

Wendy's Way: Can we begin by you telling me why Mr. Gordon has decided to deviate from the Wendy's Way standard prices?

Robert Gordon: Pure and simple—profit! Actually, the absence of profit. Because his rent doubled under the new lease, Bob's modest profit disappeared completely. He was working for salary only. Now that he's increased prices, he's able to turn a small but steady profit.

Wendy's Way: Has Mr. Gordon done an analysis of his expenses? I mean has he checked to be sure he can't cut in other areas to ensure a return? You know, instead of boosting prices?

Robert Gordon: Look, Bob Gordon is one of your most experienced and one of your better franchisees. Don't you think he checked all other avenues before embarking on what he called the "calculated risk" of raising prices? As a matter of fact, Bob has reduced his expenses in relation to gross by two percentage points since he increased prices. I know and you know that he's at the low end on expenses as compared to other franchisees. And more important than "how" or "where" Bob is getting his small profit is what Wendy's Way intends to do about it! He has every right to charge what he thinks is appropriate in his business judgment. He doesn't appreciate the regional rep threatening to yank his franchise. And he doesn't appreciate being hassled on his local advertising and the local purchase of his ancillary products. We've advised Bob that any attempt by Wendy's Way to force him to conform prices by threatening to cancel his franchise or by unreasonably refusing to let him exercise his contract rights is vertical price-fixing. Bob won't hesitate to bring an antitrust action if Wendy's Way refuses to back off.

Wendy's Way: We're here to resolve problems, not create them. No one is threatening anything at this point. Wendy's Way wants to know what needs to be done to put Bob Gordon back in the black.

Robert Gordon: He's in the black right now, thank you.

Wendy's Way: I understand that, but he's there at the expense of the entire Wendy's Way organization. Long-term success in the franchise industry depends on cooperation among all franchisees. By upping his prices, particularly during our costly national media campaign, Gordon jeopardizes the collective effort. Other franchisees are complaining that . . .

Robert Gordon: Come on! You can't seriously maintain that one franchisee poses a risk to the thousands of Wendy's Way franchisees who make up the national organization.

Wendy's Way: But it's true. We've had dozens of customer complaints that Gordon is overcharging them; we've had an inquiry from the consumer protection division of the AG's office; there's been a recent article in the trade paper labeling Gordon a "maverick" who's threatening the price advantage Wendy's Way has worked so hard to create. We view this as a serious matter that must be corrected.

Robert Gordon: Well, it can't be corrected by asking Bob Gordon to sacrifice his profits so that Wendy's Way and its other franchisees can maintain their own! It can't be corrected by refusing his legitimate requests under the franchise agreement! And it can't be corrected by threatening his gross sales with an invasion of his exclusive franchise territory!

Second Negotiation Excerpt

Wendy's Way: Let's see if we can agree on what each party needs to reach a satisfactory conclusion. Mr. Gordon must be able to make a reasonable profit, although we haven't defined precisely what that profit must be. As I understand it . . .

Robert Gordon: Oh, we can define what we mean by a reasonable profit!

Wendy's Way: OK, we'll get to that. As I understand it, Mr. Gordon is not wedded to the higher prices or to his other contract demands—local ads and supplies—so long as he maintains a profit margin. Correct?

Robert Gordon: That's right. Profit is the key.

Wendy's Way: Finally, Mr. Gordon believes he's entitled to some compensation if Wendy's Way goes forward with a franchise at the Calvert Street location.

Robert Gordon: Absolutely.

Wendy's Way: OK. On the other hand, Wendy's Way needs to protect its marketing strategy, preserving the comparative price advantage it has built vis-à-vis its competition. To achieve that goal, Wendy's Way wants Mr. Gordon to return to the standard prices and to conform his local advertising to the group approach. It would also like Gordon to continue purchasing his supplies from Wendy's Way and to participate in the corporate promotions. In obtaining this goal, both sides are very conscious of the limitations imposed by the antitrust laws.

Robert Gordon: That's right.

Wendy's Way: Also, because a franchise at Calvert Street will provide Gordon with a long-term advantage, Wendy's Way doesn't see the need for compensating Gordon.

Robert Gordon: With that proposition we take strong exception.

Wendy's Way: I understand your position. But do you understand why not compensating Gordon on the territory question is a need that Wendy's Way has?

Robert Gordon: I've heard what you said about your pattern in the six or so other cases where a franchise has been placed within an exclusive territory. I simply disagree with your reasoning.

Wendy's Way: OK. Let's concentrate on the profit/standard prices issue. Wendy's Way is willing to make some adjustments to preserve Gordon's profits. How much profit does Gordon need?

Robert Gordon: Well, Gordon shouldn't make less profit than Wendy's Way. They're collecting 4 percent of gross, and that's what we believe is a fair return for Bob.

Wendy's Way: OK, you want to tie Bob's profits to the profits of Wendy's Way—right? That's one approach we can consider. Of course, you're assuming that 4 percent is the Wendy's Way profit. In fact, it may be a lot less. The 4 percent figure is the standard franchise fee collected by Wendy's Way. Out of that must come all corporate expenses, such as corporate employee salaries, dividends to stockholders, and the like. I suspect a parity arrangement on profit would yield Gordon a lot less that 4 percent.

Robert Gordon: Oh, I see. Well, why don't we gear it to average franchisee profit. After ten years in the business, Bob should expect the high end of that. Let's use the 3 percent figure.

Wendy's Way: All right, let's use average profits. Three percent is the high end and applies to those franchisees who have low fixed costs. And we'll have to take into account . . . .

F. SELECTION OF A STYLE-STRATEGY COMBINATION

On the subject of choosing a combination of lawyer style and strategy, we want to emphasize two important points. First, we do not believe that a particular merger of style and strategy is better than any other combination. Second, the selection of a combination during the pre-negotiation planning stage does not mean that a lawyer-negotiator must maintain that union of style and strategy for an entire negotiation. Each of these propositions deserves some explanation.

Many experts on lawyer negotiation are identified with a particular model or theory of effective bargaining. There are those experts who believe that only adversarial bargaining fits with the traditional model of the lawyer as advocate and will produce outcomes that achieve client goals. Some experts in this group go so far as to say that a competitive/adversarial blend is preferred because it is likely to maximize client gains. On the other hand, a significant number of scholars argue that only a problem-solving strategy will meet client needs on a consistent basis. Within this group, some assert that only cooperative problem-solving is acceptable because only it is designed to meet the significant needs of all parties.

Our presentation of four combinations of style and strategy suggests that we are uncomfortable with any recommendation that a particular negotiation model will serve you well in any and every bargaining situation. Indeed, we believe you should select the mixture of style and strategy best suited to the circumstances and setting of your negotiation.[10] Factors you should consider in selecting the negotiation model include:

1. The goals of the client and the needs of the opposing party. For example, if the client's only goal is to obtain as much of the only fungible commodity at issue as is possible, then an adversarial strategy is likely to produce the greater gain. On the other hand, if a continuing relationship between the parties is their primary aim, problem-solving may be more appropriate.

2. The configuration of shared, independent, and conflicting needs of the parties. For example, if the needs of the parties do not conflict but are shared or independent, it suggests that a cooperative problem-solving strategy could be very successful.

3. The resources, including money, personnel, time, and the like, available to your client and to the opposing party.

4. The ability of the parties to creatively generate additional issues and resources to expand the subject matter of the negotiation. The greater the number of issues and the amount of resources involved in the negotiation, the easier it is to move from adversarial to problem-solving.

5. The comfort or discomfort you (and your client) experience when you behave as a competitive versus cooperative bargainer. While we encourage you to experiment with the four unions of style and strategy, we acknowledge it is difficult to successfully use a negotiation model with which you are uncomfortable. Your client's needs must also be considered. The angry client in a wrongful death case, for instance, may not be satisfied with a cooperative problem-solving approach.

6. The style and strategy combination selected by your opponent. Professor Williams, for example, found that effective competitive negotiators were quite successful when matched with cooperative bargainers.[11]

---

10. For example, Professor Menkel-Meadow, an articulate advocate of problem-solving negotiation, candidly admits that the model is difficult if not impossible to operate in "strict pricing problems, or a situation requiring a definite and authoritative ruling." Thus, in a situation where one party's sole interest is to obtain the highest price for an item and the other party's only goal is to pay the least amount of money, Professor Menkel-Meadow concedes that problem-solving is likely to be an unacceptable strategy. To be sure, Professor Menkel-Meadow also argues that there are few pure pricing negotiations and in many of those cases additional issues can be created to make problem-solving a viable bargaining alternative. Menkel-Meadow, Toward Another View of Legal Negotiation: The Structure of Problem Solving, 31 U.C.L.A. L. Rev. 754, 785 n.120 (1984).

11. Professor Menkel-Meadow has an extensive list of factors that one might consider when deciding between competitive and cooperative styles, some of which are included in our list. Id. at 828 n.288.

Is a style and strategy combination binding once it is selected? You are aware, of course, of the emphasis we have placed on planning before interviewing, counseling, or negotiating as a lawyer. Planning implies that when a plan is thoughtfully organized and mapped out, it ought to be carried through to its conclusion. On the other hand, we also have stressed flexibility, the need to respond to the factual, legal, and interpersonal situations presented by client or opponent. Our view of how fettered a negotiator should be by his or her style and strategy choice straddles these potentially conflicting concepts of planning and flexibility.

Negotiation plans ought to be pursued long enough to test the hypotheses on which the plans were based. If not, the time and creative energies expended in planning would be wasted. Thus, if you have determined to follow a cooperative adversarial approach in bargaining over the sales price of a business, it should be pressed to the point where gains have diminished, if not disappeared, and deadlock appears possible. But negotiation plans should be abandoned and alternatives sought when it is clear that the bargaining design was based on inaccurate or inappropriate information or that the intended purposes are not being achieved.

We are mindful that some experts on negotiation have postulated a strategic-choice model of bargaining. The strategic-choice concept suggests that negotiators constantly find themselves in the position of choosing among making a cooperative, unilateral concession, proposing a problem-solving solution, engaging in competitive adversarial behavior, or selecting another conduct combination at every stage and with every issue in the negotiation. Having observed hundreds of lawyers and law students engaged in real and simulated negotiations, we have reached the conclusion that most attorneys apply a sort of rough strategic-choice model. For example, many attorneys we have observed appear to begin the bargaining as cooperative adversarials; if linear concessions do not produce a settlement, the lawyers shift to competitive problem-solving; and, finally, once they have identified a problem-solving formula for settlement, they return to the cooperative adversarial approach to maximize gain and minimize loss. We do not endorse this shifting but, in fact, very rigid model of negotiation. We cite our experience, however, as support for the proposition that movement among models during bargaining is a common and acceptable approach. Indeed, flexibility in negotiation style and strategy is a process we heartily support.

What all of this suggests is that as a lawyer-negotiator you should examine each issue in the negotiation and decide which style and strategy package ought to be adopted to facilitate an agreement acceptable to your client. Upon examination, you may conclude that a single bargaining model can be pursued. Then again, you may reason that certain issues require a particular combination while others deserve different configurations of style and strategy. Finally, you should consider which alternative ought to prevail if your planned style-strategy approach proves unsatisfactory. Considering how you will measure the effectiveness of your plan and the possible options enhances flexibility yet preserves the value inherent in detailed preparation.

G. CONCLUSION

To be an effective lawyer-negotiator in any particular case, you must be able to conceptualize a sound negotiating theory, a theory that is consistent with the client goals identified during counseling. Creating that theory in a given setting requires the selection of the most appropriate negotiating strategy and bargaining style. You must be able to identify the available strategies and styles and you must understand what behavior is likely to follow from the choice of a certain combination. Only when you have decided upon your negotiating strategy and style can you turn your attention to specific tactics. Without a sensible conceptual framework, even proven negotiating maneuvers will be of little avail. By exploring the implications of adversarial and problem-solving negotiation and considering the behavioral aspects of competitive and cooperative styles, you will gain the confidence to select the combination appropriate for your negotiation situation.

17

The Assessment Stage

A. INTRODUCTION

Although almost all negotiations go through phases or stages that have relatively clear and identifiable characteristics, the experts cannot seem to agree on either the number of stages or the nomenclature to be applied to these stages.[1] We have nevertheless chosen the staging breakdown of one of those experts[2] because we believe it best captures the essential planning and implementation processes of lawyer negotiation. That expert asserts, and we agree, that negotiation consists of assessment, persuasion, and exchange phases. The remainder of this book analyzes each of these three stages in the negotiation process. Our examination includes commentary on both the planning and the action levels of bargaining. During our discussion of the three stages, we will distinguish between adversarial and problem-solving strategies when that is appropriate.

---

1. See, e.g., C. Craver, *Effective Legal Negotiation and Settlement* (1986) (information, competitive-distributive, and cooperative phases); D. Gifford, *Legal Negotiation: Theory and Application* (1989) (planning, orientation, initial proposals, information bargaining, narrowing of differences, and closure); B. Scott, *The Skill of Negotiating* (1981) (exploration, bidding, bargaining, settling, and ratifying); G. Williams, *Effective Negotiation and Settlement* (1981) (Stage One: Orientation and Positioning; Stage Two: Argumentation, Compromise, and Search for Alternative Solutions; and Stage Three: Crisis, Wrap-Up, or Deadlock); I. Zartman & W. Berman, *The Practical Negotiator* (1982) (diagnostic, formula, and detail phases).

2. R. Condlin, Cases on Both Sides: Patterns of Argument in Legal Dispute-Negotiation, 44 U. Md. L. Rev. 65, 67, 67 n.6 (1985).

By identifying negotiation's stages and placing them in a specified order, we do not want to mislead you. While, generally, negotiations tend to proceed in the order given—that is, beginning with assessment, moving to persuasion, and concluding with exchange—the stages also tend to intertwine. Thus, during assessment, the negotiators may well be trying to persuade each other; while engaged in persuasion, negotiators may propose an exchange of fungible or nonfungible items; and during an explicit exchange, the parties may be primarily engaged in an appraisal of the opponent's value structure. In sum, negotiation is fluid and negotiators should be flexible, prepared to follow the winding ways of bargaining.

Before turning to the first of the three negotiation stages, we must remind you about the importance of planning and its relationship to implementation. In Chapter 1 we emphasized that to be successful as a lawyer in the use of interpersonal skills you must conscientiously prepare. That is certainly the case with negotiation. Identifying goals, probing for information gaps, developing reasons, and creating an acceptable exchange structure all require preparation in terms of time, detail, and thoroughness. We have found that if the groundwork for negotiation is adequate then implementation follows naturally. That is, effective technique is a by-product of sound planning based, in turn, on a solid conceptual foundation. Technique without theory and tactics without preparation are seldom successful. Therefore, our focus will be on negotiation preparation and, in that context, our position on various tactics will be obvious.

B. ASSESSMENT: THE INFORMATION STAGE

The study and observation of negotiations involving lawyers and other bargaining professionals suggest strongly that control of the critical information during the assessment stage is one of the keys to negotiation success. That should not surprise you. It seems obvious that the side that learns more about the opponent, communicates better the facts it wants known, and better prevents the opponent from learning about its own weaknesses is likely to have an outcome advantage at the end of the bargaining. Yet that measure of the importance of information to negotiating success applies only to adversarial strategy; that is, the adversarial bargainer who controls information "more" and "better" gains an advantage in a zero-sum environment. Is information as important to a problem-solving negotiator? We believe mastery of the available information can dramatically affect outcomes obtained by problem-solving bargainers. While not necessarily the only or the most important factor, effective information exchange leads to the discovery and acceptance of integrative solutions, outcomes that are more likely to meet the needs of all of the parties.[3]

Both adversarial and problem-solving negotiators should concentrate on the information exchange process that forms the assessment stage. Dur-

---

3. D. Pruitt & S. Lewis, The Psychology of Integrative Bargaining, in *Negotiations: Social-Psychological Perspectives* 161, 170-171 (D. Druckman ed. 1977).

ing this stage, the parties share information and assess each other. While giving and receiving information in what sometimes may appear to be only small talk or preliminary bargaining, the parties actually engage in a critical evaluation of one another. Professor Condlin describes the process in this way:

> In assessment a negotiator identifies the principal meaning of an adversary's communication, determines whether it accurately predicts what the adversary will do, and measures the importance the adversary attaches to the predicted behavior. Call these the questions of meaning, trustworthiness and valuation. Because these questions are about topics that have strategic importance, answers must be discovered indirectly [by the negotiators], on the basis of circumstantial evidence, and usually as an interpretive by-product of a discussion about the substance of the dispute [or the transaction].[4]

Thus, in the assessment stage, you evaluate the style and substance of your opponents' communications to decide what the opponents mean when they describe historical facts, assert legal positions, or comment on other matters important to the negotiation. Likewise, you evaluate opponents' communications to decide under what circumstances and with what caveats you will believe them. Finally, you evaluate opposing negotiators' declarations to decide what they and their clients value highly and not so highly. You must remember, of course, that while you are amassing circumstantial evidence to answer the questions of meaning, trustworthiness, and valuation, your opponent is conducting an identical examination of your communication style. This information interchange, which begins with the first contact between negotiators and continues through to settlement or deadlock, constitutes the first critical phase of bargaining, the assessment stage.

C. THE MEANING, ROLE, AND MANAGEMENT OF INFORMATION

It is impossible to catalog all that is included within the term "information" as it relates to legal negotiations. Simply stated, information in a particular negotiation is anything that relates in any conceivable way to the matter being bargained or to the parties to the bargaining, both principals and their legal representatives. Information, then, is negotiation-specific and must be understood in its broadest sense. In every negotiation, information must include all relevant historical facts relating to the matter being negotiated. Thus, depending on the case, information may include financial data, business history, medical records, work experiences, past conduct, trade practices, economic studies, event chronologies, personal reputations, and family traditions. In addition to the retrospective focus of

---

4. Cases on Both Sides: Patterns of Argument in Legal Dispute-Negotiation, 44 U. Md. L. Rev. 65, 67-68 (1985).

historical evidence, negotiation information includes details of a prospective and attitudinal nature. Thus, the negotiator must prepare for an information exchange covering the needs, goals, plans, resources, options, emotions, fears, strengths, and weaknesses of the principals and their lawyers.

When the key element—information—of the first critical phase of negotiation—the assessment stage—is defined so broadly as to be virtually measureless, how does a negotiator go about bringing the element under control? Is there a conceptual foundation on which you can base your planning for the information exchange? Can the substance of the assessment stage be divided into segments so you can more easily work with it?

With an understanding of the role it plays in the process, you can place negotiation information in manageable categories. Remember that, from a conceptual perspective, information in a negotiation is the subject of explicit and implicit bargaining by the lawyers. Knowingly and unknowingly, they gather, give, and guard information relevant to the bargaining process. As they assess their respective bargaining power, the negotiating parties are constantly making critical decisions about the information they will share, the form in which it will be shared, and what information they will demand that others share in return. To prepare for the assessment stage and gain control over the information-bargaining process, you need to plan for each of the tasks of getting, giving, and guarding information.

The first step in planning is to divide a paper into three columns. Label these columns as follows: Information We Need; Information We Must Protect; and Information We Want to Give. Next, using a broad and negotiation-specific definition of information, analyze and then place the data in the case into one of these three categories. All the information relevant to the case that you have or must obtain will fit into one of the three columns. To make the information fit properly, you will have to combine parts, subdivide others, recategorize some, and prioritize all of it. But once you have positioned all of the relevant information into one of the columns, you will have your agenda for the assessment stage of the negotiation.

≣≣≣ **PROBLEM 1** ≣≣≣
Creating the Information Agenda

Set forth below is background information in the matter of Eugene Weber.[5] Assume that you are the lawyer who wrote the following file memo and that you represent Weber in a forthcoming negotiation with Jones &

---

5. The Weber-Jones & Jones problem is based on a teaching videotape included in J. Harbaugh, *Lawyer Negotiation Training Materials: The Basics of Negotiation Video* (Practising Law Institute 1988), and available in an expanded version in J. Harbaugh, *Basics of Negotiation* (video, Practising Law Institute 1984). The problem is a particularly good example because it combines a dispute with a transaction and because it can be negotiated effectively using either an adversarial or a problem-solving strategy. Therefore, we will use this problem several times in the chapters on negotiation to illustrate the theories and concepts, and the tactics and techniques, of lawyer bargaining. You will want to refer back to the information contained in the following memo several times as you deal with aspects of the Weber-Jones & Jones problem.

Jones, the firm that bought the WEBCo business from Weber two years ago. Based on the material contained in the memo, create an information agenda for the assessment stage. As you fill in the columns relating to getting, giving, and protecting information, prioritize the items in each category.

MEMORANDUM

To: Eugene Weber File

FROM: Attorney

We have agreed to represent Eugene Weber, age 57, in establishing a new business to be known as Executive Counseling Service. The usual business planning matters must be set aside until we can resolve a potential dispute with Jones & Jones.

Until two years ago, Weber was the president and principal stockholder in a closed corporation (Weber's wife was the other owner) known as WEBCo (Weber Employment Bureau Company), an employment agency that served clients in the five-county metropolitan area. After serving as personnel director for a large manufacturer of appliances for six years, Weber began the WEBCo business 15 years ago. The business prospered as the area expanded its high-tech industries and Weber was able to capitalize on his experience and his contacts with the leaders of the commercial and corporate community. In the end, WEBCo handled a substantial portion of the employment needs of virtually all of the area's major employers, particularly at the executive, professional, and technical levels.

Jones & Jones is the largest nationwide employment placement firm with branches in most major population centers in 33 states. Jones often penetrates new geographical markets by acquiring existing local employment agencies and converting them into operating units of the Jones organization. That is the pattern it followed with Weber, approaching him and reaching an agreement on a buy-out of WEBCo. Weber agreed to sell because his wife had encouraged him to retire early and enjoy life and because he feared that if he did not sell, Jones would enter the market in competition with him.

Jones paid Weber $875,000 for the business, $115,000 of which was allocated to a noncompetition clause in the assets purchase agreement. That clause reads as follows:

> "Seller agrees that for a period of ten years he will not, directly or indirectly, engage in the business of or own, manage, invest in, be employed by, or participate in any other way in any business directly or indirectly engaging in employment placement within [thirteen named states]."

Weber was represented at the closing by an attorney who has since died. Jones was and is represented by John Frank, a member of a large local firm. While our firm has had dealings with Frank's firm, none of us has dealt directly with Mr. Frank.

Weber says that although he negotiated with Jones about the ultimate price and some other matters, he doesn't recall how the allocation to the noncompetition clause was made except that it had something to do with taxes. He believes that inclusion of a noncompetition clause itself was "standard" in all of Jones's acquisition agreements. Weber doesn't know why the thirteen states are listed because he never did business of any kind in half of those named. In fact, the only business he did in any jurisdiction other than our own was to advertise for executive, professional, and technical workers interested in relocating in the metropolitan area.

Weber now wants to start Executive Counseling Services (ECS), a business that will advise, instruct, and retrain executive and professional people who, because of layoffs or interests, want to take advantage of new jobs in a rapidly changing economy. Weber claims that the proposed new business is significantly different from WEBCo and, therefore, it shouldn't be covered by the noncompetition clause. He cites as distinguishing ECS features the fee involved (will be a substantial flat fee up to $10,000, rather than a percentage of salary); the structure of the relationship (will represent individuals seeking a new job, not businesses looking for employees); the duration of the relationship (will represent client up to five years after obtaining a new job, instead of short period until employee finds job); and the work involved (will include career and psychological counseling, resume drafting, interviewing style, and the like, but it will not include finding a job for the client). It has been difficult getting Weber to understand that Jones may not share his view on the nonapplicability of the clause to ECS. Jones may be particularly concerned about his plans because Weber reports there are rumors that Jones is thinking about experimenting with adjunct counseling centers attached to some of their placement offices.

Another apparent distinction is that Weber claims he wants to start this business for his son, Bobby, age 28, who is about to graduate from an MBA program. The son has an undergraduate degree in industrial psychology and worked as a personnel counselor for a large business before going back to school. Weber claims he has no intention of being involved in the day-to-day operation of the new business, although he intends to advise and guide Bobby and give him the benefit of Weber's long-time business experience and contacts in the community.

I must say I am skeptical about Weber's claim of noninvolvement with ECS. I believe Weber is bored with retirement and is just itching to get back in business. Perhaps more important, Weber apparently dissipated a significant portion of his nest egg through bad investments and market fluctuations. I am convinced he needs to replenish his funds. That view is reinforced by our discussion of financing the new business and the amount he is willing to pay Jones for a buy-out from the noncompete clause.

Research on the law of noncompetition clauses in our jurisdiction leads to the following conclusions. Because noncompetition clauses are a restraint on trade, our courts hold such a clause can extend only for the time and under the circumstances necessary to protect the buyer of the business. We apply a reasonableness rule as it relates to the scope, duration, and area encompassed in the clause. I am concerned we would not prevail in litigation because the courts also adopt the "blue pencil" approach. Under the "blue pencil" method, if the court finds the seller's new business is covered by the clause but the time is too long or the prohibited area too large, it will rewrite the contract provision to make it reasonable. Thus, if "executive counseling" is covered by the term "employment placement," a court could reduce the period to less than ten years or eliminate some of the thirteen states, but Weber would still be effectively precluded from operating his business.

At a counseling session with Weber, we reviewed the above information. Weber rejected filing a declaratory judgment action and beginning the business with the possibility Jones would seek an injunction. He did so because we concluded a court action was too costly and too risky. Weber also rejected starting ECS outside the prohibited geographic area or beginning a totally unrelated venture. He did that because his business contacts are here, and neither he nor his son has expertise in any other field. In the end, Weber decided to negotiate with Jones on beginning ECS and, if necessary, pay Jones for the privilege. He authorized me to spend not more than $28,000 for the buy-out. Although I believe that is an unrealistic figure, Weber claims that more than that amount will mean he does not have sufficient funds for start-up expenses.

―――――――――――――――

With your assessment agenda in the Weber problem in front of you, something we discussed earlier is now obvious. The game theorists' assumption of perfect information is manifestly a false premise. Even with all the preparation that has gone into the creation of your agenda, the best you have been able to achieve is what the bargaining theorists call "confident expectations." Because you do not have complete or perfect information about the other side's needs, fears, and the like, you cannot fully predict or anticipate the actions of your adversary representing Jones & Jones.[6] Thus, no matter how effective your pre-negotiation preparation is, there will always be information you need to confirm or to contradict your planned bargaining strategy and tactics.

That extensive pre-negotiation planning does not guarantee absolute control over the assessment stage does not reduce the importance of preparation. It does mean, however, that the creation of the information agenda cannot close the book on the work in advance of assessment. Because you are subject to the opponent's maneuvering during negotiation, you

―――――――――――――――

6. S. Bacharach & E. Lawlor, *Bargaining* 208 (1981). As the authors note, the absence of perfect information means that you are subject to manipulation by the opponent, including bluffs, deceptions, threats, and promises.

must devise detailed plans to implement the information agenda. Implementation plans increase the likelihood that you will effectively acquire, give, and protect information, thereby reducing your opponent's ability to manipulate.

D. OVERCOMING SOME NATURAL TENDENCIES

Before we more thoroughly discuss how to plan to get, give, and block the information set out in your assessment agenda, a brief but relevant aside is in order. We have noticed two tendencies among lawyers that can interfere with two of these three information tasks. First, many attorneys do not like to ask certain questions. Second, most attorneys answer questions.

Dr. Samuel Johnson once noted, "Questioning is not the mode of conversation among gentlemen" (and, we add, gentlewomen). That observation explains the many lawyers who are uncomfortable asking questions that seek sensitive information or that may cause another embarrassment. As a result, these attorneys either avoid such inquiries altogether or preface the question with an apology, thereby inviting an evasion or a refusal to answer. This tendency obviously hinders obtaining needed information from the other side.

As a group, lawyers are high achievers. At a young age, these high achievers learned to give information in response to questioning. Many future lawyers could be seen in the primary grades waving their arms wildly in the hope of answering the teacher's question and receiving an appropriate commendation. Answering fully and honestly is a habit developed early and nurtured throughout a lawyer's academic career. It is a habit, however, that can impede the protecting of sensitive information from the probes of an opponent.

As you cultivate your negotiating skills, you should conduct a self-assessment to determine if you have developed these two tendencies. If so, try to repress them during the time you are bargaining on behalf of clients. Simultaneously, you should be conscious that your opponent may have acquired these habits, habits you may be able to exploit.

E. PLANNING TO OBTAIN NEEDED INFORMATION

As the Weber exercise indicated, every negotiation involves seeking information from the opponent during bargaining. In transactional matters, the most intensive advance investigation will not be sufficient to answer all the questions you have concerning the other side. Even in litigation cases, where you can invoke the mandated discovery process, there will always be data that can be obtained only from the opponent. Usually, again as in the Weber problem, the missing information is crucial to the outcome of the bargaining. Unless you fill these information gaps, you cannot measure the accuracy of an opponent's statements; cannot know what arguments will persuade, what promises are valued, and what threats will be feared; cannot effectively determine the opponent's bargaining ranges and rationales; cannot know whether a potential solution meets the opponent's needs; and cannot decide when to accept an offer or press for more. Without all of the necessary information, you are effectively handcuffed, locked into your client's position, and unable to recognize the opponent's goals, needs, and concerns.

You require two basic skills to obtain the data your pre-negotiation planning has identified as necessary and outstanding. Luckily, these are skills you already have studied and practiced. To get the negotiation information you need, you must be able to probe effectively and you must be an active listener. You should now reconsider earlier sections of the book dealing with the two competencies.[7] As a supplement to that reconsideration, the following discussion alerts you to the primary fact-gathering pointers relating to negotiation.

Except when a party on a pure fishing expedition gets very lucky, narrow, directed, and leading questions do not produce a significant amount of information. Instead, as you learned from what we have said and from experiments of your own, inquiries of that sort only confirm the details already in the possession of the questioner. To get the negotiation information you need, ask broad, nondirected, and nonleading questions. As in interviewing, the funnel technique ought to be used to identify a topic and to stimulate your opponent to talk about the subject in terms that are important to the other side. Follow up your initial question slowly, moving without haste to the narrow portion of the funnel. As you receive the knowledge you need, you can use more directed questions to confirm what your opponent has said, as well as to fill in information gaps. Remember, you must avoid—even when using very open-ended probes to introduce a topic—unclear, ambiguous, compound, or otherwise deficient questions. Do not forget to use the appropriate probing techniques to follow up the early answers. Keep in mind that you have a choice between neutral and directed probes. Use the former earlier in the process; the latter have their greatest utility later in the assessment stage.

Analyze the following questions by Weber's lawyer and the responses by the attorney from Jones & Jones. In your judgment, does the probing address an important information topic? Why or why not? Assuming the topic is important enough to pursue during negotiation, what would you do to make inquiry into Jones's business intentions in the counseling area more productive?

Weber: Tell me about Jones's general business plans over the next few years.

Jones: I'm not sure how those plans relate to this thing with Weber, but . . . well, I suspect they'll continue to expand. There are 17 states

---

7. On probing, see Chapter 7, Sections D through G. To review active listening, see Chapter 5, Section B. See also Chapter 3, Sections B and C, and Chapter 4, Sections D and E.

in which there are no Jones's outlets. We ought to try to move into most of those. And in the states we're in, we have to increase the number of outlets. I'm confident they'll follow the proven formula of acquiring ongoing employment agencies where they can. If not, they'll start up their own rather than see a good market go untapped. Actually, I'd like them to continue the acquisitions practice because we expect to continue representing them and we've got these acquisition contracts down almost to a sci . . .

Weber: Are they going to keep to the narrow line of employment placement or will they do what so many other service companies are doing, expanding horizontally and developing related and new areas?

Jones: I've not been privy to all their discussions, but I kind of feel they're on a "steady as she goes" routine for a few years. There are some people making noises that if Jones does not take a bold step soon, the business will become stagnant and top heavy with management. Except for some related stuff, I think they'll . . .

Weber: You know, Weber tells me that Jones & Jones is interested in the counseling business. Is that why they're so concerned about Weber coming back in?

Jones: Look, I'd hardly call it an overwhelming concern, but they are adamant about protecting their contract rights. And I have to tell you I think they're absolutely correct because if they don't guard those contract provisions, they're going to get burned. You know, they've acquired about fifty businesses in the past year, more than forty of which have been totally reorganized and are now operating as functional Jones's outlets. If we don't watch those former owners, they'll be back in the business and challenging Jones during the vulnerable early years in a new locale.

Oftentimes lawyers who have learned to be excellent active listeners in interviewing and counseling ignore that skill in negotiations. Instead of listening well, these lawyers tend to talk more, dominating the communication process where possible. By doing so, they disregard the lessons of active listening and act contrary to their informational interests.

Remind yourself of the steps to effective active listening. Pay close attention to all the communication of the other side, not only the opponent's responses to your probes but to the information volunteered. Maintain good eye contact with the other lawyer, taking few notes, certainly no more than the occasional word to remind yourself of important information. Be keenly aware of both the precise language used by your adversary and all of the nonverbal cues that are emitted, including pace, pitch, tone, and volume.[8]

At bottom, active listening is about understanding, trying to determine exactly what the other side means, wants, and values. Therefore, you should do as much as you can to comprehend the opponent's message and

---

8. Professor Charles Craver has a list of common nonverbal communicators that he has observed in negotiation settings. While we are leery of a rigid classification of nonverbal responses, review of Craver's list may alert you to the meaning of your opponent's expressions. C. Craver, *Effective Legal Negotiation and Settlement* 19-30 (1986).

to let opposing counsel know that you are serious about comprehending. To prove that you are paying attention, confirm often what the other side has said by restating it in your own words. Introductory phrases such as "As I understand it," "So that you mean," "Did you just say that," and "Let me see if I can explain what" should become part of your negotiation vocabulary. Being sure you understand an opponent does not mean you concede the validity of the fact asserted or the argument made. Indeed, the only concession involved in active listening is to let the other side know that it has been heard.

On the other hand, you cannot allow opposing counsel to avoid continuously your requests for information without abandoning your prenegotiation plans. If the opponent fails to answer your question, you must analyze why. Is it possible the other lawyer does not understand what material you sought? If that is the case, it is your responsibility to restate the inquiry to ensure the opponent's understanding. It is also possible, however, that opposing counsel knows quite well what you were seeking but does not wish to provide an answer. In that case, a number of conclusions and options are open to you. You may want to seek immediate clarification and elaboration, wait until later and use retrospective probes,[9] or abandon the area completely, content that you have identified a sensitive point. Evasion and dissembling signal you have touched a soft spot. But assume you clarify your question, then seek immediate elaboration, and later probe again, all to no avail. What do you do when the opponent refuses repeated requests for the data? If the information is not essential, you may certainly abandon the inquiry. If it is critical, you have at least two options. First, you can tell the opponent the information is pivotal and failure to supply the requested matter will cause a cessation of bargaining. Before taking such drastic action, however, you and your client must conclude that the information is crucial. A less extreme approach is to confront those on the other side with your awareness of their continued evasion and ask them why they refuse to cooperate. You could also explain their evasion has convinced you their situation must be very bleak indeed. Then paint the worst-case scenario for the opponent and announce you will proceed on the assumption the disaster you have conjured is reality. This may induce opposing counsel to assure you that things are not nearly so bad as you have painted them and to finally provide you with the requested information.

≡ PROBLEM 2 ≡
Evaluating the Acquisition of Information

In the following excerpt from the Weber-Jones & Jones negotiation, evaluate the Jones lawyer's use of the funnel technique and active listening in getting needed information.

---

9. In Chapter 7 we discussed the use of probes, such as immediate and retrospective clarification and elaboration queries. However, our attention there was directed toward the client, not someone like opposing counsel whose goal it is to keep information from you. To prepare yourself for the follow-up questions of the negotiation opponent, review the material in Chapter 9 on witness interviewing (see especially pages 215-218).

Transcript of Negotiation	*Nonverbal Conduct*
Jones: I was surprised to receive your call. I remember Weber from the closing and he was one of the sellers who was happiest to be getting out and retiring.	**Moderate pace, pitch, tone, and volume. Maintains very good eye contact.**
Weber: Oh no, you've misunderstood. Weber's not coming back to the business. His plan is to get Bobby started. See, the kid got his MBA and has background in industrial psychology. Weber really wants to get him going.	**Abrupt change in pace, pitch, tone, and volume; all faster, higher, and louder. Leans back in chair. Eye contact broken for first time in the negotiation.**
Jones: Do you mean that Weber isn't going to be involved in the daily operations?	
Weber: No, no, no, not at all. He has no plans for coming out of retirement. Well. That doesn't mean he's, uh, going to have absolutely no contact with the business. Weber has a good background, a lot of experience, and he wants to pass that on to his son.	**Pace quickens, volume increases at outset. Drops back and resumes eye contact at "That doesn't mean."**
Jones: What's he going to pass on to his son?	
Weber: Huh? Oh, well, you know, experience and things like that. You know, how he succeeded and stuff. The usual.	**Look of surprise. Hesitation in voice, as if searching for an answer.**
Jones: How is he going to pass it on to his son?	
Weber: Oh, you know. The regular way. I'm not specifically sure. I'll get back to you on this.	**Hesitation still present.**

F. PLANNING TO PROTECT SENSITIVE INFORMATION

In addition to getting information from their opponents, lawyer-negotiators need to prevent disclosure of damaging information to their opponents. Certainly, the adversarial bargainers, those who are always trying to get a leg up on opposing counsel, must protect sensitive information. Unless adversarial negotiators are careful, such material could be used as leverage against them.

But what about problem-solving negotiators? Surely, you may say, those that follow a "win-win" strategy do not hide information from their opponents. Although there may be a misunderstanding on the part of some that good problem-solving negotiators always respond openly and completely to the questions posed by an opponent, that is simply not the case. Problem solvers need to guard damaging data just as much as their adversarial colleagues do. But is it not the essence of the problem-solving strategy that the parties share needs and concerns honestly with each other? Can the open relationship required of problem-solving survive a damage control mentality?

Fisher and Ury do not hesitate to instruct problem solvers that helpful information should be shared but that damaging information should be protected.[10] They also make it clear that there is a substantial difference between outright lying and a reluctance to share everything with an opponent. "Less than full disclosure is not the same as deception . . . [and] good faith negotiation does not require total disclosure."[11] There is no need for problem solvers to bare their souls and expose their warts to maintain an open relationship with opponents.

Because all negotiators need to protect sensitive matters from their adversaries, you must develop a response strategy to deal with inquiries on matters that could be damaging. Constructing such a response approach requires first an appreciation of your options.[12] What types of answers can a negotiator give to the information-seeking probes of an opponent? There are, as it turns out, only three answers you can give to such questions by an adversary. First, you can give an honest answer; that is, you can totally disclose the sensitive information, baring your soul and exposing your warts, as it were. Second, you can affirmatively misrepresent; that is, you can lie to the other side, a course of conduct that has significant ethical ramifications and major credibility risks. Third, you can block the probe of the other lawyer; that is, you leave an opponent with the impression that you have answered the question or you communicate a reason why you will not answer the question. These alternatives need to be examined a bit more.

The honest response to a piercing probe by an opponent has neither the ethical nor the credibility risks of a lie, but it does mean sharing with an opponent information that might be used as leverage against you. For example, consider the following interchange between the Weber and Jones & Jones lawyers:

Weber: The job placement business is booming. I understand that Jones & Jones has really expanded rapidly in the last few years, acquiring a large number of businesses very similar to WEBCo.

Jones: Yes, that is the case. I think we're now the largest employment placement firm in the country. And we got to that point by buying out local competitors rather than going in and butting heads.

---

10. For example, these experts make it clear that disclosure of a problem-solving negotiator's BATNA (the best alternative to a negotiated agreement) depends on whether the alternative is favorable or unfavorable to the negotiator and how the other side would react. If the BATNA is favorable to the negotiator, Fisher and Ury urge disclosure. "However, if your best alternative to a negotiated agreement is worse for you than they think, disclosing it will weaken rather than strengthen your hand." R. Fisher & W. Ury, *Getting to Yes* 109 (1981).

11. Id. at 140.

12. Doing nothing is not one of the realistic options to dealing with touchy matters. Too often, we are afraid, lawyers follow the ostrich approach to the problem of sensitive information. "Oh, no," says the attorney, "if they learn about the raskin, they'll really have me over a barrel. I sure hope they don't ask about it!" Unfortunately, burying your head in the sand will not make the sensitive fact go away and hoping will not stop the opponent from inquiring about it. If you have identified something as being susceptible to exploitation, you always should assume that your opponent will ask about it. Proceeding in that manner will force you to consider the real choices you have when the question is popped.

Weber: Has your firm represented Jones in all these acquisitions all over the country?

Jones: Not all, but a substantial number of them. I know we've handled all of them in our 16-state region and some even beyond that.

Weber: Given all those ongoing acquisitions, you probably had to work up standard clauses in the purchase agreements for things like noncompetition to protect yourselves from slipping up in any given buy-out.

Jones: Yes, that was really the only efficient way. If not, we would have spent all our time drafting the contracts. I must say that I was surprised when you called. I remember Weber from the closing and . . .

In this scene, the Jones attorney gave an honest answer to Weber's inquiry about standard contract clauses. By telling Weber that the noncompetition clause was boilerplate, Jones has given opposing counsel the leverage of what is known as the multiplier effect. Because all of the acquisition agreements contain the identical clause, any litigation over the WEBCo contract subjects Jones's other deals to a similar ruling. Thus, Jones, in fact, may be risking more than one contract if it litigates and loses the WEBCo matter. Could Jones have done anything other than give an honest answer to such a straightforward question? Consider the following replay of the earlier scene:

Weber: The job placement business is booming. I understand that Jones & Jones has really expanded rapidly in the last few years, acquiring a large number of businesses very similar to WEBCo.

Jones: Yes, that is the case. I think we're now the largest employment placement firm in the country. And we got to that point by buying out local competitors rather than going in and butting heads.

Weber: Has your firm represented Jones in all these acquisitions all over the country?

Jones: Not all, but a substantial number of them. I know we've handled all of them in our 16-state region and some even beyond that.

Weber: Given all those ongoing acquisitions, you probably had to work up standard clauses in the purchase agreements for things like noncompetition to protect yourselves from slipping up in any given buy-out.

Jones: No, every clause is boringly different but unique. It would have been a heck of a lot more efficient to do boilerplate phrases but the client wouldn't have it. I can tell you that it seemed as if we were spending all of our time drafting these contracts. I must say that I was surprised when you called. I remember Weber from the closing and . . .

A misrepresentation, such as the one above, in response to an opponent's question is very, very dangerous. First, it may violate professional standards (not to mention general ethical principles). Rule 4.1 of the ABA Model Rules of Professional Conduct precludes the making of "a false statement of material fact or law to a third person." The Commentary to the rule makes it unmistakably clear the rule applies to legal negotiations.

Thus, even though negotiation is an arm's-length relationship, material misrepresentations are ethically unacceptable. But then the Commentary opens the door to doubt by noting that "[u]nder generally accepted conventions in negotiation, certain types of statements ordinarily are not taken as statements of material fact." The Comment then elaborates: "Estimates of price or value placed on the subject of a transaction and a party's intentions as to an acceptable settlement of a claim are in this category. . . ." These caveats require further explanation.

The specific exceptions as to price, value, and intention as they relate to an item being negotiated are quite understandable. If you could not "misrepresent" these items, negotiation as we know it could not exist. Picture a negotiation between lawyers representing two beneficiaries of an estate. The two clients have been jointly left a very valuable diamond ring. One of the parties would like to keep the ring. The other party is solely interested in receiving 50 percent of the value of the jewelry. Both have had independent appraisals of the ring and both have instructed the lawyers as to their bottom lines on the dollar value. In this setting, one lawyer asks the other, "Look, let's not pussyfoot around. Your client can keep the ring so long as we get our fair share. Based on your valuation, what is the highest price you intend to offer for our half of the ring?" If the other attorney is required to answer that question "honestly," the negotiation is effectively concluded. Indeed, in all situations where value or price had to be placed on an item to be exchanged, the "negotiation" would turn into a race to see which lawyer could ask the other the "bottom line" question first. The model rule's approach is the only one that makes sense if we want to continue the present process of discussion leading to agreement. Thus, the model rule stands for the proposition that a lawyer who receives information from an opponent on the price or value of the subject of the negotiation or on a party's intention to sell an item or settle a dispute is not normally entitled to take that as a material representation. Puffing and manipulation are to be expected in bargaining.

The Commentary's broad reference to "generally accepted conventions" is more troublesome because it is not so easily explained nor dealt with in practice. The rule suggests that certain types of lawyers or those in particular specialties or those practicing in certain localities speak in "codes" that others of the same group understand, but those outside the group probably would misinterpret. To use an "Alice in Wonderland" type of example, if in a specific group of attorneys "up" actually meant "down," it would not be an unethical misrepresentation to answer a question about the location of the sun with the response, "Why, it's down, of course!" On the other hand, a lawyer outside the group who asked the same question and received the same answer would conclude that a misrepresentation had been made. A problem exists when a lawyer from one group negotiates with an attorney from another group. Whose code governs? For example, most litigators would say an "I don't know" answer means just that—that the attorney has no knowledge of the subject of the question. Many corporate lawyers would say that the "I don't know" response was a code for "I know, but I don't want to tell you. Don't push me on it unless it's critical to your case and you're prepared to get pushed in return."[13] Thus, when a litigator negotiates with a corporate lawyer, there is a distinct possibility of miscommunication that the former would label a lie. Other than making you aware of the existence of the "generally accepted conventions" exception to the material misrepresentation rule, there is little we can advise except to learn if your opponent speaks in "codes" and to avoid misleading use of your own codes, especially when negotiating with someone from outside your own circle.[14]

A second problem with a false statement in negotiation is that it may expose you to legal liability. Of growing concern to lawyers is the danger of legal malpractice actions. Various legal theories support malpractice suits for misrepresentations in negotiation. For example, when you negotiate on behalf of a client you are acting as an agent. The law of agency may hold your principal liable for your misrepresentations to the other side. Then, in an action against you, the client may seek recompense for your allegedly unauthorized lies to the opponent.[15]

From a very pragmatic perspective, however, your decision to lie in a negotiation should not be based on a risk analysis of the chances of ethical or legal action being based on your material misrepresentations. Quite frankly, the chances of ethical or legal penalties being imposed for the negotiation lie are not very great. The chances are much greater, however, of being "caught" in the lie at the time or later and losing credibility with your opponent. And that is but the beginning of the credibility ramifications of being trapped in a misrepresentation. Your reputation as a lawyer-negotiator will spread and your misrepresentation will become known to others that you will meet in the future. As either an adversarial or a problem-solving negotiator, your most important asset is your credibility. Unless the other side believes that what you say is true, you will be asked to prove everything, your arguments will be dismissed, and your promises will be discounted. If you lose your credibility, you lose not only the assessment stage of the negotiation, but very likely the entire bargain.

Given the gloomy side effects of telling the truth and lying, luckily there is a third alternative available when opposing counsel asks that feared question about the existence of the "smoking gun." Instead of risking leverage with an "honest" response or risking credibility with an untruthful answer, you may choose to block your opponent's inquiry. As a form of evasion, an effective block leaves your opponent with the impression the question has been answered. In alternative blocking technique, you give your opponent a satisfactory reason why you are unable to reply to the request. Blocks are not without risks, however. Continued evasion on a particular subject or the continuous use of the same evasive tactic dur-

---

13. For a discussion of this example, see Freund, Lying in Negotiation Process Can Be Perilous, Legal Times, June 3, 1985, at 18, 20.

14. For a complete and thoughtful discussion of this issue, see T. Guernsey, Truthfulness in Negotiation, 17 U. Rich. L. Rev. 99 (1982).

15. In an article that you should consider, Professor Rex Perschbacher documents a number of cases based on a variety of theories where lawyers have been held liable for material misstatements during negotiation. R. Perschbacher, Regulating Lawyers' Negotiations, 27 Ariz. L. Rev. 75 (1985).

ing a negotiation indicates to your opponent that a soft spot in your defenses has been located. The perception by an opponent that you are vulnerable in a particular area can be very damaging. Although not quite as dangerous as admitting the weakness or being caught in a lie, the discovered block is information that can be used as leverage by an attentive opponent.

To reduce discovery and maximize the efficacy of your blocks, you should prepare them in advance of the negotiation. In that way, when you use them during the negotiation, you are less likely to stumble over your words, to give a series of "uh, uh" responses, to break eye contact, to fumble with your pen, or in some other nonverbal way signal that the opponent has touched a soft spot. In addition, preparing your blocks prior to the negotiation allows you to pick the best one under the circumstances and to vary them so that you do not fall into the natural habit of using the same type of block over and over again, thereby increasing the risk an opponent will identify your response as an evasion. Finally, and at least equally important, advance preparation allows you to craft your answer so that your block does not stretch over the misrepresentation line while it still camouflages the sensitive data.

It is easy enough to say prepare your blocks in advance, but it is much harder to actually do it. Before we give you some suggested blocking formats, you should try to formulate some on your own. Listed below is some sensitive information identified by both sides in the Weber-Jones & Jones problem. Assume the role of counsel for Weber and then Jones and prepare one or two blocks for each piece of information. Assume further that in a forthcoming negotiation the opposing counsel will ask you about each item. Remember, from a conceptual perspective, you are striving to convince the opponent that you have answered the question or have given a good reason why you decline to do so.

≡ **PROBLEM 3** ≡
Preparing Blocks for Weber and Jones

Weber's Sensitive Information

(1) Insufficient Funds.   Because of bad investments, Weber does not have enough resources to accomplish all of the following: pay more than $45,000 for a buy-out of the noncompetition clause, including attorney's fees (or finance litigation to clear the way for ECS); invest at least $100,000 in the new business; and retain a retirement nest egg of at least $500,000.

(2) Weber's Involvement with the New Business.   Weber claims that he will not be involved in the operation of the new business. He does say, however, that he wants to help his son get started, giving the young man the benefit of his extensive experience. Counsel does not believe Weber. Instead, counsel believes Weber is projecting this position in the belief it will be easier to avoid the reach of the noncompetition clause if he, as the former owner of WEBCo, is not involved with ECS. Counsel is strength-

ened in the belief that Weber will be immersed in the new business because of two other facts. First, Weber's financial situation suggests that he needs to replenish his losses. Second, Weber appears to regret retiring at an early age and finding himself without something interesting to occupy his time.

Jones's Sensitive Information

(1) Boilerplate Noncompete Clause. The lawyer for Jones is very concerned that the standard noncompetition clause is vulnerable to a reasonableness analysis by the courts. Counsel is worried that ten years is longer than Jones needs to become competitive; that states are included in the clause even though the prior owner did not operate there; and that the term "employment placement" may be overly broad. Even if the clause survives a court challenge, it could be substantially modified to Jones's disadvantage through "blue penciling." Counsel does not want Weber to know that litigation in this case could negatively affect dozens of other purchases of employment agencies where the same form was used. Counsel fears that if Weber knows there is a potential multiplier effect of litigation, his lawyer will find that option more attractive.

(2) Jones's Counseling Plans. Jones is planning to launch a number of experimental executive counseling units in the next six months, including one in Weber's community. Counsel is concerned that Weber will use this information to argue that counseling and job placement are two entirely different functions. Certainly, if placement includes counseling, it is strange that Jones is considering the addition of the operation an "experiment." Moreover, if Jones is just now exploring this activity and planning to create new units in existing placement offices, it is strong evidence that the parties did not contemplate or intend to cover this specific business enterprise when they signed the assets purchase agreement two years ago.

Now that you have tried your hand at preparing some information blocks, we will explain five forms of them that are commonly used in legal negotiations. After you read the explanation of each block and consider the example, review the blocks you developed to see if they fit into any of the categories. As you read about our blocks, you may question whether such simple devices can really work. But they do. They are effective because too many negotiators are not good listeners. Active listeners, on the other hand, can overcome even well-planned blocking attempts because they are working at understanding exactly what the opponent is (and is not) saying.

We turn, then, to the five basic blocks:

(1) Answer a Question with a Question. Asking another question, one of the most effective blocks, plays on the tendency of lawyers to respond to inquiries put to them. This technique works well because it is not merely a form of evasion. Asking another question also involves clarification or elab-

oration, a legitimate negotiating goal. To be most convincing, you should plan for an initial and at least one follow-up question in response to an opponent's probe for sensitive information. Evaluate the following two questions by Weber's lawyer as answers to Jones's question about Weber's involvement in the new business:

Jones: Is Gene Weber intending to have any involvement in the normal operation of this ECS business?

Weber: Are you saying that it's important to Jones whether Weber is connected with the day-to-day management?

Jones: Well, of course it's important. First of all, we paid a lot of money to Weber so that he wouldn't compete with us in this metropolitan area. Second, we assume he's a more formidable competitor than his son, Bobby, who has no track record.

Weber: Does that mean that if we can demonstrate that Weber won't be involved with the everyday operation of ECS, that it'll only be Bobby running the show with his Dad rooting him on and shouting advice from the sidelines, that Jones & Jones will withdraw their objections?

Jones: Oh no, our objections rest on our contract rights. Counseling is included in the noncompete clause because it's clearly related to placement and, therefore, covered. No, you're going to have to . . .

(2) Over- or Under-Answer a Question. With this blocking technique, you try to give opposing counsel more information than has been asked for or you try to give information on only a small and nonsensitive part of the topic contained in the question. Thus, you can give every possible answer to the question or you can give the narrowest possible answer to the question. Another way of conceptualizing this block is to think about responding generally to a particular question and particularly to a general question. Watch how this block can be applied by Jones to Weber's question about standard clauses:

Weber: The job placement business is booming. I understand that Jones & Jones has really expanded rapidly in the last few years, acquiring a large number of businesses very similar to WEBCo.

Jones: Yes, that is the case. I think we're now the largest employment placement firm in the country. And we got to that point by buying out local competitors rather than going in and butting heads.

Weber: Has your firm represented Jones in all these acquisitions all over the country?

Jones: Not all, but a substantial number of them. I know we've handled all of them in our 16-state region and some even beyond that.

Weber: Given all those ongoing acquisitions, you probably had to work up standard clauses in the purchase agreements for things like noncompetition to protect yourselves from slipping up in any given buy-out.

Jones: Well, as you know, every contract is unique. Weber is a unique person, his business was different from other ones we've bought, the price we paid was specific to his assets, the timing was special, his inventory was distinct. Based on the dozens of deals that we've done, no two have been the same. You just can't grab a complete form contract these days and slap it down on the table and have everyone just endorse it.

In this last answer, you will notice that the theme of Jones's block is a general answer to a particular question. Of course it is true that all contracts are unique. That truism does not, however, answer Weber's question about standard clauses, particularly noncompete clauses. Jones continues by over-answering, providing evidence of uniqueness as to a number of factors that were not specifically addressed in Weber's question. Jones ends his answer with two more generalities. All in all, Jones gave the appearance of answering but, on close analysis, never did face directly Weber's inquiry.

(3) Answer Another Question. When the opponent has propounded a specific question, how do you create another one to answer? There are at least three ways to do so. First, you can explicitly reframe the pending question in a way that the answer will not be damaging to you. Introductory comments such as the following signal a rephrased inquiry: "As I understand your question, you want to know . . ."; "I'd be pleased to tell you about . . ."; "If you're asking about . . . then I can tell you. . . ." A second method of developing another question to answer is simply to answer the question as if it had been asked. For this to work, the one you respond to must at least be in the same part of the ballpark as the question posed by the adversary. Finally, you can answer a question that was recently asked and answered. So long as you change your words and perhaps your focus, your response is not quite the same as what went before. Opposing lawyers who are distracted, fumbling around with papers, or making extensive notes are particularly vulnerable to this approach. Note how the answer to the following question by Jones about Weber's financial situation focuses on Weber's money, but it is about future rather than present cash flow:

Jones: I realize, of course, that we paid Weber a lot of money for the WEBCo business only two years ago, but even so, does Weber have the money that it takes to get started in business today?

Weber: This isn't going to be a mere money drop on the kid. Weber intends that Bobby will pay him back out of the proceeds of the business over a relatively short period. He has no intention of making a gift out of the start-up funds. There'll be none of this, "Here, kid, take the money and run." Of course, this isn't a capital intensive business to begin with, but, in any event, Weber intends that it's coming back his way.

(4) Rule the Question Out of Bounds. The first three blocks involve attempts to get the opponent to believe that the question has been answered. The out-of-bounds block differs because you tell the other side that you will not answer the question. For the block to work, your reason for not answering must be reasonable. The most obvious out-of-bounds block for a

lawyer is one that rests on the confidential nature of the attorney-client relationship. See how Jones tries to use the block on Weber's inquiry about Jones's plans for a counseling program:

Weber: We hear rumors that Jones is about to go into the counseling business itself. Can you confirm that for us?

Jones: Like any sophisticated business, Jones spends a lot of time and money on research and development, generating multi-year plans, analyzing where it's going, what activity it ought to be engaged in, and when it ought to do it. Jones's competitors would love to have access to its "what if" projections. That would make life for the other guys a whole lot easier. Jones has no intention of releasing information about its business plans until the appropriate time. Even if I were privy to information about the business options it's considering, I'm not in any position to share it with you or anyone else. I'm sure you understand why I can't answer your question.

(5) *Ignore the Question and Change the Topic.* This is a favorite block among lawyers and among little children when asked if they have done something wrong. This form of evasion works because the listener gets so caught up in the information being provided that the original question is forgotten. When using this block, it is best to change to a topic in which the opponent is likely to have some real interest. See how the lawyer for Weber tries that ploy as he turns away from Jones's inquiry into Weber's involvement with ECS:

Jones: Is Gene Weber intending to have any involvement in the normal operation of this ECS business?

Weber: The most difficult issue confronting Weber as he figures out how ECS is going to operate is how to structure the financing. It's not cheap to get into business today and he's not in a position to just turn to Bobby and say, "Here, kid, I'm giving you a gift of so many thousands of dollars. Run off and play at being a businessman." On the other hand, Weber doesn't want to tie the kid's hands. He's got to have the flexibility to move if things develop and they can't spend weeks considering every dime of financial implications. As you know, the most serious problem with a start-up business today is underfinancing. Everyone thinks he can get by on a shoestring. Well, Weber's not going to let that happen with ECS. It's not yet finalized, but he's . . .

Now that you have worked through the five basic blocking techniques, go back to the problem dealing with Weber's and Jones's sensitive information. Try to develop new blocks for this data, using the models set out above. Compare these blocks with those you generated earlier. Are your earlier or later ones more likely to be successful in protecting your information? Why?

You will not be surprised to learn that blocking is not a tactic reserved to lawyer-negotiators and the negotiating table. Quite often people prefer to evade rather than answer the questions put to them. Consciously or unconsciously they apply blocks to avoid discomforting subjects. As you participate in ordinary conversations, listen to others as they evade by blocking. Sort the blocks you hear according to the preceding five categories or by an arrangement of your own. You will find that this is an interesting and important negotiation exercise. A significant analytical process is subsumed when one identifies and classifies a complex thing. For example, when in a set of facts you are able to recognize res ipsa loquitor, or a life estate, or mens rea, or a third party beneficiary, it suggests that you understand the concept completely and are able to process the data almost instantaneously. It is very helpful to be able to analyze quickly the communication tactics of your opponent. It allows you to look for patterns while still concentrating on the substance of counsel's statements. So use the conversations of friends and associates as a practice field to test your blocking-recognition skills.

Bear in mind a block is only the least unattractive choice among a poor set of alternatives for protecting sensitive information. Because they are a form of deception and evasion, blocks are dangerous. To the skillful opponent, blocks can reveal a soft spot in your position. The good lawyer will hover in the vicinity of your block, developing additional information about your weakness. Because blocking is a hazardous negotiation practice, be absolutely positive that the information you list in your Need to Protect column is truly sensitive and cannot be revealed. Our experience is that attorneys tend to overreact, recording far too many items as sensitive topics. The more often a negotiator must develop and apply a block, the greater the chance that the pattern of blocking will be discovered by the opponent. Your Need to Protect list should be reviewed carefully, therefore, to determine if some matters could be handled with an honest response and a persuasive explanation. That could be more advantageous and less dangerous than developing and applying a block.

G. PLANNING TO GIVE INFORMATION

Many litigation experts say direct examination is more important than cross-examination, that a party's case-in-chief influences the outcome far more than does destruction of the other side's case. A similar judgment applies to negotiation. The information you present to the other side may well be more powerful in the long run than either the damage you do to its arguments or the information you so carefully protect. Unless you give information to your negotiation opponents that influences them in a positive way, you are unlikely to achieve your bargaining goals.

While emphasizing the critical importance of giving information, we address it only briefly at this point. The next chapter, which covers the persuasion stage of negotiation, thoroughly discusses how to organize and deliver convincing details to opposing counsel. Thus, we include this section here primarily to ensure both completeness and your awareness that when organizing information in advance of bargaining, isolating the information you need to give the opponent is an essential corollary to the getting and protecting of data.

Although it is here at the giving-of-information phase that assessment blends with the persuasion stage, two points are worth making independent of this next step. First, you will have information to give your opponent that would be difficult to include under argument, appeal, threat, or promise, the major categories you will consider under persuasion. The information we refer to here is background in nature—the circumstances and conditions that surround the main bargaining event. These are the facts that, in the appropriate negotiation, create the business environment, explain the emotional atmosphere, or untangle the family setting. This information is essential but may get lost in the planning unless you pay special attention to it. If this information is absent or poorly organized and presented, you will detract from the power of your persuasion.

The second comment deals with presenting the information you wish to give to the other side. When you make plans to communicate information to others, we suspect you think in terms of delivering the information directly. To continue the earlier analogy to the trial process, we believe you will plan to make something akin to an opening statement, a soliloquy of sorts during which you will tell opponents what you believe should influence them to do what you want them to do. If that is the approach you take to the task, you will find yourself in the company of most other lawyers.

Yet use of an opening statement in a negotiation carries certain risks. First, the statement pressures you into trying to speak extensively and continuously. When you are speaking, you are not listening to the other side. When you have a "statement" to deliver, you concentrate more on what you are saying than on what and how the opponent is hearing. Second, the longer you speak, the greater is the chance of leakage. Leakage is an unconscious undercutting of your arguments or your offers. Either through lack of preparation or because of a subconscious awareness of the flaws in your reasoning, you "leak" your shortcomings to the other side. Consider the following excerpt from a "statement" by the lawyer for Weber. See if you can detect the leakage.

Weber: The work involved in placement, the activity covered by the clause, is simply finding a job for someone. Executive counseling, on the other hand, doesn't include the finding of a job, but does include a full range of supportive activities. The type of client, the fee arrangement, the length of the relationship, and the work done with the client make counseling entirely different from placement. Let me explain each of those differences in detail. [Lawyer explains alleged differences.] This situation is even more removed from the contract umbrella because Weber's not going to be involved in the business. His son, Bobby, will own and operate ECS. You should understand that Weber will only be advising his . . . [lawyer discusses business arrangements at length]. The law is quite clear that a noncompetition clause must be judged by its reasonableness. I'm sure you're aware of our Supreme Court's opinion in *Voices, Inc.* That set the legal standard at . . . [lawyer analyzes the legal implications of the reasonableness test]. At the very least, you will have to admit the courts will blue pencil this agreement. In light of the questionable length of time and geographic prohibitions that exceed where Weber operated, there is no question that the contract will be modified. I suspect that the time period will be reduced to two or three years and the area cut back to the metropolitan region. You can see why the courts would be sympathetic to our argument that . . . [lawyer sets forth blue pencil position].

The negotiator would probably be interrupted during such a lengthy presentation of information. Nonetheless, preparing to give such an extensive statement encourages leakage such as that present above. The Weber lawyer leaked, of course, with the blue penciling argument. In classic fashion, the attorney undercut Weber's initial, and most beneficial, argument that the contemplated business fell completely beyond the contract provision. Because blue penciling occurs only when a noncompetition clause does cover the proposed enterprise (the contract is judicially reformed, not set aside), Weber's counsel demonstrated lack of faith in the most important argument in the case, the applicability of the contract clause. Leakage such as this allows an opponent to reevaluate the risks of deadlock in a way that weakens the negotiator's position.

Fortunately, you have alternatives to presenting the information you want to give directly either in an indirect fashion and in opening statement form. Consider delivering a portion of the material you want to convey to the other side by responding to questions asked by the opponent. You can be sure opposing counsel will have a number of information requests for you. Indeed, in preparation for protecting sensitive information, you have anticipated some of those questions. Go the added step of predicting questions beyond those that are touchy. Then plan how to insert background, favorable, and persuasive facts in your answers to the queries of opposing counsel. In addition to ameliorating the dangers of not listening and leakage, you actually may enhance the influence your information will have on the other side. Some studies have revealed that indirectly presented information is more powerful than its counterpart because questioners are likely to give greater credibility to information they participated in obtaining.

Of course, another means for getting across your background and essential material is to put it in a letter. Although you lose information by sacrificing your ability to observe the other side's spontaneous verbal and nonverbal responses to your statements, you more effectively organize your thoughts, present detailed data, and are able to tightly control your disclosures, thus preventing leakage.

Chapter

18

≡≡≡

The Process
of Persuasion

A. THE GOALS OF PERSUASION

1. Introduction

Whether your style is competitive or cooperative, whether your strategy is adversarial or problem-solving, to be an effective negotiator you must persuade your opponent. Persuasion involves the manipulation of the decision-making process of someone who controls decisions that can affect the achievement of the goals identified by your client.[1] Usually the manipulation is designed to convince an adversary to view a matter in issue as you and your client view it. When you persuade the opponent to view the subject of negotiation as you and your client view it, you increase dramatically the chances of reaching an agreement. If you and another share the same basic perspective about a matter, then you are likely to concur on an appropriate outcome. Perhaps even more important, the form of the agreement is more likely to meet the needs you and your client defined during your

---

1. R. Stuckey, Planning for Persuasion: A Lawyer's Guide to the Basics, 30 Santa Clara L. Rev. — (1990). Professor Stuckey emphasizes that the decisions of another at which the lawyer's persuasion is aimed must involve some degree of uncertainty. By that he means that the opponent has alternative courses of action available and the best alternative is not self-evident. (In preparing this chapter, we have consulted the manuscript of Stuckey's forthcoming article.)

counseling sessions. Effective counseling suggests that client needs will specify the shape of the solution. Thus, if you persuade your opponent to view the competing needs and solutions as you view them, you will maximize the satisfaction of your client.

While all negotiators persuade their opponents, adversarial and problem-solving bargainers differ on the specifics. Adversarial negotiators following a zero-sum strategy try to persuade the opponent to view the matter at issue most favorably to them. They may therefore distort client needs and narrowly limit the acceptable solutions as part of the persuasion process. When adversarial negotiators succeed in persuading the opponent to view the matter in that fashion, they likely gain an advantageous distribution of the fungible items being negotiated.

Problem solvers, on the other hand, try to persuade the opponent to see and appreciate the problem-solving negotiator's world and to understand how that world interfaces with that of the opponent. Thus, the problem solver encourages the other side to view the matter at issue in a "fair" manner by focusing on the parties' needs and on solutions that can meet those needs and be measured by objective, as opposed to subjective, criteria. Although the problem solver's persuasion goal appears to be less selfish and more open, be aware that "fair" often is dependent on how the problem solver defines the term. To ensure a better understanding of persuasion's role in the negotiation process, we must examine more closely adversarial and problem-solving negotiators and their underlying goals.

2. The Adversarial Negotiator's Persuasion Goals

We begin by reminding you that adversarial negotiators want to obtain as much of the fungible item at issue as they can. From an extreme theoretical perspective, adversarial bargainers want to "take it all," leaving nothing on the table for the other side. In the simplest terms, to facilitate such a distribution of the goods at issue, your fundamental goal as an adversarial negotiator is to manipulate your opponent's assessment of the resistance level (or "bottom line") of each side. Thus, you want your opponent to misassess your resistance level and to reassess its own resistance level. In a negotiation over the division of 100 widgets, for example, you want your opponent to think your bottom line is obtaining 60 widgets (when your client will settle for 40). If that occurs, your opponent has misassessed your resistance level. At the same time, you want your opponent to reconsider its bottom line of a fifty-fifty split of the widgets in light of your apparent final demand of 60 units. If your opponent does reconsider the final division, you have achieved the goal of having the other side reassess its resistance level.

≣≣≣ **PROBLEM 1** ≣≣≣
Persuading Jones & Jones

To further illustrate the goal of an adversarial negotiator's efforts to persuade, we return to the WEBCo and Jones & Jones negotiation. As you recall, Gene Weber wants to start a new "executive counseling" business and is concerned that the noncompetition clause in the agreement of sale of his old business, Weber Employment Bureau Company (WEBCo), may preclude the contemplated activity. Weber and his lawyer have agreed to negotiate with the purchaser, Jones & Jones, a large, nationwide employment placement company. Suppose Weber is willing to pay Jones as much as $60,000 to buy out so much of the noncompetition clause as would allow Weber to operate the new counseling enterprise. Although Weber will pay up to $60,000, he would prefer to pay as little as possible. Thus, if you are Weber's lawyer one of your goals is to convince the attorney representing Jones & Jones that your client will not pay more than an amount that is considerably less than the $60,000 bottom line. Assume you have made an offer to Jones of $45,000.

Turning to the other party in the negotiation, suppose that Jones & Jones is willing to "sell" to Weber the limited right of operating his executive counseling business. Assume Jones wants, among other conditions, at least $57,500—or half of the $115,000 allocated in the assets purchase agreement to the noncompetition clause—for the partial buy-out. Now, to complete our example, assume Jones has demanded the $57,500 and you believe it represents the company's bottom line.

As the attorney representing Weber, you know what you want to happen in this situation. Even though you know the overlap of bottom lines has produced a settlement zone of $2,500, you would like to maximize the outcome for your client by paying less than the $57,500 Jones is willing to take for the partial buy-out. Thus, you want to manipulate your opponent's assessment of the respective bottom lines so that it misassesses your resistance level at $45,000 and reassesses the Jones resistance level at a figure below $57,500.

To successfully manipulate opposing counsel's assessment of the respective resistance levels, you need to persuade the Jones negotiators of, among other things, your strengths and their weaknesses; the economic correctness of your analysis and the incorrectness of theirs; and the advantages of your proposal combined with the disadvantages of theirs. As an adversarial negotiator representing Weber, you must persuade the lawyer for Jones that an acceptable outcome is something different from and less advantageous than the other side anticipated. You must alter the opponent's perception of the respective resistance levels and that perception is altered through the process of persuasion.

≡≡≡≡≡≡≡≡≡≡

3. The Problem Solver's Persuasion Goals

Problem-solving, as suggested earlier, involves a persuasion process quite different from that of an adversarial strategy. Both competitive or cooperative problem solvers are engaged in a search for the underlying needs of each party and the development of objective criteria to measure the adequacy of proposals to meet those needs. As a problem-solving negotiator, you are not immune from the need to persuade your opponents, although the objectives of your persuasive efforts differ from those of your adversarial colleagues. Your goals may include persuading the opponent about the nature of your client's needs; for example, you might argue that your client's needs are real (as opposed to feigned), legitimate (as opposed to unreasonable), and capable of being met (as opposed to being unanswerable for economic or other reasons). Correspondingly, you may want to persuade opponents about the nature of their clients' needs, that those expressed needs are not, for example, real, legitimate, or capable of being met. As a problem-solving negotiator, you may also be required to persuade the opponent about the nature of the proposed solutions, such as whether they objectively, efficiently, and effectively satisfy the demands of all parties.

≡ PROBLEM 2 ≡
The Demolished Auto

To picture the persuasion responsibilities of the problem-solving negotiator more clearly, consider the following based on an example used by Fisher and Ury.[2] Assume that the plaintiff properly parked her six-month-old automobile in a legal on-street parking place. Further assume that the defendant negligently operated his vehicle, which smashed into and totaled plaintiff's car. In this dispute, where there is no question of liability, the primary issue is the amount of damages to which plaintiff is entitled. As a problem-solving negotiator representing plaintiff, you have searched for objective criteria to measure the adequacy of payment to your client instead of simply trying to squeeze the most money possible out of the defendant. Your search for solutions has yielded the following apparently objective proposals for compensating your client:

1. The original cost of the car less depreciation, that is, the standard "Blue Book" value (assume that to be $20,000 original cost less $5,000 in depreciation, or $15,000).
2. The amount the car could have been sold for in a private sale based on a random sample of newspaper ads ($17,500).
3. The trade-in value of the car in the condition it was in before the accident ($18,250).
4. The out-of-pocket cost to replace the car with a comparable one ($21,850 less $3,000 "salvage" value of the demolished auto or $18,850).
5. The amount that a court might award as the value of the car if litigation were pursued to conclusion (based on a survey of recent verdicts, between $19,000 and $22,000 less $4,500 in fees and costs or $14,500 to $17,500).

As can be seen from this example of "objective" solutions, there is a 30 percent difference between the most favorable and the least favorable out-

---

2. R. Fisher & W. Ury, *Getting to Yes* 88-89 (1981).

come for the plaintiff. Thus, even when the problem-solving negotiator employs objective criteria to measure settlement proposals, hard choices among competing options can occur. As a problem solver representing the plaintiff, you will be required to persuade an opponent that one of these "objective criteria" is a better solution under the circumstances of your case than any of the others.

In addition to selecting among contending objective criteria, problem solvers are likely to face the task of persuading some opponents about aspects of the articulated needs of the parties. Alter the earlier example in the following way. Assume that the plaintiff you represent did not own but had borrowed the now demolished auto. Assume further that the defendant has satisfied the demands of the car's owner. Your client claims, however, that she witnessed the crash and that she has been traumatized because her dog, though uninjured, was in the vehicle at the time of the wreck. Your opponent's client admits his vehicle struck the parked car but asserts he was not the "cause" of the mishap. Rather, he claims he was forced off the road by a speeding, reckless driver of another auto that fled the scene. The opponent rejects your client's "need" for compensation on two grounds: Based on the jurisdiction's case law, the plaintiff is not entitled to an award for "emotional distress" under these circumstances; and defendant is not "morally" bound to satisfy the plaintiff's need. If, as a problem-solving negotiator, you are to reach an agreement acceptable to your client in this situation, your skill in the art of persuasion will be severely tested.

B. THE ROLE OF ARGUMENT IN NEGOTIATION

Persuasion in negotiation is applied in a number of conceptual forms, the most important of which are argument, appeal, threat, and promise. This chapter, though not a substitute for an in-depth study of persuasive communication, appropriately elaborates on the elements of these four forms of persuasion, which are so common in lawyer bargaining.[3]

In an important article analyzing the role of argument in legal negotiation, Professor Robert Condlin defines negotiation argument as "the invocation and reasoned elaboration of authoritative norms . . . to support a negotiation position or to rebut an adversary's position."[4] This definition highlights what one would suppose to be the obvious tasks of the lawyer-

---

3. Because we classify promise as the obverse of threat, it will be mentioned only briefly.

4. "Cases on Both Sides": Patterns of Argument in Legal Dispute-Negotiation, 44 Md. L. Rev 65, 69 (1985). Condlin studied the videotapes of about 100 teams of lawyers and law students who negotiated simulated but very realistic legal problems. One of the problems used in Condlin's study is very familiar to us. See the Whitmore and Rice problem in Harbaugh, *Lawyer Negotiation Training Materials* (Practising Law Institute 1988). Condlin explicitly limits his analysis to dispute negotiations and to legal arguments. However, we believe that what he says can be applied to transactional negotiations and to factual and policy arguments as well.

negotiator who advances an argument. The first step in the argument process is to identify a norm that can be applied to an issue in the negotiation. That norm can be based on positive or decisional law; on legal, economic, or social policy; on fact or custom; or on other legitimate standards that can be used to analyze, measure, and influence the pending issue. Once identified, the next step in the development of a negotiation argument is to expand on the normative standard, demonstrating how it applies to the issue in question and either advances the negotiator's cause or counters the reasoning of the opponent.

These tasks may seem obvious, but too often negotiators refer to the applicable norms in such a vague, imprecise, and offhand manner that it is difficult, if not impossible, to determine what impact the standard has on the negotiation. Just as frequently, a normative standard that could influence the opponent's perception of an issue is merely identified and invoked, but not elaborated on, by the negotiator. It is as if the lawyer-negotiator assumes that just mentioning the norm will persuade an opponent.

In the absence of effective invocation and elaboration, it is not surprising that clearly relevant normative standards do not pack the persuasive punch of forceful argument. When the opponent does not respond to such ineffective arguments, many lawyer-negotiators abandon this form of persuasion altogether, most of them rushing prematurely to the exchange stage. When lawyers on both sides of a negotiation engage in this form of argument, it can be described as "volley, volley, truce."[5] One side advances a poor and undeveloped argument in support of or in opposition to a proposition. The other side responds with an equally weak and poorly formed contention. The parties then agree, usually tacitly, to abandon argument as a form of persuasion and to move on to more productive enterprises, usually throwing money at the issues.

To be effective, you must understand how to construct a persuasive negotiation argument. This construction is based on a premise assumed by Professor Condlin in his article: The ordinary rules of rationality must apply to arguments advanced during a negotiation by and among lawyers. As a consequence of this assumption, an attorney who introduces an argument in support of a position during a negotiation is required to support that argument with relevant reasoning and evidence that are, at least arguably, internally consistent and logical. If, as Condlin asserts, the parties cannot agree to abide by the canons of rationality, argument, as we know it, is not possible. It is because of a deviation from the ordinary rules of rationality, for example, that we have such difficulty negotiating with terrorists. In many hostage situations where representatives of Western governments are negotiating with the kidnappers of innocent persons, it is not altogether clear that the negotiating parties share the same view of rationality. Without such a common analytical base, it is much less likely that the "arguments" put forward by each side's representative will influence the outcome of the negotiation.

---

5. This phrase has been used by Professor Condlin and other legal educators (including one of the authors) to describe ineffective negotiation argument. It is difficult to determine who first applied the term to the persuasion phase of bargaining.

Assuming rationality and based on his analysis of the videotapes of legal negotiations, Condlin identifies six characteristics of a convincing negotiation argument: detail, multidimensionality, balance, subtlety, emphasis, and emotionality. Following is our review, with examples, of these characteristics of an influential negotiation argument.

1. The Detailed Argument

To measure up to the detail standard, your negotiation argument must be fully and completely developed. If your argument is based on fact or logic, analogy or rule, legal principle or social policy, detail demands that your argument be comprehensive. For example, if you set forth a factual contention, you must marshal and advance all the facts that bear on your argued conclusion. If your argument rests on analogy, you must isolate the elements of the analogous situation and demonstrate how those elements apply to the matter being negotiated. If your argument is based on custom, you must justify the existence of the custom and then explain how your case falls within the orbit of the custom. Detail means that your negotiation argument must have depth to it. Whether your argument is grounded in facts, rule, logic, or custom, detail requires that you exhaustively research and systematically organize the supporting material. Your detailed argument persuades an opponent because its specificity teaches the other side that which it did not know or, at least, communicates that you are aware of all the appropriate particulars. When it is detailed, your argument convinces because the opponent sees it whole, without gaps or defects that can be exploited.

Examine the following argument in the WEBCo and Jones & Jones dispute. The lawyer for Weber is arguing that executive counseling does not fall under the employment placement language in the noncompete clause. The attorney from Jones responds that the proposed new business is precluded by a contract provision that prohibits activities "related . . . to employment placement." The arguments of both lawyers obviously lack the detail required to make their points compelling. What detail should be developed by these lawyers to improve the persuasiveness of their positions?

Weber: Placement means finding a job for a client. Executive counseling, on the other hand, is simply not included within the contract provision. The fee arrangement, the type of work done for the client, and the length of the relationship with the client are entirely different in counseling than they are in placement. And this situation in particular is outside the agreement because Weber is not going to be involved in the business on a day-to-day basis. It's Weber's son who will be operating the business. Weber is only going to be advising and guiding the new venture.

Jones: I understand all that, but counseling is related to placement. Employment placement involves some counseling of the client about the job options he or she may have. As such, executive counseling is covered by the "related to" language of the agreement. And the fact that Weber may only be an investor or adviser doesn't take the business itself outside the scope of the clause.

2. *The Multidimensional Argument*

In addition to being detailed, a good negotiation argument is also multi-dimensional. As mentioned above, arguments can depend on fact or logic, analogy or rule, legal principle or social policy, as well as consequences or custom, economic theory or ethical norm, and a variety of other dimensions. Your best negotiation arguments will be constructed in as many of these dimensions as possible. By presenting a multidimensional argument, you erect a wall of logic, rule, policy, and the like, building argument on argument, extending through varied dimensions, completely outflanking the opponent. Your multidimensional argument persuades because your opponent is convinced that it cannot be breached no matter where the attack is mounted and what slant is taken. If the effective detailed argument rests on depth, the effective multidimensional argument rests on breadth. You appear thoroughly prepared, having considered the full range of matters that could affect the issues involved in the negotiation.

Compare the following argument, in which Weber's lawyer explains why the noncompetition clause does not apply to the proposed new business, with the one put forth by the same attorney in the preceding section. Identify what it is that makes this argument more persuasive. Could the argument be made even more convincing?

Weber: The clause in the assets purchase agreement doesn't apply to the counseling business for a broad assortment of important reasons. In the first place, the operation of the new business will be entirely different from the way an employment agency functions. For example, there is a 180-degree distinction in the two fee structures. In an employment agency, the employers pay the agency in more than 90 percent of the cases and the fees are set as a percentage of the new employees' salary. In the new counseling business, the client will pay a large, one-time set fee that has no relationship to salary. In the employment placement situation, the relationship ends when the client is placed in a job. In the new counseling business, the relationship between the client and the counselor extends for a set period, well beyond the time the client finds a new position. Most important, there is a fundamental difference that lies at the core of the relationship with the client. The relationship of the employment agency and the client is single focused. On the other hand, the relationship between the counselor and client has many dimensions. The counselor is concerned about the client's business or professional skills, interpersonal skills, self-esteem, family relationships, and much more.

And these factual distinctions are simply the beginning. For example, there is a widespread custom in the employment agency business that the real "client" is the employer. That custom dictates that the agency is searching for people to fill the stated needs of the employer. If a potential employee doesn't fit the qualifications listed by a pending employer, that potential employee goes to the bottom of the pile. That custom shows how different the two businesses are.

Of course, the long-standing legal rule on the applicability of noncompetition clauses supports our position. The courts and the legislature in this state are united in their view that noncompete provisions ought to be narrowly construed. Thus, the courts in a series of cases [citing case names] have said that if the activity is not clearly prohibited by the noncompete clause, then the courts will not step in and forbid it. Indeed, in [citing specific case], the court criticized as overbroad the "related to" and "indirectly as well as directly" language your client put into our agreement.

The economic policy against a broad interpretation of noncompete clauses is clear. There are two legislative reports in the last seven years that have argued against policies that restrain trade and economic development. Noncompetition clauses are one of the specific examples mentioned in both reports issued by the General Assembly.

In addition, there is a strongly analogous situation when we consider the way another industry has dealt with this very question. In the sister business of . . .

3. The Balanced Argument

In addition to being detailed and multidimensional, a good negotiation argument must be balanced. In very few legal negotiations do all the arguments favor one side as against all other parties to the dispute or transaction. In litigation matters, the further along the path toward trial the case proceeds, the more likely it is that each side's position has some merit. It is rare in transactional matters, as well, that only one party can call on law and equity to support its view. If your argument distorts the issues by failing to acknowledge your opponent's appropriate contentions, it will be unpersuasive. Those on the receiving end of such reasoning will discount your legitimate arguments because their arguments have not been considered. To enhance your persuasiveness, first acknowledge the other side's obvious and authentic support for its interests. Follow your acknowledgment with a reasoned response or a pertinent distinction that indicates why the opponent's contentions are less forceful in this situation than had been supposed. By balancing your opponent's arguments against your own, you make your position more credible and more influential.

Review the following argument advanced by the attorney for Jones & Jones. In the argument Jones's counsel concedes there is some validity to Weber's claim that counseling and placement are factually distinct. Has the lawyer struck an appropriate balance? Has the lawyer gone too far in crediting the position of the opponent? Would you have constructed your balanced argument differently?

Jones: In reaching our opinion that the noncompete clause precludes Weber from beginning the executive counseling business, we carefully considered the factual differences in the operation of the two enterprises. We understand there are distinctions between the businesses, but we believe strongly that those distinctions are superficial and not fundamental.

To be sure, a counseling program doesn't have the same fee structure as an employment agency. Nor does the relationship between the business and the client usually last as long in job placement as it does in job counseling. But those differences don't go to the heart of the business. No matter who pays the fee or how long the relationship lasts, an executive who seeks job counseling is looking for a new job. That is, while counseling is ongoing, when it has concluded, the client has to be placed in a new position. Thus, the end product of the relationship is identical.

We realize that Weber might argue that the work done on behalf of the client is quite different in counseling and placement. We believe that contention ignores the breadth of the work done by the sophisticated people running Jones & Jones. Our clients are counseled now. We teach them how to write resumes, dress for success, prepare for and participate in a variety of interviews, and follow up the positive interview to maximize impact. We use written materials and videotape techniques that rely heavily on advances in psychology and communication. In addition to the counseling, of course, we are very adept at getting our clients productive interviews and good jobs. We are convinced that what Weber plans to do is exactly what we're already doing in the placement business and, therefore, is precluded by the agreement.

4. The Emphasized Argument

Not all the points that you assemble into your complete negotiation argument on behalf of your client are going to be of equal weight or influence. Some parts will be extremely important, some will be of lesser rank and influence, while others will serve only to bridge the major points or address ancillary matters. To maximize the persuasiveness of your arguments, be organized and focused to emphasize your key points. (For example, recall the lesson from Chapter 6 (page 143 note 4) that the principles of primacy and recency give special emphasis to the first- and last-mentioned items.) Design the argument so that all of the lesser components are set in relevant perspective and in their appropriate places. During the negotiation, you should occasionally review your argument for your opponent to be sure that he or she understands the whole and appreciates all the parts. Your suitably focused argument will convince an opponent because your important points are highlighted and will be remembered.

Have another look at the multidimensional argument (pages 436-437) made by Weber's lawyer. This time ask yourself whether the attorney has met the emphasis standard. Could the argument be restructured to make it more convincing? Could other points be added to the argument to increase its persuasiveness?

5. *The Emotional Argument*

The fifth and final[6] characteristic of the effective legal argument identified by Professor Condlin is emotionality. The effective negotiator adds the appropriate dose of emotion to the presentation of the argument. Most of your negotiation arguments will be grounded on a claim of right, a call for justice, or a demand for reason. But right, justice, and reason have both emotional and logical elements. By including a measured amount of controlled emotion, your purely analytical argument becomes a touch more trustworthy and believable. For those fans of *Star Trek*, the added element of emotion explains why in the most difficult situations confronting the Star Ship Enterprise, the passion-tinged judgment of Captain Kirk is more convincing than the always sterile analysis of Dr. Spock.

The emotion that persuades, however, is seldom excessive. To the contrary, it is moderate but sincere. This is not to say you must believe in each part and every element of your client's argument to project the appropriate degree of emotion. But if you have mastered advanced levels of empathy, you can bring to the bargaining table the feelings of your client and introduce them in proper proportion. Moreover, in appropriate cases you will have your own sense of right and justice that you can communicate to the opponent in a controlled yet convincing manner.

In the following excerpt from the Weber and Jones & Jones negotiation, the emotional content of the argument made by Weber's lawyer

---

6. Condlin posits a sixth element of effective negotiation argument: The argument should be subtle. He suggests certain pieces of your argument should be left implicit, calling on your opponent to think through your contentions to fully understand them and, perhaps, discover aspects of your rationale that you did not appear to have seen. Because the opponent takes an active hand in shaping the ultimate contention, the subtle argument appears less one-sided and more like well-reasoned analysis. It is therefore more convincing.

While there may be some sense in these propositions, we are not certain how consistently they control. For example, opponents may be more impressed by an argument that had *not* occurred to them. Moreover, use of subtlety presents practical difficulties. Trying to achieve subtlety creates a tension with efforts to make your argument detailed and multidimensional. It is no easy task to offer a detailed, multidimensional, organized argument while leaving out a major premise for the other side to articulate. Nor is it clear to us just how you select the aspects of your argument for opponent discovery or how you create the opportunity for discovery.

Using subtlety can be risky, too. Suppose the opponent does not grasp the argument? Granted, you can always articulate it later, but that may compromise emphasis, organization, and clarity. And if the other side does pick up on the argument you have left for it, how will you know? Will your opponent admit it? Describe the argument with detail, multidimensionality, and proper emphasis? Can you be sure the opponent has, in fact, picked up on all the implications of your contentions? You also run a risk that the opponent will see the argument and conclude, since it has apparently escaped you, that your analytical skills are not fully developed. That counters the impression you want to give that you are completely in control of your case and have fully, accurately, and carefully considered all of its permutations.

Thus, subtlety competes with other, and we think more important, characteristics of effective negotiation argument.

changes dramatically. Assume that in Weber's initial statement, the lawyer's voice and gestures are moderate and well controlled. In the next statement, you can detect a slight change in tone and the pace moves up a notch. In the third statement, the attorney's voice rises in pitch and volume, the pace quickens markedly, and the tone is more harsh. At the conclusion of the excerpt, the attorney's language has undergone a transformation; his facial expression is tight and he is shouting, pounding the table, and pointing his finger at the opponent. What do you deduce from the alteration of emotion from the beginning to the end of the excerpt? How does the change affect the power of the lawyer's argument? Look back to one of the earlier examples of negotiation in this chapter and analyze it from the perspective of the emotional aspects of argument. Describe what emotion (through what verbal and nonverbal methods) you would add to the argument to enhance its persuasion.

Weber: Placement means finding a job for a client. Executive counseling, on the other hand, is simply not included within the contract provision. The fee arrangement, the type of work done for the client, and the length of the relationship with the client are entirely different in counseling than they are in placement. And this situation in particular is outside the agreement because Weber is not going to be involved in the business on a day-to-day basis. It's Weber's son who will be operating the business. Weber is only going to be advising and guiding the new venture.

Jones: I understand all that, but counseling is related to placement. There isn't an employment placement situation that doesn't involve some counseling of the client about the job options he or she may have. As such, executive counseling is covered by the "related to" language of the agreement. And the fact that Weber may only be an investor or adviser doesn't take the business itself outside the scope of the clause.

Weber: Look, you're familiar with the case law in this jurisdiction. You're familiar with cases like *Kutash* and *Swygert*. They make it clear that a covenant not to compete can only be as long as necessary to protect the buyer, and the geographic area has got to be limited to where the old business was.

Jones: But I'm also familiar with cases like *Voices, Inc.* and that *Irving Investment Company* one. They approved noncompetition clauses that went on for 50 years and throughout the entire United States.

Weber: At the very least, you'll have to concede that the courts will "blue pencil" this damn agreement. There isn't any doubt that the number of years—ten years—is simply too long under the law in this jurisdiction. And my guess is that it's going to be brought down to two or three years. And on top of that, WEBCo never operated in about half of those states listed in the agreement.

Jones: I'm not persuaded that the law is as clear as you say. We both reviewed the same cases and we reached different conclusions about their impact on this situation.

Weber: Now, damn it, if your people are going to remain this damn obstinate, then you leave me no other choice. If that's the way you're going to treat this damn thing, I have no other course but to go and file suit and get a declaratory judgment. Gene Weber isn't going to sit still and let your client control his economic destiny. He can't afford to forgo this opportunity. And you have to understand something. You have to understand that this isn't just this case. This involves every damn contract that you've written; every one of those standard clauses is at risk here. And I'm telling you—we'll nail you to the wall on this one!

6. Evidence, Presumptions, and "Customary Proofs"[7]

As a lawyer, you should evaluate each of the propositions that form your negotiation argument to determine if the five elements are present in appropriate measure. In reviewing your arguments, be sure to consider the importance of factual evidence, presumptions, and "customary proofs" in constructing convincing contentions. These items deserve some explanation.

It is quite obvious that you will need to refer to facts that bolster your negotiation arguments. Whether you are attempting to resolve a dispute or conclude a transaction, your negotiation arguments will rest on facts. How should you go about building facts that make your case most persuasive?

First, at the center of each of the propositions in your argument, you should seek to place one or more incontestable or virtually incontestable facts. Leading off your reasoning with even relatively minor facts that are not subject to challenge will give your argument greater vitality. Second, these incontestable facts should be surrounded by strong facts, facts that can resist the opponent's inevitable attempts to chip away at them. Because the strong facts you identify are likely to form the core of your negotiation argument, you must be prepared to defend their integrity in the face of your adversary's queries and probes. Third, you must ensure that the proposition on which your argument rests is not inconsistent with or runs counter to any incontestable fact. Nothing is more damaging to a negotiation argument than incompatibility with factual reality. Fourth, your argument should be constructed so that unfavorable facts are recognized and then explained away in a plausible manner.[8] If you marshal your facts according to this conceptual model, your negotiation arguments should be more compelling.

Presumptions persuade, but all too often applicable factual presumptions are not built into negotiation arguments by lawyer-bargainers. Valid presumptions, those considered normal and likely to occur, are as power-

---

7. Professor Stuckey lists these items among a lawyer's tools of persuasion. R. Stuckey, Planning for Persuasion: A Lawyer's Guide to the Basics, 30 Santa Clara L. Rev. — (1990). The phrase "customary proofs" is ours. Stuckey employs the term "*loci* of the preferable," an expression used by C. Perelman & L. Obrechts-Tyteca, *The New Rhetoric: A Treatise on Argumentation* (1971). We will explain the meaning of "customary proofs" in this section.

8. R. Stuckey, Planning for Persuasion: A Lawyer's Guide to the Basics, 30 Santa Clara L. Rev. — (1990), citing G. Vetter, *Successful Civil Litigation: How to Win Your Case Before You Enter the Courtroom* 27 (1977). We have reordered Vetter's references to the importance of facts in developing winning litigation theories.

ful as incontestable facts. Indeed, a sound presumption can be the starting point of your argument and the very underpinning of your reasoning. By invoking a factual presumption, you reduce or eliminate entirely the need to justify that portion of your position and you cast on your opponent the burden of setting the presumption aside. An example of the power of presumption is in order.

Although it has fallen into disfavor, there existed in criminal law the proposition that a person found in possession of property that had been recently stolen was presumed to be the thief. If the state established possession of recently stolen property by the defendant, the jury was instructed that they could presume the defendant stole the goods and could cast on the defendant the burden of proving that the items were obtained in a legitimate manner.[9] You should not be surprised that such an instruction given to the jury made it difficult for a defendant to stand mute, asserting the right to remain silent and refusing to explain the circumstances of possession. Even now when the presumption is no longer specifically called to the attention of the trier of fact, it can still play a role in the outcome of a case. One or more jurors may come to the recognition that unexplained possession of recently stolen items is extremely probative of thievery. Specifically mentioned, on the other hand, the presumption can be the ultimate basis of persuasion as to the defendant's guilt.

Closely related to presumptions are what we call "customary proofs." While presumptions are based on facts, customary proofs rest on beliefs and values that are accepted with little or no objection by members of the reference group that includes your opponent. Because they express the preferences of the community, customary proofs do not require supporting evidence. Customary proofs can be quantitative or qualitative in nature. We are stating a proof relating to

> quantity when we assert that what is good for the greatest number is preferable to what profits only a few; that the durable is preferable to the fragile; or that something useful in varied situations is preferable to something that is of use in highly specific ones. If we give as our reason for preferring something that it is unique, rare, irreplaceable, or that it can never happen again . . . , we are stating [a customary proof] of quality. It is a [customary proof of quality] that prefers the elite over the mass, the exceptional over the normal, that values what is difficult, what must be done at the very moment, what is immediate.[10]

It should be obvious that evidence, presumptions, and customary proofs will aid in the development and impact of your negotiation arguments. Giving them appropriate attention during the planning and implementation of your persuasion strategies is essential.

---

9. Herein the legal problem: Invocation of the presumption creates a burden on the defendant that is in conflict with another presumption, one of constitutional dimension—the presumption of innocence that attaches to a criminal defendant and that remains with him or her throughout the trial.

10. R. Stuckey, id., citing C. Perelman, *The Realm of Rhetoric* 30 (1982).

C. APPEAL AS A FORM OF ARGUMENT

1. Introduction

Professor Condlin and others distinguish arguments from appeals by limiting the latter to requests made of an adversary for a gratuitous concession. So defined, an appeal is similar to the practice of animals going "belly-up" when faced with certain defeat by a more powerful enemy. Condlin, for example, describes the typical appeal of a lawyer-negotiator as one where an attorney, unsuccessful in persuading the opponent to concede anything, pleads with the other side: "I don't want to go home to my client empty-handed. Could you just let me have such-and-such?"[11] In this instance, an appeal is nothing more than a petition for mercy, a request that the opponent grant a token as a mere act of grace. If that is all appeal means, then a negotiator need only be aware of the role that begging can play in an interpersonal situation such as bargaining.

We believe, however, that appeal plays a larger role in the process of persuasion in legal negotiation. Appeal is like argument because both involve a bargainer's attempt to convince her opponents to view the subject of the negotiation just as she has characterized it. But an appeal differs from argument because appeal relies on persuasive approaches that are strictly personal or emotional in nature, as opposed to the characteristics of argument described earlier. Appeal is nonrational persuasion, but it need not be ineffective.

Aristotle and the classical rhetoricians claimed that the personal appeal of the presenter was the most important factor in persuasion. While modern studies have cast doubt on that proposition,[12] it is clear that the personal attributes of the persuader play an important role in the process. Professor Stuckey lists three qualities that a lawyer ought to display when attempting to appeal to another: good sense, good will, and good moral character.[13] The lawyer's good sense conveys to the opponent a complete knowledge of the topic and the ability to identify and make practical decisions that will bring the matter to closure. To communicate good will, the advocate must seem to appreciate the interests of the audience, to speak their language, share their aspirations, and, when required, to understand their biases and prejudices.[14] Finally, the attorney must give clear evidence of sincerity and trustworthiness, must appear as a person who would not deceive the decision-maker.

Exhibiting these characteristics will enhance a negotiator's emotional appeals. We need to remember, however, that conscious thought does not control our emotions; we cannot will ourselves to feel an emotion. Emotions are aroused when people think about something that stirs them:

---

11. Condlin, "Cases on Both Sides": Patterns of Argument in Legal Dispute-Negotiation, 44 Md. L. Rev. 65, 69 (1985).

12. R. Stuckey, Planning for Persuasion: A Lawyer's Guide to the Basics, 30 Santa Clara L. Rev. — (1990).

13. Id.

14. Id.

The lawyer's goal is to cause the decision-maker to feel emotions which will lead to the decision desired by the lawyer. Lawyers who wish to arouse emotions must do so by describing scenes or people or events which will stimulate the desired emotion. It is essential to be specific. General notions and abstract schemes have hardly any effect on the imagination. The more specific the terms, the sharper the image they conjure up, and, conversely, the more general the terms, the weaker the image.[15]

While this advice is sound, it does not provide us with a conceptual foundation on which to build our negotiation appeals. Perhaps there is an arena outside of law that can inform us about the appeal process.

We are all constantly exposed to, and influenced by, appeal as persuasion. The mass of advertising that assaults us daily relies on various forms of appeal. After all, the major objective of advertisers is to persuade, to predispose persons to buy a particular product or service. Not surprisingly, then, the literature on marketing theory suggests a framework for analyzing the use of appeal in legal negotiations. As in prior instances when we have borrowed from other disciplines, the transfer of theory is not exact, but is nevertheless enlightening.

Advertisers try to persuade by appealing to people's basic motivations and relating those motivations to consumer experiences with the advertised product. Marketing theorists have used many different schemes for classifying the basic motivational appeals. One system we find helpful lists four such appeals:

- Rational Appeals (strict presentation of factual information)
- Sensory Appeals (promise of taste good, smell good, feel good, and related rewards)
- Social Appeals (promise of prestige, love, acceptance, and related rewards)
- Ego-Attitude Supports (bolstering of self-image or "appropriateness for my role in life" feelings)[16]

Advertisements show how using the product will pay the consumer back in one or more of these motivational areas. To do that effectively, advertisers try to determine how people experience—that is, how they think about and interact with—the product. The consumer's experiences can be of three kinds:

- End-Product-of-Use Experiences (results of having used the product)
- Product-in-Use Experiences
- Incidental-to-Functional-Use Experiences[17]

---

15. Id.

16. Taken from J. C. Maloney, Marketing Decisions and Attitude Research, in *Effective Marketing Coordination* 595, 601 (G. Baker ed. 1961). Maloney's work provides most of the framework for the text's discussion of appeals. Although his article dates to the early sixties, it is still relied on in current marketing texts. See, e.g., P. Kotler, *Marketing and Management: Analysis, Planning, Implementation and Control* 623 (6th ed. 1988); P. Kotler, *Principles of Marketing* 456-457 (2d ed. 1983).

17. Taken from Maloney, Marketing Decisions and Attitude Research, in *Effective Marketing Coordination* 595, 603 (G. Baker ed. 1961).

The familiar "tastes great, less filling" pitch can be analyzed using these concepts. It relies on promises of sensory rewards for product-in-use experience ("tastes great") and for end-product-of-use experience ("less filling"). In addition, the ad suggests incidental-to-functional-use experiences supporting ego attitudes. Because it is less filling, the consumer can drink more of it (and thus become more like a loveable ex-jock); and because there are one-third fewer calories, use of the product will not ruin the consumer's figure.[18] The new long neck bottles add an incidental-to-functional-use sensory appeal ("looks great").

One marketing theorist has arranged these "modes of evaluation" into a framework of twelve different attitudes that consumers might use to judge a product[19]—called here Chart A.

Chart A
BASIC MOTIVATION APPEALS

PRODUCT-RELATED CONSUMER EXPERIENCES	Presentation of Factual Information	Promise of Sensory Rewards	Promise of Social Rewards	Support of Ego Attitudes
End-Product-of-Use Experiences	I	II	III	IV
Product-in-Use Experiences	V	VI	VII	VIII
Incidental-to-Functional-Use Experiences	IX	X	XI	XII

The adaptation that follows on page 446—called here Chart B—uses illustrative examples to add further meaning to the various classifications.[20]

The basic framework allows advertisers to more effectively persuade consumers by matching the product's strengths with consumer attitudes and market competition factors. In addition, the matrix facilitates adherence to certain advertising axioms. People's attitudes, according to those precepts, are created, reinforced, and changed gradually. The shaping of attitudes is best accomplished by consistent targeting of a few well-defined attitudes. That calls for recognizing how attitudes relate to each other, which attitudes fall within the same "attitude constellation," and how particular appeals relate to attitudes. By visualizing their marketing strategy

---

18. Note that those two appeals persuade two entirely different groups. "Less filling"/"drink more" targets blue collar/male/macho/neighborhood-bar types, while the "one-third less calories"/"stay trim" appeal lures the professional/female/yuppie sets.

19. Maloney, Marketing Decisions and Attitude Research, in *Effective Marketing Coordination* 595, 604 (G. Baker ed. 1961).

20. Taken from P. Kotler, *Principles of Marketing* 457 (2d ed. 1983).

BASIC MOTIVATION APPEALS

PRODUCT-RELATED CONSUMER EXPERIENCES	*Presentation of Factual Information*	*Promise of Sensory Rewards*	*Promise of Social Rewards*	*Support of Ego Attitudes*
End-Product-of-Use Experiences	Get clothes cleaner	Settle upset stomach completely	When you care enough to serve the best	For the skin you deserve to have
Product-in-Use Experiences	The flour that needs no sifting	Real gusto in a great light beer	A deodorant to guarantee social acceptance	The shoe for the young executive
Incidental-to-Functional-Use Experiences	The plastic pack keeps the cigarette fresh	The portable TV that's lighter & easier to lift	The furniture that identifies the home of modern people	Stereo for the man with discriminating taste

within this matrix, advertisers can ensure that their messages regarding a particular product are consistent with prior, planned, and contemporaneous ads and are effectively focused.[21]

In applying the marketing theory to persuasion in negotiations, we have altered some of the categories, but retained the underlying conceptual structure. As should be clear from the brief description given above, the marketing theorists' references to "rational appeals" and "presentation of factual information" correlate with the preceding section's discussion of argument. Thus, our use of the term "appeal" confines us to the latter three categories of the matrix's basic motivational appeals, and we eliminate for present purposes the "factual information" category. In addition, we have translated the "Experience" categories into language that is more descriptive of the negotiation process. We see the relevant classifications as comprising the experiences the participants have (1) during the negotiation and (2) following settlement. The resulting framework appears at the top of page 447.

Note the "experiences" that are relevant here are those of both the negotiator and the client. As we shall see, some appeals are designed to work on only the negotiator, while others focus on the client, and still others target both. Be aware, too, that negotiation appeals, like advertisements, can influence their targets on both conscious and unconscious levels.

---

21. Maloney, Marketing Decisions and Attitude Research, in *Effective Marketing Coordination* 595, 599-600 (G. Baker ed. 1961).

BASIC MOTIVATION APPEALS

NEGOTIATOR/ CLIENT EXPERIENCES	Promise of Sensory Rewards	Promise of Social Rewards	Support of Ego Attitudes
Experiences During Negotiation	I	II	III
Post-Settlement Experiences	IV	V	VI

We now apply the reconstructed matrix to the persuasion process in negotiation.

2. Experiences During Negotiation

a. Introduction

Almost by definition, the appeals relating to experiences that occur during the negotiation primarily affect the individuals actively participating in the negotiation. In legal negotiations, then, these appeals usually target the lawyer, though they could also have an impact on clients who are present and involved in the bargaining.

As we will see, the appeals described in this section tend to manipulate the target, sometimes rather deviously. They have been characterized by commentators as "tactics," "techniques," "dirty tricks," and "psychological warfare."[22] We find some of these appeals to be silly and counterproductive, while others, under appropriate circumstances, may have some value. In any event, you should be aware of their use, how they work, and how to respond to them. Remember, too, that, like all appeals, they are effective only if their target is predisposed to certain attitudes.

b. Category I: Promise of Sensory Rewards

Many negotiators try to create different forms of physical discomfort for their opponents during a negotiation. By doing so, these negotiators

---

22. See, e.g., C. Craver, *Effective Legal Negotiation and Settlement* 113-144 (1986); C. Karrass, *The Negotiating Game* 170-198 (1970); R. Fisher & W. Ury, *Getting to Yes* 134-150 (1981).

Elsewhere in this book, we discuss a variety of negotiation maneuvers that other commentators have categorized under the general rubric of "tactics." See, e.g., "threats" in Section D (pages 454-465); "deception" in Chapter 17, Section F (pages 418-421); and "high/low openers," "Boulwareism," "limited authority," "false demands," and "escalating demands" in Chapter 20 (pages 493-500, 515-518). The latter set, of course, relate to particular aspects of the exchange process, which is the subject of Chapter 20. Chapter 21 also describes several situation-specific strategies.

perceive that they will be better able to persuade the opponent to compromise more quickly and concede more in order to alleviate the unpleasant physical sensation. For example, a sneaky negotiator may turn the heat (or the air conditioner) way up or way down, place the opponent in an uncomfortable chair or in a direct light, or negotiate for extended periods of time without food or a break.

In this instance, the "promise of sensory reward" is the negotiator's silent "promise" to the opponent, "If you make concessions and settle quickly, the physical discomfort will stop and you will feel better." The appeal can work only if the target is predisposed to being nonassertive and is unaware of either the source of the perceived discomfort or the opposing negotiator's ability to control the situation.

We do not recommend that you make much use of this tactic. If exposed, it damages your credibility and risks a deterioration in relations with your opponent and a corresponding increase in the likelihood of deadlock. We must slightly qualify those general views, however. It does not seem inappropriate to us for you to gain advantages by simply wearing down your opponent through persistence or superior stamina.

If you perceive physical discomfort during a negotiation, such that it could affect your judgment or encourage hasty concessions, you should either refuse to continue negotiating until the condition has been relieved or, at least, refuse to make any concessions. If a pattern develops with a particular opponent over several sessions, or if you are otherwise confident the opponent has intentionally caused your discomfort, then you may want to put your suspicions on the table and confront the opponent. Refuse to negotiate unless the other side stops playing games.

c. Category II: Promise of Social Rewards

At least two tactics commonly used in negotiations act on people's predisposition to avoid socially disturbing situations. One of those is variously described as "Mutt and Jeff," "Good Guy-Bad Guy," and "Good Cop-Bad Cop." You have undoubtedly watched crime movies or read crime novels in which a police interrogator exhausts a suspect with a barrage of questions and insults but then gives way to a mild-mannered questioner who offers the suspect a cigarette and a cup of coffee. The suspect's natural inclination is to trust the latter and open up in responding to his questions. (Thus, "Good Cop-Bad Cop.") The same principle applies in the negotiating context. One member of the team is a stubborn, unpleasant bulldog, while his co-counsel appears to be conciliatory and forthcoming. The team conspires to induce its opponent to avoid arousing the bad guy and inciting another socially unpleasant experience. While the bad guy fumes, the good guy gains control of the opponent's confidence and suggests compromises that might appease the bad guy but which would otherwise have been unacceptable to the opponent. The bad guy makes the good guy *seem* reasonable.

Similarly, some negotiators will bluster and feign anger in order to browbeat their opponents into concessions. If the opponents are predisposed to avoid socially discomforting situations, they will make unwarranted concessions rather than risk further antagonizing the irrational person with whom they are negotiating.[23]

The "promise" made in these instances is, again, an implied one: Give us what we want and you will not have to further endure these unpleasant encounters. Naturally, such tactics are the work of competitive-adversarial negotiators. If you find yourself the target of one of these or similar measures, you have several options available in making your response. First, you can simply ignore the disruptive behavior and proceed in the negotiations as you have planned. Presumably, the other side will eventually wear itself down. Second, you can expose the tactic and ask the other side to stick to the merits. That, it is hoped, should defuse the tactic. Third, separately or in combination with the second response, you can threaten to walk out if such outbursts recur. Fourth, you can, in fact, walk out and vow you will not return to the bargaining table unless the other side gives assurance that it will behave and negotiate in good faith.

d. Category III: Support of Ego Attitudes

Several strategems of negotiators play on their opponent's ego. The first of these operates on the theory of "divide and conquer." Prior to a session with two or more lawyers representing an opposing client, the negotiators using this ploy target one member of the other team for personal attack. During the session, they insult and embarrass their victim while showing respect to—and bargaining with—the other members of the team. This demoralizes the target of the derision while inflating the egos of the other team members. The effect splinters their negotiating team, leaving it with weakended resourcefulness and resolve. Defensive and bewildered, the attacked opponent becomes preoccupied with salvaging his or her own self-esteem, and the "respected" opponents become more willing to see the "reasonableness" of the other side.

The tactic is also sometimes used in combination with "Good Guy-Bad Guy." Thus, one member of Team A may act like a wild man, bullying and insulting a targeted member of Team B, while a second member of Team A engages in a conciliatory aside with a second member of Team B, explaining that the latter two, who are reasonable people (in contrast to the other two), can better reach an accord. That second member of Team B will then be caught up in unconscious motivations to see the "reasonableness" of Team A's good guy (who, after all, has just shown he can recognize reasonable people) and to avoid antagonizing Team A's bad guy.

Other bargainers, dubbed "Belly-up" negotiators by Charles Craver,[24] essentially fool opponents by goading them into believing in their "natural" superiority. Craver offers as an example the character of Lieutenant

---

23. Hitler used this tactic repeatedly, and with frightening success. For numerous examples, see W. Shirer, *The Rise and Fall of the Third Reich* 325-330, 385-386, 392-395, 415-417, 444-448, 570-571, 577-579 (1960).

24. *Effective Legal Negotiation and Settlement* 137-141 (1986).

Columbo in the television detective series. Show after show, Columbo manages to convince the criminals that he is a bumbling, disorganized, dim-witted, police hack who is no match for the brilliance of his adversaries. Before the criminals catch on, they have made a fatal mistake and are being escorted to their booking.

The Belly-up Bargainer does an "Aw shucks" routine that causes opponents to overestimate their control of the negotiation and underestimate their counterpart: "Geez, I'm just an old country lawyer. You city boys have so much more knowledge and experience in this stuff than I do. I hope you won't take unfair advantage of me." The city boys (and girls) are lured into a false sense of security and bend over backwards not to take advantage of the country lawyer. Meanwhile, if they remain so gullible, the country lawyer fleeces them. The obvious defense to such a tactic is to never underestimate your opponent.

Finally, there is what Craver calls the "Brer Rabbit" tactic,[25] based on the life-saving ploy used by Brer Rabbit in the Uncle Remus stories. When cornered by the fox, Brer Rabbit pleads to his captor:

> I don't care what you do with me, so long as you don't fling me in that brier-patch. Roast me, but don't fling me in that brier-patch. . . . Drown me just as deep as you please, but don't fling me in that brier-patch. . . . Skin me, snatch out my eyeballs, tear out my ears by the roots, and cut off my legs, but don't fling me in that brier-patch.[26]

The fox, desiring to punish the rabbit, throws him into the brier-patch, thus allowing Brer Rabbit to escape.

You can successfully use this bit of negative psychology only against certain opponents. They must be so caught up in the competition and their egos that they not only want to "win" the negotiation, but also want to annihilate you and your client. It helps a lot, too, if your opponent is stupid.

3. Post-Settlement Experiences

a. Introduction

Another set of appeals directs the opposing side to rewards that will accompany settlement. These appeals differ from the "promises" discussed in Section E, page 465. That section's promises concern offers made that require some sacrifice from the offeror (e.g., "If you agree to this settlement, I promise to buy you season tickets to the opera"). The rewards discussed in this section inure to the benefit of a party by the mere fact of settlement, without any additional concession or sacrifice by the appealing party. The rewards derive from offers previously or simultaneously made.

---

25. Id. at 132-133.
26. Id. at 132, quoting Joel Chandler Harris, *Uncle Remus, His Songs and His Sayings* (1880).

As with the tactics relating to experiences during negotiation, the success of appeals aimed at post-settlement experiences often depends on the predisposition of the negotiator and client at whom the appeals are directed.

b. Category IV: Promise of Sensory Rewards

Although legal negotiations do not allow for a wide variety of post-settlement sensory rewards, lawyer-bargainers do frequently use at least one of them. Settlements in legal negotiations typically give the parties and the lawyers a great psychological lift. They may eliminate uncertainty, guarantee an end to an unpleasant dispute, relieve anxiety and tension, or excite with the prospect of the settlement's payoff. Reaching settlement makes those involved feel better. Negotiators can thus use that reward to encourage agreement, especially with opponents who are particularly anxious about their alternatives to settlement.

As an example, assume you represent an employer who has been sued by a former employee for wrongful discharge. In attempting to settle the lawsuit for a reasonable amount, you could rightly indicate to the opponent how much better the plaintiff would feel if she could avoid an ugly trial, get this unhappy experience behind her, and start her professional life anew. Indeed, the desire to "get it over with" and experience the accompanying sense of relief may be compelling for many persons. You can appeal to that predisposition to your advantage.

There are other sensory reward possibilities. A defense counsel trying to coax a settlement might point out the variety of pleasure the offered money could buy (fine food, a sauna, tropical cruise, etc.). Or in negotiations for the lease of a new office complex, the lawyer representing the lessor could direct the other side to consider the aesthetic benefits of the building.

c. Category V: Promise of Social Rewards

Legal negotiations often allow opportunities to promise social rewards as an inducement to settle. Appeals to altruism, friendship, good will, and the like are both common and appropriate among bargainers. The "pay-off" for the party to whom the appeal is made comes in the form of enhanced social relations or simply personal gratification. Thus, a lawyer's pitch for a concession based on the parties' long-standing friendship promises continued friendship. A legal services attorney might appeal to a creditor's desire to help the needy or maintain good public and customer relations by granting an extension on a loan to a poor widow with eight children. Or a lawyer representing a public interest organization may be able to coax concessions from an attorney or party who is in sympathy with the organization's causes.

The "bandwagon appeal" offers another example of this method of persuasion. Here the lawyer calls on the opponent to act in a certain way because others are doing so, urging the opponent to bow to peer patterns to avoid being left behind. Appeals to shame, bias, guilt, fear, and embarrassment are among the other forms of this negotiation technique you will encounter from time to time.

d. Category VI: Support of Ego Attitudes

The final category involves appeals that explain how settlement would, in some way, enhance the opponent's status. The attorney for the employer sued by a discharged employee could contend, in arguing for a relatively low, but confidential, figure, that settlement would appear to others to vindicate the plaintiff. (Conversely, losing at trial would severely damage the plaintiff's professional standing and self-esteem.) In a negotiation over a book contract, the lawyer for a highly regarded publishing house could convince the author and his agent that any association with this publisher would enhance the prestige of both the author and the agent and would therefore support a concession from them. Perhaps a manufacturer's lawyer trying to settle a products liability case could benefit by pointing out to the plaintiff's lawyers that they would be the first in the country to reach a negotiated agreement in this particular kind of case (rather than being another in a long string of failures at trial). In practically any case, painting the other side as a "winner" in the negotiation acts as an appeal supporting both the client's and the lawyer's ego.

Most negotiations, in fact, require consideration of the impact a settlement offer would have on the ego of each of the parties. In particular, the parties will be very reluctant to settle a litigation matter in a way that impeaches their underlying contentions or that fails in some fashion to vindicate them. You should, therefore, assess how your offers can be framed to give some credence to the opponent and appease his or her pride.

≡ **PROBLEM 3** ≡
Use of Appeals to Persuade Weber

The Weber-Jones & Jones attorneys very tentatively explore below a possible alternative solution to their clients' dispute: Jones will give Weber an executive position with Jones if he forgoes his proposed venture into professional counseling. See if you can identify the use of appeals in the excerpt and evaluate their potential effectiveness:

Jones: Before we break up, let me suggest an idea for your client to consider. What if Jones offered Mr. Weber a high-level position with the company, perhaps heading up the task force on executive counseling? Would he agree to give up his idea of starting his own business in the field?

Weber: I don't know. Certainly, that would depend at least in part on the terms of such an offer.

Jones: I think we could offer him $75,000 a year salary, plus the full range of benefits and a comfortable annuity package.

Weber: I'm not sure. He's a very independent and proud man; I just don't know if he'd want to work as an underling in a large corporation.

Jones: Well, you can tell him he'd have free reins to run the operation in this district. Plus, we'll give him the title of Senior Vice President for Executive Counseling. That would put him in an exclusive club in the corporate hierarchy.

Weber: Perhaps. But don't forget Mr. Weber is very much concerned, too, about his son's business future, and I think Weber relishes the idea of working together with his son. What's the possibility of a position for Bobby?

Jones: I can't promise anything on that; I'd have to talk it over with my people.

Weber: When you do, I think you ought to point out that having both Webers on board would assure you of a couple of very contented, as well as competent, executives in important positions who would certainly be able to work well together. Your people could also take into account they would be enriching the life of one of their senior persons, giving Weber a chance to work with his son in building a business operation in a new field.

Jones: Perhaps. Of course, at Weber's age, I imagine it would be important for him to be relieved of the uncertainties of starting up a new business, let alone one that could be subject to a lengthy and sticky court challenge. The security he could gain with us should be a real benefit to him.

Weber: I will inform him of your offer, and I assume you will broach the possibility and the benefits of also hiring on Bobby.

Jones: Will do.

4. Conclusion

To fully understand how appeals can be effectively used in legal negotiations, we return to the basic marketing principles sketched at the beginning of this section. The "modes of evaluation" framework categorizes the possible attitudes that might predispose your opponents to grant concessions.[27] You select particular attitudes for the focus of your appeals by analyzing several factors.

First, you must assess your opponents. Are they likely to be receptive to sensory, social, or ego gratification? While you can create attitudes, success is more likely and easier if you can build on preexisting attitudes. This assessment requires you to consider the values and personality of both the opposing client and the opposing attorney. (The analogue in advertising would be completion of a market analysis of the attitudes of potential consumers.) In the above discussion from the Weber-Jones & Jones problem, Jones's lawyer probably had a good basis for concluding that Weber is a proud person who would be receptive to ego-supporting appeals. In fact,

---

27. Maloney, Marketing Decisions and Attitude Research, in *Effective Marketing Coordination* 595, 605 (G. Baker ed. 1961). Our analysis is adapted from id. at 598-601 and 605-607.

Weber's lawyer confirms his client is "very independent and proud." On the other hand, one would not ordinarily expect a large (and impersonal) corporation, with diffused responsibilities and relations, to be all that receptive to Weber's promises of social rewards.

Second, you must fit any use of appeals into the larger pattern of your negotiation. Your appeals should be compatible with your own overall negotiation style and strategy. Mixed signals in that regard would diminish your effectiveness. You must also ensure that the appeals match the arguments and the outcome you are trying to sell. For example, the appeals from Jones's lawyer in the above excerpt correlated well with the company's arguments about the validity of its noncompetition clause and with its desired outcomes of avoiding test litigation and preventing Weber from starting up his new business. Moreover, you want your appeals to be as consistent as possible with prior and potential arguments and appeals. Remember, attitudes change gradually and are most affected by a succession of consistent, well-focused messages.

Finally, for your appeals to be effective they must be preceded by, or joined with, the facts and effective argument. Persuasion, as we have already seen, has both cognitive and motivational properties. If your opponents do not have the facts necessary to evaluate the extent of the rewards promised by your appeals, they are not likely to be influenced. Your pleas with a local bank president on behalf of the indigent widow with eight children are unlikely to be effective if you have not proved that the client is, in fact, poor and overburdened.

D. THE ROLE OF THREATS IN NEGOTIATION

1. Introduction

When you consider what will persuade the other side in a negotiation, you ask yourself: What is it that my opponent fears most? What is it that my opponent wants most? As you fashion the answers to these questions you may find yourself constructing threats and promises to induce the action you desire from your adversary. Threats as a form of persuasion, of course, play on your opponent's fears; promises, on the other hand, go to the opponent's desires. The effective negotiator understands the elements of threat and promise and how to use and respond to both. Let us first consider the role of threat as a form of persuasion in negotiation.

When you employ a threat in bargaining, you hope it will induce your opponent to act or not act in a way that conforms to your needs and interests. The inducement that constitutes the core of threat is the avoidance of damage to the opponent's interests that you, the threatener, have the ability and the willingness to inflict. In theory, a threat will be successful if a threatened opponent can be made to understand that it is less costly to comply with your demands than suffer the damage that would follow if you carried out the threat.

In *Getting to Yes*, Professors Fisher and Ury assert that "threats are one of the most abused tactics in negotiation."[28] Too often, those authors suggest, threats are counterproductive; instead of producing compliance with the demands of the threatener, threats may stimulate counterthreats or a determined resistance. The escalating tension or "bunker" mentality that results from such responses to a threat may endanger settlement or ruin the relationship between the parties.

With reservations and explanation, we agree with Fisher and Ury that threats pose some risks to the success of the negotiation process. At the same time, however, we recognize that threats can work: They will frequently convince a negotiator to adopt the threatener's perspective.[29] We agree with Fisher and Ury that threat is abused as a tactic, particularly, in our view, by lawyer-negotiators. But we posit another and somewhat different explanation for our conclusion that threat is ineffectively used by lawyer-negotiators. Too often we have observed attorneys inject threats into a negotiation without realizing that their statements constitute a threat or without the intention of carrying through with the threat if the opponent ignores the notice of consequences. The failure of lawyers to recognize that a threat has been made is caused by a lack of understanding of the elements of threat. The absence of the will to implement the threat signifies a failure to understand the risks to the threatener's credibility produced by such lack of commitment. The remarkably widespread failure of attorneys to identify these negative implications of threat as a persuasive device suggests our next topic.

2. Analysis of a Threat

In this section we set forth the elements of an effective threat. By effective we mean a threat that maximizes the likelihood that an opponent will be persuaded to conform his or her conduct to that demanded by the threatener. In moving ahead with a discussion of effective threats, put to one side Fisher and Ury's previously mentioned concern that a threat increases the risk of a deadlocked negotiation. Although the statement is true as a general proposition, it should not deter a lawyer-negotiator from analyzing the risk of threat in a specific negotiation. Risk analysis of that type, however, is situation-specific and benefits from the informed judgment of an experienced negotiator.

a. Potential Costs to the Threatening Party

Before listing the specific elements of an effective threat, we urge you to keep in mind the fundamental proposition that every threat involves an identifiable cost to the threatening party. Most people evaluating a threat

---

28. R. Fisher & W. Ury, *Getting to Yes* 142 (1981).
29. Moreover, as more fully explained in note 30, below, every negotiator in every negotiation expresses or implies at least one threat—that is, if a satisfactory accord is not reached, the negotiator will break off bargaining and pursue an alternative.

focus only on the potential damage to the threatened party. This instinctive concentration on the injury that is threatened diverts attention from the consequences that will be suffered by the threatening party if the threat has to be carried out. But if you step back for a moment, you will realize that from a conceptual perspective no threat can be made without potential costs to the threatener. Put yourself in a number of different settings and think of some threats you might use in that context to obtain what you want. Whether it is international politics, a business situation, a neighborhood dispute, or a family matter, if you develop a threat to use against another you have created possible costs to yourself. Indeed, unless the consequences of the threatened action involve some costs to the threatener, there would be no threat. The threatener would have no reason to delay the action and its implementation. Thus, a threat can be seen as an act of hesitation, an act of self-restraint on the part of the threatener caused by a conscious or intuitive understanding of the potential price of implementing the threat.

Consider, for example, a classic threat where the costs to the threatener are routinely communicated to the party threatened. A parent says to the child, "Don't do that. If you do, I will spank you even though the spanking will hurt me more than it will hurt you." If you were ever confronted with such a threat as a child, it is not likely that you believed that the spanking would hurt your parent more than it hurt you. Now you are in a much better position to understand that a spanking may indeed involve substantial cost to parents in terms of feelings, image, philosophy, and more.

In the following negotiation excerpts, identify the costs to the threatening party if the opponent fails to act and the threat must be implemented:

1. In a labor-management negotiation over a new contract, the lawyer representing the union says, "As you know, we've been working without a contract for two months and the membership authorized a strike. Unless you are willing to make a move on the wages and job security, the members will walk off the job at midnight. The economic cost to the company of even a few days of a strike could be severe."

2. In a negotiation between the search committee for a major metropolitan museum and the number one candidate for the position of museum director, the candidate says, "As you know, I'm very interested in your institution and the exciting propects for growth. But I can only take the position if I believe I have the key people around me who I am confident will get the job done. Therefore, if you cannot make room for my Associate and Assistant Director, then, reluctantly, I will decline your offer."

3. In a negotiation between the general manager of a professional baseball team and the lawyer-agent of a ballplayer, the general manager says: "Look, your client has a lot of fans in this town, he's been a superstar, he's got a lock on the Hall of Fame, and we'd love to have him finish out his career with the team. But if he doesn't stop second-guessing the manager and the front office in the press every day, then we'll have to let him go. There's no other team around interested in a trade. That'd be a tragic ending to 14 years with this team, a lot worse than sitting on the bench and getting some 'at bats' as a pinch hitter."

4. In a negotiation between lawyers representing the plaintiff in a personal injury case and the defendant's insurance carrier that takes place two weeks before the scheduled trial, the plaintiff's lawyer says, "I don't believe you and the company understand how solid our case is and the risks if we go to trial. I am extremely confident we'll prevail and the verdict will be well into seven figures. Moreover, when we win it will open the floodgates to dozens of other suits just like this one. If I walk out of this room without an offer in excess of $350,000, I will take this case to trial and verdict no matter what you offer later."

These four examples illustrate the important principle that the potential costs to a threatener can be substantial. They also illustrate the first thing you should do before making a negotiation threat or after receiving such a threat: You must identify and total the downside costs of any threat to the threatener. Only when you have isolated all categories of costs that flow from threat and you have tabulated the value of those costs (in economic, social, psychological, or other relevant terms), can you evaluate whether the threat is likely to be a form of effective persuasion. Without such a worst-case scenario analysis from the perspective of the threatener, you will not be in position to examine the five elements of any threat.

b. Elements of a Threat

(1) A Threat Must Be Communicated

The first element, so elementary that it appears ludicrous to even state it, is that the threat must be communicated to the other side. An opponent must be aware that a threat has been made. If the target of the threat does not realize that a threat is pending, it is impossible for the threatened party to be convinced of a need to change position or attitude. Because many attorneys have not conceptualized the factors making up a threat, they do not perceive the importantance of the actual communication of the threat. Indeed, we have observed numerous instances of lawyers making a threat in an offhand manner or as a mumbled aside. If you are serious about persuading through the use of a threat, you must get the opponent's attention and signal that the threat that follows is a significant event in the bargaining.

(2) A Threat Must Be Understood

The second element of an effective threat is almost as evident as the first. A threat must be understood by the party being threatened. If the opponent does not appreciate what is at stake, the threatener is less apt to induce compliance with the demand. Some negotiators would argue that vagueness about the outcome is more effective, allowing the threatened party to conjure a parade of horribles that will encourage submission to the demands. We believe that is mere wishful thinking in most negotiation situations. To return to the parent-child situation, consider which is more effective: "Unless you do what I want you to do I will do something to you that you surely will regret" or "Do what I want you to do or you'll not be allowed to go to your best friend's birthday party."

To ensure understanding, you, as an effective negotiator, must determine that the other side comprehends exactly what action or nonaction on the opponent's part will trigger the threatened result; that the opponent appreciates the full extent of the threatened consequences; and that the opponent grasps exactly who it is that controls the trigger of the threat, either the threatener or a third party under the threatener's influence. If the other side has full knowledge of such details, you have increased the chances of the threat producing the hoped-for response.

(3) A Threat Must Be Valued

A threat that is heard and understood must also be valued by the recipient. If the consequences of action or nonaction are not valued by the threatened person, there is little chance that the party under threat will comply with the threatener's demand. This third element of an effective threat requires you to understand in detail the opponent's value structure. When the opponent's fears and needs are fully appreciated, you are better able to select a consequence of reasonable significance, thereby increasing the probability that the threat will achieve its goal.

(4) A Threat Must Be Believed

The fourth factor considered by the effective negotiator before using a threat is whether the opponent will believe that the threatener will act as promised. Your threatened opponent will not accede to your demand unless it is probable that you truly will go to the trouble and cost of acting as you have vowed to act. In other words, if the opponent considers your threat empty, compliance is not likely.

It is obvious, but it bears repeating: The most effective threat is one that is never implemented. To secure the benefit of this adage, the threatened party must believe the threatener will act as promised and, as a result, give in to the demand. The maxim's downside occurs when the threatened party does not believe the threatener will act as promised and, therefore, refuses to acquiesce. In the latter circumstance, the threatener must choose between two unpleasant alternatives. First, the threatener can implement the threatened conduct, thereby imposing costs on both parties. Second, the threatener can ignore the opponent's noncompliance, thereby imposing significant damage to his or her credibility. In either event, the injury to the threatener can be great. The possibility of being confronted with this dilemma makes the opponent's disbelief one of the great risks in using a threat.

To avoid that, you, as an effective negotiator, must proceed carefully. At the outset, you should evaluate candidly and completely the costs of implementing the proposed threat. To do this, you should first assume the worst-case scenario, that your opponent will refuse to comply with the demand contained in your threat. Next, you should analyze the exact steps that you must take to execute the threat. Only in this way can you be sure that the threatened result is actually achievable even if action is taken. With these action steps fixed firmly in your mind and the threatened outcome guaranteed, you are now in a position to total the downside price of opponent refusal to be moved by your threat. At this point, you can compare the costs to self and the costs to the opponent of threat implementation. Except in unusual circumstances, if the costs to your opponent are not greater than the costs to your client, the probability of opponent disbelief is increased. Even if the balance sheet is tipped in your favor, if the ultimate cost to your side is disproportionate to the possible gain, the opponent still is more likely to disbelieve. In any event, you must conduct a detailed cost-benefit analysis before making an injudicious threat.

(5) A Threat Must Be Prospective

The final element of the effective threat is that it must be prospective. The threatened action and the result of that action must take place in the future. Action in the past, action that is now complete, cannot threaten anyone. That does not mean, of course, that past secret acts of a party cannot be revealed sometime in the future. There, however, the conduct threatened is the revelation, not the acts themselves. An aside to the required prospectiveness of a threat is the ability of the threatener to control the threat's trigger. As we alluded in enjoining you to consider the action steps necessary to implement the threat, a threat cannot be effective unless the threatener or some entity under the threatener's control, guidance, or influence has the power and ability to initiate the threatened conduct. Thus, you must communicate to your opponent that you can cause the threatened conduct at a timely future moment.

In connection with this fifth element of threat, we should mention that some negotiation theorists distinguish threats from warnings. Fisher and Ury, for example, suggest that effective problem solvers do not threaten; instead, they warn opponents of the consequences of unacceptable conduct. We have compared the elements of warning and threats and do not find a meaningful conceptual difference. To be effective, a warning, for the reasons mentioned above in connection with threat, also must be heard, understood, valued, believed, and prospective. Only on the control of the trigger do we find a potential theoretical distinction between a warning and a threat. Fisher and Ury suggest that in a warning the trigger is removed a step or two, out of the hands of the issuing party.[30] Because, how-

---

30. Fisher and Ury indicate that "good negotiators rarely resort to threats . . . [because] there are other ways to communicate the same information." R. Fisher & W. Ury, *Getting to Yes* 143 (1981). Warnings, they suggest, are more appropriate because they involve consequences that "will occur independently of your will rather than those you could choose to bring about." The example that follows these statements explains, we believe, the lack of a real distinction between threats and warnings. In the example, the opponent is warned that failure to reach agreement will result in the publication of "the whole sordid story" by the media. While characterized as outside the hands of the warning party in the text, the warner in the example goes on to tell the opponent who is being "warned": "In a matter of this much public interest, I don't see how *we* could legitimately suppress information." (Emphasis added.) Id. at 143. It is obvious that although the press would be the ultimate actor, the warning party can choose

ever, the negotiator can influence significantly the pulling of that trigger in all of the warning examples we have encountered, we do not believe the distinction is significant. Therefore, whether you are an adversarial negotiator using a threat or a problem solver delivering a warning, you are subject to the element analysis set out above.

3. The Responses to Threats

Undoubtedly you will participate in negotiations with opponents who will threaten you and your client. You need, therefore, a framework around which to build a set of responses to threats. Without a conceptual framework, your rejoinder to the threat may not place the opponent's pressure in perspective, leading you to accede rather than dismiss. The responsive framework we commend to you is built on our earlier analysis of threats as a form of persuasion. The underlying characteristic of costs to both parties and the five elements of effective threats create an outline for our reply to an opponent's threat.

As mentioned earlier, before responding directly to any threat of another party, you should analyze the underlying costs to the threatener. Instead of concentrating on what injury your opponents can do to your side, focus first on what price they will have to pay to implement the threat. The problem with this approach, of course, is that it is difficult to conduct such a detailed analysis during the heat of negotiation exchanges. Our natural tendency when threatened is to concentrate on self-protection (the defensive reaction) or on mounting a counterattack to discourage our opponent (the counteroffensive reaction). Because of these typical inclinations and in keeping with our basic premise that the effective use of the skills discussed in this text depends on extensive advance preparation, we urge you to plan as much as possible your response to threats before the actual bargaining. To accomplish this, you should ask yourself (and, during counseling, your client): "What do we fear most and how could the opponent threaten us with that outcome?" By answering these questions, you can anticipate many of the threats an opponent could introduce during negotiation. It also will allow you time to conduct the required cost-benefit analysis when all of the implications of the threat can be figured carefully.

If your analysis of relative costs to your side and to your threatening opponent suggests that the harm to each is closely balanced or that the opponent's suffering may be greater than your client's if the threat is executed, you should entertain doubt that your adversary actually will carry out the

---

to cooperate or not cooperate with the media. We suggest that most warnings issued in negotiations are not notifications to the other side about possible acts of God or the works of independent parties. They involve actions that the warning side controls or influences. The distinction between warning and threat is semantic, in our judgment, rather than substantive.

Moreover, as Fisher and Ury inform us, every negotiator has a "Best Alternative to Negotiated Agreement"—the negotiator's "BATNA." It may be filing a lawsuit, going to trial, or buying a particular product elsewhere. The possibilities are limitless, but there is always at least one. Correspondingly, in every negotiation each side—explicitly or implicitly—communicates to the other: "If you don't settle on terms agreeable to me, I'll break off negotiations and pursue my BATNA." That is a threat.

threat. Do not, however, challenge your opponent's commitment to retaliation if you fail to acquiesce. At most, you may want to question whether the other side understands the extent of self-destruction that will follow execution of the threat. Perhaps the most effective way to accomplish this is to use clarification and elaboration probes to focus precisely on what conduct of your client the opponent wants altered and exactly what will occur if your client refuses. By forcing the other side to particularize the conduct and the consequences, you may get the adversary to appreciate the foolhardiness of carrying out the threat.

But before any other response to threat, you should consider ignoring it. Remember, the first element we identified above is that a threat must be "heard" to be effective. By interfering with the communication of a threat—in other words, by not "hearing" it—you may prevent the threat from existing as a meaningful part of the negotiation. Because many lawyers who issue negotiation threats or warnings are neither aware of nor committed to implementing them, ignoring a threat can be a very effective reaction.

An opponent's threats can be misunderstood. Particularly when you have anticipated the threat, you may be in a position to recharacterize it and then deal with it as you have refashioned it. Thus, you can diminish the costs to your client and elevate the costs to the other side. Also, you could misinterpret the action demanded, the action to be taken, or the triggering mechanism. As slight variations on this response, you can treat the threat as unsanctioned by the opponent's principal or as the product of the intense emotion of the moment. Once you have misconstrued the opponent's threat, you should proceed based on your misunderstanding.

An example of recharacterizing the threat may be appropriate. In the Weber-Jones & Jones problem, assume that counsel for Weber has learned during the assessment stage that the noncompetition clause is boilerplate language used in at least a dozen other acquisition contracts. Suppose Weber now threatens Jones & Jones with the multiplier effect, a technique designed to increase the costs and risks to the party on the receiving end of the intimidation. Notice how counsel for Jones deals with the threat in the following excerpt from a negotiation:

Weber: You know, this case involves a lot more than this single contract. It involves all your other acquisitions where this "boilerplate" noncompete language was used. We think the other sellers will be very interested in joining our request for a declaratory judgment. A positive ruling for us will open a Pandora's box for you. Why, you could have sellers in competition with you in dozens of locations around the country!

Jones: To be sure, an adverse ruling would be unwelcome, but not on the basis you've just mentioned. I am acquainted with all the sellers of employment agencies where we used the standard noncompete clause. I can't think of one who would be remotely interested in going back into business. But to get to the point that other sellers would have even the remotest interest in the matter, you have to get through a very costly legal process with a case that has little chance of success. Naturally, you don't expect any other sellers to contribute to the cost of litigation that benefits your client. Thus, Mr. Weber is facing trial costs that we estimate at a minimum of $23,000 and, in the unlikely event he's fortunate enough to prevail, appellate costs of double that amount. More important, we've told you in considerable detail why we don't believe you will be successful in a declaratory judgment action to narrow the clause. And, of course, the risk to us is entirely dependent on your winning a weak case. Why, we've confronted this type of . . .

The lawyer for Weber stated that other sellers were expected to contribute to the costs of the litigation. Counsel for Jones, however, "misconstrued" that portion of the threat and gave a rationale for the "misunderstanding." Simultaneously, Jones's lawyer went on to increase the costs to Weber of carrying through the now recharacterized threat. With this type of response to a threat, counsel forces the threatening opponent to look on the bleak side of the potential action.

The other responses to a negotiation threat follow the structure of the remaining elements of this form of intimidation. Thus, you can demonstrate to the opponent that the threatened action is not valued by your client. For example, in response to a threatened lawsuit, you might say to the other side, "My client is insured" or "My client is judgment proof." Even if you cannot credibly deny the threatened conduct is valuable to your client, you may be able to say that something else is more valuable and, therefore, must be protected. For instance, you might answer a threat with, "My client has been threatened similarly in the past and has not bowed to that kind of pressure. Her standing in the industry depends on her continuing to act based on an objective analysis of the situation, not in response to threats." You can maintain that you do not believe the opponent will take the threatened steps, although as mentioned above, that could goad the other side into acting to maintain credibility. Thus, in an appropriate circumstance you might say, "You can't expect us to believe that your client is willing to jeopardize its economic stability by launching such a costly hostile takeover." A final reply based on the elements is to communicate to your adversary that the essence of the threat is behind your client and, therefore, not prospective. As an example, you may be able say, "My client's reputation has been ruined already, so the information you plan to release can't hurt him any more than that released in the special investigator's report."

Of course, there is another rejoinder to an opponent's threat. You can counterthreat. There is something comforting in fighting fire with fire, even in a negotiation. Our ego is salved when we respond to an opponent's warning with one of our own. But as suggested earlier, this can be a very dangerous tactic. Threat-counterthreat quite often leads to an escalating spiral of even more threats, which produces deadlock and engenders bad feelings. In most situations, an alternative answer will deal better with the opponent's attempt to persuade by use of threat. Even when you have planned to introduce a threat of your own into the negotiation, timing it as a rejoinder to the opponent's threat may be counterproductive. Because there is so much risk in a negative tit-for-tat interchange, delaying or abandoning use of your warning may be more appropriate.

These are examples of the reactions you can formulate to the threats of another party. If you concentrate on the elements of threat as a negotiating tactic, you will find additional effective responses. Preventive analysis, however, is the most productive defense. Anticipating the threats that an opponent may use and planning your response in advance will hinder an opponent's attempt to manipulate you by the use of threats.

4. Responses to a Threatening Style

We have concentrated to this point on analyzing the underlying strategy that supports the use of threats as a persuasive device. Of the lawyers who rely on threats, the most impressive ones are those who deliver the threats with cool, calculating precision, in a low key and often with an almost apologetic manner that says, "I wish I could avoid doing this, but I can't." Sometimes, however, a competitive adversarial will accompany the substantive threat with a threatening style, a style designed to intimidate the opponent, to get the other side to make concessions to avoid the unpleasant confrontation.

You should consider the range of reactions available to you in responding to such a bombastic bargainer. To test what you might do when the opponent adopts a threatening style, consider again the excerpt from the negotiation between the attorneys representing Weber and Jones & Jones that we presented earlier in connection with the discussion of emotional arguments (pages 440-441). Put yourself in the position of the lawyer for Jones. Remember, as the scene ends, the Weber lawyer's facial expression is tight, and he is shouting, pounding the table, and pointing his finger at the other lawyer. Isolate the elements of the substantive threat. Consider the response options open to you following the final retort of Weber's counsel.

Weber: Placement means finding a job for a client. Executive counseling, on the other hand, is simply not included within the contract provision. The fee arrangement, the type of work done for the client, and the length of the relationship with the client are entirely different in counseling than they are in placement. And this situation in particular is outside the agreement because Weber is not going to be involved in the business on a day-to-day basis. It's Weber's son who will be operating the business. Weber is only going to be advising and guiding the new venture.

Jones: I understand all that, but counseling is related to placement. There isn't an employment placement situation that doesn't involve some counseling of the client about the job options he or she may have. As such, executive counseling is covered by the "related to" language of the agreement. And the fact that Weber may only be an investor or adviser doesn't take the business itself outside the scope of the clause.

Weber: Look, you're familiar with the case law in this jurisdiction. You're familiar with cases like *Kutash* and *Swygert*. They make it clear that a covenant not to compete can only be as long as necessary to protect the buyer, and the geographic area has got to be limited to where the old business was.

Jones: But I'm also familiar with cases like *Voices, Inc.* and that *Irving Investment Company* one. They approved noncompetition clauses that went on for 50 years and throughout the entire United States.

Weber: At the very least, you'll have to concede that the courts will "blue pencil" this damn agreement. There isn't any doubt that the number of years—ten years—is simply too long under the law in this jurisdiction. And my guess is that it's going to be brought down to two or three years. And on top of that, WEBCo never operated in about half of those states listed in the agreement.

Jones: I'm not persuaded that the law is as clear as you say. We both reviewed the same cases and we reached different conclusions about their impact on this situation.

Weber: Now, damn it, if your people are going to remain this damn obstinate, then you leave me no other choice. If that's the way you're going to treat this damn thing, I have no other course but to go and file suit and get a declaratory judgment. Gene Weber isn't going to sit still and let your client control his economic destiny. He can't afford to forgo this opportunity. And you have to understand something. You have to understand that this isn't just this case. This involves every damn contract that you've written, every one of those standard clauses is at risk here. And I'm telling you—we'll nail you to the wall on this one!

The essence of the threat by Weber's lawyer is the multiplier effect of this matter on other acquisitions by Jones & Jones. According to the lawyer, Weber will be successful in a declaratory judgment action. Moreover, this success will throw into doubt the standard noncompetition clause used in the "boilerplate" assets purchase agreements written by Jones.

To be sure, the substantive threat must be measured by the underlying cost to Weber and the five elements of threat to determine whether it should persuade Jones to alter its bargaining position. But Jones must consider separately whether and how to respond to the shouting, pounding, and pointing. Assume for the moment that you represent Jones and have determined that Weber's lawyer is using this threatening style to intimidate you as counsel for Jones and to add power to the substance of the threat.[31] What choices are available to you on the issue of intimidating style? List and explain those choices. Compare your ideas with the following thoughts we have on this subject.

One response to the intimidating negotiator is to ignore the attempt to manipulate you. You could refuse to acknowledge the threatening style by remaining calm and maintaining unflinching eye contact. When the oppo-

---

31. We have assumed for the purposes of these comments that the attorney for Weber had adopted a threatening style in order to intimidate counsel for Jones. Reading the excerpt, however, we believe it is more probable that Weber's lawyer became frustrated with the progress and direction of the negotiation. Frustration led to loss of control and the resulting tone, gestures, and language. If your opponent appears to be acting in a threatening manner out of anger, disappointment, and sense of futility, you should concentrate very closely on the exact words the opponent is using. It is at a moment like this, when prepared guards may be down, that you can learn much about the other side's real needs and fears. Be careful that you are not diverted by the powerful nonverbal signals of threat and frustration. It is one of the few occasions in negotiation that you should ignore the overwhelming nonverbal communication in favor of only the spoken language itself.

nent's tirade is complete, you could go on with the substantive discussion as if the explosion had never occurred. The implicit message of this response is that such behavior is an aberration and irrelevant to a productive discussion.

Akin to ignoring intimidating behavior is treating it with humor, a valuable tactic throughout the negotiation process. With an accompanying smile, comments such as "Wow! With that kind of acting ability, you'd be terrific on the afternoon soaps" or "Gee, when I need to blow off steam I usually kick things" may send the most appropriate message to the intimidating adversary. Humor communicates that you do not consider the attempted intimidation seriously.

Another option is to fight fire with a momentary flare-up of your own. You could respond to the opponent by blowing up yourself, using the same tone and gestures for a brief period. Following this temporary explosion, you could return abruptly to your normal calm discussion of the issues. This response is most effective if your change in tone can come in mid-sentence or halfway through a longer substantive comment. This reaction gives notice that two can play the intimidation game but that it is not likely to advance the bargaining process.

Another response is to treat the opponent's conduct as a breach of negotiation etiquette, criticizing the adversary on the threatening style. If you choose this form of reply, be sure not to include any hint of criticism on the substance of the threat or the overall negotiation. While you have the right to be indignant about the process of intimidation, that criticism must be separated from the discussion of the merits.

Obviously, there are other responses to an opponent's intimidating manner. Here, as in other parts of the negotiation process, you ought to select reactions with which you are personally comfortable. But you should not foreclose a set of options before experimenting with them to be sure they cannot be adapted for your use. As with a substantive threat, planning your reaction to intimidation in advance is advantageous.

E. PROMISE AS A FORM OF PERSUASION

The final type of persuasion we will briefly consider is promise. Promises in bargaining are intimately related to threats. Indeed, it is fair to say that promises are the obverse of threats. As we have discussed, a threat is a commitment to do something to make life unpleasant unless the other party complies with a demand. A promise, on the other hand, is a commitment to do something to make life more pleasant if the opponent agrees to what is being asked. The relationship is so close that the element analysis of promise is the same as that of threat. Thus, there is an underlying cost to the promisor and, to be effective, a promise must be heard, understood, valued, believed, and prospective.

As warning is the close relative of threat, prediction is the cousin of promise. The narrow distinction between promise and prediction mirrors the other persuasive pair. The maker does not appear to exercise exclusive or absolute power over the triggering mechanism. Thus, when you predict an outcome, you suggest that a benefit to the opponent will probably, but not necessarily, occur if the other side acts as you have outlined.

F. CHOOSING THE CORRECT APPROACH

Threat and warning, promise and prediction are all designed to stimulate an opponent to act in conformity with the negotiator's announced preferences. But the four approaches involve different costs and risks. Because predictions and promises involve positive rewards to the opponent, they are likely to be well received by the other side. Promises are likely to cost the maker more than predictions since the former are in the exclusive control of the negotiator and require the actual conferring of the benefit. Conceivably, a prediction will cost the negotiator nothing because the benefit will be the direct effect of the cause, the opponent's action. We have analyzed earlier the costs of threats and suggested that warnings may be less costly to the maker.

By their negative nature, threats are identified more with negotiators who adopt competitive styles and who follow adversarial strategies. Promises, on the other hand, are positive gestures and are more apt to be employed by those choosing a cooperative style and applying a problem-solving strategy. But we are dealing with methods that can be mixed. Therefore, negotiators of both styles and strategies ought to be familiar with each technique of convincing an opponent to view the negotiation issues as the threatener (warner) or the promisor (predictor) demands. Flexibility of this type is required because the research on the persuasive effectiveness of threat versus promise is inconclusive; that is, the use of one does not clearly stand out above the other. However, the overall results of the studies of threat and promise are quite clear. Threats and promises do increase the incidence of compliance and concession.[32]

To test yourself on your ability to distinguish among the four techniques, review the following announcement by a negotiator representing the manufacturer of a new, high-tech product line. Isolate which statements are threats, warnings, promises, or predictions. Evaluate how persuasive each statement is in its present form. Decide whether modification or elimination of any of the statements would make the complete presentation of the negotiator more persuasive.

"You know that in this age of sophisticated communications our device will take the high-end market by storm. Following introduction next month in New York and Los Angeles, the up-scale retail market for this product will explode. If your client buys in now, it will reap the benefits of being identified early as a prime source. Unless you lock us up as your steady supplier now, however, your client could be in a damn tough market position when demand increases

---

32. I. W. Zartman & M. Berman, *The Practical Negotiator* 182 (1982), citing the research published by J. Rubin & B. Brown, *The Social Psychology of Bargaining and Negotiation* (1975).

overnight and it has to scramble around to see if we or the one or two other manufacturers can fill orders. Look, if you conclude this deal on the terms we've suggested, we will guarantee that your client will be treated in a very special way in the future. You'll be entitled to preferential treatment on all future orders in the next year when demand will be the highest. In addition, we'll lock in the price for the first six months. But, if you're not going to make a commitment to us now, we won't even answer your phone calls next week."

G. PREPARING FOR PERSUASION

Just as you need to prepare for the assessment and exchange stages of negotiation, so too must you prepare to persuade your opponent to view the bargaining subjects as you and your client do. Whatever combination of argument, appeal, threat, and promise you ultimately employ in a particular negotiation, you must plan the form, the language, the organization, and the timing of your persuasion package. Your preparation is not complete, however, when you have made detailed plans concerning your efforts to influence the other side. Once you have readied your side of the matter, you must turn your talents to anticipating your competitor's persuasive techniques. Your opponent will present a collection of arguments, appeals, threats, and promises to sway you. Predicting how the adversary will try to convince you and preparing replies will help you to reflect on your positions, to modify those that are inappropriate, and to better match the final outcome to your client's needs.

As you prepare your persuasion and forecast your opponent's, you should be aware of two phenomena. First, the arguments, appeals, threats, and promises you envision in support of your client's position during the preparation stage are likely to appear better than they actually are when you finally offer them during the negotiation. Second and conversely, the counterarguments, appeals, threats, and promises you imagine will be made by your opponent are likely to be weaker than they turn out to be when presented by the opponent. Why is this so? Professor Condlin gives us his insight:

> If a private contest takes place in every negotiator's head, in which one's own arguments are compared with another's, the other starts off with the deck stacked against him. [Our own] arguments in [our own] head are seen as exquisite, and complete, filled with detail, multidimensionality, subtlety, and balance. It is not that one's own arguments are regularly this good, just that it is the private myth of most that they understand more deeply than their words express. When they introspect, they see this depth, or think that they do, but when they [imagine] another express[ing] his equivalent . . . vision they do no such filling in.[33]

---

33. R. Condlin, "Cases on Both Sides": Patterns of Argument in Legal Dispute-Negotiation, 44 Md. L. Rev. 65, 85 n.46 (1985).

Another factor contributes to this over- and underestimation. When lawyer-negotiators do take the time to plan their persuasion, the process they follow tends to mirror preparation for an appellate brief. Though the argument may not be written out, lawyers act as if the argument will be delivered in its entirety, whole and integrated, with an introduction and summary. In reality, of course, arguments made during negotiation are interrupted, incomplete, and disjointed because the opponent asks questions, makes retorts, and injects counterarguments.

To overcome the debilitating impact of these phenomena and enhance your preparation for persuasion, you can use a process of combining and separating that some consider the essence of effective thinking. We have in mind an approach that in its most sophisticated form is similar to holding a moot court prior to actually arguing a case before an appellate court. In the combination phase of the process, you construct your negotiation arguments, appeals, threats, and promises. The construction can be in outline form or another model so long as you are comfortable and the persuasion package is complete. Once constructed, you ought to record on audio- or videotape the words you intend to use when making your persuasive points during negotiation.[34] After each of your major subjects, or where it is likely the other side will interrupt, you should assume the role of your opponent and make the best possible counterargument. Be sure to say something in response to each of your own arguments, even if that response is merely a token "Sez you!"[35]

When you are finished recording the whole argument, go back and listen to it in its entirety. With your arguments, appeals, threats, and promises combined with your opponent's anticipated rejoinders, you should hear a fabricated dialogue closely resembling the persuasion stage of your forthcoming negotiation. If you are like most of us, you probably will have two reactions to this recording. First, you will be dismayed to realize that some of your exquisite arguments and persuasive promises have obvious weaknesses that need to be strengthened. Second, you will conclude grudgingly that in your role as your opponent you have advanced some telling responses and you will think of others that could be made by the real adversary. When you have reached this stage, it is time to go through the separating process. Pull apart the arguments of both sides by questioning the logic, identifying missing evidence, selecting more persuasive language, reordering the points, eliminating losers, and adding winners. When the arguments have been separated and recombined, repeat the process. When you listen to this second recording of the persuasion stage you should be

---

34. Even more effective than your recording the entire argument of both parties is to have a colleague role-play your opponent. Give your colleague the outline of your position and have him or her respond to your points, interrupting your presentation in a natural way. Because your colleague will have advance notice of your persuasive views, somewhat more pressure will be placed on you to present your arguments effectively. Moreover, the involvement of the colleague also adds the element of brainstorming to your preparation, always a valuable contribution to the development of negotiation strategy. Finally, extremely difficult intellectual gymnastics are required to construct a set of arguments and then to fashion challenging retorts. The responses of your colleague are more likely than your own to mirror what the adversary will say.

35. The token response is simply a reminder that you will have to think harder about what your opponent is likely to say in answer to your point. Seldom does an adversary completely ignore a major argument. Neither can you in preparing for negotiation.

pleased by the improvement in the substance and the presentation of your arguments. Finally, you ought to use this process for the anticipation of the opponent's affirmative attempts to persuade you and the formulation of your responses to those arguments. Your reactions the first time through the recording are apt to be that the other side's positions may have some merit and that your answers can use some shoring up. A second run-through should do much to reduce your concerns about the opponent's arguments.

H. RECOGNIZING WHEN THE OPPONENT HAS BEEN PERSUADED

At the outset of this chapter we told you that your goal at the persuasion stage of negotiation was to convince your adversary to view the matters in issue as you and your client view them. Although we noted differences between the precise ends of the adversarial negotiator and the problem-solving bargainer, we emphasized that if you are successful in persuading your opponent to perceive the dispute or the transaction as you and your client perceive it, you increase substantially the chances of agreement. What conduct on the part of your adversary will signal that you have been successful in your persuasive attempts? Does your opponent have to concede defeat in whole or in part for your persuasion to have accomplished its intended purpose? Are there signs that fall short of total capitulation that will give you indications that your arguments have hit their mark?

You undoubtedly are acquainted with the long-running television series, *Perry Mason*. You recall how that brilliant TV trial lawyer climaxed most of his segments. Picture Perry making a speech in open court to judge, jury, and audience (the speech never seemed connected with any pending question and neither was it an opening statement nor a closing argument). In the speech, Mason explains why the guilty party could not be his innocent client. Mason slowly builds the facts and circumstances that will lead even the most stupid of us to the inevitable conclusion that another has committed the dastardly deed. A moment before Perry completes his persuasive argument, the guilty party jumps up from the back of the courtroom and shouts, "All right! It's me. I did it, and I'm glad!" Hamilton Burger, the hapless prosecutor, bows his head in disgust at losing again as Mason smiles benignly at Della Street whose face shines in admiration.[36]

Week after week, Perry Mason persuades someone guilty of a heinous crime to openly concede that the lawyer's argument is uncontestably correct. In negotiation, on the other hand, it would be absolutely astonishing

---

36. Sometimes this denouement is played out in another locale, such as Mason's office or the scene of the crime. To be sure, not all of the episodes followed this exact formula. For example, on occasion the person jumping up to confess is attempting to shield a loved one. Then Perry must explain patiently that the perpetrator is another, and then all heads in the room turn slowly to glare at the true villian. And the authors do remember one or two shows where Mason lost at trial but was successful on appeal when new evidence was found by Perry's private detective and sidekick, Paul Drake. Nonetheless, in every segment, Perry Mason's astute arguments win over all doubters, audience, prosecutor, trial judge, and, on occasion, even the appellate court.

for an attorney to admit that the opponent's arguments are accurate and decisive on the pending matters. Nonetheless, effective persuasion has a dramatic impact on the outcome of bargaining.[37] While you cannot expect your adversary to jump up and say, "You're right! I'll advise my client to do all that you've asked of us," you can anticipate that your opponent will alter his or her position in the face of well-constructed, persuasive presentations.

If these altered positions do not occur directly and openly in response to your argument during the negotiation, when and where do they take place? Most likely changes will happen back in the opponent's office as your adversary mulls over what you said and privately acknowledges you have made some valid points. In the counseling that follows a negotiation session, the opponent advises the client of what occurred in the discussions with you and suggests perhaps that demands and conditions should be altered in light of what has transpired. In subsequent rounds of the negotiation, you will see the fruit of your persuasive labors as your adversary modifies his or her position and becomes more accepting of your suggestions, even as the adversary refuses to admit the validity of your reasoning.

Sometimes the persuasion has an immediate impact, though still not equal to a Perry Mason-type scenario. For example, after discussing a competing analysis of a point, your opponent simply may not put forth a final response. Some short time later, when the adversary makes a concession, you may be able to see the link between your argument and the opponent's actions. Other signs of persuasive success include a change in topic, the abandoning of an argument, or the alteration of the agenda.[38]

While lawyers will agree that factual and policy persuasion influences changes in opponent conduct, many attorneys believe legal argument in negotiation is a waste of time. They contend that persuasion based on the interpretation of law ought to be left for the courtroom where a judge or jury can and will make a definitive decision. All attorneys realize, they claim, that cases, statutes, and regulations can be found to support virtually any position, and thus opposing counsel will not accept an argument grounded on disputed claims of law. These same lawyers concede, however, that when the law is overwhelmingly in their favor, they will advance powerful legal arguments in support of their contentions. In most situations, where the law is more evenly balanced, they prefer the classic "volley, volley, truce" approach we mentioned earlier. In such cases, the lawyers on each side will refer to the legal authorities in support of their position to let the other side know they understand the nature of the argument and then call a "truce" on the matter, abandoning all attempts at legal persuasion.

We and Professor Condlin disagree strongly with that approach. The law is one of the most powerful normative standards to be brought to bear on a legal dispute or a transaction with legal implications. Abandoning its potential impact, in our judgment, is a mistake. To be sure, a definitive ruling cannot be produced in a negotiation setting. But you can convince others that the outcome is more likely to be the position that you are sug-

---

37. Review the conclusions of Professor Condlin's study of almost one hundred legal negotiations in "Cases on Both Sides": Patterns of Argument in Legal Dispute-Negotiation, 44 Md. L. Rev. 65 (1985).

38. Id. at 71-72.

gesting than that being put forward by the other side. Indeed, when an opponent refuses to discuss the application of legal principles,[39] there are two valid hypotheses: First, the opponent does not know the law; and, second, the opponent knows the law but does not believe it favors his or her side. In either one of those situations, continued attempts to persuade based on legal principles will prove to be quite fruitful.

I. CHOOSING THE MOST EFFECTIVE PACKAGE OF PERSUASION

When and under what circumstances should you choose an argument, employ a threat, resort to an appeal, or pick a promise? Is there a rule for selecting a certain form of persuasion? Unfortunately, there are no guidelines for deciding on the most effective combination of persuasive devices. The forms of persuasion must be prepared and applied in a situation-specific manner after evaluation of the issues, the parties, the negotiators, and the setting.

Are there risks and consequences connected with doing a poor job of selecting or implementing the models of persuasion? To be sure, your failure to persuade your opponent may solidify the other side's view of the situation, giving the opponent a greater sense of confidence about the validity of the case or the correctness of the deal. If done without skill, the most serious danger of ineffective persuasion is that the opponent will conclude the negotiator is incompetent, perhaps inducing the adversary to attempt to take advantage of the negotiator. On the other hand, there is little or no risk associated with effective persuasion.[40] It adds to a negotiator's credibility and encourages an opponent to reevaluate the respective positions of the parties.

J. CONCLUSION

Earlier we stated that in a negotiation there are factors that draw the parties together and others that force them apart. A number of strategic and tactical devices can be used to narrow the gap between the parties. In

---

39. We emphasize a discussion of "principles" as opposed to the mere citation of cases. String-citing cases as in the footnote to a brief will not, of course, persuade a negotiation opponent. The failure to persuade, however, is not caused by the fact that the subject matter of the string cites is law. Rather, mere reference to court decisions fails to persuade because it does not fulfill any of the five elements of effective argument. For example, a detailed, multidimensional, and balanced discussion of the principles set forth in those cases will, nonetheless, have an appropriate persuasive impact.

40. One cautionary note is appropriate. A significant number of litigators are reluctant to reveal certain information in negotiation, even though it could well persuade the opponent to settle, if the information is powerful evidence that would be a surprise to the other side and could be the decisive factor at trial (e.g., the "smoking gun," the undiscovered appellate court decision directly on point, and the surprise witness). Although one of us was once "burned" by revealing such information during negotiation when the other side had time before trial to adjust to the surprise evidence, we believe communicating the persuasive data is better in most instances. Recall that about 90 percent of all civil cases are resolved without trial.

an adversarial negotiation, each side can make concessions along the continuum of fungible items. In a problem-solving negotiation, the pie can be enlarged so that each party gets as much as it needs. But in either type of negotiation, persuasion is necessary. The parties make concessions when persuaded they are necessary. The negotiation pie is enlarged in a particular way because the parties are persuaded that doing so can then satisfy their combined needs. Without persuasion, the contenders may stumble into a settlement. With effective persuasion, they are more likely to achieve settlement based on a rational analysis of the situation that is pushing and pulling them.

Chapter 19

The Exchange Stage: Preparation

A. INTRODUCTION

The third and final phase of a legal negotiation—what most would call its heart—is the exchange stage. Indeed, many people consider the exchange stage to be the entire negotiation. For them, negotiation is simply the division of the resources, the cutting of the pie, the trading of compromises. But, as you by now appreciate, assessment and persuasion are also critical to the process. Without effective control of information and productive persuasion, a negotiator is not fully prepared for the exchange process. If the bargainer reaches the exchange stage unprepared, success as measured by objective criteria or client satisfaction may prove to be elusive.

Preparation does not end, however, when persuasion is complete. In reality, planning intensifies for the exchange stage. For that reason, we divide the exchange stage into two parts. In this chapter, we focus on the preparation aspects of the exchange process. In the second part, Chapter 20, we will turn our attention to implementation, to the tactics and the techniques of effective exchange.

In our discussion of both the planning and implementation aspects of the exchange stage, we will continue our practice of differentiating adversarial and problem-solving negotiation where that is appropriate. Indeed, it is here, in the final phase of the bargaining process, that the difference between the two strategies is the greatest and where the divergence in tactics is the most obvious. As we go through these two chapters, an interesting phenomenon will become apparent to you. It is much more difficult to plan a problem-solving strategy than it is to prepare for adversarial negotiation. On the other hand, it is much more difficult to implement an adversarial strategy than it is to carry out a well-prepared problem-solving approach. The reasons for this curiosity will become apparent as we progress.

B. PLANNING FOR EXCHANGE AS AN ADVERSARIAL NEGOTIATOR

Before we delve into the specifics of planning for an adversarial strategy, recall the conceptual goal of the adversarial bargainer and then picture what an adversarial negotiation looks like. First, the recollection. An adversarial negotiator wants to maximize the client's gain or minimize any loss. The competitive adversarial tends to want to "go for broke," defeating the opponent in an absolute sense by accumulating more of the finite item being negotiated than the other side does. The cooperative adversarial is more individualistic, maximizing the gain for the client without regard to what is retained by the opponent. Given these descriptions, the planning of adversarial bargainers must involve an itemization of the issues, a calculation in some mathematical way of the value of each issue, and the creation of some means to measure the client's gains and losses by issue.

Now picture an adversarial negotiation. As you draw this picture, assume that the negotiators have completed their mutual assessments and used their persuasive wiles on each other. Thus, we are left with nothing but the exchange.[1] What do you see? We suspect you have one negotiator making an offer, the opponent scoffing at it, a discussion ensuing, a counteroffer being made and rejected, more argument, a concession, another concession, more discussion, and so on as the parties march toward either agreement or deadlock. Your picture is much like a tug-of-war between two strong parties who have dug in their heels and resist moving toward the other with all their might. The rope strung between them is an appropriate representation of the continuum on which the fungible item being negotiated is placed. Given this vision of the adversarial negotiation, planning for it must involve advance thinking about the moves of both parties (including where, how, and why), how to resist further moves, and when the game should be called because a party has been dragged into the mud.

Based on all this, an adversarial negotiator must plan for four categories of moves along the bargaining continuum: the opening offer, the target point, one or more commitment points, and the resistance level. Each of these items deserves some explanation.

---

1. This is, of course, an unrealistic picture. Both assessment and persuasion are likely to continue throughout the exchange process.

(1) Opening Offer. The opening offer needs little discussion. It is that point along the bargaining continuum at which one of the parties believes the negotiating should begin. When we discuss implementation, we will establish some guidelines for setting the opening offer. For now, however, you should keep in mind that adversarial negotiators set their opening offers beyond both their resistance levels and their target points.

(2) Target Point. The target point is that spot on the continuum where the bargainer believes the matter will settle. Negotiators choose a target point based on their experience in similar cases, an analysis of the particular problem, and information obtained before and during assessment. As we will soon see, most negotiations involve more than one issue and, therefore, multiple target points, one for each issue. Because issues are interrelated, the ultimate outcome in a multi-issue problem is naturally more difficult to project than a single issue target point.

(3) Commitment (or Concession) Points. The distance between opening offer and resistance level is typically marked by one or more commitment (or concession) points. The negotiator plans to move to a commitment point, rest there for some period, and persuade the opponent to misassess it as the resistance level. How to get from one commitment point to another is a subject we address in the next chapter.

(4) Resistance Level. Better known as the "bottom line," the resistance level is that point on the bargaining continuum beyond which negotiator and principal have determined they will not pass. To select the resistance level, the client, with the lawyer's assistance, determines the point at which it would be better to deadlock than to concede any more. Thus, the lawyer and client resolve that it is better that the dispute continue (perhaps to trial) or that the transaction fall through than to exceed this predetermined position.

While we strongly encourage you to plan for these four types of moves if you adopt an adversarial strategy, we recognize that many lawyer-negotiators do not prepare as carefully as we suggest. Many attorneys think in advance about nothing more than their opening offer and their resistance level—that is, the two ends of the bargaining range. Those who prepare less than we advise appear to reason that extensive planning for the exchange process will limit their flexibility, their ability to respond to the dynamics of the negotiation.[2] They are supported in that view by Fisher and

---

2. There is also the claim that preparation of a detailed bargaining range will reduce the capacity of the adversarial negotiator to apply pressure to the opponent since all the moves have been charted in advance. An excuse that is given by some is that most negotiations, certainly most of those involving lawyers, are complex, multi-issue affairs. It is too difficult, they argue, to make such plans; it is better to use a gestalt approach and think about a probable outcome ballpark. See F. Ikle & N. Leites, Negotiation: A Device for Modifying Utilities, in *Game Theory and Related Approaches to Social Behavior* 247-249 (M. Shubik ed. 1964).

Ury.[3] The authors of *Getting to Yes* argue that precise predetermined positions reduce your ability to react to what you learn during bargaining; inhibit your imagination by excluding your consideration of unique solutions produced by "brainstorming" during the negotiation; and tend to set your sights too high, thereby fostering deadlock.

We believe these critics are wrong. As we will explain in some detail in the next chapter, if you are going to follow an adversarial strategy, you must make detailed exchange plans. Without them, you will fumble for a principled rationale as you move along the continuum and communicate a lack of commitment to your opponent. Without a delineation of your positions along the continuum, it is almost impossible to manipulate your opponent's assessment of the respective bottom lines.

Based on these planning points, let us construct a pre-negotiation bargaining chart[4] on the buy-out issue for Eugene Weber in the Weber-Jones & Jones negotiation. Assume that Weber has authorized his lawyer to begin with an offer of $28,750, based on an accelerated depreciation theory. Attorney and client set a target point based on an analysis of the case and the lawyer's judgment that a realistic price on the buy-out is $57,500, half of the amount allocated to the noncompetition clause in the earlier assets purchase agreement. Following an analysis of all of his finances, Weber concludes that his resistance level is $70,000. Finally, the two of them agreed on a concession at $45,000:

	Opening Offer [OO]	Concession Point [CP]	Target Point [TP]	Resistance Level [RL]	
$0	$28,750	$45,000	$57,500	$70,000	$115,000 +

As you can see, we have set Weber's plans along a dollar continuum that ranges from zero dollars to $115,000 with a following plus sign. The total bargaining range, then, is from a possibility of Weber paying Jones nothing because the noncompete clause does not cover "executive counseling," to $115,000-plus, the amount allocated to the noncompetition clause in the contract plus an amount that might be added by Jones on resale.

The adversarial negotiator representing Weber has not finished preparing for the exchange stage when this portion of the bargaining chart is completed. Next the adversarial negotiator must anticipate specifically what will be the opponent's opening offer, target point, commitment points, and resistance level. Based on whatever information is available in advance of the negotiation, Weber's adversarial attorney needs to plan for Jones's position on each of these items. Let's assume that Weber and his lawyer estimate that Jones will advance a straight line depreciation approach and an opening demand of $92,000. Further, they think Jones expects to get $75,000

---

3. Though they address only the issue of the predetermined "bottom line," by implication the authors condemn the type of planning we suggest for adversarial bargainers because of the high costs. It is not surprising, of course, that they would be critical. After all, they reject the adversarial approach completely. R. Fisher & W. Ury, *Getting to Yes* 102-103 (1981).

4. The problems and charts are similar to those in the "Primer on Negotiation" in J. Harbaugh, *Legal Negotiation Training Materials* (Practising Law Institute 1988).

from Weber, thus the Jones target point. If Weber refuses a $75,000 demand, Weber believes that Jones will move to a commitment point of $57,500. Finally, lawyer and client agree that Jones will not take less than a resistance level of $50,000.

When we add this information to the bargaining chart on the buy-out issue, the result is the completed diagram set out below:

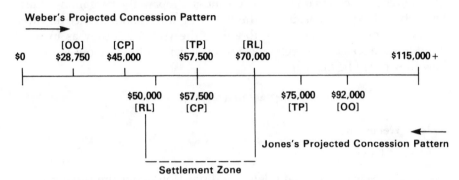

Notice that the chart includes a "settlement zone," that amount between the two overlapping resistance levels. Thus, the adversarial negotiator representing Weber anticipates this issue can be settled by the parties at some amount between $50,000 (the lowest amount Weber believes Jones will accept for a buy-out) and $70,000 (the highest amount Weber is willing to pay for a buy-out).

Pre-negotiation planning does not always produce a settlement zone. For example, assume that Weber's financial analysis revealed $50,000 was the top amount he could offer Jones. Based on this, Weber and his lawyer reduced their commitment point to $40,000. The target point remains the same, however; the lawyer still believes that $57,500 is a reasonable settlement point. Now change Jones's figures as follows. The anticipated opening demand is $134,000, based on a theory that the value of the clause has increased at a rate of 8 percent a year (inflation plus value added by the existence of the Jones operation). Concession points are projected at $115,000 and $92,000. Weber and his attorney believe the new Jones target point is also at $92,000, and they set the resistance level at $75,000. Given these figures there is no overlapping settlement zone. Instead, there is a gap of $25,000 between the two resistance levels. In this instance, Weber anticipates the parties cannot resolve this issue based solely on the exchange of money. Something will have to be done to bridge the dollar gap if the parties are to reach a negotiated settlement.

Before leaving this discussion of the planning required of an adversarial negotiator, three additional points must be made. First, in multi-issue bargaining, the adversarial negotiator should create a bargaining chart for each issue. When all of the bargaining charts are completed, the negotiator and client can decide how to value trade-offs among the issues. With all the charts in front of them, attorney and client are better able to see what exchanges are possible and how the offers and concession can be constructed. It is at this stage that a gap on one issue, such as that suggested above, might be overcome by substituting another commodity.

≣ **PROBLEM 1** ≣
Creating Bargaining Charts for an Adversarial Negotiator

The Weber adversarial negotiator needs bargaining charts for at least three other issues: the delay before beginning the ECS business; the length of a newly negotiated noncompete clause relating to placement; and the geographic restrictions on the new business. Prepare the bargaining charts for Weber's lawyer according to the following information. Once all three charts are completed, be ready to advise the Weber attorney as to what trade-offs are feasible to overcome a $25,000 gap on the buy-out issue and how they might be made.

MEMORANDUM

To: Weber File

From: Lawyer

Mr. Weber and I had a lengthy discussion about the three non-monetary issues in the forthcoming negotiation with Jones & Jones. We reached an agreement on the following positions for our side and projections as to how Jones is likely to respond.

1. Delay before beginning ECS: Weber would prefer to begin immediately. However, he agrees it will take some time to get the business off the ground (leasing space and equipment, hiring staff, training, advertising, legal work, etc.). He believes all of that will take three to four months, six months at the outside. However, if all of his other conditions are satisfied, he's willing to delay the new business for up to one year.

We believe Jones will try to hold up Weber's entry for as long as possible. If rumors about Jones going into counseling are correct, they will need at least six months, more likely nine months, to get a running start.

2. Length of a new noncompete clause: Weber insists that he and his son will not be doing any placement. Therefore, he is willing to agree to another ten-year term so long as the definition of employment placement clearly excludes executive counseling and all matters relating to that work.

Weber believes Jones & Jones would like to keep the existing time period intact. However, he believes they will agree to a new noncompete provision with a two-year term because their metropolitan placement office has done very well in its first two years. He suspects they would like to protect themselves for five years from now if that is possible.

3. Geographic restrictions on ECS: Weber wants no restrictions on ECS. Thus, if he can get it, he wants to operate ECS worldwide. While he admits that such a plan is grandiose, a nationwide business is not unrealistic. He is, however, willing to start smaller. Moving backwards, a five-state region is acceptable, then just this state, and finally his bottom line, the five-county metropolitan region. The closer he

comes to his bottom line, the more he wants time limits imposed on his geographic restrictions. Thus, if it's the metropolitan area, no more than one year; the state, two years; five-state region, three years.

On this issue Weber is less confident about his projections. If Jones is opening its own counseling operation, he suspects they will press to narrow his geographic reach. If they are not going into counseling, he does not believe they will care. On the assumption that the rumor is correct, however, he believes they will press to keep him local or statewide for as long as possible.

The second point we must make before closing this section concerns how the bargaining chart can help you place in perspective an issue addressed in earlier chapters. You will recall our discussion of the economic bargaining theorists' concept of "confident expectations" in connection with the assessment stage and the bargaining over information. The bargaining charts are used to measure the confident expectations of the adversarial lawyer. Relying on the pre-negotiation information, the attorney produces the charts; information-bargaining during the assessment stage of the negotiation confirms or denies the confident expectations reflected by the charts; based on the confirmation or denial, the lawyer modifies, if necessary, the bargaining plans. The bargaining chart, therefore, becomes a baseline for the adversarial negotiator to measure progress and fashion changes during bargaining.

The final comment also relates to the bargaining charts and a matter previously discussed. Now that you have seen and developed bargaining charts, the fundamental goal of the adversarial negotiator, first considered in the chapter on persuasion, should be obvious. Remember that the intent of the adversarial is to manipulate the opponent's assessment of the parties' respective resistance levels. Looking again at the Weber-Jones & Jones chart on the value of the noncompete clause, it is apparent that persuading the opponent to misassess your bottom line and to reassess his or her own resistance level would alter the payoff in your favor. Indeed, the bargaining chart gives you a scorecard to measure how misassessment of resistance levels by your adversary pays off for your client.

C. PLANNING FOR EXCHANGE AS A PROBLEM-SOLVING NEGOTIATOR

Before we set out a planning model for problem-solving negotiation, we once again ask you to recall and visualize. Recall the theory we discussed as the underpinning of problem-solving: The problem solver seeks to identify each party's basic needs and interests. Once they are identified, the problem solver searches for ways to meet those needs and interests. Where necessary, the problem solver measures the solutions by objective criteria to determine whether they are fair to all parties or whether they favor some at the expense of others.

With this explanation of the problem solver's goal recalled, picture in your mind what a problem-solving negotiation will look like. What do you see? The problem-solving negotiator asks a lot of clarification and elaboration questions to be sure there is mutual understanding of the parties' needs. A number of possible solutions are put on the table, many at the same time. The parties rummage through the proposals, working together where possible in brainstorming sessions. The picture is one of shared interests and responsibilities, although the negotiators are adamant about satisfying their own clients' needs.

Given this goal and this picture of the problem solver, some planning needs become apparent. First, we need to facilitate the identification, classification, and comparison of the needs of all the parties. Second, we need to stimulate questions that will clarify and elaborate on the essential requirements of the other side. Third, we need to encourage and assist creative thinking, the kind of thinking that can generate proposals for mutual gains. It will be no small task to develop a planning model that accomplishes these three tasks.

With all that has been published recently about problem-solving negotiation, surprisingly little has been written about planning for problem-solving bargaining. Much has been said to convince you to use a problem-solving strategy; somewhat less, but still quite a bit, has been written on the tactics of problem-solving. What is missing, to a large extent, is helpful material on the middle, on getting you from the decision to follow a problem-solving format to the negotiation table where you will bargain in a principled way.

Fisher and Ury do express a number of planning ideas, and we encourage you to review them.[5] One of their models is similar to the one we suggest as useful. Called the "Circle Chart,"[6] it includes four basic steps in inventing options that can later be used in a negotiating session. Each step leads to the next and the fourth feeds back into the first, thereby providing a review of what has been generated and stimulating another walk through the theoretical loop. The four steps are summarized below:

Step I. Problem:	Ask what is wrong and what are the current symptoms of that condition.
Step II. Analysis:	Sort symptoms into categories and identify causes; identify what blocks resolution.
Step III. Approaches:	Generate ideas about strategies and cures that theoretically could be done.
Step IV. Action Ideas:	Specify steps to be taken to deal with the problem.

---

5. Most of their suggestions are contained in Chapter 4, "Invent Options for Mutual Gain," particularly in the section on brainstorming with people from the negotiator's side. R. Fisher & W. Ury, *Getting to Yes* 58-83 (1981). Some of their ideas are unrealistic for many legal negotiation matters. For example, their suggestion of collecting five to eight colleagues for a brainstorming session is likely to strain the client's budget and the law firm's time. On the other hand, the overall approach to problem-solving preparation is very helpful.

6. Id. at 70. The chart and a portion of the accompanying discussion suggest that it was designed only for conflict resolution and not transactional negotiation. We believe the steps are valuable in both types of bargaining.

Although the Circle Chart is helpful, it does not provide sufficient structure for the negotiator who is just testing the problem-solving strategy for the first or second time. For that needed guidance, we recommend four somewhat different steps. To plan for a problem-solving negotiation, you should inventory, classify, compare, and satisfy the needs of the parties.

The first step, *inventory*, requires you and your client to answer the question: What are all of the needs and interests of all of the parties? Much of the inventorying can be accomplished in the counseling sessions described earlier in this text. To make inventorying most useful for negotiation, you and the client should independently list the needs and interests on separate pieces of paper. Be sure to include everything you can possibly think of; there will be time enough to pare the inventory during joint review. Do not worry at this stage about developing succinct phrases that describe the need or interest. If you must, use a single word that will stimulate your recall or a fulsome sentence that says it all. When each of you has completed your lists, compare and review them. Then work together to produce a single list of the parties' needs and interests. Finally, develop appropriately descriptive phrases that capture the essence of the needs and that can be used in the negotiation.

Your next step is to *classify* the parties' needs. We suggest a threefold classification system: absolutely essential, important, and desirable. You must differentiate between those needs on which the negotiation is likely to turn and those that are closer to the fringes. Thus, we equate *absolutely essential* needs and interests with those that are apt to be true deal-breakers. *Important* needs are high on the parties' lists but probably will not force a deadlock if they cannot be obtained in the exact form they are sought. Finally, the *desirable* classification means that the parties can live without satisfying these interests. You can use a different set of labels, expand your list to five classes, rank them from high to low, or do any other thing that allows you to accurately group your needs and those of the other side.

We have two thoughts on where to begin the classification. Because you understand them better, it seems obvious that you should begin with the needs of your client. The downside of this approach is the tendency of clients to bunch all of their own needs at the absolutely essential level. Although it is more difficult to predict and arrange the opponent's needs and interests, you and the client may be more objective in your characterization of the other side's rankings. With the pattern developed in working on the other case, you and the client may be in a better position to tackle the client's needs.

The third step *compares* the needs of the parties. To do this, you must have a system that allows you to see if the separate needs are compatible, that is, are they subject to a similar problem-solving strategy. The classification scheme above will not work because it merely rank orders each side's needs; you must also develop a grouping that addresses the nature of the needs in a comparative way. The needs of two or more parties can be shared, they can be independent of each other, or they can be in direct conflict. The third step thus calls for you to arrange the parties' interests into those groups, each of which requires a brief elaboration.

Every negotiation involves a *shared* interest. If at least one common goal drawing the parties together did not exist, a negotiation would not be contemplated. Usually there is more than a single shared interest. Unfortunately, what the parties share may not be easily spotted. This means you may have to look behind the labels you placed on the needs during the inventory stage. You and your client must ask yourselves a lot of questions. What, specifically, do we (the parties) each really want? More generally, are there any principles on which we each agree? What do we want to avoid? What do we have in common? Can we accomplish anything together, even something we could do on our own? Asking yourselves these and other hard questions about the possibility of mutual gains will produce a list of shared needs and interests. Try to express what the parties share in terms of a shared goal. It makes it easier to develop solutions.

Almost every negotiation also includes *independent* needs—each party typically wants items that are unrelated to any of the other party's wants. If you are able to identify these divergent interests, you are almost guaranteed to be able to give each side something it wants. Therefore, begin by looking for the apples that are sought by one party and the oranges desired by the other. Fisher and Ury propose that problem solvers check for differences in interests, priorities, beliefs, values, forecasts, and risk aversion.[7] Think in terms of George Homan's maxim: "Goods valued more by one party than they cost the other [should be exchanged] for goods valued more by the other party than they cost the first."[8] As you search for independent needs to compare, be on the lookout for items of low value to you and of high value to the other side. At the same time, examine the opponent's inventory for things that cost the other side little but are quite valuable to your client. Finally, consider creating additional independent needs of the parties. Adding independent needs is likely to result in increased satisfaction to the parties and a pattern of success for the negotiatiors.

As you can see, identifying shared and independent needs is not an easy task. In comparison, the recognition of conflicting interests is simple. *Conflicts* are like shared needs, however, in that there is at least one of them in every negotiation; without a conflict, there would be nothing for the parties to negotiate over. Although you will find conflicts easy to spot, do not be too eager or impulsive in collecting and comparing them. Examine apparent conflicts to be sure that underneath all the emotion, the verbiage, and the labels they are not independent needs masquerading as confrontations.

Once you have identified needs and interests as shared, independent, or conflicting, you must organize them in a way that facilitates comparison. We suggest the problem solver's chart set out at the top of page 483 as an efficient device for matching and contrasting the needs. The three classifications—essential, important, and desirable—form the rows and are listed to the left. The three comparison groups—shared, independent, and conflicting—are the columns set across the top of the chart. Remember, the independent and conflicting needs require a separate column for each party. The use of a chart or list will help you to visualize, refine, and under-

---

7. Id. at 77.
8. G. Homans, *Social Behavior: Its Elementary Forms* 62 (1961).

	SHARED NEEDS	INDEPENDENT NEEDS Party #1	Party #2	CONFLICTING NEEDS Party #1	Party #2
ESSENTIAL					
IMPORTANT					
DESIRABLE					

stand the underlying needs and interests of the parties. In other words, the chart will help you compare needs and interests, shaping a prelude to discovering problem-solving solutions to satisfy them.

Now begins the truly hard part of problem-solving negotiation, the fourth step, the *search for solutions* to meet the shared, independent, and conflicting needs and interests of the parties. With the parties' concerns set out in their appointed places on the chart, the creative part of lawyering is in front of you. Where should you begin your hunt for resolutions? We suggest you begin in the upper left-hand corner of the chart and spread your attention and your ideas slowly toward the lower right corner. Begin with the essential and important shared interests of the parties, looking for common answers to identical needs. Move next to the essential and important independent needs, searching for differences that can be matched or otherwise met. After these, focus on the shared and independent needs that are merely desirable to the parties. Here you may discover "goodies" for each side that can sweeten the deal. Be sure as you work your way through these cells of the chart that essential needs take precedence over important interests and that the latter take greater priority than those listed as desirable. If resolution of an important need interferes with meeting an essential need, the latter prevails.

As you may have noticed, we have thus far avoided discussion of the conflicting needs. In part, that is because they are the most difficult. In part, however, it is because we believe your initial planning efforts should aim at developing solutions that can be introduced at the outset of bargaining to set a positive tone for the negotiation. Matters in conflict are less likely to be solved quickly and easily and, therefore, can provoke a negative tone. More important, success in discovering resolutions of shared and independent needs stimulates ideas for compromising conflicts that might otherwise go unnoticed. Although there is no formula for creatively resolving conflicts in the limitless variety of legal settings, we have learned that working on the shared and independent needs before tackling the conflicting interests is a more productive process. Understand that the solutions you devise may overlap and even contradict each other. Because you are trying to develop responses in advance of bargaining that are acceptable to another party, multiple proposals are to be encouraged. Remember also that you do not have to enter the negotiation with answers to all the needs and interests of the parties. Brainstorming with your opponent after you have jointly explored the needs of both sides is often the most constructive process.

≣ PROBLEM 2 ≣
Creating a Bargaining Chart for a Problem-Solving Negotiator

Assume the role of the attorney for Jones & Jones and complete a problem-solving bargaining chart based on the following information. Although it is not all of the information that normally would be available in a case like this, there is sufficient material for you to inventory, classify, compare, and satisfy the needs of the parties. When you have filled in the chart as far as possible (not all cells, however, should contain information), try to develop two or three proposals that may satisfy Weber and are not disruptive of Jones's interests.

MEMORANDUM

To: Jones & Jones File

From: Attorney

Received call from lawyer representing Eugene Weber, former owner of WEBCo, an employment agency in the metropolitan area. We represented Jones when it bought out WEBCo two years ago. Counsel informed me that Weber wants to start a new business for his son, Robert, called Executive Counseling Services (ECS). The new company will advise executive and professional persons on new skills, job opportunities, how to interview and write resumes, and the like. Counsel says that there will be no job placement activities on behalf of their new clients. Just calling as a professional courtesy because of the existence of our standard noncompete clause in the assets purchase agreement.

Told counsel for Weber that I suspected Jones would be opposed to Weber's new venture because counseling was clearly related to placement and, as such, was covered by the noncompete clause. The attorney appeared to be feigning surprise when I said this. The lawyer said Weber planned to announce and open the new business as soon as possible, perhaps in the next month. Therefore, we arranged to meet next week to discuss the matter.

Spoke with the Jones officials who filled me in on Weber's proposal. Jones's folks heard a rumor of this a week ago. They believe Weber is in serious financial difficulty and is looking for a way to bail himself out. They do not believe Weber has the funds to start up the new business and cover heavy litigation expenses. Thus, the son may be nothing more than a ruse to divert the attention of the people at Jones. They just cannot believe Weber will not be involved in the day-to-day operation of the business. Not only do they think that Weber will be involved in the counseling business, they are convinced that he will edge over into placement. That is totally unacceptable to Jones. Weber must be kept out of placement for at least another three years to protect Jones's local operations.

It is important to Jones that Weber stay out of the counseling business for as long as possible. Jones intends to introduce, as early as the next three months, an experimental counseling program identical to Weber's. The plans include one in the metropolitan office. Co-opting the Webers into one of the Jones operations is preferable to them competing with Jones in placement or counseling. In any event, try to keep Weber out of counseling long enough to give the Jones experiment a chance to get off the ground. On the other hand, Jones wants to stay out of court if at all possible. Jones has no interest in a legal test of their boilerplate noncompete clause. It could affect more than two dozen acquisitions in the past two and one-half years.

Did you get all of this information sorted out and placed in a bargaining chart? If so, you should see that Weber and Jones & Jones share some of the same interests. For instance, both of them want to avoid litigation. Jones wants to stay out of court because of the risk of the multiplier effect. Weber, on the other hand, has financial woes and cannot afford a costly trial. They also share an interest in making a success out of a counseling business. That "shared" interest could eventually lead to a conflict, since separate businesses may be in competition with each other. But that is not necessarily the case, and various options may permit both parties to pursue success in the same business without direct confrontation. Other important needs are in conflict. For example, Weber wants to start his business ASAP, while Jones would like to keep Weber out of counseling for as long as possible and at least long enough for a solid head start. These and other interests should appear on your bargaining chart.

Did you find any possible solutions? How about Jones offering a management job to Bobby Weber in its new metropolitan counseling office? If not counseling, what about a job for Bobby in its employment placement operation here or elsewhere? Or, instead of a position for Bobby, what about a job for Eugene Weber, perhaps as a consultant in the new counseling operation? Would each of these solutions satisfy the needs and interests that are set out in your chart? But wait a moment. The third proposal appears to be in conflict with the other two. Does that mean one or more should be discarded? Are there any other solutions that you can see now that were not visible before?

D. CONCLUSION

Planning for the exchange stage is an important aspect of effective legal negotiation. By thinking through your choices in advance of bargaining, you very likely will enhance the outcome for your client and, perhaps, the other side. To skip planning for the exchange phase because you want to keep your options open or remain flexible is oftentimes an excuse for not doing the hard work that is involved. Planning does not mean you cannot be flexible or pursue options that develop during bargaining. Indeed, with planning you can better evaluate whether flexibility is productive and whether options are worth following. Moreover, the planning models we have suggested build in the capability to be adaptable during negotiation.

Although planning for exchange is essential, planning for adversarial trading is very different than preparing for a problem-solving interchange. Developing the assurance that you can work with either planning model will allow you to choose the bargaining strategy that is most appropriate to your particular negotiation. Comfort with your planning as an adversarial or a problem solver will give you, in turn, confidence during the face-to-face implementation stage, a topic we turn to next.

Chapter
20

The Exchange Stage:
Implementation

A. INTRODUCTION

In this chapter, we address the implementation of the exchange stage of legal negotiation. As before, we give separate consideration to adversarial and problem-solving bargaining, although, for reasons you will discover shortly, more of this section focuses on the role of the adversarial negotiator than on the conduct of problem solvers. Implementation is to be contrasted with planning, the subject of the preceding chapter. Earlier we concentrated on getting ready for the exchange phase of the negotiating session. Now we will attend to some of the interplay between the bargainers as they attempt to apportion resources. To be sure, this means we will discuss specific negotiating tactics and techniques. Notice, however, that we are not promising to present you with a set of sure-fire negotiating maneuvers, an assortment of all-occasion, snappy bargaining retorts, or a collection of crafty ploys to overwhelm your opponent.[1] Instead, we will

---

1. We do not mean to deprecate in any way books that include sections on negotiation maneuvers or bargaining ploys. They serve the important purpose of giving negotiators the opportunity to compare how they have handled certain specific and often difficult bargaining situations with the methods used and observed by experts. We believe, however, that a grasp of basic negotiation theory and sound bargaining fundamentals should precede the search for narrow answers to equally narrow questions. We also believe that, with an understanding of theory and fundamentals, you will develop your own set of effective tactics and techniques. If,

raise some of the major exchange issues that confront all negotiators, suggest ways to analyze those issues, and indicate some general tactics to consider in advancing your client's position.

As we go through these exchange issues you will notice that we devote more time to the tactics of adversarial negotiators. To be successful, adversarials need to mislead and manipulate their opponents, to employ bargaining sleight-of-hand at all times. Deception, manipulation, and sleight-of-hand are heavily dependent on effective technique. During exchange, adversarial negotiators strain to present a consistent image, to maintain the proffered position, and to be ever alert to avoid missteps. Problem solvers do not operate under the same pressures. While there are tactics and techniques that problem solvers should be aware of and use, they need far fewer of them and the cost of misuse is not nearly as great as that of the adversarial.

B. THE ROLE OF THE AGENDA IN NEGOTIATION

1. Introduction

In every negotiation, there are a number of issues that must be resolved, a number of tasks that must be accomplished, and a schedule that must be set for resolving or accomplishing them. The definition of those issues and tasks and the order in which they are addressed by the negotiators constitute an important part of the bargaining process known as the agenda. Thus, describing and sequencing the topics of negotiation is what we will consider in this first section of exchange implementation.

Three things about the agenda process must be recognized at the outset of our discussion. First, the matters that fall within the term "agenda" are important in all stages or phases of negotiation.[2] Whether the bargainers are working on the assessment, persuasion, or exchange aspects of the process, defining and arranging the topics can be matters of some moment. Second, in every negotiation and in every one of its phases, there will be an agenda; that is, the parties must define and arrange the matters to be bargained, or the parties will deadlock. Whether the agenda is tacit, ad hoc, and de facto, or is explicit and the product of negotiator planning, analysis, and discussion, there will be either an actual agenda or an im-

---

after completing this text, you feel the need to review the negotiating advice of others, you may want to consider one or more of the following well-known and favorably regarded books: H. Cohen, *You Can Negotiate Anything* (1980); C. Craver, *Effective Legal Negotiation and Settlement* (1986); R. Fisher & W. Ury, *Getting to Yes* (1981); P. Hermann, *Better Settlements Through Leverage* (1965); C. Karrass, *Give and Take* (1974), and *The Negotiating Game* (1970); E. Levine, *Negotiating Tactics* (1980); G. Nierenberg, *Fundamentals of Negotiating* (1973); S. Schweitzer, *Winning with Deception and Bluff* (1979); and T. Warschaw, *Winning by Negotiation* (1980).

2. We have deferred our discussion of this topic until now because agenda fights in lawyer negotiations seem to occur most often or to be most bitter during the exchange phase. We urge you to apply the principles of agenda analysis discussed here to other facets of the bargaining process.

passe caused by the failure to reach agenda accord. Third, disagreement and disputation over the agenda occur often in negotiation. Battles over agenda can take the shape of a fight over the parties who will be represented during an international political negotiation, an assertion that certain matters are "non-negotiable" in a labor-management dispute, or an argument about whether liability or damages should be the first item of discussion in a personal injury negotiation.

Is it worthwhile clashing over the agenda? Is there a payoff to planning for the agenda? Does it matter whether one topic is discussed before or after some other one? If you are influenced by the research on negotiation, you are likely to conclude that agenda control is important, particularly for adversarial bargainers. There is persuasive evidence that command of the agenda by adversarials may positively affect their final outcomes. Furthermore, it is our distinct impression that problem solvers who master the techniques of agenda control increase the likelihood that the final payoff will be mutually advantageous to the parties. Based on both our study and our perceptions, therefore, consideration of the role of agenda in bargaining is a productive process.

2. *Agenda Control*

In judging the value of a confrontation on the agenda, you need to know how control of the process can affect the negotiation. Agenda control influences bargaining through issue characterization and prioritization. Each of these aspects of agenda management requires explanation.

The negotiator who sets the agenda is able to identify, describe, distinguish, and illustrate the issues in dispute. There is an adage among appellate lawyers that goes, "If I can't control the facts and I can't control the law, I can still win the case if I gain control over the statement of the issues." Control over the definition of the matters being negotiated gives a lawyer power in bargaining similar to that in the appellate lawyer's maxim. For example, the negotiator who controls the agenda can clarify problems by the use of precise language. The same attorney can create issue ambiguity by selecting words capable of multiple interpretations. Issue clarity and ambiguity are factors that can lead to quite different negotiated outcomes, and they are but two illustrations of the capacity of the agenda controller to exploit issue definition.

By controlling the agenda, a negotiator also gets to sort, rank, and order the issues. There are two implications that flow from control over the chronology of the issues. First, an opponent's perception of what are the adversarial negotiator's "blue chip" and "bargaining chip" issues or what are the competitive problem solver's "absolutely essential," "important," and "desirable" needs can be manipulated by the sequence in which they are discussed. Moreover, by gaining an opponent's agreement to the negotiator's agenda, the negotiator is in a position to know in advance the placement of key issues, allowing the negotiator to concentrate persuasive discussion and emotional energy on major items of importance to the client. Because of the advantages that flow from agenda control, an effective adversarial or problem-solving negotiator has a bargaining agenda pre-pared in advance of a meeting and often resists efforts by an opponent to advance another order of issues.

The second implication of the order-of-issue bargaining involves how the agenda can be used to facilitate or impede progress toward agreement. The issues that comprise the typical lawyer bargaining problem come in various shapes and sizes, both in difficulty and importance. Quite often there are one or more matters that are particularly difficult or of greater im-portance to the parties while the remaining issues are viewed as relatively easy and minor. In adversarial bargaining, the tougher, important issues are called "blue chips"; the easy, minor ones are known as "bargaining chips." In problem-solving negotiation, we learned earlier how to classify the needs of parties as "absolutely essential," "important," and "desir-able." How should the adversarial or problem-solving negotiator place the issues on the agenda? Which comes first, hard issues or easy ones? Those that are essential or merely desirable? There are arguments in favor of, and risks associated with, beginning at either end of the respective spectrums.

In support of beginning the exchange phase of bargaining with issues that are easy or desirable—that is, with those matters that are perceived to be of lesser importance to the client—is the expectation that such an ap-proach can help to generate an atmosphere of trust, mutual respect, and conciliation between and among the parties. By their very nature, issues of this type are more likely to result in relatively rapid agreement rather than a long, drawn-out deadlock. Most legal bargaining is marked by momentum and the resolution of minor matters that separate the parties can establish a positive momentum of success moving toward final agreement. Thus, a competitive adversarial negotiator who opts for starting with those lesser issues known as "bargaining chips" may use this approach to test the op-ponent's commitment and skill by employing a variety of confrontational tactics and examining the other side's responses. At the same time, the competitive adversarial expects that these issues will culminate in grudging agreement and set a pattern for the remainder of the negotiation. A co-operative adversarial, on the other hand, will select an agenda that begins with easy issues to emphasize a willingness to be reasonable, to compro-mise in search of agreement. A problem-solving negotiator of either style begins with a "desirable" issue for reasons somewhat different than those of an adversarial counterpart. A problem solver uses less challenging issues at the outset of negotiation to teach the opponent the advantages of this bargaining strategy and how successful the parties can be if the approach is adopted for the remainder of the dispute or transaction resolution.

While there are advantages to creating an agenda that begins with easy issues, there also are disadvantages. The primary risk to both the adver-sarial and the problem-solving negotiator is the perception of being too flexible, too accommodating, or too anxious to reach agreement. An issue that is classified as a "bargaining chip" or as merely "desirable" is one to which a negotiator may not be strongly committed. A lawyer opponent, particularly one with a natural but strongly adversarial tendency, may conclude that an early "victory" on such an issue is evidence that the negotiator is uncommitted to principle or position, soft on preparation or experience, or otherwise prepared to be exploited. Such an inaccurate but strongly held perception may lead an opponent to make negotiation demands and take negotiation risks that are inappropriate and that lead the parties toward deadlock. Thus, an agenda strategy that begins with the easier issues must guard against an opponent's misconception about the bargainer's intentions.

A negotiating agenda that proceeds from "blue chip" or "absolutely essential" issues to those of lesser importance is one grounded on a quite different negotiating strategy. The adversarial bargainer who begins with the toughest issues is issuing a challenge to the opponent, demanding that the other side be flexible enough to allow the parties to resolve the most difficult matters separating them. The adversarial negotiator knows there is an inclination among many lawyers to act reasonably at the outset of bargaining, to view the relationship between the parties as positive, and to reach agreement if at all possible. Thus, the adversarial wants to take advantage of the other side by getting as much as possible at the outset of negotiating and considerably more than the opponent intended to offer.

The adversarial strategist of either a competitive or cooperative style whose agenda is consistently headed by a "blue chipper" is often an impatient negotiator. Unwilling to engage in protracted bargaining, this negotiator insists that the tough issues ought to come first so the parties can learn quickly whether settlement is likely or deadlock inevitable. If the negotiators cannot resolve the difficult items, this adversarial bargainer would rather walk away from the table than waste time on a futile goal.

The problem solver who leads with items classified as "absolutely essential" is not pursuing the same high-risk strategy as the adversarial who begins with "blue chips." Both competitive and cooperative problem solvers are working to develop solutions that will satisfy the needs of all parties. By recognizing at the outset of bargaining the "absolutely essential" needs of an opponent, the problem solver sends the message that he or she is trying to resolve those matters that could be viewed as deal-breakers by the other side. At the same time, the problem solver communicates that his or her client has "absolutely essential" matters that also must be addressed if agreement is to be reached. Thus, the mutual obligation of the parties to confront each other's most important needs is the underlying message of the problem solver who begins the bargaining with the "absolutely essential" issues.

An obvious risk to the adversarial negotiator who begins with the "blue chip" issues is that of premature deadlock. Either because of the negotiator's impatience or the opponent's belief that the parties cannot break through on a big issue, the bargainers may abandon the process before giving it a chance to work its course. Another risk to the adversarial is that "bargaining chips" not listed early on the agenda may lose their value as items that can used to sweeten the proposal on a "blue chip" issue. If the "blue chippers" are resolved initially, the adversarial may not get to use the "bargaining chips" to their full advantage.

When selecting an approach to the agenda, the negotiator must remember that resolution of any disputed issues, even minor ones, means the parties have made an investment in the process. Like the ante in a poker game, one loses the up-front investment in the negotiation if one drops out of the game.

The investment analogy can be carried over to an analysis of reasons favoring initiating the negotiation with the "big issue." If the ante for a poker hand were $5 but the rules dictated that the players could bet no more than $1 during the play of the hand, once a player had committed the ante he or she would be more likely to remain in the game until the end of play. So, too, with adversarial bargaining where the parties have settled the most important matter and have only minor issues remaining to be settled.

Other arguments in favor of placing major issues before minor ones involve the risks associated with delay. Putting off the big issue until the end of bargaining may mean most other issues have been resolved and the adversarial negotiator does not have any trade-off items with which to bargain. This means that the effective negotiator must balance the agenda with "blue chips" (those that mean the most to the client) and "bargaining chips" (those which mean little to the client). Moreover, there is the danger that physical and psychological fatigue may set in as the negotiation drags on, diminishing the negotiator's skill when the "blue chip" is still to be negotiated.

A key factor dictating against tackling the "blue chip" issue early is that the parties may be unable to resolve it because of substantive or interpersonal roadblocks, bringing an abrupt and premature end to the bargaining.

As with many of the exchange process issues we've discussed, the problem-solving negotiator is less concerned with agenda control than is his or her adversarial colleague. As long as the negotiators are addressing the real needs and interests of the parties, the problem-solving negotiator is not overly concerned about order and timing. Indeed, many problem-solving negotiators encourage their opponents to "set the agenda" in hopes of learning what's truly important to their clients by the agenda they choose.

It is only when the opponent deviates from discussion of the parties' needs and interests that the problem-solving negotiator is motivated to control the agenda. For example, assume that a problem solver's opponent resorts to threats, "take it or leave it," or personal attacks on the negotiator or the negotiator's client. At this point, the problem solver would insist on dealing only with the parties' interests and not the positions announced by the opponent, would insist on the use of objective criteria to measure proposals, and reject outright the opponent's hard-line tactics. Unless the problem solver grabs control of the agenda in this situation and forces the discussion back to needs and interests, it is likely the negotiation will fall into an adversarial model and it may deadlock.

C. MAKING AND MEETING OFFERS

The assessment stage may be extensive, with negotiators giving, getting, and protecting information. The persuasion stage may be intense, with bargainers swapping arguments, presenting promises, and even trading threats. But at some point in the negotiation process, somewhere along the bargaining line, one of the parties will address the other side with something like, "Look, will your client agree to accept $345,000?" Someone, sometime during the bargaining has to make an offer to the other side. Counteroffers, clarifications, and concessions will likely follow, but always there is a first. The first offer, then, is an important tactical moment in the negotiation. It is a tactical moment we explore at some length.

When the issue of the opening offer is considered there are five important questions that must be addressed. Those questions are:

1. Who should make the first offer?
2. When should the opening offer be made?
3. How much should the first offer be?
4. How should the first offer be made?
5. What response should be given to the first offer?

Each of these questions will be considered from the adversarial and the problem-solving perspectives. Also, much of what we say about first offers applies equally well to second and subsequent offers. Counteroffers are made of the same conceptual stuff as the original model.

1. Who Makes the First Offer: Adversarial

There is a saying in the world of adversarial negotiation that goes "Old negotiators never die . . . unless they make the first offer." While there is often much wisdom in ancient expressions, this is *not* one of those adages with a golden nugget of truth. In fact, the persuasive research on adversarial negotiation is in direct conflict with the implication of the maxim. There is no apparent correlation between who makes the first offer in an adversarial negotiation and the outcome of the bargaining. That is, who gains more or loses less is not affected by the making of the first offer. Making or not making the first offer is thus not an issue on which the negotiation should turn; effectively, who makes the first offer is a neutral event. There is evidence, however, of a relationship between who makes the first concession in adversarial bargaining and the outcome of the negotiation. Research studies suggest that the party making the first concession does less well. Based on the research findings, then, an adversarial negotiator should not be reluctant to make the first offer, but may be hesitant to be the first to modify an offer.

Our experience coincides generally with the experimental studies of adversarial bargaining. The side making the first move during the exchange phase does not seem to be penalized for having opened the exchange dialogue. Indeed, certain advantages, mentioned below, can flow from the initial offer. On the other hand, while we believe there is a connection of some significance between first concession and a poorer adversarial outcome, the reason for the relationship requires explanation. The initial adjustment of an offer is not a stigma that leads inevitably to a negative result. Indeed, a well-prepared and effective negotiator can make the opening concession and go on to "win" the bargain by any objective measure. But many negotiators who are first to modify their opening offer are those who concede not only early, but also often and in substantial amounts. These tend to be, in our observations, bargainers who are ill-prepared and have an insufficient sense of the dynamics of adversarial negotiation. While our subsequent discussion cautions adversarials about the dangers of the concession process, we do not advise that making the initial change in offer necessarily leads to a negotiation loss.

If you subscribe to the bargaining cliché concerning first offers, you should be aware there are negotiation situations that make it difficult to follow the maxim. There are many negotiation settings where one of the parties is a natural first offeror. For example, the seller of an item is the one who is expected to set a price, and the plaintiff in a personal injury case is presumed to be the one to place a value on settlement by making a demand. Because an offer is expected or presumed does not mean, of course, that a seller or a plaintiff is required to make the opening offer. There are techniques you can use to avoid the position of natural first offeror. For example, answering a question with a question, an approach used in the assessment stage to divert an opponent's attention, can be used to duck making the opening proposal. Thus, if you represent the seller of an item and your opponent says, "How much are you asking?" you can respond with, "How much do you think it's worth?" If there are tactics to evade making the first offer even in those situations where most negotiators foresee that you will present the original proposal, one thing should be clear: You have the freedom to decide if you want to be the initial offeror or would rather respond to the opponent's proposition.

If negotiators can exercise control over the offer process and the research suggests so strongly that the first proposal does not translate into success or failure, why did "never make the first offer" become a proverb in the adversarial bargainer's bible? There are at least two reasons why experienced negotiators urge offer restraint. First, many adversarials are afraid to appear too eager to reach an agreement and believe that the first offer is an obvious sign of such eagerness. Second, adversarial bargainers are apprehensive about making an opening offer that is within the opponent's settlement zone. We need to consider both of these fears.

An adversarial negotiator ought not to appear too anxious to reach an agreement. It can affect the negotiator's credibility and can encourage an opponent to hold out for future concessions by the overeager negotiator. Making the first offer, however, is not necessarily a sign that a negotiator is unusually anxious. Agreement anxiety is not demonstrated merely by making an offer; it can be evidenced, however, by how the offer is made. Moreover, the too-eager negotiator is apt to communicate settlement impatience long before the first offer is placed on the table. For example, consider the seller of an item who asks few questions during the assessment stage and answers queries about tight delivery schedules, stringent warranties, and similar tough requirements with assurances of full compliance. Consider also that this seller is unconvincing during the persuasion phase, seemingly agreeing with the opponent's arguments. Consider further that the opponent makes a patently low opening offer and the seller's counteroffer includes a rationale for a higher price than seller eventually presents. Finally, consider that seller concludes the presentation of the counteroffer with, "I have to tell you one important thing. I want our discussion to conclude with a deal." If you were bargaining with this seller, you no doubt would conclude that your opponent was too earnest about making a sale. Your conclusion, however, would not be based on who made the first-offer but on how your opponent handled the early stages of the negotiation, how the opponent introduced the issue of price, and how the offer actually was made.

Because most adversarial negotiators soon learn how to control the outward signs of agreement anxiety, it is the second fear—of making an offer that falls within the opponent's settlement zone—that motivates most lawyers who follow the "no first offer" rule. The primary cause of negotiator fear of opening too close to the other side's bottom line is a lack of confidence in the valuation of the case or the deal. The most effective way to overcome valuation insecurity is to engage in a client-centered counseling session. The client rather than the lawyer is more likely to have information that can relieve uncertainty. If, however, an effective counseling round does not dissipate a negotiator's genuine doubts about the value of the case or the value of the deal being negotiated, then he or she may have some legitimate concerns about opening within the opponent's settlement zone. In that situation, it may be better for the adversarial negotiator to refrain from making a first offer. Instead, a negotiator who has valuation doubts should consider inviting the opponent to make the first offer.

In a significant number of legal negotiations, we have observed what we call the "ping-pong" effect, where each lawyer urges the other to make the first-offer and each invitation is refused. As the first-offer ball bounces back and forth across the negotiating table, the bargainers seem to be saying to each other: "Here it is, you make the first offer;" "No, no, I don't know enough about how much this matter is worth so you set the range." Finally, one of the adversarial lawyers, often too embarrassed to refuse any longer, stumbles into an ineffective first offer. If you are following an adversarial strategy and are in bona fide doubt about the value of your case or your deal, we believe it makes sense to invite your opponent to make the first offer. In that way, you may avoid inadvertently opening the exchange debate too close to or even within the opponent's settlement zone. If, however, the opponent refuses your invitation, it is very possible that the other side has as many doubts about case or deal valuation as you have. In that event, it becomes safer for you to move ahead and make the first offer. If the reservation is mutual, your first offer may influence the opponent's assessment of the case or deal. In such a situation, it may be tactically advantageous to alter your planned opening by moving it an appropriate distance along the bargaining continuum in your favor. To be sure, you must quickly develop and communicate a credible justification[3] for this modified position to avoid undermining your entire adversarial exchange strategy. But if you are able to adjust your opening offer by pushing it advantageously along the continuum, you are likely to increase the value of the outcome for your client.

Adversarial negotiators should keep in mind that there may be a distinct advantage in making the properly constructed and delivered first offer. The first offeror is in position to observe the opponent's reaction to

---

3. See the subsection "How to Communicate the Offer," page 504, for an explanation of the importance of justification in making effective adversarial offers.

the initial volley in the exchange battle. By scrutinizing the opponent's response—the precise language and the accompanying nonverbal communication—the adversarial negotiator may learn much about the opponent's bargaining range. Thus, when you have adopted an adversarial strategy, you may want to plan to make the first offer to ensure that you have the opportunity to evaluate the other side's response. The ability to closely monitor your adversary's reply to an initial offer, seeking clues to the opponent's exchange plans, can be of great tactical advantage.

2. Who Makes the First Offer: Problem Solver

In contrast to the adversarial negotiator, the problem solver worries little about who makes the opening offer. Because a problem-solving strategy treats the early steps in the exchange process as a continuation and refinement of the assessment and persuasion stages, problem solvers are more likely to make opening offers. Indeed, problem-solving bargainers are likely to treat making the initial set of offers as an important part of their overall negotiation strategy.

Although we know of no research data to support this conclusion, we believe differences exist among problem solvers concerning who will make the opening offer, differences that depend on the configuration of the style-strategy match-up. When a problem solver—competitive or cooperative—negotiates against an adversarial, the problem solver is more likely to initiate the offer stage. The problem-solving negotiator uses the offer process to influence the adversarial opponent to adopt a joint problem-solving approach. Moreover, the problem solver seeks to head off the possibility of the adversarial negotiator becoming locked into positional bargaining by advancing an offer along the zero-sum continuum. Therefore, the problem solver is apt to rush to be the first offeror.

On the other hand, when a cooperative problem solver meets a competitive problem solver, our experience suggests the cooperative tends to go first. The effective competitive problem solver, with a limited solution approach, more often seems to hold back, preferring to be in a reactive position. If negotiating theory prevails, the cooperative problem solver will propose all possible solutions, including those that favor the competitive negotiator's client and eventually would be advanced by the competitive problem solver. The competitive negotiator tends to respond only to those solutions suggested by the cooperative bargainer that favor his or her client. To be most effective, the cooperative problem solver must demand that the competitive opponent analyze all resolutions that are suggested. If this is not insisted on, the competitive problem solver will succeed in limiting the discussion to those outcomes that clearly advantage only one side.

3. When Should the First Offer Be Made: Adversarial and Problem Solver

Many lawyer negotiations reveal an impatience by the bargainers to initiate the exchange process. Assessment and persuasion seem to be viewed as annoying preliminaries to the main event, the division of resources by adversarials and the acceptance of solutions by problem solvers. Thus, both types of negotiators have the tendency to hurry through information-bargaining and efforts aimed at convincing the opponent about the state of factors crucial to the negotiation. The goal of rushing through the first two phases of negotiation by these bargainers appears to be to get quickly to the first offer. It is at the exchange stage, claim the anxious negotiators, that the "real" bargaining occurs. We suggest, however, that the clients of both types of impatient bargainers would be better served if their lawyers would delay initiation of the exchange stage until after the planned assessment has been completed and effective persuasion employed.

The adversarial negotiator risks more than the problem-solving colleague by pushing toward the exchange process. The adversarial bargainer's exchange strategy is predicated on a set of "confident expectations" about the opponent developed during counseling and pre-negotiation planning. The adversarial's opening offer, target point, and commitment points bear some relationship to the comparable positions of the opponent. The timing of and justifications for moves along the continuum depend in part on an assessment of the opponent's strengths, weaknesses, needs, fears, resources, and the like. If the adversarial negotiator confirms his or her "confident expectations," then it is with some comfort that the negotiator's planned opening offer can be made. If the adversarial's "confident expectations" are contradicted during the assessment and persuasion stages, an appropriate adjustment must be made before the negotiator can put an effective opening offer on the table. In either event, it is important for the adversarial negotiator to postpone initial offers until substantial assessment and persuasion have occurred.

Timing of the opening offer is certainly important but somewhat less critical for the problem-solving negotiator. Because the construction of effective solutions depends on the accumulation of critical information, the problem solver also should delay the first offer until assessment is virtually complete and some persuasion has taken place. On the other hand, this type of negotiator often uses offers as an important and integral part of the assessment process. By analyzing the opponent's response to several possible solutions that are advanced, the problem solver gains a better understanding of the adversary's underlying needs. Moreover, the most effective persuasion by the problem solver is the explanation of how a proposed solution meets the essential needs of the contending parties. Since the first two stages of the negotiation process often blend with the exchange stage in the problem solver's strategy, the actual timing of the first offer does not have the same significance it does for the adversarial negotiator.

4. The Size of the Opening Offer: Adversarial

One of the most troubling questions for the adversarial bargainer is how much should an opening offer or demand be? The question's importance is understandable, given our earlier discussion of situations in which the bargainer is uncertain about the value of the case or transaction. Indeed, concern about the size of the opening offer or demand appears to increase in direct proportion to a negotiator's lack of confidence in case or deal valuation. But even when an adversarial negotiator is certain about valuation, there can be apprehension over the appropriate amount of the first offer. The need for negotiating room between the first offer and the client's resistance level, the number and the size of concessions that can be made between those two points along the bargaining continuum, and the actual distance between the opening positions of the parties are tactical issues that are affected by the determination of the original offer. As a result, the adversarial negotiator is likely to devote a fair amount of time to the question of the size of the opening offer or demand.

From a conceptual perspective, there are only three first-offer options for the adversarial negotiator. The first demand can be: unreasonably high/low; "fair"; or moderately high/low. For our purposes, the unreasonable opening can be defined as one that cannot be justified by the usual objective criteria. For example, in a litigation case an initial demand that is completely out of sync with comparable jury verdicts would be unreasonable. In a transactional matter, a price that bears virtually no relationship to the acceptable economic and financial analysis of the situation likewise would be termed unreasonable.

A moderately high/low opening position, on the other hand, has a clear relationship between the offer and some objective standards. Though tied to some neutral criteria, the moderately high/low opening stretches the criteria in favor of the side making the offer. Thus, in a litigation the adversarial negotiator who adopts a moderately high/low opening will push the data from parallel cases to and slightly beyond the edge of most favorable comparison. In a transactional matter, the negotiator who adopts the moderate high/low opening will put forth an initial offer or demand justified by information that just barely supports the position.

Finally, a "fair" initial demand is one that in an unbiased and impartial way is totally in accord with the applicable objective criteria. In either a dispute or transactional setting, the adversarial negotiator who advances a fair opening position will take into account his or her strengths, weaknesses, resources, needs, and interests and those of the opponent.

There has been a considerable amount of research on the relationship between the size of the opening offer or demand and negotiation outcome as measured in such fungible items as dollars. These studies include analysis of both dispute and transactional negotiations where the parties adopted adversarial strategies. The data in these experimental settings are drawn from situations where the negotiators have settled their dispute or reached an agreement in their transaction. A reasonable reading of the research literature suggests that the adversarial negotiator who makes an unreasonably high/low initial demand maximizes the return for the client. A "fair" opening offer, on the other hand, produces the least favorable return of the fungible commodity for the client. Given these two research outcomes, it is not surprising that the negotiator who opens with a moderately high/low position fits somewhere in between the negotiators who adopted the other two opening strategies.

Such research results should not be a surprise although they may be disappointing. Many have hoped that dealing "fairly" with others during a negotiation would produce a "golden rule" response on the part of adversarial opponents. Alas, that does not seem to be the case. Those who make "fair" opening offers appear to settle for substantially fewer of the dollars or other fungible items being negotiated. Those who act in the most aggressive and outrageous fashion seem to receive the greatest reward.

Assuming the accuracy of such research data, does that end our analysis of the size of the initial offer or demand in adversarial negotiations? Does it mean that you should initiate the exchange process in any adversarial negotiation with an unreasonable opening position? The answer to both questions is an emphatic "no!" Recall that the study results mentioned above apply only in those situations where the bargaining parties reached agreement. Is there important information to be gained from those experimental negotiations where adversarial bargainers deadlocked? Indeed there is.

The research data indicate an extraordinarily high incidence of deadlock in adversarial negotiations where the original offers were unreasonable. Deadlock occurred in these experiments even though the negotiating parties had sufficient authority to reach an agreement. In contrast, "fair" initial positions produced a very high percentage of settled negotiations. Finally, the moderately high/low opening resulted in a deadlock/settlement outcome in between the other two conclusions.

Once again, these outcomes should not be surprising. The reasons for the settlement consequences in the first two situations seem to be straightforward. In the case of the unreasonable opening position, it often causes the opposing negotiator (a) to use threats or other high-risk adversarial tactics to pressure the bargainer into substantial concessions; (b) to conclude that the parties are so far apart that it is not worth a good faith effort to reach a settlement; and (c) to decide that the lawyer presenting such a position is so inexperienced or incompetent that an increase in the negotiator's settlement expectations is justified.[4] On the other hand, while the greatest number of negotiations with "fair" first offers settle, the opponent has so much to gain that it is unlikely that deadlock will result. "[A] demand which is too low will usually raise opposing counsel's estimates of the probable settlement outcome and may force concessions which approach counsel's minimal settlement point."[5]

Based on both research results and our own observations, the moderately high/low opening position in an adversarial negotiation best balances the normally competing desires to maximize the return and to avoid a deadlock. Beginning with the moderate strategy, an adversarial negotiator can adjust toward a tougher or softer position depending on the variables present in the negotiation. For example, if the client is more interested in achieving success than avoiding failure, a higher risk strategy may be ap-

---

4. G. Bellow & B. Moulton, *Negotiation* 100 (1981). The authors also point out that the unreasonable offer or demand may adversely affect influential third parties (e.g., a judge in a litigation situation or a potential lender to the parties trying to form a joint venture). On the other hand, the authors recognize that an unreasonable opening may be "dismissed and have no effect on opposing counsel's decisions."

5. Id.

propriate. In that case, the moderate opening can be moved toward the un-reasonable position. On the other hand, if the client deems it virtually essential that an agreement be struck, movement toward the "fair" open-ing posture might be a more suitable strategy.

≡ **PROBLEM 1** ≡
Setting the Opening Demand of an Adversarial

It is one thing to conceptualize the opening position of the adversarial negotiator as limited to but three choices. It is quite another matter to select the most advantageous opening from among those three options in an ac-tual negotiation situation. The difficulty, of course, is that the particular facts and circumstances of each negotiation determine what is meant by unreasonable, fair, and moderate. Thus, the real meaning of each choice changes with each and every negotiation.

Try your hand at setting the opening demand as an adversarial nego-tiator representing Jones & Jones. In doing so, consider the following facts. Jones purchased the WEBCo business two years ago. The $875,000 pur-chase price included the following components: the ten-year noncompete clause had a $115,000 price tag; goodwill was set at $210,000; all remain-ing aspects of the business were valued at $550,000. Similar employment placement firms in WEBCo's region have been purchased by Jones over the past three years. The prices paid in those acquisitions have ranged from $625,000 to $1.2 million. In each assets purchase agreement, there was a noncompetition clause identical to the one in the WEBCo contract except for time and geographic limitations. The amount allocated to the clause ranged from 10 percent to 25 percent of the purchase price. The combina-tion of noncompetition and goodwill ran between 25 percent and 45 per-cent of the total paid by Jones for the acquired business.

Jones plans to begin operating executive counseling units in key loca-tions around the country within six months. Middleburg, the location of the acquired WEBCo business, is one of the branch locations targeted for a counseling division. Therefore, Jones would prefer to keep Weber out of the field permanently or for as long as possible. On the other hand, Jones wants to prevent a court test of its "boilerplate" noncompete clause for fear that an adverse ruling might encourage other sellers to challenge its provi-sions. Jones is nervous about an unfavorable judicial response because it believes counseling is an operation that is independent of the placement business.

The Jones operation in Middleburg has flourished since the purchase of WEBCo. The Jones branch has retained more than 90 percent of WEBCo's former clients and has made significant penetration into the em-ployment market formerly controlled by others. As a result of its successes in Middleburg, Jones fears little from a return by Weber in the placement field. On the other hand, Jones is wary that Weber's entry into counseling could provide strong competition to Jones's proposed experimental opera-tion. Jones worries that the executives and other professionals of Weber's former institutional clients might turn to him for counseling services because of the rapport he developed with them on a personal level.

QUESTIONS

In light of these facts, set an unreasonable, a moderate, and a fair opening demand for Jones in its negotiation with Weber.

1. If you actually were engaged in a negotiation with Weber, which of the three opening positions would you maintain? Why?

2. What facts would have to change (and in what way would they have to change) or be added for you to begin the bargaining by maintaining each of the other two demands you set?

3. Why are those facts crucial to your opening position as an adversarial negotiator?

5. The Number of Opening Offers: Problem Solver

One of the critical questions posed by an adversarial negotiator is "how much should my opening offer be?" But a problem-solving negotiator is not faced with that question because, unlike the adversarial, achievement of the problem solver's underlying goal is not dependent on the manipulation of a finite amount of fungible items. Instead, the problem solver inventories, classifies, and compares the needs of the parties to develop solutions for satisfying the demands of the principals. The process of inventorying, classifying, and comparing is designed to produce enough information for the problem solver to "see" possible solutions to the joint needs of the parties. Thus, the pertinent question for the problem solver is "how many opening offers should I make simultaneously if my goal is to understand and meet the real needs of the parties?" Once the question is posed in that fashion, the answer is fairly obvious. The problem solver should try to make multiple offers on each issue or "need" that has been identified during pre-negotiation preparation and during the information-bargaining aspects of the assessment stage.

A multiple offer approach is constructive to problem solving because it facilitates the clarification and elaboration of the opponent's real needs and the exposure of any feigned needs that have been articulated by the opponent to mislead the problem solver. The opponent who has received multiple offers from a problem-solving negotiator must be forced to respond to the offers by rejecting proposed solutions that are unacceptable, modifying those that meet less than all of the opponent's needs, and tentatively acquiescing to any that appear to be acceptable. Effective problem-solving negotiators listen carefully to the opponent's varying responses to multiple offers, measuring each response to determine how closely it appears to meet a real need of the opponent. Thus, effective evaluation by the problem solver of the responses to multiple offers is one of the keys to negotiation success. Accurate assessment of responses to offers increases the likelihood that the problem solver will understand the opponent's true needs and determine how those needs fit with those of the problem solver's client. Precision in evaluation will result in the refinement of the solutions the problem solver proposes.

Because offers and their evaluation are so important in clarifying the opponent's real needs, the effective problem-solving negotiator often creates additional issues or subissues. These added issues or subissues become new "needs" of the opponent that must be met through the negotiation process. The existence of added needs means that the problem solver can put more offers on the table. More offers by the problem solver will produce more responses by the opponent. More responses by an opponent mean a further clarification and elaboration of the other side's actual needs.

≡ PROBLEM 2 ≡
Multiple Offers by the Problem Solver

To illustrate how the problem solver may use multiple opening offers, reconsider our discussion in Chapter 19 about the solutions that a Jones & Jones problem-solving negotiator might propose (page 485). We have incorporated into the following dialogue between bargainers the three offers we suggested earlier. Notice how an introduction of these specific proposals advances the problem solver's assessment goals while supporting the negotiator's persuasive efforts. To reinforce our discussion earlier in this chapter of how timing of the opening offer affects the problem solver, assume that the conversation takes place in the beginning phase of a negotiation between lawyers representing Eugene Weber and Jones & Jones.

Weber: So, you can see that the executive counseling business will be quite different from an employment placement operation. I can't see why Jones would object to Weber's plans. In any event, ECS is certainly outside the noncompete clause.

Jones: Based on what you've told me, there are some options available to Weber that could be attractive to both of our clients. As I see it, Weber wants his son, Bobby, to have the opportunity to get into a business where the kid can use his training and experience in industrial psychology. He also wants Bobby in a field where the old man can pass on his wealth of experience to his son. This leads me to think Jones may be able to find Bobby a position in its existing placement business or in its new counseling operation. If, on the other hand, it's Gene Weber who's looking to run a new business, perhaps Jones could find a place for him in its organization.

Weber: I'm not sure I understand. You mentioned three or four different things there and they sound like they're colliding with each other.

Jones: Let me try to explain each one of my ideas. What if Jones can find a management-level position for Bobby in its employment placement operation? It's the same field the father excelled in and it's one that the kid's background qualifies him for. Moreover, Bobby gets to work for one of the most dynamic employers in the personnel field in the country.

Weber: I don't think that's going to meet my client's needs. Weber is convinced that counseling executive-level personnel is a critical and under-explored field. He has his heart set on Bobby choosing a career that offers real growth opportunities. Weber sold WEBCo because he thought the business was peaking. Counseling, on the other hand, is at the front end of its development.

Jones: OK, I understand better now what your client's needs are. Let's consider the other idea I had. What about a position for Bobby in the counseling division Jones expects to test market within the next six months? Why, we may even be able to get him a management-level job in the counseling office Jones expects to open in Middleburg. If Weber wants Bobby to get experience in counseling, he couldn't ask for more than the chance to work with the national leader in employment placement as it expands into what you've described as this rapidly developing field.

Weber: Maybe, but Weber doesn't have the opportunity to work alongside his son, passing on his expertise and experience to the kid. He doesn't want to work full-time but he feels the need to be part of Bobby's career. He can't do that unless he has the chance to do real, meaningful work that is like the job Bobby is doing. Jointly developing ECS satisfies that goal. Watching Bobby, even here in Middleburg, is simply not the same as starting a new business. If you start your own business, you have the possibility of reaping great rewards. As part of a large corporate group, you have neither the opportunities for making it a real success nor the risks associated with failure. Working for Jones just isn't the same.

Jones: The more I hear you talk, the less important becomes a job for Bobby and more important becomes providing Gene Weber himself with the chance to influence development of a business. If that's the case, what about a position for Eugene Weber himself, perhaps as a consultant in Jones's new counseling operation?

Weber: I don't think he'd go for just a consultant's job. You know, a consultant is on a fixed salary for a limited term. Also, a consultant is on the outside looking in; he's not a part of the leadership team that develops the new business. Gene needs something without a closed end, and he needs the opportunity to nurture a counseling operation from idea to successful venture. And there has to be the chance to reap a significant share of the rewards if the venture blossoms as he expects. No, I don't see the consultant's route as a profitable option.

Jones: OK, but what I hear you saying is that Weber is interested in playing a major role in the development of an executive-type counseling business and the chance to share in the profits. Is that right?

Weber: Well, I suppose you could reduce it to that. Oh, and the chance to work with Bobby.

Jones: All right; if Bobby's part of the development and management team, that need would be satisfied, wouldn't it?

Weber: Maybe. Now, I'm not sure any of this would work. I don't have any authority to commit him to any kind of relationship with Jones & Jones. Besides, there are too many gaps for this idea to work. I haven't heard anything about compensation, the security of position, a place for Bobby. This is all too speculative.

Jones: Well, I don't have specific authority for much of this, either, but I think it's worthwhile seeing where it goes. Look, a relationship with Jones could reduce the risks to Weber. Perhaps it will cost less in start-up if they're working together. Remember also that Jones & Jones has a steady supply of folks—including executive and professional types—looking for positions. They're coming into Jones & Jones offices every day, all over the country. That's a pretty good client base on which to build a counseling business. On the other hand, Jones is going to need someone with a background in employment placement at the head of its counseling division. Weber would bring a lifetime of very successful experience in placement to the Jones counseling enterprise. Joining forces could benefit both parties.

Weber: Well, I admit there could be some advantages in Weber and Jones collaborating on counseling. That doesn't mean Weber has to be an employee of Jones. There are other ways to work together. Even so, there are lots of problems. Have you considered the ramifications of . . .

QUESTIONS

1. What did the problem-solving negotiator representing Jones & Jones learn from Weber's lawyer?

2. What role did the solutions proposed by Jones's lawyer play in the learning process?

3. Identify the attempts at persuasion made by Jones. How successful were these persuasive efforts?

4. What other proposals can Jones make that may satisfy the needs that were expressed by Weber during this dialogue?

6. How to Communicate the Offer

During much of the preceding discussion on first offers, we focused on the strategic choices available to the adversarial and the problem-solving negotiators. While tactics and technique were mentioned, they did not play the major role. We now move to a topic that is dominated by tactical considerations. In answering the question, "How should an opening offer be made to maximize its impact?" we will concentrate on techniques to assist the adversarial and the problem solver.

Once again, we isolate the differences between the two types of bargainers. First, we will address the presentation maneuvers that enhance the offers made by adversarials. Then we will contrast those techniques with others that can assist the problem solver in delivering a proposal to an opponent. In each case, hypothetical problems will be used to reinforce our tactical analysis.

≡ **PROBLEM 3** ≡
Comparing Adversarial Offers

Set out below are two examples of an opening offer by an adversarial negotiator. In each, the lawyer representing Weber offers to purchase from Jones & Jones the right to operate Executive Counseling Service. Consider the two offers and decide which is the more effective presentation of Weber's position.

E x a m p l e 1

Jones: Let's assume for the moment that the noncompetition clause precludes Weber from operating his ECS business. How much would he be willing to pay Jones for the right to begin the enterprise?

Weber: This would be a purely hypothetical discussion, you know. Because we don't believe Weber is obligated under the contract.

Jones: I understand, I understand.

Weber: [During the following statement, the Weber lawyer looks at a legal pad on which he finally writes in large figures the numbers that comprise his offer. Toward the end of the statement, he increases pace, pitch, and volume.] Well, if Weber could get the right to begin his business immediately, unhindered by Jones in any way . . . well, we would consider offering . . . Understand, of course, we're not obligated to do this. We would be able to offer, uhm, let's say about . . . in the range of, ah, ah, $20 to $28,000 . . .

Jones: [Vigorous negative shaking of head and holding forehead with hand.] There's no way . . .

Weber: [Hand up, palm flat, and facing opponent.] Now, now, let me tell you where the offer is coming from. Jones has had two full years under the contract to get its business off the ground. And if we're going to be paying that much, there can't be any question in the future about Weber himself being involved in the new business as well as his son Bobby. Moreover, if we adopt your theory that counseling is a part of employment placement, remember that we're not buying back the whole business, just a part of it. That's a heck of a lot of money to pay to get back only a small portion of the total business.

Jones: There's no way Jones is going to take $28,000! Why, we paid $115,000 for the noncompete clause. I can't take back less than a quarter of that amount after only two years of . . .

Example 2

Jones: Let's assume for the moment that the noncompetition clause precludes Weber from operating his ECS business. How much would he
be willing to pay Jones for the right to begin the enterprise?

Weber: This would be a purely hypothetical discussion, you know. Because we don't believe Weber is obligated under the contract.

Jones: I understand, I understand.

Weber: [During following statement, Weber looks directly at Jones and
maintains an even pace, pitch, tone, and volume.] Weber will pay
Jones $28,750 for the right to begin ECS immediately, unhindered in
any way by Jones, including Gene Weber's freedom to be actively involved in the business.

Jones: [Vigorous negative shaking of head and holding forehead with
hand.] There's no way Jones is going to take $28,000! Why, we paid
$115,000 for the noncompete clause. I can't take back less than a quar-
ter of that amount after only two years of protection. You're going to
have to come up with a lot more than that!

Weber: Let me tell you the reasoning behind that figure. As courts have
said and common sense confirms, the economic value of a noncompetition clause is greatest at the beginning of the protected term and
tapers off dramatically during the remainder of the noncompete period. Thus, Jones has received the primary benefits from the clause
during these last two years. Based on this economic reality, an accelerated depreciation analysis is the way to determine the present value of
the clause. If half the value of the clause was used during the first year,
that brings it down to $57,500. If half of that is attributed to the second
year, it makes the clause worth $28,750 now as we enter the third year.
At the end of this year, it'll be worth only $13,875.

QUESTIONS

1. In which example did the Weber lawyer do a better job of communicating the offer to Jones? What factors influenced your conclusion?

2. How could the lawyer who did the better job of conveying Weber's
offer have improved on the presentation?

3. How would you assess the effectiveness of the responses from
Jones's lawyers?

4. Can you derive any tactical "rules" from these examples that you
can apply to other adversarial bargaining situations?

7. Communicating the Offer: Adversarial

We expect that you determined the first demonstration of an adversarial
offer was not as effective as the second proposal of Weber's lawyer. In
deciding in favor of the second example, we assume you identified certain

factors, including the following, that made the latter bid more persuasive: The second lawyer was "smoother"; used nonverbal communicators to enhance the presentation; responded directly to the opponent's objections; and gave a better reason for the offer that was made. Even if you concluded that the second example was better and you recognized a number of the components that made the offer more convincing, you may have had difficulty extracting tactical principles that you could use in delivering other adversarial offers. If that is so, let us suggest three "rules" of adversarial offer-making: Be brief; be specific; and justify every offer. Each of these concepts needs to be expanded on.

Before we explain these three "rules," recall what your goal is as an adversarial negotiator. Remember that you want your opponent to misassess your resistance level and, as a result, to reassess his or her bottom line, moving along the continuum in your favor. With that principle held firmly in mind, particularly the first half of it, our discussion of brevity, specificity, and justification will make more sense.

Underlying the misassessment-reassessment design is the need on the part of the adversarial negotiator to place the parties along the bargaining continuum. The more the adversarial knows about the opponent's place on that continuum, the greater the advantage. Thus, the offer process should be used, if possible, to obtain information about the other side's resistance level. An adversarial offer that is presented concisely reduces the opponent's opportunity to prepare a thoughtful, reasoned rejection. Instead, the opponent must react instinctively, giving the adversarial negotiator a better opportunity to measure the response and increasing the possibility of locating the rival's resistance level. Slips of the tongue and revealing nonverbal signs are sometimes the helpful by-products of an opponent's hurried answer to the briefly presented adversarial offer.

To maximize the possibility that the opponent will expose information through the response, all adversarial offers should include as few words as possible. Although brief, the offers should be complete, containing references to the major elements of the proposal. When making the offer, the negotiator should maintain strong eye contact to better evaluate the opponent's nonverbal reactions. In addition to enhancing the negotiator's ability to "read" the other side, continuous eye contact improves the credibility of the offer. Credibility is further strengthened by delivering all adversarial offers in an even pace and pitch, with a moderate tone and volume.

In the first example above, the lawyer for Weber violated virtually all of the brevity guidelines. The negotiator rambled, broke eye contact, altered the nonverbal oral communicators, and hesitated as the number associated with the offer was approached. The lawyer in the second example, however, was more conscious of the need to make the offer concise. That attorney's actual offer was presented in but a couple of dozen words and the nonverbal signals reinforced offer credibility.

In addition to being brief, the effective adversarial negotiator tries to make every offer specific. You have learned that one of the tell-tale signs of an adversarial negotiator is that most issues are reduced to fungible items that can be placed along a bargaining continuum. When translated into negotiation offers, these fungible items are usually conveyed to the opponent in terms of numbers, such as dollars or units of production. Precision in the communication of these numbers is what we mean by specificity in the adversarial offer process.

Why is specificity important to the adversarial bargainer? Because the adversarial wants the other side to believe that the offer is the negotiator's resistance level, the negotiator must appear to be committed to the position. An offer that is specific reinforces commitment. An offer that lacks the requisite precision communicates a willingness to concede. Thus, an offer that includes a specified number of items, such as dollars or units of production, conveys the impression that the negotiator making the offer has thought it through carefully and is bound to remain firm. On the other hand, an offer that includes "weasel words" in proximity[6] to the number strongly suggests that there is some give in the negotiator's position. Such phrases as "in the neighborhood of," "we would be willing to pay, say . . . ," "around," and "about" accompanying the offer are prime examples of "weasel words." Any expression, however, that imparts the sense that the negotiator is not completely committed to the offer qualifies as "weasel words."

In our two earlier examples, the second Weber lawyer was quite specific in communicating an offer of exactly $28,750. In contrast, the attorney in the first example violated the rule of specificity in a number of ways. When the offer included phrases such as "well, *we would consider* offering" and "we *would be able to* offer, *uhm, let's say about*," the Weber lawyer might just as well have shouted to the opponent that the number of dollars that followed was but one step in a march along the bargaining continuum toward the position of Jones. The lawyer's hesitancy, indecision, and qualifications made it clear that the offer was not the negotiator's resistance level.

The same lawyer compounded the specificity error by one of the common negotiating mistakes—the improper use of a range—by saying, "in the range of, ah, ah, $20 to $28,000." A range sends the message that the negotiator is not committed to either of the mentioned positions. The sophisticated opponent immediately discards the end of the range that does not favor the opponent's position and, henceforth, only recognizes the other point of the range, the one closer to its side of the bargaining range. You will note that the Jones lawyer in the first example ignored the $20,000 end of the range, acknowledging only the $28,000 offer.[7]

The third and final rule relating to how an adversarial negotiator

---

6. By "proximity" we mean within a short period of time before or after identifying the number that makes up the offer. While leakage of this type can occur at any time in the bargaining, we have noticed a pronounced tendency for "weasel words" to occur within three to five minutes of the offer, particularly when the adversarial negotiator making the offer rambles on with an explanation of the proposal.

7. A range can be used effectively by the adversarial bargainer when it is tied to specific variables. For example, the Weber lawyer might have said, "We'll offer $20,000 if Weber has to delay opening his new business for more than one month. On the other hand, we're willing to pay Jones $28,000 if Weber can open the business immediately." When communicated in this manner, the range is really a pair of contingent offers. Unless the points of the range are linked to separate factors of the same issue or to different issues, a good negotiator on the other side will always assume that the end of the range that favors him or her is the only "real" offer being made.

should present an offer probably is the most important one. To be effective, all adversarial offers must be justified. By that we mean the specific amount of the offer must be supported by precise and persuasive reasons. An unjustified offer by an adversarial negotiator should be treated as merely the prelude to a future concession. A well-justified offer, on the other hand, actually could be the adversarial negotiator's true resistance level.

By making justified offers, you convey commitment to your position. Unless a legitimate reason is advanced that undercuts or destroys your articulated justification,[8] you can comfortably resist moving from the amount offered. To make your offer appear to be final and to give the appearance of resolute commitment to it, furnish your opponent with a specific reason for the precise number that you have offered. If your justification rationale does not fit the exact number contained in your offer, you communicate a willingness to move from your position. If you fail to give any justification for your offer, you proclaim that you have no commitment whatsoever to the specific number contained in your offer.

In the first example, the lawyer for Weber promised to tell the opponent the underlying basis of the offer. The attorney broke that promise by failing to give any justification whatsoever for the offer of $28,000. To be sure, the lawyer said "now, let me tell you where the offer is coming from," but then went on to articulate a condition of, not a reason for, the offer. Certainly, whether Weber himself has the right to participate in the new business is not linked in any rational way to the precise figure of $28,000. While the Weber lawyer in the first example went on to explain that the client was proposing to buy back far less than the business activity covered by the noncompete clause (just counseling, not all of employment placement), this explanation bore no specific relationship to $28,000. Of course, if one purchases less than the complete product, one is justified in paying less than full price. Assuming that full price for the noncompete clause is $115,000, the amount allocated in the assets purchase agreement of two years ago, that rationale justifies only an amount less than $115,000. It does not justify, however, $28,000 any more than it justifies $38,000, or $51,000, or $66,000 or any given number under that amount. Contrast these attempts at justification with the presentation of the lawyer in the second example. Consider again the explanation given by Weber's lawyer for the offer of $28,750:

Weber: Let me tell you the reasoning behind that figure. As courts have said and common sense confirms, the economic value of a noncompetition clause is greatest at the beginning of the protected term and

---

8. Either your opponent or you can present legitimate reasons for you to move off of your stated offer and further along the bargaining continuum to another position. Your opponent will attempt to persuade you that your justification does not survive close analysis. If the adversary does present reasoning that casts severe and legitimate doubt on your rationale, it is time for you to make a concession, a topic dealt with subsequently. But there are occasions when you will want to make a concession (see page 516) even though your opponent has failed to articulate a logical argument that undermines your reasoning. Simply conceding may destroy your commitment credibility. In that situation, therefore, you will have to mount an attack on your own justification (disguising it, if possible, by attributing it to the opponent) so that there is a good reason for abandoning your offer.

tapers off dramatically during the remainder of the noncompete period. Thus, Jones has received the primary benefits from the clause during these last two years. Based on this economic reality, an accelerated depreciation analysis is the way to determine the present value of the clause. If half the value of the clause was used during the first year, that brings it down to $57,500. If half of that is attributed the second year, it makes the clause worth $28,750 now as we enter the third year. At the end of this year, it'll be worth only $13,875.

Here, the lawyer begins the justification with a principle (that the worth of a noncompetition clause diminishes with time). The lawyer supports the principle with a reference to external authority ("courts") and reliance on reasoning ("common sense"). To implement the principle, the attorney proposes a formula ("an accelerated depreciation analysis"). Finally, Weber's negotiator applies the formula, demonstrating how the exact amount of the offer, $28,750, is reached. Thus emerge the elements of adversarial justification: articulation of a principled position; as much multidimensional support for that principle as can be marshaled; and employment of the principle in a way that demonstrates the precise relationship between the principle and the specific offer.

An adversarial offer that is justified in this manner communicates that the negotiator is committed to the position. When an offer appears to rest solidly on flawless reasoning, it follows that the negotiator who makes it will be unwilling to move from the spot. Therefore, unless and until the supporting rationale is tested and shown wanting, the bargainer comes across to an opponent as bound firmly to the offered position.

While you can readily see how an effective justification enhances the credibility of an adversarial offer and can appreciate the simple logic of the justification model, do not underestimate the difficulties faced by the adversarial negotiator attempting to develop multiple justifications for a single negotiation. Generating justifications is perhaps the most difficult task confronting the negotiator who adopts an adversarial strategy. Assuming the bargainer plans for an opening offer, one or more concession points, and a resistance level, a justification must be created for each of these positions. Moreover, to be most effective, the multiple justifications should be consistent with each other, demonstrating a congruous quality in the underlying reasoning. Though many justifications are merely rationalizations for the positions espoused, they must appear to be truly principled if they are to be effective. Conceiving justifications, then, can be the sternest test of an adversarial lawyer's creativity and ingenuity.[9]

---

9. To appreciate the difficulties involved in the development of persuasive justifications for adversarial offers, set and support two other offers that the lawyer in the second example could submit to Jones & Jones. Make one of these offers less than the $28,750 tendered in the example; make the other offer more than that amount. Try to have the reasoning articulated by the lawyer in the second example be the underpinning for the two offers you develop.

As an example of a low-end opening offer by Weber, $11,500 could be justified by claiming that executive counseling is an activity that would account for no more than 40 percent of the revenue in a joint placement-counseling operation. Therefore, 40 percent of $28,750 (the present value of the noncompete clause) is the maximum amount to which Jones is entitled. Hence, an offer of $11,500. On the other hand, as a concession from $28,750, Weber's lawyer

8. Communicating the Offer: Problem Solver

For the problem solver, the answer to the question "how should I make my opening offers" is: Do the exact opposite of what the adversarial negotiator has been advised to do. If the adversarial should be brief, then the problem solver should be expansive. The adversarial must be specific, but the problem solver should be general. And as the adversarial must justify the offer to appear committed, the problem solver must come across as uncommitted. The stark contrast between adversarial and problem-solving negotiation requires some explanation.

Remember that the adversarial bargainer tries to get a leg up on the opponent, searching for tidbits of information about the other side's resistance level by reducing the adversary's opportunity to prepare a thoughtful, reasoned response to an offer. In place of the adversarial's hope for an instinctive reaction, the problem solver looks for a thoughtful and reflective answer by the opponent to the multiple offers made by the problem solver. Therefore, the problem-solving negotiator must be expansive in presenting offers, taking the time to explain how each offer meets the joint needs of the parties as those needs are perceived by the problem solver. The problem solver's detailed explanation of how a proposed solution meets needs has two important benefits. First, it allows the problem solver to reveal and reinforce the needs of his or her client. Thus, the message that the problem solver's needs must be satisfied for there to be an accord is delivered in a firm yet nonthreatening way. Second, the explanation allows the problem solver to say to the other side that its needs are recognized as being significant and that a serious attempt is being made by the problem solver to address them. Acknowledgment of and attention to the needs of the opponent are crucial to stimulating a response from the other side that will help clarify those needs. Clarification of the opponent's needs leads to understanding on the part of the problem solver; understanding leads to the creation of possible solutions; multiple solutions, in turn, lead to the settlement of differences.

The adversarial presents a specific offer, an enumeration of a precise amount of a fungible item that the negotiator asserts will satisfy the respective claims of the parties. Ideally, on the other hand, the problem-solving negotiator begins with the most general statement of solutions to joint needs and moves slowly to more specific statements only as the needs of the opponent become clarified. As the other side elaborates on its needs and the problem solver determines if those needs are shared, conflicting, or independent of the needs of the problem solver's client, the presentation of solutions becomes clearer, more precise, and specific. The approach of

---

could offer $51,111. That figure is reached by reducing the accelerated loss of value in the noncompetition clause from 50 percent per year to one-third per annum.

Both of these additional offers retain the fundamental principle of accelerated depreciation that was enunciated in the original example. Two different spins on that principle allow the adversarial negotiator to move backward or forward along the bargaining continuum. It should be emphasized, however, that each of those spins needs to be justified. That is, the 40 percent factor of the lower offer and the one-third depreciation of the higher offer must be supported by some data or reasoning.

the problem solver to offers is akin to the funnel approach to information-seeking questions: Begin generally, with an open-ended statement of the solution, narrowing the proposal only when sufficient information has been produced about the needs of the parties to allow the problem solver to fashion a detailed offer.

The goal of the adversarial bargainer is to appear totally committed to the pending offer, creating in the opponent the impression that the proposal on the table is the adversarial's bottom line. Because the problem solver's aim is diametrically opposed, the offer tactics of this negotiator must be the reverse of the adversarial's tactics. The problem solver tries to convey a commitment to a joint search for mutually advantageous answers to problems. While committed to an open search for solutions, the problem solver should not appear committed to any one of the multiple offers he or she advances. Indeed, at least for the cooperative problem solver, no hint of preference should be expressed among the solutions advanced. If the other side gets the impression that the problem solver prefers a single solution and that the others are being presented as a sham, a resistant response to the favored proposal is likely. Such a response is apt to interfere with the process of clarifying and elaborating on the real needs of the opponent. We insist that the problem-solving negotiator must avoid treating his or her suggested solutions with a self-centered "pride of offership." Instead, the problem solver should invite honest and legitimate criticism of all proposals because it will illuminate the parties' needs, increasing the likelihood of discovering an acceptable agreement.

With the principles of expansiveness, generality, and noncommitment in mind, revisit the earlier problem of multiple offers by the problem-solving negotiator (page 502). Did the problem solver representing Jones & Jones adhere to these precepts during this offer segment? How might this negotiator have improved the offer presentation?

9. Responding to Offers:
Adversarial and Problem Solver

The final question we address about offers is how to respond to offers made by an opponent. You will not be surprised to learn, once again, that adversarial and problem-solving negotiators are at polar opposites. Consider the following sequence of offers by a lawyer representing Jones and responses by an attorney for Weber. Try to isolate the essential features of each reply. Which responses do you believe to be more consistent with the underlying strategy of the adversarial? Of the problem solver? Why?

Jones: Based on what you've told me about Weber's goals for his son, I think Jones & Jones can be helpful. How about Bobby coming to work with Jones in their placement operation here in Middleburg? If that doesn't appeal to him, how about waiting a few months and then have Bobby head up one of Jones's new counseling operations, perhaps the one they plan for this area?

Weber: [With a look of incredulity, a sarcastic tone of voice, and distinctly negative shakes of the head.] Those are the silliest suggestions I've ever heard! Where did you get the idea that Bobby was coming to Jones & Jones looking for employment placement assistance? Weber's going to start a business. He intends that his son will take over that business. He plans to pass on to the kid a lifetime of experience. It's insulting for you to offer Bobby a job. If he wanted just a job, he could get one on his own or with the help of his dad. The Webers don't need handouts from Jones & Jones.

Jones: We certainly didn't mean to insult either Gene Weber or his son. We understood from you that Mr. Weber wanted to get Bobby started in business. We believe that a management position with Jones & Jones is a heck of a way to start a business career. On the other hand, I'm now hearing a slightly different purpose on Weber's part. It sounds like he wants to be very actively involved in the business, at least at the beginning. In that way, he can be sure to give Bobby the benefit of his business background. If that's the case, would Weber and Bobby consider serving as consultants to Jones as it starts the new counseling venture?

Weber: Look, Weber isn't interested in some kind of make-believe consulting operation. Consultants by definition are controlled and limited by those with whom they consult. Weber believes the executive counseling business is virtually boundless. The chance to set the pace in a new, exploding field can't be compared with running a consulting firm tied to a plodding giant like Jones & Jones. Now, you did get one thing right. Weber wants the freedom to take an active role in the business, at least through the start-up period, to make sure Bobby gets off the mark and moving in the right direction. So, we intend to begin ECS with Gene Weber at the helm and Bobby standing by, ready to take over as soon as his father gets the business past the difficulties it will inevitably face at the outset.

Jones: OK, Weber wants to take an active role during the early stages of a new business that has almost unlimited potential. How would he react to a joint venture with Jones & Jones in the counseling business? Jones puts in money and a tie-in with all of its placement operations around the country. The Webers add money and their "sweat equity." Another possibility is a somewhat looser arrangement between the two whereby Jones refers its clients to Weber for counseling and Weber refers his clients to Jones for placement. Each party gets a substantial cut from the placement or counseling charges of the other as a referral fee.

Weber: Both of those proposals are worth considering because they meet some of Weber's most important goals. The business we're talking about is executive counseling, the field Weber believes is primed. In each option, Weber is in business for himself. Bobby can work with his dad, gradually assuming more control. That doesn't mean there aren't some problems connected with your suggestions. The joint venture puts some constraints on Weber's control of ECS that might limit his sound business judgment. In the referral alternative, if the fee Weber has to pay Jones is based on a percentage, it could endanger his cash flow during the early stages of the business. That's especially true because it'll take longer for him to develop his own clientele, the ones where he'd be getting a fee back from Jones.

Jones: Yeah, there might be some problems with one or both of my suggestions, but let's pursue each one and see where it goes. Now, in thinking about the joint venture we need to keep in mind that the best way to . . .

The lawyer representing Weber in this example responded three times to offers made by Jones & Jones. It should be obvious that the first two replies were those typical of the adversarial negotiator and the third answer was similar to that given by effective problem solvers to an opponent's offer. The characteristic that dominates the adversarial's reaction to offers is the negative focus. Noteworthy in a problem solver's reply to the proposals of the other side is the emphasis on the positive features of the suggestions.

An adversarial's negative response to an opponent's offer, signaling that the proposal does not meet the negotiator's needs, can be either very strong or more moderate in tone. The very strong negative reply, such as the first answer given by Weber both verbally and nonverbally, indicates that the opponent is not even close to the adversarial negotiator's settlement zone. A more moderate negative response, similar to the second one made by Weber's attorney, suggests that the other side is on the right track but still has a way to go before an agreement can be reached.

Selection of a negative response to an opponent's offer sends two critical messages to the other side. The first message is an unhesitating rejection of the opponent's proposal. Failure to answer the other side quickly and firmly may give the opponent hope that the offer comes close to the adversarial bargainer's settlement zone, increasing the possibility that the offer eventually will be accepted. The second signal sent by the negative answer is that the adversarial negotiator is concerned primarily and perhaps exclusively with achieving the goals of his or her client. The needs of the opponent are declared to be of secondary interest at best and, perhaps, completely irrelevant. Thus, the adversarial negotiator says to the other side, "You are responsible for satisfying my needs but I have no obligation to fulfill any of your conditions."

The response of the problem solver to an opponent's offer, in contrast, concentrates on the positive aspects of the suggestion. The problem-solving negotiator has two goals in focusing on the constructive portions of the proposal. First, the problem solver must communicate the needs of the client and make sure the opponent understands those needs. To be sure this has been accomplished, the problem-solving bargainer tells the opponent how the offer specifically satisfies those needs, in whole or in part. Second, the response is designed to reinforce the problem solver's view that all parties to the negotiation are accountable for the attainment of their own goals and the satisfaction of the needs of the other side. This message of mutual responsibility for the needs of all parties is the opposite of the communication contained in the adversarial's response to an offer.

To be sure, the problem solver's reply to the opponent's proposition is not always totally positive. If the opponent's offer meets only a portion of the negotiator's needs, the problem-solving negotiator must then point out specifically how and why the proposal falls short. Thus, in the third response in the preceding example, the lawyer for Weber advises Jones that certain of the client's needs are unmet by the two alternative offers. Although the problem solver clarifies needs by directing attention to inadequacies in a suggested solution, the initial emphasis on the satisfying aspects of the proposal maintains a positive momentum at this stage of the exchange process.

After achieving the goals inherent in the initial negative or positive response, both adversarial and problem-solving bargainers, depending on the negotiating strategy, should consider exploring the opponent's offer using elaboration and clarification probes. The neutrality of these two inquiry techniques will allow the negotiator to obtain information about the opponent's intentions without further tainting of the bargaining process. Detailed data about the other side's proposals are necessary if the effective adversarial or problem solver is to fashion future responses that advance the negotiator's strategy.

D. CONCESSIONS

Why would an adversarial lawyer ever make a concession? Instead, would it not be more convincing to follow the "no concession" strategy known as "Boulwarism"? If a concession is a permissible tactic, when should it be employed by an effective negotiator? How can a concession be made by an adversarial bargainer without destroying the credibility created in the earlier phases of the negotiation? What should the alert adversarial be watching for in the concession pattern of an opponent?

1. The Need to Make Concessions

Lemuel R. Boulware, a vice president of the General Electric Company in the 1950s, had an approach to negotiating with labor unions that appears consistent with an effective adversarial strategy. Boulware first analyzed the issues separating labor and management in advance of face-to-face bargaining. He then formulated for each issue a single offer that he determined was fair to all parties. Once he made that offer to the team representing the union, Boulware never budged unless the union adduced information he had overlooked. No matter what else the union negotiators argued, promised, or threatened, Boulware refused to engage in what many call a "concession charade," the process whereby the parties move inexorably toward each other. You should not be surprised to learn that the General Electric Company had more than its share of strikes during Boulware's time as its negotiator. You also may be interested to learn that the

National Labor Relations Board found that Boulware's bargaining conduct violated the employer's statutory duty to bargain in good faith.[10]

Even though a Boulwarian "take it or leave it" offer system has the advantage of never risking erosion of the adversarial negotiator's credibility, it is not an acceptable approach to the bargaining process.[11] Indeed, a "no concession" method is the antithesis of negotiation. Instead, premised as it is on issuing ultimatums, Boulwarism rejects the give-and-take expectations of the parties to bargaining. The expectation of changes of position during the course of negotiation forms one of the most powerful normative factors in adversarial bargaining.

An adversarial negotiator must be confident of having the ability to exert influence over and move an opponent. The negotiator's ability is measured by the rival's position changes during bargaining, changes known as concessions. These changes in position fill the negotiator's inherent need to earn the respect and positive regard of the other bargainer. This need is met because concessions by the opponent communicate to the negotiator an ability to manipulate the other's intentions, aspirations, expectations, and goals. Likewise, concessions by the negotiator send a similar message to the other side, thereby meeting the opponent's need for the same measure of bargaining achievement. Concessions of some type and size, therefore, are required in adversarial negotiations if agreements are to be reached and deadlocks avoided.

2. When to Make Concessions

In addition to meeting the psychological needs and expectations of the parties, concessions move adversarial negotiators closer to agreement. Adversarial negotiations typically begin with the parties asserting positions that separate them substantially along the bargaining continuum. One party stakes out a claim closer to one end of the continuum. The other party counters by locating itself at the opposite end of the spectrum. Settlement is reached by concessions that reduce and eventually eliminate the gap that divides the negotiators.

That concessions bring separated negotiators closer together sheds light on when a bargainer ought to make a concession. A concession is appropriate when it is required to facilitate the movement toward agreement but does not do serious damage to the adversarial's credibility. So long as a negotiator has some distance between his or her pending offer and the client's resistance level, there is the opportunity to make a concession. That opportunity should be seized when other attempts at encouraging agreement have proved unsuccessful.

---

10. National Labor Relations Act, §8(a)(5), 29 U.S.C. §158(a)(5). See *General Electric Co. and IUE*, 150 N.L.R.B. 192 (1964), aff'd, *NLRB v. General Electric Co.*, 418 F.2d 736 (1969).

11. This is not to say that adversarial bargainers, particularly those of the competitive variety, may not from time to time declare that an issue or two in a multiple issue negotiation must be treated as a Boulwarian "non-negotiable" matter. A "take it or leave it" approach to less than all of the issues in a negotiation may force the other side to accept the single offer. It is, however, a high-risk strategy that can sour the bargaining and lead to deadlock.

There are a number of situations common to adversarial negotiation when a concession may facilitate progress toward agreement. A time deadline is an example of one of those situations. If time is critical, and a negotiator perceives a concession will take less time than persuasion to prod the opponent to make a move, then a concession can be in order. A midnight strike deadline can cause a labor or management negotiator to make a concession at the eleventh hour in the hope that it will stimulate reciprocal action from the other side. An approaching trial date may prompt the lawyer representing one of the parties to consider a concession. Time is a significant external factor that often stimulates concessions.

A negotiation stalled on dead center is another typical example of when a concession may be appropriate. Oftentimes, adversarial negotiators get entrapped[12] in a position. On such occasions when an opposing party becomes overcommitted to a particular offer and the risk of premature deadlock looms, a negotiator may be better off making a concession rather than suffering the consequences of no agreement. As an illustration, consider the situation when the management of a target company subject to a hostile takeover makes public statements about the lengths to which it is willing to go to resist. Having entrapped itself, management becomes less willing to take steps to reach an agreement with the bidder that could avoid critical damage to both companies. A concession by the raider may be the negotiating gesture that prevents disaster.

The future relationships between the parties also may be cause for a move along the adversarial continuum. Thus, the preservation of good will and avoidance of hostility in future bargains may justify making a concession. For instance, if the parties are trying to reach agreement in the first of what may turn out to be a series of mutually profitable deals, an adjustment in the negotiator's offer position may prove to be advantageous over the long term although it might be viewed in a less positive fashion in the pending bargain.

Finally, consider the impact that a concession may have on powerful third parties. For example, how might a negotiator be viewed by a judge if just prior to a status conference the negotiator makes a concession that is perceived to be significant? Or how might the potential lender to a possible joint venture react if one of the adversarial bargainers concedes in a way that would increase the lender's security interest? In both cases, the third party is likely to be impressed by the seeming reasonableness of the negotiator's position and the recalcitrant attitude of the opponent. When the third party is in a position to exert pressure on the other side, the negotiator's concession may be well worth the risk.

The time is ripe for concessions when the adversarial negotiator's other tactics, such as arguments and appeals, promises and threats, have proved unsuccessful in moving the opponent and the risk of deadlock

---

12. Entrapment, a concept that has been studied by negotiation researchers, occurs when a party is locked into a particular stance, as, for example, when a negotiator convinces himself or herself of the correctness of the position being advanced; when the need to save face prevents a bargainer from giving ground; and when the length of time committed to a position makes it seem economically unsound to move.

has increased to an intolerable level. Then, if resources and patience are strained, or a time deadline nears, or an intense conflict endangers the relationship, or a powerful third party is pressuring the parties, or any similar circumstances are present, the adversarial negotiator should consider making a concession toward the client's ultimate resistance level instead of chancing the break-off of bargaining.

As an effective adversarial negotiator deciding when a concession is appropriate, you ought to keep in mind what some of the economic bargaining theorists have posited as to who will make the next concession in any negotiation. The hypothesis is that the immediately succeeding concession always will be made by the negotiator who fears most the consequences of deadlock under then current conditions. Because one message that may accompany any concession is a fear of a failed negotiation, you ought to carefully consider the timing of any move toward the opponent's position. To be sure you do not move too quickly in making a concession, you should carefully prepare a persuasive analysis of each offer stage that points out the consequences to the respective parties in the event deadlock occurred at that moment. Your analysis should demonstrate to the opponent the distinct disadvantages to his or her client if bargaining broke off. On the other hand, you should explain to the other side that, in comparison, your client will suffer less in the event agreement cannot be reached. The problem solver's BATNA (best alternative to a negotiated agreement) is a constructive model to use in developing this deadlock comparison that may persuade an opponent to make the next concession.

3. Concessions as Communication

A concession can damage the credibility you established as an adversarial negotiator when you made your opening offer brief, specific, and justified. Once you move from an initial offer position to another point on the bargaining range, you inform the opponent that your commitment to your original position was not as firm as you portrayed it to be. Therefore, if your negotiating credibility is to be protected, this message must be balanced by evidence that the new position is one to which your commitment is stronger.

That concessions damage credibility and force negotiators to regain it should help us to conceptualize them as a powerful form of communication. A concession expands on, detracts from, or otherwise alters the data previously supplied to the opponent by the negotiator. A concession sends new information to the other side about the bargainer's perceptions, preferences, and purposes. It tells the opponent more about what the negotiator intends, wants, and will settle for.

Although a conceding party gives up a portion of the fungible item being negotiated when a concession is made, the effective adversarial can use the concession process as a way to gain advantage on the opponent. The information aspects of the concession allow an adversarial negotiator to manipulate the information available to the other side, in effect to manage an opponent's impressions. Thus, facts about client aspirations, impressions about reasonableness and flexibility, and data about which issues are critical and which can be compromised are in the hands of the conceder. Such information control can be extremely influential in a negotiation.

The concession process, the actual arrangement of offers and counteroffers during the negotiation, conveys three types or pieces of information to an opponent. First, the concession process may reveal how close the conceder is to the resistance level or bottom line. By analyzing the string of concessions, carefully noting the magnitude and rate of the opponent's movement, the negotiator is in a position to reliably estimate when the other will run out of bargaining authority. Research discloses that a concession made early in the negotiation is likely to be larger than one made near the end of bargaining. Studies also suggest that concessions come more slowly during the early stages of bargaining, while the rate picks up considerably as a bargainer approaches the limits of authority. The timing and size of concessions, therefore, may tell the opponent much about an impending bottom line.

Second, an examination of the opponent's concession pattern may expose the extent to which the other side's actions appear to be contingent on the negotiator's behavior. By conscientiously monitoring the relationship between the opponent's concessions and the negotiator's arguments or other forms of persuasion, the competent adversarial may be able to determine the extent to which the other bargainer's moves are made in response to negotiator action. The concession pattern of the opponent is likely to convey information about the negotiator's ability to systematically exert influence over the other side during bargaining.

Third, aside from questions of timing, size, and sequence, concessions communicate an abundance of information about a negotiator's bargaining style. The bargainer's approach to the issue of compromise tells much about the extent to which the negotiator can be labeled a competitive or a cooperative. The more reasonable and open the negotiator is in making concessions, the more likely it is that reaching a mutually satisfactory agreement is an important value. The more rigid and resistant the bargainer is in conceding, the more probable he or she is attempting to maximize gain without regard to, or even at the expense of, the opponent.

As with all information in a negotiation, the efficient bargainer tries to control all that is communicated by and through the concession process. Understanding the nature of the messages that can be gleaned from your opponent's concession pattern will help you to better manage the information flow.

4. Making Effective Concessions

Once you have decided to concede along your adversarial continuum and have analyzed the process from an information perspective, can you as an adversarial negotiator structure your concessions to maximize the gain and minimize any loss resulting from your action? Experts from the social-psychological school of bargaining have theorized that if a party makes very small, very few, or even no concessions, then the opponent will attribute high aspirations and a tough image to the negotiator. In reaction to this approach to concessions, the theorists suggest, the opponent will reduce its aspirations. Reduced aspirations are likely to be followed by a greater number of concessions and a greater amount conceded.[13] Research into adversarial negotiation tends to support the theory that it pays to be tough on concessions. The research evidence leads to the conclusion that a grudging approach to the size and the number of concessions results in the maximum payoff to the negotiator. Some studies add to our understanding of the concession process by pointing out that linking a tough stance with a reciprocal or matching approach to offer modification is most effective in inducing settlements that favor the negotiator.[14] Positioning oneself just outside an opponent's settlement zone for a considerable period before making a final concession to the other side's area of acceptance extracts as much as possible for the negotiator's client. A cautionary note must be added to the research data. Extreme levels of toughness—that is, Boulwarism or "no concession" tactics—are counterproductive, leading to a higher incidence of reduced payoff and deadlock.

The research data suggest you can construct an effective concession pattern as an adversarial negotiator by doing the following: Be sure your rate of concession is not too rapid, nor the size of the concessions too great, nor the number too many. Consistent with the research, taking a strong stand on a moderately high or low opening offer with one or, at most, a few concessions to your resistance level will produce the most positive results.[15] Finally, you should attempt to accurately identify the minimum your opponent will accept to settle the matter and then position yourself just outside that point, resisting a further concession for as long as possible.

While the preceding is a thumbnail sketch of a positive approach to the concession process, the effective adversarial negotiator making offers of compromise must remember the rules of specificity and justification discussed earlier in connection with offers. A negotiator with a tough approach to concessions, one who makes a few small concessions, still can be manipulated along the bargaining continuum if specificity and justification are abandoned. To be sure these principles are applied in your concession process, use a two-step approach. First, give a specific reason for moving from your present position. Second, justify why you are coming to rest at a specific point farther along your bargaining range.

The first step is critical to maintaining negotiator credibility while still conceding to avoid deadlock. Unless you can give a reason why you are vacating the number you had previously maintained, your opponent is entitled to believe you are simply following a positional approach to the bargaining, merely selecting temporary resting places on an inevitable march

---

13. S. Siegel & L. Fouraker, *Bargaining and Group Decision-Making* (1960).

14. By reciprocal or matching concessions is meant symmetrical either by size or number (but not by both). Asymmetrical concessions—those where the negotiator insists that the opponent makes more concessions (number) or in greater amounts (size)—produce bigger gains for the negotiator but do so at an increased risk of deadlock.

15. This approach avoids what some experts describe as "the grinding down that multiple concessions invite, for there is no doubt that the more incremental concessions are made, the more are expected." I. W. Zartman & M. Berman, *The Practical Negotiator* 171 (1982).

of concessions. To avoid that reaction, you should persuasively explain that you have moved only for compelling reasons. One of the most effective methods of developing the specific explanations that will support your concessions is to identify and isolate your opponent's most persuasive points and to use them to excuse your moves. Thus, your opponent's best arguments, appeals, threats, and promises can be the basis for your concessions. There are two points to keep in mind when following this technique. First, it is very convincing. Opponents are so strongly committed to their own forms of persuasion that it takes little effort to convince them their persuasiveness is the basis for your concession. Second, there is a danger that a sophisticated opponent will associate your concession with his or her persuasive device and try to exploit such power by reapplying it in the hopes of inducing another concession on your part. To sidestep this attempt to manipulate you, avoid using more than once as a ground for concession any argument, appeal, threat, or promise of an opponent.

The second step in preserving your credibility while conceding is the now familiar process of justification. Once you have given a good reason to uproot yourself from your earlier position, you need to come to rest at another place. Of course, the new location must be specific and must be communicated without accompanying "weasel words." Most important, however, is a convincing explanation for the new position. Most forceful is a justification that fits with, and is a logical extension of, the rationale that supported your earlier offer. If you cannot develop a consistent justification theme to support your entire concession process, another compelling approach is to link your reasoning for the new position to the rationale you used to abandon the earlier offer.

As an effective adversarial you should be aware that if you use more flexible language in describing your concession, the easier you will find it to extricate yourself from the position and make a further concession at a later time in the negotiation. On the other hand, the firmer the language you use in describing a concession, the more credible will be your commitment to the conceded position. This is not an argument in favor of a flexible approach to the concession process. Indeed, our fear is that adversarial negotiators who want to appear more flexible will end up using inappropriate "weasel words," thereby destroying their negotiating integrity. Nevertheless, there will be occasions in multiple issue negotiations when you may want to signal your interest in further movement on a particular issue if the appropriate combination of items can be packaged. In those situations, flexible language will be useful in encouraging reciprocal action by the opponent.

Most negotiations conducted by lawyers involve multiple issues. Constructing an effective concession process in these bargaining situations is more complicated than in a single issue negotiation. There are two important questions we should consider in developing concessions in multiple issue bargaining. First, is it more effective to use an integrative or an isolation approach to the issues? Second, in building a concession strategy, how should an adversarial negotiator confront the packaging of issues that are each valued differently by the client?

There is research evidence that integrating the many issues into offer packages is more efficient and effective than isolating the items being bargained and dealing with them one by one. This is not meant to contradict the earlier discussion of "blue chips" and "bargaining chips" in the context of agenda. The issues being negotiated must be approached and analyzed in some order because it is virtually impossible to collapse them into a single discussion topic. However, when it comes to formulating an offer or making a concession, studies suggest it is better to merge the items into a combined offer package.

The secret to efficiently exchanging items of differing values to the client for items held by an opponent is contained in the maxim: "Goods valued more by one party than they cost the other [should be exchanged for] goods valued more by the other party than they cost the first." [16] Thus, the adversarial negotiator should go through a process similar to the one followed by the problem solver in distinguishing the shared, independent, and conflicting needs and goals of client and opponent. In generating an offer and concession package, the adversarial should attempt to bundle the issues in a way that the exchange maxim is exploited to the fullest extent possible.

In conclusion, the importance of planning for and executing an appropriate concession pattern is clear when the research on the "negotiation dance" aspects of adversarial negotiations is considered. The evidence is that the plurality of agreements in adversarial bargains settle at the midpoint, plus or minus 5 percent, of the opening positions of two negotiators. If the parties move in an unthinking, nonstrategic manner, they are likely to end up centered between their initial offers. If one of those parties plans and executes an effective concession pattern and is conscious of the opponent's pattern, it is likely that party will do significantly better. At the very least, that negotiator should end up with the 5 percent fudge-factor on his or her side of the table and, ultimately, in the hands of his or her client.

---

16. G. Homans, *Social Behavior: Its Elementary Forms* 62 (1961).

Chapter

21

An Afterword: Coming Full Circle

Having concluded our commentary on negotiation principles and theories, we must admit that a discussion of bargaining could continue almost indefinitely. Others, for example, have written more extensively and in greater detail than we about negotiation techniques. Much of the advice of these respected negotiation authorities is quite prescriptive and involves the presentation of the precise tactics to be applied in particular bargaining circumstances. We would be among the first to concede that many of their recommendations are often appropriate and effective in specific situations. We also recognize that the guidance they give is likely to reduce negotiator anxiety and promote bargaining confidence.

We are concerned, however, that early reliance on situation-specific tactics may be counterproductive to the development of your negotiation skills. By adhering to bargaining maxims you are apt to stifle the detailed strategic and tactical analysis that should be brought to every bargaining encounter. By selecting another's more or less exactly defined negotiation tactic, you are likely to reject other bargaining guidelines that may better fit with the style-strategy combination you have chosen. You may overlook difficult-to-spot variations in the negotiation setting and, as a result, induce in your opponent an unintended reaction to your use of the suggested bargaining approach.

After working with the materials in the last few chapters, you now have a solid conceptual foundation in the art and science of negotiation, the underpinning you need to construct effective bargaining plans on behalf of your clients and to prepare reasonable responses to the strategies of your opponents. Applying those planning and strategy theories to real and simulated negotiation situations will enhance your skills at electing and implementing effective bargaining techniques. With sufficient experience in analyzing a negotiation problem according to the principles we have discussed, you will be better prepared to study and select specific situational tactics.

To test our concern that the specific tactical advice of negotiation experts may be misleading and sometimes harmful to an effective bargaining strategy, we will apply a few of the suggestions of prominent authorities to the Weber-Jones & Jones problem. For some of the suggested tactics, we will analyze the appropriateness of the negotiation rules. With other techniques, we will ask you to provide the analysis. In that way you can measure your ability to diagnose a bargaining situation and develop a set of appropriate strategies and tactics.

≡ PROBLEM 1 ≡
Small Talk During the Assessment Stage

Donald B. Sparks, a management consultant who includes among his specialties corporate mergers, produced an interesting book that urges a "win/win approach" to negotiation. Throughout the text, Sparks sets forth "guidelines," short statements of advice to negotiators. In a section on influencing opponents, Sparks proposes the following guideline: "Negotiators who are unsure of their opponent's backgrounds, preferences, etc. should avoid discussing subjects not relative to the negotiation; these generally include dress, religion, politics, food, and other personal preference items."[1]

Let's try to apply the guideline to the Weber-Jones & Jones negotiation and see how it might affect the bargaining strategy of the lawyer for Gene Weber. Recall[2] that Weber's counsel did not represent the client during the sale of WEBCo to Jones & Jones. Recall further that the lawyer has never dealt with the attorney for Jones. In this situation, do you believe Sparks's guideline is appropriate?

You will not be surprised to learn that our response to the question is the classic, "It depends!" On the one hand, Sparks's advice to negotiators can be compared to the recommendation we gave to interviewers of new clients to "engage in small talk about common, unchallenging topics [to] overcome that brief awkwardness most people experience when meeting someone for the first time."[3] Similarly, it may make sense as Weber's lawyer

1. *The Dynamics of Effective Negotiation* 111 (1982).
2. See the background memo in Problem 1 of Chapter 17, pages 409-411.
3. See Chapter 4, page 88.

to avoid controversial topics that are not essential to the bargaining, particularly those that could cause counsel for Jones to stake out a position and then be forced to defend it. The danger Sparks sees is, of course, the premature adoption of adversarial postures that could jeopardize agreement.

There is, however, an alternative interpretation, one that would encourage you as Weber's attorney to introduce an unrelated controversial topic early in the bargaining with a lawyer for Jones with whom you have no professional or personal relationship. Your goal in initiating a discussion where the other side is likely to state a preference with which you can disagree may vary slightly depending on whether you have decided on an adversarial or a problem-solving strategy. As a problem solver, one of your goals is to force the parties to discuss their respective needs and to concentrate on solutions that meet those needs. You realize that a stubborn adversarial attitude by the opponent will impede problem-solving progress. Introduction of a controversy that is independent of the negotiation issues allows you to gauge your opponent's bargaining personality, and to assess whether the representative of Jones is likely to adopt an adversarial approach and, if so, whether the style is apt to be competitive or cooperative. Measuring the opponent on the adversariness scale may be important in deciding how or whether the other side will respond to problem-solving techniques. If you were to adopt this tactic in the Weber-Jones & Jones negotiation, you would want to reject Sparks's guideline completely. By that we mean you should be sure the controversial matter that you raise is totally unrelated to the subjects of the bargaining; by using a personal preference item as a test of the opponent's style and strategy combination, you will be less liable to infect the substantive discussion with undue adversariness.

If you have decided on an adversarial strategy, there is a goal independent of assessing the opponent's style and strategy that may dictate rejecting Sparks's guideline. As an adversarial, your strategy implies "winning" as many of the important issues as possible, giving up only that which is required to achieve an advantageous agreement. Therefore, you may want to insert an unrelated contentious issue into the process to "prove" to the other side that you are an aggressive, tough, and tenacious negotiator. Whether your style is competitive or cooperative, it can be effective in certain circumstances to convey early on that you view the process as zero-sum and that you will insist that your client "win" as much as possible. It is probably better to send these messages about your adversarial approach to negotiation via unrelated topics that are, in the scheme of things, relatively low risk when compared to the risk associated with using actual bargaining issues for this purpose. You can "lose" a debate on an unrelated topic without exposing the essence of the negotiation to unreasonable danger.

Please understand that we are not advocating that you should necessarily reject Sparks's guideline in those situations where you are unsure of the opponent's background and preferences. Rather, we urge you not to adopt it automatically in circumstances where you do not have a prior relationship with a bargaining opponent. Instead, we suggest that you analyze the unique negotiation situation with which you are confronted in light of the goals of the style-strategy combination that you have selected. That analysis will recommend the tactics you should adopt and the topics selected for the "small talk" phase of assessment.

≡ PROBLEM 2 ≡
Creating the Agenda

Herb Cohen's book, *You Can Negotiate Anything*, was listed on the New York Times best-seller list for months following its publication in 1980. Writing one of the early self-help texts on negotiation, Attorney Cohen set out to produce "a practical and readable guide for laypeople." While he claimed that the book "painted with a broad brush" to be sure readers would "understand the broad underlying concepts,"[4] on numerous occasions Cohen wrote as if there is only one way to approach a particular negotiation situation.

An example of the singleness of Cohen's bargaining mind-set involves the ordering of negotiation issues:

> If you have something difficult to negotiate—an emotional issue, or a contract item that can be stated numerically, such as price, cost, interest rate, or salary—*cope with it at the end of a negotiation, after the other side has made a hefty expenditure of energy and a substantial time investment.* What if the emotional issue or quantifiable item surfaces at the beginning of the negotiation? Acknowledge it, chat about it, but put it off till later—returning to it only after the other side has spent a lot of time with you. You'll be surprised how the other side's investment will cause them to become flexible at the end of the negotiation.[5]

It would be hard to imagine a more specific rule about how to construct a negotiation agenda when the bargaining involves a tough or fungible issue.

Consider whether the rule works when you are representing Jones in the Weber negotiation. As you do your analysis, remember that there are three obvious issues over which the parties are likely to bargain—an amount of money to be paid by Weber for a full or partial buy-out of the noncompetition clause; the timing of the start-up of Weber's new business and the length of any remaining portion of the noncompete provision relating to employment placement; and the geographic restrictions, if any, on Weber's Executive Counseling Service. The issue that best fits Cohen's rule is the price Weber will have to pay Jones for the right to operate ECS. Can you think of any circumstances when it would be advantageous for Jones to lead off with a discussion of dollars instead of postponing the topic to the end of bargaining? One of the difficulties you may encounter in applying Cohen's rule to this negotiation is that each of these issues involves a fungible matter and, therefore, can be expressed numerically (the payout declared in an exact number of dollars; time represented by the number of months or years; and geography couched in terms of a number of miles or a number of states). Can you delay all three questions until late in the ne-

---

4. H. Cohen, *You Can Negotiate Anything* 10 (1980).
5. Id. at 72-73 (emphasis in the original).

gotiation process? If so, how do you fill up the early bargaining sessions? Will Cohen's rule be easier to apply if you adopt either an adversarial or problem-solving strategy?

≡ **PROBLEM 3** ≡
Offers an Opponent Cannot or Must Refuse

A well-known writer and lecturer on negotiation, Chester L. Karrass, left no doubt that he was providing the reader with an all-inclusive review of negotiation moves when he titled one of his books *Give & Take: The Complete Guide to Negotiating Strategies and Tactics* (1974). In *Give & Take*, Karrass boldly presents the 200 strategies and tactics one must know and apply to conduct business and personal transactions successfully.[6] There are two offer strategies or tactics that Karrass contrasts. One he titles "make him an offer he can't refuse," borrowing the phrase of the Godfather in Mario Puzo's popular book. As used by Karrass, the tactic appears to involve the use of power to leverage a negotiation opponent to accept an unreasonable offer. The flip side of this technique is to "make him an offer he must refuse." Karrass explains why and when the tactic should be employed:

> But why should anyone give another person . . . an offer [he must refuse]? There are lots of reasons. Such proposals set the stage for making later offers look good by comparison. They serve to get the other man off your back or give you a chance to think things through. They can tie negotiations up, force talks to break down or postpone decisions. I have seen unacceptable offers made simply as an ego kick—just to show the opponent how independent the negotiator was.
>
> One of the best reasons for making an offer he can't accept is to help zero in on what he will accept. The magic of such an offer is that it opens up a flow of conversation. When people believe that no deal is likely, they talk candidly with one another. It is then that real motivations and goals are revealed. There is no reason why a man cannot then follow up with bargaining in good faith.[7]

According to Karrass, one of the many times this bargaining ploy should be used is when a negotiator wants to engineer a recess to review and consider developments. Consider the consequences of invoking Karrass's "must be refused" offer tactic in the context of the Weber-Jones & Jones negotiation. Suppose you are representing Jones and that thus far in the negotiation you have been employing a cooperative adversarial approach. While you have hinted that Jones may be willing to "sell" Weber a portion of the noncompete provision, you have not set a specific price. You have insisted that the remainder of the noncompetition clause be extended

---

6. Karrass organizes the book not by chapters but alphabetically by strategy and tactic, each of which is labeled with a snappy term such as "Cherry Picking: The Optimizer's Tactic" (a process of soliciting bids and then negotiating among the bidders, playing one off against the other); "Hostage Tactic" (the business kidnapper who takes something valued by the other side "hostage," holding it for trade); and "Scrambled Eggs: How Disorder Can Work Against You" (deliberately confusing the issues and other matters for tactical reasons).

7. C. Karrass, *Give & Take: The Complete Guide to Negotiating Strategies and Tactics* 107-108 (1974).

beyond the original ten-year term, that Weber delay entry into the employment counseling business for eighteen months, and that Weber limit ECS to a local operation.

Assume that the attorney for Weber has been following a cooperative problem-solving strategy. Weber's lawyer suggests that Weber and Jones set up a reciprocal arrangement whereby Jones will refer all of its clients that need employment counseling to Weber and, in return, Weber will refer all of his counseled clients to Jones & Jones for job placement. Under the terms of the Weber proposal, each party will pay the other 25 percent of the fee collected from clients referred by the other. Upon hearing this proposal, you feel the need to recess the session to review all the implications of this arrangement. While your immediate reaction is that Weber's suggestion may meet many of your client's needs, you know that there are permutations of the proposed arrangement that must be pondered. Though anxious to break off bargaining, you do not want to appear too hesitant or too interested in the proposal. You recall Karrass's "an offer he must refuse" rule and immediately counter Weber's suggestion with a demand that Weber pay Jones $415,000 for the right to begin his new business. You justify the stated amount as being equal to the portions of the original contract price allocated to the noncompete clause ($115,000) and for goodwill ($300,000). Your tactic works. Weber's lawyer rejects your demand and calls a recess in the negotiation.

Analyze the implications of your use of the Karrass tactic. Develop alternatives to the technique that will achieve your need to obtain a recess without weakening your adversarial position.

≡ PROBLEM 4 ≡
Doubling Back: A Reversal Strategy

Gerard I. Nierenberg, a lawyer who conducts seminars on negotiation throughout the country, has written a number of texts on the bargaining process. In one of those books, Nierenberg describes a negotiating technique that he calls "reversal" or "you can go forward, backward."[8] According to this strategy, you act contrary to what the other side expects. Nierenberg points out that confounding the opponent by taking a position diametrically opposed to that anticipated may seem to be a simple task. In reality, however, it is exceedingly difficult to plan and execute. The "double reversal" is a variation of the technique and, according to Nierenberg, is even more complex:

> In using [double reversal,] you intentionally send two messages forcing the opposer to accept the less onerous one. For example, if mild demands are first made and then are followed by stronger demands, the other side will react to and be more likely to accept the milder demands.[9]

8. G. Nierenberg, *Fundamentals of Negotiating* 155-158 (1973). As will be seen, there are some similarities between Nierenberg's reversal strategy and Karrass's "must refuse" tactic.
9. Id. at 157.

Nierenberg gives an example of the double reversal strategy. A major airline company was building a large complex and wanted to be accorded lower rates than those charged by the local company producing electric power. The utility refused to lower its charges, claiming that its rate schedule did not permit such reductions. When negotiations stalled, the airline hired engineers to estimate the cost of building its own independent electricity-producing plant to provide the services it needed. The cost estimate received by the airline encouraged it to go forward to create a new company. When the power company learned of these plans, it reversed its earlier position and appealed to the public utilities commission for much lower rates for this type of customer. The commission approved the new rates quickly. To the dismay of the power company, however, the airline refused the new rate schedule and insisted it was going ahead with its plans to build a generating facility. The local utility company panicked, and went back to the commission and obtained an even lower rate applicable to its largest commercial users. Only then did the airline agree to abandon its plans to build a competing company and to purchase its electricity from the existing supplier.

Although Nierenberg presents reversal as one of several strategies available for general use,[10] it should be obvious that it is a high-risk adversarial technique. Applying it to the Weber-Jones problem will demonstrate that the associated dangers should restrict its use to situations where the negotiator has little fear of deadlock.

Assume that you represent Weber and are back at the pre-negotiation planning stage. Recall that during counseling you identified a number of options available to Weber.[11] The client chose to negotiate with the buyer of the WEBCo business in the hope of creating an exception to the noncompete provisions. Negotiation in these circumstances is the approach the other party is most likely to anticipate. When reasonable people differ on the application of a contract provision to particular business conduct, it is usual for the parties to sit down to discuss the situation and seek to reach an amicable understanding.

Another alternative open to the client, however, is to make plans to begin the new employment counseling business immediately.[12] Instead of

---

10. Reversal is one of eight "when" strategies designated by Nierenberg as tools to be employed during bargaining. The term "when strategy" refers to the timing of its use and is contrasted with twelve "how and where" strategies that focus more on the method of application. According to Nierenberg, a "when" strategy such as reversal "is easier to use in a negotiation when a new element enters the picture rather than when all elements are static. But properly applied, it can change a static situation into a dynamic one." Id. at 148.

11. See the background memo in Problem 1 of Chapter 17, page 408.

12. Notice that we said to "make plans" for the new business rather than "start up" the new business. The important differences between preparing for and actually beginning ECS distinguish "reversal" and another Nierenberg tactic called "fait accompli." As you would expect from the name, fait accompli "demands that you act, achieve your goal against the opposition, and then see what the other side will do about it." In an obvious understatement, Nierenberg points out that "those who employ this strategy must make an appraisal of the consequences in case it should prove to be a failure." Id. at 152. The slight differences between these two tactics raises another concern of ours. Attempts to narrowly define and label bargaining techniques may confuse negotiators and further mislead them about the appropriateness of a given tactic.

contacting Jones or its lawyer and consulting with them on how to avoid a confrontation, Weber sends them an announcement on the new business, inviting Jones personnel to the opening of the offices of ECS. This reversal of form will communicate to the other party Weber's determination to begin the ECS operation and may induce Jones to initiate negotiations. The bargaining posture of the parties will be quite different if the reversal tactic works. Instead of Weber arguing for an exception to the noncompetition rule, Jones will be asking Weber to abandon or alter his plans. Analyzed from the perspective of the competitive adversarial, Weber will enhance at least the appearance of his power in the bargaining if he can put Jones in the position of being a supplicant.

The very statement of what Weber hopes to achieve with the use of the reversal ploy exposes the dangers and limitations of the tactic. Instead of rushing to the negotiation table, Jones may declare that the operation of ECS would be in conflict with the provisions of the noncompete clause and demand that Weber cease and desist from going forward. If Weber continues with his planned opening of the business, Jones may commit itself to seek injunctive relief, thereby moving the dispute to another level of intensity.

A tactic by Weber that induces the threat of court action by Jones places severe limitations on Weber's responses and intensifies the adversarial relationship of the parties. While that result may be justified and appropriate under certain circumstances, a move that causes such a reaction can hardly be one considered generally available and applicable in negotiations. Its use must be severely limited to extraordinary occasions. To be sure, the reversal tactic will not always risk such a menacing response by the opponent. But the use of reversal or any tactic will cause the other side to react. Because reactions vary so widely among lawyers and those they represent, the selection of a negotiation technique requires careful and thoughtful analysis according to an overall conception of the bargaining process. Negotiation tactics cannot simply be taken down off the shelf based on the labels applied by others and used without consideration of the strategic implications for the specific bargaining setting.

———————————————————

We want to emphasize that we are not recommending that you disregard the advice of bargaining experts. Indeed, we urge you to read broadly about the negotiation process, absorbing as much as you can about the art and science of negotiating. The tactics identified and explained by authorities in the field will give you ideas, stimulate your thinking, and promote the development of new alternatives. We insist, however, that you should never accept the tactical suggestions of others blindly, quickly adopting a technique that appears superficially to be just the stratagem to use in a pending negotiation. Instead, every technique must be measured against the strategy you have decided to follow and the style you have chosen to adopt for the particular bargaining situation.

This brings us full circle. Thousands of words ago in the first chapter of this book we explained our approach to learning the critical lawyering skills of interviewing, counseling, and negotiating. To develop effectiveness on these interpersonal levels we believe you must first be able to articulate and describe what has occurred, what is occurring, or what will likely occur in an interpersonal session with a client or another lawyer. To reach this level of consciousness you must understand the conceptual and theoretical underpinnings of interpersonal relationships and have a vocabulary that allows you to think about and analyze an interpersonal encounter. Next, we believe that there is a building-block approach to learning the skills of interviewing, counseling, and negotiating. All of the skills of interviewing are used in counseling and new skills are added. Those mastered in interviewing and counseling are applicable to negotiation but new skills must be learned to maximize your effectiveness. A failure to understand that one skill builds on another will limit the range of your reactions in counseling and negotiating. The third element in the learning theory on which this book rests is that a lawyer must interview, counsel, and negotiate to become proficient at interviewing, counseling, and negotiating. Reading and rereading this and other texts about these three interpersonal skills will not, without more, make you an effective lawyer. You must practice these skills in real and simulated settings, reflecting on what you have done as preparation for employing the same skills again in other circumstances.

The final point we made at the outset of this text about our approach to skills development was the importance of preparation. We emphasize as we close our discussion that there is no substitute for careful and thorough planning for these three complex professional encounters. Your natural abilities and the experience you gain as you move through your career as an attorney will reduce preparation time and effort. They will not, however, obviate the need to prepare for an interpersonal session or to reflect critically on it once it has ended as part of the preparation for a future interpersonal event.

Interviewing, counseling, and negotiating are tasks that make the life of a lawyer interesting, challenging, and rewarding. They also are the skills you will need for the effective representation of your clients.

Index